Technology&Procedures
for Administrative Professionals

Patsy Fulton-Calkins

Ph.D., CPS
Adjunct Professor, Educational Consultant
Grand Rapids, MI

THOMSON

SOUTH-WESTERN

Australia · Canada · Mexico · Singapore · Spain · United Kingdom · United States

THOMSON
™
SOUTH-WESTERN

Technology & Procedures for Administrative Professionals
By Patsy Fulton-Calkins

Vice President/Executive Publisher:
Dave Shaut

Team Leader:
Karen Schmohe

Project Manager:
Dr. Inell Bolls

Production Editor:
Carol Spencer

Acquisitions Editor:
Joseph Vocca

Production Manager:
Tricia Boies

Executive Marketing Manager:
Carol Volz

Marketing Manager:
Chris McNamee

Marketing Coordinator:
Cira Brown

Manufacturing Manager:
Charlene Taylor

Art and Design Coordinator:
Stacy Jenkins Shirley

Cover and Internal Design:
John Robb & Associates

Compositor:
Thompson Steele Production Services

Printer:
Quebecor World/Dubuque

Rights and Permissions Manager:
Linda Ellis

For permission to use material from this text or product, contact us by
Phone: 1-800-730-2214,
Fax: 1-800-730-2215, or
www.thomsonrights.com.

Library of Congress Cataloging-in-Publication Data

Fulton-Calkins, Patsy
    Technology & procedures for admnistrative professionals / Patsy Fulton-Calkins.
        p. cm.
    Includes bibliographical references and index.
    ISBN 0-538-72590-7 (alk. paper)
    1. Information technology.
    2. Management. 3. Leadership.
    4. Employees--Effect of technological innovations on. I. Title: Technology and procedures for administrative professionals. II. Title.

HD30.2 .F865 2002
658'.05--dc21

2001058193

PREFACE

The administrative professional's role in the workplace today is challenging and ever changing. Why? A major part of the answer is that we live in an age with a continuous explosion of knowledge. Advances in technology provide us with expanding communication capabilities and equipment that allow us to perform our tasks with greater speed and sophistication than in the past. Administrative professionals can produce complex reports containing graphics and tables with relative speed and efficiency. However, the explosion of knowledge, with the technological advancements it has brought, is only a partial answer to why the workplace is challenging and ever changing. We also live in a world that is more international in scope, with numerous organizations in the United States having worldwide operations. Additionally, the population of the United States is more diverse than ever before—diverse in race, ethnicity, gender, and age. This world demands that the administrative professional have not only technology skills but also a broad range of human relation skills (including verbal and written communication) and critical-thinking skills. Due to the ever-changing nature of our world, the administrative professional must also commit to continual learning. This textbook will help you be better equipped to meet the demands of that world.

TEXTBOOK ORGANIZATION

Technology & Procedures for Administrative Professionals is organized into six parts, with a total of 15 chapters.

LEARNING AIDS

To assist you in the learning process, learning aids are provided in each part and each chapter. The part learning aids are these.

- Professional profiles of administrative professionals presently working in the field who share their success stories and provide job-related situations in which they have been involved, including how they solved the situations. You are invited (before you look at their solutions) to determine how you would solve the situations.
- Part tests to reinforce your understanding of the concepts in each section of the textbook.

The chapter learning aids are as follows:

- Learning Objectives (given at the beginning of the chapter)
- At least one soft-skill objective (a business-related, nontechnical skill) at the beginning of each chapter, with the objective appearing in italic print.
- Self-Check
- Technology, Human Relations, Health, and Communication Tips
- Key terms highlighted and defined within the chapter
- Numerous illustrations and figures
- Chapter Summary
- Chapter Glossary listing the key terms and definitions
- Discussion Items
- Critical-Thinking Activity (cases and situations to be analyzed using critical-thinking skills)
- Projects that reinforce the learning objectives
- Collaborative projects that provide opportunities to work with classmates in developing team-building skills
- Projects that provide opportunities to make class presentations
- Projects that require using a CD-ROM
- Online research activities designed to reinforce the use of the Web
- English Usage Challenge Drills designed to reinforce language skills
- Assessment of Chapter Objectives

SOFT SKILLS

Soft skills (such as critical thinking; teamwork; interpersonal; and leadership) are consistently identified by organizations as critical skills that all employees must possess. Because of the importance of these skills to the administrative professional, the soft skills appear in italic print in the objectives of each chapter. You will also develop a Professional Growth Plan throughout the course that focuses on soft skills.

SUPPLEMENTARY LEARNING AIDS

To assist in learning, these supplementary items are provided.

- Student CD containing projects and forms
- Optional activities
- PowerPoint® presentation software, emphasizing key concepts in each chapter
- Chapter quizzes, part tests, and a final exam

NEW FEATURES IN THIS EDITION

- New chapter—Chapter 3: Telework
- Three new profiles of administrative professionals, with one administrative professional from outside the United States—New Zealand
- Soft skills identified and emphasized in the objectives, projects, and Professional Growth Plans
- A multinational company orientation—AmeriAsian Airlines with locations in China and Michigan
- Emphasis on critical thinking, with a Critical-Thinking Activity at the end of each chapter and new activities designed to help develop critical-thinking skills
- New projects
- Emphasis on Web research with numerous online projects
- New and current research integrated throughout the chapters
- Student CD, which includes projects and forms
- Instructor's Resource Manual on a CD
- Expanded use of color throughout the textbook

- Expanded number of PowerPoint slides for use in presenting the objectives of each chapter, an outline of each chapter, and selected text designed to encourage class discussion
- Online instruction available through Blackboard or Web CT platforms

STUDENT MESSAGE

This textbook has been written for you, the user. As the author, I have considered your learning needs throughout the book, and I have made every effort to present the material in an understandable and relevant manner. In every chapter, you have a chance to develop and expand skills that will contribute to your success as an administrative professional. It is my hope that from studying this book and completing the projects, you not only learn and grow in your abilities and skills but also have fun in the process. I extend my best wishes to you for a challenging and successful course.

THE AUTHOR

Dr. Patsy J. Fulton-Calkins' experience in the field is extensive. Her past experience in the workplace includes working as an administrative professional for large corporations for six years. Early in her career, she completed the CPS certification. Her teaching experience includes over 13 years at the university, community college, and high school levels.

In addition to her teaching experience, she has worked as an administrator in the following positions:

- Chancellor of Oakland Community College (the chief executive officer), Oakland County, Michigan
- President of Brookhaven College, Dallas, Texas
- Vice President of Instruction at El Centro College and Cedar Valley College, Dallas, Texas
- Division Chairperson of Business and Social Science, Cedar Valley College, Dallas, Texas

Her present position includes working with Tom Monaghan Associates, Inc., as a senior consultant in institutional advancement work with clients across the United States. Additionally, she is an adjunct professor at the university level.

Her educational credentials include a B.B.A., an M.B.Ed., and a Ph.D. Honors include Outstanding Alumnus, University of North Texas; Transformational Leader in Community Colleges; Who's Who in America, Outstanding Woman in Management; Paul Harris Fellow of Rotary International; Beta Gamma Sigma, National Honorary Business Fraternity; and Piper Professor.

ACKNOWLEDGEMENTS

Thanks to the following reviewers for their helpful comments as this book was being developed.

Reviewer	School Affiliation
Mitsy W. Ballentine, M.Ed.	Greenville Technical College Greenville, SC
Ann Cooper, M.Ed.	Central Carolina Technical College Sumter, SC
Gloria Smith, M.Ed.	Southern Ohio College Cincinnati, OH

CONTENTS

Technology & Procedures

for Administrative Professionals

A
Success
Profile

Bernice Fujiwara, CPS
Administrative Secretary II
First Hawaiian Bank
Honolulu, Hawaii

I attribute my success to a combination of several things: having a supportive family (including my husband, my two boys, my parents, and my sisters), working hard, being a member of the International Association of Administrative Professionals (IAAP), and being at the right place at the right time.

My educational background includes a secretarial diploma from Cannon's School of Business. I was inducted into Cannon's Business College Alumni Hall of Fame in April 1993. However, my education has not stopped. I have completed a number of courses from the American Institute of Banking: principles in banking, economics, law and banking, residential mortgage lending, and analyzing financial statements. I have also completed an in-house supervisory training program. In addition, I have attended numerous workshops and courses on various computer programs, gaining proficiency in Microsoft Word®, Excel®, IBM®, WordPerfect®, Lotus®, and Macintosh Word®. In 1986, I attained the Certified Professional Secretary rating by passing a two-day, six-part examination covering behavioral science in business, business law, economics and management, accounting, office administration and communication, and office technology. I attained recertification of the CPS in 1996.

I have been with First Hawaiian Bank since 1974. My career began as a steno-receptionist; I am currently the administrative secretary to an executive vice president. My responsibilities include assisting in customer service, being a liaison between division and regional managers, composing and editing letters and memos, coordinating bankwide branch managers' meetings, taking minutes at various meetings, preparing and following up on management reports, preparing itineraries for executive travel, and assisting the executive in nonprofit organizational activities. In addition, I supervise one secretary.

The most enjoyable part of my job is coordinating our semiannual branch manager's meeting. My responsibilities include making hotel reservations, preparing the meeting agenda, attending the meeting, and assisting with dinner arrangements. The bank has 57 branches in Hawaii and two in

Guam. I enjoy meeting and talking with our branch managers.

I enjoy the challenge of using technology to be more efficient at my job. I think administrative professionals sometimes get into a rut by doing a task the same way day in and day out. When I improve a procedure, even though it may be a simple one, I wonder why I did not think of it sooner. When I am able to save time doing mundane tasks, I have more time to organize and plan for other projects.

The most stressful part of my job is having to do ten things at once because my executive is extremely busy and needs my support. I have learned that good communication between an administrative assistant and an executive is vital to being productive. The administrative assistant needs to know the purpose or reason for a project so he or she can get organized and meet the deadline. (Many times the executive does not know the process or details necessary to get a job done.) The administrative assistant must use good judgment in deciding what to tackle first. Another stressful part of my job includes unhappy customers who scream at me over the telephone. I have learned to listen and ask the right questions. I know my company well—the organization, the people, and the products—so I can refer customers to the appropriate department.

My hobbies include needlepoint, ceramics, and Japanese washi paper dolls. I enjoy most craft work. I also enjoy taking aerobic classes, walking, going to the beach to swim, and playing basketball with my sons.

I have been a member of the Hawaii Chapter of IAAP since 1980. I have held numerous officer positions in our division and chapter, including president, vice president, and treasurer. Our club is involved in activities such as offering scholarships to students in the administrative professional field (which means we do fundraising), assisting with community service projects, and providing continuing education for our members. I am proud of the special recognition I have received through IAAP, including the following awards:

- 2001 Outstanding Division President in Membership
- 1992–1993 International Secretary of the Year for Professional Secretaries International (now IAAP)
- 1992–1993 Southwest District Secretary of the Year
- 1992–1993 Hawaii Division Secretary of the Year
- 1991–1992 Hawaii Chapter Secretary of the Year

I was also inducted into Cannon's Business College Alumni Hall of Fame in April 1993. Hall of Fame inductees receive this award because of their contributions to the college and community and because of their accomplishments since graduation.

BERNICE FUJIWARA'S CASE

The role of the administrative assistant has changed and evolved over the years, in large part because employers are doing business in different countries. When dealing with people from other countries or from other ethnic groups, ask questions if you are unsure of how to handle a situation. Most people will appreciate your efforts to make them feel comfortable. Here is a situation in which I was involved.

The Situation

The executive tells you he needs to organize a dinner within one week involving a group from an important company in Japan. The total number of people attending is 30, which includes spouses. You know very little about Japanese customs and language, although most of the guests do speak English. An important contract hinges on the outcome of this dinner. What are some factors you should focus on, and what are some items to include on your to-do list?

Decide how you would handle the situation. Then turn to the end of Part 1 (page 53) to see how I solved the situation.

CHAPTER 1
THE WORK ENVIRONMENT

LEARNING OBJECTIVES

1. Describe the changing work environment.
2. Identify the role and responsibilities of the administrative professional.
3. Determine twenty-first-century traits necessary for the administrative professional.
4. Begin the development of a professional growth plan.
5. *Develop critical-thinking skills.*

Will we ever live on Mars? This question is one that would not have entered the minds of our grandparents and may not have entered the minds of our parents. The possibility of such a happening was too remote to have entered their consciousness. Today such a question is not even unique, and the answer to this question is a possible "yes." In an article in the April 2000 issue of *Time*, the question was asked and answered with this statement:

> By 2017—about the time that children born this year approach voting age—mankind's first tiny settlement on another world may be taking hold.
>
> Scientists at NASA and in the private sector have been quietly scribbling out flight plans and sketching out vehicles that—so they say—could make manned landings on the Red Planet not only possible but also economically practical.[1]

Additionally, here are several less dramatic but nevertheless amazing changes that are projected to have an impact on our everyday life.

- Intelligent rooms in our homes with walls that can "see" us by the use of sensors and recognize our voices, allowing us to speak our requests and see the results promptly
- The ability in an emergency to call into the air "Get the ambulance!" and get an immediate response
- Clothing and household linens made of smart fabrics that clean and press themselves, making washing machines and ironing boards oddities of the past
- Electronic image spots that display Van Goghs or any other art you dial up
- Homes you can enter and exit by using voice commands, making keys and locks antiques
- Human gene therapy to revitalize damaged brain cells

---

[1] Jeffrey Kluger, "Will We Live on Mars?" *Time*, April 10, 2000, 58–62.

- Vehicles that run on magnetized tracks on the interstates, traveling bumper to bumper at 100–200 miles per hour, with no real driving involved
- Onboard computers that monitor the workings of your auto and diagnose incipient or actual failures, automatically informing the shop of spare parts you need
- Aircraft that take off vertically, reducing noise and the size of airports[2]
- Smart cards that contain such information as Website passwords and addresses, driver's license information, medical insurance data, commuter passes, to name some of the possibilities[3]

Just as our world is changing dramatically, so is the workplace and workforce. These are some of the changes you are encountering if you are presently working or you will encounter as you enter the workforce.

- A workforce that is more diverse than ever before, with diversity present in ethnicities and cultures, gender, and age
- A business environment where **multinational corporations** (corporations that operate both within and outside the United States) are the norm rather than the exception

Our nation may have a settlement on Mars by 2017.

© PhotoDisc, Inc.

- Large corporations with **merger mania** (mergers occurring nationally and internationally at rates never heard of previously) existing throughout the world
- Workplaces with **state-of-the-art technology** (the latest available), including wireless communications and voice-activated technology
- **E-commerce** (businesses that operate on the Internet) expanding rapidly
- More people engaged in **telework** (work that can be performed anywhere and at any time using technology)

To survive and thrive in this workplace, you need to acquire the knowledge, skills, and qualities that allow you to become a valued part of the organization. This chapter will help you begin that development; and throughout this course, you will continue that development.

Take a moment now to reread the learning objectives given at the beginning of this chapter. It is very important for you to begin each chapter understanding exactly what you are expected to achieve. The learning objectives will help you focus your study and use your time efficiently. At the end of each chapter, you will be asked to respond to the following:

- Did you accomplish the objectives?
- If you were unable to accompish the objectives, give your reasons for not doing so.

THE INFORMATION AGE

Why is the workplace constantly changing? A major part of the answer to that question is that you and I live in the Information Age. As the term **Information Age** suggests, we are living in a time of tremendous explosion of knowledge. As you read the introduction to this chapter, you were reminded of the changes that are

---

[2]Susan Crowley, "Hello to Our Future," *AARP Bulletin,* January 2000, 3, 14–15.
[3]Anne D'Innocenzio, "Financial Powerhouses Pushing Smart Cards," *The Grand Rapids Press,* December 25, 2000, A9.

projected in our world in the next few years—changes that our grandparents never imagined. Driving these changes is the technology that is an integral part of this Information Age.

Consider for a moment the tremendous changes that have taken place in the workplace in a few short years. The microcomputer did not exist; the mainframe computer performed all computer applications. The telephone was the standard piece of telecommunications equipment. The conference call was one of the most sophisticated techniques available when communicating with several people. Now workers use computers, voice mail, email, fax machines, and printers/copiers. Cell phones are used by many people; instant communication with the workplace and our homes is important. **Palm® organizers** (small handheld computers) allow us to make frequent changes and additions to our calendar from any location, pick up our email, store our phone numbers, download information from the Web, check our stock portfolios, and perform a number of other functions. People may work from their homes or other locations outside the traditional workplace in a **telework environment.**

When you add to the technological changes additional directions such as an increasingly diverse population and the globalization of our economy, you begin to understand why we live in a world of constant change.

A Diverse Labor Force

From the period of 1998–2008, employment is projected to increase by 23 million, approximately 13 percent.[4] This workforce will be increasingly diverse, with minorities and immigrants constituting a larger share of the workforce than they do today. White non-Hispanics will make up a decreasing share of the labor force, from 93.9 to 70.7 percent. The projected percentages for other ethnicities in the workforce by 2008 are

- Hispanics—12.7 percent
- African Americans—12.4 percent
- Asians—4.6 percent[5]

The fastest-growing population group in our country today is Hispanic. The United States

Census 2000 results show that the Hispanic population numbers 35.3 million (12.6 percent of the country's 281 million people).[6] The population numbers for Hispanics surpassed previous projections and increased 58 percent from the 1990 census. It is projected by 2050 that the distribution of our total population will change dramatically, with white non-Hispanics making up only 52.8 percent of the population; African Americans, 13.2 percent; Hispanics, 24.3 percent; Asians and Pacific Islanders, 9.3 percent; and American Indians, .8 percent.[7]

Women in the Workforce

More women are in the workforce today than in the past, and that number is projected to grow. In fact, the number of women in the workforce is projected to grow between 1998 and 2008, from 46.3 to 47.5 percent, while the men's share of the labor force is expected to decrease during this same period of time, from 53.7 to 52.5 percent.[8] Women, both single and married, continue to enter the workforce in greater numbers than in the past. Women who

© Digital Stock

Sixty percent of women are in the workforce today.

[4]U.S. Department of Labor, *Occupational Outlook Handbook* (Washington, D.C.: Bureau of Labor Statistics, 2000–01), 1.

[5]Ibid, 1–2.

[6]"Census 2000," accessed January 12, 2001; available from www.census.usatoday.com.

[7]"Futurework—Trends and Challenges for Work in the 21st Century," accessed January 12, 2001; available from www.dol.gov/dol/asp/public/futurework.

[8]U.S. Department of Labor, *Occupational Outlook Handbook* (Washington, D.C.: Bureau of Labor Statistics, 2000–01), 1–2.

have children are returning to the workforce today while their children are still preschool age. This is particularly true for families maintained by single women, a group that is growing significantly. A recent survey of 700 U.S. working men and women found the number one career-related concern for employees of the changing workplace is the ability to balance work and family demands.[9]

Senior Workers

The number of workers 45 and older is expected to increase from 33 to 40 percent of the labor force between 1998 and 2008 due to the aging baby-boom generation. As medical technology continues to make advances that allow people to live longer, we can expect people to stay in the workforce beyond the traditional retirement age of 65. In fact, the Committee for Economic Development, based in New York and Washington, states in a recent report that it will be important for older workers to stay in the workforce to avert a sharp slowdown in economic growth due to a scarcity of workers as the American population ages over the next few decades. In 1950, there were five people working for every person over 65 and retired. Today there are only three workers for every retiree, and in 30 years, it is projected that there will be approximately two workers for every person over 65. Such demographic changes will leave businesses scrambling to find workers unless traditional attitudes about retirement change.[10]

Thus, you will probably work with people aged eighteen to well over sixty. Certainly, each generation of our population grows up with differing national and local influences in their lives. For example, the generation of Americans who served in World War II and are now in their mid-seventies have been characterized by writers as a generation that was extremely patriotic and pragmatic, putting personal goals aside in order to serve the needs of our nation. That generation views the world through a very different lens than do people who have never served in a world war. Consider still another example of differences. Young people who are in their teens today have grown up in an age of technology; they are the digital generation. They probably have played video games all their lives; thus, technology has become a part of their daily existence. The Internet is not a mystery, but a way of researching, shopping, sending messages, chatting with people around the world, and exchanging digital photographs. Whereas people in their forties or fifties had to acquire technology skills as adults; these skills were not something they mastered as young children or teenagers.

These age differences in the workplace mean that we may view the world from different perspectives. In order to work together successfully, we have to listen closely to each other and accept each other's different views. Our task is to accept the individual for who he or she is.

Cultural Diversity

America has been racially and culturally diverse since its very beginning. We are a nation of immigrants—a nation who has welcomed and accepted people from countries all over the world. However, America is becoming more and more diverse. You have already learned that by 2050, it is projected that almost half of our population will be Hispanic, African American, Asian or Pacific Islander, or American Indian—with the Hispanic population growing much faster than the other groups. You will work with people who are very diverse ethnically. In fact, if you are now working in California, New York, Florida, Texas, New Mexico, or Arizona, you are probably already experiencing this diverse workforce.

Multiculturalism by definition means "relating to or including several cultures." **Culture** is defined as "the ideas, customs, values, skills, and arts of a specific group of people." As you work in this diverse workplace, you need to be aware of and sensitive to the various cultural differences and backgrounds. You must understand that individuals, because of their different backgrounds, may view situations differently than you do. Your openness to different ideas and perspectives is essential.

[9]"Office of the Future: 2005," accessed January 15, 2001; available from www.iaap-hq.org.
[10]Christopher Conte, "New Focus on Older Workers," *AARP Bulletin*, January 2000, 26.

It may not always be easy to remain open to differences, but the results will be well worth your effort. Only through awareness, understanding, and acceptance of different cultures can we expect to work in a harmonious, productive business world.

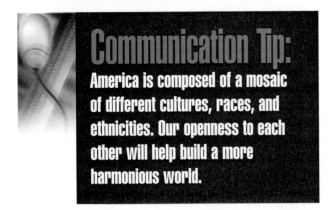

Communication Tip:

America is composed of a mosaic of different cultures, races, and ethnicities. Our openness to each other will help build a more harmonious world.

Gender Roles in the Workplace

More than ever before, women are assuming positions of greater authority and responsibility, and the positions traditionally filled exclusively by men are becoming more open to women. For example, past assumptions were that males would hold all supervisory positions. This assumption is no longer valid as more and more females are assuming management positions. As women assume higher-level positions, we must examine our assumptions about the way both men and women react in the workforce. For example, one of the fairly common assumptions about women has been that they are more emotional than men. Can we say that such an assumption is categorically true? No, we cannot. People, with different backgrounds and different cultures, react differently to situations, but it is not because they are male or female. The socialization process in various cultures often encourages men and women to develop different traits. For example, if you were born in the United States and are female, you may have been encouraged to express your feelings openly. Males may have been taught to keep their feelings to themselves. Notice that "may have" is used in both sentences.

We cannot say that all females born in the United States have been socialized in this manner. Neither can we say that all males have

been. The point of this entire section is to remind you that we cannot **stereotype** (a perception or an image held of people or things that may be favorable or unfavorable) individuals. We cannot assume that individuals have certain characteristics because of their gender. Your role in the workplace is to be aware that stereotyping can occur and not to let your attitudes or decisions be based on these stereotypes. *Your focus must be on understanding and accepting differences.*

Increased Education

Due to our ever-increasing technological world, the level of education for jobs is higher than in the past. Numerous employers require an associate degree, while others require a bachelor's degree. Education is essential in getting a job, and ongoing education is a must in keeping a job. Lifelong learning is necessary for all individuals who expect to remain productive workers. This education does not always have to take a formal route (attendance at a technical/community college or a university), although a formal education may be necessary. However, informal education through reading, attending seminars and conferences, and being active in professional organizations is essential for maintaining and improving the knowledge and skills needed as work responsibilities change.

The level of education needed for jobs is increasing.

A Changing Work Environment

Our work environment is constantly changing in numerous ways. Increasingly, there is a globalization of our economy. Mergers, both national and international, are commonplace today. Telework is growing, with the expectation that it will continue to grow rapidly in the future. Companies are placing an increased emphasis on using teams of people to deliver quality products and services. The traditional workweek is changing, and temporary employees are becoming more and more a part of the workforce environment.

Globalization of the Economy

You merely have to pick up a newspaper, read a business magazine, or listen to the news on television to see and hear the many references to our global economy. If you follow the stock market, you hear references to downturns and upturns in the market in Europe and Asia and the interrelatedness of the markets to the U.S. market. Go into an American electronic store, and you notice the number of products that are manufactured in Asia. Look at the labels on

© PhotoDisc, Inc.

Our American economy is a global one.

your clothes and shoes, and you become aware of the number of articles that are made outside the United States. Observe the automobiles that we drive, and you will notice the cars that are made by international firms. We also have a huge number of foreign investors in the United States. In fact, when the stock market takes a downward turn in the United States, you hear financial experts expressing concern that foreign investors may take their money out of the United States, thus impacting the stock market even more. Virtually everyone is affected by the rapid globalization of the world economy. It is estimated that 73 million people in today's global workforce work for foreign owners. This continued movement toward a global workforce merely increases the need to not only understand but also effectively handle cultural differences in the workforce.

Merger Mania

Although corporate mergers are not new, they have grown enormously since the late 1970s. These mergers are both national and international. One of the large international mergers was Chrysler (one of the big three of the U.S. automobile industry) with Daimler-Benz in 1998. In early 2001, America Online merged with Time Warner (a $165 billion transaction) for the largest merger in the United States to that point. The combined valuation of the two companies at the time of the merger was approximately $290 billion. All indications are that these kinds of mergers will continue in the foreseeable future. Many industries, both national and international, remain highly fragmented. It is anticipated that the increasing pressure to globalize markets will result in increased multinational mergers and larger and larger multinational corporations. These international mergers demand an in-depth understanding of global issues and cultures.

Quality Focus

Whether the organization is national or international, its effectiveness and long life depends on the production of a quality product or service. Workforce teams have become an important part of producing quality work based on the concepts of Dr. W. Edwards Deming, an American statistician who developed the quality concept. He first introduced his concepts to businesses in the United States but failed to receive their support. In the 1950s, he took his concepts to Japan, where industrialists received him and his ideas enthusiastically. Significant productivity results began to emerge in Japanese industries. In fact, Japan began to surpass the United States in certain areas of production; e.g., technology and cars. As a result, American businesses began to pay attention to the processes being used in Japan and began to apply Deming's principles in their firms. Deming's concepts stressed the principle of continued improvement through **total quality management (TQM).** This approach is also referred to as **continuous quality improvement (CQI).** Deming's 14 principles are listed in Figure 1-1.

How does TQM affect the administrative professional? How does it change your work? Here are some possibilities. You may find that you are

- More involved in decisions that affect the direction of the organization
- Part of a workforce team (perhaps even leading a team) that is responsible for improving a service or product
- Expected to be a productive member of a team, making unique contributions that

PRINCIPLES FOR AMERICAN MANAGEMENT

W. Edwards Deming

1. Create constancy of purpose toward improvement of product and service, with the aim to become competitive and to stay in business and to provide jobs.
2. Adopt a new philosophy. We are in a new economic age. Western management must awaken to the challenge, must learn their responsibilities and take on leadership for change.
3. Cease dependence on inspection to achieve quality. Eliminate a need for inspection on a mass basis by building quality into the product in the first place.
4. End the practice of awarding business on the basis of price tag. Instead minimize the total cost. Move toward a single supplier for any one item, on a long term relationship of loyalty and trust.
5. Improve constantly and forever the system of production and service, to improve quality and productivity, and thus constantly decrease costs.
6. Institute training on the job.
7. Institute leadership. The aim of leadership should be to help people and machines and gadgets to do a better job. Leadership of management is in need of overhaul, as well as leadership of production workers.
8. Drive out fear so that everyone may work effectively for the company.
9. Break down barriers between departments. People in research, design, sales, and production must work as a team, to foresee problems of production and use that may be encountered with the product or service.
10. Eliminate slogans, exhortations, and targets for the workforce, asking for zero defects and new levels of productivity.
11. Eliminate work standards on the factory floor. Substitute leadership. Eliminate management by objective. Eliminate management by numbers, numerical goals, substitute leadership.
12. Remove barriers that rob the hourly worker of his pride of workmanship. The responsibility of the supervisor must be changed from sheer numbers to quality. Remove barriers that rob people in management and engineering of their right to pride of workmanship. This means, among other things, abolishment of the annual or merit rating and of management by objective, management by numbers.
13. Institute a vigorous program of education and self-improvement.
14. Put everyone in the company to work to accomplish the transformation. The transformation is everyone's job.

Figure 1-1

Excerpted from *Out of the Crisis,* Massachusetts: Massachusetts Institute of Technology, 1993.

assist the company in improving the quality of its goods and services

■ More involved in helping to solve the problems of the organization

Downsizing

Downsizing, reducing the number of full-time employees in an organization, has become a large corporate movement. You merely have to be aware of newspaper headlines to notice this trend. Local newspapers carry downsizing stories of the area's corporations, and *The Wall Street Journal*® carries stories reflecting the national movement. Many major companies (such as General Motors®, Xerox®, and IBM) have downsized their companies in the last few years. There are two major reasons for downsizing—streamlining an organization so that it is more manageable and cutting **overhead costs** (salary and benefit costs). An employee can no longer assume that an organization is committed to lifetime employment.

Outsourcing

Outsourcing, utilizing an outside company or a consultant to take over the performance of a particular part of an organization's business or to complete a project, is a cost-cutting measure being used extensively today. For example, an outside computer firm may be hired to perform the computer operations of a company. This approach can save the organization money in salary dollars and benefits often granted to employees, such as health insurance and retirement options.

A number of organizations use the assistance of temporary agencies. These temporary agencies supply the business with various types of temporary help, including accounting assistants, administrative assistants, and human resources assistants. Statistics show that twice as many temporary workers are employed by organizations today as in the past.

Telework

Today many workers have traded in the traditional work environment for telework, work that can be performed at any place and at any

Technology Tip:
To keep current on telework trends, browse the Web for recent information and read periodicals such as *PC Magazine* and *Home Computing.*

time using technology. The telecommuting-to-work lifestyle is here to stay. It is projected that by the year 2005, there will be 30 million teleworkers in the United States.

The concept started several years ago as **telecommuting,** working from home or another established location via computer hookup. Today work can be performed using cellular phones, fax machines, modems, voice mail, email, laptop and hand-held computers, and so on. Job interviews can even be held through telecommuting centers with the interviewer, for example, being in China and the interviewee being in Michigan. Today telework is the word most frequently used. Telework is a broad term that means using telecommunications to work from a home office, a client's office, or a multitude of other locations. Telecommuting today refers to those individuals who are full- or part-time employees of an organization and work from home for part or all of the workweek. Also, **remote employment** (any working arrangement in which the worker performs a significant portion of work at some fixed location other than the traditional

© PhotoDisc, Inc.

Telework can be performed from virtually anywhere at any time using technology.

workplace) and the **virtual office** (the operational domain of any organization that includes remote workers) are terms used in describing the concept of work that is done through technology where an individual is physically present in one location and virtually present in another. You will learn more about telework in Chapter 3.

The Workweek

As you have already learned, the workplace may be the traditional office, the home office, or any number of other locations. Just as the workplace has changed, so has the workday. The workday may be nine-to-five or it may involve flexible hours. In addition to the flexible workday, the workweek may be compressed, may involve flextime, or may involve job sharing with another individual.

With a **compressed workweek,** employees work the usual number of hours (35 to 40); however, the hours are compressed into four days. For example, a 35-hour week consists of three days of nine hours each and a fourth day of eight hours.

Another departure from the workday is the **flextime** approach (the staggering of working hours to enable an employee to work the full quota of time but at periods defined by the company and the individual). Flextime helps to reduce traffic congestion at the traditional peak hours and allows employees needed flexibility in their schedules.

Still another departure from the traditional workday is **job sharing.** Under this arrangement, two part-time employees perform a job that otherwise would be held by one full-time employee. Such a plan may be suitable for a mother or father with small children or workers who want to ease into retirement.

THE ADMINISTRATIVE PROFESSIONAL'S ROLE AND RESPONSIBILITIES

With the availability of technology and the emphasis on greater efficiency and productivity through **flattened organizational structures**

(fewer management levels than the traditional structures of the past) and teams, administrative professionals of today and tomorrow will find that their role is continually shifting. With this shifting role generally comes greater responsibility.

The Shifting Role

For years the administrative professional's title was confined to secretary, receptionist, and such specialized titles as legal and medical secretaries. Although the titles mentioned here are still used to a limited extent, the emerging titles today reflect the shifting role of the administrative professional. A few of these titles are administrative assistant, executive assistant, marketing assistant, payroll assistant, human resources assistant, and office manager. The shifting role is reflected in the duties of the administrative professional, which include:

- Researching and preparing reports (using the Web, as well as traditional research methods) complete with graphics and spreadsheets
- Assisting with the planning and direction of the company through leading TQM teams and working on organizational teams
- Supervising support staff

© PhotoDisc, Inc.

The administrative professional today may have the responsibility of managing a Website.

- Administering computer networks
- Helping to upgrade and recommend office software
- Providing computer and software training
- Managing Websites
- Working with outsourcing companies such as accounting and staffing firms

Although job roles and responsibilities differ among the various positions, certain skills and knowledge sets are essential in all administrative professional roles. These skills and knowledge sets will be discussed in the next section and emphasized throughout this course.

The term **administrative professional** will be used consistently throughout the text to denote the workplace support person.

Job Responsibilities

As was mentioned in the previous section, the job responsibilities of the administrative professional have increased in complexity and accountability as compared to several years ago. With technology, many executives now answer their own voice mail and email, key certain correspondence directly on the computer, and handle much of their own scheduling using electronic calendars provided with computer software. This change frees the administrative professional to become more involved in creating correspondence and in becoming a valued member of the office team.

Job responsibilities of the administrative professional vary depending on educational level, work experience, and even the initiative of the employee. Figure 1-2 lists some of the basic responsibilities that are fairly generic to all administrative professional positions.

TWENTY-FIRST-CENTURY SKILLS AND QUALITIES

If the administrative professional is to succeed in a world of technology and rapid change, he or she needs certain skills and qualities. You should begin now to develop these skills and qualities.

BASIC JOB RESPONSIBILITIES OF THE ADMINISTRATIVE PROFESSIONAL

- Composing and keying various types of correspondence, including letters, memorandums, and reports
- Researching report information within the defined parameters set by the employer
- Participating in quality teams, with the more experienced administrative professional serving as team leader
- Administering computer networks
- Helping to upgrade and recommend office software
- Providing computer and software training
- Managing Websites
- Working with outsourcing companies such as accounting and staff firms
- Solving day-to-day problems within the role of the administrative professional
- Communicating both verbally and in writing with individuals both within and outside the office
- Scheduling appointments
- Setting up meetings and conferences
- Organizing time and work
- Maintaining correspondence and records in both electronic and manual files
- Making travel arrangements for the executive
- Using telecommunications technology, including the telephone, voice mail, and fax
- Interviewing and making recommendations on the employment of office support personnel
- Supervising office support personnel
- Taking and transcribing minutes from various types of meetings
- Making recommendations on equipment purchases
- Purchasing office supplies
- Handling incoming and outgoing mail
- Processing paperwork that involves mathematical calculations (expense reports, budgets, invoices, purchase orders, petty cash, and so on)

Figure 1-2

Success Skills

In 2000, the National Association of Colleges and Employers (NACE) identified important skills that employers seek in new hires. The top nine skills listed by employers were as follows:

- Interpersonal skills
- Teamwork skills
- Verbal communication skills
- Critical thinking/analytical skills
- Technology/computer skills
- Written communication skills
- Leadership skills
- Time, stress, and organizational management skills
- Verbal presentation skills

The next section covers these skills in detail.

Question #4

Interpersonal Skills

For years, surveys have shown that more employees lose their jobs due to poor interpersonal skills than poor technology skills. As an administrative professional, you come in contact with a number of people. Within the company, you work with co-workers, your supervisor, and other executives. Contacts outside the company include customers and other visitors to your office, all with different backgrounds and experiences. If you are to be effective, you need to understand and accept them and be able to work with them. Interpersonal skills are like most of our other skills. We must constantly develop and improve these skills if we are to grow in our abilities. Take the interpersonal skills Self-Check and compare your answers to the suggested responses at the end of this chapter. Where do you need to improve? Commit now to improving these areas during this course. You will have an opportunity to learn more about the importance of interpersonal skills and to continue to develop your skills throughout this course.

Teamwork Skills

You have learned in this chapter that organizations are using teams more and more in producing work. Obviously, if these teams are to be successful, individual team members must

Homework

Self-Check

Respond to the following comments with a yes or no answer.

		YES	NO
1.	I understand that differences exist in culture, race, and ethnicity.	☐	☐
2.	I respect others' differences in culture, race, and ethnicity.	☐	☐
3.	I expect all individuals to react to situations just as I do.	☐	☐
4.	I listen carefully when others are talking.	☐	☐
5.	I ignore body language when others are talking.	☐	☐
6.	I am conscious of the words I use in my written communications.	☐	☐
7.	I avoid dealing with conflict.	☐	☐
8.	I evaluate individuals when they are talking to me.	☐	☐
9.	I trust people who are older than I am.	☐	☐
10.	Men are better supervisors than women.	☐	☐

possess the ability to work well together. The word **team** can be traced back to the Indo-European word *deuk*, meaning "to pull." Successful teams in the work environment include groups of people who need each other to accomplish a given task. Teamwork skills are very similar to interpersonal skills in that they demand that you understand, accept, and respect the differences among your team members. Teamwork also demands that you engage in the following behaviors:

- Behave courteously to all team members
- Build strong relationships with your team members so the team's goals can be accomplished
- Learn collectively with your team. You must start with self-knowledge and self-mastery, but then you must look outward to develop knowledge and alignment with your team members
- Take responsibility for producing high-quality work as an individual team member and encouraging a high-quality team project

Verbal Communication Skills

If you are to be an effective verbal communicator, you must be able to express yourself accurately, concisely, and tactfully. Additionally, you must be a good listener. Although most of us think we spend an inordinate amount of time listening, research studies show that we only listen with 25 to 50 percent efficiency. In other words, 50 to 75 percent of what we hear is never processed. Moreover, even when we do process what we hear, we may not grasp the full implication of what has been said. As you have already discovered, the office continues to become more diverse in the ethnicity, gender, and age of the workforce. This diversity demands your constant improvement in verbal communication so you can effectively work with a diverse group of people. You will learn more about verbal communication in Chapter 2.

© PhotoDisc, Inc.

The administrative professional must have excellent verbal communication skills.

Critical-Thinking Skills

Critical thinking can be defined as "a unique kind of purposeful thinking in which the thinker systematically chooses conscious and deliberate inquiry." Critical comes from the Greek word **krinein,** which means "to separate, to choose." When we think critically about a subject, we try to see it from all sides before coming to a conclusion. Critical thinking requires us to see things from perspectives other than our own and to consider the possible consequences of the positions we take. Critical thinking is considered a **soft skill** (a business-related nontechnical skill). Other soft skills you have been introduced to in 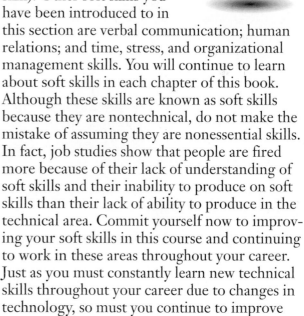 this section are verbal communication; human relations; and time, stress, and organizational management skills. You will continue to learn about soft skills in each chapter of this book. Although these skills are known as soft skills because they are nontechnical, do not make the mistake of assuming they are nonessential skills. In fact, job studies show that people are fired more because of their lack of understanding of soft skills and their inability to produce on soft skills than their lack of ability to produce in the technical area. Commit yourself now to improving your soft skills in this course and continuing to work in these areas throughout your career. Just as you must constantly learn new technical skills throughout your career due to changes in technology, so must you continue to improve your soft skills.

In each chapter throughout the course, a soft skill is emphasized. Soft skills are identified in two ways. In the Learning Objectives at the beginning of the chapter, the soft skill is italicized. Did you notice that Develop critical thinking skills is italicized in the Learning Objectives for this chapter? Within each chapter, soft skills are identified by the soft skill icon 🕎. This icon will serve to remind you of the importance of soft skills and the need for you to concentrate on developing them.

If you are to succeed in the complex world of the twenty-first century, you must be able to think critically about the day-to-day decisions you make in the workplace. The Critical-

Thinking Activities and Projects in the course require that you demonstrate your continual growth in critical thinking. At the end of each chapter, a workplace situation is given in the Critical-Thinking Activity. You will be asked to critically analyze the activity and determine how it should be handled, using a critical-thinking approach. To help you understand more about how critical thinking is approached, read the list of questions in Figure 1-3. You should ask yourself these questions when you are attempting to critically analyze an issue.

Technology/Computer Skills

Success today demands that you be technologically competent. You must be

- Proficient on a computer
- Knowledgeable about the most current software packages, including word processing, spreadsheets, databases, graphics, and presentation software
- Competent in using telecommunications equipment
- Competent in using printers/copiers
- Willing to continually learn new workforce technology

Chapters 4, 5, and 6 will help you continue to develop these important skills.

Human Relations Tip:
Commit to learning something new every day. Constantly set new goals for yourself.

Written Communication Skills

Administrative professionals spend a majority of their time communicating with others. Such communication may be in written form, such as letters, memorandums, reports, email, and faxes. Written communication skills implies that you have a mastery of the English language. The administrative professional must be able to apply the rules of grammar, punctuation, and capitalization. Many times the employer expects the administrative professional to be the English expert, relying on the professional to correct any grammatical errors that the employer may make.

Software packages today identify incorrectly spelled words and grammar errors as you are keying by underscoring the errors in color, with red used to identify spelling errors and green used to identify grammar errors. Although this function is an extremely helpful aid, you should recheck the entire document using the spell and grammar check program once you have finished keying.

The spell checker does have limitations. For example, if you key *off* when you actually mean *of*, the spell checker will not identify the error because the word is not spelled incorrectly. This means that you must be an extremely good proofreader even with the tools that are provided on your computer software. Take the time to proofread thoroughly and carefully each document you produce.

Also included in your software package "tools" are readability statistics that give you the following information on the document you have keyed:

- Number of paragraphs
- Sentences per paragraph

- Words per sentence
- Readability statistics, including passive sentences and the Flesch-Kincaid readability level of the document

These statistics are helpful in knowing how easy or difficult your document will be to read. For a general audience, you usually need to write at the eighth- to tenth-grade level. However, if you are writing technical material for a highly educated audience, you may write at the twelfth-grade level or above. You will learn more about written communication skills in Chapter 9.

Leadership Skills

Leadership skills are developed over time. They are not something that we automatically have at birth. You begin to develop your leadership skills by seeking out and/or accepting leadership opportunities. For example, accepting the chairperson position of a committee helps you develop leadership skills. Accepting an office in one of your college organizations or in a professional organization to which you belong helps you develop leadership skills. The essential strategy for you to remember is to look for leadership opportunities and take advantage of each one. As you pursue and are granted certain leadership opportunities, learn from each one. Evaluate yourself or ask a close friend to evaluate your performance. What mistakes did you make? How can you correct your mistakes?

As you are promoted to higher-level positions, you may also have the responsibility of supervising one or more employees. Being an effective supervisor, one who is able to inspire people to produce at their maximum, demands that you understand and apply effective leadership and management principles. Chapter 15 will help you learn and apply these skills.

Time, Stress, and Organizational Management Skills

As an efficient administrative professional, you must be able to organize your time, your workload, and your stress. You must be able to establish priorities, determining what needs to be done first. You must organize your workstation and files, whether they are paper or electronic. You must organize your time so your work flows smoothly and tasks are finished as needed. Chapter 8 will help you understand more about these important skills and give you a chance to practice them.

Verbal Presentation Skills

Administrative professionals today serve on project teams and may even chair a team. These project teams often make presentations of their findings and recommendations to peer groups or to executives within the workplace. You may also have occasion to speak at professional organizations to which you belong. If your presentations are to be successful, you must develop verbal presentation skills. Chapter 10 will help you develop these skills.

Success Qualities

In addition to the skills that have been identified, there are certain qualities that are essential for the success of the administrative professional. These qualities include openness to change, dependability, confidentiality, integrity/honesty, initiative/motivation, and flexibility/adaptability.

Openness to Change

Since change will continue to play such an important role in the workplace, you must learn to cope with change as well as embrace it. Embracing change means accepting and preparing for change and being creative and flexible. Try to predict the changes you will face, and prepare yourself for them. For example, since you know technology will continue to play an important role in the workplace, keep current on the latest technological changes that might impact your workplace.

Follow these steps in dealing effectively with change.

- Understand why change is necessary. Determine what circumstances have occurred that have necessitated change.
- Determine what objectives will be achieved by the changes that are proposed.
- Establish guidelines for achieving those objectives.

- Determine the benefits or rewards that will occur as a result of the change.
- Once the change has occurred, evaluate the effectiveness of the change and your effectiveness in working through the change.

Figure 1-4

Be creative when dealing with change. **Creativity** is the ability to approach existing ideas or things in new ways. When a change occurs, you can usually connect that change to some already existing idea or way of doing something. Review the steps listed in Figure 1-4 to help you understand how to deal with change.

Dependability

Dependability means being trustworthy. It means being at work on time if you are working at an established location. If you are engaged in telework, it means being productive in performing your job. Dependability is the willingness to put in additional time on important assignments. It also means doing what you say you will do and when you say you will do it.

Confidentiality

As an administrative professional, you have access to information that is extremely confidential. For example, if you are working in the personnel department of an organization, you have access to information about employees—their work history, performance evaluations, salaries, ages, and so on. If you work for a criminal attorney, you may have access to information about a client's case. If you work for an MD, you may have access to patients' files containing highly personal and confidential information about health issues. Your employer may occasionally talk with you about information that is highly confidential—perhaps a merger with another company that is pending. You may also overhear confidential conversations between executives. You must always maintain

the **confidentiality** (secrecy) of the information received or the confidences shared. To let any confidential information leak outside your office may cause irreparable damage to your employer, to others within your organization, to customers, and to your organization.

Integrity/Honesty

Integrity is defined as "the adherence to a code of behavior." In the workplace environment, the code of behavior means in part that you are honest. It means you do not take equipment or supplies that belong to the company for your own personal use. It means you spend your time on the job performing the duties of the job—not making and receiving personal phone calls or writing personal emails. It means you uphold high standards of ethical behavior. You do not engage in activities in which your morals or values may be questioned.

Initiative/Motivation

Initiative is defined as "the ability to begin and follow through on a plan or task." Initiative is taking the tasks you are given and completing them in an appropriate manner. It means having the ability to set appropriate work goals for yourself. The most highly valued administrative professional has the ability to analyze a task, establish priorities, and see the work through to completion. The professional takes the initiative to make suggestions to the employer about needed changes or revisions and is truly worth his or her weight in gold.

Motivation is closely related to initiative. Motivation means that someone is provided with an incentive to act—a move to action. In taking the initiative to begin a task, you may be motivated **extrinsically** (from outside) or **intrinsically** (from within). For example, you may be motivated to perform a task because it provides a monetary reward for you or external recognition from your supervisor. Additionally, you may be motivated to perform a task because you are committed to learning and growing. You understand that each task you perform provides you the opportunity to learn something new.

Flexibility/Adaptability

Flexibility is being responsive to change. **Adaptability** is being capable of adjusting. As you can readily determine, the two terms are closely related. In our fast-paced global and technology-driven world, we must respond and adjust to the changes that are constantly occurring not only in our work world but also in our personal life. You learned earlier in this chapter about the importance of being able to work with a diverse workforce. You also learned that mergers, downsizing, outsourcing, and telework can and often do make our work environment very different from the work environment of the past. All of these changes demand your flexibility and adaptability.

A PROFESSIONAL IMAGE

The administrative professional with a professional image constantly presents to the public the essential skills and success qualities discussed in the previous sections. In addition, the administrative professional must present a positive personal appearance. He or she dresses in appropriate business attire and is well groomed. The administrative professional pays attention to hairstyle, personal hygiene, appropriate jewelry and accessories, physical condition, good posture, and proper eating habits. Depending on the office, appropriate business attire may include a suit and tie for males and a suit or dress for females. Some workplaces may be more relaxed, allowing shirts without a tie for males and skirts or slacks and blouses or sweaters for females. A number of workplaces

© PhotoDisc, Inc.
The administrative professional dresses in appropriate business attire and is always well groomed.

have a day once a month or even once a week when casual dress is appropriate, even if the remaining days are considered standard business attire. Some organizations allow employees to dress in business casual on a daily basis. Many organizations are becoming more casual in their dress considerations than in the past. If you are uncertain about the appropriate dress style in your organization, notice how respected people in the organization dress. You can generally follow their lead.

A professional image is more than dressing appropriately, however. A positive personal appearance without the necessary skills and qualities is meaningless. If the administrative professional expects to succeed, he or she must combine the necessary skills and qualities with an appropriate personal appearance. A professional image is a combination of all of these areas.

PROFESSIONAL GROWTH

In our constantly changing world, you must be willing to continue your professional growth. This professional growth can be through

- Attending classes at a college or university
- Attending seminars and workshops provided by your company or outside firms
- Reading business periodicals
- Participating in professional organizations

Figure 1-5

Periodicals

Numerous periodicals are available with articles to assist you in enhancing your knowledge and skills. Several of these periodicals are listed in Figure 1-5. Begin now to become familiar with them by reading selected articles. Visit your school or local library to see what periodicals on this list are available.

Professional Organizations

Listed here are several professional organizations that provide growth opportunities for the administrative professional.

- IAAP (International Association of Administrative Professionals)—This organization is the world's largest association for administrative support staff, with nearly 700 chapters and 40,000 members and affiliates worldwide. IAAP administers certification programs for entry-level and advanced skills. The entry-level skills program is available through the Office Proficiency Assessment and Certification program. The advanced-level certification program awards the CPS (Certified Professional Secretary) designation on the successful passage of the exam plus the required work experience. The letters *CPS* after an administrative professional's name are indicative of the achievement of the highest professional standard within the field. Figure 1-6 gives more details about this certification. IAAP publishes a magazine called *OfficePro*. The Web address for IAAP is www.iaap-hq.org.

- National Association of Legal Secretaries (NALS) and Legal Secretaries International—NALS sponsors an Accredited Legal Secretary (ALS) examination and certification program administered by the Certifying Board of the National Association of Legal Secretaries. This organization also administers an examination to certify a legal secretary with three years of experience as a Professional Legal Secretary (PLS). Legal Secretaries International confers the designation Board Certified Civil Trial Legal Secretary in specialized areas such as litigation, real estate, probate, and corporation to individuals who have five years of law-related experience and pass the exam. The Web address for NALS is www.nals.org; the Web address for Legal Secretaries International is www.legalsecretaries.org.

- American Association for Medical Transcription (AAMT)—This organization is for office staff, assistants, and technicians employed by physicians or hospitals. It sponsors a certification program, Certified Medical Transcriptionist (CMT), and publishes a magazine called the *Journal of the American Association for Medical Transcription*. The Web address for the American Association for Medical Transcription is www.aamt.org.

- National Association of Education Office Professionals (NAEOP)—NAEOP (at www.naeop.org) sponsors a program that issues certificates based on education, experience, and professional activity. It also publishes *National Educational Secretary*.

- ARMA International, the Association for Information Management Professionals—This association sponsors the Certified Records Manager (CRM) designation. It publishes *The Information Management Journal*. Their Web address is www.arma.org.

THE CERTIFIED PROFESSIONAL SECRETARY

WHY CERTIFICATION?	**Job Advancement**—The CPS rating gives you a competitive edge for promotion and hiring.
	Professional Skills—You will learn more about office operations and build your skills by studying for and taking the CPS exam.
	Salary—An IAAP Membership Profile study shows that CPS holders earn an average of $2,228 more per year than those who do not have certification.
	Esteem—Attaining the CPS certification demonstrates to your employer and yourself that you are committed as a professional.
	College Credit—Many colleges and universities offer course credit for passing the CPS exam.
WHO IS ELIGIBLE?	You may take the CPS exam if you are employed as an administrative professional or have at least two years of work experience as an administrative professional, varying according to your level of college education. Students or teachers in a college business education program also may qualify.
WHEN AND WHERE IS THE EXAM GIVEN?	The CPS examination is a one-day exam, administered each May and November at over 250 locations across the United States, Canada, and other countries.
WHAT ARE THE PARTS OF THE EXAM?	The exam has three parts: ■ Finance and Business Law ■ Office Systems and Administration ■ Management

Figure 1-6

Excerpted from www.iaap-hq.org/cps/

COMPANY SCENE

Throughout this course, you will be working for AmeriAsian Airlines, 5519 Reeds Parkway, Grand Rapids, MI 49509-3295. AmeriAsian is the result of a merger in March 2000 between AmeriAir, founded in 1970 in Grand Rapids, Michigan, with only 30 employees, and China Airlines, founded in 1975 in Beijing, China, with 40 employees. Presently China is the world's third largest aviation market, after the United States and Japan, with airline traffic growing by 20 percent per year. Before their merger, AmeriAir had grown to the fourth largest airline in the United States, garnering 11.7 percent of the market. China Airlines had grown to the second largest airline in China, with 30 percent of the market. AmeriAsian Airlines now employs over 39,000 people. The U.S. hub office is located in Grand Rapids at the address given above. The China hub is located in Beijing. Net earnings this past year for the combined company were $5.6 billion, a slight drop in net earnings from the combined net earnings of both companies before the merger in 2000. AmeriAsian is listed on the New York Stock Exchange and currently lists for $62 per share of common stock. AmeriAsian is presently developing strategies to increase its overall market share by decreasing labor costs, increasing its on-time performance, lowering ground-handling costs, and providing certain incentives. The company is looking at adding a frequent flyer program for the China operation and improved in-flight customer service for the total company.

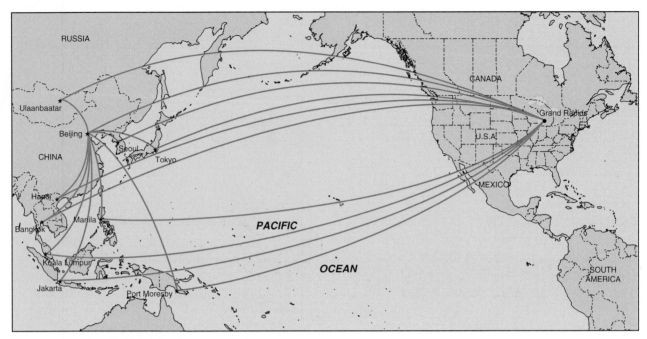

Figure 1-7   AmeriAsian Flight Hubs and Flight Patterns

Your job title is executive assistant. You report directly to Martin Albertson, Vice President of Corporate Marketing and Communications in Grand Rapids. Since the merger, executives in both companies have been discussing how they might assume more social responsibility in the hub office cities. They intend to take an active role in the educational, environmental, and social concerns of the community, both in the United States and China. Before the merger, each community saw the airline as a good corporate citizen. Executives want to assure that their companies remain respected corporate citizens. Although their profitability picture has been good since the merger, there has been a slight downturn. As a result, the Grand Rapids hub has laid off 50 employees in the corporate office. The result has been a slight morale problem. However, steps have been taken to make the employees feel more a part of the decision making through TQM.

Your duties are extremely varied. They include assisting Martin Albertson with setting up meetings with government and educational leaders within the local communities to determine issues of common concern. At one point, you traveled to China with your employer and two other support staff to help set up a community conference there. This is the only time you have traveled outside the company; however, you do communicate frequently with China through fax, email, and computer conferencing. Other duties include the following:

- Researching and preparing all types of correspondence
- Participating in TQM teams
- Organizing your employer's schedule
- Scheduling meetings
- Making travel arrangements
- Handling the mail
- Filing correspondence
- Supervising two assistants

You have two assistants that report to you—Juan Mercado (who has been working for AmeriAsian Airlines for slightly over a year) and Luyin Wu (who has been working for AmeriAsian Airlines for six months).

CHAPTER SUMMARY

The summary will help you remember the important points covered in the chapter.

- The workforce of the twenty-first century will (1) be more diverse than ever before, (2) be more global than in the past, with both national and international mergers continuing at a rapid pace, (3) have state-of-the-art technology, with e-commerce expanding rapidly, and (4) have a large percentage of the workforce engaged in telework.

- It is projected that by 2050 the distribution of our total population will change dramatically, with whites making up only 52.8 percent of the population; African Americans, 13.2 percent; Hispanics, 24.3 percent; Asians and Pacific Islanders, 9.3 percent; and American Indians, .8 percent.

- Women will continue to be a growing part of the workforce; they will occupy diverse positions in the workforce, including all levels of management.

- The workforce will be older, with workers 45 and older expected to increase from 33 to 40 percent of the labor force between 1998 and 2008. Many people will work longer than the traditional retirement age of 65, working until they are seventy or eighty.

- As you work in the diverse office, you need to be aware of and sensitive to the various cultural differences and backgrounds.

- We cannot assume that women and men react differently to situations because of their gender.

- Age differences may mean that we view the world from different perspectives.

- The level of education for jobs is increasing, with the requirement for an associate degree growing faster than all other levels of education.

- The quality concept developed by W. Edwards Deming is now used by numerous American businesses in an effort to improve quality and productivity. As a result of this emphasis, employees now operate in teams more often than in the past.

- Downsizing and outsourcing are two methods used to cut organizational costs.

- Temporary employees are used extensively to get the work of the organization done as economically as possible in an extremely competitive world.

- Today a number of workers have traded in the traditional office environment for a telework environment—one in which work may be done at any time and in any place.

- Workweeks today may be flexible, with hours varying from the traditional eight- or nine-to-five workday. The compressed workweek, flextime, and job sharing are all examples of flexible workweeks.

- The administrative professional's role is shifting due to technology, with duties that include researching and preparing reports complete with graphics and spreadsheets, assisting with the planning and direction of the company through TQM teams (and even leading these teams), supervising support staff, administering computer networks, helping to upgrade and recommend office software, providing computer and software training, managing Websites, and working in a liaison capacity with outsourcing companies such as accounting and staffing firms.

- The administrative professional needs these skills: interpersonal skills; teamwork skills; verbal communication skills; critical thinking; technology/computer skills; written communication skills; leadership skills; time, stress, and organizational management skills; and verbal presentation skills.

- The administrative professional must develop these qualities: openness to change, dependability, confidentiality, integrity/honesty, initiative/motivation, and flexibility/adaptability.

- A total professional image (including knowledge, skills, qualities and personal appearance) is essential for success.

- Professional growth can occur through attending classes or seminars/workshops, reading business periodicals, and participating in professional organizations.

CHAPTER GLOSSARY

The following terms were introduced in this chapter. Definitions are provided to help you review the terms.

- **Multinational corporations** (p. 7)—corporations that operate both within and outside the United States.
- **Merger mania** (p. 7)—mergers between business that occur nationally and internationally at rates higher than normal.
- **State-of-the-art technology** (p. 7)—the latest technology available.
- **E-commerce** (p. 7)—businesses that operate on the Internet.
- **Telework** (p. 7)—work that can be performed anywhere at any time using technology.
- **Information Age** (p. 7)—an age when there has been a great explosion of knowledge, due mainly to the technological revolution.
- **Palm organizers** (p. 8)—small handheld computers that allow us to make frequent changes and additions to our calendar from any location, pick up our email, store our phone numbers, download information from the Web, check our stock portfolios, and perform a number of other functions.
- **Telework environment** (p. 8)—work that is done outside the traditional workplace through the use of electronic equipment.
- **Multiculturalism** (p. 9)—relating to or including several cultures.
- **Culture** (p. 9)—the ideas, customs, values, skills, and arts of a specific group of people.
- **Stereotype** (p. 10)—a perception or an image held of people or things that may be favorable or unfavorable.
- **Total quality management (TQM)** or **continuous quality improvement (CQI)** (p. 12)—emphasizes continued improvement of both goods and services through team approaches within a business.
- **Downsizing** (p. 13)—reducing the number of full-time employees in an organization.
- **Overhead costs** (p. 13)—salary and benefit costs.
- **Outsourcing** (p. 13)—utilizing an outside company or a consultant to take over the performance of a particular part of an organization's business or to complete a project.
- **Telecommuting** (p. 13)—working from home or another established location via computer hookup.

- **Remote employment** (p. 13)—any working arrangement in which the worker performs a significant portion of work at some fixed location other than the employer's office.
- **Virtual office** (p. 14)—the operational domain of any organization that includes remote workers.
- **Compressed workweek** (p. 14)—regular workweek hours compressed into four days.
- **Flextime** (p. 14)—the staggering of working hours to enable an employee to work the full quota of time but at periods defined by the company and the individual.
- **Job sharing** (p. 14)—two part-time employees performing a job that otherwise would be held by one full-time employee.
- **Flattened organizational structures** (p. 14)—fewer management levels than the traditional organizational structures of the past.
- **Administrative professional** (p. 15)—a term used to denote a workplace support position. In this text, it is used as a means of clarifying the position.
- **Team** (p. 16)—Comes from the Indo-European word *deuk* meaning "to pull." Teams are people who pull together to perform a task.
- **Critical thinking** (p. 17)—a unique kind of purposeful thinking in which the thinker systematically chooses conscious and deliberate inquiry.
- **Krinein** (p. 17)—the Greek word meaning "to separate or choose."
- **Soft skill** (p. 17)—a business-related nontechnical skill.
- **Creativity** (p. 20)—the ability to approach existing ideas or things in new ways.
- **Dependability** (p. 20)—trustworthy.
- **Confidentiality** (p. 20)—secrecy.
- **Integrity** (p. 20)—the adherence to a code of behavior.
- **Initiative** (p. 20)—the ability to begin and follow through on a plan or task.
- **Motivation** (p. 20)—provided with an incentive to act, a move to action.
- **Extrinsically** (p. 21)—motivation from outside.
- **Intrinsically** (p. 21)—motivation from within.
- **Flexibility** (p. 21)—being responsive to change.
- **Adaptability** (p. 21)—being capable of adjusting.

DISCUSSION ITEMS Homework

These discussion items provide an opportunity to test your understanding of the chapter through written responses and/or discussion with your classmates and your instructor.

1. Explain how the work environment of the future will be more diverse. What does this diversity suggest for you as a future employee?
2. How is our work environment changing?
3. Where is the workplace of the twenty-first century? In your response, explain what is meant by telework.
4. How is the administrative professional's role changing?
5. What skills are needed in the twenty-first century? In your response, explain the meaning of each skill.

CRITICAL-THINKING ACTIVITY

AmeriAsian Airlines has introduced TQM in an effort to improve quality and productivity. You were asked to be part of a team that looks at the improvement of internal communication, and you took the assignment seriously. Before the first meeting, you had identified several communication problems that seem to be ongoing in the organization. You brought these communication problems up at the meeting; i.e., failure to respond to email (electronic mail) promptly, failure to respond to voice mail, and airline ticket customers who have long waits when attempting to buy tickets by phone. Two of the individuals who work in your department became upset with you. They assumed that your statements referred to situations you had encountered with them. They exploded in the meeting, making these comments:

I can't answer the email you send me within the hour. Get off my back.

The next time you have a complaint about me, talk with me personally.

The manager in charge of the airline ticket sales department asked exactly what you meant by "long waits" with airline customers attempting to buy tickets. He did not seem upset but was merely asking for clarification of your comment.

You let the two individuals in your department know that you were not talking about individual cases. You were attempting to identify problems that needed to be

addressed so the customer might be better served. You answered the manager's question with "I don't know the exact length of time; I have just heard complaints." Since the meeting did not get off to a good start, you feel responsible. You want to be a contributor to the process. What should you do? Think through the following items and prepare responses.

- What is the problem?
- Do the upset employees have cause to be concerned about your behavior?
- Should you talk to these employees before the next meeting? If so, what should you say?
- Did you have enough information about the customer ticket issue to bring it up? How should you handle this type of issue in the future?
- How should you identify problems/issues that are negatively affecting office communication?
- How can you present problems/issues at the next meeting without causing the volatility of the last meeting?

Remember, your task is to critically analyze the situation given here. Before you attempt to answer the questions, review Figure 1-4 on page 20 of your text. Additionally, study the information given on page 28 on thinking and analyzing situations critically.

CRITICAL THINKING

Critical thinking is a unique kind of purposeful thinking in which the thinker systematically and habitually

- Imposes criteria and intellectual standards upon the thinking
- Takes charge of the construction of thinking
- Guides the constructions of the thinking according to the standards
- Assesses the effectiveness of the thinking according to the purpose, the criteria, and the standards

QUESTIONS TO ASK:

- Is this belief defensible or indefensible? What is the basis for this belief?
- Is my position on this issue reasonable and rational?

- Am I willing to deal with complexity, or do I retreat into simple stereotypes to avoid it?
- Is it appropriate and wise to assume that my ideas and beliefs are accurate, clear, and reasonable if I have not tested them?
- Do I ever enter sympathetically into points of view that are very different from my own, or do I just assume that I am right?
- Do I know how to question my own ideas and to test them?[11]

RESPONSES TO SELF-CHECK

The most appropriate answers are as follows:

1.	Yes	**3.**	No	**5.**	No	**7.**	No	**9.**	Yes
2.	Yes	**4.**	Yes	**6.**	Yes	**8.**	No	**10.**	No

PROJECTS

Project 1-1 (Objective 1)
Online Project

Browse the Web for the following information:

- Articles on the changing office. At the IAAP Website (www.iaap-hq.org), check the *OfficePro* magazine for articles.
- Determine the diversity statistics in your state as reported by the United States Census 2000; here is a Web address you can use: www.census.gov/dmd/www/2Kresult.html.

Prepare a short summary of the articles, giving the Web addresses; submit your summaries to your instructor.

Project 1-2 (Objectives 2 and 3)
Collaborative Project

In teams of two or three, interview two administrative professionals. You do not have to interview these people in person; you may choose to do it by email. Ask them the following questions:

- What are your roles and responsibilities?
- What skills and qualities do you need in order to be successful?
- What types of technology changes have occurred in your organization in the last five years? two years?
- Describe the diversity of personnel within your organization. Have there been any issues in dealing with this diversity? If so, what were those issues and how were they handled?

Report your findings verbally to the class.

---

[11]Richard Paul, *Critical Thinking: How to Prepare Students for a Rapidly Changing World* (California: Foundation for Critical Thinking, 1993), 17–36.

Project 1-3 (Objective 4)

Begin the development of a Professional Growth Plan, which you will add to in each chapter. This plan should identify the periodicals you will read and/or the professional activities you will attend. For example, you might decide to attend two meetings of your local chapter of IAAP or some other professional organization. Prepare this plan and save it on a disk under "Progro1-4." You will be adding to this disk throughout the course. This portion of your Professional Growth Plan is to be titled "Improving My Knowledge of Today's Business World." You will be asked at the end of the course whether you accomplished the items listed on your professional growth plan.

Project 1-4 (Objective 5)

Read the Critical-Thinking Activity at the end of this chapter, page 27, and respond to the items at the end of the activity. Submit your responses to your instructor.

ENGLISH USAGE CHALLENGE DRILL

Correct the following sentences. Cite the grammar rule that is applicable to each sentence. Before you begin, refresh your memory of grammar rules by reviewing subject/verb agreement in the Reference Guide of this text.

1. Not only my supervisor but also the president of the company were present at the total quality meeting in June.
2. Neither Mr. Tamorui nor the Asian employees was willing to discuss the multicultural issues in the company.
3. The quality committee have agreed unanimously to recommend the adoption of a flexible workweek.
4. The number of employees who endorsed the plan suggest the consensus of opinion in the group.
5. A number of requests for written materials on total quality management was made.

ASSESSMENT OF CHAPTER OBJECTIVES

Now that you have completed the chapter and the projects, take a few minutes to review the chapter learning objectives. For your convenience, the objectives are repeated here. Did you accomplish these objectives? If you were unable to accomplish the objectives, give your reasons for not doing so.

1. Describe the changing work environment.   Yes _____   No _____

   _____

   _____

   _____

2. Identify the role and responsibilities of the administrative professional.   Yes _____   No _____

   _____

   _____

   _____

ASSESSMENT OF CHAPTER OBJECTIVES

(continued)

3. Determine twenty-first-century traits necessary for the administrative professional.   Yes _____   No _____

_____

_____

_____

4. Begin the development of a professional growth plan.   Yes _____   No _____

_____

_____

_____

5. Develop critical-thinking skills.   Yes _____   No _____

_____

_____

_____

You may submit your answers in writing to your instructor, using the memorandum form on the Student CD, SCDAP1-1.

CHAPTER 2

COMMUNICATION SKILLS FOR A DIVERSE ENVIRONMENT

LEARNING OBJECTIVES

1. Develop skills needed in a culturally diverse workforce.
2. Explain the communication process.
3. Develop and use effective verbal and nonverbal communication skills.
4. *Clarify your values.*

You cannot be effective in the workplace without being an effective communicator. Your effectiveness as an administrative professional implies effective communication skills, since the majority of the administrative professional's day involves contact with people. Effective communication is the ability to process and exchange ideas and feelings so the person originating the communication and the person receiving the communication clearly understand what is being communicated. Building and maintaining effective communications are never easy. This statement is particularly true today in our complex, diverse world. People find it difficult enough to relate successfully to others who are like them. However, when people are from different cultures and backgrounds, of different ages, and even from different countries, the task becomes even more complex.

Since effective performance in the workplace depends greatly on the ability to communicate effectively, the question you must ask yourself is this:

How well do I communicate with others?

Take Self-Check A now. Compare your answers to the suggested responses at the end of this chapter. Now ask yourself this question:

How do I become a more effective communicator?

Make up your mind to improve your communication skills throughout this course. Commit to carefully studying the concepts presented in this chapter and to using the effective communication techniques presented.

Respond to the following comments with a yes or no answer.

		YES	NO
1.	I am always aware of the nonverbal communication of others.	☐	☐
2.	I never allow my own biases to interfere with my communication.	☐	☐
3.	I pay attention to cultural differences that may be present in the communication process.	☐	☐
4.	I always listen well.	☐	☐
5.	I am nonjudgmental of others.	☐	☐
6.	I use words precisely in my communication.	☐	☐
7.	I always seek to understand the other person's point of view.	☐	☐
8.	I offer advice only after understanding the situation presented.	☐	☐
9.	I allow myself to engage in critiquing the speaker.	☐	☐
10.	I use direct, simple language in my communication.	☐	☐

COMMUNICATION— A COMPLEX ISSUE

Forces that contribute to the complexity of communication today include the following:

- Our global world
- The increasing number of multinational organizations
- The greater diversity of the people who comprise the workplace
- The number of immigrants who are entering our country
- The technological workplace

Consider the U.S. population for a moment. According to the 2000 U.S. Census (a census that is done every ten years), the foreign-born population totaled over 27 million in 2000, an increase of 8 million over the 1990 census. Census projections are that by the year 2010,

the foreign-born population of the United States will reach over 33 million and by 2050 over 54 million.[1] More than one hundred languages are spoken in the school systems of our large cities, such as New York, Chicago, and Los Angeles. If we were a global village of 100 people, North Americans would be very much in the minority. That village would be composed of the following:

- 56 Asians
- 21 Europeans
- 9 Africans
- 8 South Americans
- 6 North Americans[2]

This global world demands that we be globally literate—that we see, think, and act in ways that are culturally mindful of the vast differences in our world.

You learned in Chapter 1 that our native-born population is also changing drastically. It is projected that by the year 2050, non-Hispanic whites will make up approximately 52 percent of our population and African Americans, Asians and Pacific Islanders, Native Americans, and Hispanics will comprise the remaining 48 percent.

Communication Tip:

When you have a customer, caller, or business associate who does not speak fluent English, paraphrase what you believe the person has said. Then ask, "Is that correct?"

Our technology and the multinational nature of business add to the complexity of our communication. Our contacts with others may be through telecommunications—the Internet, fax, telephone, and virtual conferencing, for

---

[1] "Population Statistics," accessed February 20, 2001; available from www.census.gov/population.
[2] Robert Rosen and others, *Cultural Literacy* (New York: Simon & Schuster, 2000), 175.

example—in addition to our face-to-face communication. Regardless of the form the interaction takes, you must practice effective communication techniques. Effectiveness assumes that you are

- Clear concerning your own values and attitudes
- Sensitive to cultural differences
- Aware of gender and age issues

Value Clarification

The word **value** comes from the French verb *valoir,* meaning "to be worth." Values are our beliefs. They determine how we live on a day-to-day basis. For example, knowledge is a value. You probably would not be taking this course if you did not value knowledge. You want to learn. We may or may not spend much time thinking about what we value, but the decisions we make each day are influenced by the values we have.

Our early values are learned from significant people in our environment, such as our parents and other family members. In addition, values are learned from our educational, social, and religious structures, such as our schools and places of worship. However, our values are not static; that is, as we grow and change, our values may change. Figure 2-1 graphically depicts a set of values that an individual may have. In this illustration, a tree is used to depict the growing and changing individual. The roots of the tree are the people and social and religious structures that have helped shaped the person's values. The branches of the tree contain the values by which the person operates. As the person continues to grow and change mentally, psychologically, and physically, an expanded root system may include other factors that shape the values of the individual, resulting in new values (branches) being added to the tree and even old values (branches) being chopped off the tree. As you study the material in this course and perform the tasks given, you should come to understand your value system. Your value system shapes what you believe, how you live and work, and how you relate to others.

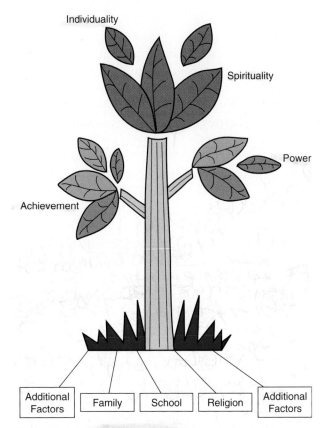

Figure 2-1   Values are learned.

Self-Check B

Stop for a moment and think about your values. List your top five values.

1. _____
2. _____
3. _____
4. _____
5. _____

Values are not inherently good or bad. However, the way in which you live your values may involve behaviors that are either acceptable or unacceptable in our society. We sometimes say if we encounter someone who is not behaving appropriately for the values we hold, "That person has no values." Such a statement is incorrect; everyone has values. However, the values a person holds may not match our values or may not match the values of the society in which we live. For example, one might say that Adolph Hitler was value-centered, with one of his values being to build a superior race. In his attempt to do so, he engaged in one of the greatest atrocities of our history, killing over eight million Jews.

One of your values may be to become economically independent. To accomplish this value, you may decide to obtain an education and then seek a job in an organization that provides you the opportunity to move to higher levels of responsibility. Conversely, you could decide to rob a bank, become involved in drug trafficking, or engage in some other type of criminal behavior to satisfy your need to become economically independent. In other words, the principles that you hold, the attitudes that you exhibit, and the behaviors that you demonstrate in living your values are legally and socially acceptable or unacceptable.

Attitude Clarification

Generally, we do not give much thought to how our values may be different from other people's values. We sometimes assume that everyone has the same values and then operate from this assumption. Obviously, that assumption is not true, and it can cause communication difficulties if it is not understood. Also, we do not give much thought to the attitudes we demonstrate in pursuit of our values. **Attitude** is defined in the dictionary as "position, disposition, or manner with regard to a person or thing." Consider an example of a value you might have, recognizing differences. You value the importance of recognizing the differences of all individuals with whom you work. Yet recently, when one of your co-workers from Mexico got "right in your face" when talking with you, you became irritated with her behavior and asked her not to violate your space. She went away in puzzlement, not understanding that most North Americans do not stand extremely close to each other to talk unless they have an intimate relationship.

The attitude you demonstrated to this person did not reflect that you value recognizing the differences of all individuals. It reflected rudeness and even lack of consideration to the person from Mexico. Just as you need to understand what you value, you also need to be clear about the attitudes you reflect to others. In the workplace, a great deal of attention is paid to the attitude of employees. In fact, during the formal evaluation process, an individual is often evaluated on his or her attitude. A positive attitude is always an asset, whereas a negative attitude is always a detractor.

Communication Tip:
Treat each co-worker as a unique individual, recognizing that all individuals are different.

Cultural Differences

With our population becoming more diverse and our organizations becoming more multinational, we must continue to be alert to the differences among the people with whom we work. We must be tolerant of these differences, not expecting that all people will react to situations the same way. We must understand and

© Digital Stock

Diversity can mean that significant differences exist among our values, our assumptions, and our attitudes.

accept that diversity can mean that significant differences exist among our values, our assumptions, and our attitudes. Consider some of the cultural differences among people.

Trust is earned differently in various countries. For example, if an employee in the United States performs well on his or her job, the individual earns trust quickly. Superior performance equates to trusting the individual to do the job well. In contrast, in Japan and Germany, trust is earned over a long period of time. For the Japanese and the Germans, trust may in fact be a result of family relationships or long-term knowledge of an individual.

Respect also is viewed differently in various cultures. For example, in Asian countries, great respect is given to the older generation. Respect is also given to people in authority, such as political officials. In the United States, we tend to believe that respect must be earned; it is not automatically given to specific people or groups of people.

Nonverbal communication varies greatly among countries. A Japanese member of a work team may smile in a friendly but noncommittal manner. A North American usually takes the smile as an expression of agreement with what is being said. The German team member may interpret the smile as disagreement. An Italian may agree to a deadline without ever meaning to adhere to it. The Italian is merely being agreeable. When the Italian does not meet the deadline, the North American takes the behavior as a sign of disrespect or lack of interest.

United States' students learn from the time they enter school that class participation is important. We are taught to give our opinions. If students do not participate in class, they are considered to be uninterested or even unprepared for the class. In contrast, Asians regard teachers so highly they find it difficult to voice their own views in class. Doing so is almost a sign of disrespect to the teacher.

North Americans are considered demonstrative. Generally, we show our feelings easily. If we are happy, we smile a lot. If we are sad, we seldom smile. We are taught from an early age to make eye contact with people. To look down at the floor while someone is talking to you can mean disrespect for the individual or signify a lack of confidence on the part of the person looking down.

North Americans have certain concepts of time and space. For example, in the United States, it is important to be on time for business appointments. A certain amount of space distance is maintained when talking with people. When talking to an acquaintance, we generally maintain a distance of from two to three feet. Only when talking with someone with whom we have an intimate relationship do we get close to that person. Figure 2-2 highlights how these same behaviors are viewed very differently in certain other countries.

CULTURAL DIFFERENCES

- In Korean culture, smiling can signal shallowness and thoughtfulness.
- Asians, Latin Americans, and Caribbeans avoid eye contact as a sign of respect.
- Avoidance of eye contact in Japan means that the person is being polite and nonconfrontational. Mothers often scold their children for staring into peoples' eyes when they speak.
- In France and Mexico, being 30 minutes late to an appointment is perfectly acceptable.
- Latin Americans stand very close to each other when talking; the interaction distance is much less than in the United States.

- Open criticism should be avoided when dealing with Asian employees, as this may lead to loss of face.
- In Japan and China, "yes" does not always mean "yes."
- Japanese are taught to withhold their personal opinions. An old Japanese proverb says, "Silence is a virtue."

Figure 2-2

Source: Norine Dresser, *Multicultural Manners: New Rules of Etiquette for a Changing Society* (New York: John Wiley & Sons, 1996).

Due to a lack of understanding of our global cultural differences, we make mistakes. These mistakes are costly not only to our interactions with others but also to businesses. Here are some examples of cultural illiteracies that were costly to business.

■ McDonald's took 13 months to realize that Hindus in India do not eat beef. When it started making hamburgers out of lamb, sales flourished.
■ In Africa, companies show pictures of what is inside bottles so that illiterate customers know what they are getting. When a baby food company showed a picture of a child on its label, the product did not sell very well.
■ A U.S. television ad for deodorant depicted an octopus putting antiperspirant under each arm. When the ad flopped in Japan, the producers realized that octopuses do not have arms there; they have legs.
■ A U.S. firm sent an elaborate business proposal to Saudi Arabia bound in pigskin. Since pigs are considered unclean by Muslims, the proposal was never opened.
■ Kentucky Fried Chicken's "finger lickin' good" translated to "eat your fingers off" in Chinese.[3]

In the future, remind yourself not to expect people from different cultures to behave as you do. Educate yourself about other cultures. Here are some suggestions about how to do so.

■ Read books on different cultures that are available in bookstores and/or your local library.
■ Join a global "chat group" on the Internet.
■ Talk with individuals from different cultures with whom you work about their life and the differences they see in various cultures.
■ Set a goal to make it one of your top priorities to develop appropriate cultural expectations.

Gender Issues

The gender of an individual in all societies has significant importance in job roles, social responsibilities, family responsibilities, and even education and socialization. People are born female or male, but they learn to be girls and boys who grow up to be women and men. We are taught values, attitudes, behaviors, and roles based on what our particular socialization group (parents, teachers, significant others) believes are right and appropriate for the male and the female. The appropriate roles and behaviors vary depending on what country we are born in and the position in society of the group teaching the behaviors (professional role or occupation, education attainment, and so on). The roles taught also may vary within a particular part of the country or within various communities in the same part of the country (ethnic communities). For example, with our diverse population, a city may have large numbers of various ethnic groups, with these groups having different cultures and backgrounds that socialize men and women in very different ways. Also, boys and girls who grow up in large cities as opposed to more rural environments may be socialized differently.

Gender roles are not static but change in response to events in our world. Very few women in the United States worked outside the home before World War II. Their role was one of wife, mother, and caretaker of the home and family. Since many men were in the armed services in WWII, women were needed to fill essential jobs in business and industry. That experience for women of working outside the home not only changed the way many of them viewed work roles but also changed the way many businesses and industries viewed the role of women in the workforce. Today, as you have already learned, we have greater numbers of women in the workforce than ever before in our history, with those numbers expected to increase in the future.

An important concept that business and industry learned about more women being in the workforce is that different gender voices are needed. These different voices provide the opportunity for analyzing situations in various ways, often resulting in better decisions for the organization. For example, in producing and marketing products, different gender voices provide perspectives that can allow the organization to meet the needs of a greater number of

---

[3]Robert Rosen and others, *Global Literacies* (New York: Simon & Schuster, 2000), 174.

people, with the likelihood of increasing the profit margin.

Before moving on, take a few minutes to reflect on gender roles in your own community. Using Self-Check C, respond to the items given.

Self-Check C

1. List the different professional roles carried out by men and women in your community.

_____

_____

2. List the professional roles you identified in number 1 in order of status in your community.

_____

_____

3. In your opinion, does one gender carry more status in professional roles than the other? If so, explain how.

_____

_____

4. List the home activities carried out by men and women; e.g., cooking, cleaning, child care.

_____

_____

5. Is one gender responsible for more of the home activities than the other? If so, what are they?

_____

_____

6. If you could change the way gender in your community is viewed, what would you do?

_____

_____

Age Issues

With the U.S. population over 50 years of age increasing, it is expected that people will stay in the workforce beyond the traditional retirement age of 65. Thus, workforce teams will be made up of people with large variations in age. Just as people who grow up in different cultures and environments have different values and expectations, so do people who are of different ages. To help you think about the various generations and some of their characteristics, look at how various generations have been categorized by writers in the field.

Birth Dates	Generation Name
1930–1945	Silent Generation
1946–1964	Baby Boomers
1965–1980	Generation X
1981–2000	Net Generation or N-Geners

As writers have categorized these generations by age groups, they have also studied how these generations behave and have assigned certain values/characteristics that seem to be common to the group. For example, in his best-selling book entitled *The Greatest Generation*, Tom Brokaw discusses the common values held by the men and women who came of age during the Great Depression and the Second World War, the Silent Generation. Some of the values he lists are duty, honor, courage, service, and responsibility for oneself.

Characteristics/values that have been identified for the Baby Boomer generation include these:

- Are committed to education
- Are more individualistic than the Silent Generation—always take care of themselves
- Are skeptics—skeptical about status quo and politics
- Believe in themselves

In contrast, Generation X values/characteristics have been identified as follows:

- Have less belief in self
- Are more tolerant than previous generations—accepting of most everything except narrow-mindedness
- Are spiritual
- Are nonworkaholics—a job is what one does to earn money
- Are relational—value good friends

Tapscott in *Growing Up Digital* defines the N-Gen values in these terms.

They are the young navigators. They doubt that traditional institutions can provide them with the good life and take personal responsibility for their lives. They do value material goods but they are not self-absorbed. They are more knowledgeable than any previous generation and they care deeply about social issues. They believe strongly in individual rights such as privacy and rights to information. But they have no ethos of individualism, thriving, rather, from close interpersonal networks and displaying a strong sense of social responsibility.

They appear very determined and even optimistic about the future, but are unsettled about the difficulties facing them including obstacles to a rewarding adult life. They are quite alienated from formal politics and depending on age, there are growing discussions about the need for fundamental social change.[4]

As can be seen through analyzing these different generations, individuals who grow up in different times may have different values. However, recognizing these different values does not give one the right to characterize or make judgments about individuals based on their ages. The information is given here to help you understand some of the differences in values that can occur due to the societal events that are happening during our lifetime. The importance of this information in the workforce is that people recognize possible differences due to age and address the differences in positive ways.

An Action Agenda

Your task as you work in a diverse world in which value differences, cultural differences, and gender and age issues exist is to

- Recognize that these differences occur
- Constantly seek to understand these differences
- Understand their implications for communication
- Grow in your ability to communicate with all people

In order to grow in your ability to communicate, you must understand the communication process and the barriers to effective communication. Additionally, you must continually practice effective communication techniques. The next sections of this chapter will help you gain these skills.

THE COMMUNICATION PROCESS

In understanding a culturally diverse workforce, you have already learned the importance of communication. Now consider the elements of the communication process—the originator, the message, the receiver, and the response.

The Originator

The **originator** is the sender of the original message. The originator transmits information, ideas, and feelings through speaking, writing, or gesturing. Although the originator is often a person, the originator may be a company, a committee, or even a nation. For example, in the advertisements you see on television about a particular product, the company is the originator of the communication.

The Message

The **message** is the idea being presented by the originator. Words are usually used in communicating the idea; but hand signals, gestures, or a combination of words and gestures may also be used. The transmission of these words or gestures usually takes the form of face-to-face exchanges, telephone conversations, voice mail, or written correspondence such as email, faxes, Web correspondence, and letters and memorandums. Other forms of transmission are radio, television, video cassette, audio cassette, CDs, and DVDs.

The Receiver

The person for whom the message is intended is the **receiver.** The receiver transfers the message into meaning. For example, if the message

---

[4]Don Tapscott, *Growing Up Digital: The Rise of the Net Generation* (New York: McGraw-Hill, 1998), 9.

were "Please send this letter out immediately," the receiver would develop a meaning based on his or her understanding of the words and previous knowledge of the originator. The receiver may decide that the letter should be sent out in 30 minutes, for example; in another situation, the receiver may decide that two hours is the appropriate time frame.

The Response

The **response** (feedback) of the receiver lets the originator know whether the communication is understood. The response may be verbal or nonverbal (such as a nod of the head, a smile, or a shrug of the shoulders.) If the response of the receiver indicates to the originator that the communication was misunderstood, the originator can send the message again, perhaps in a different manner. For example, in the situation of the letter to be sent out, assume the originator meant for the letter to go out within 10 minutes and the receiver did not send it out for 30 minutes; as a result, the letter missed the morning mail. In the future, the originator could frame the message in this manner, "Please see that the letter makes the morning mail." A communication model is shown in Figure 2-3.

Each element of the communication process is important. If the originator does not clearly state his or her message, problems can occur. If the receiver interprets the message incorrectly and responds inappropriately, there may be problems. Each person in the communication process has an obligation to communicate as clearly as possible, to frame his or her message well, and ask questions if the message or response is unclear.

VERBAL COMMUNICATION

Verbal communication is the process of exchanging ideas and feelings through the use of words. Initially, the concept of verbal communication seems simple. We all understand words and know what they mean. In actuality, verbal communication is not simple at all. Words, although they may be spelled the same, have different meanings for different people. Add to this situation the complexity of a diverse workforce, and the relevance of words often having very different meanings becomes clear.

Verbal Barriers

Barriers do exist whether we are communicating with others of the same culture or of different cultures. Several of these barriers are given here.

Listening

Listening is the complete process by which verbal language, communicated by a source, is received, recognized, attended to, comprehended, and retained. The listener attends to the verbal language of the source with the intent of acquiring meaning. Thus, the main components of listening are not located in the ears, just as the main components of seeing are not located in the eyes. Our ears hear the sound vibrations to which we attend and comprehend; but our listening is based on our needs, desires, interests, previous experiences, and learning. As you can see, listening is a complex phenomenon involving the total individual. As we listen, our process of thought, which is composed of many separate and independent concepts, flows into ideas and emotions and affects what we hear.

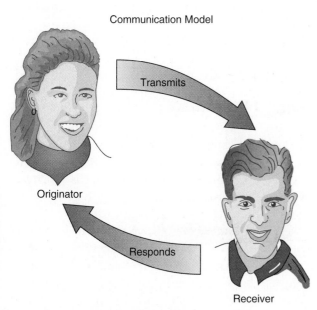

Communication Model

Transmits

Responds

Originator

Receiver

Figure 2-3   Communication Model

Studies show that the average person spends 70 percent of the day communicating with others, with 45 percent of that communication time spent listening to others. However, listening is considered one of the weakest links in the communication process. Research studies show that immediately following a conversation, a listener retains approximately 50 percent of what was said. However, after 48 hours, the percentage drops to only 25 percent. In other words, 50–75 percent of what we hear is never processed.

Do you consider yourself a good listener? Complete Self-Check D to determine your present listening effectiveness. Rate yourself by answering the statements with "always," "sometimes," or "never."

How did you do? Did you recognize yourself as an ineffective listener? If you are like most of us, your score can probably be improved. Improvement comes by understanding what causes poor listening and then working on effective listening techniques. Numerous characteristics produce poor listening behaviors. Consider the following ineffective listeners:

The talker—Unfortunately, many of us are so intent on discussing what has happened to us that we have difficulty waiting for the other person to finish so we can begin talking. In fact, many times the eager talker will interrupt the speaker to get his or her point across. Such individuals absorb little of what the other person says. In addition, they usually are planning their story while the other person is talking.

The attention faker—Have you ever talked with someone who seemed to listen to every word you said, but when it came time for the person to respond, you realized she or he had not heard a word? Have you ever sat in a classroom and intently watched the instructor during an entire lecture but were unable to answer any questions about what was said? Most of us are good at adopting an outward posture that leads the speaker to believe we are listening when actually we are thinking of something else.

The easily distracted—Most people speak at approximately 135–175 words a minute, yet it is believed the brain can process information at about 500 words a minute. Listening allows plenty of time for the mind to wander. Unless the listener is committed to hearing the speaker, he or she can easily become distracted. Distraction can be in the form of **external noise** (physical sounds that hinder the listening process) or movement, either inside or outside the room. Distractions can also be in the form of **internal noise** (distractions that occur inside the listener), such as a problem that is bothering you. You may be thinking about your problem and miss the speaker's point totally.

The outguesser—Have you ever known someone who would never let you finish a sentence but always finished it for you? That person may have assumed time was being saved when time was actually lost. Many times the outguesser makes an inaccurate assumption

You can miss vital information when you do not give the speaker your full attention.

© PhotoDisc, Inc.

concerning your message. You, therefore, have to stop and explain to the outguesser that he or she has made a wrong assumption.

Language Usage

The language we use often prevents clear communication. Words in isolation have no meaning. They have meaning only because people have agreed upon a particular meaning. You may say, "But what about the dictionary? Doesn't it contain the correct meanings of words?" Yes, it contains the correct meaning as agreed to by **etymologists** (specialists in the study of words). This meaning can be called the objective meaning of a word, and we use the dictionary to determine it. However, cultural differences impact the meaning of certain words. Although people in England speak the same language as people in the United States, they may use words in different ways. For example, when people in the United States have to wait in line, they refer to this behavior as "standing in line"; the British refer to it as "queuing up." In England, an elevator is called a "lift." *Napkins* in England mean "diapers." The word *scheme*, for most North Americans, has a negative implication. In England, it is merely a synonym for the word *plan*.

Meanings of words also change with time. New words come into existence, and other words become obsolete because of lack of usage. The computer era has generated different applications for certain words. Remember when a bulletin board meant only a board that was hung on a wall to which notes were attached? Now a bulletin board can mean a public-access message system through computer linkage. A chat room in computer terminology does not mean a room at all in the standard definition of the word, but a location where people all over the world, connected by the Web, can "talk" with each other via computers.

Evaluation

One of the major barriers to communication is the tendency to judge the individual making a statement and then to accept or reject the statement based on the **evaluation** (to judge carefully) of the individual. This evaluation is made from the listener's frame of reference and experience. If what is said agrees with the listener's experience, the listener tends to make a positive evaluation. If what is said does not agree with the listener's experience, he or she may make a negative evaluation.

Inference

Inference is the process of deriving logical conclusions from premises known or assumed to be true. The problem that can be caused from making inferences is that individuals may act upon what they believe to be true when it is in fact not true.

Consider Figure 2-4 shown on page 42. What do you see in the illustration? Do you see a woman? Is she young or old? What is she wearing? You may have answered that she is a young woman with a small nose and a choker around her neck. What if I tell you that you are wrong? It is an old woman with a large nose and her head tucked down into a fur coat. Who is right? Look at the picture again. We are both right. Both a young woman and an old woman are in this picture.

Each of us thinks we see things exactly as they are; in other words, we are objective in our assessment of what we see. When other people disagree with us, we immediately think

Figure 2-4   What do you see?

something is wrong with them. In actuality, we see the world through our own filter—a filter that has been established through our values, our culture, our background, and our teachings.

Noise

Noise in our environment creates distortion in the message being sent and prevents us from understanding the message as it was intended. Noise can come from any number of sources. It may be external noise, such as telephones ringing, a construction crew sawing and hammering, and traffic noise. It may be the internal noise of the receiver, such as having a sick child or anticipating a pending holiday. When we have numerous issues or problems on our mind, the internal noise blocks what the sender of the communication is attempting to say. The time of day the communication is delivered can also constitute noise. For example, if it is late on a Friday afternoon, we may not be able to hear a complex communication.

Cultural, Gender, and Age Differences

The cultural, gender, and age differences of our diverse workplace can and many times do make our communication even more complex. Due to the differences in values, backgrounds, and beliefs these differences often bring with them, major barriers can occur.

In addition to the verbal communication barriers that have been mentioned, there are numerous other barriers. Study Figure 2-5 to understand these barriers.

Effective Verbal Communication

In order to communicate effectively, we must learn to reduce communication barriers. Due to the number of people with whom we communicate each day and the different situations in which we find ourselves, it is impossible to reduce all barriers. However, we can make significant improvement in our verbal communication by using a variety of techniques. Study the ones presented in Figure 2-6 on page 44. Commit yourself to practicing these techniques as you communicate each day. The improvement you see in your communication will be more than worth the effort you expend.

Understand the Other Person's View

In *The Seven Habits of Highly Effective People*[5], Covey states that in all communication it is important to seek first to understand the individual, then to be understood. This approach is not consistent with what most of us do. Generally, we try to explain our position first. Often we do a sales job on it. Once we have finished, we then turn to the person for his or her response. The ability to listen first requires respect for the other individual and the ability to stop talking and truly listen. It requires active listening—the type of listening that is explained in the next section.

---

[5]Stephen R. Covey, *Principle-Centered Leadership* (New York: Summit Books, 1990), 45–46.

- Hearing the Expected. We are often guilty of sizing up an individual and then only hearing what we think that individual should say.
- Ignoring Conflicting Information. If you have predetermined feelings about a subject, you tend to ignore new information on the subject. This new information may be valid, but you have made up your mind otherwise.
- Evaluating the Source. It is difficult to separate what we hear from our feelings about the person speaking. If you like the person, you tend to accept what the person is saying. If you dislike the person, you tend to ignore what the person is saying.
- Viewing Things Differently. Individuals may view the same situation in different ways. For example, if one person sees people in an office laughing and telling jokes, the person may decide they are goofing off and no work is being accomplished. Another person may interpret the office as a happy place and one where work is accomplished easily in teams.
- Using Word Barriers. Words have different meanings for different people. Even such simple words as *great, small, good,* and *bad* are open to interpretation by the listener. Communication theorists say that a word in and of itself has no meaning. A word only has the meaning given to it by the communicator. To counter word barriers, communicators must always clarify the meaning attached to words.
- Noticing Differences in Position. Breakdowns often occur because of differences in position. For example, your supervisor may tell you something you do not understand. Yet you do not ask for clarification because you fear he or she will think you are stupid.

Figure 2-5

Listen Actively

Active listening requires that you listen for the meaning as well as the words of the speaker. Here are some suggestions for becoming an active listener.

- Prepare to listen. Drive distracting thoughts from your mind, and direct your full attention to the speaker.
- Listen for facts. Mentally register the key words the speaker is using, and repeat key ideas or related points. Relate what the speaker is saying to your experiences.
- Minimize mental blocks and filters by being aware of them. Know your biases and prejudices. Do not let them keep you from hearing what the speaker is saying.
- Take notes. When listening to a presentation or lecture, taking notes can be beneficial in jogging your memory later. Write only the main points of the message; do not attempt to record each word.
- Question and paraphrase. Ask questions when you do not understand what you have heard. Paraphrase by putting the speaker's communication in your own words and asking the speaker if you have understood correctly.

Be Nonjudgmental

Try to understand the message as the speaker intends it. Be **nonjudgmental;** do not attempt to judge the individual's culture, values, background, intelligence, appearance, or other characteristics. Listen to what the speaker is saying. In other words, give the person a chance to get his or her message across, without forming judgments.

Communication Tip:
Listen for feelings. Search beneath the surface. Listen to what is and is not being said.

Since communication is so important in effective human relations, how can you communicate better? Here are several techniques that will help you become a more effective communicator.

- Paraphrase if you do not understand. **Paraphrase** means to restate the concept in your own terms. Then ask the speaker "Is this what you mean?"
- Get ready to listen. Stop paying attention to the miscellaneous thoughts that constantly run through your mind. Direct all your attention to the speaker.
- Listen for facts. Use the differential time between how long it takes the speaker to say the words (an average of 130 words a minute) and how long it takes you to comprehend them (approximately 500 words a minute) to review the key ideas presented. Raise questions in your mind about the material. Relate what the speaker is saying to your own experience. Mentally repeat key ideas, or associate key points with related ideas.
- Watch for nonverbal communication. Observe the speaker's eyes, hands, and body movements. Do the nonverbal communications agree with what the speaker is saying?
- Use mnemonic devices to remember key ideas. A **mnemonic device** is a formula, word association, or rhyme used to assist the memory. For example, if a person says that his objections to a jogging program include boredom with the activity, exhaustion in the process, and the time required, you might develop the mnemonic device of BET to remember these ideas.
- Minimize your mental blocks and filters. All of us have certain biases and prejudices. However, if we are aware of these blocks, we can control them. You may have heard people say, "You can't talk to CPAs; they are only number crunchers" or "All athletes are stupid." In such statements, you can hear prejudices. **Stereotyping** is taking place; an entire group of people or things is being evaluated based on a perception or an image held, which may be favorable or unfavorable. In this case, the image was unfavorable. Listening behaviors are improved if you become aware of your own blocks and filters, as well as the speaker's blocks and filters.
- Use direct, simple language. Never attempt to use big words and long sentences to try to impress the listener or the reader.
- Utilize feedback. When communicating with someone, listen to what that person is saying in its entirety, not only to the words. Remember, there are many ways to communicate, including the use of words, gestures, facial expressions, tone of voice, time, and space. If you believe the other person does not understand what you are saying, try to explain your point in a different manner.
- Time messages carefully. You need to be aware of what is going on in the world of the receiver. We can cause problems for ourselves by trying to communicate with someone when that person is not ready to receive our communication. Stop, look, and observe what is going on in the world of the receiver before you attempt to communicate.
- Organize what you hear. A listener who can identify the speaker's main points and the pattern of the speaker's remarks certainly has an advantage over the listener who simply listens to the words.
- Do not expect people from different cultures to behave the same way you do.
- Commit to constantly improving your communication skills.

Figure 2-6

Avoid arguing with the speaker. If you are opposed to an idea, do not argue or become emotional. Control your reaction at least until you have heard everything the speaker has to say. Regardless of your acceptance or rejection of what a speaker says, your knowledge increases when you listen—even if you only learn another person's view.

Question

If you do not understand what someone is saying to you, one of the best things to do is **question** (technique used to understand verbal communication through the use of questions) the individual. Questions can help us

- Gain information

DILBERT reprinted by permission of United Feature Syndicate, Inc.

Questioning allows you to verify information.

- Understand the other person's point of view
- Build trust
- Verify information

When asking questions, you should

- Know what you are trying to accomplish with the question
- Ask only one question at a time and keep the question easy to understand
- Try not to manipulate or trick with your questions

Give Feedback

When communicating with someone, listen to what that person is saying in its entirety, not only to the words. Remember that there are many ways to communicate, including the use of words, gestures, facial expressions, tone of voice, time, and space.

Seek **feedback** (clarifying statements and questions) from the individual with whom you are communicating. Use clarifying statements and questions such as these.

- "Let me see if I can review the main points we have discussed." Then after you have reviewed the points, ask "Is that a correct summation? Have I left anything out?"
- "I understand your major concerns are . . . Did I hear you correctly?"
- "As I understand you, your major objections are . . . Have I stated them correctly? Do you have other objections?"

NONVERBAL COMMUNICATION

Nonverbal communication can be another barrier to effective communication. However, before you consider this area, keep several points in mind.

People of different cultures give different meanings to gestures. You learned about some of these differences in the first sections of this chapter.

© PhotoDisc, Inc.

Watch for nonverbal communication, observing the speaker's eyes, hands, and body movements.

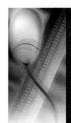

Communication Tip:

Pay careful attention to nonverbal communication; it helps you know whether your message is being received.

Here are some additional differences in the meanings given to gestures by people of different cultures.

- The "OK" sign in Germany is a rude signal. The "OK" sign in Japan is used to signal the word *money* or *change*. It means you want your money in the form of change.
- In the Middle East or Southeast Asia, never expose or point the sole of your shoe at another person. This is a grievous insult because the sole of your shoe is the lowest and dirtiest part of your body.
- In Thailand, never pat anyone on the top of the head. The Thai people believe that is where their spirits reside.
- In Russia, when entering a theater or an auditorium and walking through the row to take your seat, always face the people already seated. If you face the stage, you are being impolite by passing your derriere directly in front of their bodies or faces.[6]

You must constantly keep in mind that how you interpret gestures may not be the same as how others interpret gestures.

Conclusions cannot be drawn from only one element of nonverbal communication. For example, a person may cross his or her arms because the person is cold. You must take all elements of nonverbal communication as a whole, and you must be cautious about your interpretations.

Now consider four elements of nonverbal communication.

Body Language

Various body motions or gestures can have meaning; we refer to this as **body language.** Consider this situation. You are very intently talking with someone, and that person is leaning back in the chair with his or her arms crossed, frowning. Do you think the individual is interested in what you are saying? Believing what you are saying? Bored with the whole exchange? You probably answered "yes" to at least one of these questions and may have answered "yes" to all of them. All of the nonverbal body language signs indicate that the message is not being received. Something about the message or the speaker is blocking the individual from truly listening to what is being said.

Although body language is extremely important, one gesture alone does not have significant meaning. One gesture merely gives you a clue that something may be wrong. When evaluating body language, consider all the gestures a person makes along with what the person says. For example, when you are communicating with someone, do not make the mistake of assuming that a frown indicates the person disagrees with what you are saying. If you are concerned about the body language, ask for an explanation. You might say, "You are frowning. Is something wrong?" Such a question gives the person with whom you are talking a chance to explain his or her behavior.

Voice Quality

A loud tone of voice is usually associated with anger; a soft tone of voice, with calmness and poise. Two people talking softly with each other usually indicates they are at ease. **Voice quality** (the loudness or softness of the voice, the pitch of the voice, and the enunciation of the words) is a nonverbal behavior that reveals something about an individual. A person's voice is usually pitched higher when he or she is tense, anxious, or nervous. Also, a person usually talks faster when angry or tense. If a person is nervous or upset, he or she may not enunciate clearly. In

---

[6]Roger E. Axtell, *Do's and Taboos of Humor Around the World* (New York: John Wiley & Sons, Inc., 1999), 99–100.

contrast, a low pitch and a slow pace usually indicate a relaxed tone. Other forms of nonverbal voice communication include the nervous giggle; a quivering, emotional voice; a breaking, stressful voice; and a whiny (upset) voice. Voice quality is so important that individuals whose voices are important to their success or failure on the job, such as TV and radio newscasters, spend time and effort to be certain their voices do not cause people to switch to another station. For example, a nasal voice or a very high-pitched voice is irritating to the listener.

Time

Another important nonverbal communicator is **time.** You have already learned in the first part of this chapter that not all cultures treat time in the same way. However, in the United States, we have learned to treat time in certain standard ways. For example, as a student, you have probably learned that turning in a paper or project late usually results in a grade penalty. In a business situation, people who are habitually late with reports or who are constantly late for work may find themselves fired. An applicant who is late for a job interview may forfeit the chance to get the job.

Space

Space is also treated differently in different cultures. However, in the United States, we have defined space expectations. For example, at home, do you have a special chair that is considered yours or a special space that is considered yours? We tend to lay claim to a certain territory and defend it if someone else takes *our space*, which is defined as **territoriality.** In the office, we also use space in special ways. For example, people who have the same level or position are generally allocated the same amount of space. The president's office is usually larger than the vice president's office. The vice president's office is generally larger than a supervisor's office. An administrative assistant to the president generally has a larger space than an administrative assistant to the vice president.

COMMUNICATION IMPROVEMENT

If we are to develop effective relationships in the workplace, we must constantly work on communication in all forms. We must understand that our workforce is diverse; that different cultures exist; and that because of our cultures and backgrounds, we view situations differently. We must work to overcome the numerous communication barriers that exist, including discriminatory barriers. We must recognize that constant attention and effort to improving communication are essential. The process of improvement must be an ongoing, ever-present one. If we are diligent in our efforts, a fairer and more effective workplace will be the result.

CHAPTER SUMMARY

The summary will help you remember the important points covered in the chapter.

- You cannot be effective in the workplace without being an effective communicator. Effective communication is the ability to process and exchange ideas and feelings so the person originating the communication and the person receiving the communication clearly understand what is being communicated.
- Forces that contribute to the complexity of communication in our world include globalization, multinational organizations, diversity of our population, the number of immigrants who are entering our country, and technology.
- All of us have values, which are not inherently good or bad. The way we set about to accomplish our values involve behaviors that are either acceptable or unacceptable in our society. An understanding of our own values and the recognition that others may not have our values are crucial in the communication process.
- The way we carry out our values often reflects the attitudes we have. A positive attitude is always an asset; a negative attitude is always a detractor.
- Understanding cultural differences demands that we understand that people from other cultures may have values different from our own.
- The gender of individuals in all societies has significant importance in job roles, social responsibilities, family responsibilities, and even education and socialization.

- As the traditional age of retirement extends beyond 65, it is important to understand that people of different ages often have different values.
- The elements of the communication process include the originator, the message, the receiver, and the response. Each element is important.
- Verbal communication is the process of exchanging ideas and feelings through the use of words.
- Verbal barriers to communication include listening; language usage; evaluation; inference; noise; and cultural, gender, and age differences.
- In order to be an effective verbal communicator, you should consider the other person's view, use active listening, resolve conflicts, be nonjudgmental, question, and give feedback.
- Nonverbal communication can be a barrier to effective communication. The four elements of nonverbal communication include body language, voice quality, time, and space.
- Communication effectiveness is a process; improvement is ongoing and ever present.

CHAPTER GLOSSARY

The following terms were introduced in this chapter. Definitions are provided to help you review the terms.

- **Value** (p. 33)—our beliefs that determine how we live on a day-to-day basis.
- **Attitude** (p. 34)—position, disposition, or manner with regard to a person or thing.
- **Originator** (p. 38)—the sender of the original message.
- **Message** (p. 38)—the idea being presented by the originator.

- **Receiver** (p. 38)—the person for whom the message is intended.
- **Response** (p. 39)—feedback; lets the originator know whether the communication is understood; may be verbal or nonverbal.
- **Verbal communication** (p. 39)—the process of exchanging ideas and feelings through the use of words.

- **Listening** (p. 39)—the complete process by which verbal language, communicated by a source, is received, recognized, attended to, comprehended, and retained.
- **The talker** (p. 40)—a person who in communicating has difficulty waiting for the other person to finish so he or she can begin talking.
- **The attention faker** (p. 40)—a person who seems to listen to every word but actually does not hear much, if any, of what was said.
- **The easily distracted** (p. 40)—a person who is distracted by external or internal noises while another person is talking.
- **External noise** (p. 40)—physical sounds that hinder the listening process, such as traffic noise.
- **Internal noise** (p. 40)—distractions that occur inside the listener that are due to different backgrounds, experiences, and perceptions that cause a person to interpret a communication in a certain way or are due to problems or issues the listener is concerned about at the time of a communication.
- **The outguesser** (p. 40)—someone who always tries to finish the statement or thought of the individual communicating.
- **Etymologists** (p. 41)—specialists in the study of words.
- **Evaluation** (p. 41)—judge carefully.
- **Inference** (p. 41)—the process of deriving logical conclusions from premises known or assumed to be true.

- **Noise** (p. 42)—external or internal; creates distortion in the message being sent and prevents the receiver from understanding the message as it was intended.
- **Active listening** (p. 42)—requires an individual to listen for the meaning as well as the words of the speaker.
- **Nonjudgmental** (p. 43)—care taken *not* to judge an individual based on culture, values, background, intelligence, appearance, or other characteristics.
- **Paraphrase** (p. 44)—restate the concept in your own terms.
- **Mnemonic device** (p. 44)—a formula, word association, or rhyme used to assist the memory.
- **Stereotyping** (p. 44)—evaluating an entire group of people or things on a perception or an image held, which may be favorable or unfavorable.
- **Question** (p. 44)—a technique used to understand verbal communication through the use of questions.
- **Feedback** (p. 45)—the use of clarifying statements and questions in an attempt to be better understood.
- **Body language** (p. 46)—various body motions or gestures.
- **Voice quality** (p. 46)—the loudness or softness of the voice, the pitch of the voice, and the enunciation of the words.
- **Time** (p. 47)—a nonverbal communicator.
- **Space** (p. 47)—a nonverbal communicator.
- **Territoriality** (p. 47)—laying claim to a certain space and defending that claim.

DISCUSSION ITEMS

These discussion items provide an opportunity to test your understanding of the chapter through written responses and/or discussion with your classmates and your instructor.

1. What is meant by value clarification? Do all individuals have values? Explain.
2. List ten cultural differences between the U.S. population and people who live outside the United States.
3. Identify and explain five verbal communication barriers.

4. Identify and explain five effective verbal communication techniques.
5. List and explain four elements of nonverbal communication.

CRITICAL-THINKING ACTIVITY

Yuan Liang is a manager for AmeriAsian Airlines. He was transferred from China shortly after the merger of the two companies. He speaks English; however, he has never lived outside China although he had visited the United States several times before his transfer. He is having difficulty understanding the culture. Although you do not report to Mr. Liang, your employer, Mr. Albertson, has assigned you to work on a quality team with Mr. Liang. Mr. Liang is chairing the team. In the first meeting with the team, you made several suggestions to Mr. Liang and the committee. Mr. Liang smiled and nodded in agreement with your suggestions; the team also voiced agreement with your suggestions. However, when the minutes from the meeting were sent out, you found no indication that your suggestions were going to be implemented. During the second meeting, Mr. Liang started the discussion with the same problem that was discussed at the last meeting—the one you thought had been resolved. After some discussion within the group (without your participation), you stated that you did not understand why the topic was being discussed again since you thought the group had agreed on a resolution at the last meeting. Mr. Liang only smiled and continued the discussion. However, after the meeting, he contacted your manager and told him you had embarrassed him before the group. Mr. Albertson called you in and asked you to explain the situation; he stated that you should have told him your concerns about the meeting. You are angry and also defensive—angry with Mr. Liang because he did not talk with you and angry with your supervisor because he seems to be questioning your integrity.

Using several of the critical-thinking techniques presented in the last chapter, ask yourself these questions:

- Am I recognizing the cultural differences that are involved?
- Is my position on this issue reasonable and rational?
- Have I tried to understand the situation from Mr. Liang's point of view?

With those critical-thinking concepts in mind, answer these questions:

- How should I have handled the situation?
- What can I learn from this situation?
- Should I talk with Mr. Liang about my feelings?
- What should I say to Mr. Albertson?

RESPONSES TO SELF-CHECK A

The most appropriate answers are as follows:

1. Yes
2. Yes
3. Yes
4. Yes
5. Yes
6. Yes
7. Yes
8. Yes
9. No
10. Yes

RESPONSES TO SELF-CHECK D

The most effective listeners would have responded with "never" on the first eight items and "always" on the last three items.

PROJECTS

Project 2-1 (Objective 1)
Online Project

Browse the Web for articles on the culture of Asians and Hispanics. Summarize two articles, giving the Web addresses, and submit your summaries to your instructor. You might want to use this browser as you search— www.google.com.

Project 2-2 (Objectives 1 and 2)
Collaborative Project

With a team of three or four of your classmates, discuss the case given here; then answer the questions given at the end of the case by writing a memorandum to your instructor, using the memo form on the Student CD, SCDP2-2. List the members of your team in the From section.

CASE

In your position at AmeriAsian, you have two assistants who report to you. They are Juan Mercado and Luyin Wu. Luyin has been having some personal problems that she has talked with you about. She has come in late twice during the last month. Each time Juan has made a remark (that the entire office heard) about Luyin coming in late. Luyin has not responded to Juan's remarks. Last week Luyin called in sick, but that evening Juan saw Luyin at the grocery store. The next morning (again while the entire office listened) Juan said, "It's a shame you were sick yesterday; but you weren't so sick last night, were you?" Again Luyin said nothing; she merely lowered her head and kept walking to her desk. Today Luyin was late again. When she came in, Juan remarked, "I wish I were the office pet." Luyin remained silent.

You think Luyin will soon solve her personal problems; she has been a good employee. You want to continue to give her a chance to work out her problems and get back on track at work. You know the situation cannot go on indefinitely, but she has indicated that the problem should be resolved within the next three weeks. You are very concerned about Juan's actions. Juan's work is also good, but he is out of line on this matter. Luyin does not want anyone to know about her personal problems. You are beginning to believe you cannot let Juan continue to disrupt the entire office with his remarks.

1. Who is the originator in this communication situation? Who is the receiver?

2. Explain the communication problem between Juan and Luyin.
3. Is there a communication problem between you and Juan? If so, what is it?
4. How should you handle the situation?

Project 2-3 (Objective 3)

Keep a five-day log of the time you spend speaking and listening. You cannot be accurate to the minute, but make a concentrated effort to record the amount of time spent on both speaking and listening. Also, record the effective and ineffective behaviors you engage in while listening and speaking. At the end of the five-day period, analyze your log. How much time did you spend speaking? How much time listening? What effective behaviors did you engage in? What ineffective behaviors occurred? Determine ways in which you can improve your communication. Write a report identifying improved communication techniques you plan to follow. Submit your report to your instructor.

Project 2-4 (Objective 4)

In this chapter, you were asked to list your five top values. Add to this list your next five values. You will have ten values when you finish, listed in order of importance to you. Next, list the attitudes you think you demonstrate to others. Once you have listed your attitudes as you understand them, check with a trusted friend or family member. Ask that person to tell you what attitudes he or she believes you demonstrate. Save a copy of your values and attitudes on the Professional Growth disk you began in Chapter 1. Title your list "Values and Attitudes." Save it under "Progro2-4." This project is a continuation of your Professional Growth Plan, which you will be adding to in each chapter.

Here is a list that may help you complete your top ten values.

- Knowledge
- Honesty
- Dependability
- Cooperation
- Tolerance
- Justice
- Honor
- Responsibility
- Peace
- Sharing
- Freedom

ENGLISH USAGE CHALLENGE DRILL

Correct the following sentences. Cite the grammar rule that is applicable to each sentence. Before you begin, refresh your memory of grammar rules by reviewing number usage in the Reference Guide of this text.

1. Two hundred seventy-five dollars per credit hour is the tuition rate for in-state residents.
2. We have ten volunteers for Thursday evening, 12 for Friday evening, and 16 for Saturday evening.
3. The meeting will begin at two p.m.
4. The conference will be held May 8th through May 12th.
5. We have 3 new employees in the Payroll Department and 5 new engineers in the Design Department.

ASSESSMENT OF CHAPTER OBJECTIVES

Now that you have completed the chapter and the projects, take a few minutes to review the chapter learning objectives. For your convenience, the objectives are repeated here. Did you accomplish these objectives? If you were unable to accomplish the objectives, give your reasons for not doing so.

1. Develop skills needed in a culturally diverse workforce. Yes _____ No _____

   _____
   _____
   _____

2. Explain the communication process. Yes _____ No _____

   _____
   _____
   _____

3. Develop and use effective verbal and nonverbal communication skills. Yes _____ No _____

   _____
   _____
   _____

4. Clarify your values. Yes _____ No _____

   _____
   _____
   _____

You may submit your answers in writing to your instructor, using the memorandum form on the Student CD, SCDAP2-1.

BERNICE FUJIWARA'S CASE SOLUTION

You will have many tasks to do on the job that you do not learn how to do in school. My success in doing these tasks well means using common sense and being sensitive to individual differences. Hawaii is known to be a melting pot of ethnic groups, and I feel fortunate to be exposed to so many different cultures and backgrounds. Many times I take for granted my ability to get along with people of various ethnicities. However, I understand how miscommunication can occur between different cultural groups. The important thing to remember is to treat others with respect, as you would like to be treated. Here is a list of items I consider when working with a group from another country.

- Find a person with the foreign group who will be helpful. Ask your executive if you can contact someone from the company.
- Inquire if anyone has diet restrictions and/or are vegetarians. Ask your contact if you need to know anything about how a food dish is prepared or if certain foods should not be served due to cultural or religious beliefs.
- Determine if someone from your company who speaks the language should be present.

- Prepare seating arrangements and name cards, which are less awkward than open seating. Determine the guests of honor, and seat them accordingly to the right and left of your executive or the company's highest ranking executive. To do this, you need a list of attendees and titles. In many Asian cultures, the location of the seat is most important and is a sign of respect.
- After the draft of the seating arrangement is made, check with your contact to ensure that the seating is appropriate. In some cultures, a wife of a deceased partner is still considered important and, therefore, should sit at the head table.
- Find out if your guests are comfortable with the time of the dinner and the location of the restaurant. If appropriate, check with your executive about arranging a limousine to pick up the guests, especially if they are coming from the airport.
- Determine if guests are to be formally introduced during the dinner and if a toast to the guests is appropriate. Check to see if background music is appropriate.
- Check with your executive or others in your company to see if small gifts are appropriate.

A Success Profile

Narressa Ross Lee

Former Coordinator, Risk Management
Howard University,
Washington, D.C.

I enjoy sharing with anyone who will listen that my mother, Nancy L. Ross, a former secretary for Howard University, was my mentor and the reason I got in the field. I would often go to her office, watch her at work, and ask many questions. Sometimes I would sit in her chair and pretend I was a secretary. I was awed by the respect she received from her executive and others throughout the university. I recognized early that if I chose to follow in her footsteps,

MASTERING TECHNOLOGY

I could become a part of a management team responsible for day-to-day operations of an organization. Initially, I aspired to be an elementary school teacher but found working as a secretary to be more rewarding.

I began and maintained a successful career in the health-care profession as an administrative professional. I was employed for 32 years at Howard University Hospital, Washington, D.C. I had various positions, including Unit Clerk, Secretary, Administrative Assistant, Staff Assistant, and Coordinator of Risk Management. I had numerous responsibilities in my risk management role. In addition to management responsibilities, I performed several administrative professional functions.

My educational background includes two years of college in areas of educa-tion and business management. I am also certified as a paralegal. I am presently seeking to complete a two-year degree in Business Administration from Strayer University, Maryland. Prior to attending Strayer, I continued to learn through classes, seminars, and workshops on subject matter related to the administrative assistant profession. I have taken classes sponsored by the International Association of Administrative Professionals (IAAP) for the Certified Professional Secretaries Examination. I aspire one day to take the exam to become a CPS.

If you want to excel as an administrative assistant, executive assistant, or office manager, research the company/firm for which you want to work. Also, take classes related to the field of business. Be certain the field you choose matches your values and personal work

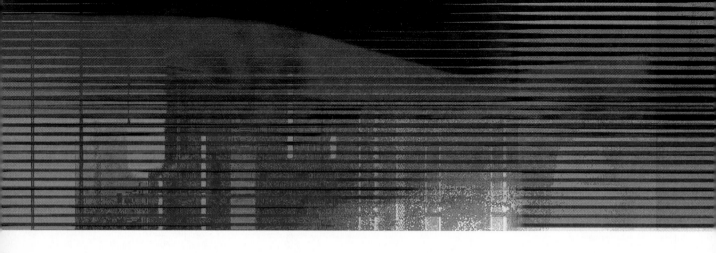

style. This is the computer age; learn to be a part of it, or you will be left behind. Although you may receive little credit or recognition for jobs well done, the rewards do come. Be patient. Realize as you begin work in this field that it is *your beginning to a promising future.*

I am extremely active in the community in which I live, being a chaplain with my husband in the Married Couples Ministry of Ebenezer AME Church, Fort Washington, Maryland. My professional associations and rewards include the following:

- Active member of International Association of Administrative Professionals (IAAP)
- Active member of District of Columbia Chapter, IAAP
- Elected on the international level as a 2001–2003 Trustee, Retirement Trust Foundation
- Portrait of Excellence Award, U.S. Department of Education, Washington, D.C., 1991
- Via FedEx (Federal Express) Administrative Excellence Award, 1994
- Employee of the Year, Howard University Hospital, 1997
- International Who's Who of Professional Managers, 1997
- Contributed to a news article in *The Washington Post* (3-11-96) on the Administrative Professional Association

- Contributed to "The Exceptional Assistant," *Administrative Assistant Adviser* and "Respect: The Best Gift This Week," *Washington Times*

The loves of my life are my husband, Robert, and daughters, Nancie and Kimberly. I also enjoy the challenge of new tasks and responsibilities. I appreciate and thank my family for standing with me as I have walked from one room to another during my 30 years in the business world.

NARRESSA ROSS LEE'S CASE

Here are two situations I encountered during my years as an administrative assistant. My intent is to help you see that understanding why problems occur is just as important as solving them. After reading my situations, decide what you would do. Then turn to the end of Part 2 (page 163) to see how I solved each situation.

Situation 1
I was in a rush to complete numerous assignments that included mailing several letters and lawsuit summaries to an insurance carrier. The information was to be completed as soon as possible. My computer keyboard locked up two to three times that day. This can be a simple problem to solve once you know what to do. Why was my keyboard locking up?

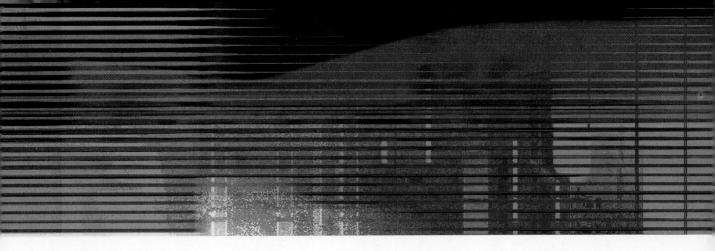

Situation 2

The A: drive on my computer would not permit me to read a disk. I tried rebooting the computer, which did not work. I removed the disk and inserted it back in the A: drive. It still would not read the disk. I needed to retrieve several documents and did not have time to rekey the entire set of minutes, announcements, special-assignment letters, and new committee policies. What should I have done?

CHAPTER 3
TELEWORK

LEARNING OBJECTIVES

1. Define telework and explain the various terms used.
2. Identify the advantages and disadvantages of telework.
3. Describe the individual qualities and skills necessary for success in telework.
4. Describe the essentials of a telework space.
5. Explain the organizational commitment and techniques required to manage and support teleworkers.
6. *Determine and practice the qualities and behaviors necessary in self-management.*

A continually growing segment of the U.S. workforce is choosing to work in locations outside of the traditional office. Research in 2000 conducted by the International Telework Association & Council indicated that there were 2.8 million new teleworkers from 1999 to 2000, with a projection by 2004 of 30 million teleworkers.[1] The growing number of people in telework is not limited to the United States. In the UK, there are over 1 million employees teleworking, with the projection that by the year 2010, 52 percent of the population will be in some form of telework.[2] A survey of 15 member nations of the European Union showed that the United States is behind three of the EU countries (Finland, Netherlands, and Sweden) in per capita telework participation. This survey also projected that the EU countries may reach 40 million teleworkers before the United States does.[3] Clearly, telework is not only a national phenomenon, but also an international one.

© PhotoDisc, Inc.

It is projected that by 2005, there will be 30 million teleworkers in the United States.

---

[1]Ginger Kaderabek, "Office Sweet Office," *Computer, Buyer's Guide and Handbook*, January 2001, 80.

[2]Ibid.

[3]"Telework America (TWA) 2000—Research Results," accessed March 3, 2001; available from www.telecommute.org/twa2000/research_results_summary.shtml.

Teleworkers work from home, from telework centers, from satellite offices, from client's offices, from airport lounges, from hotel rooms, from their cars, or even from the local Starbucks®. Many public places now accommodate this work style. For example, a number of airports have enclosed workspaces with desks, telephones, and plugs for notebook computers. Hotels often have desks built especially for computers in the guest rooms, and many have fax machines/printers/copiers as permanent equipment in the rooms. Even places we traditionally think of as vacation spots (such as ski lodges and cruise ships) now have workstations. Literally, our society is one that understands, promotes, accepts, and even demands support for an anyplace and anywhere work style.

TELEWORK DEFINED

You learned some basic definitions of telework in Chapter 2. However, before studying this chapter further, you need to understand the terminology. *Teleworking* and *telecommuting* have often been used interchangeably. However, there are differences between the two. In this text, the traditional definition of telecommuting is used. **Telecommuting** is the workstyle of salaried employees (employees paid by organizations for either full- or part-time work) who work at home for part or all of the workweek rather than going to a business office. Telecommuting was the original term used when virtual work was first introduced.

Telework is a broader term that means using telecommunications to work from a home office, a client's office, or a multitude of other locations. **Mobile telework** is a term used to describe the arrangement of individuals who spend a great deal of time traveling and/or on customers' premises (for example, consulting or sales work). The **virtual office** for purposes of this text means the operational domain of any organization that includes remote workers. One of the later iterations of telework is the **virtual company,** a company in which all or most all of the staff members work from home. This model is a relatively common one for small start-up companies since it requires minimal expenditures for office space and equipment. Figure 3-1 gives several Web addresses that will help you learn more about telework.

Why telework? The advantages to the individual and to the organization are many. However, there are distinct disadvantages also. Before an organization decides to support telework or before an individual decides to become a part of the rapidly growing teleworker group, a careful analysis should be made of the advantages and disadvantages.

Advantages to the Individual Worker

Here are some of the advantages cited by individuals who are teleworkers.

- Fewer distractions, with the result being greater productivity

RESOURCES FOR TELEWORKERS

- www.att.com/telework—AT&T's Website
- www.ecatt.com—Status of telework worldwide
- www.gilgordon.com—A variety of teleworking resources
- www.nepi.org—National Environmental Policy Institute that is studying telework
- www.intlhomeworkers.com—Work From Home Jobs Digest

- www.gdinet.com—General information about remote employment
- www.cot.org—Center for Office Technology
- www.telecommute.org—International Telework Association & Council

Figure 3-1

- Greater flexibility of work times and work style
- Decreased driving, with resultant decreases in gasoline costs—no long commute to the traditional office
- Access to family when working at home
- Increased flexibility in daily schedule
- Autonomy
- Freedom to make mistakes and correct them on your own
- Deliverance from office politics
- Flexibility for two-career couples to work for different employers many miles apart (even cities or states apart)
- Financial savings from at-home versus restaurant lunches and business wardrobe costs
- Elimination of commuting aggravations, such as rush-hour traffic and parking
- Opportunity to remain in work despite moving from one part of the country to another

In a survey done by AT&T®, teleworkers identified additional advantages of telework. Some of the results of this survey, along with the demographics of teleworkers, are shown in Figure 3-2. If you know someone who is a teleworker or you have done telework, you may add your own list of advantages to the ones listed. Each person's particular set of values determines whether the individual finds telework attractive. For example, if you value flexibility, autonomy, and freedom, you may find telework to be the right job for you. Also, if you have small children and you value having greater accessibility to them during the day, telework may be what you decide to do.

Disadvantages to the Individual Worker

Some of the disadvantages for the teleworker are as follows:

- Isolation from the office team—can be a lonely environment
- Lack of organizational identity—few or zero ties with an organization
- No support group—teleworker is responsible for all aspects of his or her job
- Little or no support for telecommunication problems
- Lack of access to necessary equipment
- Loss of fringe benefits, such as paid vacations and insurance coverage, if you are a **self-employed teleworker** (a individual owner not employed by an organization)
- Fewer opportunities for development and promotion
- Conflict between work and home responsibilities
- Interruptions and distractions if in a home environment

As is apparent from the lists of advantages and disadvantages, the telework environment is

TELEWORKER STUDY RESULTS

- 74 percent were married.
- 28 percent had a child in the house under 6 years old.
- 32 percent had a child in the house between the ages of 6 and 12.
- 25 percent had teenagers in the house aged 13 to 17.
- 73 percent said they have a more satisfying personal and family life than they had before telecommuting.
- 63 percent said telecommuting has positively affected their careers.
- 24 percent said they have gained more responsibility because they telecommute.

- 71 percent said the job is more satisfying now that they telecommute.
- 68 percent say they communicate less with co-workers.
- 30 percent say their productivity has increased an average of 22 percent.
- 71 percent said they have more uninterrupted time and better concentration.

Figure 3-2

Source: Study commissioned by AT&T of 12,000 U.S. households; in-depth interviews were done with 400 teleworkers.

not a perfect one. It has its downsides, just as working in the traditional office does. Each individual considering telework must determine his or her goals, career directions, priorities, and needs. Also, consideration needs to be given to personality and work style. The Myers-Briggs, an instrument developed from the work of the noted psychologist Carl Jung, purports to classify individuals according to a typology derived from their preferences on how they come to know and understand the world. For example

- An individual who prefers to be energized by the outside world is classified as an extrovert.
- An individual who prefers to focus attention on the inner world is classified as an introvert.

Additionally, the instrument classifies people according to intuition/sensing, thinking/feeling, and judging/perceiving. As an example of how these personality classifications may be used in determining your interest in telework, a person high in extroversion is more likely to be successful in telework if there is a high degree of communication with outside individuals. For example, a consultant who works from his or her home but often visits the site of the customer probably enjoys the work more than a person who is high in introversion. A person high in introversion probably requires little communication with others. That person, for example, may enjoy telework that involves the production of documents, such as setting up Web pages, writing reports, and so on. Although a detailed explanation of the Myers-Briggs inventory is outside the scope of this textbook, if you are serious about telework, you may want to consider your personality type as defined by the inventory. Many colleges and universities offer the instrument to their students.

Advantages to the Organization

Advantages to organizations in pursuing telework options include

- Greater productivity of employees. For example, the use of teleworkers can increase employee retention and productivity by approximately 20 percent
- Greater flexibility in staff size changes since facilities are less sensitive to teleworker staff size
- Greater flexibility in allocation of on-site facilities
- Financial savings from reduced office space; some studies report a savings of between $5,000 and $10,000 per year on real estate costs.[4]
- Access to highly skilled workers across the nation. For example, high-tech companies dependent on technological skills are less concerned about where individuals work than about finding individuals with the necessary skills.
- Improved accuracy in employee performance evaluations based on net productivity and quality of work[5]
- Flexible employment opportunities. For example, women in their childbearing years may be provided telework in order to retain their expertise for the organization.
- Opportunity for work to be done outside traditional office hours
- Opportunity for work to be done at remote locations
- Greater competitiveness in a global economy
- Increased productivity when workers are freed from meetings and office socializing
- Type of work can be done better in isolation

As unlikely as it may seem, a fire chief in Fairfax County, Virginia, determined that teleworking on certain aspects of his job improved productivity. Report writing was one of his main activities. This task, since it demanded concentration and accuracy, was one that clearly could be done better in isolation than at the firehouse. When he began to telework from his home office for certain periods of the week, his productivity shot up 20 percent because he produced reports more immediately (shortly after the incident) and more accurately.[6]

[4]Ginger Kaderabek, "Office Sweet Office," *Computer, Buyer's Guide and Handbook*, January 2001, 81.

[5]"Arevo: Advocates for Remote Employment and the Virtual Office," accessed March 3, 2001; available from www.globaldialog.com/~morse/arevo/index.htm.

[6]"Telecommuting (or Telework): Alive and Well or Fading Away?" accessed March 6, 2001; available from www.telecommute.org/aboutitac/alive.shtm.

Disadvantages to the Organization

Disadvantages to the organization may be as follows:

- Managing teleworkers
- Experiencing increased selection and training costs
- Developing policies for teleworkers
- Determining performance/evaluation methods
- Assuring that teleworkers remain part of the total workforce team
- Providing technological support

These disadvantages are generic ones that are particularly true for organizations in the infancy of their efforts in telework. If an organization is going to commit to long-term telework, planning must be done to avoid these disadvantages. The supervisors of teleworkers must manage these workers differently than traditional workers. The next paragraph offers suggestions concerning management techniques.

When providing telework opportunities, the organization must think differently about the management role. How can managers not only measure the productivity of the worker, but also help the worker to feel a part of the total organization while working in isolated locations? Consideration must be given to employing the right people in telework situations and then giving them the proper support. There are no easy answers, but many organizations are making the arrangement work effectively. Organizations are using video conferencing, telephone conferencing, and computer conferencing to link individuals from their remote locations to individuals in the traditional office setting. Also, a number of organizations include teleworkers in biweekly or monthly staff meetings on site at the organization. **Virtual teams** are also used, dispersed workers who come together through telecommunications technology to accomplish a task. Before the teleworker begins any task, both the manager and the teleworker must be clear about project expectations and timelines. Since teleworkers receive less informal feedback than do other employees, they must receive adequate information during formal evaluation sessions.

The concerns and techniques given here address only a few of the myriad management issues. An organization that supports teleworkers must continually study and improve its support structures to assure the productivity of its teleworkers.

Societal Advantages

Societal advantages include

- Increased entrepreneurial activity
- Increased community stability
- Less pollution

Telework encourages entrepreneurial activity. Individuals can set up and maintain home offices at relatively low costs. Technology and the Internet provide new business opportunities that were not available in the past. To understand the relevance of this statement, just scan the Web to discover the number of entrepreneurs who have beginning ventures. Additionally, more opportunities are available for women since telework allows them to maintain a successful business operation while juggling family and home responsibilities.

Telework also provides for increased community stability and less pollution of our environment. In a study conducted of their workers in 2000, AT&T reported the following:

- Teleworkers are more satisfied with their jobs and personal/family lives than the traditional worker. Of the teleworkers, 77 percent reported much greater satisfaction with their current career responsibilities than before teleworking; 83 percent said the same of their personal/family lives. Employee satisfaction results in lower turnover for the company and thus greater community stability; employees tend to stay with a company rather than move to a new area. In fact, AT&T teleworkers reported they had declined offers from other companies, with approximately 67 percent of the teleworkers saying the reason for the decline was their satisfaction with telework.
- According to AT&T research, telework practices produce a significant environmental quality contribution. For example, in 2000, AT&T teleworkers avoided

© PhotoDisc, Inc.

Telework reduces the number of miles driven and reduces the emission of air pollutants.

110 million miles of driving, saving 5.1 million gallons of gasoline. This prevented the emission of air pollutants, including 1.7 million tons of carbon monoxide, 220,000 tons of hydrocarbons, 110,000 tons of nitrogen oxides, and 50,000 tons of carbon dioxide.[7]

TELEWORK SUCCESS

As you already learned, the benefits of telework are many. However, before an individual considers telework, he or she should carefully examine the qualities and skills needed to be a happy, productive teleworker. A study done at the University of Michigan in 1997 listed the following personal qualities a teleworker should have:

- Maturity and self-discipline; ability to work with little supervision
- Flexibility
- Appropriate knowledge of technology, such as computers, email, faxes, and so on
- Consistent, productive, and organized work habits[8]

Listed here are several additional qualities and skills that are necessary.

Strategic Thinking

Individual **strategic thinking** involves the application of your experience and your wants and needs to determine your future directions. It demands the ability to separate yourself from the day-to-day issues for a period of time and take a hard look at what you want to accomplish in the next five or ten years of your life. Two major elements of strategic thinking are values and vision. In Chapter 2, you began to clarify your values. Think for a moment about your top five values. What are they? Did you list such values as freedom, empowerment, independence, responsibility, and family? If so, you may be interested in pursuing telework.

Stephen Covey, a well-known authority in the area of establishing goals, suggests asking these questions as you begin to think strategically about your directions.

- What do I feel are my greatest strengths?
- What strengths have others who know me well noticed in me?
- What have been my happiest moments in life? Why were they happy?
- When I daydream, what do I see myself doing?
- When I look at my work life, what activities do I consider of greatest worth?
- What quality-of-life results do I desire that are different from what I now have?[9]

---

[7]"Telework Reaches All Time High at AT&T," accessed March 6, 2001; available from www.att.com/telework/artlib/alltime-high.html.

[8]L. Bolletino and others, accessed March 6, 2001; available from www.itd.umich.edu/telecommuting.

[9]Stephen R. Covey, Roger Merrill, and Rebecca R. Merrill, *First Things First* (New York: Simon & Schuster, 1994) 307–314.

Once you ask and answer these questions, Covey suggests that you write a **mission statement** (a statement that lists what an individual or organization values and the future direction intended) to clarify your goals. A thoughtful mission statement

- Fulfills your own unique capacity to contribute
- Includes fulfillment in physical, social, mental, and spiritual dimensions
- Is based on quality-of-life results
- Deals with both vision and values
- Deals with all the significant roles in your life—personal, family, work, community
- Inspires you to achieve[10]

To understand more about how a mission statement is written, look at Figure 3-3, which shows one person's mission statement. If you are self-employed and have established a company, you also may want to write a mission statement for your company. Such a statement helps you remain focused on the direction

PERSONAL MISSION STATEMENT

My mission is to:

Discover and use all of my talents and abilities
Treasure my family
Live true to the principles I hold dear (self-sufficiency, honesty, integrity, and giving)
Be an outstanding worker—one who contributes to my employers and clients
Provide adequate income for my family

Figure 3-3

you have determined for the company. An organizational mission statement is shown in Figure 3-4.

Productivity

To be an effective teleworker, you must be productive. You must accomplish the job tasks to the satisfaction of your employer if you are a telecommuter or to the satisfaction of your clients or customers if you are an entrepreneur. If you are a telecommuter, your supervisor needs to be very clear with you about what is expected on each job and when that job is to be completed. If he or she does not provide you with adequate instructions, ask for clarification. Know what is expected to avoid doing a job incorrectly or missing a deadline. If you are working with a client or customer, you need to be certain you understand that person's expectations for the completed job and the timeline for completion. Repeat what you believe the expectations are. Then if there is a misunderstanding, the client or customer can correct you.

Communication Tip:
Check your email at specific times during the day—once at midmorning and once at midafternoon.

Productivity demands discipline. Certainly a large part of your discipline is driven by external sources—that is, your paycheck depends on discipline. If you are an independent worker, you understand the relationship of discipline and productivity. Those individuals who are not disciplined enough to deliver the product the customer/client needs soon find themselves with no customers/clients. You may have a little more flexibility as a telecommuter, since a team of individuals is usually involved on a project. However, if you continue to fail to produce, you eventually will be unemployed.

---

[10]Stephen R. Covey, Roger Merrill, and Rebecca R. Merrill, *First Things First* (New York: Simon & Schuster, 1994), 307–314.

Merck & Co., Inc.

Merck & Co., Inc. is a leading research-driven pharmaceutical products and services company. Merck discovers, develops, manufactures and markets a broad range of innovative products to improve human and animal health.

Our Mission

The mission of Merck is to provide society with superior products and services—innovations and solutions that improve the quality of life and satisfy customer needs—to provide employees with meaningful work and advancement opportunities and investors with a superior rate of return.

Our Values

1. Our business is preserving and improving human life.
2. We are committed to the highest standards of ethics and integrity.
3. We are dedicated to the highest level of scientific excellence and commit our research to improving human and animal health and the quality of life.
4. We expect profits, but only from work that satisfies customer needs and benefits humanity.
5. We recognize that the ability to excel—to most competitively meet society's and customers' needs—depends on the integrity, knowledge, imagination, skill, diversity and teamwork of employees, and we value these qualities most highly.

Figure 3-4

Source: www.merck.com

Discipline involves knowing when to tell friends you cannot talk on the phone—you have work to get done. One concern of the home-based worker is that society does not understand the implications of working at home. Individuals often call and say such things as, "Did I get you out of bed?" when it is 8:00 a.m. If you respond, "Of course, I am up; I am working," many people still do not get the picture. Somehow it is more difficult for the general public to envision you are actually working if you are at home. Fortunately, that image is beginning to change. However, you must be clear with your friends and relatives when they call; tell them

you are working. Additionally, be sensitive to the needs of the caller; ask if you can call back at a better time. If you are pleasant but firm, callers will soon understand the situation.

A way of ensuring more discipline and thus greater productivity is to set objectives for yourself each day. Just as you would set objectives if you were working in the traditional office, you need to set them at home. In fact, before you quit work in the afternoon, you might write down (on your computer or palm pilot) the objectives you need to accomplish for the next day. Another key to helping you remain disciplined is to put timelines by each

Human Relations Tip:

When a personal call interrupts your work time, tell the caller politely but firmly "I am sorry, but I cannot talk now. I am working on an important project. I will be free at 8 this evening. Are you available then?"

objective. Obviously, some projects take more or less time than you had envisioned, but establishing estimated times helps keep you focused the next day. When you turn on your computer in the morning, you are immediately reminded of your tasks.

Do not let distractions interfere with your focus. Distractions for the home-based worker are numerous—household chores, children, and errands, to name a few. Formulate a plan for dealing with them. For example, if you have small children, you may need to hire some help during the day. When your children are school age, help them understand when you can and cannot be disturbed.

You also need to be disciplined about when to quit work. High achievers may be tempted to work 14 hours a day. You may be able to keep that schedule for a few days, but burnout and sleep deprivation eventually will occur.

Self-Management

Self-management is the soft-skill objective for this chapter. What does **self-management** mean? It means that you

- Have self-knowledge—you know your personal and professional strengths and weaknesses
- Are able to manage your time effectively
- Are able to handle stress
- Are able to balance your work and your personal life
- Understand your values
- Are able to articulate your goals

Self-management is no small task for any one. It requires constant attention and self-nurturing. Take a few minutes now to evaluate your self-management skills by completing Self-Check B.

Creativity

In the traditional office setting, you generally have someone you can go to for help in solving problems. You are part of a team that can help you, and you soon learn each team member's

Self-Check B

Answer these questions with a yes or no answer.

		YES	NO
1.	I know what my values are.	☐	☐
2.	I am able to articulate my goals.	☐	☐
3.	I know my strengths.	☐	☐
4.	I understand my weaknesses.	☐	☐
5.	I seek to minimize my weaknesses.	☐	☐
6.	I maintain an appropriate balance between my work and my personal life.	☐	☐

strengths and weaknesses. You know what individual to go to for help. Not so in most telework situations. You have to be a creative problem solver. You have to figure out how a report should be written, what format is most effective, and what graphs and charts to include. The old proverb "Necessity is the mother of invention" is particularly true for the teleworker. Whatever occurs, you must be creative enough to find a solution.

Technology Skills

Technology skills are essential in many jobs today, including that of an administrative professional. However, the role that technology plays in the life of a teleworker cannot be overstated. Remember what telework means: using telecommunications to work from a home office, a client's office, a car, a satellite center, or a multitude of other locations. Much of the time, a teleworker performs his or her job in isolation, with no readily available help when a problem with technology occurs. The teleworker must figure out the problem or get some assistance from an outside source. Many sources are available today to help with telecommunications problems. Microsoft®, AOL®, and Xerox®, for example, have telephone help lines available many hours of the day. Some help services even offer assistance 24 hours a day. Many manufacturers of telecommunication equipment offer online services. But using these services demands more understanding of telecommunications on the part of the teleworker than is demanded of the worker in

A teleworker must be able to troubleshoot technology problems.

the traditional office. For example, many traditional offices have a telecommunications department that provides assistance when problems occur. The assistants from this department generally can correct the problem for you. As a teleworker, you have to be able to understand the problem well enough to describe it accurately and to follow instructions from the online or telephone assistant. Also, you have to be able to apply what you read in manuals in order to prevent problems from occurring. In other words, you have to be your own troubleshooter.

As telecommunication equipment becomes more sophisticated, you, as a teleworker, must continue to upgrade your knowledge and skill. You can do so by reading computer periodicals, by checking upgrades on equipment through the Web, and by talking with other teleworkers about what they are using. Chat rooms exist for teleworkers to communicate with each other on a variety of topics. You can find chat rooms by using a search engine such as Yahoo® or Google™ and entering the keywords *Teleworker Chat Rooms.* Another option for keeping up to date on equipment is to enroll in a distance education course. Many community colleges and universities offer these courses. They allow you the flexibility of learning from your own home.

SUCCESS DETRACTORS

Being a successful teleworker demands that you conquer isolation, noise, and family concerns. You also have to develop an appropriate balance between home and work responsibilities.

Isolation

To a great degree, the environment of a teleworker is one of isolation. If you have been accustomed to working in a traditional environment, you understand the differences immediately. You are not able to get a cup of coffee with a co-worker and exchange small talk. You do not have access to someone with whom you can discuss a work problem. You miss little things, such as walking into work with someone from the parking lot. The degree to which isolation bothers you depends to a degree on your personality traits. Are you an introvert or an extrovert by nature? As you learned earlier, the Myers-Briggs instrument can help you discover several of your personality traits, including introversion and extroversion. However, Self-Check C on page 68 will offer you some insight as to whether you are an introvert or an extrovert. Take that quiz now.

If you discover you are more extroverted, you can still enjoy telework and be successful at it. However, you will need to seek more contact with others than someone who is introverted. Here are suggestions for feeling less isolated.

- Join a health club; exercise with people; sign up for an aerobics class.
- Make arrangements to have lunch occasionally with someone in a similar business.
- Go to a deli or coffeehouse where you can chat with people.
- Exchange pleasantries with the merchants with whom you deal; for example, your mailing service, your office supply store, and your grocery store.

Are You an Introvert or Extrovert?

Both a strong introvert and a strong extrovert will have some difficulty adapting to telework. Answer each question by recording R for "rarely," S for "sometimes," F for "frequently," or A for "always." Score your responses using this rating: Rarely = 1, Sometimes = 2, Frequently = 3, Always = 4. When you finish the quiz, go to the end of the chapter and read the comments that pertain to the type you most closely resemble.

1. I turn on the TV as soon as I get home. _____
2. I do my best work with others around. _____
3. Time goes more quickly when I am with others. _____
4. I would rather walk in the city than in the woods. _____
5. On my own, I get bored easily. _____
6. I would rather go to a party than stay at home. _____
7. I feel restless after a day spent alone. _____
8. I do not like to eat alone. _____
9. I get a lot of energy from others. _____
10. I need colleagues to problem-solve. _____
11. Frequent feedback helps me enjoy a project. _____
12. When things go wrong, I call a friend right away.[11] _____

- If you are a telecommuter, take advantage of company-sponsored professional development activities and company social events.
- Turn on the television to a news program during your lunch to get in touch with what is happening in the outside world.
- Schedule jogs or walks with a neighbor who also exercises.
- Go to an occasional movie in the afternoon.

If you are extremely introverted, you probably need to work on enjoying interactions with others. For example, if your business involves working with clients or on teams, you may need to work on communicating with your contacts and enjoying your interactions.

Noise

Noise around the home can be a problem due to the following:

- Noisy neighbors
- Garbage trucks
- Car and ambulance alarms
- Incessant barking of dogs outside the home
- Pets within the home making noise—dogs, birds, and cats
- Airplanes
- Neighbors doing yard work or having pool parties

Since noise can be a distraction when you are trying to work, you should try to lower the noise level around the house. Some of these solutions are more costly than others. Adding more insulation to your home is one solution, although a costly one. You can install acoustic foam on your walls, put in double-pane glass windows, and add wall-to-wall carpeting. Here are some less costly ways to lessen the noise:

- Add noise-reducing ceiling tiles
- Seal electrical fixtures with electric switch sealers
- Install self-stick foam weather stripping to windows

Family Issues

If you have decided to become a teleworker and you are married, have a family, or live with other family members, you must talk with your family members about this arrangement. First of all, many people have misconceptions about what working from home means. To some, it means you are not really working or you have time to take on additional responsibilities around the house. Of course, these are gross misconceptions. You need to talk with your family about what teleworking is. Explain that you are serious about your work and that you cannot be a full-time parent or housekeeper and maintain a full-time work schedule. Each member of the family needs to understand his

---

[11]Alice Bredin, *The Home Office Solution* (New York: John Wiley & Sons, 1998), 38–42.

or her role in the new arrangement. Determine a division of household tasks. What are the spouse's responsibilities? What are the children's responsibilities? Who does the cooking? Who does the cleaning? Who buys the groceries? Once the responsibilities have been determined, write them down and post them in a place that is readily accessible to all family members. Other suggestions for keeping family issues to a minimum include the following:

- Find a house-cleaning service or an individual who can come in when needed; hire someone full-time if the workload becomes overwhelming.
- Decide if you need someone to help with the children either full-time or after school. If you do, call a child-care referral service and/or ask friends for recommendations. You need to be assured that you have a competent, caring individual looking after your children.

© Corbis

Clarify the role expectations of family members through a meeting.

- Keep the lines of communication open with your family. When you believe someone is not doing his or her fair share, communicate your feelings.
- Do not expect perfection from your family as they perform their tasks. Be grateful they are chipping in to do their share of the work.
- Try to keep your home a low-maintenance one. Do not buy furniture or carpet that requires constant cleaning—such as glass tables or white carpet.

With both family and friends, continue to communicate what your needs and expectations are. Be sure they know your working hours, as if you were going to the traditional office each day. To help your family understand when you cannot be disturbed, you may

- Close your office door
- Put a "Do not disturb" sign on the door
- Put a sign on a bulletin board in a place the family uses frequently to indicate your working hours for the day or week

Refer to your home office as your workplace. Do not let family and friends think you can take on extra community projects because you are a teleworker. Give a business reason for your refusal; for example, "I am sorry but I have an important project to finish. I simply do not have the time." Answer your business phone professionally with your name and/or your company name.

Work/Life Balance

Just as you cannot let family and friends interrupt your work to the point that you get nothing done, you also cannot ignore family and friends to the point that all you do is work. There must be a balance between family and work. What is that balance? You must answer that question for yourself. What is important is that you understand what a healthy balance is and maintain that balance. You may have heard the old saying "All work and no play makes Jack [or Jill] a dull person." The statement has great validity. If you allow work to become all-consuming, you can develop stress levels that make you physically and emotionally sick. If you never read a book, listen to a news program, read a magazine, or learn something new outside of your job, you may find that you have fewer good ideas and less creativity in your work projects. Several questions about balancing work and life are given in Figure 3-5; if you answer "yes" to four or more of these questions, your life may be out of balance.

HOME WORKSPACE

Before considering what type and size of workspace you need, ask yourself these questions: What type of work will I be doing? How much space do I need to accomplish the work? What furniture and equipment do I need? Will I be working on highly technical material that requires a distraction-free workspace? Will I be meeting clients or customers in my workspace? What environmental factors are important to me; for example, do I need to be close to a window?

Once you ask and answer these questions, you are ready to consider the location and size of your workspace.

Workspace Size and Location

If you need a distraction-free workspace, locate your office away from the family living area of your home. A spare bedroom or a basement room may be the answer. If clients, customers, and/or co-workers will be meeting with you occasionally, the space should be close to an outside entrance. If you have extremely noisy neighbors on one side of you, locate your workspace on the opposite side of the house or as far away from the noise as possible. Ask yourself this question: How large does my space need to be? If you are a telecommuter who is working at home only one or two days per week, you can be less concerned about workspace. Your space may be a small area you set up with a minimum amount of equipment in a corner of a room. If you are working at home full-time, consider what type and size of desk you need and the space required for a copier, a computer, a printer, and any other equipment. Also consider the number and size of filing cabinets needed and whether you need bookshelves.

The location you choose must have adequate lighting for your equipment. You do not want to locate your computer so close to a window that the outside light causes a glare on your computer screen. Your location also needs to have sufficient electrical outlets and telephone jacks to accommodate your equipment. The electrical outlets must be in proximity to your equipment. Stringing extension cords across a room can be dangerous.

You want to be able to control the heating and cooling in the room. Working in an environment that is too hot or too cold contributes to lessened productivity.

The color of your office can make a big difference in your productivity. Because you are going to spend a major portion of your time in the office, color is important. We know from color research that colors affect our well-being. Tones of gray tend to put workers to sleep. Cool colors, such as light greens and light blues, produce a calm and tranquil atmosphere. Red is an aggressive color and is not appropriate when you need to concentrate for long periods of time. Warm colors, such as yellow, are cheerful and inviting. Color research shows that people have more clarity of thought when working in yellow environments. Yellow also stimulates creativity and mental activity.

Furniture and Equipment

When determining the type of furniture and equipment you need, pay attention to ergonomic factors. You will learn more about ergonomics in Chapters 4 and 7. **Ergonomics** refers to furniture and equipment that is psychologically sound so you remain healthy as you use it. For example, your chair should have an adjustable back and seat so it is the right height and fits your back; otherwise, the chair can cause you health problems. Your desk should also be ergonomically correct. Ideally, your desk should be height-adjustable and have an adjustable keyboard pad offering keyboard and mouse support. The illustration on this page shows one configuration of office furniture and equipment.

Your equipment purchases should include the basics—a computer, printer, fax, copier, and scanner. Multifunction machines (such as a fax, printer, copier, and scanner all in one machine) are available and may meet your needs. To help

© PhotoDisc, Inc.

Furniture and equipment should satisfy your needs and be ergonomically sound.

you determine what equipment will best meet your needs, do the following:

- Read computer periodicals such as *Home Office Computing*, *PC World*, and *PC Computing*.
- Conduct online research; many equipment and software manufacturers advertise their products through the Internet. Figure 3-6 provides several online resources.
- Shop your local computer stores.
- Talk with people who use the technology. For example, discuss the best buys with other teleworkers, computer technicians, or friends who are computer-literate.

ONLINE RESOURCES FOR EQUIPMENT

- www.athome.compaq.com
- www.dell.com
- www.epson.com
- www.fujifilm.com
- www.gateway.com
- www.hp.com/all-in-one
- www.kodak.com
- www.lexmark.com
- www.minolta-qms.com
- www.qps-inc.com
- www.umax.com/usa
- www.viewsonic.com
- www.zdnet.com/computershopper

Figure 3-6

Workplace Safety

Be conscious of the need for security. Since you are often working home alone using computer technology and other expensive hardware, you want to do what you can to maintain a theft-proof environment. Here are several suggestions for keeping your workplace safe:

- Install simple locks on windows so they cannot be forced open from the outside.
- Install a security system that contacts the police if there is a break-in.
- Install a deadbolt on the office door.
- Draw the shades when you are working at night.
- When traveling for a few days, leave a few lights on and put other lights on automatic timers.
- Be certain your office furniture and equipment is insured for the proper amount.

Health, Life Insurance, and Retirement Benefits

If you are a self-employed teleworker, you need to purchase health and life insurance and set up a program for retirement. Talk with several health and life insurance companies, and research the benefits available. If you have a friend who has a trusted insurance agent, you might start with that person. You must be concerned about providing adequately for you and your family during your retirement years. Options include **IRAs** (individual retirement accounts) and investments in **mutual funds** (funds that include a combination of stocks and bonds purchased through a mutual fund company) or individual **stocks** (ownership in a company) and **bonds** (a debt owed by an organization). Consult with an investment counselor about your long-term plans and needs.

SURVIVAL STRATEGIES

As a teleworker, these skills are essential.

- Creativity
- Self-management
- Productivity

- Strategic thinking
- Technology
- Continual learning

Certainly these skills are many of the same ones the traditional workplace demands. However, in the traditional workforce, you have the luxury of receiving input from your co-workers about your strengths and weaknesses and taking advantage of organization-sponsored staff development events if needed. As a teleworker, these opportunities are not as easily available to you. Thus, it behooves you to take care of yourself. You cannot keep up a pace of constant, effective work production if you do not also give yourself the opportunity for renewal. You do not want to become **insular** (narrow or provincial in outlook). How do you provide that opportunity of renewal? Here are some suggestions.

Take a Walk in the Woods

Give yourself breaks—breaks of 30 minutes and breaks of an hour or two. These breaks do not reduce your productivity; they improve it by giving you a chance to renew and think more creatively. Take a walk in the woods for an hour; notice the beauty of nature. Go to a park; observe the children playing and the dogs enjoying their walks. Let your mind be free of the stresses of work for a period of time.

Reward yourself with longer breaks where you have the chance to enjoy a beautiful setting and also work. That setting may be a week in a cottage on the shores of Lake Michigan or two weeks on Kona Beach in Hawaii. Remember, the teleworker can work from almost any setting as long as he or she has access to telecommunications. You may be surprised at how much work you actually accomplish and how creative and refreshed you feel for allowing yourself the opportunity for renewal. Growth comes when we let ourselves thoroughly experience the world.

Schedule Relaxation

If you are not very good at taking that walk in the woods—you never quite find the time or you just forget about it—schedule the walk on your calendar, along with other relaxation activities. Schedule 30 minutes to read or watch television every evening, or schedule an hour at a local club every week to play tennis with a friend. Although scheduled relaxation appears to be an **oxymoron** (a combination of contradictory terms), many of us have become so conditioned to accomplishing what is on our calendars that the only way we take advantage of a relaxing activity is to schedule it.

Exercise

Numerous studies have shown the importance of regular exercise for our bodies and minds. Yet most Americans ignore the studies and fail to exercise on a regular basis. Here is why exercise is so important. The task of the cardiopulmonary system is to pump oxygen into your blood and then to pump the blood to all parts of your body. When you are sitting and breathing quietly with your heart at rest, less oxygen and blood are flowing to your brain than when you exercise. Your brain activity naturally slows because blood and oxygen are in lower supply.

The exercise should be **aerobic.** Aerobic exercise means the body uses oxygen to produce the energy needed for the activity. In order for an activity to be aerobic, it must meet three criteria: It must be brisk, be sustained, and involve a repeated use of large muscles. Walking, jogging, swimming, stationary cycling, and jumping rope are examples of aerobic exercise.

Both starting and maintaining an effective exercise program are hard tasks but well worth the effort—the payoff not only being a healthier body but also a more creative, productive brain. Here are some tips to help you sustain an exercise program.

- Write on a calendar the days you plan to exercise each week.
- Mark off the days you exercise as the week goes by.
- At the end of the week, count up the number of times you exercised. Did you meet your goal?
- Make arrangements for family or friends to exercise with you.
- Find an indoor location where you can exercise in extreme weather conditions.

Eat Properly

Eating properly may be more of a challenge for the teleworker than the traditional office worker. Why? It is easy to take a break in the kitchen and reach for whatever snack is available. It is also easy to get involved in a project

Leave your cell phone at home while exercising.

and reach for a snack to break the tension. Most of us use food in a variety of ways—to feel better, to be sociable, to reduce boredom. Although food cannot solve our emotional and mental issues, we attempt to fool ourselves that it can. Certainly a major part of the way we treat food has to do with what we learned about food growing up. Did our parents allow us candy if we cleaned our room? Were we rewarded with a special meal celebration if we brought home good grades? To get our eating under control, we may have to undo the patterns we learned as children.

One of the tricks to getting your eating under control is to refrain from buying candy, cookies, and other snacks at the grocery store. If the food is not in the house, you cannot eat it. As you or another family member prepares the weekly grocery list, make certain it is replete with fruits and vegetables. Learn to cut out a major part of the fat that is in your diet, and reduce sugar and caffeine consumption. Excessive intake of fat, sugar, salt, and caffeine contributes to poor health and to certain diseases, such as hypertension and heart disease. The average cup of regular coffee contains 100 to 150 milligrams of caffeine. Nervousness, insomnia, and headaches have been related to as little as 250 milligrams of caffeine. The average American consumes more than 126 pounds of sugar a year. Excessive sugar consumption can lead to an increase in triglyceride levels in the blood, which can lead to cardiovascular disease. Too much salt can lead to an increase in blood pressure and to the development of hypertension.

Sleep

The proper amount of sleep is essential to mental and physical health. Studies show that many Americans have **sleep deprivation;** they have denied their bodies the proper amount of sleep for so long that it is affecting their physical health. Although the amount of sleep needed varies among individuals, studies show that most people need from seven to nine hours of sleep per night.

A number of us have problems getting the proper amount of sleep due to our busy schedules and stressful lives. The teleworker may go back to the "office" at the end of the day for another three or four hours of work. Teleworkers may also go to bed thinking about the projects for the day or the projects planned for the next day and find that sleep does not come for an hour or so after hitting the pillow. Practicing the following techniques will help you fall asleep easily:

- Set aside the hour before bed for quiet activities such as reading.
- Take a hot bath.
- Turn off the TV in the bedroom and/or turn down the TV in an adjoining room.
- Practice deep-breathing exercises.
- Create a relaxing scene in your head—waves rolling up on a beach or a mountain stream.
- Be certain your mattress and pillow are right for you—the proper firmness or softness.
- Pay attention to the amount of coffee, tea, cola, and chocolate you are consuming; these drinks can lead to sleep deprivation.

Reward Yourself

In the traditional work setting, rewards can come from your supervisor or from your co-workers in the form of a smile and a thank you or a pat on the back, with the statement "Good job," or from a promotion and/or increase in salary. When you are a teleworker, you must remember to give yourself rewards. That may not be easy for you to do. However, being successful in life demands that you not only recognize your strengths but also reward yourself for them. You need to feel good about your work and your accomplishments. How do you reward yourself? Try these techniques.

- Make a to-do list of what you plan to accomplish each day. Then mark off your accomplishments at the end of the day. Say a mental "thank you" for your ability to stick to the task.
- Share your accomplishments with others. Tell your spouse, your children, and your close friends about what you have achieved. For example, if you have completed a complicated Web page project and the public response has been favorable, brag about it a

little. Your family and close friends can be proud of your accomplishments also and share your successes.

- Reward yourself. Give yourself a night out at the theatre or buy something for yourself you have been wanting. Take the time to read a novel, go to a concert, or enjoy a meal at a restaurant with family or friends.

MANAGEMENT OF THE TELEWORKER

With the number of teleworkers increasing and the expectation that the numbers will continue to increase, the experienced administrative professional may have the responsibility of supervising a teleworker. Although this chapter has focused on the role, responsibilities, and success factors necessary for being an effective teleworker, some consideration needs to be given to the management of teleworkers. You learned earlier in this chapter that disadvantages to an organization in managing teleworkers include developing policies for them and determining performance/evaluation methods. In addition, the management techniques used are, by necessity, somewhat different than the regular management ones. You will learn more about regular management responsibilities in Chapter 15. Although a detailed discussion of telework management is beyond the scope of this chapter, an overview is presented here for your understanding of some of the unique management responsibilities.

Some of the issues that must be managed with the teleworker are

- Socialization
- Communication
- Selection of teleworker[12]

Socialization

Since the teleworker is not at the same location with the traditional worker, the socialization process is very different. However, the teleworker still must understand the values and directions of the company and meet individuals who are part of the company. The manager of a teleworker should

- Help the teleworker understand the values of the company and determine if there is a match between the individual's values and the company values.
- Introduce a mentoring system that allows the teleworker a contact person to help him or her understand the organization and assist when a problem or an issue comes up. Such a system helps the teleworker feel less remote.
- Bring teleworkers into the organization to engage in team meetings, professional development, and socializing activities of the organization, such as company picnics.

Communication

In managing the teleworker, the manager must determine the most appropriate communication styles, which may vary with the particular job assignment. For example, if the teleworker is beginning a new project with a team of people, it may be appropriate to have a team meeting at the organization's office to go over the objectives and expectations of the project and discuss assignments for each member of the team. As the team members begin to work in their home workspaces, they may communicate through email, teleconferences, or conference calls. The manager of the project may choose to schedule monthly team meetings at the organization's office or participate with the team in email discussions or conference calls. The manager must understand the various communication processes available and what will work best in each situation. Communication between the manager and the teleworker is important and should result in work that is produced effectively with little confusion.

Selection of Teleworkers

You have already learned that if teleworkers are to be successful, they must possess certain characteristics, such as motivation, persistence, and

---

[12]Kevin Daniels, David A. Lamond, and Peter Standen, ed., *Managing Telework* (United States: Thomson Learning, 2000).

technological competencies. As organizations are expanding into telework situations, managers need to give consideration to the variables that impact teleworker selection. Omari and Standen[13] identifies these variables.

- Organizational environment—business goals, corporate culture, management style, co-workers/clients
- Type of telework—knowledge intensity, internal contact, external contact
- Teleworker—work motivation, personality, telework competencies, performance record

- Remote environment—physical, social, psychological
- Task characteristics—autonomy, variety, social integration, sense of value, clarity of goals

If you manage teleworkers, understand that your management role is different and that you must give consideration to the unique variables of the teleworker's environment. The success of the organization's telecommuting efforts and the success of the individual teleworker depend on it.

---

[13]Kevin Daniels, David A. Lamond, and Peter Standen, ed., *Managing Telework* (United States: Thomson Learning, 2000).

CHAPTER SUMMARY

The summary will help you remember the important points covered in the chapter.

- It is projected that by 2004, there will be 30 million teleworkers in the United States. There is also a growing number of people in telework outside the United States; the UK projects that by 2010, 52 percent of its population will be involved in teleworking.
- Advantages of telework for the individual include greater productivity, greater flexibility of work times and work style, decreased driving, greater access to family, autonomy, freedom, and opportunity to remain in work.
- Disadvantages of telework for the individual are isolation, lack of organizational identity, no support group, lack of access to equipment, loss of fringe benefits, fewer opportunities for development and promotion, and conflict between work and home responsibilities.
- Advantages of telework for the organization include financial savings, access to highly skilled workers across the nation, flexible employment opportunities, opportunity for work to be done outside traditional office hours, greater competitiveness in a global economy, and increased productivity.

- Disadvantages of telework for the organization are managing teleworkers, experiencing increased selection and training costs, developing policies for teleworkers, determining performance/evaluation methods, and providing technological support.
- Societal advantages of telework include increased entrepreneurial activity, increased community stability, and less pollution.
- To be successful in telework, the individual must be able to think strategically, be productive, manage oneself, be creative, and use technological skills.
- Detractors to telework success include isolation, noise, family issues, and work/life balance.
- The teleworker must consider home workspace and equipment and furniture needs.
- The teleworker must also consider workplace safety and health, life insurance, and retirement benefits.
- Survival strategies include both short and long breaks, relaxation, exercise, proper nutrition, sleep, and rewards.
- The teleworker must be managed differently than the traditional worker. Managers must consider socialization, communication, and selection of teleworkers.

CHAPTER GLOSSARY

The following terms were introduced in this chapter. Definitions are provided to help you review the terms.

- **Telecommuting** (p. 59)—the workstyle of salaried employees (employees paid by organizations for either full- or part-time work) who work at home for part or all of the workweek rather than going to a business office.
- **Telework** (p. 59)—a broader term than telecommuting that means using telecommunications to work from a home office, a client's office, or a multitude of other locations.
- **Mobile telework** (p. 59)—a term used to describe the arrangement of individuals who spend a great deal of time traveling and/or on customers' premises.
- **Virtual office** (p. 59)—the operational domain of any organization that includes remote workers.
- **Virtual company** (p. 59)—a company in which all or most all of the staff members work from home.

- **Self-employed teleworker** (p. 60)—individual owner not employed by an organization.
- **Virtual teams** (p. 62)—dispersed workers that come together through telecommunications technology to accomplish a task.
- **Strategic thinking** (p. 63)—the application of experience and wants and needs to determine a future direction.
- **Mission statement** (p. 64)—a statement that lists what an individual or organization values and the future direction intended.
- **Self-management** (p. 66)—have self-knowledge, able to manage time and stress, able to balance work and personal life, understand values, and able to articulate goals.

CHAPTER GLOSSARY

(continued)

- **Ergonomics** (p. 71)—refers to office furniture and equipment that is psychologically sound so the user remains healthy while using it.
- **IRAs** (p. 72)—individual retirement accounts.
- **Mutual funds** (p. 72)—funds that include a combination of stocks and bonds purchased through a mutual fund company.
- **Stocks** (p. 72)—ownership in a company.
- **Bonds** (p. 72)—a debt owed by an organization.

- **Insular** (p. 72)—narrow or provincial in outlook.
- **Oxymoron** (p. 73)—a combination of contradictory terms.
- **Aerobic** (p. 73)—exercise that causes the body to use oxygen to produce the energy needed for the activity.
- **Sleep deprivation** (p. 74)—denying the physical body the proper amount of sleep for a long period of time, resulting in deterioration of physical health.

DISCUSSION ITEMS

These discussion items provide an opportunity to test your understanding of the chapter through written responses and/or discussion with your classmates and your instructor.

1. Define telework. List five advantages and five disadvantages of telework for the individual. List five advantages of telework for the organization.
2. List and explain five qualities and skills necessary for success in telework.
3. Explain what is meant by self-management.
4. List what to consider when setting up a home office.
5. List and explain five survival strategies for the teleworker.

CRITICAL-THINKING ACTIVITY

Aaron Stapleton has been working for A&I Telecommunications as an administrative professional for five years. His work involves researching and preparing reports, managing a Website, providing computer and software training, and working on TQM teams. Recently, he was offered the chance to telecommute two days per week, with the rationale being that researching and preparing reports plus managing a Website require a work environment free from interruptions. The company believes he can be more productive by working on these projects from a home office. A&I will provide him with the computer equipment he needs.

Aaron is married and has two children—one ten years old and one two years old. Aaron's wife works full-time away from the home. Aaron has now finished his first two weeks of telecommuting. Although Aaron thought his wife understood that he has a full-time job the two days he is home, she begins making additional demands of him. She suggests that he keep the two-year-old on the two

days he is home. She also expects him to cook on those two nights. He tries keeping the two-year-old, but he cannot get any of his work done. However, since his wife is insisting on the arrangement, he is going to give it more time.

Aaron considers himself an extrovert. Although he enjoys the freedom of working on his own the two days each week, he misses the hubbub of the workplace. He also is getting a lot of email and telephone calls from his supervisor and co-workers about work issues. The report he prepared his first two weeks took more of his time than usual. He had to work from 8 a.m. until 10 p.m. each day to finish the report; his child-care duties and meal preparation also interfered with his work time. He believes his productivity is decreasing rather than increasing. Aaron wants to continue with the telecommuting, but he is not sure the hassles he is facing are worth it. What advice would you give Aaron? Using critical thinking, suggest how the issues Aaron is facing should be handled.

RESPONSES TO SELF-CHECK C

Explanation of Score

12-20 Strong Introvert. You may need to get out more than you are doing now. The critical aspects of working at home, such as communicating with customers or co-workers, may feel like chores to you.

21-30 Moderate Introvert. You probably do not have many problems coping with the relative isolation of working at home. However, make regular interaction breaks a priority.

31-35 Introvert/Extrovert. You enjoy solitary and social time in a balanced way. You have trouble with isolation when a deadline or major project keeps you from your usual regimen of socializing.

36-41 Moderate Extrovert. You often feel cooped up and lonely. The good news is that you are not likely to let that happen very often. As an extroverted person, you probably initiate contact whenever you feel you need it.

42-48 Strong Extrovert. You may have trouble handling the isolation that comes with working at home.

PROJECTS

Project 3-1 (Objectives 1, 2, and 3)
Online Project

Research three articles on the Web to discover the advantages and disadvantages of telework, current telework directions, statistics, and qualities and skills needed by the teleworker. Use the Web addresses given in Figure 3-1 or additional resources that you discover. Write a short summary of your findings, listing at least three sources. Submit your keyed report to your instructor.

Project 3-2 (Objectives 3 and 6)

Using your answers to Self-Check B, write a plan for improving your self-management skills. This plan is part of your ongoing Professional Growth Plan that you began developing in Chapter 1. Concentrate on only one area of self-management. For example, if stress is a problem for you, concentrate on improving your ability to handle it. Identify the actions you will take. Also, briefly address how the weakness you have identified relates to your values and attitudes. Save your self-improvement plan on your Professional Growth Plan disk as "Progro3-2." Develop an appropriate title for this portion of your plan.

Project 3-3 (Objective 4)

Research two articles using periodicals such as *Home Office Computing* and *PC World* or the Web addresses in Figure 3-6 to determine how teleworkers should configure their workspace and how they should use furniture and equipment. Submit a short keyed summary of the articles to your instructor, listing the resources you used.

Project 3-4 (Objective 5)
Collaborative Project

With two or three of your classmates, interview a manager of teleworkers. You may do this interview in a conference call or email the manager with your questions. It does not have to be a personal interview. Ask him or her the following questions:

- How do you select teleworkers?
- How many teleworkers does your organization have presently? Do you expect to have more teleworkers in the future?
- What characteristics and skills do you look for in teleworkers?
- How do you introduce teleworkers to the organization's goals?
- Are there special issues that you have with managing teleworkers? If so, what are they?

Present an oral report of your findings to the class.

ENGLISH USAGE CHALLENGE DRILL

Correct the following sentences. Cite the grammar rule that is applicable to each sentence. Before you begin, refresh your memory of grammar rules by reviewing the rules on the use of common gender language and collective nouns in the Reference Guide of this textbook. In the past, grammatical convention specified using masculine pronouns to refer to indefinite pronouns. Today people are aware that the masculine pronouns exclude women who comprise more than half the population. Correct sentences 1, 2, and 3 by replacing the masculine pronoun to include both males and females.

1. Everyone hopes that he wins the scholarship.
2. Since the technology age has resulted in a proliferation of information, a physician usually has time to read only in his specialty.
3. Each of the employees performed his job well.
4. The audience was cheering as they stood to applaud the speaker.
5. The class presented their report as a group.

ASSESSMENT OF CHAPTER OBJECTIVES

Now that you have completed the chapter and the projects, take a few minutes to review the chapter learning objectives. For your convenience, the objectives are repeated here. Did you accomplish these objectives? If you were unable to accomplish the objectives, give your reasons for not doing so.

1. Define telework and explain the various terms used.   Yes _____   No _____

_____

_____

_____

2. Identify the advantages and disadvantages of telework.   Yes _____   No _____

_____

_____

_____

3. Describe the individual qualities and skills necessary for success in telework.   Yes _____   No _____

_____

_____

_____

4. Describe the essentials of a telework space.   Yes _____   No _____

_____

_____

_____

5. Explain the organizational commitment and techniques required to manage and support teleworkers.

Yes _____ No _____

_____

_____

_____

6. Determine and practice the qualities and behaviors necessary in self-management.

Yes _____ No _____

_____

_____

_____

You may submit your answers in writing to your instructor, using the memorandum form on the Student CD, SCDAP3-1.

CHAPTER 4
COMPUTER HARDWARE AND SOFTWARE

LEARNING OBJECTIVES

1. Explain the functions of computer hardware components.
2. Utilize the Internet to research information on the Web.
3. Explain the difference between operating systems software and applications software.
4. Troubleshoot software problems.
5. Explain the importance of computer ergonomics to physical health.
6. Identify ethical computer behaviors.
7. *Demonstrate a commitment to continual learning in our technological age.*

The computer revolution has occurred. We live with the evidence of this statement daily as we work, shop, attend educational classes, and operate household appliances. Certainly computers will continue to get more powerful and less expensive, with new advances coming constantly. However, the revolution that promised computing power for everyone has occurred. Technology is an integral part of our world. So too has the Internet revolution occurred. Today the **Internet** (the world's largest group of connected computers) and the **Web** (a huge collection of computer files scattered across the Internet) are a part of our daily lives. For example, as a society, we use the Internet and the Web to

- Send email to our friends
- Buy numerous types of products—airline tickets, books, clothes, gifts, computer software and equipment, stocks, groceries, and prescription drugs, to name a few
- Research all types of information, from the latest in software to health issues to job information
- Take college classes

At work, the Internet is invaluable in

- Sending email
- Providing research information
- Allowing businesses to make information available to the public through Web pages
- Selling products
- Connecting businesses worldwide

Just as new advances will continue to occur with computers, so too will there continue to be new advances with the Internet and the Web. The task today and for the future is to fully utilize the changes that will occur in computer and Internet technology to make work and home lives more productive and efficient—no easy task. We must engage in **lifelong learning** (a commitment to continue to learn throughout life), realizing that as technology continues to become more powerful and to offer us more services, we must continue to learn how to utilize these changes effectively in our work and home lives.

The purpose of this chapter is not to teach you a software program or to make you an expert on the interworkings of a computer. No doubt you have already taken software courses in which you learned word processing and possibly spreadsheet, graphics, and presentation programs. The purpose of this chapter is to assist you in understanding the basics of computer operations and to be conversant with current computer and software terminology, along with computer ergonomics and ethics. Review the objectives at the beginning of this chapter so you clearly understand the goals you are to accomplish.

COMPUTER CLASSIFICATIONS

The **microcomputer** (more commonly known as the PC) is the one you will be using in your work. However, you should also have a general understanding of the various other computers and their classifications. Computers are classified by their storage capacity and speed of operation. The classifications are as follows:

- Supercomputers
- Mainframe computers
- Minicomputers
- Workstation computers (supermicros)
- Microcomputers (PCs)

Supercomputers

The mightiest and most expensive mainframes are called **supercomputers.** Although the price of computers fluctuates, supercomputers sell for $27 million and up. They are used in organizations that process huge amounts of information.

For example, biotech and high tech are teaming up today in projects involving the **genome** (determining the genetic blueprint of humanity) and **high-end protein analyzers** (identifying the sequence of the amino acids that make up proteins). Both of these projects require supercomputers. The convergence of medicine and computing is definitely here. Additionally, the federal government uses supercomputers for tasks that require mammoth data manipulation. Examples include national census data processing (for example, the United States Census 2000), worldwide weather forecasting, and weapons research. The present supercomputers operate at a speed of over 12 **teraflops** (one teraflop equals one trillion operations per second). With one trillion bytes of memory and more than 160 **terabytes** (one terabyte equals one trillion bytes) of disk storage, a supercomputer can hold six times the information contained in all the books in the Library of Congress. This capacity allows researchers to develop new drugs, improve airline safety, and continue to engage in human gene research. However, researchers are not satisfied with the

Supercomputers operate at speeds in excess of 12 teraflops per minute, with the projection that by 2003 or 2004, their speeds will increase to 100 teraflops per minute.

speed and capacity of the present supercomputers. The goal of the Accelerated Strategic Computing Initiative (ASCI), under the U.S. Department of Energy in conjunction with IBM, is to build a 100-teraflop supercomputer by 2003 or 2004. In fact, IBM is spending $100 million to design Blue Gene, a supercomputer 1,000 times as powerful as Deep Blue, which defeated chess champion Gary Kasparov in 1997.[1]

Mainframes

Mainframes are large computers capable of processing great amounts of information at fast speeds (although the speed is less than the supercomputer). Mainframes can support a number of auxiliary devices, such as terminals, printers, disk drives, and other input and output equipment. They are commonly found in large businesses and government agencies. However, the market for mainframes is not as great as in the past. Although these old computer giants helped the United States put men on the moon in the years following World War II, they have major competitors today—namely, the supercomputer and PC client-server networks. Even in the Internet business, where traditionally the mainframe has been used extensively, smaller, more flexible machines are threatening it. Although it is projected that the mainframe will continue to be used to a degree by large organizations, its use will be limited.

Technology Tip:
If you misplace a document you have worked on, click the Start button and go to Documents in the pop-up menu. You will see a list of your documents; click on the one you want to open.

Minicomputers

The **minicomputer** (a midrange computer) was introduced in the 1960s and generally was used in midsize organizations. It is slower, has less storage capacity, and is less expensive than the mainframe computer. Although some minicomputers still exist in medium-sized organizations, most minicomputers became obsolete when the **microprocessor** (a single miniature chip that contains the circuitry and components for arithmetic, logic, and control operations) was introduced. Some minicomputers eventually grew to mainframe size and some became microcomputers.

Workstation Computers (Supermicros)

Workstation computers (supermicros) are the upper-end machines of the microcomputer (explained in the next section). They have a large amount of processing power, approaching the power of a mainframe. They have a high-speed microprocessor, significantly increased memory, and hard disk storage capacity. Supermicros are **multiuser** computers (able to serve several users at the same time).

Microcomputers (PCs)

The microcomputer is the smallest of the computer systems. Microcomputers were made possible by the advances in technology in the 1970s that permitted the manufacture of electronic circuits on small silicon chips. In the work environment of today, administrative professionals, managers, and executives have PCs on their desks. PCs are very powerful, having more capabilities and storage capacity than the early mainframes, with the capacity of these machines continuing to grow as technological advances occur. One technological invention that has greatly increased the power of the PC is the **processor chip** (a type of microprocessor) that provides for increased speed and performance capability. Today's processor chips are known as the **Pentium®** processor (manufactured by Intel®), the Advanced Micro Devices **Athlon** for Windows®, and the **PowerPC** processors for the Mac™. Organizations use PCs to run basic applications such as word

[1]Pamela Sherrid, "Bytes and Bits Meet Biotech," *U.S. News & World Report,* April 16, 2001, 33.

processing, spreadsheet, and email programs and to connect employees to the company network and the Internet.

Due to the relative low cost of PCs, they are also purchased extensively for home use. PCs are used to balance personal checkbooks, to pay bills, to assist in investment strategies, to do homework assignments, to review news articles on the Internet, to talk with people all over the world, and even to play games. With the price of PCs decreasing, the home market is expected to continue to grow. Figure 4-1 gives you some tips on caring for your computer.

In addition to the desktop PC, portable computers (**notebooks** or **laptops**) are used extensively. Although notebooks and laptops are smaller than the traditional desktop PC, their power (which is continually increasing), capabilities, and portability make them very popular. For example, someone who travels frequently may use the notebook on a plane, in a hotel room, or in the car. The power of notebooks allows you to crunch data and handle graphics at speeds that are close to the low-end PCs. While on the road, you can also send and retrieve email, check and record calendar events, and do research. You can transfer information from your desktop PC to your note-

book. The administrative professional may use a notebook to take notes at a meeting and format the notes into minutes that are later distributed throughout the organization.

One of the latest additions to the portable PC market is the **PDA** (personal digital assistant). The PDA, at its most basic, serves as an appointment book, an address book, a to-do list, and a calculator. You can also

- Check your email
- Retrieve telephone calls
- Transfer data from personal-information managers such as Microsoft Outlook®
- Read newspaper headlines
- Check the financial markets
- Beam professional information that has traditionally been on business cards to clients or business contacts

Although many PDAs operate on batteries, wireless PDAs are now being produced. The Internet is also becoming wireless, which makes it possible to display Web pages from the wireless Internet to wireless PDAs. In addition, PDAs can become cellular phones and digital cameras. For personal use, we may soon be able to scan supermarket items with our PDAs and pick up the items at the checkout.

COMPUTER CARE

- Keep your computer clean. Dust is a problem because it causes heat buildup in the components it covers. Vacuum every horizontal surface of your computer on a regular basis.
- Keep the keyboard clean. Purchase a can of compressed air to spray between the keys to remove dust. You also can purchase tiny computer vacuums that are specially designed for this task.
- Keep the mouse clean. Use alcohol on a cotton swab to wipe the rollers clean. Clean the ball inside the mouse with lukewarm soapy water and dry it thoroughly.
- Do not have food or drink near your computer. Spilling a soda or getting crumbs inside the keyboard may require a costly visit from a computer repairperson.
- Periodically turn off the monitor and wipe your screen clean with a static-free cleaner.

- Periodically delete files you no longer need from your hard drive. If you think you might need the files at a later time, save them to a floppy disk.
- Periodically defrag your drive. The **defragmenter** is a utility that gathers the fragments of files that the operating system has scattered across the surface of your hard disk and reassembles them so each file's data is **continuous** (with no empty spaces between files). Defragging improves disk performance.
- Make certain you have a **surge suppressor** or an **uninterruptible power supply (UPS)** so power fluctuations do not cripple your computer equipment.

Figure 4-1

© PhotoDisc, Inc.

PDAs provide individuals with the flexibility of checking email, maintaining calendars, and making phone calls on a computer that can be held in the palm of their hand.

PDAs are also called **Palms,** since the industry leader in the field has been Palm®, Inc. As the name suggests, Palms can be held in the palm of your hand. The very small and powerful computers are inexpensive, costing from slightly over $100 to approximately $500. The growth in the number of PDAs in use is phenomenal, with continued growth and expanded applications expected. For example, in 1998, there were slightly over 3 million PDAs in use; by 2004, it is expected that there will be almost 21 million PDAs in use. Some experts in the field are projecting that we will eventually use PDAs to make purchases through infrared or other wireless technology. In other words, PDAs will take the place of cash, checkbooks, and credit cards. In the Scandinavian countries, for example, it is already commonplace to pay for candy and other small items with a cell phone.

INFORMATION INPUT

Information for the computer is input in a variety of ways, including the following:

- Computer keyboard
- Scanners
- Voice recognition technology
- Touch screens
- Digital cameras

Computer Keyboard

You probably use a computer keyboard many hours each day. Obviously, it is the most frequently used input device and is expected to remain so indefinitely. Although voice recognition technology is growing and will continue to grow, the days of speaking into a computer as the only means of inputting information are a long way off and may never be commonplace.

Ergonomic Health Issues

Individuals who sit at a computer keyboard each day for more than two hours should take special care to ensure the workstation is user-friendly. If it is not, health problems may result. **Ergonomics** is the term used to denote the fit between people, the tools they use, and the physical setting where they work. Ergonomics comes from the Greek words **ergos** (work) and **nomos** (natural laws). Due to the amount of time individuals spend at computer keyboards, **RSIs** (repetitive stress injuries) can occur. RSI is a generic name given to injuries that occur over a period of time and are known as overuse disorders. **OSHA** (Occupational Safety & Health Administration) reports that approximately two million workers annually have ergonomic-related injuries, and thousands of these workers miss some work as a result. Thus, RSIs impact workers' health and cost businesses dollars in lost work and insurance claims. A type of RSI is **carpal tunnel syndrome.** This condition occurs due to the compression of a large nerve, the median nerve, as it passes through a tunnel composed of bone and ligaments in the wrist. Symptoms include a gradual onset of numbness and a tingling or burning in the thumb and fingers. Other types of overuse injuries, which occur as a result of sitting at the computer for long periods of time, include the following:

- **Computer vision syndrome** (vision problem associated with screen glare)
- Back problems (from chairs that are not the right height or configuration for the user)

Figure 4-2 gives several tips for helping to avoid RSIs.

- Be certain the light on your computer screen is bright enough. Position monitors parallel to overhead lights and perpendicular to windows.
- Place your computer monitor directly in front of you, with the top of the screen at eye level.
- Position keyboards and mice low enough so your shoulders are relaxed.
- Get a desk light if you are squinting while reading at your desk.
- Take frequent breaks—a one-minute break every 20 minutes.
- Take a short rest period (10–15 minutes) every two–three hours.
- Stand up every 30 minutes.
- Take more frequent breaks to increase circulation if you are stiff when you get up from your chair.
- Be certain your chair is adjusted properly for you. Adjust the angle and height of the backrest of the chair so it supports the hollow in your lower back. Your chair should also have armrests adjusted to the same level of your desk to take the pressure off your neck and shoulders.
- Use proper keyboarding techniques. Always sit up straight. Sit close enough to the keyboard so you do not have to stretch to reach it and close enough to the monitor so you do not have to stretch to see it. Your wrists should be in a straight line with your forearms. Your wrists should never be bent to the side or resting on anything.
- Organize your workstation.
- Be certain that your keyboard is at an appropriate height for you. For most adults, the keyboard should be 24–25 inches from the floor.
- Use good posture.
- Keep wrists relaxed and straight, using only finger movements to strike the keys.
- Look away from the screen for a short period of time every 30 minutes.
- Focus on distant objects occasionally as an exercise to relieve strain on eye muscles.
- Maintain a viewing distance of 24–28 inches from the eye to the computer.
- Use proper hand and wrist position when keyboarding.
- Place the mouse at the side of the keyboard and at the same level. Have it close enough so you do not have to reach a long distance; a mouse pad or rest may help. Choose a mouse that fits your hand.

Figure 4-2

Ergonomic Computer Equipment

In addition to following the tips in Figure 4-2, you may wish to check out ergonomic keyboards, trackballs, and mice. Some of the features of ergonomic keyboards are as follows:

- Split keyboards
- Built-in wrist rest
- Detachable wrist rest
- Chair-mounted keyboards
- Foot-switch support
- Mouse functions through keys

Trackballs are the device of choice for many people whose hands cramp when they use a conventional mouse device. Microsoft manufactures a trackball whose internal moving parts are replaced with an optical sensor that provides the user with a precise pointer that stays stationary on the desk. Also available is a mouse that vibrates, helping the user to find an exact location on cluttered Web pages and Windows screens with less hand motion.

© Eyewire

Ergonomic keyboards offer split keyboard designs and built-in wrist rests, along with other features.

Scanners

Scanners allow information to be input directly into a computer without the traditional key-stroking. Scanners can scan text, drawings, graphics, and photos. You may also modify the copy by

- Adjusting the image size
- Retouching, cropping, and manipulating the copy in various ways
- Editing the scanned copy

Multifunction scanners allow you to print, copy, fax, and scan. These scanners are designed for small offices and home use.

Courtesy of International Business Machines Corporation. Unauthorized use not permitted.

Scanners allow information to be input directly into the computer without keying.

Voice Recognition Systems

Although voice recognition technology has been used with mainframes and minicomputers for over 20 years, it has not been a real option for the PC user until the last few years. It has become an option due to **continuous speech recognition,** which allows you to speak almost naturally in complete phrases and sentences without needing to pause between individual words. In contrast, the older technology, **discrete speech recognition,** required you to pause between individual words. However, even with continuous speech recognition systems, you need to modify your speech patterns to a certain degree. For example, you get the best results if you enunciate words clearly and speak at a consistent rate and volume. With practice and proper speaking patterns, voice

systems can now achieve an accuracy rate of more than 95 percent, with some reports of 98 or even 99 percent accuracy. In addition to accuracy, the systems are fast, allowing the speaker to talk at speeds of 160 words a minute. In contrast, good keyboarders can key approximately 100–120 words a minute; excellent keyboarders, 140 words per minute. In addition to speed and accuracy, other advantages of voice recognition systems include the following:

- Fewer problems with carpal tunnel syndrome because strain to your wrist is reduced
- An alternative for people who have difficulty using their hands to operate a keyboard
- An alternative for people who have difficulty spelling

The systems use headset microphones, which keep the recording element a fixed distance from your mouth and make it easy to alter your position without affecting the recording quality. Here are some of the voice recognition systems that are on the market.

- Dragon NaturallySpeaking®—Allows you to move the mouse by voice and correct a word by saying "correct" followed by the correct word.
- ViaVoice® Millennium—Offers natural language commands for Word, Excel, Outlook, and Internet Explorer®.
- Philips FreeSpeech 2000™—Offers language models for 13 other languages, including French, German, Spanish, and Dutch.
- AOL's Point and Speak®—Allows you to send email without touching a single key. It also works with Windows-based word processing and spreadsheet programs to allow you to prepare reports and papers.

Touch Screens

With a **touch screen,** the user touches the desired choice on the screen with his or her finger rather than using a mouse or trackball. Touch screens are used in a variety of settings, including the following:

- Hospitals, where the M.D. can use it to sign a virtual prescription for a patient
- Fast-food restaurants, where employees input food items ordered and compute the amount of the bill
- Gasoline stations, where customers start the pump by punching in the appropriate type of gasoline
- Office buildings, where visitors find the location of a particular office

Digital Cameras

Digital photography is evolving, but it already gives individuals more options than regular film. The **digital camera** becomes an input device when paired with a PC, allowing the user to print pictures in a variety of formats. Photographs may be inserted into email documents, posted on a Website, and used in other office applications (such as on letterhead and in reports). Digital cameras have quickly evolved from gadgets to serious photography tools designed for business users and professional photographers. You learned in Chapter 1 that the role of the administrative professional may now include designing and managing a Web page. The use of a digital camera provides a great amount of flexibility in designing the page. The quality of a camera depends mainly on the amount of information the camera's sensor can record. The number of **pixels** (picture elements) registered by the sensor measures **resolution** (the quality of the picture). One pixel is a spot in a grid of millions of spots that form the image. The current standard of image quality is the three-megapixel, or 3MP, camera.

With the assistance of photo-editing software, such as Adobe's Photoshop®, photographs can be edited, altering color and contrast, position, and features, for example. You can also add voice annotation to photos and enhance them with special effects. In addition, it is possible to convert already existing prints or transparencies to digital images by using scanners. Photographs may be stored on Zip drives or CDs. You will learn more about these storage devices in the next section of this chapter.

Since this chapter contains a lot of technical information, take a few minutes now to answer the questions in Self-Check A. Once you have completed the Self-Check, refer to the answers at the end of this chapter. If you do not do very well, you might want to reread the first part of this chapter before preceding to the next section.

© PhotoDisc, Inc.

With a digital camera, the user can include photographs in various types of electronic documents.

Self-Check A

1. What are the five major computer classifications?
   _____
   _____

2. What is a PDA and how is it used?
   _____
   _____

3. How is information input to the computer?
   _____
   _____

4. What is the meaning of ergonomics, and why is it important?
   _____
   _____

STORAGE DEVICES

Both internal and external storage are important when working with a computer. The internal storage capacity, or memory, of computers is referred to as primary storage. Memory capacities are expressed in million-byte units called **MB** (megabytes), billion-byte units called **GB** (gigabytes), and trillion-byte units called **TB** (terabytes). For example, your PC may have 124MB or 10GB of **RAM** (random access memory). This memory works very fast and is used to run software packages. Before you purchase a new software program, you need to know if your computer can handle it.

A second type of internal storage on a computer is known as **ROM** (read-only memory). Storage memory is much slower than RAM memory. Both hard disks and CD-ROMs are considered storage memory. Your computer uses storage memory the way you use a file cabinet—to organize, store, and retrieve information. Before buying a new software package, you also need to know how much ROM you have. Your computer uses the ROM to store the software.

The internal storage capacity of computers has continued to increase over the years and will continue to increase. However, internal capacity is always finite. Thus, it is important

to have secondary storage devices. Some of the most common secondary storage devices for the PC are as follows:

- Floppy disks
- Zip and Jaz disks and SuperDisks
- CDs
- DVDs

Floppy Disks

Floppy disks are indispensable storage mediums for the computer. The term *floppy* originated from the first size available (a 5.25-inch disk rarely used today) because it flopped when you waved it. Although floppy is a misnomer for the 3.5-inch disk used now (since it is housed in a rigid case), the term continues to be used to refer to this smaller disk. The amount of data that can be stored on a disk is expressed in terms of **density.** The density of disks is referred to as double-sided and high-density. For example, a double-sided high-density 3.5-inch disk may store 1.44MB (megabytes). To give you an idea of what this means, a typical printed page, using single spacing, contains 2,500 to 3,000 characters. Thus, 1MB holds 400 pages of single-spaced text. Proper care must be taken when using and storing disks. The care of floppy disks is presented in Figure 4-3.

Zip, Jaz, and SuperDisk External Storage

Zip disks are available in 100 and 250MB capacities (the equivalent of 70 to 175 floppy disks) and allow the user to

- Store large files with graphic images
- Archive old files that are not used anymore but must be maintained
- Exchange large files with other users

Removable **Zip drives** are also available that are reasonably inexpensive, portable, and easy to install. The capacity on a Zip drive is from 100MB to 2GB.

The **SuperDisk** holds 120MB of data and solves one of the problems of the Zip

---

Self-Check B

Stop! Take a few minutes to go to your computer and check out how much RAM and ROM you have.

- To find out how much working memory you have, go to My Computer on your desktop. Right-click on the right mouse button and select Properties. The General Tab in the bottom right-hand corner will show you how much RAM you have.

- To find out how much storage memory you have on your computer, go to My Computer on your desktop. Double-click your left mouse button. Right-click on the C: drive; then left-click on Properties. You will see how much used and free space you have on your ROM.

- When labeling a disk, write on an adhesive label before applying it to the disk cover. Remove old labels on a disk before applying a new label.
- Store disks in a specially designed container. Such containers keep the disk free of dust and smoke particles. One smoke particle on the surface of a disk can cause a problem for the disk drive read head.
- Keep floppy disks away from water and other liquids. Dry them with a lint-free cloth if they get wet.

- Keep floppy disks out of direct sunlight and away from other sources of heat.
- Write-protect a disk if it contains data you do not want changed. On a 3.5-inch disk, there is a tiny latch in the lower left-hand corner, which is usually closed. To write-protect the disk, turn the disk over and slide the latch downward so a small window appears in the corner of the disk.

Figure 4-3

format. Zip drives can read only Zip disks; the SuperDisk format can read floppies as well as SuperDisks. The **Jaz disk** provides the same portability as the Zip disk but holds more data than the Zip does. The Jaz disk holds 1GB of data (the equivalent of 850 floppy disks). All of these disks (the Zip disk, Jaz disk, and SuperDisk) are used in portable drives.

CD-ROMs

Besides being used as internal storage for your computer, CD-ROMs are also used as external storage. For example, software packages that you purchase are on CD-ROMs. To install the software, you place the **CD-ROM** (compact disk read-only memory) in the CD drive of your computer. You also may choose to store information on a CD. A good solution for sharing files is the **CD-R** (compact disk recordable). The **CD-E** (compact disk erasable) allows you to rewrite over the data already on the disk. Most PCs now have internal **CD-RW** (compact disk read and write) drives as standard equipment. The CD disk, which holds 550MB to 650MB, allows you to put more data on a disk than the floppy allows at less than $1 per disk.

DVDs

DVD-ROM (digital versatile disk read-only memory) is expected to eventually replace the CD-ROM disk. The DVD disk is the same

diameter as a CD-ROM disk, but it has much more capacity than the CD. It can hold as much as 17GB of data, 24.84 times the data that one CD is capable of holding. DVD-ROMs are also faster than CD-ROMS, and they can take advantage of the high-quality video and multichannel audio capabilities being added to many DVD-ROM-equipped computers. All major PC manufacturers now have models that include DVD-ROM drives.

The first DVD adopters were corporate users who used CD multimedia for training and sales presentations. The disks allowed organizations to make longer and higher-quality full-screen multimedia presentations. DVDs are used in airports and public places (kiosks in lobbies of hotels) where music and video are important parts of the presentation.

INFORMATION OUTPUT

The main two output devices are monitors and printers. If you want **soft copy** (copy shown on the monitor only; a printed copy is not necessary), the video display monitor or **CRT** (cathode ray tube) is appropriate. If you want **hard copy** (printed on paper), the printer is appropriate. A good example of soft copy is the sending of email messages. Most of the time the receiver of the email merely reads the message on the monitor and then saves it in the computer or destroys it. No printed copy is needed.

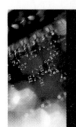
Monitors

Although computer technology advances quickly and major equipment changes are common, computer monitors have been the exception to the rule. Monitors have stayed basically the same for years with the changes being mainly in size and color, with today's monitors offering full color. However, we now have **LCD** (liquid crystal display) monitors in addition to the traditional CRT (cathode ray tube) monitor. The major selling point of LCDs is their size. Traditional CRT monitors are a foot or more deep and take up a lot of space on a desktop. Flat-panel displays are only a few inches deep, making them practical for normal desktops and for cramped quarters such as cubicles. Another advantage of the LCD is its color accuracy. For example, if you send a digital signal for a certain shade of blue, the LCD will always produce that precise shade. CRTs are less accurate in comparison. The major

disadvantage of the LCD has been its price. However, there is very little price differential between CRTs and LCDs now.

Printers

The most commonly used output device is the printer. The two printers in use today are the inkjet and laser printer. In the past, there was a vast difference in the quality of the inkjet printer and laser printer, with the laser printer being far superior in quality. However, inkjet printers have seen the most significant technological advancements of the two, with the results being almost imperceptible differences in the quality of the two printers. Prices of both laser and inkjet printers have decreased significantly; however, inkjet printers remain less expensive than laser printers.

Inkjet Printers

Inkjet printers work by spraying ink onto the paper. These printers are available in black and white or color, with the color printing requiring additional ink cartridges. Inkjet printers produce high-quality graphics and text, with the quality and speed being close to that of a laser printer. Inkjet printers have become inexpensive, with the price ranging from $100 to $300. However, other considerations are the cost of ink/toner products and the number of pages that can be printed with an ink/toner cartridge. Inkjet printers generally have operating costs of 5–10 cents per page for black and white and 10–20 cents per page for color. Inkjet printers produce approximately 12 pages per minute and are capable of producing vivid colors and high-quality graphics.

© Eyewire

Two of the major advantages of a LCD monitor are its thin size and color accuracy.

Laser Printers

The **laser printer** uses a beam of light to form images on paper. Laser is actually an acronym for <u>L</u>ight <u>A</u>mplification by <u>S</u>timulated <u>E</u>mission of <u>R</u>adiation. Laser printers, in general, have faster printing speeds than inkjet printers, with some lasers capable of printing 30 pages per minute. Most businesses use laser printers due to their speed. Although you may purchase a laser printer for approximately $500, most high-end lasers, particularly for networked printers, cost more. However, laser printers typically have operating costs of a few pennies per page, as opposed to 5–20 cents per page for the typical inkjet printer.

Networked Printers

A number of businesses use **networked printers** (attached to a local area network). Depending on the needs of the business, networked printers can be a cost savings to the business. For example, if color or specialized functions are required in one department of a company but not for each individual within the department, the department might use a networked printer. This printer can provide the capabilities needed for a group of people.

Multifunction Peripherals

A multifunction peripheral is a machine that combines two, three, or four functions. Generally, these functions are printing, faxing, copying, and scanning. When considering a multifunction peripheral, consider these factors:

- Space available—One multifunction device takes up far less space than the machines it

replaces and can be installed more easily since one hookup takes care of numerous functions.
- Capability needed—Multifunctions are available with various speeds, print resolutions, and capabilities.
- Cost—The cost can range from a low of several hundred dollars to a high of several thousand dollars, depending on the capabilities and speed of the machine.
- Downtime—When a multifunction device goes down, you lose all functions—the copier, printer, scanner, and fax. This is an important factor to consider, especially in a small business or home office where there are no backup machines.

Take a few minutes now to respond to the items in Self-Check C. Once you have answered the questions, turn to the end of this chapter and check your answers.

Self-Check C

1. List the external computer storage devices.

_____

_____

2. What are the two major types of printers used today?

_____

_____

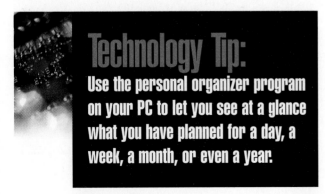

Technology Tip: Use the personal organizer program on your PC to let you see at a glance what you have planned for a day, a week, a month, or even a year.

COMPUTER NETWORKS

Computers and other peripheral equipment, such as printers, can be linked through networks. These networks may be

- **LANs** (local area networks), which link various types of technological equipment within a building or several buildings within the same geographic area
- **MANs** (metropolitan area networks), which link technological equipment over a distance equal to the size of a city and its surroundings

- **WANs** (wide area networks), which link technological equipment over an area of hundreds of thousands of miles

The Internet

The growth of technology and the need for sharing information worldwide have spawned worldwide networks. The Internet is the world's largest group of connected computers, allowing people from all over the world to communicate. The Internet was created in the 1960s as a project of the U.S. Department of Defense. Since that time it has grown exponentially, with approximately 300 million Internet users worldwide. Internet capability has changed the way we live and work, and the number of users will continue to grow. Access to the Internet can be gained in the following ways:

- Cable
- **DSL** (digital subscriber line)
- Fixed wireless
- Satellite
- Analog dial-up

In the past, the only access to the Internet was through a modem attached to a telephone line (the analog dial-up option mentioned above), and this type of access is still used extensively around the world. However, telecommunications is moving rapidly; in addition to analog dial-up, the options mentioned above (cable, DSL, fixed wireless, and satellite) have become available. All of these options promise faster service than the analog dial-up option. However, where you live does affect the availability of various services. For example, **broadband** service (cable, DSL, wireless, and satellite) may not be available in your area at the present time. Service providers are working to make the services available, but there are still areas of the country where certain broadband services are not available. You will learn more about these various telecommunication services in Chapter 5.

The Web

The World Wide Web is one of several features of the Internet. The Web is a huge collection of computer files (more than 800 million Websites and growing daily) scattered across the Internet. The Web is a portion of the information available through the Internet. For example, in addition to the Web, the Internet contains news articles, weather information, entertainment (games), email messages, and encyclopedia information, to name a few. Helpful Web terminology is given in Figure 4-4.

The Web was created by Tim Berners-Lee, a consultant at the Swiss research laboratory CERN, as a tool for physicists to share research data. The general public did not use it until the creation of Mosaic™, a **Web browser** (an application program that provides a way to look at and interact with all the information on the World Wide Web). From this first browser, a number of other browsers have

WEB TERMINOLOGY

- Browser—An information retrieval tool. Some of the Web browsers available are Internet Explorer®, Netscape®, Neoplanet®, and Opera®.
- Home page—A top-level document of an organization in which information about the organization is given, including the company's direction.
- HTML—Hypertext Markup Language; the rules that govern the way we create documents so they can be read by a Web browser.
- HTTP—Hypertext Transport Protocol; the protocol used by Web servers.
- Hyperlink—A link in a given document to information within another document.
- Protocol—A planned method of exchanging data over the Internet.
- Server—A computer that serves information and software to the Internet community.
- URL—Uniform Resource Locator; the address to a source of information.

Figure 4-4

been developed, including Internet Explorer, Netscape, Neoplanet, and Opera.

One of the biggest challenges, with the millions of pieces of information available on the Web, is finding data that meets your needs. Search engines have been developed to help with this process. These search engines are updated frequently and keep up with the new pages being submitted every minute. Figure 4-5 lists several search engines you might find helpful as you surf the Web.

Web Ethics

With the relative newness of the Web and the millions of people and organizations that use the Web daily, Web ethics has become an issue. Richard Spinello, author of *Cyberethics: Morality and Law in Cyberspace*, observes the following about the Web.

> If it is easier to publish and spread truthful and valuable information, it is also easier to spread libel, falsehoods, and pornographic material. If it is easier to reproduce and share digitized information instantly, it is also easier to violate copyright protection. And if it is easier to build personal relationships with consumers, it is also easier to monitor consumers' behavior and invade their personal privacy.[2]

The Electronic Signatures Act (E-Sign), signed into law on October 1, 2000, is an example of the convenience the Internet brings to us, but it also presents the possibility of misuse and even fraud. This law makes it possible for people to sign legal agreements online. Although it clearly has its advantages, there are many details to be worked out. For example, no standards were set for the technology to be used. It also does not require that electronic signatures match wet ink signatures in functional characteristics. Early adopters of electronic signature technology are expected to be banks and other financial institutions. However, as the use of electronic signatures becomes widespread, the risk of fraud will increase.

Clearly, the power of the Internet can be abused. Here are additional examples of possible abuse.

- **Proprietary data** (data owned/originated by people or organizations) is being sent and received at extremely fast speeds and in very high volumes.
- Customer information is easier to collect, analyze, and use for purposes not covered in typical privacy agreements.
- As health care goes digital, patient information can be inadvertently released; medical inquiries can be directed to the wrong people.
- Mailing lists may be sold, with the result being unsolicited advertisements from retailers.
- College and university students may purchase term papers from the Web and then submit the term papers as their own.

Some work is now being done in Web ethics, with various organizations writing and

[2]Richard A. Spinello, *Cyberethics: Morality and Law in Cyberspace* (Massachusetts: Jones and Bartlett Publishers, 2000), 120.

"I sold his unlisted phone number to telemarketers."

posting their codes of ethics. However, the Web is the responsibility of all of its users, and everyone using the Web (both organizations and individuals) should behave ethically.

Intranet

The **intranet** is a private network that belongs to an organization and is accessible only by the organization's employees. To help you understand the relationship between the intranet and the Internet, think of the Internet as a worldwide network of computers and the intranet as an organization or business network of computers with a **firewall** (prevents unauthorized outside individuals from using an intranet or an extranet [discussed in the next section]) in between. People from the intranet can break through the wall to access information from the Internet. However, individuals from the Internet (outside individuals) cannot break

Technology Tip:

Keeping current on technologies that impact your office means reading technology publications such as *Modern Office Technology* and *PC World*. Commit to reading at least one technology publication each month.

through the wall to access the information on the intranet. Intranets are used to share information that needs to be quickly and easily disseminated, such as company policies and in-house newsletters.

Extranet

An **extranet** also operates behind a firewall, but the firewall allows the inclusion of selected individuals, companies, and organizations outside the company. You can access an extranet if you have a valid user name and password. Your identity determines the parts of the extranet you can view. An extranet, for example, may be used by

- Financial institutions to provide clients with account information and performance reports
- Health institutions to access medical records
- Businesses to allow stockholders to view their finances

SOFTWARE

You have probably had fairly extensive experience using several software packages, including word processing, presentation, and graphics. This portion of the chapter is not designed to teach you a software package. It is designed to help you

- Understand the difference between operating systems software and applications software
- Troubleshoot software problems
- Understand the importance of computer ethics in relation to software
- Learn how to avoid computer viruses

Operating Systems Software

An operating system is a program that enables your computer to read and write data to a disk, send pictures to your monitor, and accept keyboard commands. Without an operating system, you cannot perform any of the tasks required in your word-processing program or in other applications software programs. In understanding how an operating system works, consider this analogy. When you turn the key in your car, the motor starts. You merely perform the one function, without being aware of the various electronic parts and the interrelationship between them that it takes for the motor to start. Once the motor starts, you are ready to perform a whole series of other steps—putting the car in gear, stepping on the gas, turning on the heat or air conditioning, and so on. When you turn on your computer, the operating system begins working for you. It gets the computer ready to receive your additional commands, which generally come from applications software programs, presented in the next section.

A number of operating systems are available. The following list includes the major ones:

- Windows® XP
- Windows® Millennium
- Windows® 2000
- Windows® NT
- Linux®
- UNIX®

Operating systems are continually being modified and revised. As you are studying this text, newer operating systems are probably available.

Applications Software

Through applications software programs, you tell the computer how to perform a specific task you need done. For example, you can produce a report with graphics by using a word-processing program. You can add tables to the report by using a spreadsheet program. You can develop a presentation using graphics with presentation software. Numerous software programs are available; several of them are listed below.

- Microsoft Office® XP
- Microsoft Office® 2000
- Microsoft Works® Suite 2001
- Money® 2001
- Excel® 2000
- FrontPage® 2000—a package to help you develop a Web page
- PowerPoint® 2000
- Outlook® 2000—a personal calendaring and scheduling package

- Publisher® 2000—desktop publishing
- Lotus® 1-2-3—a spreadsheet package

Just as operating systems are continually revised and updated, so are applications software programs. For example, Microsoft has revised its word-processing suite approximately every two years.

Technology Tip:
Think of your computer as a filing cabinet, and store your work items in folders (like you store paper records in folders).

Free Software

Thousands of free software packages are available on the Web. Some of these packages, by categories, are shown in Figure 4-6 on page 98.

Troubleshooting

As you work with both computer hardware and software, problems are going to occur. One of your tasks as an administrative professional is to solve as many of your problems as possible. You need to become adept at **troubleshooting** (tracing and correcting computer or software problems). To be an effective troubleshooter, you should have the following general information:

- The operating system your computer uses
- The amount of RAM and ROM on your computer
- The functions of software packages you are using
- The assistance available to you within the organization in which you work (Is there a computer technician who can help you? If not, is there an administrative professional who is competent on the package you are using?)
- The services available from the software vendor

FREE SOFTWARE PACKAGES AVAILABLE ON THE WEB

Here are a few of the free software packages, by category, available on the Web.

Business
Accounting
Calculators
Databases
Fax utilities
Finance, investments
Word processing

Internet
Web browsers
Web servers
Message boards

Education
Astronomy
Chemistry
Teaching tools

Graphics
Clip art
Animation, video

Home/Hobby
Genealogy
Health and fitness
Sports
Religion

Figure 4-6

When you are working on a particular software program and encounter problems, you can take certain troubleshooting steps. As an example, the following troubleshooting assistance is available for most software programs:

- A help button allows you to ask questions. The help button provides a wide array of information about many topics.
- Online and telephone help from the software manufacturer is often available. Microsoft and AOL both have online and telephone help.
- Manuals are available that have answers to many questions you might have. These manuals are available in most bookstores; for example, *Word 2000 for Dummies* is one source.

COMPUTER VIRUSES

A **computer virus** is a program with unauthorized instructions that is introduced without permission or knowledge of the computer user. It is called a virus because it is contagious. It can pass itself on to other programs in which it comes in contact. Viruses range from annoying but harmless, causing messages to pop up on your screen, to destructive, deleting all the data on your hard drive and crashing your computer. Basically, viruses are of two different types.

- Boot sector viruses reside on the part of your hard disk where the computer stores the files it needs to start up. These viruses become active each time you turn on your computer.
- Program infectors that attach themselves to any file that runs a program. Program viruses can be contracted from floppy disks.

Here is one example of how a computer can get a virus. A computer hacker inserts a few unauthorized instructions (either carelessly or maliciously) into a computer operating system program. The disk with the infected operating system is used and copied onto other files. The virus spreads to another disk, and the process is repeated. After the infected disk is copied a number of times, the virus can cause all data in the files affected to be erased.

The first computer viruses crept into the world of computing in 1987. Since that time there has been a growing awareness of the need for security. Here are some suggestions on how to protect against viruses.

- Educate yourself about computer viruses.
- Make backups of your files immediately—before you have a virus.
- **Download** only from sources you trust. Download means to receive a file from another source and transfer the information to your hard drive or to receive a file via email, a bulletin board, or an online service.

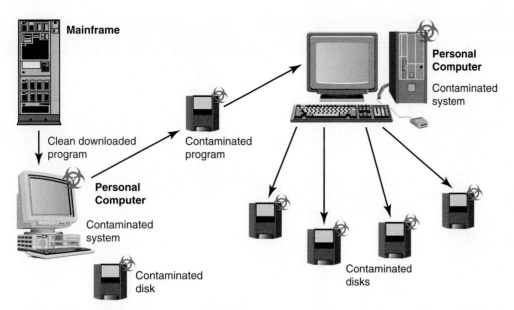

Figure 4-7 Infection from a computer virus can occur when a program with unauthorized instructions is introduced into the system.

- Install antiviral software. Installing such a program is the single most important action you can take to protect against viral attack. Two widely used programs are McAfee® and Norton™. Antiviral software is available as part of the package when you buy a computer. Antiviral software is also free on the Internet, with two packages being F-Prot® and Trend Micro™.
- Purchase all software programs in tamper-proof packaging.

COMPUTER ETHICS

Computers have spawned behaviors by some individuals that are unethical or questionable. Just as we need to be ever vigilant about behaving ethically within our workworld, we need to be certain we are living the organization's values and our personal values as we perform computer work. One problem that has become pervasive with computers is the illegal copying of software. People often rationalize that computer software companies are getting rich anyway so it is okay to copy software for their personal use. According to information reported in various journals, as much as 40 percent of business software in the United States is obtained illegally.

Organizations and individuals who illegally copy software can be tried under both civil and criminal law. Title 17 of the United States Code specifies that it is illegal to make or distribute copies of copyrighted material, including software, without authorization. Title 18, passed in 1991, instituted criminal penalties for copyright infringements of software. Penalties include imprisonment for up to five years and fines of up to $250,000 for the unauthorized reproduction or distribution of 10 or more copies of software with a total retail value exceeding $2,500. There is one exception to copying—one backup copy of software may be made. In addition to the copying of software being unethical and illegal, copying can bring viruses into the system. Also, companies and individuals who copy software deprive themselves of the benefits of technical support and training provided by many software companies and the ability to buy upgrades at reduced rates.

It is unethical to use a computer to gain entry into a company's data bank; in fact, it is theft. You might ask, "If I produced the data for the company, isn't it my property to do with as I please?" The answer is no; it is not your property unless you have specifically negotiated an arrangement with your company that allows you to retain the rights to the property. The property rights belong to the company that has used its resources to develop the product—in

TEN COMMANDMENTS FOR COMPUTER ETHICS

1. Thou shalt not use a computer to harm other people.
2. Thou shalt not interfere with other people's computer work.
3. Thou shalt not snoop around in other people's files.
4. Thou shalt not use a computer to steal.
5. Thou shalt not use a computer to bear false witness.
6. Thou shalt not use or copy software for which you have not paid.

7. Thou shalt not use other people's computer resources without authorization.
8. Thou shalt not appropriate other people's intellectual output.
9. Thou shalt think about the social consequences of the program you write.
10. Thou shalt use a computer in ways that show consideration and respect.

Figure 4-8

Source: Arlene Rinaldi, Florida Atlantic University, 1998.

other words, paid you or others within the company a salary or a commission to develop the product. To usurp any property rights, including the right to use the property, is a form of property theft and is unethical.

It is also unethical to use workplace computers to send and receive personal email, to take an Internet class unless the company authorizes the class, and to use the computer in any way for personal use. Employees sometimes believe it is acceptable to use a computer after the workday has ended for personal use or even to take a few minutes during the day to send an email to a friend. It is not okay unless permission is granted by the organization. An employee should never assume that the absence of a policy regarding acceptable behavior implicitly gives the employee the right to do as he or she pleases. Figure 4-8 provides "Ten Commandments for Computer Ethics."

CONTINUAL LEARNING

This chapter reinforces the importance of continual learning in our technological age. Even though great care was taken to include the latest information available when this chapter was  written, technology moves quickly, with changes occurring constantly. You can no longer assume that once you learn a body of information, that information will be cor-

rect for a lifetime. All of us must be continual learners if we are to be productive workers and citizens in our society. Years ago Alvin Toffler said in his book *Future Shock* that the educated person of tomorrow is the person who has learned how to learn. That statement is particularly relevant today and will be relevant throughout your lifetime. Here are some suggestions for you as you commit yourself to continual learning.

■ Since none of us can keep all the information that is generated in our heads, learn where to look for information. For example, you have been given a number of sources of information in this chapter; namely, the Web, computer periodicals, and books.

■ Develop an inquiring mind. Ask questions when you do not understand something. Do not be afraid to admit that you do not have all the answers. Part of ongoing learning is accepting what you do not know and being willing to do something about it.

■ Commit to continuing your formal education. Take classes offered by your organization or classes offered at a college or university. Take a course though distance learning. Most colleges and universities now offer a wide variety of these courses that you can complete in your home at a time that is convenient for you.

■ Devote time to learning. Learning does take time, but the results are well worth the time spent.

CHAPTER SUMMARY

The summary will help you remember the important points covered in the chapter.

- Computers are classified as supercomputers, mainframe computers, minicomputers, workstation computers (supermicros), and microcomputers (PCs).
- Information is input to the computer by computer keyboards, scanners, voice recognition technology, touch screens, and digital cameras.
- Storage devices include floppy disks, Zip disks, Jaz disks, SuperDisks, CDs, and DVDs.
- Information is output from the computer by monitors, inkjet printers, laser printers, networked printers, and multifunction peripherals.
- Networks used within business organizations include local area networks, metropolitan area networks, and wide area networks.
- The Internet and the Web are computer networks that are used worldwide by organizations and individuals.
- The emergence of the Web nationally and internationally has brought with it the need to pay attention to ethical issues, such as maintaining confidentiality of individual's financial and health records and not selling lists of names for marketing use.

- The intranet and the extranet are private networks used by organizations for internal uses and selected external uses.
- Operating systems software enables a computer to read and write data to a disk and to accept commands from applications software.
- Applications software tells the computer how to perform a specific task, such as write a report, use graphics, and so on. Word-processing suites are one example of applications software.
- Numerous free software packages are available on the Web.
- Computer viruses can result in the trashing of all data on the hard drive and result in the crashing of your computer.
- Computers have spawned behaviors by some individuals that are unethical or questionable.
- Due to our fast-paced information age, it is important that we commit ourselves to continual learning of technological issues.

CHAPTER GLOSSARY

The following terms were introduced in this chapter. Definitions are provided to help you review the terms.

- **Internet** (p. 82)—the world's largest group of connected computers, allowing people from all over the world to communicate.
- **Web** (p. 82)—a huge collection of computer files scattered across the Internet (more than 800 million Websites and growing daily).
- **Lifelong learning** (p. 83)—a commitment to continue to learn throughout one's life.
- **Microcomputer** (p. 83)—the smallest of the computer systems, commonly called a PC (personal computer).
- **Supercomputers** (p. 83)—the mightiest and most expensive of the mainframe computers.
- **Genome** (p. 83)—the genetic blueprint of humanity.
- **High-end protein analyzers** (p. 83)—the sequence of the amino acids that make up proteins.
- **Teraflop** (p. 83)—one trillion operations per second.

- **Terabyte** (p. 83)—one trillion bytes.
- **Mainframes** (p. 84)—large computers capable of processing great amounts of information at fast speeds (although the speed is less than the supercomputer).
- **Minicomputer** (p. 84)—a midrange computer.
- **Microprocessor** (p. 84)—a single miniature chip that contains the circuitry and components for arithmetic, logic, and control operations.
- **Workstation computers (supermicros)** (p. 84)—the upper-end machines of the microcomputer.
- **Multiuser** (p. 84)—able to serve several users at the same time.
- **Processor chip** (p. 84)—a type of microprocessor that provides for increased speed and performance capability of the PC.

CHAPTER GLOSSARY

(continued)

- **Pentium processor** (p. 84)—a type of processor chip manufactured by Intel.
- **Athlon** (p. 84)—a type of processor chip manufactured by Advanced Micro Devices.
- **PowerPC** (p. 84)—a type of processor chip manufactured by MacIntosh.
- **Notebooks** or **laptops** (p. 85)—portable computers.
- **PDA** (p. 85)—personal digital assistant; a small PC that can be held in the palm of your hand.
- **Defragmenter** (p. 85)—a utility that gathers the fragments of files scattered across the surface of the hard disk and reassembles them so data is continuous.
- **Continuous** (p. 85)—no empty spaces between files.
- **Surge suppressor** and **uninterruptible power supply (UPS)** (p. 85)—devices that keep power fluctuations from crippling your computer equipment.
- **Palms** (p. 86)—one of the leading manufacturers of PDAs.
- **Ergonomics** (p. 86)—a term used to denote the fit between people, the tools they use, and the physical setting where they work.
- **Ergos** (p. 86)—a Greek word meaning "work."
- **Nomos** (p. 86)—a Greek work meaning "natural laws"; *ergos* and *nomos* were combined to coin the word *ergonomics*.
- **RSI** (p. 86)—repetitive stress injury, a generic name given to injuries that occur over a period of time and are known as overuse disorders.
- **OSHA** (p. 86)—Occupational Safety & Health Administration.
- **Carpal tunnel syndrome** (p. 86)—a major occupational illness that occurs due to the compression of a large nerve, the median nerve, as it passes through a tunnel composed of bone and ligaments in the wrist.
- **Computer vision syndrome** (p. 86)—develops from screen glare.
- **Continuous speech recognition** (p. 88)—a computer voice recognition process that allows the user to speak in complete phrases and sentences to a computer.
- **Discrete speech recognition** (p. 88)—a computer voice recognition process where the user is required to put pauses between individual words when speaking to a computer.
- **Touch screen** (p. 88)—a computer screen that allows the user to input to the computer by touching the finger or a pointer to the screen.
- **Digital camera** (p. 89)—a camera that can become an input device with a PC, allowing the user to modify and print photographs in a variety of formats.
- **Pixels** (p. 89)—picture elements.
- **Resolution** (p. 89)—the quality of the picture.
- **MB** (p. 90)—megabytes; million-byte units.
- **GB** (p. 90)—gigabytes; billion-byte units.
- **TB** (p. 90)—terabytes; trillion-byte units.
- **RAM** (p. 90)—random access memory; stored on the hard drive of a PC.
- **ROM** (p. 90)—read-only memory; stored on the hard drive of a PC.
- **Floppy disks** (p. 90)—small external storage mediums for a PC.
- **Density** (p. 90)—the amount of data that can be stored on a disk; double-sided and high-density disks hold 1.44MB of data.
- **Zip disk** (p. 90)—external storage for a PC; holds 100 and 250MB of data.
- **Zip drives** (p. 90)—removable drives for a PC that hold from 100MB to 2GB of data.
- **SuperDisk** (p. 90)—external storage for a PC that holds 120MB of data.
- **Jaz disk** (p. 91)—external storage for a PC that holds 1GB of data.
- **CD-ROM** (p. 91)—compact disk read-only memory.
- **CD-R** (p. 91)—compact disk—recordable.
- **CD-E** (p. 91)—compact disk—erasable.
- **CD-RW** (p. 91)—compact disk read and write.
- **DVD-ROM** (p. 91)—digital versatile disk—read-only memory.
- **Soft copy** (p. 91)—copy shown on the monitor only; used when a printed copy is not necessary.
- **CRT** (p. 91)—cathode ray tube.
- **Hard copy** (p. 91)—copy printed on paper.
- **LCD** (p. 92)—liquid crystal display; type of computer monitor.

- **Inkjet** (p. 92)—a type of computer printer that works by spraying ink onto the paper.
- **Laser** (p. 93)—a type of computer printer that uses a beam of light to form images on paper.
- **Networked printers** (p. 93)—attached to a local area network.
- **LANs** (p. 93)—local area networks; link various types of technological equipment within a building or several buildings within the same geographic area.
- **MANs** (p. 93)—metropolitan area networks; link technological equipment over a distance equal to the size of a city and its surroundings.
- **WANs** (p. 94)—wide area networks; link technological equipment over an area of hundreds of thousands of miles.
- **DSL** (p. 94)—a telecommunications network that uses a digital subscriber line.
- **Broadband** (p. 94)—a telecommunications service that uses cable, DSL, wireless, and satellite connections.
- **Web browser** (p. 94)—an application program that provides a way to look at and interact with all the information on the World Wide Web.

- **Proprietary data** (p. 95)—data owned/originated by people or organizations.
- **Intranet** (p. 96)—a private network that belongs to an organization and is accessible only by the organization's employees.
- **Firewall** (p. 96)—prevents unauthorized outside individuals from using an intranet or an extranet.
- **Extranet** (p. 96)—a private network that belongs to an organization and provides for the authorization of selected external people to use the network.
- **Troubleshooting** (p. 97)—tracing and correcting computer or software problems.
- **Computer virus** (p. 98)—a program with unauthorized instructions that is introduced without permission or knowledge of the computer user.
- **Download** (p. 98)—receive a file from another source and transfer the information to a hard drive or to receive a file via email, a bulletin board, or online service.

DISCUSSION ITEMS

These discussion items provide an opportunity to test your understanding of the chapter through written responses and/or discussion with your classmates and your instructor.

1. Explain the differences in the Internet, intranet, and extranet.
2. List and explain computer input devices.
3. Explain the difference between operating systems software and applications software.
4. What is meant by computer ergonomics? Give five ergonomic tips.
5. Explain two ethical problems involving the computer that may occur in organizations.

CRITICAL-THINKING ACTIVITY

Juan has been working for AmeriAsian Airlines for slightly over a year as your assistant. When he started with the company, you gave him the Policy and Procedures Manual for AmeriAsian, which included a section on computer ethics. This section makes clear that all computers are the property of AmeriAsian and not to be used for the personal use of employees. Yesterday your supervisor, Martin Albertson, asked you why Juan

was working overtime the evening before. Mr. Albertson said that he had worked until about 7 p.m. As he was leaving, he noticed that Juan was still at his desk. He walked over to say goodnight and noticed that Juan was writing some type of paper that did not appear to be related to AmeriAsian work. You had to answer that you knew nothing about it but that you would look into it. You asked Juan this afternoon why he was working late that

CRITICAL-THINKING ACTIVITY

(continued)

evening. He stated he had a paper to do for a class he was taking but he did not have a computer at home. You thanked him for giving you the information and left to "mull over" what you should do. Juan has been an exceptional employee—he never misses work; he is always on time; his work is done promptly and accurately; he is polite and understands confidentiality. In fact, in his yearly review last month, you gave him an outstanding rating.

When you gave him the Policy and Procedures Manual, you did not go over it with him, but you did ask him to read it. After thinking about it overnight, you went back to Juan the next morning and asked him if he had read the Policy and Procedures Manual. When he answered yes, you asked him why he violated the company policy on

using computers for personal business. Juan told you the manual did not discuss personal use of computers. He pulled it from his desk and showed you that there was no section on computer ethics. Now you are in a real quandary. Address the following items:

- Do you believe you made a mistake in giving Juan an incomplete Policy and Procedures Manual? Do you believe Juan is lying to you? Explain your answers.
- How should you handle the situation?
- How can you be certain in the future that employees understand and adhere to what is in the Policy and Procedures Manual?
- What will you report to Mr. Albertson after talking with Juan?

RESPONSES TO SELF-CHECK A

1. Supercomputers
   Mainframe computers
   Minicomputer
   Workstation computers (supermicros)
   Microcomputers (PCs)

2. A PDA is a personal digital assistant. At its most basic, it serves as an appointment book, an address book, a to-do list, and a calculator. You can also check your email, stock quotes, newspaper headlines, and so on.

3. Computer keyboard
   Scanners
   Voice recognition technology
   Touch screens
   Digital cameras

4. Ergonomics is the term used to denote the fit between people, the tools they use, and the physical setting where they work. Ergonomics is important when working with computers so you do not damage your physical health.

RESPONSES TO SELF-CHECK C

1. External computer storage devices include floppy disks, Zip disks, Jaz disks, SuperDisks, CDs, and DVDs.

2. The two major types of printers used today are inkjet and laser.

PROJECTS

Project 4-1 (Objectives 1 and 2)
Online Project

Using one of the search engines listed in this chapter (such as www.askjeeves.com or www.google.com) research the function of the microprocessor and the status of voice recognition systems. Write a short summary of your findings, identifying your sources. Submit your summary to your instructor.

Project 4-2 (Objectives 2, 3, and 5)
Online Project

Search the Web for the following information:

- The newest office suite software available and the latest antiviral package available
- The most current operating systems in use
- Office/computer ergonomics

Write a summary of your findings, identifying your sources. Submit your summary to your instructor.

Project 4-3 (Objective 4)

Refer to the document on Student CD, SCDP4-3a. Numerous changes must be made. If you do not know how to make the changes, use the help icon on your software package to troubleshoot. Print out a copy of the document with the changes you made. Using the memorandum form on Student CD, SCDP4-3b, write a memorandum to your instructor and provide the readability level.

Project 4-4 (Objectives 2 and 6)
Collaborative Project

AmeriAsian plans to write a computer ethics policy to distribute to the staff. Working with two or three of your classmates, surf the Web for company policies that may be available and articles on ethics. From your research and information in the textbook, write a draft of an ethics policy for AmeriAsian. Submit your draft policy with a cover memorandum to Mr. Albertson. Use the memorandum form on Student CD, SCDP4-4. Additionally, you have been asked to research what other organizations are doing concerning policies on computer ethics for a section to be included in the Policy and Procedures Manual. Using the Web, see what you can find on the subject. Summarize your findings, citing your sources, and submit your findings to your instructor.

Project 4-5 (Objective 7)

Prepare another section of your Professional Growth Plan; describe how you will commit to continual learning throughout this course. Refer to the suggestions in your text on continual learning before you prepare your plan. Save your self-improvement plan on your Professional Growth Plan disk under "Progro4-5." Develop an appropriate title for this portion of your plan.

ENGLISH USAGE CHALLENGE DRILL

Correct the following sentences. Cite the grammar rule that is applicable to each sentence. Before you begin, refresh your memory of grammar rules by reviewing the rules on pronouns in the Reference Guide of this text.

1. The contest winner was me.
2. May I speak to Nancy? This is her.
3. Who does Ann admire?
4. The instructor and myself had a long talk.
5. She invited my girlfriend and myself to the concert.

ASSESSMENT OF CHAPTER OBJECTIVES

Now that you have completed the chapter and the projects, take a few minutes to review the chapter learning objectives. For your convenience, the objectives are repeated here. Did you accomplish these objectives? If you were unable to accomplish the objectives, give your reasons for not doing so.

1. Explain the functions of computer hardware components.   Yes _____   No _____

_____

_____

_____

2. Utilize the Internet to research information on the Web.   Yes _____   No _____

_____

_____

_____

_____

3. Explain the difference between operating systems software and applications software.   Yes _____   No _____

_____

_____

_____

4. Troubleshoot software problems.   Yes _____   No _____

_____

_____

_____

5. Explain the importance of computer ergonomics to physical health.   Yes _____   No _____

_____

_____

_____

6. Identify ethical computer behaviors.   Yes _____   No _____

_____

_____

_____

7. Demonstrate a commitment to continual learning in our technological age.   Yes _____   No _____

_____

_____

_____

You may submit your answers in writing to your instructor, using the memorandum form on the Student CD, SCDAP4-1.

CHAPTER 5
TELECOMMUNICATIONS

LEARNING OBJECTIVES

1. Discover how information is transmitted electronically.
2. Develop and use proper telephone techniques.
3. Use proper email communication techniques.
4. *Recognize the importance of email ethics.*

Although the word *telecommunications* **is sometimes not understood,** we actually use telecommunications daily. For example, when you access the Internet and send email, you are using telecommunication technology. Additionally, when you use the fax and the telephone, you are using telecommunication technology. **Telecommunications** is defined as "the electronic transmission of text, data, voice, video, and image (graphics and pictures) from one location to another."

Today the telecommunications field is involved in a revolution that is rapidly changing the traditional ways we have employed these services. For example, systems at various stages of development are breaking down the barriers between the computer and the telephone, allowing us to communicate with anyone at any time over a wire line or a wireless path. Use of the cellular phone is an example of communication over a wireless path. However, new developments in telecommunications are now making possible the integration of the cellular phone and PDAs (personal digital assistants), with Internet access over wireless technology rather than a wire modem. These examples are merely two ways in which our telecommunication capabilities are changing. The revolution promises to change and expand drastically our telecommunication capabilities.

This chapter is designed to help you understand the relationship among various telecommunication technologies and to understand some future telecommunication possibilities. For your day-to-day activities as an administrative professional in the workplace of the twenty-first century, an understanding of the human element of telecommunications is also important. Although we communicate daily with numerous individuals without ever seeing or talking to them, we cannot forget that a human being is on the receiving end of our communication. This understanding brings with it the importance of communicating our message using effective human relations skills. Additionally, the rapid advances in telecommunications have contributed to the emergence of ethical issues that demand we not only be cognizant of the issues but also behave ethically.

TELECOMMUNICATIONS— THE REVOLUTION

Traditional telephone companies are in the process of transforming themselves from delivering a service that only connects *people to people* to one that connects *people to people* and *people to machines* through a wide range of telecommunication devices. Organizations that we never before thought of as providing telephone service are getting into the market. For example, computer companies such as Compaq®, Hewlett Packard®, and Dell™ are now providing telephone access through computers with the assistance of software. Additionally, telecommunication companies are merging with companies that are in a different business (for example, AOL and Time Warner) to garner more of the market and provide a variety of services. In other words, the market lines among companies have become blurred. Gone are the days when one supermonopoly owned the whole network support infrastructure. Couple these directions with the technology that is becoming available through **broadband** (short for broad bandwidth) and there is indeed a revolution in the field. Broadband allows phenomenal changes in what can be sent to people from machines. Websites are available that move, talk, and sing. The information available from these sites can be sent to numerous machines—computers, cellular phones, PDAs, televisions, and a combination of these machines. Consider what AT&T presents as its directions for the future.

According to a spokesperson for AT&T, it has redefined itself from a domestic long-distance provider to a global all-distance provider of broadband communications services. In the future, AT&T plans to build and operate the following:

- A new network with the circuit-switched, connection-oriented network of the past 125 years being replaced by a **packet-switched network** (one in which each signal, [whether it carries music, video, or email] is chopped into tiny digital parcels that are commingled with other packets and routed to their destinations)

- New access methods with the narrowband voice channels replaced by broadband channels
- New services with the traditional voice and data services enhanced by real-time communications, messaging, finding people and information, selling/buying items, entertainment, distance learning, storage and access to records, photos and videos, and creation of a sense of virtual community
- New operations with automated operations services utilizing Web-based interfaces for billing and payments, as well as customer care, and attendant functions realized using natural language voice dialogues with machines[1]

To help you understand some of the telecommunications terms, refer to Figure 5-1.

In redefining themselves and providing a variety of new services, the traditional telephone companies, along with new service providers entering the market, are using a number of telecommunication pipelines. The major ones are cable, DSL, fixed wireless, satellite, and ISDN. Analog dial-up (the traditional pipeline) is still used, but the future projection is a drastic decrease in its use. All of the pipelines are referred to as broadband, which encompasses many different technologies— some mainstream, some **moribund** (state of dying)—and others immature at the present time. It is projected that by 2004, more than half of all firms and 15 percent of all households will have broadband connections (cable, DSL, wireless, and satellite).[2]

In addition to making more information available at faster speeds through pipelines, the broadband revolution is about making the information easier to retrieve when it gets to the other end of the pipeline. **Bluetooth**™ (named for a tenth-century Danish king), a new technology standard for short-range wireless communication, was developed by a consortium of companies including Ericsson®, IBM, Intel, Lucent®, Microsoft, Motorola®, Nokia®, 3Com®, and Toshiba®. It helps laptops

---

[1] Larry Rabiner, "Research Vision, Challenges, Endstate," accessed March 15, 2001; available from www.att.com.
[2] Stewart Alsop, "How Broadband Adds Up," *Fortune*, October 9, 2000, 30.

TELECOMMUNICATION TERMS

Backbone—The part of the network used as the main path for carrying traffic between network endpoints.

Broadband—Short for broad bandwidth. A high-speed network able to carry video as well as voice. Bandwidth describes the throughput of a network per unit of time, measured in kilobits, megabits, or gigabits per second.

Crosstalk—Interference on analog lines created by cables that are too close together.

Firewall—Software or hardware that filters or blocks traffic from a public or private network, preventing unauthorized or unrecognized access.

Packet-switched network—One in which each signal, whether it carries music or video or email, is chopped into tiny digital parcels that are commingled with hordes of other packets, routed to their destinations, and then reassembled. The Internet is a packet network. The phone system is a circuit network, where each signal travels unbroken on its own end-to-end pipe.

Streaming media—In theory, like listening to radio or watching television but with a signal that travels over the Internet. The quality is not excellent at present, but it is getting better as bandwidth increases.

VoIP (Voice over Internet Protocol)—Software and hardware that allow voice signals to be carried over an IP-based network, with Plain Old Telephone Service (POTS) quality and reliability.

VPN (virtual private network)—An authentication, encryption, and data-packaging technology that lets private network traffic travel over the public networks.

Walled garden—The practice by which an Internet service giant like AOL gives customers easier access to its own and its partners' content than to that of its competitors.

WLL (wireless local loop)—A broadband connection system that uses high-frequency radio links to deliver voice and data.

Figure 5-1

---

communicate with printers, cell phones with headsets, palms with vending machines, and each of these devices with the Internet, all through the air (wireless). It uses microwave radio to transmit data over short distances.

© *PhotoDisc, Inc.*

The future will provide us with increased wireless communication possibilities.

Presently, at least one company is working on a way to let people buy sodas from a vending machine simply by clicking on a PDA. A discussion of broadband is given in the next section. Although you are not expected to have a detailed knowledge of the telecommunication pipelines, a general understanding will help you be conversant with the terminology and direction of telecommunications.

Analog Dial-Up

Modem technology that uses analog dial-up has been around for many years. The modem allows computers to communicate with each other by converting their digital communications into an analog format to travel through the public phone network. Then the information is changed back to a digital format that the computer can understand. The word *modem* is an acronym that stands for modulate/demodulate. A computer modem "modulates" data so it can be transmitted on telephone lines in analog form, and it "demodulates" incoming signals so the computer's digital processor can understand them. Modems exist in the computer, and a regular telephone line connects the modem from the computer to the external telephone line.

Modem technology is the slowest of the technologies available today. However, it still has some advantages over newer technologies. Some of its advantages are listed here.

- It is less expensive than other telecommunication pipelines.
- Dial-up is available everywhere phone lines are available.
- A modem is safer. It does not stay on 24 hours a day as other broadband connections do. Since your computer spends less time connected to the Internet, it is safer from computer hackers. Other broadband technologies discussed here are "always on," meaning the user does not have to dial in to the server and wait for a connection (as is presently the case with AOL). However, even though computer hackers are definite threats to "always on" pipelines, the ability exists to protect the company and individuals through firewalls.

Cable

Cable is another way of accessing the Internet. A **cable modem** is an external device that connects to the computer and to a service provider's coaxial cable line. Although cable has been available for years as a modem for TV sets, these cable modems were not designed for data traffic, particularly high-speed data traffic. They were also designed only for one-way television programming communications; that is, from the programmers to the consumer. Internet communications require two-way service. Thus, the cable has required extensive upgrading. This two-way service cable is just recently becoming available to people over most areas of the United States, with the projection that by 2004, there will be 13.7 million subscribers to cable as compared to 3.4 million in 2000.[3] Many rural areas may not have cable broadband for a period of time, if ever.

Cable is fast. Figure 5-2 shows a comparison of the download time and some of the pros and cons of the different broadband technolo-gies. Notice that with cable, the time to download a 10MB file is 1.4 minutes compared to an analog time of 28.4 minutes. However, cable is not consistently fast. Because cable modems use shared connections, they are prone to slow-downs if too many users along a particular stretch of cable are online at one time. Speedy access is not guaranteed at any time.

DSL

DSL (digital subscriber line) superficially is much like cable. It is fast and it uses wires that run to the organization or home. However, these are the only similarities. DSL users report more consistent speed than cable users. Notice in Figure 5-2 that the download time for a 10MB file is approximately the same as cable—1.8 minutes as opposed to 1.4 minutes. DSL is available in **ADSL** (asymmetric digital subscriber line), **SDSL** (symmetric digital subscriber line), or **IDSL** (Internet digital subscriber line). In most cases, ADSL and SDSL connections must be located within 18,000 feet of the service provider's central office. Consequently, they tend to be most widely available in urban and thickly populated suburban areas. ADSL download rates are higher than the other two, but upload rates are capped at lower rates. The faster the rate, the more expensive the service. The majority of DSL users are businesses that already have telephone service in place. Most of the time DSL service can be purchased from the same company that provides telephone service to the business. However, the local telephone company does not have a monopoly on DSL service; it is available from multiple providers. It is estimated that by 2004, there will be 12.2 million subscribers to DSL as compared to 1.97 million in 2000.[4] Figure 5-3 illustrates how DSL works.

Fixed Wireless

Fixed wireless, or **WLL** (wireless local loop), technology is making the transfer of data and voice readily available at relatively fast transfer

---

[3]Cassimir Medford, "Pipe Dreams," *PC Magazine,* February 6, 2001, 144.
[4]Ibid.

PIPELINE COMPARISONS

Technology	Time to Download 10MB file (min.)	Pros	Cons
Analog dial-up	28.4 min.	Cheapest Internet connection.	Provides a fraction of broadband speed.
Cable	1.4 min.	Very quick downloads; comparatively quick installation.	Limited upload speed; bandwidth sharing can degrade performance.
DSL	1.8 min.	Variable-bandwidth services can be tailored to your needs and budget.	Higher bandwith tends to cost more; long waits for installation at present time.
Fixed wireless	2.7 min.	Nice, if available.	Not yet widely available.
Satellite	3.4 min.	New bidirectional services bring DSL-like speeds to rural users.	Inexpensive one-way service requires dial-up modem for upstream communication.

Figure 5-2

Source: Scott Spanbauer, "Cable vs. DSL vs. Everything Else," *PC World*, January 2001, 94–95.

speeds. Notice in Figure 5-3 that the download transfer time on fixed wireless is 2.7 minutes for a 10MB file, slightly slower than cable and DSL but faster than satellite or analog. However, before presenting more information on fixed wireless, the distinction needs to be made between fixed and mobile wireless.

Mobile wireless service has been available for a period of time and is the service that has been used by cellular phones. With cellular phones, you move in and out of service areas. **Cellular technology,** or **mobile wireless service,** breaks a large service area down into smaller areas called cells. When a customer

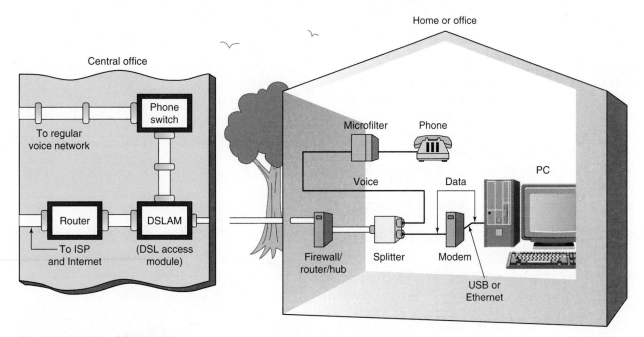

Figure 5-3   How DSL Works

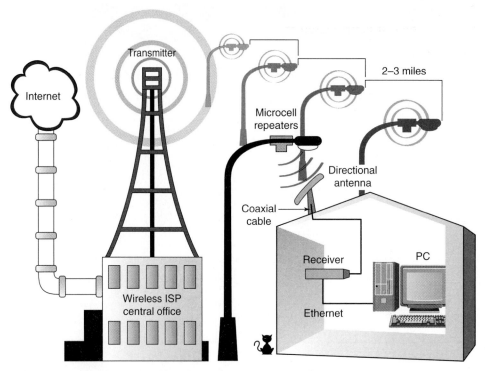

Figure 5-4   How Fixed Wireless Works

Source: Cassimir Medford, "Pipe Dreams," *PC Magazine*, February 6, 2001, 156.

places a call from a mobile unit, the nearest cell or transmitting station relays it to a central computer that in turn directs the call into the local telephone system. When a customer leaves one cell area and enters another, the computer automatically switches the transmission to the next nearest cell. Today voice communications and messaging are no longer sufficient for businesses and consumers. Access to the Internet, and through it access to corporate networks, is now just as important. Although data from the Web is available over mobile wireless technology, the speed of the data transfer is slow. However, new mobile wireless technology is being introduced that includes voice (with improved quality), messaging, location tracing, and data transmission. This technology could make mobile wireless a contender in the broadband market.

Fixed wireless technology is simpler than mobile wireless because it does not utilize client devices moving in and out of coverage areas. WLL is offered primarily to businesses and homes in areas where the infrastructure is not in place to deliver broadband through cable or DSL. Data is converted to wireless signals

and relayed to customers through a network of transceivers mounted on utility poles, streetlights, and so on. Each WLL subscriber has a small radio receiver and directional antenna oriented toward the nearest microcell. Fixed wireless offers a short installation time, greater installation flexibility, and performance equal to or greater than many wireline options. WLL costs more per month than cable or DSL. However, as more organizations and people subscribe to WLL, equipment prices should fall. It is estimated that by 2004, the number of users of fixed wireless will be 1.3 million as compared to 144,000 in 2000.[5] Figure 5-4 illustrates how fixed wireless works.

Satellite

Although satellite service has disadvantages over cable and DSL in the higher cost, the degrading of transmission due to heavy rain or high wind, and download time, it is the only broadband service presently available for a

---

[5]Scott Spanbauer, "Cable vs. DSL vs. Everything Else," *PC World*, January 2001, 94–95.

number of homes and businesses, particularly those in rural areas. In fact, it is projected that it will be almost ten years before the majority of homes and businesses will be wired for other broadband services. It is anticipated that the number of users of satellite will increase to 2.4 million by 2004 as compared to 75,000 in 2000.[6] Since satellite is a shared service, as more people use the service, the speeds will inevitably be slower. However, companies are working to increase bandwidth that will increase the upload and download times. Presently satellite is slower than cable, DSL, and fixed wireless on download time at 3.4 minutes for a 10MB file.

Before you move on to the next section, take a few minutes to reflect on your understanding of the telecommunication technology that has been described here and answer the questions in Self-Check A. Check your answers with those at the end of this chapter.

Self-Check A

1. How is the telecommunications revolution changing how we live and work?

   _____

   _____

   _____

2. Explain how traditional telephone providers are changing their services.

   _____

   _____

   _____

3. Explain the differences between cable, DSL, and fixed wireless.

   _____

   _____

   _____

FAX

A telecommunications device that has been in use for a period of time is the **fax machine** (facsimile). It is a type of copier that electronically sends an original document from one location to another via communication networks. With a fax, you may communicate with other people within the same building, in the same city, across the nation, or across the world. The fax machine has become a standard piece of office equipment. However, with the download and upload capability of email, some of the documents that in the past would have been sent by fax are now being sent through email at less cost to the organization. If you are sending a document that has already been keyed, fax remains a viable option. Fax machines are often multifunction machines, combining printing, faxing, copying, and scanning or two or three of these functions into one machine. The multifunction machines are inexpensive and particularly useful in teleworker environments where cost and space are considerations.

Confidential documents and/or documents that should be viewed only by certain individuals within the organization should not be faxed. These documents include social security numbers, financial statements, contracts, legal matters, and sensitive personnel items—evaluations, terminations, salaries, and so on.

EMAIL

Telecommunications has revolutionized the way we communicate. Most correspondence to individuals within an organization today is written as **email** (electronic message). Email is also used extensively in the home. Many families choose email as their preferred choice of communication. It allows them immediate access, at a reasonable cost, to family members who may be scattered across the world. In fact, some email services are free, with others having a low monthly cost. Also, with the emergence of the digital camera, family photos can be sent through email. Additionally, students use email as a communication tool with their peers and their instructors.

An iteration of email is **IM** (instant messaging). IM avoids the delay of email, which

---

[6]Scott Spanbauer, "Cable vs. DSL vs. Everything Else," *PC World*, January 2001, 94–95.

can stay unanswered for days if an individual does not check his or her email box. With IM, a line keyed on one computer is seen almost instantly in a window that appears in one corner of the sender's computer and the computer of one or more recipients. AOL was the first to market IM in the form of its buddy lists. Now other vendors have come into the market. In 2001, more than 60 million people worldwide were using IM regularly. It is projected that by 2004, approximately seven billion people per day will use IM. However, concerns do exist in the workplace about the use of IM. For example, it opens up potential security loopholes in office computer networks. Workers may tap IM for corporate business, thus using the Internet to chat with a fellow employee about an issue and possibly sending company secrets across public networks.

When email messages are sent in the workplace, email guidelines, ethics, and etiquette must be considered. If not, major mistakes can be made at great cost to the organization and the individual writing the email.

Technology Tip:
Ethical practices must be followed when email messages are sent.

Email Guidelines

When composing email, adhere to these guidelines.

- Be certain you have thought through the purpose of your email before you begin writing; in other words, know what you are trying to achieve with your email.
- Be succinct. Before you send your email, reread it. Delete unnecessary phrases, words, or sentences.
- Be polite. Think of your email as a short letter and follow etiquette rules. Use *please* and *thank you*.
- Be appropriately formal when writing email. The rule of thumb is to be almost as formal in email as you are in standard memorandums to your employer and/or co-workers. The message below is too informal.

Inappropriate

jim, we need to have a meeting soon—can you arrange? I'm free next mon. thks.

Appropriate

Jim,

We need to meet soon to discuss our division's projected budget for the next six months. Are you available on Monday, November 14, from 9 a.m. until 10 a.m.? If so, let me know by this afternoon. We can meet in my office.

Ed

"You've got mail."

EMOTICONS

\<G\>	I'm grinning as I write this sentence.
\<LOL\>	I'm laughing out loud.
☺	I'm smiling.
;-)	I'm winking.
☹	I'm unhappy.
;->	Indicates a comment is intended to be provocative

Figure 5-5

Always capitalize the appropriate words, be specific about needs, and use a proper closing.

- Avoid using **emoticons** (faces produced by the Internet counterculture in answer to email being devoid of body language). Figure 5-5 illustrates a few emoticons. Save emoticons for communications with your close friends or family.
- Use the Subject line that is provided on the email form. This line should be concise yet give enough information so the receiver knows at a glance what the message is about. For example, if you are sending an email about a TQM meeting, the subject should read "TQM Meeting, 2:30 p.m., November 1," rather than "Meeting."
- If you are replying to a message but are changing the subject of the conversation, change the subject also. Better yet, start a new message altogether.
- Organize the message and tightly construct it. Email should not be longer than one screen. If the length of your memo is longer than one screen, send a hard-copy memorandum.
- Edit and proofread carefully. Do not send out an email that contains inaccuracies or incorrect grammar.
- Use complete sentences.
- Capitalize and punctuate properly.
- Do not run sentences together; it is difficult to read email constructed in this manner.
- Insert a blank line after each paragraph.
- Check your spelling.

- Always include your name and title (if appropriate) when replying to an email.
- Assume that any message you send is permanent. The message can be sitting in someone's private file or in a tape archive.

Email Ethics

Throughout this course, there has been an emphasis on ethics, with the hope that you will understand the importance of ethics and accept the responsibility of behaving ethically. Although email is fairly new, there is a growing body of ethical issues in regard to email. Some organizations  have even developed a code of ethics for using email. Figure 5-6 on page 116 shows a portion of the code of ethics for Massey University. Figure 5-7 on page 117 lists several suggestions that cover both ethics and etiquette on the Web. As you send and receive email, you must be ethical in your responses and your use of email. Here are some suggestions for maintaining a solid ethical stance.

- Do not send personal email from your office computer.
- When people send you inappropriate email, let them know politely that you cannot receive it. You might say, "I would enjoy hearing from you, but please send any personal email to my home."
- Do not use email to berate or reprimand an employee.
- Do not use email to terminate someone.
- Do not use email to send information that involves any type of legal action; third parties that should have no knowledge of the action may obtain the information.
- Do not forward junk mail or chain letters; both are inappropriate in an office.

Technology Tip:
Do not use email to send information that involves any type of legal action.

CODE OF ETHICS FOR THE USE OF ELECTRONIC MAIL

Massey University

Forged email. No electronic mail may be sent so as to appear to originate from another person, with the intention of thereby deceiving the recipient or recipients.

Menacing email. No electronic mail may be sent that is abusive or threatens the safety of a person or persons.

Harassing email. No electronic mail may be sent such that a person or persons thereby suffers sexual, ethnic, religious or other minority harassment or in contravention of the Human Rights Act 1993. The charge of harassment may be based on the content of the electronic mail sent or its volume or both.

Privacy of email. No person may access or attempt to access electronic mail sent to another user, without the permission of that user, except when necessary as part of that person's duties in respect of the operation of the electronic mail system.

Privacy Act. No electronic mail may be sent that contravenes the rights of a person or persons under the Privacy Act 1993.

Figure 5-6

Source: Massey University Computing Services Email Ethics and Good Practice, accessed March 2, 2001; available from www.massey.ac.nz/~/wwits/emailpol.htm.

- Do not forward unwanted or junk email to a mailing list. This practice is known as **spamming,** and some organizations have established email policies that result in loss of computer privileges for individuals who engage in spamming.
- Do not forward an email unless you know it is true. For example, you may think you are being helpful forwarding a message about a computer virus. However, when you receive ten email messages concerning misinformation about the viruses, you understand the importance of being certain that an email is true before forwarding it.
- Do not include credit card numbers in email messages. Email can be intercepted in transit; an unscrupulous individual can use a valid credit card number.
- Do not criticize or insult third parties.

Email Etiquette

- Do not use different types of fonts, colors, clip art, and other graphics in email. Such an approach merely clutters your message and takes longer to send and receive, particularly if you include numerous graphics.

- Do not key your message in all uppercase. It is okay to emphasize a word or phrase in all capitals, but use the Caps Lock button sparingly.
- Avoid sending messages when you are angry. Give yourself time to settle down and think about the situation before you send or reply to an email in anger. Take a walk around your office, drink a cup of hot tea to soothe

© PhotoDisc, Inc.

Never send an email when you are angry.

- Observe the Golden Rule in cyberspace; treat others as you would like to be treated.
- Act responsibly when sending email or posting messages to a discussion group. Don't use language or photographs that are racist, sexist, or offensive. Be careful when using humor or sarcasm as they can be misunderstood.
- Use a style and tone that are appropriate to the intended recipient of your message. Observe proper spelling, punctuation, and grammar. Make sure the information you convey is accurate to the best of your knowledge.
- Conserve resources. Don't add to network congestion by downloading huge files, sending long-winded email messages, or engaging in spamming.

Figure 5-7

Excerpted from "Netiquette Tips," *Keying In*, The Newsletter of the National Business Education Association, Volume 11, Number 2, November 2000.

your nerves, or wait 24 hours. Avoid expressions such as "You must be stupid if you do not understand that . . ." Such expressions contribute to "flaming" and "flame wars." In some cases, you may want to make a telephone call to or have a personal conversation with the person, rather than writing or responding to his or her flaming email.

- Before you reply to an email, ask yourself if you really need to reply. For example, a message to a list server that only says "I agree" should be sent only to the person who wrote the original email or perhaps not sent at all. If the message was only for your information, no reply is needed.
- If another person needs to know about the information contained in an email, send a copy of the email to that person.
- If you send a message in haste and then immediately realize you should not have done so, use the "unsend" option.
- Answer your email promptly. However, promptly does not generally mean you should respond within five or ten minutes. Your job involves more than answering your email. The general rule is to read and respond to your email once or twice a day (depending on volume).

TELEPHONES

As you have learned, the entire telecommunications field is changing quickly. Telephones in the past have used **Plain Old Telephone Service (POTS)** that carries signals through standard line technology that has been in existence for years. Today, however, broadband technology, with its numerous pipelines for sending and receiving video, sound, text, and graphics, is providing options that have not been available in the past. One technology that promises to change telephone service drastically is **Voice over Internet Protocol (VoIP).** By routing phone calls over the Internet, VoIP will be a focal point of the commingling of voice and data. It also has the capacity to change our notion of what a phone company is and how the Internet works. You learned earlier in this chapter that telephone service providers are changing drastically, with new players in the market that have never before been considered telephone providers. With IP, Internet service providers become telephone providers also. Here are some examples of this concept.

- With call waiting, a subscriber surfing the Web will see a small window pop up identifying callers and showing what they want.
- Cisco's® IP phone will include a virtual assistant who can screen calls and send them to you or to voice mail, depending on the caller.
- The Internet will be permeated by voice. Chat in chat rooms will gain new meaning when you can click on someone's Web or email address and start talking instead of keying.

Additionally, software such as NetMeeting® or CUseeMe® and digital video cameras allow us to see each other over our PC monitors while we are talking.

Free Internet telephone calls can be made from PC to phone or PC to PC.

It is predicted that the number of calls routed over the Internet will increase from 1.4 percent of U.S. long-distance traffic in 2000 to over 13.7 percent in 2004.[7]

Today many of the Internet-based telephone services offer free PC-to-phone or PC-to-PC calls from almost any place in the world. It is predicted that free service will soon be available all over the globe. In addition, for those individuals who do not want the potential inconvenience of being tethered to a computer, many vendors sell phone cards, which allow phone-to-phone traffic to be routed over the Internet. When using phone cards, however, you may incur additional connection fees and per-minute fees, in addition to possibly paying phone surcharges. Technological advances will continue to push this field, with new services

Communication Tip:

Good human relations remain extremely important as the needs of clients and customers are facilitated through the use of technology.

available in the future. Internet-based telephone services also make it possible to enjoy video phoning and videoconferencing options.

Multifunction units are beginning to be used that are a combination of cell-phone technology and data technology, available through a wireless pipeline. Disposable cell phones are being marketed, where it is possible to make a few calls at a relatively low cost and throw away the cell phone after use.

Cell phones, combination cell phones and PDAs, video phoning and videoconferencing, and voice technology will be discussed in the next section. However, regardless of what happens with technology, human beings must be able to use this technology well and organizations must be able to facilitate the needs of their clients and customers through the technology. Thus, good human relations remain crucial. If administrative professionals are to succeed in this world, they must constantly improve their communications and human relations skills.

Cell Phones

Cell phones, which use mobile wireless technology (discussed earlier in this chapter), have become standard equipment for most people, both in their work life and their home life. It is estimated that by 2003, more than one billion people will be using cell phones internationally—more than use the standard telephone. As a population, we enjoy the ability to send and receive calls from any location at any time. In fact, cell phones are so popular that many people carry a cell phone with them constantly, whether for business or personal use. It is common to see people making calls from airplanes and theatres. In fact, many theatres now make an announcement asking people to turn off their cell phones during the show.

One technological change that has occurred with cell phones is the combination of cell phones with PDAs (personal digital assistants). Some of the capabilities available on these units are as follows:

---

[7]Stewart Alsop, "Voice on the Net—Tip of the Iceberg," *Fortune*, October 9, 2000, 58.

- Phone, fax, and email messages delivered into a single mailbox reachable from the phone
- Corporate mail accounts and databases
- Weather forecasts
- Digital assistants to forward messages and manage how and when you can be reached
- Web browsing
- Audio services that enable you to play your favorite soundtracks
- **PIM** (personal information management), including managing contacts
- Speakerphone for hands-free calls
- Speed-dial numbers
- Call waiting and call forwarding
- Complete transactions initiated from the desktop browser
- IM (instant messaging) email
- Voice recording
- Text messaging (short messages—160 characters or so)
- Handwriting recognition systems

© PhotoDisc, Inc.

Cell phones are becoming PDAs.

Video Phoning and Videoconferencing

The videophone, its possibilities touted for decades, really never became a technology that was widely used or perceived to have much benefit. Part of the problem was cost effectiveness, while getting it to work well enough to attract a broad audience. Today, with all businesses and many homes equipped with computers, video phoning and videoconferencing are more an issue of software and connection speed. With the increasingly global world, there is a need to network groups of people in real-time conferences. With a video camera and a connection to the Internet via broadband, video phoning and videoconferencing are available to both the business and home market at very reasonable costs.

Voice Technology

Voice messages used with our telephones have been commonplace since the 1980s. However, today we are seeing a phenomenal increase in the use of voice technology, with much wider application than voice mail. The future promises an even greater increase in voice technology. You will be able to use voice commands to mine the Internet for just about any kind of information. Today, while standing in line at an airport, you can use your PDA to access the following:

- Stock quotes
- Weather forecasts
- Email
- An electronic calendar
- A customer's order
- An Internet-based bookstore
- Directions to a meeting location

All of this can be done without touching a keypad—all by voice command. Both wireless broadband and voice recognition technologies are fueling this increase in voice technology.

Of relevance to you now in your day-to-day functioning in the workplace is the proper use of voice mail. Many times we dial a business, are asked to speak or key into the receiver our information or request, and are answered by a computerized voice. There is never any actual contact with a human being. In organizations, voice mail is used extensively. It has been estimated that only 25 percent of all calls placed reach the person for whom they are intended on the first try. Voice messaging has become an efficient way of answering the phone when an employee is unable to do so. It allows the caller to leave a message or be routed to another individual who can take the call. If the caller leaves a message, the individual receiving the message can then return the call as soon as possible. Some advantages of voice messaging include

- Greater productivity of workers by eliminating repeated telephone calls when the individual called is not available
- Less extraneous conversation (Voice messages average 30 seconds; normal phone conversations average 4 or 5 minutes.)
- Providing the frequent traveler with the ability to communicate with the office at any time
- Increasing delivery speed on communications by getting messages through even with time zone differences (Even if the organization being called is closed for the day, a voice message can be left. The receiver can listen to it upon arriving at work the next morning or from the home office.)

If voice messaging is to be effective, attention must be paid to the message content, length, and branching system. It is very disconcerting to be branched to several computerized voices and never get your question or issue resolved. If you, as an administrative professional, are involved in helping to design a voice message system, you must be certain that it is both effective and efficient. You must always consider first the ability of the system to respond to the needs of the clients or customers. Listed here are some of the disadvantages of voice messaging and suggestions for how to counter them.

- Voice messaging is often misused by the employee who consistently puts his or her phone on voice mail, even when in the workplace. Certainly there are times when

it is essential to use voice messaging while in the office. For example, if work must be done with no interruptions and there is no one else to take the calls, voice messaging may be used. However, this situation should be rare. Do not hide behind a voice messaging system. An employee can save both parties time by answering the phone when in the office.

- A voice message may be poorly designed—too long and ineffective in routing the individual calling. The voice message needs to be succinct, clearly stated, and able to route an individual quickly and efficiently. With each step of the routing system, give callers no more than four options. Instructions should be short—under 15 seconds if possible. Give the most important information or answer the most frequently asked questions first. Tell the caller what you want him or her to do first, then the key to press; for example, "To transfer to our receptionist, press zero." If you give the number first, the caller may forget what number to press.
- A voice message may not allow the caller to talk with a person. Be certain your system allows the caller to talk with a person if necessary. No one likes to be lost in a voice message system that never allows the caller to be heard by a human being.
- The voice on a voice message may not sound pleasant. Remember, the sound and tone of your voice message greeting must create a favorable impression. On a voice message, vary your vocal tone; do not talk in a monotone. Be careful, also, of background sound when recording a message.

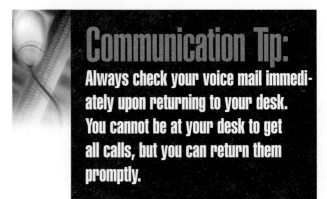

Communication Tip:
Always check your voice mail immediately upon returning to your desk. You cannot be at your desk to get all calls, but you can return them promptly.

Telephone Techniques

Telephone techniques remain extremely important in the effectiveness of all organizations. Attention must be paid to handling both outside and inside callers well. Business can be gained or lost due to effective or ineffective telephone procedures. You may be thinking "Why should I study effective telephone techniques? I already know how to use the telephone." Chances are you do make errors when using the phone; we all do. You also probably have been the recipient of ineffective telephone techniques used by others. Before you begin this section, take a few minutes to think through some of your own telephone behaviors. Do so by responding to the statements given in Self-Check B.

Self-Check B

Answer each statement with a yes or no answer.

	YES	NO
1. I am always pleasant with every telephone caller.	☐	☐
2. I greet telephone callers with a friendly salutation.	☐	☐
3. I give callers my full attention.	☐	☐
4. I say "please" and "thank you" often.	☐	☐
5. I keep a smile in my voice.	☐	☐
6. I am attentive to the caller's needs.	☐	☐
7. I avoid slang.	☐	☐
8. I take messages accurately and completely.	☐	☐
9. I use the caller's name frequently.	☐	☐
10. I ask questions tactfully.	☐	☐

Be Aware of Time Zone Differences

Due to the multinational nature of business today, calls are made frequently to places around the world. Obviously, time zone differences must be taken into consideration when making calls. In the United States, the time zones are Eastern, Central, Mountain, and Pacific. A time zone map for the United States is shown in Figure 5-8 on page 122. Time zones for international cities are shown on the Web at www.worldtimezone.com.

Keep a Smile in Your Voice

When you have customers or visitors in your office, a cheerful smile, a cup of coffee, and a magazine usually keeps the in-person callers happy, even when they have to wait. Since these services cannot be provided over the telephone, you must rely on your voice and your manner to make the voice-to-voice contact as pleasant as the face-to-face contact.

A voice that makes the caller feel as if a smile is coming through the receiver is a winning one. How do you develop such a smile in your voice? One way is to smile as you pick up the telephone receiver. When you are smiling, it is much easier to project a smile in your voice. Treat the voice on the other end of the line as you would treat a person who is standing in front of you. Let the individual know you are interested in him or her. Maintain a caring attitude. Never answer the phone in a curt or rude manner. Do not speak in a monotone; vary your voice modulation.

Be alert to what you are saying. Sometimes when we are tired or busy, we say things we do not intend. Here are some blunders that have been made on the telephone. Your experiences with the telephone will, no doubt, allow you to add to this list.

- Good morning. Account Services. Lori screaming.
- You can go to any bank that is inconvenient for you.
- Thanks for holding me.
- We're open between 12 and noon.

Good for a chuckle? Yes, but similar things can happen to any of us if we are not alert at all times.

Be Attentive and Discreet

Listen politely to what the other person says. Do not interrupt. If the caller is unhappy about some situation, allow him or her to explain why. Most of a person's anger can be vented in telling the story. It is easier to handle an unhappy person after you have listened to the problem. Use good listening skills.

- Listen for facts and feelings.
- Search for hidden or subtle meanings.

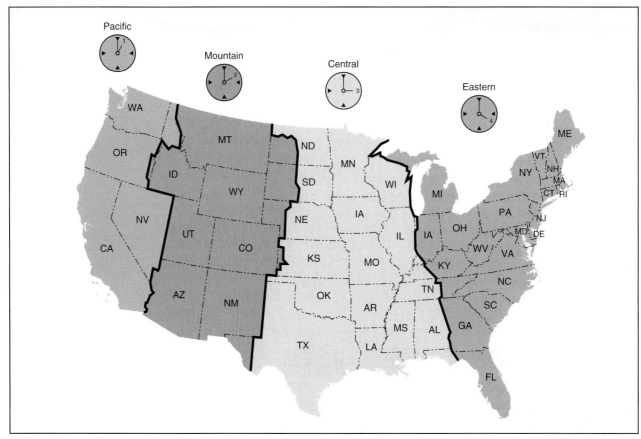

Figure 5-8   United States Time Zone Map

- Be patient.
- Do not evaluate.
- Try to understand what the speaker is saying, both from the words and from the tone of voice.
- Help the caller; respond to what the caller wants or asks. Do not just try—do it! As a customer, which response would you prefer to hear—"I will try" or "I will get the document faxed to you immediately"?

Be discreet if your employer is unavailable. Carefully explain why your employer cannot answer the telephone. You may say, "Mr. Albertson is away from the office now. I expect him back in approximately an hour. May I have him call you when he returns?" Never say, "Mr. Albertson is not here yet" (at 10 a.m.), "He's gone for the day" (at 3 p.m.), or "He's playing tennis" (at any time of day). A good rule to remember is to be helpful about when your employer is returning but not specific about where he or she is.

Use Correct English

Pay attention to using correct English and pronunciation. Anyone who has a good grasp of the English language would be uncomfortable to hear "This is her" or some similar grammatically incorrect statement.

Avoid Slang

Using slang is neither businesslike nor in good taste.

Avoid	Say
Yeah	Certainly
OK	Yes
Un-huh	Of course
Bye-bye	Goodbye
Huh?	I beg your pardon. I did not understand.
	or
	Would you please repeat that?

Take Messages Completely and Accurately

Incomplete messages are frustrating. Always get the necessary information. If you are not given all the information, ask the caller. Repeat the message to the caller so you can be certain it is accurate. You need the following information:

- the caller's name spelled correctly (Ask the caller to spell his or her name if you are not certain of how it is spelled.)
- company name
- telephone number (with area code if long distance)
- time of call
- message—exactly

Organizations supply message pads for recording the information. These message pads may be in single or duplicate sheets so the assistant has a copy of all messages.

Use the Caller's Name

It is flattering to the caller to be recognized and called by name. Frequent responses such as "Yes, Mr. Valentine. I will be happy to get the information" and "It was nice to talk with you, Ms. Keiba" indicate to callers that you know who they are and that you care about them as individuals.

Ask Questions Tactfully

Care should be used in asking questions. Ask only necessary questions, such as "May I tell Mr. Albertson who is calling?" or "When Mr. Albertson returns, may I tell him who called?" Never ask "Who's calling?" People are offended by such a blunt question. If your employer is not in or cannot take the call for some reason,

ask about the nature of the call so you can handle the call or refer it to someone else. For example, you may say, "If you tell me the nature of your call, perhaps I can help you or refer you to someone who can."

Speak Distinctly and Clearly

Make sure the caller can understand what you say. You cannot speak distinctly with gum, candy, or a pencil in your mouth. Also speak in a voice that can be heard. You do not want to shout or whisper.

- Place the receiver firmly against your ear.
- Place the center of the mouthpiece about an inch from the center of your lips.
- Speak in a normal voice. Watch the speed of your voice. Do not talk too fast or too slow. Speak at a moderate rate.

Handle Problem Calls

Most individuals are pleasant over the telephone, especially if you are courteous to them. Occasionally you may have a caller who has had a difficult day or for some other reason is unhappy. Many angry callers have been defused by an administrative professional taking the time to let them tell their story. Do not become emotionally involved in the situation. Remember that they are not angry with you, but rather with a situation or an event.

Once you have listened to the person, try to assist the individual in getting the problem solved. This approach may mean that you suggest a solution or that you tell the person you will have someone who can solve the problem call him or her back. Do not put the person on hold or mishandle the call by transferring it to

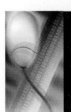

Communication Tip:

If you have regular callers with last names that are difficult to spell, store a list of difficult names on your computer. When the person calls, you can look up the name quickly without having to ask for the spelling.

an individual who cannot help. Such approaches merely make the person angrier.

Sometimes you have callers who refuse to give their name. You should have an understanding with your employer about what to do in such a situation. However, if you do not, put the person on hold while you tell your employer you are unable to get the caller's name. Your employer can then decide whether or not to speak to the individual.

Use Words to Identify Letters

Use words to identify letters in the spelling of names and places when necessary. Some letters are difficult to understand over the telephone. Figure 5-9 gives you some examples.

USE WORDS TO IDENTIFY LETTERS

A as in **A**lice	**F** as in **F**rank
B as in **B**ertha	**G** as in **G**eorge
C as in **C**harles	**H** as in **H**enry
D as in **D**avid	**I** as in **I**da
E as in **E**dward	**J** as in **J**ohn

Figure 5-9

Do Not Discriminate

Have you ever found yourself being nicer over the telephone to the president of the company than to a client you do not know? If the answer is "yes," make a point of being friendly before you know who is on the other end of the line. Try saying to yourself before answering the phone "A friend is calling."

Avoid Gender Bias

Some people still assume that all assistants are female and all executives are male. If you answer the telephone and the voice on the other end is female, do not assume she is an assistant and ask to speak to her employer. When addressing anyone, use terms that connote respect. Do not refer to a woman as a girl, a young lady, as a

© PhotoDisc, Inc.
Adopt a friendly attitude before answering the phone.

beautiful young thing, a gal, or any other term that can be construed as gender biased. Do not refer to a man as a boy, a hunk, or a guy.

Keep a List of Frequently Called Numbers

A file of frequently called numbers is an excellent time saver. For quick reference, these numbers should be kept on your PIM software. You may also program the most frequently used numbers into your telephone.

Incoming Calls

The techniques you learned in the previous section apply to all calls. Here are some special techniques for handling incoming calls.

Answer Promptly

When your telephone rings, answer promptly—on the first ring if possible and certainly by the third ring. You may lose a potential customer if you are slow in answering the telephone.

Identify Yourself and Your Organization

The organization for which you work will usually instruct you as to how to answer the telephone. If you work in a large organization, chances are you will not be the first person to answer the telephone. The first person answering identifies the company; then the caller will ask for a specific person or department. As an administrative professional for Mr. Albertson, you might answer "Mr. Albertson's office, Rebecca Martinez." If you need to identify the organization, you might say "Good morning. AmeriAsian Airlines."

Transfer Calls Carefully

Before you transfer a call, explain to the caller why you must transfer it. Make sure the caller is willing to be transferred. For example, you may say "Mr. Albertson is out, but Travis Figimara can give you the information. May I transfer you to Mr. Figimara?" You may also want to give the caller the extension number of the person to whom the caller is being transferred in case the transfer is not completed. The caller can then call the number without having to call you again.

Be certain you know how to transfer calls. Callers dislike being told they are going to be transferred and then getting disconnected due to incorrect transferring procedures.

Place Calls on Hold Only After Requesting Permission

A caller may sometimes request information that you do not have at your fingertips. You may need to check with someone else or go to your files to get the information. When this happens, do not place the caller on hold without permission. You may say "I need to pull the information from my files. Would you like to hold for a moment while I get it, or shall I call you back?" If the caller agrees to hold, try to get back to the person as soon as possible. Nothing irritates a caller more than to be left on hold for a period of time. When you return to the line, let the caller know you are back by saying "Thank you for waiting." If you are delayed in getting the information, go back to the person on hold and ask if she or he wants to continue to hold; apologize for the length of time it is taking.

Handle Multiple Calls

You may have more than one telephone line that you are responsible for answering. If so, at times you will be answering a call on one line when another line rings. When this happens, you must remember that the caller on the second line does not know you are already on the phone. The caller is expecting to get an answer immediately. Excuse yourself politely by saying to the first caller, "May I place you on hold for a moment? I must answer another phone." If the second call is going to take awhile, ask the caller for a number so you can call back as soon as you finish the first call. Then go back to the first caller with "Thank you for waiting." Your responsibility is to handle all calls as quickly and efficiently as possible.

Handle Cell Phone Calls

If you are working off-site with a client or customer and you receive a cell-phone call, interrupting your work to answer the cell phone may seem discourteous to the client or customer. Taking these outside calls conveys the impression that you have something more important to do than helping the client. Therefore, turn your cell phone to silent mode when assisting an in-person client. If you must keep your cell phone plugged in due to an urgent call you are expecting, be sure the client you are talking with knows about it. You may say, "We may be interrupted by a call I must take, but I promise to be as quick as possible." If the call comes through, excuse yourself and keep the conversation as brief as possible.

Screen Calls

Many executives have one telephone number that is published for callers and another inside number that is not published. The executive uses the inside number to make outgoing calls; the number also may be given out to close friends or family members. The administrative professional usually is expected to screen calls that come from the published number. For example, when the executive receives a call, the administrative professional is expected to determine who is calling and why. The executive may refuse to take certain calls. If someone else in your company can handle the call, transfer it to that person after requesting permission from the caller to transfer the call. If no one is available to take the call let the person know courteously that your employer is not interested. One response might be "I appreciate the information; however, Mr. Albertson is not interested in pursuing the matter at the present time."

Leave a Message When You Leave Your Desk

If you have to leave your desk, arrange for someone else to answer your telephone. You may forward it to a co-worker. Tell the co-worker where you can be reached and what time you will be back. If your employer is also gone, tell the co-worker in general terms where your employer is and when he or she will be back. You might say, "Mr. Albertson is in a meeting and will be available around 3 p.m."

Follow Through on Promises

If you make a promise to call back with information, do so. A broken promise can cause a canceled order or a lost customer. A kept promise can enhance a reputation for reliability and trustworthiness. Help your employer remember promises made. If you know of information that your employer has promised a customer but has not followed through on, provide a tactful reminder of the need to follow through. Your employer will appreciate your assistance.

Outgoing Calls

As an administrative professional, you are often responsible for placing calls for your employer or for making business calls yourself. Just as incoming calls must be handled effectively, so must outgoing calls. Tips are provided in this section.

Place Calls Properly

Supervisors usually place their own calls to save time and to create favorable impressions. You may, however, work for someone who does not wish to place calls. If so, identify your supervisor's name before you transfer the call. For example, you may say, "Mr. Albertson of AmeriAsian Airlines is calling." Then transfer the call to Mr. Albertson.

If your supervisor is not available or makes another call after you place one, make some subtle suggestions to your supervisor. For example, before you place the call, you might say, "Mr. Albertson, are you going to be available for a few minutes? I want to place the call you requested to Mr. Chen." Your supervisor may just be unaware that his or her habits are discourteous and irritating to the person being called.

Plan Your Call

Take a few minutes to plan your call before you make it. Know the purpose of your call and what you intend to say. Once you get the person on the telephone, state your purpose clearly and concisely. For example, you may say, "This is John Chin of AmeriAsian. I'm calling to verify your attendance at the sales meeting tomorrow at 3 p.m. in Conference Room A." You may exchange pleasantries with the individual you are calling. However, the main purpose is to get your message across without wasting the time of the individual called.

Self-Check C

In Self-Check B, you considered some of your own telephone errors. Take a few minutes now to consider the mistakes others have made with you over the telephone. List those mistakes here, along with correction suggestions.

_____

_____

_____

_____

_____

THE FUTURE OF TELECOMMUNICATIONS

Twenty years from now today's high bandwidth solutions and scenarios will likely be irrelevant due to pure fiber-optic networks. These fiber-optic networks promise to deliver bandwidth that is far greater than what cable, DSL, or satellite can offer. It is also predicted that fiber-optic connections, in addition to being the major network used by businesses, will also be widely used in homes. Eventually there will be fiber network interfaces in our homes that provide for virtual reality, DVD-quality streaming media, and almost anything else one can imagine—all provided over a fiber pipe. This broadband revolution will eventually result in ultra-fast Internet connections that will be as common as telephone service today.

As broadband connectivity becomes widely used, providers will begin differentiating themselves by offering extra services. For example, some broadband companies now offer flexible subscription services for software and games. Broadband in public spaces, including airports and convention centers, is burgeoning. According to some sources, this segment will grow from $18.5 million a year to nearly $1.2 billion in 2004.[8]

Telecommunications will continue to affect our life outside the workforce. Wireless technology is transforming our automobiles into a multimedia data center and productivity tool. With a connected car, you will be able to

- Receive data from roadside sensors that will alert you to traffic bottlenecks
- Direct you to empty parking spaces at the airport, where sensors and bar-code readers will automatically produce a rental-car receipt
- Determine whether or not your flight is on time or has been delayed
- Access a virtual advisor that will allow you to access information, including your email, and information delivered through synthesized voice

The revolution of telecommunications promises to continue, with access to all types of data, video, audio, text, and graphics at faster speeds than we are presently experiencing due to fiber-optic networks. In addition, companies will continue to both merge and expand their services. Telecommunication companies will not consider themselves merely a provider of broadband pipelines, but a deliverer of telecommunication services that connect people to people and people to machines in a multitude of ways.

---

[8]Cassimir Medford, "The Future: Broadband's Next Trick May be Fiber-Optic," *PC Magazine*, February 6, 2001, 160–161.

CHAPTER SUMMARY

This summary will help you remember the important points covered in the chapter.

- The telecommunications field is involved in a revolution that is rapidly changing the traditional ways we have employed these services. Systems at various stages of development are breaking down the barriers between the computer and the telephone.
- Traditional telephone companies are in the process of transforming themselves from delivering a service that only connects people to people to one that connects people to people and people to machines through a wide range of telecommunication devices.
- Telecommunications companies are merging with companies in different businesses to garner more of the market and provide a variety of services. Gone are the days when one supermonopoly owned the whole network support infrastructure.
- The telecommunications field is experiencing a revolution, with numerous broadband pipelines available to organizations and individuals. These pipelines (in addition to standard analog dial-up) are cable, DSL, fixed wireless, and satellite. Information (including text, music, graphics, and pictures) can be retrieved from these pipelines at faster rates than in the past.
- Analog dial-up modem technology is the slowest technological pipeline. However, it is less expensive than other telecommunication pipelines and is available everywhere phone lines are available.
- Cable is a means of accessing the Internet. Cable is fast and is becoming available to people in most areas of the United States.
- DSL is available in ADSL, SDSL, or IDSL. The majority of DSL users are businesses that already have telephone service in place.
- Fixed wireless technology is simpler than mobile wireless technology (the technology used by cell phones) because it does not utilize client devices moving in and out of coverage areas. Fixed wireless (WLL) is offered primarily to businesses and homes in areas where the infrastructure is not in place to deliver broadband through cable or DSL.
- Satellite has disadvantages over cable and DSL (higher cost, degrading of transmission in heavy rain or high wind, and download time); however, it is the only broadband service presently available for a number of businesses and homes, particularly those in rural areas.

- Fax is a telecommunications device that electronically sends an original document from one location to another via phone lines. It is an old technology, and the fax machine has become a standard piece of office equipment in businesses and homes.
- Email has revolutionized the way we communicate. Email is used extensively in businesses as well as homes. When email messages are sent, email guidelines, ethics, and etiquette must be considered.
- Behaving ethically when sending email is extremely important. Do not send personal email from your office computer. Do not use email to berate or reprimand an employee. Do not use email to terminate someone. Do not use email to send information that involves any type of legal action.
- Etiquette is most important when sending email. Never send an email when you are angry, and answer your email promptly.
- It is predicted that the number of calls routed over the Internet will increase from 1.4 percent of U.S. long-distance traffic in 2000 to over 13.7 percent in 2004. The broadband revolution promises to change telephone service drastically. For example, telephone calls can now be sent free from PC-to-phone or PC-to-PC to most global locations.
- Cell phones have become standard equipment for most people, both in their work life and their home life.
- Cell phones are now available as combination units with PDAs (personal digital assistants). These units are capable of sending phone, fax, and email messages; retrieving corporate mail and databases, weather forecasts, and news headlines; and browsing the Web.
- With the ability to use computers to make telephone calls, video phoning and videoconferencing are now available. For example, by using a digital camera and an Internet connection that allows you to send a phone call through the Internet, video phoning and videoconferencing can be accomplished relatively easily.
- Voice technology is becoming widely available, and the future promises an even greater increase in voice technology.

- Voice mail should be used properly in the workplace. For example, a voice messaging system should be designed so the caller does not get lost in the system without ever being able to talk with a person. Also, voice messaging should not be misused by the employee who is responsible for answering the phone.
- Proper telephone techniques are important to the effectiveness of all organizations.
- The telecommunications revolution will continue. Twenty years from now today's high bandwidth solutions and scenarios will likely be irrelevant due to pure fiber-optic networks. These fiber-optic networks promise to deliver bandwidth that is far greater than what cable, DSL, or satellite can offer.
- As broadband connectivity becomes widely used, providers will begin differentiating themselves by offering extra services.
- Telecommunication companies will not consider themselves merely a provider of broadband pipelines, but a deliverer of telecommunication services that connect people to people and people to machines in a multitude of ways.

CHAPTER GLOSSARY

The following terms were introduced in this chapter. Definitions are provided to help you review the terms.

- **Telecommunications** (p. 107)—the electronic transmission of text, data, voice, video, and image (graphics and pictures) from one location to another.
- **Broadband** (p. 108)—short for broad bandwidth, as in a high-speed network able to carry video as well as voice; describes the throughput of a network per unit of time, measured in kilobits, megabits, or gigabits per second.
- **Packet-switched network** (p. 108)—one in which each signal (whether it carries music or video or email) is chopped into tiny digital parcels that are commingled with other packets and routed to their destinations; the Internet is a packet network; the phone system is a circuit network, where each signal travels unbroken on its own end-to-end pipe.
- **Moribund** (p. 108)—state of dying.
- **Bluetooth** (p. 108)—a new technology standard for short-range wireless communication.
- **Cable modem** (p. 110)—an external device that connects to the computer and to a service provider's coaxial cable line.
- **DSL (digital subscriber line)** (p. 110)—a technology that provides high-speed data communications over analog phone lines.
- **ADSL (asymmetric digital subscriber line)** (p. 110)—a form of DSL that supports peak downstream speeds of 144 Kbps to 2.2 Mbps and upstream rates from 90 Kbps to 640 Kbps.
- **SDSL (symmetric digital subscriber line)** (p. 110)—a form of DSL that transfers data upstream and downstream at symmetric rates of up to 2.3 Mbps over a single copper twisted-pair line.
- **IDSL (Internet digital subscriber line)** (p. 110)—a form of DSL that transfers data upstream and downstream at rates of 144 Kbps and does not have the strict distance limitations that ADSL and SDSL have.
- **Fixed wireless,** or **WLL (wireless local loop)** (p. 110)—a broadband connection system that uses high-frequency radio links to deliver voice and data.
- **Cellular technology,** or **mobile wireless service** (p. 111)—a technology that uses cells to relay information to a computer that in turn directs the call into the local telephone system; when a customer leaves one cell area and enters another, the computer automatically switches the transmission to the next nearest cell.
- **Fax machine** (p. 113)—facsimile; electronically sends an original document from one location to another via communication networks.
- **Email** (p. 113)—electronic message; a message that is sent from the computer via a broadband pipeline to another computer.
- **IM** (p. 113)—instant messaging; an iteration of email in which messages are sent instantaneously from one computer to another computer.

CHAPTER GLOSSARY

(continued)

- **Emoticons** (p. 115)—faces produced by the Internet counterculture in answer to email being devoid of body language.
- **Spamming** (p. 116)—forwarding unwanted or junk email to someone who has not requested it.
- **Plain Old Telephone Service (POTS)** (p. 117)—carries signals through standard telephone line technology from one telephone to another.

- **Voice over Internet Protocol (VoIP)** (p. 117)—software and hardware that allow voice signals to be carried over an IP-based network, with POTS quality and reliability.
- **PIM** (p. 119)—personal information management software.

DISCUSSION ITEMS

These discussion items provide an opportunity to test your understanding of the chapter through written responses and/or discussion with your classmates and your instructor.

1. Define telecommunications.
2. List and explain five telecommunication pipelines.
3. Explain the importance of Internet ethics and etiquette. Give five examples of good practices for both ethics and etiquette.

4. Explain the relevance of VoIP to the telephone.
5. List ten effective telephone techniques.

CRITICAL-THINKING ACTIVITY

You asked one of your assistants, Juan, to send an email to a group of managers setting up a meeting with the superintendent of schools in Grand Rapids to discuss a mentoring program AmeriAsian wants to begin with the public school system. The meeting is to be held on Monday, January 20, in Conference Room C, beginning at 8:30 a.m. and lasting approximately one hour. The managers are to forward written suggestions for a mentoring program to Mr. Albertson on Thursday, January 16. You did not review the email Juan sent. His email, a response from one of the managers, and Juan's response to the manager is on the Student CD, file SCDCTA5-1, SCDCTA5-2, and SCDCTA5-3. Juan comes to you very upset. He says one of the managers is angry with him, and when he tried to handle the situation, it became worse.

Review the email exchanges. Has Juan made errors? If so, what are they? How should the present situation be handled? What advice would you give Juan on preventing such a situation in the future?

RESPONSES TO SELF-CHECK A

1. The telecommunications revolution is changing the way we communicate, allowing us to

   - Make telephone calls from PC to PC or PC to telephone over the Internet
   - Send information through voice technology (speaking into the computer)
   - Hold computers in the palm of our hands, speak into them, and make phone calls; get data from our PCs; get stock quotes; and get newspaper headlines

   All of this can be done at faster and faster speeds over pipelines that are both wired and wireless.

2. Traditional telephone providers are changing their services by providing various broadband pipelines; providing voice and data services enhanced by real-time communications; and providing new services such as Web-based interfaces for billing and making payments, as well as customer care, and attendant functions realized using natural language voice dialogues with machines.

3. The differences between cable, DSL, and fixed wireless are as follows:

   - Cable is a broadband pipeline that operates at very fast speeds in downloading information. A cable modem connects to the computer and to a service provider's coaxial cable line. It has limited upload speed, and bandwidth sharing can degrade performance. Because cable modems use shared connections, they are prone to slowdowns if too many users along a particular stretch of cable are online at one time.
   - DSL is also a broadband pipeline that operates at a fast speed, slightly slower than the cable pipeline for downloads. However, DSL users report more consistent speed than cable users. DSL stands for digital service line. Most DSL service can be purchased from the same company that provides telephone service.
   - Fixed wireless (also referred to as wireless local loop) converts data to signals and relays it to customers through a network of transceivers mounted on utility poles, streetlights, and so on. Each WLL subscriber has a small radio receiver and directional antenna oriented toward the nearest microcell. Fixed wireless at this point is slower in receiving and sending data than cable and DSL.

PROJECTS

Project 5-1 (Objective 1)
Online Project

Surf the Web for the following information:

- The status of cable, DSL, and fixed wireless broadband. Attempt to discover the capabilities of each of the telecommunication pipelines and the numbers of users of each service.
- The status of fiber-optic broadband. Attempt to discover projections of when this telecommunications pipeline will be available to large segments of the population.

In searching the Web, you might want to use www.google.com as your search engine.

Additionally, review periodicals such as *Fortune, PC World,* and *PC Magazine* in your search for information.

Present your findings orally to the class, or write a report of your findings, documenting your resources. Submit your report to your instructor.

Project 5-2 (Objective 2)

Four situations are provided on Student CD, SCDP5-2. Respond to each situation. Print a copy of your responses, and submit to your instructor.

PROJECTS

(continued)

Project 5-3 (Objective 2)
Collaborative Project

Choose a member of your class to work with on this project. Call each other, re-creating situations 1, 2, 3, and 4 in Project 5-2, which are on Student CD, file SCDP5-2. Complete each of the situations twice. One of you should be the caller and the other the administrative assistant; then switch roles and replay the situations. Print out a copy of the Telephone Voice Rating Form (Student CD, file SCDP5-3). Complete the form and submit it to your instructor.

Project 5-4 (Objective 3)

Three emails are on Student CD, SCDP5-4a, 5-4b, and 5-4c. Review these emails, determining what is wrong with each one. Then rewrite each email as it should be written, using the email forms on SCDP5-4d, 5-4e, and 5-4f. Make a copy of your email, and submit to your instructor.

Project 5-5 (Objective 4)

Add to the Professional Growth Plan you began in Chapter 1 by developing your own behavior guidelines for using email ethically. Save your plan on your Professional Growth Plan disk as "Progro5-5." Develop an appropriate title for this portion of your plan. Before you begin your plan, review the email ethics section in your text and Figure 5-7.

ENGLISH USAGE CHALLENGE DRILL

Correct the following sentences. Cite the grammar rule that is applicable to each sentence. Before you begin, refresh your memory of grammar rules by reviewing punctuation rules in the Reference Guide of this text.

1. Ruth Rogers who is in excellent physical condition enjoys swimming.
2. Some people, who are in excellent physical condition, enjoy swimming.
3. Her replies, that were given entirely in Spanish, amazed the visitors from Spain.
4. Individuals living in the Midwest according to studies do not have as pronounced an accent as people living in the South.
5. According to his thinking therefore the only way to overcome fear of flying is to fly.

ASSESSMENT OF CHAPTER OBJECTIVES

Now that you have completed the chapter and the projects, take a few minutes to review the chapter learning objectives. For your convenience, the objectives are repeated here. Did you accomplish these objectives? If you were unable to accomplish the objectives, give your reasons for not doing so.

1. Discover how information is transmitted electronically.   Yes _____   No _____

_____

_____

_____

2. Develop and use proper telephone techniques.   Yes _____   No _____

_____

_____

_____

_____

3. Use proper email communication techniques.   Yes _____   No _____

_____

_____

_____

4. Recognize the importance of email ethics.   Yes _____   No _____

_____

_____

_____

You may submit your answers in writing to your instructor, using the memorandum form on the Student CD, SCDAP5-1.

LEARNING OBJECTIVES

1. Define records management and explain how it is used within an organization.
2. Identify and use records storage systems.
3. Use the basic indexing rules.
4. *Increase decision-making skills.*

Technology has significantly impacted the manner in which records within an organization are handled. We now have the ability to create, use, maintain, and store records technologically without ever making paper copies. However, the paperless office that was touted as a possibility as well as a probability has not become a reality. In fact, we are seeing an explosion in the amount of paper records *and* electronic records generated. We seem to want both. Think about this statement from your personal perspective for a moment. How many times have you read an email and then printed out a paper copy even though your software allows you to maintain an electronic copy? According to studies done by Hewlett-Packard, workers who say they regularly print pages from the Internet print an average of 32 pages a day.[1] How many times have you transferred a piece of correspondence to a disk for electronic storage and also made a paper copy for a manual file? We seem to have difficulty giving up paper even when we have excellent technological records management capabilities.

What does this mean for the administrative professional in today's workplace? It means you have to be proficient in both electronic and manual (paper) records management systems. And that is not an easy task. A major complaint of executives is that it is often difficult and sometimes impossible to find essential information when it is needed. This inability to find a record or to find one quickly is not only a frustrating process but a costly one as well. It can

- Cost the organization hundreds or thousands of dollars
- Force the management of a company to make decisions based on incomplete information
- Result in the loss of a valuable client
- Hinder a legal case due to lack of information

The administrative professional is the individual most often held responsible for not finding a record or for not finding it in a timely manner. An understanding of records

---

[1]Dianna Booher, *E-Writing* (New York: Simon & Schuster, Inc., 2001), 51.

management procedures and techniques can simplify the process for you and allow you to become known as the person who can locate needed materials instantly—a skill that can make you invaluable to your supervisor and the organization. This chapter will help you learn the basics of records management. Your ongoing task regarding records management is to keep current on new developments in the field.

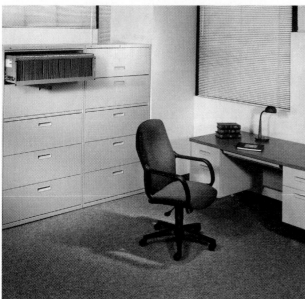

Photo courtesy of The Hon Company.

The successful administrative professional is able to locate records quickly.

RECORDS MANAGEMENT DEFINED

A **record** is any type of recorded information, whether that information is an email message, a letter, a report, a spreadsheet, a contract, a personnel record, or any other type of organizational record. **Records management** is the systematic control of records from the creation of the record to its final disposition. In order for a records management system to function, there must be information, equipment, and people. Information is generated by many sources and can appear in many forms—as a paper record or

as an electronic record that is stored on a disk, a videotape, a microfilm, or on numerous other electronic media. Equipment in a records management system includes all of the hardware used in processing documents. People include the necessary personnel to get the right documents to the right individuals at the lowest cost. *Since both electronic and paper systems are used in most organizations today, this chapter will emphasize both manual and electronic procedures.*

RECORDS MANAGEMENT COMPONENTS

If a records management system is to be effective, it must include these essential components.

- An organizationwide records structure
- A records storage system
- Alphabetic and numeric indexing rules
- Appropriate filing supplies
- Necessary equipment and media
- Retention schedules
- Active to inactive file procedures
- Procedures for updating the management system
- Records management manuals and ongoing training for personnel

These components are necessary for an electronic system, a manual system, or a system that combines the two (prevalent in most organizations). These processes are shown graphically in Figure 6-1 on page 136. The components of the records management system are explained in detail in the next sections.

Organizationwide Records Management System

The records management department or the person in charge of records management must clearly state the organization's file structure. This structure should be comprehensive in approach; that is, the structure should include how records are to be filed, how long they are

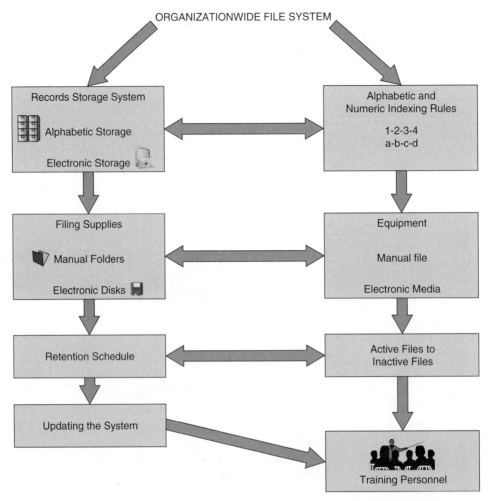

ORGANIZATIONWIDE FILE SYSTEM

Records Storage System

Alphabetic Storage

Electronic Storage

Alphabetic and Numeric Indexing Rules

1-2-3-4
a-b-c-d

Filing Supplies

Manual Folders

Electronic Disks

Equipment

Manual file

Electronic Media

Retention Schedule

Active Files to Inactive Files

Updating the System

Training Personnel

Figure 6-1   Records Management Components

to be kept in active status, and how inactive records are to be stored. Without such clarity, personnel within each department may file records in very different ways, with the result being great confusion, mishandling of records, and loss of important records.

Records Storage Systems

An important consideration in any records management system, whether that system is electronic or manual, is how the records are stored. **Records storage systems** include alphabetic (alphabetical order) and numeric (numerical order). Both of these systems have several variations that are explained in the following paragraphs. Records in a manual or electronic system may be stored by either of these methods.

Alphabetic Storage Methods

The **alphabetic storage** method uses letters of the alphabet to determine the order in which the record is filed. This is the most common

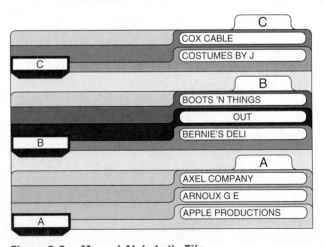

Figure 6-2   Manual Alphabetic File

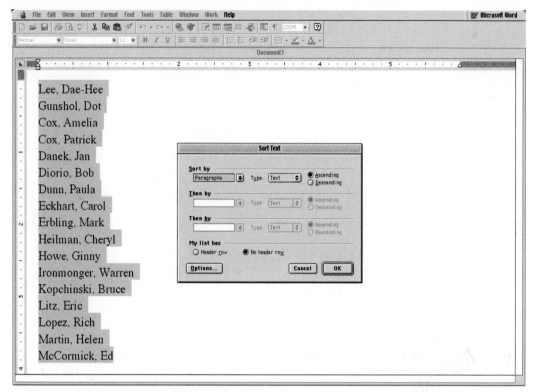

Figure 6-3   Electronic Alphabetic Screen

method used and is found in one form or another in every organization. Figure 6-2 illustrates a manual alphabetic file. An electronic alphabetic screen is shown in Figure 6-3. Documents are filed according to the basic alphabetic filing rules, which are given in a later section of this chapter.

Advantages of an alphabetic system are as follows:

- It is a **direct access** system. There is no need to refer to anything except the file to find the name.
- The dictionary arrangement is simple to understand.
- Misfiling is easily checked by alphabetic sequence.

Variations of the alphabetic storage method include **subject filing** (arranging records by their subject) and **geographic filing** (arranging records by geographic location).

Subject Filing. Subject filing is used to some extent in most organizations. An illustration of a manual subject file is shown in Figure 6-4.

Although subject order is useful and necessary in certain situations, it is the most difficult

classification to maintain. Each record must be read completely to determine the subject—a time-consuming process. It is a difficult method to control since one person may read a record and determine the subject to be one thing

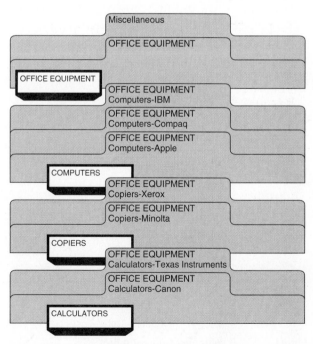

Figure 6-4   Manual Subject File

and another person may read the record and decide the subject is something entirely different. For example, one person classifying records concerning personnel grievances may determine that the subject is *grievances* while another person may determine that the subject is *personnel—grievances.*

You learned earlier that an alphabetic system is a direct system—a file can be found by going directly to the name of the file. A subject system can be considered direct or indirect. When the system is direct, the subject file is a simple one (with few subjects consisting of only a single sheet of titles) and access can be obtained directly through its alphabetic title. However, most subject systems are more complex and demand some type of index. For electronic systems, cross-reference terms can be incorporated within the index. Without an index, it is almost impossible for the subject storage method to function satisfactorily. This index may include several levels or several cross-references. Figure 6-5 illustrates two- and three-level subject indexes. The index should be kept up to date as new subjects are added and old ones eliminated. When new subjects are added, the index provides guidance to avoid the duplication of subjects.

The index to the Yellow Pages of the telephone directory is a good example of a subject index. Take a few minutes now to look at your Yellow Pages. Notice the index that precedes the directory. The index gives you the subject areas. If this subject area is not where the information is located, the user is given the correct subject area. Here are some examples.

> Advertising Art & Layout Service
> See Artists—Commercial; Graphic Designers
>
> Doctors
> See Chiropractic Physicians; Clinics; Dentists; Hospitals; Optometry, Physicians & Surgeons—M.D.; Physicians & Surgeons—DO; Physicians & Surgeons—Podiatrists

One of the major advantages of the subject method is that all records about one subject are grouped together. For example, notice above that all dentists are grouped together; all hospitals are grouped together, and so on. If this information was filed using a straight alphabetic method, each individual dentist would be listed by name and each individual hospital would be listed by name. Obviously, such a system is not helpful in finding information if you do not know the name of a hospital or a dentist.

Geographic Filing. Another variation of an alphabetic system is the geographic method, with related records grouped by place or location. Geographic filing is considered a direct method if you know the location of the file needed. If you do not, it is an indirect system and requires a separate geographic file in a manual system or the appropriate **keywords** (unique identifiers) set up for an electronic system so you can query the system in a variety of ways. Geographic filing is particularly useful for the organizations listed here.

- Utility companies where street names and numbers are of primary importance in troubleshooting
- Real estate firms that have listings according to land areas
- Sales organizations that are concerned with the geographic location of their customers
- Government agencies that file records by state, county, or other geographic division

In a manual geographic file by state and city, file guides are used to indicate the state and city. File folders are arranged alphabetically

Figure 6-5   Three-Level Subject Index

Chapter 6: Records Management

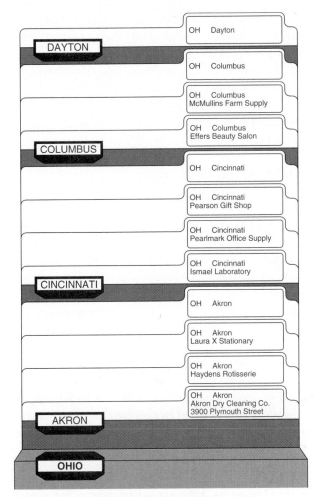

Figure 6-6   Manual Geographic File

behind the guides, with tabs indicating the company or individual. Figure 6-6 shows a manual geographic arrangement.

Numeric Storage Methods

Under the **numeric method,** records are given numbers that are arranged in a numeric sequence when stored. The numeric method is particularly useful to the following organizations:

- Insurance companies that keep records according to policy numbers
- Law firms that assign a case number to each client
- Real estate agencies that list properties by code numbers

The manual numeric file has four basic parts.

- Numeric file
- Alphabetic general file

- A file containing the names of the clients, customers, and/or companies with the number that has been assigned to the individual or company
- A file containing a list of the numbers that have been used

In practice, here is how the manual numeric method works.

1. When a document is ready to be filed, the file containing the names of the clients and customers is consulted to get the number of the particular client or customer.
2. The number established is placed on the document; the document is placed in the numeric file.
3. If the client or customer is new and no number is established, the document may be placed in the alphabetic file until the client or customer has enough documents to open an individual numeric file.
4. If it is necessary to establish a new numeric file, the file containing the list of numbers is consulted to determine the next number to be used.

Figure 6-7 illustrates the manual numeric method. Here are three variations of numeric filing.

- Chronological filing
- Terminal-digit filing
- Alphanumeric filing

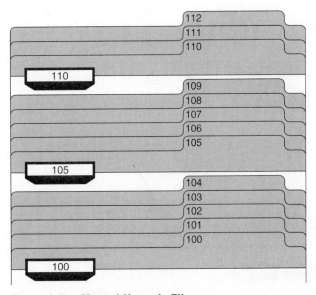

Figure 6-7   Manual Numeric File

Chronological Filing. Chronological filing is the arrangement of records by date, usually by year, month, or day. Additionally, other calendar divisions (such as weeks, months, or quarters) may be used as key sort fields for document groupings. Chronological filing is also used for **tickler files** (files used to tickle your memory and remind you to take certain actions). An example of a tickler file is the calendar file that is used on PIM software. The to-do items are arranged by the date the item is due. Once the items have been keyed into the PIM system, you can readily call up what you are to accomplish each day.

Terminal-Digit Filing. In the basic numeric method, as the files increase, the numbers assigned become higher. When the numbers become several digits long, it becomes difficult to file items correctly. One remedy to this difficulty is the use of **terminal-digit filing,** in which the final digits of a number are used. For example, assume that you are setting up a file, with the file number being 129845. The document would be filed first by the last two digits, 45. The next digits used would be 98, with the final digits being 12.

Alphanumeric Filing. Alphanumeric filing combines alphabetic and numeric characters. For example, RM-01 Records Management may be the main directory, with the subdirectories being RM-01-01 Manual Filing Methods and RM-01-02 Electronic Filing Methods.

Manual Filing Procedures

When filing manual records, certain procedures should be followed before placing the record in the file, including:

- **Inspecting**—Checking to see that the correspondence is ready to be filed. A release mark (such as the supervisor's initials, a file stamp, or some other agreed upon designation) lets you know the record is ready to be filed.
- **Indexing**—Determining the way the record is to be filed—the name, the subject, the number, or the geographic location.
- **Coding**—Marking the record by the name, subject, location, or number that was determined in the indexing process.

When filing records electronically, you must also follow certain procedures. For example, if you are using a subject file, you must have the appropriate keywords so the system can display information in a variety of ways. Software database and document management software are particularly helpful in filing electronic records.

Database and Document Management Software

Database programs include dBase IV®, FoxPro®, and Microsoft Access®, among others. Free database programs are also available on the Web.

With **database software** programs, the user can organize, enter, process, index, sort, select, link related files, store, and retrieve information. Data can be shared within the organization, across the organization's intranet, and over the Internet. **Electronic indexing** sorts the records and stores the information based on one or more key fields. The keyword is a unique identifier chosen by the user. For example, if you are working in a human resources department and entering employee information, the keyword might be the employee's social security number. In this case, you would be using a numeric filing system. This system is similar to the inspecting, indexing, and coding mentioned previously that is necessary when filing documents manually. You can **query** (ask) the database to display information in a variety of ways. For example, you might ask for employees who are making a certain salary level or employees who have been employed for a specified period of time. Information may be stored on a variety of media, including DVDs and CDs. **Integrated packages** combine database software with spreadsheet and word-processing software so users can easily move stored information from one application to another. Figure 6-8 illustrates the cycle.

Document management software is also available to assist you in managing electronic, microimage, and paper systems. One document management program is Step2000®, a program available from Universal Document Management Systems, Inc. Document management programs are helpful if an organization decides

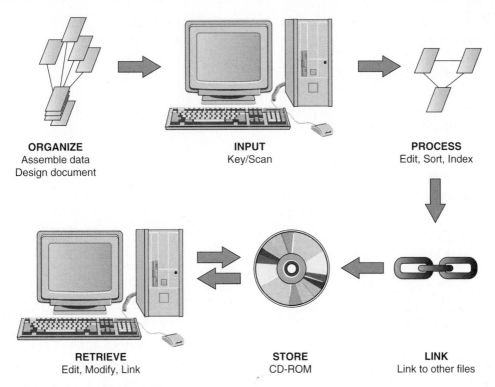

ORGANIZE	INPUT	PROCESS
Assemble data Design document	Key/Scan	Edit, Sort, Index

RETRIEVE	STORE	LINK
Edit, Modify, Link	CD-ROM	Link to other files

Figure 6-8   Database Cycle

to move from a manual to an electronic system. For example, with document management software, paper documents can be digitized and stored on a variety of media, including CDs, optical media, and hard drives or even online.

Some of the advantages of a document management system are as follows:

- Retrieving documents faster
- Reducing labor costs involved in processing files
- Viewing, printing, faxing, emailing, or annotating any document from your PC
- Recovering manual filing and storage space for other business use
- Storing backup copies of all files in a safe location
- Generating activity reports by department and user
- Generating records retention and disposal guidelines

You have already learned that you must perform certain functions before filing a record manually, such as inspecting, indexing, and coding. So too must you perform certain functions before filing an electronic record. You must determine how you want the information sorted. For example, do you want to sort by name, by location, or by number? If you want to sort by location, will you sort by state, by city, and then by name? In other words, you have to pay careful attention to setting up your electronic file system in a manner that lets you retrieve the data quickly and accurately.

Alphabetic and Numeric Indexing Rules

The rules for filing may vary slightly from organization to organization based on the specific needs of the entity. The organization must be clear about its indexing rules and make these rules clear to all administrative professionals through written documents. ARMA International, the Association for Information Management Professionals, has set forth rules. These rules are given in a later section of this chapter. You will want to become familiar with these rules. ARMA provides additional services, some of which are listed here.

- *The Information Management Journal* and *InfoPro* are published quarterly, offering assistance to professionals in the records management field. *InfoPro Online* is also available.

- A bookstore offers recent publications on records management.
- Information concerning how to obtain the CRM (Certified Records Manager) designation is given.
- Through ARMA International's Career Placement Services, employers may post a position and applicants may search for a position.

You may obtain more information about ARMA from their Website at www.arma.org.

Storage Supplies, Equipment, and Media

Storage supplies, equipment, and media are very different, depending on whether the document management system is a manual or an electronic one. As you have learned earlier in this chapter, most organizations have both types of systems today. You need to be knowledgeable about the systems and equipment used in both.

Basic Manual Filing Supplies

Basic manual filing supplies include file folders, suspension folders, file guides, and labels.

File Folders. A file folder is generally a manila folder either 8½ by 11 inches or 8½ by 14 inches in size. Other colors of folders are available including blue, yellow, green, red, and so on. The filing designation for the correspondence placed in the folder is keyed on a label that is then affixed to the tab of the folder. The tab may be at the top of the folder for traditional drawer files or on the side of the folder for open-shelf filing. Folders are made with tabs of various widths, called **cuts.** The cuts are straight cut, one-half cut, one-third cut, and one-fifth cut. File folders may be purchased with these cuts in various positions. For example, if you are buying folders with one-third cuts, you may want to have all the tabs in first position. Or you may want to have the tabs in first, second, and third positions. By choosing tabs in three positions, you are able to see the

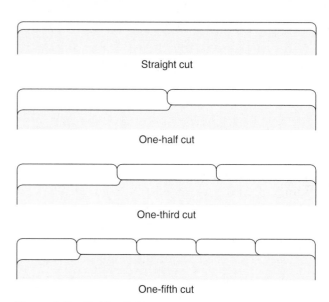

Straight cut

One-half cut

One-third cut

One-fifth cut

Figure 6-9   Folder Cuts

file captions on three folders at once. Figure 6-9 illustrates the cuts in various positions.

Suspension Folders. In addition to standard file folders, suspension folders are available. These folders are sometimes called hanging file folders because small metal rods attached to the folders allow them to hang on the sides of the file drawer. Plastic tabs and insertable labels are used with the folders. These tabs and labels may be placed in any position using the precut slots on the folder.

File Guides. A file guide is usually made of heavy pressboard and is used to separate the file drawer into various sections. Each guide has a tab on which is printed a name, a number, or a letter representing a section of the file drawer in accordance with the filing system. Guides with hollow tabs in which labels are inserted are also

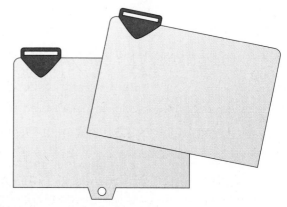

Figure 6-10   File Guide

available. The filing designation is keyed on the label and inserted in the table. Figure 6-10 illustrates one type of file guide. Guides are always placed in front of the file folders.

File Folder Labels. File folder labels may be purchased in various configurations, including continuous folder strips, separate strips, rolls in boxes, or pressure-sensitive adhesive labels. Different colored labels can speed up the process of filing and finding records and eliminate much misfiling. It is easy to spot a colored label that has been misfiled since that color stands out from the other colors that surround it.

Some of the ways in which colored labels may be used are to

- Designate a particular subject (e.g., green labels may designate budget items; blue labels, personnel items)
- Indicate geographic divisions of the country
- Designate particular sections of the file

When preparing labels for files, consistency should be observed in keying them. Suggestions for preparing labels are given here.

- Key label captions in all capital letters with no punctuation.
- Begin the caption two spaces from the left edge of the label; key any additional information five spaces to the right.
- Always key the name on the label in correct indexing order.
- Use the same style of labels on all folders. For example, if you decide to use labels with color strips, be consistent. If you decide to use colored labels, be consistent.
- Key wraparound side-tab labels for lateral file cabinets both above and below the color bar separator so the information is readable from both sides.

Manual Equipment

Vertical drawer cabinets are the traditional storage cabinet, with the most common vertical file having four drawers. Lateral files are similar to vertical files except the drawer rolls out sideways, exposing the entire contents of the file drawer at once. Less aisle space is needed for a lateral file than for a vertical file.

Photo courtesy of The Hon Company.

Lateral files use less space than vertical files.

Movable-aisle systems consist of modular units of open-shelf files mounted on tracks in the floor. Files are placed directly against each other. Wheels or rails permit the individual units to be moved apart for access. The movable racks are electrically powered. Because these movable systems take up less space than standard files, they are being used more and more today. Movable systems may be manual, mechanical, or electrical. Manual systems are small, with two to four carriages. They require no power; the user merely pushes the files apart. Mechanical systems operate by turning a crank. Electrical systems move carriages with motors. Features that provide safety both for

Communication Tip:

To keep your desk clean and improve your organization, keep a small file beside your desk. Place all ongoing projects and pending files in order of importance in this file. You can quickly retrieve the important work without having to rummage through numerous papers on your desk.

Movable-aisle systems consist of modular units of open-shelf files mounted on tracks in the floor.

the administrative professional using the system and for the file contents are a top priority of companies. Protection devices are available for all systems. The most basic device is a key-operated carriage lock that prevents the system from rolling on the rails. Another safety device is a strip that runs the length of the file cabinet at floor level. Pressure of more than a few ounces stops cabinet movement. Still another safety device is an infrared photoelectric beam. If a person or an object breaks the beam, the system stops moving. When the person or object is no longer breaking the beam, the system resets itself. To ensure safety of materials, users may have a badge that is swiped through a badge reader to allow entrance to the system or they may enter a password code. Also, some systems can be fitted with locking doors.

Electronic Equipment

The personal computer has become a major electronic filing equipment component. With database and document management software, which you learned about earlier, the personal computer that is networked with other PCs can

- Provide electronic document storage
- Serve as an access device for scanned and electronically generated documents
- Maintain records inventories
- Retrieve paper and electronic documents based on the same file code
- Store records retention and destruction data

Also, larger computers, such as supercomputers and mainframes, serve as electronic filing equipment.

Electronic Media

In addition to electronic records being stored on the hard drive of a computer, they may be stored on a variety of external storage media. (The major ones are listed here.) The storage capacities shown were correct at the time this book was published. However, storage capacities are constantly being increased with the introduction of new electronic media.

- Floppy disks—double-sided and high-density 3.5-inch disks store 1.44MB
- Zip disks—250MB
- Jaz disks—1GB
- A variety of **CD** (compact disk) technology, including **CD-R** (CD-recordable) and **CD-RW** (CD-rewritable). CD-R is **WORM** (write once, read many) technology. This technology has become popular in digital archiving since information stored in this manner cannot be modified or erased but can be read any number of times. If the information stored on the CD needs to be revised, then CD-RW technology is used. CDs provide 650MB of storage.
- A variety of **DVD** (digital versatile disk) technology is available, including **DVD-ROM** (read-only memory), **DVD-R** (write once), and **DVD-RAM** (random access memory-rewritable) and **DVD-RW** (rewritable). The storage capacity for DVDs is 17GB. DVDs are more expensive than CDs, but the cost is dropping rapidly. It is expected that DVD storage will replace CD storage.

Microform Storage

In addition to the storage of records in paper and electronic form, microforms have been used to store records. For example, personnel departments have stored personnel records of former employees on microforms and libraries have stored research information on microforms. There are two types of microforms—**microfilm** (a roll of film containing a series of frames or images) or **microfiche** (a sheet of film containing a series of images arranged in a grid pattern). Today many organizations are moving to **COLD** (computer output to laser disk) technology to organize information that was historically stored on microforms. A COLD system indexes data and places it on an optical disk, making the data much easier to find and display. The users define indexing fields, and searches may be done based on single or multiple indexes. The software allows for a fast search and retrieval of files.

COLD technology includes these advantages.

- A dramatic reduction in cost associated with the creation of microforms and printed reports
- Instant access to information and the elimination of the cumbersome and time-consuming tasks associated with microform retrieval
- Reduction of repetitive and time-consuming tasks of administrative personnel
- Reduction in space required to store microforms
- Instant access in branch offices or remote sites to COLD data through network storage
- Confidentiality of information controlled through information security systems

New versions of COLD technology are constantly being released. The latest version at the time this book was published was 4.20.

Retention Schedules

In both electronic and manual systems, it is important to know how long records should be retained by the organization. The cost of maintaining documents that are no longer of any use can be significant, particularly in manual systems, due to the floor space necessary for the files. Additionally, even though electronic storage is not nearly so space-intensive, there is some cost to maintaining unneeded documents.

The retention schedule should identify

- The period of time a record should be retained

- How long records are needed in the active area of the organization
- The length of time records should be retained in inactive storage

As an administrative professional, you generally will not make retention schedule decisions. The general approach is to consult with the legal counsel of the organization (or if it is a small organization, use an outside legal firm), then develop appropriate retention schedules. A sample retention schedule is shown in Figure 6-11. If the company does not have a records retention schedule, the administrative professional should check with the supervisor before making any decisions about how documents should be transferred or destroyed.

The United States government provides initiatives and publications concerning records management; some of these initiatives are listed here.

Major Initiatives

- Records Management Guidance for Agencies Implementing Electronic Signature Technologies
- Electronic Records Archives (ERA) Program

Publications

- *Disposition of Federal Records: A Records Management Handbook*
- *NARA Basic Laws and Authorities*[2]

RETENTION SCHEDULE			
Record Category	Retention Period	Retained in Active File	Retained in Inactive File
Personnel files (terminated)	6 Years	2 Years	4 Years
Payroll records	8 Years	3 Years	5 Years
Patents	Indefinitely	Indefinitely	--

Figure 6-11 Retention Schedule

To understand more about retention control, consider the following categories into which records can be classified:

---

[2]"Records Management" accessed April 11, 2001; available from www.nara.gov/records.

Vital Records

Records that cannot be replaced and should never be destroyed are called **vital records.** These records are essential to the effective continued operation of the organization. Some examples of vital records are corporate charters, deeds, tax returns, constitutions and bylaws, insurance policies, procedures manuals, audited financial statements, patents, and copyrights.

Important Records

Records that are necessary to an orderly continuation of the business and are replaceable only with considerable expenditure of time and money are known as **important records.** Such records may be transferred to inactive storage but are not destroyed. Examples of important records are financial statements, operating and statistical records, physical inventories, bank statements, and board minutes.

Useful Records

Useful records are those that are useful for the smooth, effective operation of the organization. Such records are replaceable, but their loss involves delay or inconvenience to the organization. These records may be transferred to inactive files or destroyed after a certain period of time. Examples include letters, memorandums, reports, and bank records.

Nonessential Records

Records that have no future value to the organization are considered **nonessential.** Once the purpose for which they were created has been fulfilled, they may be destroyed. For example, a memorandum that is written to arrange a meeting generally has no value once the meeting has occurred.

Active to Inactive File Procedures

At some point in the life of a record, based on records retention information, you either decide to destroy it, retain it permanently, or transfer it to inactive storage. Two common methods of transfer are perpetual and periodic.

Perpetual Transfer

With the **perpetual transfer,** records are continuously transferred from the active to the inactive files. The advantage of this method is that all files are kept current, since any inactive material is immediately transferred to storage. The perpetual transfer method works well in offices where jobs are completed by units. For example, when a lawyer finishes a case, the file is complete and probably will not need to be referred to at all or certainly not frequently. Therefore, it can be transferred to the inactive files.

When distinguishing between active and inactive records, the following categories should be used:

- Active records—Used three or more times a month; should be kept in an accessible area.
- Inactive records—Used less than 15 times a year; may be stored in less accessible areas than active records.
- Archive records—Have historical value to the organization; are preserved permanently.

Periodic Transfer

With **periodic transfer,** active records are transferred to inactive status at the end of a stated period of time. For example, you may transfer records that are over six months old to the inactive file and maintain records that are less than six months old in the active file. Every six months you follow this procedure.

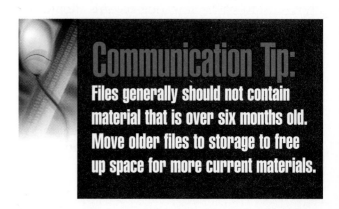

Communication Tip:
Files generally should not contain material that is over six months old. Move older files to storage to free up space for more current materials.

Maintaining and Updating the File Management System

The records management needs of an organization change over time. Additionally, new manual and electronic systems, equipment, and storage possibilities become available. Organizations must keep current on what is available and change systems as appropriate. Although changing systems can be expensive in the short term, new systems often save money in the long term by offering improved speed and accuracy and requiring less staff time to operate. For example, with electronic filing of records, new software is available that offers more features for improving a records management system. New features can save the organization considerable dollars and provide for more efficient management of records. If the organization is a large one, generally at least one person in a management position is responsible for the ongoing maintenance and updating of the system.

Ongoing Training of Personnel

With changes in records management systems and new equipment, ongoing training should be provided to those personnel involved in records management. The organizational person in charge of records management generally provides this training.

INDEXING RULES

In order to store and retrieve records effectively, a set of rules must be followed. ARMA has published a standard set of rules for filing documents. These rules include alphabetic indexing and cross-referencing. These same rules are used whether you are working with an electronic or manual system.

If you are presently working in an organization or when you begin your career, you may find that the indexing rules used are slightly different from the ones presented in this text. At times, organizations deviate from these rules for reasons that support their own internal needs. At other times, deviation from the rules may merely mean the individuals setting up the filing system were not aware of the most recent indexing rules. You might want to call attention to the differences if they are significant. However, wait until your supervisor has come to respect your competence.

Alphabetic Indexing

The rules in this chapter are compatible with ARMA's *Alphabetic Filing Rules.*

Rule 1: Indexing Order of Units

A. *Personal Names.* A personal name is indexed in this manner.

- The surname (last name) is the key unit.
- The given name (first name) or initial is the second unit.
- The middle name or initial is the third unit.

If determining the surname is difficult, consider the last name as the surname. A unit consisting of just an initial precedes a unit that consists of a complete name beginning with the same letter—*nothing comes before something.* Punctuation is omitted. See Table 6-1 (Rule 1A) for examples of indexing personal names.

B. *Business Names.* Business names are indexed as written, using letterheads or trademarks as guides. Each word in a business name is a separate unit. Business names containing personal names are indexed as written. See Table 6-1 (Rule 1-B) for examples of indexing business names.

Rule 2: Minor Words and Symbols in Business Names

Articles, prepositions, conjunctions, and symbols are considered separate indexing units. Symbols are considered as spelled in full. When the word *the* appears as the first word of a business name, it is considered the last indexing unit.

Examples of articles, prepositions, conjunctions, and symbols that are commonly found in business names are given here. See Table 6-1

Index Order of Units in Personal Names

Name	Key Unit	Unit 2	Unit 3
Walter Kingscott	KINGSCOTT	WALTER	
Walter A. Kingscott	KINGSCOTT	WALTER	A
Walter Andrew Kingscott	KINGSCOTT	WALTER	ANDREW

Index Order of Units in Business Names

Name	Key Unit	Unit 2	Unit 3	Unit 4
Beaumont Health Center	BEAUMONT	HEALTH	CENTER	
Beaver Creek Golf Club	BEAVER	CREEK	GOLF	CLUB
Chuck Beaver Pharmacy	CHUCK	BEAVER	PHARMACY	

Index Order of Units in Minor Words and Symbols in Business Names

Name	Key Unit	Unit 2	Unit 3	Unit 4	Unit 5
A Bit of Honey	A	BIT	OF	HONEY	
At Home Laundry	AT	HOME	LAUNDRY		
The $ and ¢ Shop	DOLLARS	AND	CENTS	SHOP	THE

Index Order of Units with Punctuation and Possessives in Personal and Business Names

Name	Key Unit	Unit 2	Unit 3	Unit 4
Abbey's Grooming	ABBEYS	GROOMING		
A-Z Video Company	AZ	VIDEO	COMPANY	
North/South Printing	NORTHSOUTH	PRINTING		

Index Order of Units for Single Letters and Abbreviations in Business and Personal Names

Name	Key Unit	Unit 2	Unit 3	Unit 4
J. V. Hildebrand	HILDEBRAND	J	V	
Jas. W. Hildebrand	HILDEBRAND	JAS	W	
Wm. R. Hildebrand	HILDEBRAND	WM	R	
J K of Texas	J	K	OF	TEXAS
KRLD Television	KRLD	TELEVISION		
U.S.A. MOTORS	USA	MOTORS		

Table 6-1 Examples of indexing rules 1–7.

Examples of Rule 5A

Index Order of Units for Titles and Suffixes in Personal Names

Name	Key Unit	Unit 2	Unit 3	Unit 4
Father James	FATHER	JAMES		
S. R. Harrold II	HARROLD	S	R	II
S. R. Harrold III	HARROLD	S	R	III
S. R. Harrold, Jr.	HARROLD	S	R	JR
S. R. Harrold, Sr.	HARROLD	S	R	SR
Frederick Johns, MD	JOHNS	FREDERICK	MD	
Ms. Helen Johns	JOHNS	HELEN	MS	

Examples of Rule 5B

Index Order of Units for Titles and Suffixes in Business Names

Name	Key Unit	Unit 2	Unit 3
Doctors' Hospital	DOCTORS	HOSPITAL	
Dr. Pepper Bottling	DR	PEPPER	BOTTLING

Examples of Rule 6

Index Order of Units for Prefixes in Personal and Business Names

Name	Key Unit	Unit 2	Unit 3	Unit 4
Paul Alan LaFaver	LAFAVER	PAUL	ALAN	
MacDugal's Meat Market	MACDUGALS	MEAT	MARKET	
McDouglas & Edwards	MCDOUGLAS	AND	EDWARDS	
Mary Lou St. Marie	STMARIE	MARY	LOU	

Examples of Rule 7

Index Order of Units for Numbers in Business Names

Name	Key Unit	Unit 2	Unit 3	Unit 4
4-Cent Copy Center	4	CENT	COPY	CENTER
4th Street Garage	4	STREET	GARAGE	
400-410 Daniels Court	400	DANIELS	COURT	
Four Seasons Health Spa	Four	SEASONS	HEALTH	SPA
Highway 30 Café	HIGHWAY	30	CAFÉ	
Highway Service Station	HIGHWAY	SERVICE	STATION	

Table 6-1 *(continued)*

(Rule 2) for examples of indexing minor words and symbols in business names.

Articles:	a, an, the
Prepositions:	at, by, for, in, of, off, on, out, over, to, with
Conjunctions:	and, but, or, nor
Symbols:	&, #, $, %

Rule 3: Punctuation and Possessives

All punctuation is disregarded when indexing personal and business names. Commas, periods, hyphens, apostrophes, dashes, exclamation points, question marks, quotation marks, and slash marks (/) are disregarded, and names are indexed as written. See Table 6-1 (Rule 3) for examples of punctuation and possessives in indexing.

Rule 4: Single Letters and Abbreviations

A. *Personal Names.* Initials in personal names are considered separate indexing units. Abbreviations of personal names (*Wm., Jos., Thos.*) and nicknames (*Liz, Bill*) are indexed as they are written.

B. *Business Names.* Single letters in business and organization names are indexed as written. If there is a space between single letters, index each letter as a separate unit. An acronym (a word formed from the first or first few letters of several words) is indexed as one unit regardless of punctuation or spelling. Abbreviated words (*Mfg., Corp., Inc.*) and abbreviated names (*IBM, GM*) are indexed as one unit regardless of punctuation or spacing. Radio and television station call letters are indexed as one unit. See Table 6-1 (Rule 4) for examples of single letters and abbreviations in indexing.

Rule 5: Titles and Suffixes

A. *Personal Names.* A title before a name (*Dr., Miss, Mr., Mrs., Ms., Professor*), a seniority suffix (*II, III, Jr., Sr.*), or a professional suffix (*D.D.S., M.D., Ph.D.*) after a name is the last indexing unit. Numeric suffixes (*II, III*) are filed before alphabetic suffixes (*Jr, Sr.*).

If a name contains both a title and a suffix, the title is the last unit. Royal and religious titles followed by either a given name or a surname only (*Father John*) are indexed and filed as written. See Table 6-1 (Rule 5A) for examples of titles and suffixes for personal names.

B. *Business Names.* Titles in business names are filed as written. See Table 6-1 (Rule 5B) for examples of titles and suffixes in business names.

Self-Check A

Complete Self-Check A to determine if you understand the first five indexing rules. Determine the following: key unit, second unit, third unit, and fourth unit. Check your answers with those at the end of the chapter.

		UNIT		
	Key	2	3	4
Henry Hubert Bowers, Jr.	____	____	____	____
Roger Alan Le Feve	____	____	____	____
500 Cafeteria	____	____	____	____
The 500, Inc.	____	____	____	____
Z. T. Glasier, III	____	____	____	____
U-R Rental Company	____	____	____	____
NBC Television	____	____	____	____
Sister Mary Vanetta	____	____	____	____
Physicians' Hospital	____	____	____	____

Rule 6: Prefixes—Articles and Particles

A foreign article or particle in a personal or business name is combined with the part of the name following it to form a single indexing unit. The indexing order is not affected by a space between a prefix and the rest of the name, and the space is disregarded when indexing.

Examples of articles and particles are *a la, D', Da, De, Del, De la, Des, El, Fitz, L', La, Las, Le, Lo, Los, Mac, Mc, Saint, San, Santa, St., Ste., Ten, Van, Van der, Von,* and *Von der*. See Table 6-1 (Rule 6) for examples of prefixes.

Rule 7: Numbers in Business Names

Numbers spelled out in business names (for example, *Seven Seas Restaurant*) are filed alphabetically. Numbers written in digit form are filed before alphabetic letters or words (*B4 Photographers* comes before *Beleau Building Co.*). Names with numbers written in digits in the first units are filed in ascending order (lowest to highest) before alphabetic names (*229 Club, 534 Shop, Bank of Chicago*). Arabic numerals are filed before Roman numerals (2, 3, II, III).

Names with inclusive numbers (33–37) are arranged by the first digit(s) only (33). Names with numbers appearing in other than the first position (*Pier 36 Café*) are filed alphabetically and immediately before a similar name without a number (*Pier and Port Café*).

When indexing numbers written in digit form that contain *st, d,* and *th* (lst, 2d, 3d, 4th), ignore the letter endings and consider only the digits (1, 2, 3, 4). See Table 6-1 (Rule 7) for examples of numbers in business names.

Rule 8: Organizations and Institutions

Banks and other financial institutions, clubs, colleges, hospitals, hotels, lodges, magazines, motels, museums, newspapers, religious institutions, schools, unions, universities, and other organizations and institutions are indexed and filed according to the names written on their letterheads. See Table 6-2 (Rule 8) for examples of organizations and institutions as indexing units.

Rule 9: Identical Names

When personal names and names of businesses, institutions, and organizations are identical (including titles as explained in Rule 5), filing order is determined by the addresses. Compare addresses in the following order:

- City names
- State or province names (if city names are identical)
- Street names, including *Avenue, Boulevard, Drive, Street* (if city and state names are identical)
  a. When the first units of street names are written in digits (*18th Street*), the names are filed in ascending numeric order and placed together before alphabetic street names.
  b. Street names with compass directions are considered as written (*South Park Avenue*). Numbers after compass directions are considered before alphabetic names (*East 8th, East Main, Sandusky, SE Eighth, Southeast Eighth*).
- House and building numbers (if city, state, and street names are identical)
  a. House and building numbers written as figures (*912 Riverside Terrace*) are considered in ascending numeric order and placed together before alphabetic building names (*The Riverside Terrace*).
  b. If a street address and a building name are included in an address, disregard the building name.
  c. ZIP Codes are not considered in determining filing order. See Table 6-2 (Rule 9) for examples of identical names.

Rule 10: Government Names

Government names are indexed first by the name of the governmental unit—country, state, county, or city. Next, index the distinctive name of the department, bureau, office, or board. The words *Office of, Bureau of,* and so on, are separate indexing units if they are part of the official name. Note: If *of* is not part of the office name as written, it is not added.

A. *Federal.* The first three indexing units of a United States (federal) government agency name are *United States Government.* See Table 6-2 (Rule 10A) for examples of federal government names as indexing units.

B. *State and Local.* The first indexing units are the names of the state, province, county, parish, city, town, township, or village. Next, index the most distinctive name of the department, board, bureau, office, or government/political division. The words *State of, County of, Department of, Board of,* and so on, are added only if needed for clarity and only if they are in the official name. They are considered separate indexing units. See Table 6-2 (Rule 10B) for examples of state and local government names.

Examples of Rule 8

Index Order of Units for Organizations and Institutions

Name	Key Unit	Unit 2	Unit 3	Unit 4
Bank of DeSoto	BANK	OF	DESOTO	
First United Christian Church	FIRST	UNITED	CHRISTIAN	CHURCH
Horace Mann Elementary School	HORACE	MANN	ELEMENTARY	SCHOOL

Examples of Rule 9

Index Order of Units for Identical Names

Name	Key Unit	Unit 2	Unit 3	Unit 4	Unit 5	Unit 6	Unit 7
Liz Bowman 212 Luther Dallas, Texas	BOWMAN	LIZ	DALLAS	TEXAS			
Liz Bowman 818 Oak San Diego, CA	BOWMAN	LIZ	SAN DIEGO	CALIFORNIA			
Brother's Pizza 1120 14 Street Detroit, Michigan	BROTHERS	PIZZA	DETROIT	MICHIGAN	14		
Brother's Pizza 8010 Apple Street Detroit, Michigan	BROTHERS	PIZZA	DETROIT	MICHIGAN	APPLE		
Brown Computers 500 Forrest Building Detroit, Michigan	BROWN	COMPUTERS	DETROIT	MICHIGAN	500	FORREST	
Brown Computers Five Hundred Building Detroit, Michigan	BROWN	COMPUTERS	DETROIT	MICHIGAN	FIVE	HUNDRED	
Elder Market 213 Arch Street Troy, Michigan	ELDER	MARKET	TROY	MICHIGAN	213	ARCH	STREET
Elder Market 944 Arch Street Troy, Michigan	ELDER	MARKET	TROY	MICHIGAN	944	ARCH	STREET

Table 6-2   Examples of indexing rules 8–10.

Examples of Rule 10A

Index Order of Units for Federal Government Names
(Units 1, 2, and 3 are UNITED STATES GOVERNMENT for each example)

Name	Unit 4	Unit 5	Unit 6	Unit 7	Unit 8	Unit 9	Unit 10	Unit 11
General Services Administration	GENERAL	SERVICES	ADMINISTRATION					
Federal Protection and Safety	FEDERAL	PROTECTION	AND	SAFETY				
Health and Human Services Department	HEALTH	AND	HUMAN	SERVICES	DEPARTMENT			
Social Security Administration	SOCIAL	SECURITY	ADMINISTRATION					
Internal Revenue Service	INTERNAL	REVENUE	SERVICE					
Department of the Treasury	TREASURY	DEPARTMENT	OF	THE				

Examples of Rule 10B

Index Order of Units for Local Government Names

Name	Key Unit	Unit 2	Unit 3	Unit 4	Unit 5	Unit 6
Department of Commerce State of Alabama	ALABAMA	STATE	OF	COMMERCE	DEPARTMENT	OF
Montgomery, Alabama	MONTGOMERY					
Leon County	LEON	COUNTY				
Department of Public Welfare Tallahassee, Florida	TALLAHASSEE	PUBLIC	WELFARE	DEPARTMENT	OF	

Examples of Rule 10C

Index Order of Units for Foreign Government Names

Name	Key Unit	Unit 2	Unit 3
Canada	CANADA	DOMINION	OF
Polska Rzecapospolita Ludowa	POLISH	PEOPLES	REPUBLIC
Estados Unidos Mexicanos	UNITED	MEXICAN	STATES

Table 6-2 *(continued)*

C. *Foreign.* The distinctive English name is the first indexing unit for foreign government names. This is followed by the remainder of the formal name of the government, if necessary. Branches, departments, and divisions follow in order by their distinctive names. States, colonies, provinces, cities, and other divisions of foreign governments are followed by their distinctive or official names as spelled in English. See Table 6-2 (Rule 10C) for examples of foreign government names.

Self-Check B

Check your knowledge of rules 6–10 by completing Self-Check B. Determine the key unit, second, third, and fourth units. Check your answers with the correct ones given at the end of the chapter.

		UNIT		
	Key	2	3	4
Los Angeles Cleaners	___	___	___	___
3rd Street Movie	___	___	___	___
43-47 Rogers Road Materials	___	___	___	___
7 Seas Restaurant	___	___	___	___
Joe Dee, 712 Elm, San Diego, CA	___	___	___	___
U.S. Labor Department	___	___	___	___
Department of Commerce, State of Texas	___	___	___	___

Cross-Referencing

Cross-referencing should be done when a record may be filed under more than one name. Here are some rules for cross-referencing personal and business names.

Cross-Referencing Personal Names

Cross-references should be prepared for the following types of personal names:

1. *Unusual Names.* When it is difficult to determine the last name, index the last name first on the original record. Prepare a cross-reference with the first name indexed first.

Original	*Cross-Reference*
Andrew Scott	Scott Andrew
	See Andrew Scott

2. *Hyphenated Surnames.*

Original	*Cross-Reference*
Sue Loaring-Clark	Clark Sue Loaring
	See Loaringclark Sue

3. *Similar Names.* SEE ALSO cross-references are prepared for all possible spellings.

Baier	Bauer	Bayer
See also	See also	See also
Bauer, Bayer	Bayer, Baier	Baier, Bauer

Cross-Referencing Business Names

Cross-references should be prepared for the following types of business names:

1. *Compound Names.* When a business name includes two or more individual surnames, prepare a cross-reference for each surname other than the first.

Original	*Cross-Reference*
Peat Marwick and Main	Marwick Main and Peat
	See Peat Marwick and Main
	Main Peat and Marwick
	See Peat Marwick and Main

2. *Abbreviations and Acronyms.* When a business is commonly known by an abbreviation or an acronym, a cross-reference is prepared for the full name.

Original	*Cross-Reference*
YMCA	Young Men's Christian Association

3. *Changed Names.* When a business changes its name, a cross-reference is prepared for the former name and all records are filed under the new name.

Original	*Cross-Reference*
DaimlerChrysler	Chrysler
	See DaimlerChrysler

4. *Foreign Business Names.* The name of a foreign business is often spelled in the foreign

language. The English translation should be written on the document and the document stored under the English spelling. A cross-reference should be placed under the foreign spelling.

Original   *Cross-Reference*
French Republic   Republique Francaise

EFFECTIVE DECISION MAKING

Effective decision making is clearly important in all areas of your work as an administrative professional. To help you improve your decision-making skills in records management, read the following section carefully.

A **decision** is the outcome or product of a problem, a concern, or an issue that must be addressed and solved. The process by which a decision is reached includes five steps, which are shown in Figure 6-12. You should systematically follow these steps in making a decision.

Define the Problem or the Purpose

This step may sound simple, but it is usually the most difficult of the steps. When attempting to define the purpose or problem, ask yourself a series of questions.

- What problem am I trying to solve?
- Why is this decision necessary?
- What will be the outcome of this decision?

Establish the Criteria

The next step in the decision-making process is to determine the criteria you need to make a sound decision. When setting your criteria, ask yourself the following three questions:

- What do I want to achieve?
- What do I want to preserve?
- What do I want to avoid?

Generate Alternatives or Possible Solutions

The next step in the decision-making process is to begin generating alternatives or possible solutions. What do you think you can do to solve the problem or make the decision? What alternatives are available to you?

Test the Alternatives and Make the Decision

The effective decision maker tests each alternative using this system.

- Eliminate alternatives that are unrealistic or incompatible with the needs of the organization.
- Select the alternative that appears to be the most realistic.

Evaluate the Decision

The last step in the decision-making process is evaluating the decision. In evaluating the decision, here are some questions to ask.

- What was right about the decision?
- What was wrong about the decision?
- How did the decision-making process work? What improvements are necessary? What changes need to be made for the future?

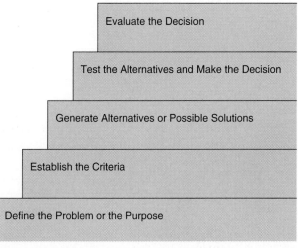

Figure 6-12 Effective Decision-Making Steps

Now using a records management situation, apply the steps. Assume you are the records management professional. You recently have been hired by a small company to assist in setting up a coordinated records management program. The company has been in existence only two years, but it is growing rapidly. A manual file system has been used in the past, with a few individuals filing information on their computers in certain situations. Each individual has decided how he or she would file the documents electronically. There is no overall records management strategy. In using the decision-making model, you make these decisions.

- The problem is to establish an *effective*, *coordinated* records management program.
- In establishing the criteria, you determine that you want to establish both a manual and electronic filing system that can be used by all employees in storing and finding materials quickly and easily. You want to avoid a high-cost system, but you also need to provide a system that can grow as the company grows.
- The alternatives you generate are as follows:
  (a) Establish a manual system with the assistance of internal staff.
  (b) Establish an electronic system with the assistance of internal staff.
  (c) Employ a firm to assist with both the manual and the electronic system.
  (d) Determine the type of database and document management software available and implement the system with limited internal support.

- After reviewing the alternatives, you decide to use database and document management software to implement the electronic system and provide detailed standards for manual filing. You have extensive experience in database and document management software; you have also identified two experienced individuals within the company who can assist you. Additionally, you have identified one individual who can assist with setting up the manual filing system.
- Once the records management system is designed, implemented, and used for six months, you evaluate its effectiveness. The system is working well, so you feel the correct decision was made. However, you discover that you did not provide enough training on the electronic system for some individuals within the organization. You immediately implement an ongoing training program, and you begin writing a comprehensive document management manual.

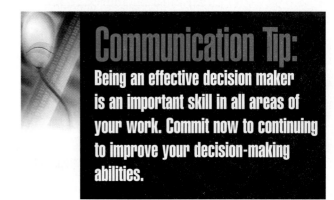

Communication Tip:
Being an effective decision maker is an important skill in all areas of your work. Commit now to continuing to improve your decision-making abilities.

CHAPTER SUMMARY

The summary will help you remember the important points covered in the chapter.

- A record is any type of recorded information, whether that information is an email, a letter, a report, a spreadsheet, a contract, a personnel record, or any other type of organizational record.
- Records management is the systematic control of records from the creation of the record to its final disposition.
- An effective records management system has these components:
  (a) An organizationwide records structure
  (b) A records storage system
  (c) Alphabetic and numeric indexing rules
  (d) Appropriate filing supplies
  (e) Necessary equipment and media (electronic and manual)
  (f) Retention schedules
  (g) Active to inactive file procedures
  (h) Procedures for updating the management system
  (i) Records management manuals and ongoing training for personnel
- Document management systems may be manual, electronic, or a combination of the two.
- There are two basic records storage systems—alphabetic and numeric.
- The alphabetic storage method uses letters of the alphabet to determine the order in which the record is filed. Variations of the alphabetic storage method include subject filing (arranging records by their subject) and geographic filing (arranging records by geographic location).
- Numeric records are given numbers that are arranged in a numeric sequence when stored. Variations of a numeric file include chronological filing, terminal-digit filing, and alphanumeric filing.
- In the filing of manual records, the procedures to be followed include inspecting, indexing, and coding.
- In the filing of documents electronically, database and data management software are available to assist you.
- Consistent filing rules should be used. ARMA has developed indexing rules that are widely used.

- Basic manual filing supplies include file folders, suspension folders, file guides, and file folder labels.
- Manual equipment includes vertical drawer cabinets, lateral files, and movable-aisle systems.
- Electronic filing equipment includes PCs and larger computers such as supercomputers and mainframes.
- Electronic filing media include floppy disks, Zip and Jaz disks, CDs, and DVDs.
- Microform filing media includes microfilm and microfiche.
- COLD technology allows the organization of information that was historically stored on microforms. A COLD system indexes data and places it on an optical disk, making the data much easier to find and display.
- Retention schedules (providing the length of time a record should be maintained) are essential to effective records management systems.
- Vital records are those records that cannot be replaced and should never be destroyed.
- Important records are those records necessary to an orderly continuation of the business.
- Useful records are those that are useful for the smooth, effective operation of the organization.
- Nonessential records have no future value to the organization once the purpose for which they were created has been fulfilled.
- Records may be transferred to inactive files through perpetual or periodic transfer.
- Cross-referencing is necessary when a record may be filed under more than one name.
- The steps in effective decision-making are
  (a) Define the problem or the purpose
  (b) Establish the criteria
  (c) Generate alternatives or possible solutions
  (d) Test the alternatives and make the decision
  (e) Evaluate the decision

CHAPTER GLOSSARY

The following terms were used in this chapter. Definitions are provided to help you review the terms.

- **Record** (p. 135)—any type of recorded information.
- **Records management** (p. 135)—the systematic control of records from the creation of the record to its final disposition.
- **Records storage systems** (p. 136)—a method of filing records that includes alphabetic, numeric, and alphanumeric systems.
- **Alphabetic storage** (p. 136)—uses letters of the alphabet to determine the order in which a record is filed.
- **Direct access** (p. 137)—a system that does not require referring to anything but the file to find the name.
- **Subject filing** (p. 137)—arranging records by their subject.
- **Geographic filing** (p. 137)—arranging records by geographic location.
- **Keywords** (p. 138)—unique identifiers.
- **Numeric method** (p. 139)—records are given numbers that are arranged in numeric sequence.
- **Chronological filing** (p. 140)—the arrangement of records by date, usually by year, month, or day.
- **Tickler files** (p. 140)—files used to tickle your memory and remind you to take certain actions.
- **Terminal-digit filing** (p. 140)—a numeric filing order in which the final digits of a number are used as the first filing unit.
- **Alphanumeric filing** (p. 140)—using a combination of alphabetic and numeric characters in filing.
- **Inspecting** (p. 140)—checking to see that the correspondence is ready to be filed.
- **Indexing** (p. 140)—determining the way the record is to be filed—the name, the subject, the number, or the geographic location.
- **Coding** (p. 140)—marking the record by the name, subject, location, or number that was determined in the indexing process.
- **Database software** (p. 140)—allows the user to organize, enter, process, index, sort, select, link to related files, store, and retrieve information.
- **Electronic indexing** (p. 140)—sorts the records and stores the information based on one or more key fields.
- **Query** (p. 140)—to ask the electronic system to display information in a certain way.

- **Integrated packages** (p. 140)—combine database software with spreadsheet and word-processing software so users can easily move stored information from one application to another.
- **Document management software** (p. 140)—assists in managing electronic, microimage, and paper filing records.
- **Cuts** (p. 142)—tabs on folders made in various widths.
- **CD** (p. 144)—compact disk.
- **CD-R** (p. 144)—CD-recordable.
- **CD-RW** (p. 144)—CD-rewritable.
- **WORM** (p. 144)—write once, read many.
- **DVD** (p. 144)—digital versatile disk.
- **DVD-ROM** (p. 144)—read-only memory.
- **DVD-R** (p. 144)—write once.
- **DVD-RAM** (p. 144)—random access memory—rewritable.
- **DVD-RW** (p. 144)—rewritable.
- **Microfilm** (p. 144)—a roll of film containing a series of frames or images.
- **Microfiche** (p. 145)—a sheet of film containing a series of images arranged in grid patterns.
- **COLD** (p. 145)—computer output to laser disk.
- **Vital records** (p. 146)—records that cannot be replaced and should never be destroyed.
- **Important records** (p. 146)—records that are necessary to an orderly continuation of a business and are replaceable only with considerable expenditure of time and money.
- **Useful records** (p. 146)—records that are useful for the smooth, effective operation of an organization.
- **Nonessential records** (p. 146)—records that have no future value to an organization.
- **Perpetual transfer** (p. 146)—records are continuously transferred from the active to the inactive files.
- **Periodic transfer** (p. 146)—active records are transferred to inactive status at the end of a stated period of time.
- **Decision** (p. 155)—the outcome or product of a problem, a concern, or an issue that must be addressed and solved.

DISCUSSION ITEMS

These discussion items provide an opportunity to test your understanding of the chapter through written responses and/or discussion with your classmates and your instructor.

1. List the essential components of a records management system.
2. Identify and explain records storage methods.
3. Explain the features of database software and document management software.
4. What is COLD technology and how is it used?
5. List and explain the decision-making steps.

CRITICAL-THINKING ACTIVITY

AmeriAsian has a relatively good companywide records management program. Both manual and electronic management systems are maintained, with individual offices filing their records manually as long as they are active and moving to electronic storage after the active period has passed. No companywide records management manual has been produced. The records manager has encouraged individual offices to move to electronic filing for most active records; however, most offices have not followed the recommendation. You have moved to electronic filing for almost all records. A number of the administrative professionals have seen your system and have asked for help in transferring their files to an electronic system. Mr. Albertson gave his permission for you to work with them. Using the decision-making model presented in this chapter, describe the problem and the steps you would take to assist them in filing and managing their records. What suggestions, if any, would you make to the records manager?

RESPONSES TO SELF-CHECK A

Name	Key Unit	Second Unit	Third Unit	Fourth Unit
Henry Hubert Bowers, Jr.	Bowers	Henry	Hubert	Jr
Roger Alan Le Feve	LeFeve	Roger	Alan	
500 Cafeteria	500	Cafeteria		
The 500, Inc.	500	Inc	The	
Z. T. Glasier, III	Glasier	Z	T	III
U-R Rental Company	UR	Rental	Company	
NBC Television	NBC	Television		
Sister Mary Vanetta	Sister	Mary	Vanetta	
Physicians' Hospital	Physicians	Hospital		

RESPONSES TO SELF-CHECK B

Name	Key Unit	Second Unit	Third Unit	Fourth Unit
Los Angeles Cleaners	LosAngeles	Cleaners		
3rd Street Movie	3rd	Street	Movie	
43-47 Rogers Road Materials	43	Rogers	Road	Materials
7 Seas Restaurant	7	Seas	Restaurant	
Joe Dee, 712 Elm, San Diego, CA	Dee	Joe	SanDiego	California
U.S. Labor Department	United	States	Government	Department
Department of Commerce, State of Texas	Texas	State	of	Commerce

PROJECTS

Project 6-1 (Objective 1)
Collaborative Project

Team with three of your classmates on this task. Interview one administrative professional concerning records management; your interview may be done by email. Ask the questions listed below. Report your findings orally to the class.

1. What records management system(s) do you use (manual, electronic, or a combination of these systems)?
2. What storage methods do you use (alphabetic, numeric, or alphanumeric)?
3. If you use alphabetic, do you use subject and/or geographic?
4. What is your role in document management?
5. Do you use document management software? If so, what packages?
6. Does your company have a records retention schedule? If so, may I have a copy?
7. What aspect of records management is the most difficult for you?
8. What suggestions do you have for the beginning administrative professional as to how to handle records management?

Project 6-2 (Objectives 2 and 3)

Load Student CD, file SCDP6-2. For each group of names, indicate the indexing units and place the names in correct alphabetical order. The correct response is given for the first group as an example. Using the form on the disk, key your responses, and submit your work to your instructor.

Project 6-3 (Objectives 2 and 3)

Load Student CD, file SCDP6-3. Print the list of names as a working copy. Then key the list in proper alphabetic sequence. Print out and hand in a copy of your work to your instructor.

Project 6-4 (Objectives 2 and 3)

Load Student CD, file SCDP6-4. Print the list of customers as a working copy. Then key the list in proper alphabetic sequence. Print out a copy of your work.

Next, key the list in proper geographic sequence. Print out a copy of your work. Hand in both printouts to your instructor.

Project 6-5 (Objectives 2 and 3)

Load Student CD, file SCDP6-5. Indicate the subject you would use in storing the correspondence listed. Place your answer to the right of each item. Print out and hand in your answers to your instructor.

Project 6-6 (Objectives 2 and 3)

Load Student CD, file SCDP6-4 from Project 6-4. Print the list of names as a working copy. Create a database and enter the customer names. Add a field for the ZIP Code. Also add a field for the customer number. (The number is listed in parentheses to the left of the name.) Retrieve the list by ZIP Code; print out a copy of the list. Next, retrieve the list by customer number; then print out a copy of the list. Turn in both printouts to your instructor.

Project 6-7 (Objective 4)
Online Project

Using the Web, find the latest database and document management software available. Determine which packages you would recommend if you were setting up an electronic storage system. Write a memorandum to your instructor using the form on the Student CD, file SCDP6-7. Explain what packages you would use and why. Identify the Web sources you used.

Project 6-8 (Objective 4)

Add to your Professional Growth Plan by determining how you will continue to increase your decision-making skills. File your plan on your Professional Growth Plan disk as "Progro6-8."

ENGLISH USAGE CHALLENGE DRILL

Correct the following sentences. Cite the grammar rule that is applicable to each sentence. Before you begin, refresh your memory of grammar rules by reviewing the rules on subject and verb agreement in the Reference Guide of this text.

1. The number of senior citizens in the area have increased in the last ten years.
2. A number of employees has called in ill with flu symptoms.
3. One of the guests was the one hundredth visitor to the new theme park.
4. The Canary Islands have been their favorite vacation site for several years.
5. The Hawaiian Islands has something unique on each island.

ASSESSMENT OF CHAPTER OBJECTIVES

Now that you have completed the chapter and the projects, take a few minutes to review the chapter learning objectives. For your convenience, the objectives are repeated here. Did you accomplish these objectives? If you were unable to accomplish the objectives, give your reasons for not doing so.

1. Define records management and explain how it is used within an organization.   Yes _____   No _____

_____

_____

_____

ASSESSMENT OF CHAPTER OBJECTIVES

(continued)

2. Identify and use records storage systems.   Yes _____   No _____

_____

_____

_____

3. Use the basic indexing rules.   Yes _____   No _____

_____

_____

_____

_____

4. Increase decision-making skills.   Yes _____   No _____

_____

_____

_____

You may submit your answers in writing to your instructor, using the memorandum form on the Student CD, SCDAP6-1.

NARRESSA ROSS LEE'S
CASE SOLUTIONS

Situation 1

Some administrative professionals key so rapidly that they move their fingers faster than the keyboard permits. When upgrading your computer, ask about the number of strokes per minute that apply to your keyboard. If necessary, change the keyboard.

Situation 2

Since I needed the information from the disk immediately, I went to another computer to complete the task. Then I called a computer technician for help. The drive was not permitting my disk to lock in place, so I could not read it. The computer technician had to check my A: drive to determine if it needed to be replaced or rebuilt.

A
Success
Profile

Debra L. Trahair
Executive Assistant
Traverse City Area Public Schools
Traverse City, Michigan

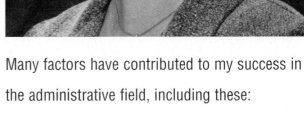

Many factors have contributed to my success in the administrative field, including these:

- Technical skills
- People skills
- Education
- Mentoring
- Drive and ambition
- Loyalty

My first priority was to develop strong keyboarding and computer skills. While developing the technical skills necessary to obtain a position in the administrative professional field, I earned an associate degree in Office Information Systems. In addition to office systems classes, my courses included English, government, mathematics, economics, and general education, all helping to broaden my education.

Once employed, my advancement was rapid. Within five years, I rose from an entry-level administrative professional to the assistant to the CEO of a large community college. Although technical and people skills, a college degree, and hard work were necessary for success, the mentoring I received from my supervisors was the key element for my success. I was fortunate to work for intelligent, caring individuals who were confident and trusting of my abilities.

I graduated magna cum laude with a degree in Office Information Systems. While working on my associate degree, I became a member of Phi Theta Kappa, a national honorary fraternity, and received the Mildred C. Storch Scholarship Award. Since college, I have continued to grow and learn on the job. I have taken advantage of numerous professional development seminars, including total quality management, time management, and diversity training. Through on-the-job training, I am now proficient in Word, Lotus, Excel, and PageMaker®. In my role as an assistant to the CEO of a community college, I worked closely with the administration and board of trustees. My responsibilities included attending board meetings, taking and preparing the official minutes, and making travel arrangements for the board, to name a few. The workload was heavy, overseeing the needs of the board, which required constant attention to detail. I was also responsible for supervising one secretary. My responsibilities in my present position include scheduling interviews, maintaining degree and certification records for teachers and administrators, and taking minutes during collaborative bargaining contract negotiations.

The most enjoyable and stressful parts of my job are intertwined. My job includes recording minutes for collaborative bargaining meetings and negotiating employee contracts. Although the meetings are interesting, coming to a mutual agreement can be difficult. A particular topic may be discussed by many people for as long as two hours. Individuals give a variety of input. I find it helpful when the facilitator reiterates the consensus reached, allowing me to clearly understand the agreement. I enjoy participating in the meetings, but I also find them quite challenging.

I suggest that anyone seeking a career in the administrative professional field continue to develop communication, human relations, and technical skills. In addition, an individual entering the field should be willing to work hard, be reliable, and follow through on each project. I also believe a college degree is important. My immediate professional goal is to be a conscientious, courteous, and caring employee.

My hobbies include physical activities that are good sources of stress relief. I enjoy swimming, skiing, and roller-blading. Having moved to northern Michigan, I have found it easy to enjoy a variety of physical activities. An eight-mile bike trail and public beach are within walking distance of my home, encouraging me to exercise. I also enjoy traveling and reading.

DEBRA L. TRAHAIR'S CASE

I have prepared a case from my experiences as an administrative professional. Decide how you would handle the case by answering the questions at the end of the situation. Turn to the end of Part 3 (page 215) to see how I solved the case.

The Situation

At one point in my career, I worked with a particularly strong-willed individual who had a personal agenda. The individual criticized everything, regardless of the time and attention someone put into a task. The individual was excessively demanding and treated others with little respect.

The working relationship was difficult for me for many reasons. Throughout my career, I have always strived to be competent, organized, and thorough, always doing more than was expected of me. However, in this working relationship, there was absolutely no task

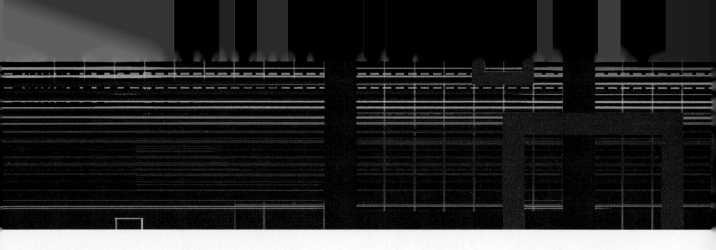

I could complete successfully. At one point during the situation, I found myself carrying the stress home. I did not sleep well, and my children did not understand why I was so stressed.

How would you handle this stressful situation? What suggestions do you have for improving communication? Where could I get help in handling the situation?

CHAPTER 7
ETHICAL BEHAVIOR

LEARNING OBJECTIVES

1. *Recognize the importance of ethical behavior.*
2. Identify characteristics of an ethical organization.
3. Identify traits of an ethical employee.
4. Define the steps necessary for ethical change.
5. *Demonstrate a commitment to community involvement.*

The ethics of business enterprise, the dominant institution in America and in the world, affects our society greatly. Highly successful business leaders are quoted in the news, and their behavior is observed and often emulated by others, not only in the business world but also in the nation and the world at large.

However, the influence of business on society and the influence of corporate leaders on individuals are not always positive. Inferior products and services, environmental pollution, unsafe working conditions, unfair treatment of employees, and various other unethical behaviors are sometimes the outcomes of poorly run businesses and leaders who misuse their power and authority. When business leaders are irresponsible, our society and individuals within it are often the losers.

In this chapter, ethics is considered a **pragmatic** topic—one not only to be understood conceptually but also to be practiced in the day-to-day operation of a business and in the lives of employees within the business.

BUSINESS ETHICS

Ethics is a systematic study of moral conduct, duty, and judgment. Certainly ethical behavior has always been important for organizations and individuals. However, today more and more attention is being paid to ethical concerns. Why? Here are two answers to that question.

- Due to the coverage given to business through television, radio, and newspapers, we are more aware of unethical practices. For example, if an airline crash kills hundreds of people and the cause is faulty equipment due to improper maintenance by the airlines, the public knows that information quickly, due to extensive media coverage. If a company puts a food product on the market with an additive that may cause illness or even death, the public is informed through television, radio, and newspapers. The result of instances such as these is public demand of improved safety and health regulations and management accountability.

■ Technology has advanced so far today that horrendous uses of it are possible. For example, medical science has expanded to the point that ethics are of major consideration. Some of the questions we hear debated are these.

1. Does an individual have the right to determine when he or she dies and to seek assistance with death?
2. How long should a seriously ill patient be kept alive through artificial means?
3. With the genetic work being done to determine links between genetics and diseases, is it ever "right" for parents to decide to abort a fetus?
4. Is it ethical to insert growth hormones into children who have no growth-hormone deficiency but who may be on growth curves shorter than their parents would like?
5. With the cloning of Dolly the sheep in 1997, the possibility of cloning humans may be imminent. In fact, an article in *Time*, February 2001, reported that several scientists are forming a consortium to produce the first human clone.[1] If we have the ability to clone human beings, is it ethical? Here are several other questions that were asked in the *Time* article: What if cloning becomes popular and supplants natural selection? Will that skew the course of human evolution? What if a clone develops unforeseen abnormalities? Could the clone sue the parents for wrongful birth?

All of these questions have implications not only for individuals but also for the various health professions and pharmaceutical businesses.

Obviously, these ethical questions are only a few of the issues we are facing. As technology opens new vistas for all of us, ethical questions will continue to occur. The point here is that

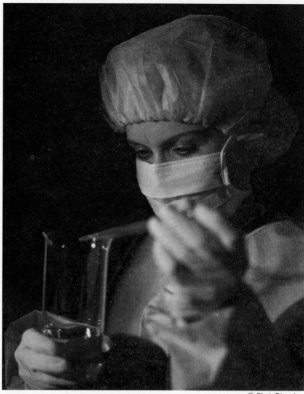

© PhotoDisc, Inc.

Advances in medical science are raising ethical questions.

wisdom on the part of business leaders and individuals who are employed by business is required now and in the future to face and solve the ethical issues that will confront us. An important aspect of this wisdom is **morality** (a set of ideas of right and wrong). All of us must strengthen our own ethical understandings and **moral integrity** (consistently adhering to a set of ideas of right and wrong), both within and outside the workplace.

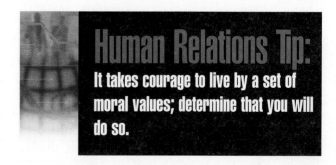

Human Relations Tip:
It takes courage to live by a set of moral values; determine that you will do so.

[1]Nancy Gibbs, "Baby, It's You! And You, And You . . . ," *Time*, February 19, 2001, 47–57.

THE ETHICAL ORGANIZATION

Ethics has become so important that it is the topic of numerous books, the subject of seminars, the basis for consulting businesses, and a concern of executives daily. A company can succeed or fail due to its ethical behavior.

Each year *Fortune Magazine* prints a list of the "100 Best Companies to Work For." The Container Store was No. 1 on the list in 1999 and 2000. The statements made about The Container Store that supported this designation were ethical in nature; they were not about the size of the company or the amount of profit it makes. Here are some of the statements.

- People care about each other.
- The employees are the driving forces behind the success of our business; and therefore, we strive to create a place where our employees enjoy getting up in the morning and coming to work.
- The Container Store is guided by their "do unto others" business philosophies.[2]

Cisco Systems, No. 3 on the list of the "100 Best Companies to Work For" in 2000, makes this statement on its Web page.

- Cisco Systems actively supports a wide variety of local, statewide, and national charities, nonprofit organizations, and educational programs.[3]

These statements show a commitment to employees and community involvement, both characteristics of ethical organizations. Many organizations today are writing vision or mission statements that make clear the directions and values of the organization. Such statements let the employees know the directions of the organization, what it values, how it intends to live those values, and what is and what is not ethical behavior within the organization. Although the scope of this book will not allow for an exhaustive treatment of all the characteristics of an ethical organization, a number of ethical characteristics are covered in the next section.

Socially and Environmentally Responsible

Certainly we have examples in our society where business has been socially and environmentally careless and irresponsible. According to the American Petroleum Institute: "Protecting the environment while producing, transporting, refining and marketing fuel is a challenge the petroleum industry must meet every day. While seeps are natural, we have an obligation to protect nature from accidental oil spills from our operations that can damage an ecosystem."[4] A major oil spill that caused environmental damage was the Exxon Valdez. On March 24, 1989, the Exxon Valdez grounded on Bligh Reef and spilled nearly 11 million gallons of oil into the biologically rich waters of Prince William Sound. Exxon was fined $150 million for this spill, the largest fine ever imposed for an environmental crime. As restitution for the injuries caused to the fish, wildlife, and lands of the spill region, Exxon agreed to pay $100 million. As a result of this high-profile spill and the damage caused to the environment, the oil industry is paying greater attention to the reduction of spills. In 1997, Coast Guard statistics reported that the volume of oil spilled in United States waters declined by two-thirds compared to the year before, representing the lowest amount of spill recorded since the Coast Guard began publishing data in 1973. This case, including the reactions by citizens, our government, and the courts, reinforces our national expectations of environmentally responsible businesses.

Business executives who are socially and environmentally responsible are constantly aware of the possible dangers in their businesses. Responsible executives take all necessary precautions to see that the environment is not polluted. They pay attention to government regulations regarding careful disposal of waste

---

[2] "The Container Store Tops Fortune's 100 Best List for Second Year in a Row," accessed May 10, 2001; available from www.containerstore.com.

[3] "Company Overview," accessed May 10, 2001; available from www.ciscosystems.com.

[4] "Oil Spill Prevention and Response—It's in Everyone's Best Interest," accessed May 10, 2001; available from www.google.search.

products. When building new buildings, they give top priority to cutting down as few trees as possible and protecting wetland areas and other areas that are environmentally important.

Internationally Aware

When opening businesses in other countries or buying or selling products in other countries, ethical business organizations understand the importance of learning and respecting the culture and business customs of the country. You learned about several of these cultural differences in Chapter 2. Take time now to go back to that chapter and review some of the differences.

Here are some additional differences for you to consider. A basic precept of Japanese culture is to put the best face on even the worst situation. Consequently, a smile, a nod, even a spoken affirmative in business negotiations may merely mean a reluctance to disappoint. Business is also never conducted at the beginning of a meeting. There is a set ritual that includes introductions, the pouring of tea, and the exchange of business cards. In contrast, the French get right down to business matters quickly; but they may be slow in coming to decisions. However, whether the decision is good news or bad, they state their intentions unambiguously. In Latin America, you may behave as you like as long as you are comfortable with Latin ways. Eye contact must be unflinching; conversation must be nose to nose. Hugs and two-handed handshakes are common among mere acquaintances. Siesta is sacred, which means that almost all businesses, including stores and banks, close for two or three hours in early afternoon. Late arrival at meetings is customary, from a quarter of an hour to an hour or two.

Committed to Diversity

The ethical organization is committed to diversity in its hiring, promotion, and treatment of employees. The ethical organization

- Is intolerant of discrimination—racial/ethnic, gender, and age
- Maintains a policy against sexual harassment
- Provides for the physically challenged

Intolerant of Discrimination

Unfortunately, discrimination is ever present in our society. Businesses are made up of people who bring their own particular prejudices to the workplace. What does *prejudice* mean? **Prejudice** is defined as "a system of negative beliefs, feelings, and actions." These beliefs, feelings, and actions are based on *learned* categories of distinctions, *learned* evaluation of these categories, and *learned* tendencies to act according to the beliefs and feelings held. Prejudice can lead to acts of **discrimination** (treatment or consideration based on class or category rather than individual merit).

Discrimination may occur in many forms; race or ethnicity, gender, and age are some of the most likely forms. Discrimination may also involve sexual harassment. Discrimination has been so prevalent in our society that laws have been enacted in an attempt to eliminate it. For example, Title VII of the Civil Rights Act of 1964 made it illegal to discriminate on the basis

© PhotoDisc, Inc.

We must respect the cultural differences between individuals.

of race, color, religion, gender, or national origin. Since that time, other acts have been passed that address age, disability, equal pay, and pregnancy discrimination. Figure 7-1 lists some of these acts.

LAWS GOVERNING DISCRIMINATION

It is unlawful to discriminate against applicants, employees, or students on the basis of

- Race
- Religion
- Color
- National origin
- Gender
- Age
- Height, weight
- Marital status
- Disability or handicap

The following acts ensure that sexual harassment will not be tolerated:

Civil Rights Act of 1964, Title VI and VII

Title IX of the Education Amendments of 1972

The Age Discrimination Act of 1975

The Americans with Disabilities Act of 1990

Civil Rights Act of 1991

The following acts make pay discrimination based on sex and discrimination on the basis of pregnancy, childbirth, or related medical conditions unlawful:

The Equal Pay Act of 1963

The Pregnancy Discrimination Act of 1978

The Family and Medical Leave Act of 1993

Figure 7-1

Race/Ethnic Discrimination. Racial/ethnic tensions have occurred in the United States from the time the first white settlers drove Native American Indians from their land and set up a system of labor based on black slavery. However, the existence of discrimination is no reason to accept it. Ethical businesses and individuals seek to eliminate discrimination. The ethical organization sets an example for its employees of nondiscriminatory behaviors and demands that its employees behave in nondiscriminatory ways. The ethical organization has a procedure for handling discrimination and provides the information to its employees.

Gender Discrimination. Title VII covers gender discrimination as well as racial/ethnic discrimination. Employers may not advertise a job specifically for a man or woman unless the employer can prove that it is necessary that a person of a specific gender is needed. In other words, the question of gender may be asked only if it pertains to a bona fide occupational qualification; for example, a model for men's clothing. We recognize in our society today that there are very few gender-specific occupations. A person may apply for any job, and the hiring decision must be based on whether the individual has the knowledge and skills needed for the job, not on whether the person is male or female.

Neither can employee pay be based on whether a person is male or female. The Equal Pay Act, a 1964 amendment to the Fair Labor Standards Act, prohibits pay discrimination because of gender. Men and women performing work in the same establishment under similar conditions must receive the same pay if their jobs require equal skill, effort, and responsibility.

Although sexual orientation is not covered under Title VII, most businesses today recognize that there can be no discrimination based on sexual orientation. Gay and lesbian organizations have become active in helping to ensure that the rights of individuals are not violated based only on their sexual preference.

Age Discrimination. No distinction can be made in age, either in the advertising or hiring process or once an employee is on the job. For example, an organization cannot print a job vacancy notice that specifies a particular age or age range for applicants. Additionally, under the provisions of the Mandatory Retirement Act, an employee cannot be forced to retire due to his or her age.

STEPS FOR HANDLING DISCRIMINATION

- Know your rights and know the laws. Know your organization's position on racial discrimination and sexual harassment, what is legal under the EEOC (Equal Employment Opportunity Commission) guidelines, and what your employer's responsibility is.
- Keep a record of all sexual harassment and racial discrimination infractions, noting the dates, incidents, and witnesses (if any).
- File a formal grievance with your company. Check your company policy and procedure manual or talk with the Director of Human Resources concerning the grievance procedure. If no formal grievance procedures exist, file a formal complaint with your employer in the form of a memorandum describing the incidents, identifying the individuals involved in the sexual harassment or racial discrimination, and requesting that disciplinary action be taken.

- If your employer is not responsive to your complaint, file charges of discrimination with the federal and state agencies that enforce civil rights laws, such as the EEOC. Check your local telephone directory for the address and telephone number of the EEOC office in your city. Your state may also have civil rights offices that can assist you. Check your local directory for these offices.
- Talk to friends, co-workers, and relatives. Avoid isolation and self-blame. You are not alone; sexual harassment and racial discrimination do occur in the work sector.
- Consult an attorney to investigate legal alternatives to discriminatory or sexual harassment behavior.

Figure 7-2

Maintains a Policy Against Sexual Harassment

Sexual harassment has been defined by the Equal Employment Opportunity Commission (EEOC) as "persistent torment arising from sexual conduct that is unwelcome by the recipient and that may be either physical or verbal in nature." Three criteria for sexual harassment are set forth.

- Submission to the sexual conduct is made either implicitly or explicitly as a condition of employment.
- Employment decisions affecting the recipient are made on the basis of the recipient's acceptance or rejection of the sexual conduct.
- The conduct has the intent or effect of substantially interfering with an individual's work performance or creates an intimidating, hostile, or offensive work environment.

The Civil Rights Act makes the organization responsible for preventing and eliminating sexual harassment. The organization is liable for the behavior of its employees whether or not management is aware that sexual harassment has taken place. The organization is also responsible for the actions of nonemployees on the company's premises. Because of these liabilities, many organizations have published policy statements that make it clear to all employees that sexual harassment is a violation of the law and of company policy. These statements generally include a clearly defined grievance procedure so an employee has a course of action to take if sexual harassment does occur.

Provides for the Physically Challenged

Physically challenged individuals (persons with physical handicaps) often face biases based on their physical challenges. They may be treated differently due to their disabilities. The ethical organization

- Provides access for the physically challenged to all facilities
- Provides proper equipment and workspace
- Ensures that initial employment practices do not discriminate against the physically challenged

In summary, the organization that values diversity

- Is intolerant of any type of discrimination—racial/ethnic, gender, age, physically challenged, and sexual harassment
- Upholds its clearly stated policies and procedures that are committed to equal employment
- Has a personnel department with expertise in assisting minorities and women with special issues
- Publishes grievance policies that are clearly stated and distributed to all employees
- Provides diversity sensitivity training for its employees
- Holds managers accountable for consistently supporting and ensuring diversity within the environment

Committed to the Community

The ethical organization understands its social responsibility to the community. Dell® is an example of one corporation that accepts that

responsibility. The following statements are made on Dell's Web page.

- The Dell Foundation is a corporate charitable foundation recently rechartered to focus on equipping youth for the digital economy primarily in Texas and Tennessee, the company's United States base of operation.
- The Employee Giving Program is Dell's annual program to promote philanthropy among its employees and executives. The program, one of the top employee campaigns in Central Texas and one of the most successful Web-enabled campaigns nationwide, has generated significant support for charities around the globe.
- Volunteerism efforts at Dell mobilize thousands of employees each year to support community needs worldwide. Dell is taking advantage of Web-based tools to help make immediate connections between Dell employees and charitable organizations.[5]

The ethical organization is cognizant of the needs of its community and assists with

[5] "Dell Community Initiatives," accessed May 8, 2001; available from www.dell.com.

meeting these needs when possible. For example, the organization might

- Provide tutors for elementary and high school students
- Engage in mentoring programs for troubled youth
- Work with colleges and universities in providing intern experiences for students
- Provide computers (or other technology the business manufactures) to schools
- Serve on community boards and commissions
- Participate in the local Chamber of Commerce
- Contribute to community charities
- Provide leadership to solicit funds for worthy causes, such as disabled children, health care of the indigent, and shelters for the homeless
- Assist with arts programs by providing leadership and/or monies

Respects the Needs and Rights of Employees

Promoting employee productivity is important to the ethical organization. An ethical organization understands that employees have needs. They need to know the values and directions of the company, what is expected of them, and so on. Here are some ways the organization can meet the needs of employees.

- Provide employees with a copy of the values and goals of the organization; ask that managers go over these documents with the employees.
- Encourage managers to consistently distribute important information about the organization.
- Help employees set achievable goals that are consistent with the goals of the organization.
- Administer employee performance evaluations fairly.
- Support employees in learning new skills.
- Reward employee creativity.
- Challenge employees to generate new ideas.
- Encourage collaboration and cooperation among employees.

- Establish teams who work on significant organizational issues.

An ethical organization also understands that employees have rights. Two such rights are a right to due process and a right to privacy.

Right to Due Process

Generally, employees make a conscientious effort to contribute to an organization. In return, they expect to be treated fairly by an organization. People would not choose to work for an organization if they did not think they were going to be treated fairly. **Employment at will** (the doctrine that allows employees to be fired for good cause or for no cause) has been and still is an employment doctrine upheld by some organizations. In an unethical organization, adherence to such a doctrine can cause irreparable harm to employees. For example, companies have been known to call long-time employees into a supervisor's office, tell them they no longer have a job, and send them home immediately with no severance package and loss of all benefits. The doctrine of employment at will has come under considerable attack and is being replaced in most organizations by the right to due process. **Due process** means that managers impose sanctions on employees only after offering them a chance to correct the organizational grievance. An ideal system of due process is one in which employees are given

- A clearly written job description
- Organizational policies and procedures
- The assurance that all policies and procedures will be administered consistently and fairly without discrimination
- A commitment by top management that managers will be responsible for adhering to the values and morals of the organization
- A fair and impartial hearing if the rules are broken

Right to Privacy

Another right that the ethical organization grants to individual employees is the right to privacy. Certainly an organization has the right to information about an employee that affects the individual's performance. For example, if an individual has developed some type of physical illness that no longer allows the person to perform his or her job, the employer has a right to know about it. However, the employer does not have the right to know about illnesses that do not affect job performance. An employer does not have the right to know about a person's political or religious beliefs. In fact, in a job interview, the employer cannot ask questions about marital status, age, organizations to which the person belongs, where the person was born, what the spouse does, and so on. These questions are illegal. If an organization acquires information about an employee's personal life while doing a legitimate investigation, the organization has an obligation to destroy the information, especially if the data would embarrass or in some way injure the employee. Also, an organization must give employees the right to give or withhold consent before any private aspects of their lives are investigated.

© PhotoDisc, Inc.

An employer does not have the right to know about a person's political beliefs, personal life, or religious beliefs.

Establishes and Lives Organizational Values

Many organizations today establish vision and value statements and make these statements available to their employees and to the public by posting them on Websites and distributing them in organizational publications. Here are excerpts of mission/vision/value statements from two companies—Merck® and Herman Miller®.

Merck

The mission of Merck is to provide society with superior products and services—innovations and solutions that improve the quality of life and satisfy customer needs—to provide employees with meaningful work and advancement opportunities and investors with a superior rate of return.

- Our business is preserving and improving human life.
- We are committed to the highest standards of ethics and integrity.
- We recognize that the ability to excel—to most competitively meet society's and customers' needs—depends on the integrity, knowledge, imagination, skill, diversity, and teamwork of employees, and we value these qualities most highly.[6]

Herman Miller

At Herman Miller, we believe that our greatest assets are the gifts, talents, and abilities of our employee-owners. Our corporate culture develops and rewards those who acquire new skills and take charge of their careers. We foster a sense of community throughout our organization that respects a diversity of perspectives, opinions, talents, and backgrounds.[7]

Once you know the company mission/value statement, it is your responsibility to behave in ways that support the mission. If you find yourself in a company where you cannot support the mission/values, it is time for you to find another position.

Maintains a Safe and Healthy Environment

The ethical organization is committed to providing a safe and healthy organization for the community it serves. Johnson & Johnson®

---

[6]Mission Statement, Merck, accessed May 8, 2001; available from www.merck.com.
[7]Corporate Culture, Herman Miller, accessed May 8, 2001; available from www.HermanMiller.com.

exhibited commitment to a safe and healthy community environment in their handling of the Tylenol® crises of 1982 and 1986. Someone from outside the company tampered with Tylenol bottles, lacing them with cyanide. Several deaths occurred as a result. Johnson & Johnson immediately removed all Tylenol capsules from the United States market (even though the deaths were confined to one area of the United States) at an estimated cost of over $100 million. They also mounted a massive communication effort to alert the public and deal with the problem.

Another company, Bridgestone/Firestone®, faced enormous criticism over its failure to be forthcoming about dozens of fatal accidents that may have been linked to the company's tires. Firestone did go public on the situation, but documents obtained by The Associated Press showed the Company had data indicating safety problems years before the August 9, 2000, recall of 6.5 million tires. Firestone is also facing numerous lawsuits filed by individuals with family members who were killed or disabled as a result of the accidents allegedly caused by the tires. At separate House and Senate hearings in 2000, lawmakers admonished the tire maker and Ford®, which uses Firestone tires on its popular Explorer® and other models, for not notifying the public about a problem even though complaints about the tires had been made worldwide for years.[8]

The public expects organizations to behave in ways that protect and maintain a safe and healthy environment for its customers. Additionally, the ethical organization is also committed to providing and maintaining a safe and healthy environment for its employees. For example, an ethical organization upholds the Occupational Safety and Health Administration's (OSHA) requirements that employers furnish a place of employment free from recognized hazards that can cause death, injury, or illness to its employees. Figure 7-4 gives a few of the guidelines that should be followed to keep the workplace safe.

Smoking

Smoking can be extremely dangerous to an individual's long-term health. Although the public is well aware of the dangers of smoking, some individuals within our environment continue to smoke. Nonsmokers complain of eye, nose, and throat irritations resulting from secondhand smoke. Studies have shown that breathing secondhand smoke is unhealthy and can cause emphysema and lung disease. Thus, most businesses have adopted smoking policies to protect the nonsmokers. These policies prohibit employees from smoking inside the building; smoking is usually allowed at a designated place (for example, a separate room for smokers).

SAFETY GUIDELINES

Ask these safety questions about your workspace.

- Is the space sufficient to perform tasks?
- Is the space sufficient for equipment?
- Can all items that are used frequently be easily reached?
- Does flexibility exist to rearrange the workstation if needed?
- Is the lighting sufficient?
- Is the height of the work surface appropriate?
- Is the height of the chair appropriate?
- Can the chair be adjusted easily?
- Does the chair feel sturdy?
- Can the work surface height be adjusted easily?
- Is the computer screen free of glare?
- Can the computer screen be tilted?
- Is the work surface depth adequate to allow the computer screen to be placed at an appropriate distance?
- Is the computer keyboard two inches lower than the desk surface?
- Are document holders provided?
- Is the furniture light in color?
- Is the equipment suitable for the work to be done?
- Is adequate storage space provided?

Figure 7-4

---

[8]"Firestone Knew About Tire Problems," accessed May 8, 2001; available from www.eastsidejournal.com.

Substance Abuse

Substance abuse is a huge problem in our society. **Substance abuse** refers to the use of alcohol or drugs to an extent that is debilitating for the individual using the substance. Drug and alcohol users are absent an average of two to three times more than other employees. Drug and alcohol users also perform at about two-thirds of their actual work potential. Thus, productivity in the workplace is lowered. Shoddy work and material waste are also evident with individuals who abuse substances. Mental and physical agility and concentration deteriorate with substance abuse. Chronic drug abuse creates wide mood swings, anxiety, depression, and anger. Employees who abuse drugs are more likely to steal equipment and materials to get money for their substance abuse habit. Substance abusers are also over three times more likely to cause accidents. Even small quantities of drugs in a person's system can cause deterioration of alertness, clear mindedness, and reaction speed.

Provides an Ergonomically Sound Environment

In Chapter 4, you were reminded of the importance of ergonomics in relation to the computer. You learned the importance of protecting yourself from RSIs by engaging in sound ergonomic practices while inputting data. Additionally, management of an organization has responsibilities in relation to ergonomics. The responsibilities consist of providing an environment where factors such as lighting, acoustics, and other ergonomic factors are carefully considered. Although this chapter cannot provide an in-depth approach to ergonomics (entire books are written on the subject), several areas are addressed here. Figure 7-5 provides a workstation check list.

Lighting

For employees to process information in an organization, an adequate lighting system must be maintained. Improper lighting can cause headaches, eye fatigue, neck and shoulder strain, and irritability. If improper lighting conditions continue over a period of time, productivity and morale are lowered, which in turn can cost a business considerable dollars.

Since the administrative professional spends a large amount of time looking at a screen, glare from a computer screen can be a major problem. Glare is caused by a number of factors, including light bouncing off objects such as picture frames, mirrors, and even glossy periodicals. Techniques used to reduce glare include

- Relocating items on the wall or framing artwork with nonglare glass
- Reorienting workstations
- Replacing overhead lighting with flexible systems so lights can be easily repositioned and brightened or dimmed
- Using screens and draperies that diffuse light and deflect glare

Acoustics

Sound in the workplace can be good or bad. Soft background music and subdued conversations do not disrupt the workday. Street sounds and loud machines can disrupt the workday, even causing employees to become irritable. Also, an employee's efficiency and productivity may be decreased by offensive noise. For example, noise interferes with communication, makes concentration difficult, and causes fatigue. The long-term effect of offensive noise can cause serious health problems for employees, including hearing impairment, sleep loss, and emotional damage.

These methods may be used to control noise.

- Install partitions with acoustical panels between workstations.
- Place noisy equipment in separate rooms.
- Provide conference rooms for small and large group meetings.
- Install carpet, draperies, and acoustical ceilings.

Color

Color can impact the productivity and morale of employees. Attractive, cheerful, and efficient-looking workplaces tend to inspire

- Eliminate glare from your computer and your work-station.
- Be certain you have adequate light for reading without squinting.
- Adjust your chair to fit your height.
- Be certain your chair is sturdy.
- Place your computer keyboard two inches below your desk surface.

- Eliminate loud noises from your workstation environment.
- If the color of your workstation is depressive, ask your employer if it can be changed.

Figure 7-5

confidence and trust. In contrast, drab or poorly painted workplaces can arouse doubt or mistrust. Tones of gray tend to put workers to sleep. Warm colors (such as yellow, red, and orange) create cheerful surroundings. Cool colors, such as green and blue, produce a calm and tranquil atmosphere. Studies have shown that productivity increases and absenteeism is reduced as a result of improved color in the workplace.

Furniture

Much of the workplace furniture today is modular. Desktops, shelves, and cabinets attach to partitions. These units can be adjusted for height, efficiency, and attractiveness. Ergonomic chairs should be purchased that are fully adjustable for seat height and back height. Chair arms should be height-adjustable. It is also important that the chair's seat and back move independently of each other so necessary adjustments can be made.

Honest

An ethical organization is honest. It makes its policies and procedures clear to both its customers and its employees. For example, its pricing policies are made clear to buyers; its product warranty is upheld. Employees understand salary and promotion policies. Executives within the organization are honest. The ethical executive does not appropriate excessive and lavish perks to himself or herself. The ethical executive's word can be taken seriously;

employees know and understand the direction of the company.

Visionary

The visionary organization has the ability to look beyond the day-to-day activities of the organization. Executives within the ethical organization can help managers and employees understand where the company will be in 5, 10, or 15 years and assist others in formulating policies and objectives that will help the company achieve its goals. The organization, through its leadership, consistently articulates the vision of the company and constantly evaluates the daily operations of the company in relation to meeting the vision.

Self-Check A

Stop and take a few minutes to list six of the characteristics of an ethical organization. When you finish, check your answers with those given at the end of the chapter.

1. _____
2. _____
3. _____
4. _____
5. _____
6. _____

THE ETHICAL EMPLOYEE

Now that you have discovered some of the ethical characteristics of an organization, consider certain ethical characteristics of employees within the organization.

Respects the Organizational Structure

The organization today has fewer layers than in the past. Many organizations use teams to deliver products and/or services. However, there is still an organizational structure and a reporting line. Usually, an organization chart spells out the reporting structure. Being respectful of the organization means you do not circumvent your supervisor with issues or concerns. If you have an idea that you believe will help the productivity of the office, share it with your supervisor. If you cannot meet a deadline on a project, let your supervisor know. If you have problems with someone who reports to you, talk with your supervisor. Keep your supervisor informed on all significant items. The rule of *no surprises* between employee and employer is a good rule to follow.

© PhotoDisc, Inc.

Do not circumvent your employer; talk with your supervisor about issues.

Makes Ethical Decisions

Your own ethics are influenced by the following:

- Your religious beliefs
- Your philosophical beliefs
- The culture in which you grew up

The convergence of these factors plus the culture and expectations of the business organization where you are employed can make it difficult to determine what truly is right and wrong in a particular situation. Asking these questions can help you decide what is ethical.

- What are the facts in the situation?
- Who are the stakeholders, or who will be affected by my decision?
- What are the ethical issues involved?
- Are there different ways of looking at this problem? If so, what are they?
- What are the practical constraints?
- What actions should I take?
- Are these actions practical?

If you are still unclear about what you should do, ask yourself these questions.

- If my actions appeared in the newspaper, would I feel all right about everyone reading about what occurred?
- Is what I anticipate doing legal?
- Could I proudly tell my spouse, my parents, or my children about my actions?
- Will I be proud of my actions one day, one week, and one year from now?
- Do my actions fit with who I think I am?

Accepts Constructive Criticism

Your supervisor is just that—your supervisor. He or she has not only the right but also the responsibility to help you do your job well. You should be willing to accept constructive criticism; i.e., criticism that can help you learn and grow. If your supervisor recommends that you do something differently, do not view his or her remarks personally. For example, assume you recently set up a meeting for your employer at a hotel where lunch was served. This was the first time you planned such a meeting, and you thought you did a good job. However, after the meeting, your employer told you the room arrangement was not satisfactory and the food was not good. How do you respond to such criticism? First of all, you deal with the issues at hand. You might say, "Can we talk about it further? How should the room have been arranged? What type of meal would you suggest?" Keep an open mind; realize that you have much to learn and that everyone makes mistakes. You might also suggest reviewing the arrangements with your supervisor before the next meeting.

Always avoid an emotional response to criticism. Try to separate the issue from the critic; realize the critic is merely concerned with improving the situation. If you respond emotionally to the critic, you may succeed only in upsetting yourself (and possibly the person who is doing the criticizing). Do not dwell on criticism and carry it around with you. Learn what you can from the situation, determine never to make the mistake again, and then move on.

Respects Diversity

As the ethical organization is committed to diversity, so is the ethical employee. The ethical employee understands that the world is very diverse and that it will continue to become even more diverse in the future. The ethical employee accepts and respects the diversity of all people—whether that diversity is in ethnicity, race, gender, or age. The ethical employee understands that there is no place in the office for telling jokes that have racial, ethnic, or gender overtones.

Aware of Workplace Politics

Workplace politics are fed by networks of individuals where who you know can be more important than what you know. Favors may be handed out based on the existing networks. In a truly ethical world, office politics would not exist. Unfortunately, we do not live in such a world and probably never will.

So what do you do about workplace politics? When you begin a new job, notice what is happening around you. Be aware of the power bases. Be aware of who knows whom and what

the relationships are. Then hold on to your own value system. Do your job to the best of your ability. Do not gossip about office politics. Use your awareness of the power bases to get your job done. In other words, do not fight a power base when you know you cannot win. Spend your energies in doing what is right. Generally, if you hold on to your values and perform your job extremely well, you will be recognized and respected for who you are.

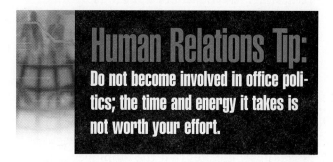

Human Relations Tip:
Do not become involved in office politics; the time and energy it takes is not worth your effort.

Respects Others' Privacy

Respect the privacy of others within the office. If someone confides a personal matter to you, do not spread the "juicy gossip." If you have access

© PhotoDisc, Inc.

If someone confides a personal matter to you, do not spread the "juicy gossip."

to personnel files that contain confidential information about others, keep the information confidential. You may at times be given information that is not specifically labeled "confidential," yet it should not be passed on to others. Also be sensitive to the handling of this information. Do not hide behind the rationale "But I was not told it was confidential." Use common sense here. Ethical conduct dictates that you are always discreet. Remember the golden rule: Treat others as you would want to be treated.

Honest

Being honest means the employee does not take anything that belongs to the company, is conscientious about using time wisely, and gives the company eight hours of productive work (or whatever the office hours may be) each day.

Honesty dictates that the employee *not*

- Send email to family or friends on the office computer
- Take home office supplies such as paper, pens, and notepads
- Use the Internet for personal research or "chats"
- Use the telephone for personal calls
- Use the computer for preparing personal correspondence
- Take longer than the time allocated by the organization for lunch or breaks
- Spend an inordinate amount of time repairing makeup or eating breakfast upon arriving at work
- Use the copier for personal use

Dependable

Do what you say you will do when you say you will do it. Do not make excuses for poor performance. Your employer or peers are not impressed with excuses. A survey done by Accountemps and reported in *From Nine to Five* polled 150 executives and asked them to list the most unusual excuses they had heard for someone being late to work or absent. The responses included the following:

- The wind was blowing against me.
- My favorite actress just got married. I needed time alone.
- I thought Monday was Sunday.
- I had to sort socks.
- I forgot to come to work.

In addition to providing a good laugh, these excuses point to the ridiculousness of trying to find a reason for irresponsible actions.

Cooperative

You may believe that when your particular job is finished, you need not worry about helping anyone else. However, you are an employee of the company. Just because you have completed your tasks does not mean you can sit and do nothing; there is still other work that must be done. Remember, the time may come when you have more work than you can do and need the help of a coworker. When you help someone else, do not make that person feel obligated to you. Offer your help in the spirit of cooperation and with a desire to further the interests of the company.

TO ASSURE YOUR FAILURE AS A PROFESSIONAL AND TO ALWAYS BE SEEN AS UNCOOPERATIVE, follow these simple guidelines.

- Always have an excuse ready for why you cannot help someone else.
- Point out why the individual needs help. Obviously, the individual is incompetent or lazy.

Human Relations Tip:

Deal honestly and directly with any mistakes you make. Inform the necessary people of the error, and state how you will correct the error.

- Forget about the importance of office productivity and customer satisfaction.
- Always look out for yourself. (You cannot possibly help because you have to go home early to take your sick pet to the veterinarian.)

Respects Clients and Customers

As an administrative professional, you must be respectful of your clients and customers. The old adage that "the customer is always right" is true. Stop and think about that statement for a moment. Literally a customer may be wrong; he or she is human and makes mistakes. However, what the statement means is that in the context of service to the customer, he or she is always right. As an administrative professional, you may need to listen to numerous unhappy clients and customers. Let the clients and customers get their anger out; then proceed to address the issue. At times, you will not be able to say "yes" to the customer. When you cannot say "yes," explain the rationale of the company. Always act as your client's advocate within the company, getting the information or providing the service (if at all possible) your client needs. Value the client's time. Do not waste the client's time by keeping him or her on the phone for an inordinate amount of time or by being late for an appointment. Deal with irate clients calmly and professionally. Do not be defensive. Treat every client and customer as a VIP (very important person). Without clients and customers, the company would not be in business and you would not have a job.

Keep the customer informed. If there are production problems, material shortages, or other problems that prevent the customer from getting an order on time, tell the customer. Keep a computer file on the clients and customers with whom you work. Record important information in your file, and review it if a client calls. Remember that all clients are important, whether you deal with them once a year or once a month.

You may have occasion to help entertain customers and clients. For example, you may be asked to take an out-of-town customer to dinner. If so, keep the situation on a purely profes-

sional basis. You also may occasionally receive gifts from clients and customers. Certainly a small gift may be appropriate, and you can accept it graciously. However, as a matter of ethics, you should not accept an extremely expensive gift, and some organizations have a policy prohibiting you from accepting *any* gifts.

© PhotoDisc, Inc.

Always treat the customer with respect.

Take a few minutes now to complete Self-Check B on page 184. When you finish, check your answers with those given at the end of the chapter.

ETHICAL CHANGE

We do not live in a world in which all individuals and organizations are ethical. Such a statement is not meant to be negative. It merely suggests the inevitable—we do not live in a perfect world. We do live in a world in which employees make ethical mistakes but, in the majority of instances, consistently strive to improve themselves and the organizations in which they work. Ethical organizations require people within the organization to behave ethically, including top management as well as all individuals throughout the organization. The process of achieving ethical change requires understanding, a systematic approach, commitment, cooperation, and hard work. Consider the following factors that impede ethical change as well as certain pragmatic steps that produce ethical change.

Factors Impeding Ethical Change

Our backgrounds and beliefs often stand in the way of ethical change. As you read the statements in Self-Check C, ask yourself if you believe these statements to be true or false. Now examine each of these statements individually.

Organizations Are Amoral

Amoral is defined as "lacking moral judgment or sensibility, neither moral nor immoral."

Generally, we readily accept that individuals should have ethics, but we are not so clear about what that means within the organizational framework. You may hear a statement such as: "The organization has no right telling me how to behave." Yet if an organization is to be ethical, its employees must be ethical. The two are inexorably linked—the organization is the people who comprise the organization, and the people within the organization are the organization. Managers have a right and an obligation to hold employees responsible for upholding the ethics of the organization and to hold them accountable for maintaining the skills required to produce the product or service of the organization.

Organizational Leadership Is Unethical

Certainly there are organizations in which the leadership does not behave ethically. However, to assume automatically that all management is bad is negatively stereotyping management. If we do not want to behave ethically, it is easy to shift the blame for our lack of ethical behavior to management. Your first obligation is to uphold the organizational ethics yourself. Then if you find through repeated incidences that management does not uphold the organizational ethics, you may decide to leave the organization. When organizational ethics are not embraced by management, the organization may not be a good place to work.

Values Cannot Be Changed

Clearly, we have difficulty changing our values since they are beliefs we have generally held from childhood. However, change is possible.

Consider this example. Edgar learned at an early age that gender roles are fixed in our society—a female holds the more menial positions; a male, the management positions. Edgar has a female supervisor and has discovered that women can indeed hold high-level positions and be extremely competent in these positions. He has altered his view of women as a result of having a competent female supervisor. Organizations, by upholding a set of values and giving support to changes a person makes, can help an individual change or redefine his or her values.

Labels Accurately Describe Individuals

When we attach a label to someone, we are usually not describing that individual accurately. For example, to describe a person as a "computer nerd" or a "party animal" is restrictive of the whole person's qualities and traits. Remember that labeling hinders rather than helps the change process. Labeling individuals often restricts our view of them. We begin to see them only as the label we have attached. We ignore their other qualities. If we are committed to ethical change within an organization, we must avoid the use of restrictive labels.

Supporting Behaviors

The organization and individuals committed to ethical change can take certain practical steps to produce the change. These steps include the following:

- Determine the ethical change needed.
- Determine steps required to achieve the objective.
- Practice the new behaviors.
- Seek feedback on the change.
- Reward the individual or group involved.
- Evaluate the effects of ethical change.

Determine the Ethical Change Needed

Consider this example of a setting in which ethical change is needed and is addressed within the organization.

As an administrative professional, you have two people reporting to you—Juan Mercado and Luyin Wu. You have been asked to lead a ten-person team who will be looking at hiring practices of administrative professionals. Presently AmeriAsian's number of minorities in this category is not consistent with the number of available minorities in the area. Of the administrative professionals presently working for AmeriAsian, 7 percent are African American, 3 percent are Hispanic, and 2 percent are Asian. The statistics for Grand Rapids show that the availability of administrative professionals is African Americans, 25 percent; Hispanic, 10 percent; and Asian, 5 percent. The task of the team is to examine how AmeriAsian might change these statistics to be more representative of the area. You ask both Juan and Luyin to work with you on the team. At the first meeting, Juan makes several statements that are interpreted by the team as being negative concerning the need for change. Luyin says nothing but exhibits body language that suggests she is upset with Juan. You believe you must try to help them modify their behaviors or the team will not be successful. You determine that the ethical changes needed are these.

Juan: Demonstrate greater acceptance of *all* diversity.
Luyin: State opinions in meetings in an open, but nonconfrontational manner.

Determine the Steps Required to Achieve the Objective

After thinking through the situation, you decide to approach each person individually and discuss the following:

- Juan—Discuss with Juan the importance of AmeriAsian improving the diversity statistics and ask his opinion of how this might be done. Ask him to prepare his ideas before the next team meeting and to go over his ideas with you. In this example, the team leader recognized that the approach to Juan must be positive, not negative. The team leader did not berate him for his behavior, but asked for his help on the completion of the team report.
- Luyin—Discuss with Luyin the importance of stating her opinions in an open manner

at the team meetings. Let her know you value her opinions and want to hear from her. Remember that Luyin is Chinese, and it may not be easy for her to state her opinions openly.

You also decide to clarify the objectives with the entire group at the next meeting, presenting the objectives positively.

Practice the New Behaviors

Give Juan and Luyin a chance to behave differently than they did in the last meeting by asking Juan to share his suggestions for improvement (that you have gone over with him before the meeting). If Luyin does not voice her opinions, ask for her response. Reward Juan and Luyin for doing a good job by publicly praising both individuals.

After clarifying the objectives for the group, ask if anyone has questions and discuss whatever issues are raised.

Seek Feedback

Ask a trusted member of the committee to evaluate your behavior and the behavior of the team and to make suggestions for changes. If necessary, you might have a consultant observe the group and offer suggestions to team members for successfully completing their tasks. The team leader may also engage in team-building exercises with the group.

Reward the Individuals and the Group

Assuming Juan and Luyin show positive changes in their behavior, reward them for their growth. Let them know you appreciate their work on the committee; they did a good job; and the results of their work will make AmeriAsian a better place to work. In addition, reward yourself for your work with the team. You deserve to be proud of your insights and willingness to work with the individuals. Mentally add this success to your list of strengths.

Evaluate the Effects of the Ethical Change

Observe whether the team's recommendations result in greater diversity in the numbers of administrative professionals who are employed. If not, you might want to discuss the problem with the human resources director.

ETHICS—THE CHOICE IS YOURS

Although you cannot impact the ethics of an entire organization unless you are in upper management, you can carefully check out an organization's ethics before you accept a position. How do you check out an organization's ethics? Here are a few suggestions.

- Read the organization's Web page information. Are the ethics of the organization mentioned? Is a commitment to diversity mentioned? Is a commitment to the external community mentioned? What type of programs do they have for employees?
- Check the history of the organization. Have they ever made newspaper headlines for behaving unethically?
- Talk with acquaintances who work for the organization. Ask them to describe the ethical environment of the company.

As an individual employee, you can commit to behaving in an ethical manner. You can decide to follow the ethical stances mentioned in this chapter. You will

- Respect the organizational structure
- Make ethical decisions
- Accept constructive criticism
- Respect diversity
- Consider office politics
- Respect others' privacy
- Be honest
- Be dependable
- Be cooperative
- Respect clients and customers

You can also promise yourself that if for some reason (beyond your control) your organization begins engaging in grossly unethical behaviors, you will seek employment in another organization. Senge, in his book, *The Fifth Discipline*, tells the story of the frog: If you put a frog in a cup of tepid water, it will not jump out; the temperature is comfortable. If you continue to turn up the heat gradually over a period of time until the water is boiling hot, the frog will continue to stay in the water and die. The frog adjusts to the temperature as it is turned up and does not notice the difference in the environment or the threat to its safety. The moral of the story is this: Unless you are com-mitted to observing the ethical behavior of an organization and behaving in an ethical manner yourself, you may stay in an organization that becomes unethical and find yourself supporting those unethical behaviors to the detriment of your own value system and career growth. Commit now to "jumping out" of unethical waters before you "die" in them.

CHAPTER SUMMARY

The summary will help you remember the important points covered in the chapter.

- The study of ethics and the ethical organization have been important to our society for a number of years. The lack of ethical behavior by business can impact our society and the individuals within it.
- More and more attention is being paid to ethical concerns today due to the immediate coverage of business practices through television, radio, and newspapers and the advances in technology that have resulted in questions about ethical standards.
- The ethical organization is socially and environmentally responsible, internationally aware, committed to diversity, honest, and visionary. The ethical organization commits to the community, respects the needs and rights of employees, establishes and lives organizational values, maintains a safe and healthy environment, and provides an ergonomically sound environment.
- The ethical employee respects the organizational structure, makes ethical decisions, accepts constructive criticism, respects diversity, is aware of workplace politics, respects others' privacy, is honest, is dependable and cooperative, and respects clients and customers.
- Factors impeding ethical change include these perceptions: organizations are amoral, organizational leadership is unethical, values cannot be changed, and labels accurately describe individuals.
- Activities that help bring about ethical change include these: determining the ethical change needed, determining the steps required to achieve the objective, practicing the new behaviors, seeking feedback on the change, rewarding the individual or group involved, and evaluating the effects of ethical change.
- Although an individual cannot impact the ethics of an organization unless the person is in upper management, he or she can commit to behaving ethically and leaving an organization that is unethical.

CHAPTER GLOSSARY

The following terms were used in this chapter. Definitions are provided to help you review the terms.

- **Pragmatic** (p. 168)—a topic to be understood conceptually and practiced in the operation of day-to-day activities.
- **Ethics** (p. 168)—a systematic study of moral conduct, duty, and judgment.
- **Morality** (p. 169)—a set of ideas of right and wrong.
- **Moral integrity** (p. 169)—consistently adhering to a set of ideas of right and wrong.
- **Prejudice** (p. 171)—a system of negative beliefs, feelings, and actions.
- **Discrimination** (p. 171)—treatment or consideration based on class or category rather than individual merit.
- **Sexual harassment** (p. 173)—persistent torment arising from sexual conduct that is unwelcome by the recipient and that may be either physical or verbal in nature.
- **Physically challenged** (p. 173)—persons with physical handicaps.
- **Employment at will** (p. 175)—the doctrine that allows employees to be fired for good cause or for no cause.
- **Due process** (p. 175)—the ability of managers to impose sanctions on employees only after offering them a chance to correct the organizational grievance.
- **Substance abuse** (p. 178)—the use of alcohol or drugs to the extent that is debilitating for the individual using the substance.
- **Amoral** (p. 184)—lacking moral judgment or sensibility, neither moral nor immoral.

DISCUSSION ITEMS

These discussion items provide an opportunity to test your understanding of the chapter through written responses and/or discussion with your classmates and your instructor.

1. Why is ethical behavior important for businesses?
2. List and explain six characteristics of the ethical business.
3. List and explain six characteristics of an ethical employee.
4. Can ethical change occur? If so, how?
5. What beliefs often impede ethical change?

CRITICAL-THINKING ACTIVITY

Martin Albertson, your supervisor at AmeriAsian, gives his expense accounts to you each month. Your responsibility is to put the information on a form and return the form to him. Once he reviews and signs it, you send it to the president for signature. Last month you noticed Mr. Albertson included alcoholic beverages on the expense report (under the category of food and beverage). This month you noticed he did it again, and you remember the same thing occurring several months ago. Company policy specifically states that an employee cannot be reimbursed for alcohol. You believe it is merely carelessness on the part of your supervisor; you believe in his honesty. However, you are beginning to wonder if you are engaging in unethical behavior by not calling his attention to these items. Mr. Albertson has always been clear about your responsibility for knowing and adhering to the policies and procedures of the company.

- What is the problem?
- What is your role in the issue?
- How should you handle the situation?
- Have you been behaving ethically by not calling it to his attention? If your answer is "yes," explain your position.

RESPONSES TO SELF-CHECK A

The characteristics of an ethical organization include the following:

- Socially and environmentally responsible
- Internationally aware
- Committed to diversity
- Committed to the community
- Respects the needs and rights of employees
- Establishes and lives organizational values
- Maintains a safe and healthy environment
- Provides an ergonomically sound environment
- Honest
- Visionary

RESPONSES TO SELF-CHECK B

The most appropriate answers are as follows:

1. Always
2. Always
3. Never
4. Always
5. Never
6. Always
7. Always
8. Never

9. Sometimes (If the gift is small, it may be appropriate; each situation needs to be analyzed. Some organizations do not allow an employee to accept any gifts.)

10. Sometimes (On some issues, you may not need to involve your employer, but never circumvent him or her to a higher level.)

PROJECTS

Project 7-1 (Objective 1)

In this project, you are to examine your own ethics. Instructions are provided on the Student CD, file SCDP7-1. This project is a continuation of your Professional Growth Plan. Save your project on your Professional Growth Plan disk under "Progro7-1."

Project 7-2 (Objectives 1, 2, and 3)
Collaborative Project

Along with three of your classmates, interview two executives concerning the following:

- The importance of ethical behavior
- The characteristics of an ethical organization
- The traits of ethical employees

As you are interviewing the executives, determine if their organizations have a vision or mission statement. If so, ask if you may have a copy of the statement. Present your findings to the class. Take notes during the interviews so you can report your findings accurately.

Project 7-3 (Objective 4)

Read the following case, and respond to the questions given. Submit your answers to your instructor in a short memorandum using the memorandum form provided on the Student CD, file SCDP7-3.

CASE

Juanita Rodriquez has been with AmeriAsian for eight months. She works in the Human Resources Department as an assistant to the director. During her eight months, she has demonstrated that she is an extremely capable individual and is committed to upholding the values of AmeriAsian. AmeriAsian has a nondiscriminatory policy that it publishes for all of its employees. Included in this policy is a statement concerning sexual harassment, making it clear that there is no tolerance for any form of sexual harassment at AmeriAsian. Juanita is well aware of this policy; in fact, she assisted the director as he dealt with one case of sexual harassment. In this particular case, the employee accused of sexual harassment was terminated due to the seriousness of the charge and the finding that he was guilty of the charge.

Recently, AmeriAsian hired a new employee, Montgomery Rogers, in the Accounting Department. One day in the break room, Juanita introduced herself to him. She knew he was a new employee, and she welcomed him to AmeriAsian. Since that time she has seen him three times in the halls. He made these remarks to her: "You look great today; you are certainly a beautiful girl." "Wow! That color looks wonderful on you; you should wear blue more often." "How about coffee in the morning?" She merely smiled each time and said nothing.

She does not think he meant any harm by the remarks; she thinks he is merely trying to be friendly. However, she strongly believes that she should say something to him if he makes another remark.

1. Explain how Juanita should handle this situation. Should she report the incident to her supervisor? Why or why not?
2. Since Montgomery is a new employee, should he be helped to understand AmeriAsian's commitment to an environment that is free of sexual harassment? If so, who should help him?
3. What steps can be taken to assist Montgomery in assuring that his behaviors match the ethical standards of AmeriAsian? In answering this question, reread page 173 in your text. Then develop a plan to help Montgomery match his behaviors with the ethical commitment of AmeriAsian.

Submit your responses in writing to your instructor.

Project 7-4 (Objective 5)

Add to your Professional Growth Plan that you began in Chapter 1 by describing how you can demonstrate a commitment to community involvement. For example, if you have an interest in assisting with the education of young children, you might volunteer to help in an elementary school. Or if you enjoy working with the sick, you might volunteer to work in a hospital. The purpose of this project is to encourage you to think about the strengths and interests you have so you can assist your community. Remember, the ethical organization and individual seek to give back to the community in whatever way possible. Think futuristically and commit to working in your community in the future. You will not be engaging in this activity this semester unless you decide you want to do so. Save your plan on your Professional Growth Plan disk under "Progro7-4."

ENGLISH USAGE CHALLENGE DRILL

Correct the following sentences. Cite the grammar rule that is applicable to each sentence. Before you begin, refresh your memory by reviewing the comma rules in the Reference Guide of this text.

1. When music is the topic to be discussed the group quickly begins a lively exchange of the latest light rock hits.

2. To satisfy a craving for ice cream fearful individuals will brave the worst weather.

3. For example the course does not compare favorably to a similar one at Midwestern.

4. Culture is a way of thinking feeling and believing.

5. The huge restless crowd waited patiently for the concert to begin.

ASSESSMENT OF CHAPTER OBJECTIVES

Now that you have completed the chapter and the projects, take a few minutes to review the chapter learning objectives. For your convenience, the objectives are repeated here. Did you accomplish these objectives? If you were unable to accomplish the objectives, give your reasons for not doing so.

1. Recognize the importance of ethical behavior. Yes _____ No _____

_____

_____

_____

2. Identify characteristics of an ethical organization. Yes _____ No _____

_____

_____

_____

3. Identify traits of an ethical employee. Yes _____ No _____

_____

_____

_____

4. Define the steps necessary for ethical change. Yes _____ No _____

_____

_____

_____

5. Demonstrate a commitment to community involvement. Yes _____ No _____

_____

_____

_____

You may submit your answers in writing to your instructor, using the memorandum form on the Student CD, SCDAP7-1.

CHAPTER 8
STRESS, ANGER, AND TIME MANAGEMENT

LEARNING OBJECTIVES

1. Define the causes of stress.
2. Identify stress reducers.
3. Identify time wasters.
4. *Manage time.*
5. *Control stress.*
6. *Manage anger.*

The Information Age in which we live is producing more stress in individuals than ever before. The price for this increased level of stress is high for both the individual and the organization. Every week millions of people take medication for stress-related symptoms. Physical problems that may be the result of stress include ulcers, headaches, high blood pressure, and even heart disease. It has been estimated that 75–90 percent of visits to physicians are stress-related.[1] Additionally, many psychological disorders are related to stress. And rather than stress-related problems decreasing, they are increasing. In fact, job stress costs American businesses an estimated $150 billion each year in absenteeism, lost productivity, accidents, and medical insurance.[2]

A major cause of stress is poor management of time. Some of the errors we make are

- Trying to do too much in too little time
- Wasting time and becoming frustrated due to lack of productivity
- Not establishing appropriate priorities

Stress and time management go hand in hand, with each contributing to the other. If we are stressed out, we cannot manage our time well. If we do not manage our time well, we become stressed out.

Also, closely related to stress management is anger management. Anger, with resulting violent conflicts in the workplace, has become one of corporate America's biggest problems. National polls taken of workers have shown that two out of every ten employees have confessed to being angry enough to "hurt" a co-worker. Employees are killing and maiming each other as a result of their mismanaged and uncontrolled anger and rage.[3] Just as mismanagement of time produces stress, so does mismanagement

---

[1] Jeff Davidson, *10 Minute Guide to Stress Management* (Indianapolis: Macmillan USA, Inc., 2001), 2.
[2] Ibid.
[3] "Managing and Coping with Anger in the Workplace," accessed May 22, 2001; available from www.angermgmt.com/workplace.html.

of anger. The results of this mismanagement of anger have become so serious in our world that each of us must give careful consideration to managing our anger and thus controlling our stress. This chapter can be extremely beneficial in helping you understand how to reduce your stress, control your anger, and manage your time.

STRESS—A MAJOR MALADY

As knowledge continues to expand rapidly and ever-changing technology becomes the rule rather than the exception, we must constantly learn new ways of performing our jobs. As businesses **downsize** (reduce the number of employees) and **rightsize** (determine the most efficient and effective number of employees and organizational structure), we may lose our jobs and even change our careers. As telework becomes a reality for more and more employees, we must adjust to working in very different conditions than in the past—often by ourselves. Such situations force us to deal with change as well as embrace it if we are going to be successful workers in the twenty-first century. All of these occurrences can and often do contribute to stress.

Stress is the body's response to a demand placed upon it. Our wants, needs, and desires are derived from stress of some kind. Stress cannot be avoided; in fact, we would not want to avoid all stress. If you never felt a need to achieve, you would not go to school. If you never felt a need to contribute, you would not accept a challenging job. Stress can and does have a positive impact on our lives. However, when stress becomes chronic, it is a negative health factor. **Chronic stress** occurs when a distressful situation is prolonged, allowing no rest or recuperation for the body; it can cause physical and emotional problems.

Causes of Stress

In addition to the change factors in our society that can cause stress, there are numerous other causes of negative stress. Some of the more common causes are discussed here.

Work Overload

Productivity is a key word in all organizations today. In order to compete in an international market, organizations are experiencing the need to be more productive; at the same time they are expected to reduce costs. Employees are often asked to produce more in less time with a greater degree of accuracy than ever before. Employees find themselves working long hours. In fact, Americans work an average of a full month longer each year as compared to 20 years ago. Americans today work more hours than people in other major countries.

Dual-Career Families

In the majority of families today, both parents work. Parents must balance the pressures of the job with spending time with children and juggling the demands of grocery shopping, housework, and other responsibilities.

Communication Tip:

Set up a job jar for each member of the family. On Sunday, determine tasks that must get done for the week and assign tasks to each family member. Or make the assignment of tasks a family activity where each member volunteers for certain duties.

Single-Parent Families

The divorce rate in the United States continues to be high, and single-parent homes are prevalent. The responsibility for raising children may fall on one parent. The responsibilities at home, along with the pressure of having to make enough money to meet the needs of the family, can cause stress.

Elderly Family Members

Americans are living longer than ever before. Many times this long life means that families include elderly family members who may require special care. Adult children may have to devote time and energy to assisting elderly parents in adapting to new living arrangements. Dealing with the challenges of the elderly family members can be difficult for everyone involved.

Economic Pressures

Even dual-career families may find it difficult to make ends meet. Individuals may work longer hours or take second jobs to bring in

© PhotoDisc, Inc.

Individuals sometimes take second jobs to help with the expenses at home.

additional money for household needs. Single parents, too, may find themselves struggling to meet the financial needs of the family.

Distressing Work Conditions

Personality conflicts sometimes occur within the office. Co-workers can be unhappy in their personal lives, and this unhappiness may manifest itself on the job. You may be the innocent party who must face an unhappy individual at the office each day. You may also have to deal with a difficult supervisor—one who is neither consistent nor considerate. These situations can cause stress.

Anger—A Growing Corporate Problem

Over the past few years, incidences of violence in the workplace have increased. In fact, workplace violence has become such a large problem in the United States that the Occupational Safety & Health Administration has published specific guidelines for some industries and is holding all industries accountable for a safe and healthy environment under its General Duty Clause. Shootings at two Atlanta brokerage firms in the summer of 1999 are just two examples of workplace violence that have received national news coverage. Here are some statistics for your consideration.

- Violence is the leading cause of death at work for women and the second leading cause of death for men.
- According to estimates, domestic violence costs businesses around $3.5 billion every year due to lost productivity, absenteeism, and increased medical care costs.
- One-sixth of all crime occurs in the workplace.
- The health-care and social services industries experience more assaults than any other industry. The cause of these assaults is attributed to the high-stress atmosphere of these industries.
- The National Institute for Occupational Safety and Health has found through long-term trend analysis that an average of 20 workers are murdered each week in the

United States. An estimated 1 million workers, 18,000 per week, are victims of nonfatal workplace assaults each year.[4]

Violence is so prevalent in the workplace that many organizations have started workplace violence prevention programs, which include helping individuals learn how to de-escalate conflict and to manage their anger.

Violence in the workplace compounded by the following events shows that we are becoming an angrier, more violent country:

- The violence that is happening in our schools, including Columbine High School where 13 high school students were gunned down and Flint, Michigan, where a six-year-old killed a classmate
- Road rage, which is becoming more prevalent on our highways

Why? No one has all the answers to this question, but experts suggest that these issues may contribute to increased anger and violence.

- Ignorance of other cultures
- Belief that one is being treated unfairly
- Fear of losing a job or a promotional opportunity
- Feelings of inadequacy when faced with new procedures or technology
- Feeling out of control

Chronic Stress—Harmful to Your Health

Prolonged or chronic stress triggers the production of chemicals that cannot be broken down by our bodies. They remain in our system where they are capable of injuring our health. For example, chemicals produced by chronic stress can cause the following illnesses:

- High blood pressure
- Kidney damage
- Cardiovascular disease
- Migraine headaches
- Ulcers
- Elevated cholesterol
- Cancer

- Weakening of the immune system, which then leads to a number of illnesses

Chronic stress also can cause the following emotional problems:

motional

- Depression
- Withdrawal
- Deep-seated anger
- Loss of self-esteem
- Self-rejection

STRESS REDUCERS

Although we cannot avoid all negative stress, we must guard against it becoming a prevalent part of our lives. Healthy individuals find ways to get rid of negative stress so their bodies will not be damaged. Here are some stress reducers for you to practice.

Balance Work and Play

Many people comment that they work a 50- or 60-hour week, and the statement may be made with a sense of pride. Are these people producing a large amount of work? Maybe not. Do they have demanding and challenging jobs? Perhaps. Are they appreciated and respected for their work contributions? Not necessarily. We know there is a relationship between hours worked and productivity. Of course, individuals differ in the number of productive hours they can work. However, studies have shown that productivity decreases after extended periods of time. Most of us realize immediately when we are not being productive. When we become fatigued, the amount of work we produce goes down and our error rate goes up, signaling that it is time for us to slow down and take a break.

We actually can gain new energy by taking time to play. As adults we may have forgotten how to relax and, with complete abandon, enjoy the world around us. Some experts writing in the field of creative energy urge us to take "joy breaks"—to stop for two to five minutes to play when we feel overtired or nonproductive. We might even have toys at our desk—putty,

---

[4]"Ounce of Prevention Could Cure Workplace Violence," accessed May 23, 2001; available from www.austin.bcentral.com/austin/stories/1999.

a slinky, a kaleidoscope. These toys are small enough to keep in your desk. Just a few minutes of working the putty, moving the slinky back and forth, or looking at the various shapes in the kaleidoscope can release stress through relaxation, pleasant thoughts, and smiles.

Companies across corporate America are realizing the importance of laughter for their employees. Major companies have used humor consultants to help create joy communities. Driving this move are the business issues that people face today (such as downsizing, international competition, increasing workloads, and technological change). Companies are realizing that if their employees are going to be productive and happy, they must help their employees use humor in the workplace. Studies have shown that humor can increase productivity, decrease absenteeism, and lead to better job satisfaction. Stanford University researcher William Fry has found that laughing 100 times a day is equivalent to ten minutes of exercise on a rowing machine. A good, hearty laugh pumps air into the lungs, increases oxygen intake, and causes muscles to relax. Laughter can even cause blood pressure to drop. After a hearty laugh, a person enters a deep state of relaxation that can last as long as 45 minutes.[5] A chuckle also helps. Take a few minutes each day to read your favorite cartoon in the newspaper or to notice the funny antics of your co-workers. Laughter really is good medicine.

Another way to reduce tension quickly is to take a short exercise break. You might keep athletic shoes at your desk and during a break, spend five or ten minutes climbing stairs or walking briskly. Such physical activity allows you to release built-up tension, to open blocked thinking, and to trigger creative ideas.

Self-Check A

Take a few minutes now to write down several things that are fun for you and that you can do at the office during a two- to five-minute break from your job.

_____

_____

_____

How did you do? Were you able to come up with five or six items?

Distinguish Between Achievement and Perfection

Perfectionism is defined as "a propensity for setting extremely high standards and being displeased with anything else." Many of us believe we must do everything perfectly. Certainly, we must achieve and do things well; however, no human being can be perfect. To blame yourself continually for not doing everything perfectly is to engage in energy-draining behavior. In fact, mistakes can be beneficial. Thomas Edison was asked how he came to hold so many patents. He answered that he dared to make more mistakes than ten other people and that he learned from each mistake. Edison knew that the creative process involved trial and error—failure and success. Unless we are willing to risk failure, we will never grow and learn.

Self-Check B

Are you a perfectionist? Do you believe that everything you do must be done extremely well? Read and answer "yes" or "no" to the statements listed below.

	YES	NO
1. If I do not do something well, I feel as though I am a failure.	☐	☐
2. When I make a mistake, I spend many hours rethinking how I might have done it better.	☐	☐
3. I have a reputation of being someone who is hard to please.	☐	☐
4. When I am playing a sport (tennis, golf, baseball), I get angry with myself if I do not play my best game.	☐	☐
5. I will not start a project unless I know everything I can about what I am to do.	☐	☐
6. I do not like to try new things.	☐	☐
7. I lose patience with others when they do not do things well.	☐	☐
8. I expect every piece of work I produce to be perfect.	☐	☐

[5]Andrea Atkins, "Laughing Matters," *World Traveler*, November 1996, 53–56.

If you responded positively to all of the statements, you are probably caught up in a negative, perfectionist pattern of behavior. Begin now to rethink how you view yourself and your work.

Communication Tip:
Do not worry about things you cannot control.

Recognize Your Limits

You must recognize when you are working too hard. Everyone has a different energy level. You may be able to work ten hours a day quite successfully; someone else may be able to work productively eight hours a day. How do you know when you are working too hard? Become familiar with the symptoms of stress that include the following:

- Anxiety
- Headaches
- Panic attacks
- Muscular neck pain
- Insomnia
- Jaw pain
- Phobias

If you develop these symptoms, seek help. Most insurance programs provide for therapy sessions with psychologists or psychiatrists. These trained individuals can help you discover the causes of your stress and how you can alleviate it. You might want to check with your family physician; he or she can provide sources of assistance. *Reduce ex stress*

Exercise

Cardiovascular specialists have found that regular exercise can lower blood pressure, decrease fats in the blood, reduce joint stiffness, control appetite, and decrease fatigue. Exercise changes the body's chemistry, getting rid of toxins and producing endorphins and other hormones that increase creativity and silence negative self-talk. You will be more patient, calmer, and more receptive to others, as well as a better listener, after just 20 to 30 minutes of aerobic exercise.

What type of exercise should you do? Many exercises are good for your body—swimming, walking, and bicycling, to name a few. Participate in an exercise that you enjoy. What time of day should you exercise? It depends on you. You may prefer to exercise in the morning, while someone else may find the evening a better time to exercise. You may choose to exercise while following along with a video or a television program. You may join a health club or the local Y. Some clubs open as early as 5:30 a.m. and close as late as 11 p.m. or midnight. Most experts suggest exercising three to five times a week for a period of 30 minutes to an hour. When you begin exercising, go slowly. Train your body; do not strain it. If you have any medical problems or you are just beginning an exercise program, consult your doctor about the type of exercise that is best for you.

Health Tip:
Make taking care of yourself a No. 1 priority.

Eat Right

What you eat or do not eat affects your overall health. Excessive intake of fat, sugar, salt, and caffeine contributes to poor health and to diseases such as hypertension and heart disease. Six ounces of coffee contain 180 milligrams of caffeine, six ounces of tea contain 70 milligrams, and twelve ounces of cola contain 45 milligrams.

Excessive amounts of caffeine can cause an individual to exhibit the same clinical symptoms as an individual suffering from anxiety. Many people turn to junk food (candy, chips, and other munchies) to relieve stress. However, eating junk food increases stress. The high calorie and fat content of junk food also contributes to being overweight.

Junk food increases rather than decreases stress.

© *PhotoDisc, Inc.*

The average American consumes more than 126 pounds of sugar a year. Excessive sugar consumption can lead to an increase in triglyceride levels in the blood, causing cardiovascular disease. Too much salt can lead to an increase in blood pressure and to the development of hypertension. The wisest course of action is to lower the intake of fat, sugar, salt, and caffeine in the diet.

Your diet should include plenty of fresh fruits and vegetables, and you should drink six to eight glasses of water a day. Whole grain breads and high fiber are good for your body. Maintaining a balanced, healthy diet will help keep your energy level high and your stress level low.

Get Enough Sleep

Surveys have shown that approximately 40 percent of adult Americans suffer from stress every day of their lives and find that they can sleep no more than six hours a night. What is enough sleep? It all depends on you; however, the general rule is at least seven hours, with many people needing eight or nine hours. You need to get enough sleep to function effectively.

Manage Your Anger and Your Time

Although we cannot always prevent ourselves from becoming angry, we can learn to recognize our anger and its causes and symptoms; we can also learn how to reduce that anger. Additionally, we cannot add hours to our day to give us more time to do the many things we believe must be done. We can, however, learn to manage ourselves in relation to the time we have. As you have learned, stress is closely related to both anger and time management. When we are angry, we get stressed. When we do not have enough time to do what is important to us, we get stressed. The remainder of this chapter is devoted to helping you understand how to manage both your anger and your time more effectively.

Health Tips:

- **Stop drinking caffeinated beverages at least six hours before retiring.**
- **Drink a glass of milk before you retire to help you sleep.**
- **Read about 30 minutes before you go to sleep to help you relax.**

ANGER MANAGEMENT

Take a few minutes to answer the following questions.

Self-Check C

1. How are you feeling right now? Anxious? Hostile? Depressed? Numb? Frustrated? Sarcastic? Resentful? Paranoid? Victimized?

_____

_____

The words listed above represent some of the names given to feelings of anger. The first step in resolving an anger problem is to identify the feeling as anger. The purpose of this step is to make the anger more specific. No one can manage anger that is vague and hidden by euphemisms.

2. If you selected any of the above words, what happened to make you angry? If you focus on the specific incident that triggered your anger, it becomes more understandable and easier to manage.

_____

_____

3. Who is the focus of your anger? you? your spouse? your partner? your boss? the kids? all men? all women? other races?[6]

_____

_____

Once you have established the fact that you are angry and that your anger has a specific focus, you are ready to put your anger into a more manageable perspective and take steps to reduce it. The following techniques will help you.

Relax

Deep-breathing exercises are one of the quickest ways to relax your body. Start by finding a comfortable position; sit in a comfortable chair or lie down. You may close your eyes if that makes you feel more at ease. Then slowly inhale air through your nose until you feel your lungs fill with air. Next, exhale the air slowly, breathing out either through your nose or mouth.

Use Positive Self-Talk

If you are angry, negative self-talk can escalate your anger; positive self-talk can de-escalate your anger. For example, assume you are playing a game of tennis with a friend who is extremely good. You miss a ball and say to yourself, "I really am terrible!" You are engaging in negative self-talk, and negative self talk on the tennis court causes you to miss more shots. In other words, your negative self-talk is a self-fulfilling prophecy. You decide you are terrible and you prove yourself right. Now consider a positive self-talk response. When you miss a ball, you say to yourself, "No big deal; I'll get the next one." And, you do! You hit a terrific ball. When you find yourself engaging in negative self-talk, turn it around by

- Recognizing the negative self-talk
- Stopping it immediately
- Beginning positive self-talk

Walk Away

Walk away physically if you can; if you cannot, walk away emotionally. When you were a child, did your mother ever say, "Before you say or do anything when you are angry, count to ten"? Counting to ten allows you to interrupt your anger and cool off. It also allows you time to consider what other choices you might have. In your head, you are walking away from what is making you angry. Consider the following example, a common situation that often makes people angry.

You are waiting in line at the grocery store. The checker is slow, talking to customers as he scans their groceries. In addition, no grocery sackers are available, so the checker must sack the items. The person in front of you has forgotten

---

[6] "Anger Toolkit," accessed May 23, 2001; available from www.angermgmt.com/measure.html.

two items and asks the checker if she can go get them; the checker agrees. You have an important appointment, and you must be on time. You find you are getting angrier and angrier. You are ready to scream at the person in front of you and at the checker.

What are your choices? You can walk away mentally—count to ten, sing a song to yourself, or envision yourself at one of your favorite places having a wonderful time. Or if you are going to be late for your appointment, you can physically walk away. Leave before you become angry and emotionally upset. You can always come back to the grocery store at another time.

Talk to a Friend

If a situation at work makes you angry, talk to a trusted friend about it. That person may be able to help you understand what is causing your anger and help you decide what you can do about the situation. For example, assume you have this situation at work.

> You are chairing a team whose task is to recommend a records management system. The team has met three times, and you believe progress is being made on the task. You believe the team has worked well together. Yesterday your supervisor called you into her office, closed the door, and said that she needed to talk with you about a serious matter. She told you that two people on the records management team had complained that you were not listening to what the team was suggesting—that you apparently had already made up your mind about what the records management system should be and the team had almost no input. As she talked, you found yourself getting very angry. You believe that the accusations are totally false, and you do not understand why anyone would make such statements.

To address the issue and avoid excessive anger, you might take these steps.

- Tell your supervisor that you have not made up your mind about the records management system and that you feel the team is working well together. However, tell her you want to think about the situation carefully and develop a plan to address it.

- Spend time talking with a trusted friend in the organization about the problem. Be open to the friend's comments. Then, develop a plan to address the situation.
- Talk with your supervisor about your plan.

Solve the Problem

Sometimes the same problem occurs frequently. For example, consider this situation.

> You are the only woman in a department of men. Your job description is the same as the men's. Each time an important assignment comes up the work is given to one of the men. You do a good job, and your supervisor (who is male) has given you excellent evaluations. However, you are beginning to think he does not value your work. You believe that as long as you are passed over in the assignment of more challenging work, you will not have a chance to learn and grow on your job. You also believe that without having the opportunity to do the challenging assignments, you will not have a chance for promotion. You wonder if your supervisor is guilty of gender bias. You are beginning to feel anger not only toward your supervisor but also toward the other men in the department.

What do you do? The problem is important enough that you should attempt to solve it. You can use a problem-solving approach. Figure 8-1 illustrates the problem-solving steps, which were explained in detail in Chapter 6. You can do the following:

- Identify the problem. The problem in this case is that you are not being given any challenging assignments.
- List your alternatives. You can quit your job; you can talk to your supervisor; you can talk with the other males in the department; you can get angry and yell at everyone.
- Choose the best alternative. The best alternative in this situation is to talk with your supervisor. He is the one controlling the job assignments. Explain how you feel; attempt to understand how he feels.
- Evaluate the situation. Was the talk successful? Did the supervisor explain his rationale successfully? Is he willing to give you more

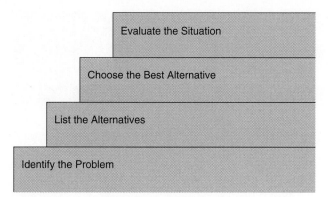

Figure 8-1   **Problem-Solving Steps**

challenging assignments? Do you believe you now have a chance to move up in the organization if you continue to do a good job? Hopefully, the answers to these questions are positive ones. If they are not, you may be in a situation that you cannot change. However, rather than getting angry, you might ask for a transfer within the organization or look for a position in another organization.

TIME MANAGEMENT

Time management is really a misnomer since none of us can control the number of hours in a day. Time is finite; we cannot increase or decrease time by managing it. But we can learn to manage the way we use our time. Thus, **time management** really refers to the

way we manage ourselves and our tasks in relation to the time we have in a day, a week, or a year.

Time Defined

Time is a resource, but it is a unique resource. It cannot be bought, sold, borrowed, rented, saved, or manufactured. It can be spent, and it is the only resource that must be spent the minute it is received. Every one of us receives the same amount of time to spend each day; we all have 24 hours each day to manage in relation to our professional and personal goals. We cannot speed the clock up or slow it down. Time passes at the same rate each minute, each hour, and each day. The difficulty with time management occurs as we try to manage ourselves in relation to the finite time we have; many of us do not understand how we spend our time. We do not understand our time wasters, and we certainly are not taking steps to manage ourselves more effectively in relation to our time. Many of us do not realize that once we have wasted time, it is gone and it cannot be replaced.

Time Wasters

Before you begin to analyze how you might do a more effective job in managing yourself in relation to your time, look at some of the common time wasters. You may find that you have been guilty of many of these behaviors.

We must manage ourselves in relation to the time we have.

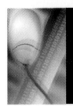

Ineffective Communication

As an administrative professional, you will communicate both verbally and in writing with people in the workplace (your employer and co-workers) and outside the workplace (customers and clients). The lines of communication between you and others must be open and easily understood. Think of the time you will waste if you must rewrite a letter because you misunderstood the instructions from your employer; think of the profits the company may lose if you make a customer unhappy and lose an account as a result of misunderstood communication.

Poor Telephone Usage

The telephone becomes a time waster when it is not used properly. Here are some of the mis-

© PhotoDisc, Inc.

The telephone can become an ineffective means of communication when it is not used properly.

takes people make that cause the telephone to be a time waster.

- Engaging in personal conversations during work hours
- Failing to give the proper information to a co-worker, client, or customer
- Failing to get the proper information from a caller; i.e., name, phone number, and reason for call
- Using the telephone when it would be more efficient to use email or a fax

Inadequate Planning

Many individuals do not plan what they need to do on a particular day. Lack of planning can cause both you and your supervisor problems. Consider this situation.

Your supervisor gives you a report on Friday afternoon that must be completed by Monday afternoon. You understand that the job is a high priority. The report is not lengthy, but you do not analyze how long you will need to produce it. On Monday morning, you have numerous interruptions; you do not begin the report until 2 p.m. Monday. As you get into the report, you see that it is very involved and that you will not be able to finish it by 5 p.m. You are embarrassed and frustrated when you have to admit to your employer that the report is not completed, and your employer is unhappy. Your lack of planning resulted in an important report not being produced in a timely manner. If such planning lapses continue, you could lose your job.

Improper Handling of Visitors

As an administrative professional, your responsibility is to make visitors feel comfortable and welcome. However, that does not mean you must entertain the visitors while they are waiting to see your employer. Also, you should not spend long periods of time chatting with co-workers who stop by your workspace to visit. Certainly if a co-worker comes by on a work-related errand, you may engage in pleasantries such as "Good morning. How is your day going?" But you should not spend a lot of time in idle chitchat.

Disorganization

Does your desk have a pile of file folders on it, with their contents spilling out? Do you have half-finished projects, half-finished memorandums, and a stack of filing sitting around? Disorganized individuals are a serious liability to their organization. They cannot be depended upon to provide information in a timely manner because they forget where the information is. They cannot meet deadlines because they forget to write them down. They waste an enormous amount of their time and other people's time searching for files, phone numbers, reports, and other necessary information.

© PhotoDisc, Inc.

When your desk is disorganized, it is difficult to get work done quickly and efficiently.

Procrastination

Procrastination is the postponement or needless delay of a project or task that must be done. Many of us are guilty of procrastination. We postpone a project because we are

- Afraid we will fail at it
- Not interested in the work
- Angry with the person who delegated it to us

Of course, we do not want to admit any of these reasons, so we make excuses. We make statements similar to the following:

- *I have too many other projects.*
- *I don't have what I need to do the job.*
- *Before I can get started, I have to consult with my supervisor.*
- *There really is no rush to begin; it's not due for three weeks.*

Procrastinators are late for meetings, put off handling projects, and do not return telephone calls. Procrastinators may be such relaxed, easy-going people that their procrastination does not bother them as much as it bothers others. However, they can create stress for themselves with their last-minute efforts, and the stress they put on other members of their work group can be significant.

Self-Check D

What are your time wasters? Do you know? Take a few minutes to consider them.

_____

_____

_____

TIME MANAGEMENT TECHNIQUES

You have considered the importance of time management, and you understand that time is a resource that must be used well. You have looked at some of the time wasters that we all face. Now you must understand how to do a better job of managing yourself in relation to time. This area requires constant work. We never become such effective time managers that we can forget about the constraints of time. However, when we pay attention to effective management techniques, we find that not only do we seem to have more time to get our tasks done, but we reduce the stress in our lives.

Set Goals

A **goal** is an objective, a purpose, or an end that is to be achieved. The idea of establishing goals makes many people feel uncomfortable—having to write them down and then being expected to achieve them. How many of us have set New Year's resolutions in good faith and then failed to reach any of them? Even thinking of these resolutions at a later date results in a vague sense of guilt about not having accomplished what we set out to do.

Goal setting can produce these same feelings of hesitancy and guilt. However, if we are to accomplish anything on our job and in our personal lives, we must set goals. An old Chinese proverb states "If you don't know where you are going, any road will take you there."

In other words, if you do not establish goals, you become undirected and may wind up someplace you did not intend to go.

Organizational Goals

Most organizations are involved in strategic and organizational planning. When these plans are written, they include definite goals to be accomplished and deadlines to meet these goals. Employees are usually brought into the planning process. In fact, companies often ask employees to write action plans that reflect what they will accomplish to meet the goals of the organization. Then during their performance evaluations, these employees are evaluated on how well they met their goals.

Personal Goals

Personal goal setting is also important. This goal setting can take the form of deciding

- What your career goals are—what you want to be doing and where you want to be in five or ten years
- When you want to purchase a house
- When or if you want to start a family
- Where you want to live

Goal Attributes

Effective goals must be achievable. They should also challenge you so you have the opportunity for growth. They should be specific and measurable. Goal attributes are explained here.

- *A goal should challenge you.* A goal should require you to do more than you have been doing. It should challenge you to reach a higher level of accomplishment.
- *A goal must be attainable.* Although goals should challenge you, they should not be unrealistically high. Goals should be achievable with hard work, appropriate skills, and dedication to the task.
- *A goal must be specific and measurable.* If your goal is too vague, you will not know when you have achieved it. For example, "to become a more effective communicator" is a goal that is too vague. How can you become a more effective communicator? You should determine behaviors in which you are going to engage to accomplish your goal. Your goal might be stated as follows:

I am going to become a more effective communicator by paraphrasing, using direct and simple language, and listening to others.

Your next step is to establish methods for measuring the accomplishment of your objective. In the communication situation, you might determine that you are going to measure the accomplishment in the following way:

In order to determine if I have accomplished my objective, I will ask three people within my work group to evaluate my communication skills.

- *A goal must have a deadline.* Deadlines allow us to see if the goal has been accomplished. In the communication example given above, you might set yourself this deadline.

Evaluation of my communication goal will occur by December 19, 2003 (within three months after it was set).

- *A goal should be flexible.* Sometimes external conditions impact your goals to the point that you cannot accomplish them. When this occurs, do not cling stubbornly to something that is no longer possible but do not be too quick to eliminate the goal. By working smarter, you may be able to offset the external factors. Also, you may be able to revise your goal or establish a different time frame for completion.

Analyze Your Time

Although you might think you know exactly how you spend your time, actually most people do not. Check periodically how you are spending your time. You might be surprised at what is taking up your time, and you might discover some time wasters.

Log Your Time

One way to determine how you spend your time is to chart on a time log the amount of time you spend in various daily activities. Certainly you should not become a slave to the log, and you do not need to be accurate to the second or minute. However, you should be faithful to the process for a period of one or two weeks so you have a realistic picture of how you are spending your time. Figure 8-2 shows a time log.

DAILY TIME LOG			
Name _____ Day _____ Date _____			
Time	Activity	Priority	Nature of Interruptions
		1 2 3	

Figure 8-2   Time Log

Analyze the Log

The next step is to analyze your time log to discover ways in which you can improve the management of your time. Ask yourself these questions.

- What was the most productive period of the day? Why?
- What was the least productive period of the day? Why?
- Who or what accounted for the interruptions?
- Can the interruptions be minimized or eliminated?
- What activities needed more time?
- On what activities could I spend less time and still get the desired results?

Prepare an Action Plan

After you analyze your log, the next step is to prepare an action plan. The purpose of the plan is to set goals for yourself as to how you will increase your time management efficiency.

Establish Effective Routines

Here are some techniques that will help you manage yourself in relation to your time. Obviously, there are numerous other effective time management techniques; only a sampling is provided here.

Set Priorities

Many times you will not be able to do everything you are asked to do in one day. Thus, you must be able to set priorities—to distinguish between the most important and least important jobs and determine the order in which they should be completed. If you are new to a job, you may need help from your supervisor to determine which tasks are the most important. When you learn more about your position and your supervisor, you should be able to establish priorities on your own.

Prepare Daily To-Do Lists

Before you leave work for the day, prepare a to-do list for the next day. List all the tasks,

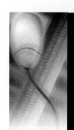

Communication Tip:

Keep your to-do list on your computer, where updating and establishing priorities can be done quickly.

activities, and projects that you need to accomplish. Then review your list. Mark the most important items A, the less important items B, and those remaining C. Use your list, with priorities in place, to

- Arrange papers on your desk in priority order, with the A's in one pile, the B's in another pile, and the C's in still another pile
- Prioritize telephone messages, marking them A, B, or C

The next day as you complete the items on your to-do list, mark them off. This step gives you a sense of accomplishment and calls your attention to what you still need to accomplish. As you prepare your to-do list for the next day,

use the present to-do list. If it still lists items you have not been able to accomplish, transfer these items to the to-do list for the next day. A sample to-do list is shown in Figure 8-3.

Simplify Repetitive Tasks

If you find yourself keyboarding a form numerous times, simplify the process. Prepare a template on your computer. Do you find yourself looking up the same address or telephone number several times? Make yourself a list of frequently used addresses and telephone numbers. Store these on your computer. Simplifying a repetitive task takes time to organize initially, but in the long run, the savings in time can be significant.

September						
Sunday	Monday	Tuesday	Wednesday	Thursday	Friday	Saturday
31	1	2	3	4	5	6
7	Labor Day 8	9	10	11 Prepare report	12	13
14	15 Send Memo on TQM meeting	16	17 Make luncheon reservations for Mr. A	18	19	20
21	22	Begin 23 presentation for community meeting	24			27
28	29	30	1			4

My To-Do List—Sept. 11

Task	Priority
Make phone calls	A
Prepare report	A
Write memo on TQM meeting	B
File	C

Figure 8-3   To-Do List

Handle Paper Once

Do you ever find yourself rereading a piece of paper or shuffling it from the top of a stack to the bottom of the stack several times? Most of us do. In fact, many time management experts claim that handling paper over and over is the biggest paperwork time waster. The basic rule is to handle paper once. Read it, route it, file it, or answer it. Get it off your desk as quickly as possible.

Conquer Procrastination

Pick one area where procrastination plagues you and conquer it. For example, assume you always put off filing. You find yourself with two or three weeks of filing stacked on your desk, and you are constantly rummaging through papers for something your employer needs. In your list of priorities, set aside 20 or 30 minutes each day (or whatever time you need) for filing; put it on your to-do list. Check it off when you have accomplished it.

Here are some additional ways you can conquer procrastination.

- Focus on one task at a time.
- Give yourself deadlines and meet them.
- Tackle the most difficult tasks first.
- Do not let perfectionism paralyze you; do not be afraid to make mistakes.
- Recognize that you have developed the habit of putting things off; then take steps to correct the habit. For example, create whatever visual reminders you need; you might make a sign for your desk reminding you not to procrastinate. Do not let yourself make exceptions by saying "It's okay to procrastinate on this task." A lapse is like a car skid; it takes much more effort to recover than to maintain control from the outset.

Organize Your Work Area

When you are working on a project, clear your desk of materials that relate to other projects. Put these materials in a file folder, label the folder with the name of the project, and place the folder in your drawer.

Keep in and out trays on your desk, and label the trays for incoming and outgoing material. If space permits, you may wish to have a tray on your desk for material to be filed. Keep frequently used supplies (such as pencils, pens, and paper clips) in your center desk drawer. Organize your paper into letterhead, plain bond, memorandum, and so on.

Reduce Interruptions

Interruptions can be frustrating time wasters. Controlling or minimizing interruptions is crucial to efficient time management. Here

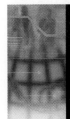

are some suggestions for reducing telephone and visitor interruptions.

Telephone

- Give and record correct information during telephone calls.
- When placing calls, identify yourself, your supervisor (if you are placing a call for her or him), and what you need.
- If the person called is not in, find out when the person will return.
- When taking incoming calls, find out who is calling and the nature of the call.
- If you are taking a call for your supervisor who is not in, let the person know when your supervisor is expected.
- If you take a message, repeat the name, phone number, and message to the caller to confirm the accuracy.
- When you have several calls to make, group them and make the calls when people are likely to be in the office. Early morning is usually a good time to reach people.
- Keep your personal calls to a minimum. Let your friends know they should not call you at the office.
- Use email and faxes as an alternative to leaving and receiving phone messages.

Visitors

- Set up appointments for visitors. Discourage people from dropping by unexpectedly to see you or your supervisor.
- Make visitors welcome, but do not make small talk for extended periods. Continue with your work.
- Discourage co-workers from dropping by to socialize. You can socialize on breaks and at lunch. Make it clear that your responsibility during working hours is to work.

Use Good Communication Techniques

If your supervisor asks you to do something, be sure you understand exactly what you are to do. Paraphrase what you believe he or she said if you are not clear. Do not be afraid to ask questions. Transmit ideas in simple, clear terms. Define terms if necessary.

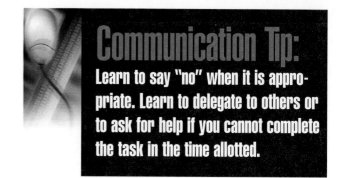

Communication Tip:
Learn to say "no" when it is appropriate. Learn to delegate to others or to ask for help if you cannot complete the task in the time allotted.

Listen carefully when someone is talking. When you are communicating with an individual face-to-face, look at her or him. Be sensitive to the person's body language as well as to the words the person is saying. Keep your mind open to new ideas; refrain from passing judgment on what the speaker is saying.

TIME MANAGEMENT SYSTEMS

A number of systems can help you use your time well. These systems may be manual or computer systems.

Manual Systems

One type of manual system is a calendar that allows you to record all appointments for the day, week, month, and year. If you use a manual calendar, keep all activities logged on the same calendar.

Planning systems are also available. These systems include calendars; but they also include places to record prioritized daily tasks and appointments, monthly planning calendars for future years, sheets for recording goals, telephone/address directories, and delegation sheets.

Another type of manual system is a tickler file. A **tickler file** is a chronological record of items to be completed. The system may be one you design yourself or one you purchase. If you are setting up the system, place a guide for the current month in the front of the file followed by a separate guide for each day of

	Wednesday, May 02, 2003			Customize Outlook Today...

Calendar	Task	Messages	
		Inbox	1
		Drafts	0
		Outbox	0

Figure 8-4   Calendar Software

the month. Place guides for each month of the year at the back of the file. To use this file, write notes on index cards of tasks that need to be accomplished and file them behind the appropriate dates.

Computer Systems

PIM (Personal Information Management) software is a popular type of software that allows you to manage a wide variety of information. For example, with PIM software, you can access the following:

- Calendar software, which manages your schedule, address book, and to-do list
- Contact management software, which lets you track your contacts and keep detailed histories of your business contacts
- Information database software, which handles documents you have downloaded from the Internet or from another source

A number of companies produce this type of software, with several of these companies listed below.

- Microsoft Outlook®—calendar software. This software comes as part of Microsoft Office XP; it also may be purchased individually.
- Lotus Organizer—calendar software.
- Above & Beyond® 2000—calendar software. This is **shareware** or **trial software,** which means you can download it from the Web

for a trial period of 21–30 days to determine if the program meets your needs. Shareware PIMs are available at ZDNet® Software Library.

- Maximizer® and GoldMine®—contact management software. You may download both programs as trial versions.
- Info Select and Zoot™—database software. Zoot is available for a trial download from Zoot Software.

A calendar software page from a computer software package is shown in Figure 8-4.

YOUR POWER AND YOUR POTENTIAL

If you are to thrive in the business world today, you must master the multitude of changes that come your way in the form of technology, be productive and happy in your work, and be able to realize your full power and potential. When you are stressed to the point of being burned out on your job, angry a large part of the time, and finding too few hours in the day to accomplish what you must accomplish, you are not able to realize your full power and potential. By putting to use the techniques presented in this chapter, you have a chance to not only succeed in your job but also thrive in the world of change.

CHAPTER SUMMARY

The summary will help you remember the important points covered in the chapter.

- Stress is the body's response to a demand placed upon it. Chronic stress occurs when a distressful situation is prolonged, allowing no rest or recuperation for the body. Chronic stress can cause physical and emotional problems.
- Factors in our society that contribute to stress are work overload, dual-career families, single-parent families, elderly family members, economic pressures, and distressing work conditions.
- Anger is a growing corporate problem. Over the past few years, incidences of violence in the workplace have increased.
- Chronic stress is harmful to your health, causing illnesses such as high blood pressure, cardiovascular disease, migraine headaches, elevated cholesterol, and cancer. Chronic stress can also cause emotional problems such as depression, deep-seated anger, and loss of self-esteem.
- Stress reducers include balancing work and play, knowing the difference between achievement and perfection, recognizing limits, exercising, eating right, getting enough sleep, and managing anger and time.
- These techniques can help you manage anger: relaxing, engaging in positive self-talk, walking away either physically or emotionally from an angry situation, talking to a friend about the situation, and solving the problem that is making you angry.
- Time is a unique resource; it cannot be bought, sold, borrowed, rented, saved, or manufactured. It is the only resource that must be spent the minute it is received.
- Time wasters include ineffective communication, poor telephone usage, inadequate planning, improper handling of visitors, disorganization, and procrastination.
- Good time management techniques include setting goals, analyzing our time, and establishing effective routines.
- Time management systems such as calendars, tickler files, and computer software can help us manage ourselves in relation to our time.

CHAPTER GLOSSARY

The following terms were used in this chapter. Definitions are provided to help you review the terms.

- **Downsize** (p. 193)—reduce the number of employees within a business.
- **Rightsize** (p. 193)—determine the most efficient and effective number of employees and organizational structure.
- **Stress** (p. 193)—the body's response to a demand placed upon it.
- **Chronic stress** (p. 193)—occurs when a distressful situation is prolonged, allowing no rest or recuperation for the body; it can cause physical and emotional problems.
- **Perfectionism** (p. 196)—a propensity for setting extremely high standards and being displeased with anything else.
- **Time management** (p. 201)—the way we manage ourselves and our tasks in relation to the time we have in a day, a week, or a year.
- **Time** (p. 201)—a resource that cannot be bought, sold, borrowed, rented, saved, or manufactured; it is the only resource that must be spent the minute it is received.
- **Procrastination** (p. 203)—the postponement or needless delay of a project or task that must be done.
- **Goal** (p. 204)—an objective, a purpose, or an end that is to be achieved.
- **Tickler file** (p. 208)—a chronological record of items to be completed.
- **Shareware or trial software** (p. 209)—software that can be downloaded from the Web for a set trial period to determine if the program meets your needs.

DISCUSSION ITEMS

These discussion items provide an opportunity to test your understanding of the chapter through written responses and/or discussion with your classmates and your instructor.

1. Is all stress unhealthy? Explain your answer.
2. List and explain five causes of stress.
3. List and explain five ways you can manage your anger.
4. List and explain five time wasters.
5. What is PIM software, and how can it help you manage your time?

CRITICAL-THINKING ACTIVITY

Claudia Shaeffer has worked in human resources at AmeriAsian for five years. Claudia is in charge of employee benefits. She is an excellent employee—very competent, knowledgeable about human resources (holds an MBA, with a specialty in management), loyal, dependable, and respected by her colleagues. Two years ago, a new director of human resources was hired. Claudia has tried to work with him, but the situation does not get better; it merely gets worse. He gives her inadequate information. He asks her at the last minute to prepare reports. He lies to her about company policies and directions. Then, he yells at her about violating the directions of the company. On several occasions, Claudia has yelled back at him. She has never felt good about the situation when she allowed this to happen. She has talked with him repeatedly about the issues from her perspective. He seems to listen but never responds. He has never complained about her performance; she believes he is satisfied with her work. Claudia has considered leaving the job; however, she has two more years until she is vested in the retirement system. If she leaves now, she loses all of her retirement benefits. Recently, Claudia began to have health problems. She went to her physician, who said her illness was the result of stress. He also recommended that she take at least three months off. Claudia did so. The three months have passed, and Claudia is ready to come back to work.

What suggestions would you make to Claudia to decrease the stress on her job?

PROJECTS

Project 8-1 (Objectives 1, 2, and 5)

Analyze the case presented here. Then respond to the items following the case in a memorandum addressed to your instructor. Use the memorandum form on the Student CD, file SCDP8-1.

A friend of yours (Johanna) works in an office in your building. She is having problems. Her situation is described here.

JOHANNA'S SITUATION

Johanna has worked for the company for three years. Recently, she was promoted to administrative assistant for the president of the company. The job is a demanding one. Her responsibilities include setting up meetings, making travel arrangements for the president and the board of trustees, arranging meals before the monthly board meetings, and responding to calls from the board members about various items. In addition, she supervises two office assistants and takes minutes at the board meetings and at the biweekly staff meetings called by the president. She is responsible for numerous other projects as well.

Johanna is attempting to employ a new office assistant. This task is taking a long time. She is using a temporary employee until she can employ someone full time.

PROJECTS

(continued)

Johanna has four children. She and her husband are in the process of getting a divorce, which has been a difficult, emotional process. The situation at home is very stressful.

Johanna likes her job, but she is not being as effective as she usually is.

1. Are there stressors in Johanna's work environment? If so, what are they?
2. What are the stressors in Johanna's home environment?
3. What might Johanna do to reduce some of the stress?

Project 8-2 (Objectives 3 and 4)

On the Student CD, file SCDP8-2a is a screen from your PIM software and file SCDP8-2b an email message from Martin Albertson. Considering both of these documents, place your to-do list in priority order, adding the necessary items from Mr. Albertson's memo. Assign an A to the items you must attend to immediately, a B to the items you should deal with this week, and a C to the items you should begin work on as soon as possible but that have no immediate deadlines. Print out your new prioritized to-do list, and submit it to your instructor.

Project 8-3 (Objectives 3 and 4)

On the Student CD, file SCDP8-3a is a time log form. Print out five copies of the form. For the next five days, use the form to log the time you spend on various activities. If you are employed, log the time you spend at workday activities. If you are not employed, log the time you spend at personal activities.

After you finish that part of the project, analyze the way you spent your time during the five days. Student CD, file SCDP8-3b contains questions to help you analyze your time. Student CD, file SCDP8-3c contains a Time Effectiveness Questionnaire, which provides general questions concerning the use of time. Respond to these items. After you have analyzed the way you use your time and considered your answers to the Time Effectiveness Questionnaire, prepare an action plan using the form on the Student CD, file SCDP8-3d. Indicate what you will be doing to make more effective use of your time. Print out

one copy of your action plan, and submit it to your instructor.

Project 8-4 (Objectives 5 and 6)

Frederick, a friend of yours who has worked for AmeriAsian for two years, is extremely unhappy in his job. He has confided in you about the office situation and has asked for your analysis of what is happening. Respond to the questions at the end of this case by writing a memorandum to your instructor, giving your suggestions. Use the memorandum form on the Student CD, file SCDP8-4.

FREDERICK'S SITUATION

Recently, several personnel cutbacks have taken place in Frederick's department. Now there are only two administrative assistants in the department; previously there were four. The other remaining administrative assistant has been with the company for only six months. Since Frederick knows the operations well, having been with the company for two years, he has been asked to assume most of the responsibilities of the two assistants who left.

Frederick has always felt good about his abilities. He is able to produce large amounts of work quickly. However, for the last two months, he has not been able to see the top of his desk. His supervisor has become irritated with him on several occasions when work was not completed on time. There never seems to be an end to the amount of work stacked on his desk; he cannot get caught up. Frederick has not been feeling well or sleeping well lately. He wakes up two or three times a night, thinking about the office. He has resorted to taking sleeping pills in order to get some rest at night.

Additionally, Frederick has been having trouble with the other administrative assistant, Maria Gustavo. Frederick has gotten very angry with her on several occasions. Frederick's anger has demonstrated itself in the following ways:

- Frederick yelled at Maria for not helping him with his workload. Maria has been doing her job, but she has not offered to help Frederick. She does not believe she has the time; she can barely keep up with her own work.

- Frederick called Maria incompetent when she asked for his help on an assignment. Frederick has always been willing to help Maria in the past; she does not understand why he is not willing to help her now. She believes she deserves the help since she has only been with the company for six months. The second time he called her incompetent, she became so upset that she screamed at him.

1. Identify the factors that have contributed to Frederick's anger and stress.
2. What steps can Frederick take to manage his anger?
3. What steps can Frederick take to control his stress?

Project 8-5 (Objectives 5 and 6)
Collaborative Project
Online Project

Work with three of your classmates on this project. Using the Web, search for three recent articles on the following:

- Controlling stress
- Managing anger

Tip: You may want to use www.google.com as your search engine.

Present your findings to the class. Turn in a written report of your findings to your instructor; cite all your references.

Project 8-6 (Objectives 5 and 6)

Add to the Professional Growth Plan that you began in Chapter 1 by describing how you can control your stress and manage your anger in the future. In preparing this plan, do the following:

- Identify the stressors that you have in your life at the present time. These stressors may be at home, at school, or at the office.
- Identify ways in which you can relieve these stressors.
- Identify situations that make you angry at the present time.
- Identify ways you can manage that anger.
- Identify ways you will seek to control stress and manage anger in the future.

Save your plan on your Professional Growth Plan disk under "Progro8-6."

ENGLISH USAGE CHALLENGE DRILL

Correct the following sentences. Cite the grammar rule that is applicable to each sentence. Before you begin, refresh your memory by reviewing capitalization in the Reference Guide of this text.

1. He gave three reasons for not being on time: (1) bad weather caused traffic slowdowns. (2) the time listed on his calendar was incorrect. (3) he had to stop for gasoline.
2. The reasons for the delay were: Bad weather, poor scheduling, and Equipment failure.
3. "Of course," she added, "The project will take time."
4. I was introduced to senator George Aikens.
5. Mr. Monroe is President of the company.

ASSESSMENT OF CHAPTER OBJECTIVES

Now that you have completed the chapter and the projects, take a few minutes to review the chapter learning objectives. For your convenience, the objectives are repeated here. Did you accomplish these objectives? If you were unable to accomplish the objectives, give your reasons for not doing so.

1. Define the causes of stress.   Yes _____   No _____

_____

_____

_____

2. Identify stress reducers.   Yes _____   No _____

_____

_____

_____

3. Identify time wasters.   Yes _____   No _____

_____

_____

_____

4. Manage time.   Yes _____   No _____

_____

_____

_____

5. Control stress.   Yes _____   No _____

_____

_____

_____

6. Manage anger.   Yes _____   No _____

_____

_____

_____

You may submit your answers in writing to your instructor, using the memorandum form on the Student CD, SCDAP8-1.

DEBRA L. TRAHAIR'S SOLUTION

As I worked with the individual, I listened intently to what was said. I tried to put my individual feelings aside and sort through what was being said to determine the facts of the situation. I completed my work to the best of my ability. I was never rude; I kept a smile on my face and a positive tone in my voice, realizing I was not the problem. I listened, listened, and listened some more.

I also worked closely with my immediate supervisor. We developed a wonderful working relationship. We worked through each negative encounter with this individual openly and honestly. My supervisor knew I had no ulterior motives. Regardless of how heated the situation became, my supervisor and I supported one another while trying to find ways to work with the person. At one point, we went together for professional counseling, which was very helpful. I learned how not to carry the situation home—at least not as overtly as I had done in the past.

Although it was a very trying time, I grew from the strength of trusting myself and being true to my beliefs. I became a stronger person. I did my very best every day and learned to let go of the negatives of the situation.

A Success Profile

Barbara D. Griggs, CPS/CAP

Administrative Assistant

Pharmacia Corporation
Peapack, New Jersey

Although I took office administration courses in high school, I really did not think I would spend the better part of my working years as an administrative assistant. In 1983, I completed a three-month course at Cittone Institute (a local New Jersey business college) where I learned Wang® word processing. After completing the course, I worked at a local towlift and machinery company for a few months as a temporary employee in the accounts payable department. The company

offered me a permanent position as the sales secretary. I supported the sales personnel and the executive vice president. Subsequently, a personnel agency arranged an interview for me at Johnson & Johnson Baby Products (now J&J Consumer Products). I was hired. In this position, I provided secretarial support to two engineering managers and between 15 and 20 chemical and process engineers. I also provided assistance for the lead secretary, who supported the director of engineering. I was responsible for typing purchase orders, collating monthly reports, making travel arrangements, and keeping the department organized. Occasionally there were conflicts; in such a large group, someone always wanted his or her purchase order or travel reservations taken care of before anyone else's. My goal was to work out those conflicts without involving the manager. Most often I was able

to do so; but with so many personalities and needs, the department manager occasionally had to intervene. However, I was paying attention. Important to being successful as an administrative assistant is the development of your interpersonal skills. Knowing how to respond to a request with efficiency, friendliness, and tact makes a big difference in an administrative assistant's career. I find interacting with different people to be challenging but interesting. I am also an observer of people.

My next position was in the national accounts department. This position was one of my favorite assignments. I supported the director of national accounts, who traveled three or four days a week. I also supported four regional directors in various locations across the country with whatever requests they had of the home office. It seemed to be the goal of

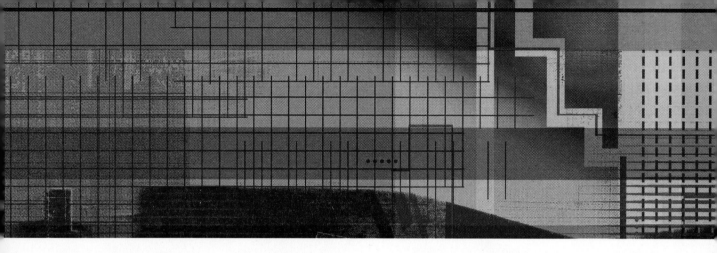

the director to teach me every administrative detail of his department so I could answer questions and assist others in his absence. Because of his attitude, my confidence as an assistant soared. I was involved in calculating commission checks, sending out products for demonstration, writing sales letters, transcribing dictation, and assisting other secretaries in the office on an as-needed basis. Looking back, it was an easy, common-sense type of position. But more important, the director seemed to be personally concerned about my success and future with the company.

During those years with Johnson & Johnson, I made a point of being involved in company initiatives and reading everything that came across my desk. I joined Professional Secretaries International (now IAAP) in 1989 and became certified as a professional secretary (CPS) in 1991. I held increasing levels of responsibility in the local PSI chapter as well as on the job. In 1996, I received an associate degree in Liberal Arts from Thomas Edison State College, which I obtained mostly via distance and online learning. In that same year, I became a Competent Toastmaster (CTM) through Toastmasters International. During the 14½ years I was employed by Johnson & Johnson, I held many interesting and challenging positions. The company generously supported my

education and attendance at other seminars related to my job.

In 1998, I accepted a position with a pharmaceutical company that was new to New Jersey—Pharmacia® & Upjohn®. I was quite apprehensive about changing employers. I had no prior knowledge about the company, but my research revealed it to be an up-and-coming company. Now after three years, I can honestly say I am glad I took the risk and changed employers.

In my present position for the vice president and development coordinator of research and development, I manage the R&D seating plan for office space, attend meetings in the vice president's stead, travel to off-site meetings to support the executives in attendance, participate in training the R&D staff when we upgrade to new software, and perform routine administrative duties. Once again I have found myself with an executive who does not mind sharing his expertise. He is an excellent coach and challenges me to pursue higher goals within the company and in IAAP. In 2001, I received the Certified Administrative Professional designation; and at the International Association of Administrative Professional's International and Education Forum, I was elected the International Director, Northeast District, for a second term.

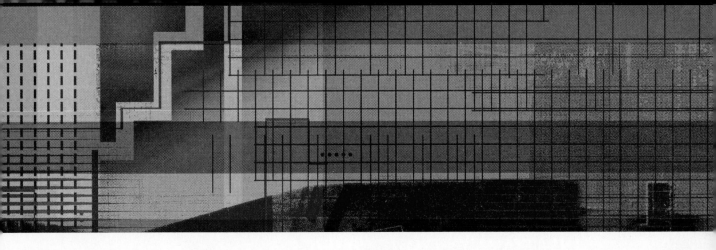

BARBARA GRIGGS' CASE

In 1998, I was working for a vice president. On my second day of employment, the company sent me (on one of the company's jets) to Kalamazoo, Michigan. I was to meet and be trained by the vice president's previous assistant.

This executive traveled much of the time, so we had few opportunities to sit and talk about the business and get to know each other. The company relied heavily on email correspondence. The vice president and I communicated by email several times a day and by telephone once or twice a day. I believed we had developed a good working relationship, but when he was in the office, it was another story. I always seemed to be a step behind. I thought I was performing my job well, but I soon came to realize I was not meeting his needs as well as either he or I had expected. I was confounded because I had just come from a company and culture where I was considered to be a proficient assistant. I just needed to find out what I could do to make his job easier. And, I really did not know where to turn.

Decide how you would have handled the situation. Then turn to the end of Part 4 (page 267) to see how I solved the situation.

LETTERS, MEMOS, AND REPORTS

LEARNING OBJECTIVES

1. Identify the characteristics of effective correspondence.
2. Compose letters and memos.
3. Research and write a business report.
4. *Observe ethical and legal obligations in written correspondence.*

The importance of communication pervades not only our verbal communications but our written communications as well. In Chapter 2, you developed skills for communicating effectively in our multicultural workforce. You learned that if you are to be effective in your job, good verbal and nonverbal communication skills are essential. Letters, memos, and reports as well as email (introduced in Chapter 5) are among the major communication documents in the workplace. Depending on the effectiveness of the writer of these documents, goodwill or ill will for the organization (and the writer) may be created. Thus, you need to add another communication skill to your list of qualifications if you are to be a truly effective administrative professional—the ability to compose effective business documents. This chapter will help you attain the necessary skills; practice will help you perfect these skills.

TYPES OF WRITTEN MESSAGES

The basic types of written messages that the administrative professional prepares are memorandums, email, letters, and reports. (Since email correspondence was covered in Chapter 5, it will not be addressed here except to cite some of its advantages. However, you may want to review that portion of Chapter 5 now.) As you begin your career, you may be asked to prepare routine correspondence, such as email and interoffice memorandums. As you learn more about the organization and demonstrate to your employer your writing skills, the complexity and number of your writing assignments will probably increase. You should establish a goal now to become an excellent communicator through the written word. No matter what type of position you hold, written communication skills are invaluable to both you and the organization.

Memorandums

Although email has become the communication vehicle of choice for most interoffice correspondence due to its many advantages, some of which are discussed here, memorandums are still written, particularly when the message is longer than a paragraph or two.

Advantages of Email over Memorandums

- Email reaches its destination in a matter of seconds, even if that destination is across the world.
- Multiple individuals may be sent the same message quickly, with all addressees receiving the information instantaneously.
- It is not necessary to make a hard copy of email, thereby saving paper.
- Email may be filed electronically on the computer and retrieved as needed, or email may be destroyed immediately after the person receiving the message reads it.
- The date and time of the email are automatically printed on the document so both the writer and the recipient have a record of when it was sent.

The hard-copy memorandum generally is written when the message is a fairly long one and will not fit on one computer screen. Although an email can be longer than one computer screen, the general rule is that an email needs to be a very short communication. An email several screens in length becomes cumbersome for the recipient who must go back and forth between screens to review the message.

Characteristics of Effective Memorandums

In memorandums, just as in letters or reports, it is essential that you adhere to the effective correspondence guidelines presented in the section of this chapter entitled "Effective Correspondence." For example, memorandums must be clear, concise, simple, complete, considerate, correct, prompt, and positive. These requirements are explained in more detail later. Additionally, certain guidelines are unique to memorandums, including the appropriate format addressed here.

Memorandums are usually written on a preprinted form. This form generally contains the word *memorandum* and the following elements:

- Organizational logo
- *To* line
- *From* line
- *Date* line

- *Subject* line
- *pc* (photocopy) or *cc* (courtesy copy) if copies are being sent to other individuals

When filling out the "To" portion of the memo, know what your company preferences are and follow them. For example, here are some general rules.

- Use the first name (or initial) and last name of the individual.
- Use the job title of the individual if it is company procedure to do so; many organizations do not use titles in memorandums.
- Do not use *Ms.* or *Mr.*
- List the names in alphabetical order or by hierarchical order within the company.
- If you are addressing a memo to ten or more people, use a generic classification, such as "TQM Team." When sending memorandums, you may use specially designed envelopes. These envelopes are reusable and are generally large enough that standard-size stationery can be inserted without folding. An example of an interoffice envelope is shown in Figure 9-1.

INTER-DEPARTMENT DELIVERY				
Note–Cross Out Entire Line When Received and Re-Use Until All Lines Are Full.				
Date	Deliver to	Department	Sent by	Department
	◯		◯	
	◯		◯	
	◯		◯	

Figure 9-1   Interoffice Envelope

- List *pc* or *cc* recipients alphabetically or hierarchically, whichever is company procedure.
- If the memorandum is more than one page, key the additional pages on plain paper. Key the names of the individual(s) receiving the memo, date, and page number at the top of all additional pages.

Figure 9-2 illustrates a memorandum. Notice the memorandum uses side headings. This approach helps the reader scan the memo quickly and easily. Such an approach also helps the writer to focus on and clarify the message.

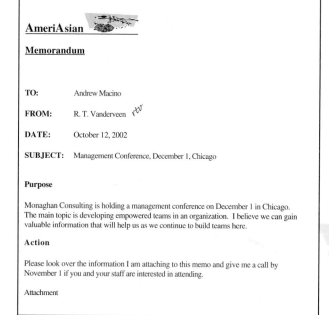

AmeriAsian

Memorandum

TO: Andrew Macino

FROM: R. T. Vanderveen

DATE: October 12, 2002

SUBJECT: Management Conference, December 1, Chicago

Purpose

Monaghan Consulting is holding a management conference on December 1 in Chicago. The main topic is developing empowered teams in an organization. I believe we can gain valuable information that will help us as we continue to build teams here.

Action

Please look over the information I am attaching to this memo and give me a call by November 1 if you and your staff are interested in attending.

Attachment

Figure 9-2   Sample Interoffice Memorandum

Letters

One of the first letters you may be asked to write as a beginning administrative professional is a routine one, such as a letter requesting information. These letters are usually very direct, with the first paragraph requesting the information, the second paragraph providing additional information needed, and the third paragraph specifying the action the writer wants and expressing appreciation to the reader for responding to the request. Once your employer is confident in your skills, he or she may ask you to compose letters in draft or final form for his or her signature. Whatever role you play in the composition of letters, the principles set forth in this chapter will help you be successful.

Reports

In addition to memorandums and letters, numerous reports are prepared in the workplace. These reports may be informal reports of two or three pages, or they may be formal reports containing a table of contents, the body of the report (with footnotes or endnotes), appendices, and a bibliography. You will learn more about writing reports in a later section of this chapter.

EFFECTIVE CORRESPONDENCE

If a written communication is to accomplish its goal, the writer must adhere to certain principles, which are presented here.

Clear, Concise, and Simple

The reader should be able to determine without a doubt the purpose of the correspondence. Writing clearly requires good organization and simple expression. Conciseness in writing

Communication Tip:

To add crispness to your business communications, avoid redundancies, such as *consensus of opinion. Consensus* is all that is necessary.

- Keep your sentences short. Sentences should vary in structure and in length but on average should be no more than 15 to 20 words. Consider the following examples of a sentence that is too long and the shortened, more effective sentence.

  Long sentence: *In answer to your letter of June 12, I wish to tell you how pleased and happy I am with your asking me to speak at the meeting on July 12 and to tell you that it will give me great pleasure to speak to your group.*

  Short sentence: *Thank you for the invitation to speak at your meeting on June 12. I will be delighted to do so.*

- Use the simple rather than the complex approach. If a shorter word will suffice, use it. You should not use business correspondence to impress the reader with the breadth of your vocabulary. The aim of business correspondence is to get your purpose across in a simple, concise manner. Write to express rather than impress. An effective writer can express complex ideas in clear, simple terms. For example, rather than writing *endeavor to ascertain,* use *try to find out.* Rather than writing *elucidate your meaning,* use *clarify your meaning.*

- Write as you speak. Ask yourself how you would say something if the reader were sitting next to you. A conversational tone is usually appropriate. (This tone may not be suitable for international correspondence. A section later in this chapter will present the principles of writing internationally.)

- Edit unnecessary words. Verbosity (using too many words) weakens writing. Make sure every word is essential. Practice editing unnecessary words. You might be able to cut as much as one-half of the length of your correspondence. Consider the following example containing unnecessary words and its concise rewrite:

  Excessive: *At this point in time, I must tell you that our plant will be closed due to the remodeling of*

our facilities. We have wanted to remodel our facilities for the last five years but have been unable to do so due to the large demands of our customers for products. We have every confidence in our ability to complete the remodeling and get your order out by July 15.*

  Concise: *Since our plant will be closed for remodeling from June 1 to June 15, your order will be shipped on July 15.*

- Use active verbs. Active verbs can bring life to your sentences by emphasizing action. For example, say "We received your order for ten modular units today," not "Your order for ten modular units was received today."

- Vary your style. Keep your writing interesting by varying your sentence structure, length, and vocabulary.

- Avoid clichés. You have probably read such phrases as a*ccording to our records, at your earliest convenience,* and *under separate cover.* These phrases are clichés; they are overused. Notice the following clichés and the improved wording.

  Cliché: *According to our files*
  Improved: *Our files indicate*

  Cliché: *At the present time*
  Improved: *Now*

  Cliché: *In view of the fact that*
  Improved: *Because*

  Cliché: *By return mail*
  Improved: *Mail today*

  Cliché: *May I take the liberty*
  Improved: Omit the phrase and make your statement.

  Cliché: *Your kind letter*
  Improved: Omit *kind*—people, not letters, are kind.

Figure 9-3

means that you express the necessary information in as few words as possible. Say what you need to say without cluttering your correspondence with irrelevant information, needless words, or flowery phrases. Simple means that you use words that are easily understood; you do not try to impress the reader with your vocabulary. Principles to assist you in writing clearly, concisely, and simply are given in Figure 9-3.

Complete

A business document is complete if it gives the reader all the information needed so the intended results are achieved. To help you achieve completeness in your writing, ask yourself these W questions.

- *Why* is the correspondence being written?
- *What* is the goal of the correspondence?
- *What* information is needed before writing the correspondence?
- *Who* needs to receive the correspondence?
- *What* information needs to be included in the correspondence?

Refer to Figure 9-4 for examples of ineffective writing when the W questions were not asked and corresponding examples of effective writing when the W questions were asked.

USE THE W QUESTIONS

Here are some examples of ineffective writing when the W questions were not asked followed by effective writing when the W questions were asked.

- Ineffective: Your order will be mailed soon. (When?)
- Effective: Your order will be mailed October 9.

- Ineffective: We will offer a seminar on May 12. (Where and what kind of seminar?)
- Effective: We will offer an effective letter-writing seminar in the Executive Conference Room at 2 p.m. on May 31.

Figure 9-4

Considerate

Being considerate in correspondence means that you use good human relations skills. Treat the reader with respect and friendliness, and write as if you care about the reader. When dealing with people face-to-face, courtesy and consideration are necessary in order to develop and maintain goodwill. The same or even greater concern must be evident in written correspondence since only the written word conveys the message; a smile, a nod, or a friendly gesture cannot be seen.

Never show your anger in business correspondence. You may be extremely unhappy about a situation, but to express your anger merely compounds the problem. Angry words make angry readers. Both parties may end up "yelling" at one another through the written word, and little is accomplished. Being considerate also means being believable. If a person asks you something, respond to the question. If you are unable to respond, explain why. If you must respond negatively, explain why. An explanation lets others know you are sincere.

Being considerate also means using *please* and *thank you* often. Do not be afraid to apologize when you make an error. We are all human; we all make mistakes. A courteous apology builds credibility and goodwill. Use these courteous phrases often.

We appreciate . . .
Thank you for . . .
Please let me know . . .
I apologize for . . .
You were very kind to . . .
You were very nice to . . .

Correct

Correctness in business writing means using correct grammar and mechanics, appropriate format, and careful proofreading. When you make errors in writing, you send a message to the reader that you are careless or, even worse, uneducated or lacking in intelligence.

Spelling, grammar, punctuation, capitalization, and sentence structure must be correct. To assist you in catching errors, use the grammar and spell check on your computer. However, remember that grammar and spell check features do not catch all errors. For example, if you use *your* rather than *you're*, the error will not be detected. Thus, you must have good grammar and spelling skills. In addition, you must be a good proofreader. Proofreading tips are given in Figure 9-5.

Correctness means using the correct format. Readers expect business letters and reports to follow recommended styles and formats. If you use a nonstandard format, you run the risk of detracting from the message by drawing the reader's attention to its layout rather than its

- Use your grammar and spell check feature.
- Proofread your document on the screen before you print. Scroll to the beginning of the document, and use the top of the screen as a guide for your eye in reading each line.
- Proofread a document in three steps.
  a. General appearance and format
  b. Spelling and keyboarding errors
  c. Punctuation, word usage, and content
- Read from right to left for spelling and keyboarding errors.
- If possible, do not proofread a document right after keying it; let it sit while you perform some other task.
- Pay attention to dates. Do not assume that they are correct. Check to determine that Thursday, June 18, is actually a Thursday, for example. Check the spelling of months; check the correctness of the year.

- Do not overlook proofreading the date, the subject, the enclosure notation, and the names and addresses of the recipients.
- Use a thesaurus if you are not certain a word is appropriate.
- Watch closely for omissions of *-ed, -ing,* or *-s* at the end of words.
- Be consistent in the use of commas.
- Be consistent in the use of capital letters.
- Check numbers.
- Be consistent in format.
- Keep a good reference manual at your desk to look up any grammar or punctuation rules you question.

Figure 9-5

contents. Standard formats for business letters and reports are given in the Reference Guide of this textbook.

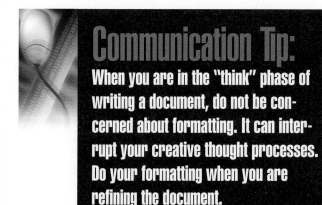

Communication Tip:

When you are in the "think" phase of writing a document, do not be concerned about formatting. It can interrupt your creative thought processes. Do your formatting when you are refining the document.

Correctness also includes accuracy. Although you cannot be perfect, you should do your best to be accurate. Get the facts before you begin the business correspondence. Check your information carefully. If you are quoting prices, be certain you have the latest price list. If you are presenting dates, confirm the dates. If you are giving sales figures, double-check the figures. Verify the correct spelling of any names used in the letter.

Prompt

The conscientious business correspondent is concerned about being on time. Prompt messages convey to the reader that the writer and organization care. Conversely, late messages convey several negative impressions, some of which are listed here.

- The writer or organization does not care about maintaining a positive relationship with the reader or the organization.
- The writer or organization is grossly inefficient.
- The writer or organization is indifferent to the needs of the reader or the organization.

In general, replies to routine letters and memorandums should be sent within three to five days. Urgent messages (such as urgent email or mail sent by overnight delivery, for example) should be answered immediately (within 24 hours).

Positive

It is easier to hear the word *yes* than to hear the word *no.* It is easier to accept a concern than it is to accept a complaint. Positivism gives the reader a favorable impression of the person, service, or product. It helps the reader respond the way the writer intends. A positive tone is set by the words the writer chooses and how she or he uses those words. For example, some words possess positive qualities while other words possess negative qualities. Figure 9-6 gives some positive and negative expressions. However, even a negative statement can be written in a positive tone. For example, "Do not litter" can be changed to "Please deposit all trash in the nearest receptacle." To which statement would you be more likely to respond?

POSITIVE AND NEGATIVE WORDS

Positive	Negative
Glad	Sorry
Immediately	Whenever possible
Pleasure	Displeasure
Satisfactory	Unsatisfactory
Please let us know.	You failed to let us know.
Please send your check.	You neglected to send your check.
Your order will be shipped.	I hate to inform you that your order has not been shipped.

Figure 9-6

Appropriate in Tone

You set the entire **tone** (the manner of expression in writing) of the letter, whether that tone is positive or negative, by considering your reader first and carefully choosing your words. You should establish a positive tone at the beginning of a letter and carry that positive tone throughout. In establishing a positive tone, you should adhere to the concepts spelled out in the previous sections. These concepts are as follows:

- Conciseness
- Completeness
- Consideration
- Correctness

- Promptness
- Positivism

In other words, as you have learned in these sections, you should write in a conversational tone—one that is appropriate for the reader. You should write to express your thoughts—not to impress the reader. You should treat the reader with respect and friendliness; you should never show anger. By using the words *please* and *thank you* and referring to the reader by name, you tell the reader that you care about him or her. Being prompt says to the reader that you care about the individual and the organization. By expressing statements in a positive rather than a negative manner, you help give the reader a favorable impression of you and your organization. If you carefully and consistently heed these guidelines, you will set a positive tone for the reader. In the process, you will have served your organization well.

Figure 9-7 illustrates the importance of tone. This figure shows a letter written in a positive tone (adhering to the concepts set forth) and a letter written in a negative tone. As a reader, to which letter would you respond favorably? Notice the first letter is written from the writer's point of view. There is no consideration of the reader; in fact, the writer is almost condescending to the reader. The overall tone of the letter is negative.

Effective in Paragraphing

Effective paragraphs possess unity, coherence, and parallel construction.

Unity

A paragraph has unity when all its sentences clarify or help support the main idea. All sentences in the paragraph must relate to the main idea. The sentence that contains the main idea of a paragraph is called the **topic sentence.** This sentence shapes the content of the paragraph. In the paragraph below, the topic sentence is the first sentence.

A management conference is being held on December 1 in Chicago. The major focus of the conference is on developing empowered

McBEE CONSULTING
811 Oakridge SE
Kentwood, MI 49512
616-555-0150

November 19, 2003

Ms. Cordelia Ramsey
AmeriAsian Airlines
5519 Reeds Parkway
Grand Rapids, MI 49509-3295

Dear Ms. Ramsey:

Do you write letters frequently? If so, are you sometimes unable to find the right words to let the customer know you care about her or him?

If you answered "yes" to these questions, you are certainly among the majority of writers. As you know, writing can be a difficult process. All of us sometimes have writer's block. We can't decide how to say what we mean or say it effectively.

Join us and a number of individuals who work in positions similar to yours for a writing seminar on Tuesday, October 25, from 9 a.m. until 3 p.m. in the conference room of our office on 811 Oakridge SE. The cost for the day is $150—a small price to pay for hearing a noted communication theorist, Abraham Gassell, and having a chance to learn from your colleagues about their writing techniques. Lunch is included in the price.

Just mail the enclosed card by October 1. I hope to see you soon.

Sincerely,

Marvin Hanley
Marvin Hanley
Communication Consultant

McBEE CONSULTING
811 Oakridge SE
Kentwood, MI 49512
616-555-0150

November 19, 2003

Ms. Cordelia Ramsey
AmeriAsian Airlines
5519 Reeds Parkway
Grand Rapids, MI 49509-3295

Dear Ms. Ramsey:

Since we at McBee Consulting know that most people have trouble writing letters, we are having a one-day seminar on letter writing that you must not miss. We have put together a program that will be beneficial for you. After our seminar, you will have no trouble explaining to your reader exactly what you expect of him or her and getting what you want.

Give my office a call at 555-0150 to register. We are looking forward to your positive response to this letter.

Sincerely,

Rhonda Edwards
Rhonda Edwards
Training Consultant

Figure 9-7   Letters with positive and negative tones.

teams in an organization. Please look over the information enclosed and give me a call by November 10 if you are interested in attending.

The topic sentence is not always the first sentence. It may be at the beginning or end of the paragraph, or it may even be implied. The point to remember is that the topic sentence helps the writer stay focused on one main idea for the paragraph.

Coherence

A paragraph has coherence when its sentences are related to each other in content, in grammatical construction, and in choice of words. Each sentence should be written so the paragraph flows from one thought to the next in a coherent fashion. The following sentences represent coherence in content and construction:

> "There is only one social responsibility of business. That responsibility is for business to use its resources and engage in activities designed to increase its profits so long as it stays within the rules of the game." Those words are fighting words today even more than when they were written nearly 40 years ago by Nobel Prize–winning economist Milton Friedman. The great debate over business's responsibility to society, which bubbled in the '60s and '70s, is exploding now.[1]

Coherence can be achieved by repeating key words in a paragraph or using certain words for emphasis. Consider the following use of repetitive words.

> The anthropologist Elena Padilla describes life in a squalid district of New York by telling how much people know about each other—*who* is to be trusted and *who* not, *who* is defiant of the law and *who* upholds it, *who* is competent and well and informed, and *who* is inept and ignorant.

In an excerpt from an article in *Fortune* on multitasking, notice how the author uses *and* and *but*, and contractions in the first paragraph. Notice also how he uses repetition in the last paragraph of the article.

> Last night I was in a Chinese restaurant. At the next table there was a young woman with a fork in one hand and a cell phone in the other, using her mouth to chew and talk at the same time . . . All of a sudden a goblet of water went flying off her table. Bang! Crash! *And* still she went on, multitasking . . . *That's* the thing about multitasking. Some people can do it in such a way that each of their multiple tasks is accomplished as if it had been the subject of unique concentration. *But* not many. Most people are as lousy at multitasking as they are at everything else . . .
>
> *I will* spend time with my family when at home . . .
> *I will not* watch TV and go online at the same time.
> *I will not* watch TV, go online, and listen to MP3s at the same time.
> *I will not* watch TV, go online, listen to MP3s, check my stocks, talk on the phone, and toast an English muffin at the same time.[2]

The writer used the conjunctions *and* and *but* to begin a sentence. At one point, we were taught not to use conjunctions to begin sentences. However, this rule no longer holds true. In fact, according to the *Harper Dictionary of Contemporary Usage*, it is perfectly acceptable to use *and* at the beginning of a sentence. Notice that the writer uses a contraction. We were taught in the past not to use contractions. However, contractions are perfectly acceptable in most writing today—in all but the most formal of writings.

Parallel Structure

Parallel structure helps you achieve coherence in a paragraph. **Parallelism** is created when grammatically equivalent forms are used within a sentence. Consider the parallel construction used in the following paragraph.

> Superstitions are *sometimes smiled at, sometimes frowned on, sometimes seen as*

---

[1]Geoffrey Colvin, "Should Companies Care?" *Fortune*, June 11, 2001, 60.
[2]Stanley Bing, "Walk Now, Chew Gum Later," *Fortune*, September 17, 2001, 61–62.

old-fashioned, and *sometimes seen as backwoods*. Nevertheless, they give all of us ways of moving back and forth among our different worlds—*the sacred, the secular,* and *the scientific.*

The following sentence illustrates nonparallel and parallel construction.

Nonparallel: The position is prestigious, challenging, and *also the money isn't bad.*

Parallel: The position offers prestige, challenge, and money.

Concerned with Readability Level

Readability is the degree of difficulty of the message. Items that contribute to a greater reading difficulty include long sentences and words with several syllables and/or very technical terms. Readability formulas such as the Gunning Fog Index and the Flesch-Kincaid Index provide readability indices. The higher the readability index is, the less readable the message. Business messages should be written to achieve a readability index between 7 and 11. This means that what you have already learned about short words and short sentences should be followed. You want the letter, memo, or report to be clearly understood by the reader. Obviously, if the document is not understood, the message is ineffective.

Formal reports that include technical or scientific terms may have a readability index of 14 or higher due to their complexity. However, these reports are not written for a general audience, but for an audience with the background and educational level to comprehend the report.

THE CORRESPONDENCE PLAN

To be effective, correspondence must be well planned and organized. For a formal report, you should make an outline before beginning. If you are a beginner at writing letters, you may find that making notes on a scratch pad will help you organize your thoughts. As you become more experienced in writing letters and informal reports, you may make only a mental outline of what you want to write. However, a formal report always requires an outline. Whatever the case, planning before writing saves you time and lessens any frustrations you may experience.

The steps in the planning process are as follows:

- Determine the objective
- Consider the reader
- Gather the facts

Determine the Objective

When writing letters or reports, determine what your objective is. Why are you writing the letter or report? What do you hope to accomplish? Business messages generally have one of three primary objectives: to inform the reader, to request an action or information, and to persuade the reader to take action or accept an idea. Some business messages have more than one objective. For example, the objectives may be to inform and persuade. What does the reader need to know about the subject? Will the reader want or need background information or support data? If your

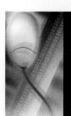

Communication Tip:
If you are trying to avoid using certain words when you are writing, delete them from your spell checker's dictionary. Then if you mistakenly use them, the computer will flag them, giving you an opportunity to change the word.

task is to persuade someone to accept an offer, consider what it would take to convince the person to say "yes."

Consider the Reader

Who will receive your letter or report? How much does the person receiving the document know about the subject? Is the reader familiar with technical jargon that might be used? What is the educational level of the reader? What effect will the message have on the reader? Will the reader react favorably or unfavorably to the message? How much time does the reader have? Is the reader a busy executive who prefers short, concise memos, letters, and reports? Or does the reader need a great deal of supporting information and detail?

Gather the Facts

Before you begin to write a letter, memorandum, or report, gather all the necessary facts. If you are writing a letter or memorandum, ask yourself the W questions: Who? What? When? Where? Why? For example, assume your employer asks you to find an appropriate video on organizational ethics. You plan to write to several video companies to find out what videos are available. What do you need to tell the company so you get the most appropriate video for your organization's needs? Ask these questions before you begin.

- Who will be viewing the video?
- What type of knowledge do these people already have about ethics?
- What price range is appropriate?

If you are writing a report, here are some W questions to ask.

- Who is the audience? Who will read the report?
- What level of expertise about the subject do the readers have?
- Where can I obtain the information needed for the report? Do I need to research the subject? Is information available through library research, or must I do original research?

- What level of detail is important to the reader?
- What level of formality is important? In other words, should there be a title page? a table of contents? a reference section? recommendations? an executive summary?
- Who should review the draft document of the report?
- Who is responsible for making recommendations? Am I responsible or should I work with someone in developing the recommendations?
- Assuming an executive summary is needed, who is responsible for writing it?

Seek Help from Software Packages

You have learned that the readability level should be between 7 and 11. If you are a beginning writer, you may want to check the readability level of your writing. Grammar software packages contain a readability formula such as the Gunning Fog Index or the Flesch-Kincaid Index. Within a matter of seconds, you can obtain the readability of your material.

You have learned that you should use the grammar and spell check feature on your word-processing software. You can quickly identify misspelled words by using the spell checker. You also know the spell checker will not detect all spelling errors. It will not detect such words as *to* for *too* and *here* for *hear*. If you are not a good speller, you may have someone who spells well proofread your material. Check your spelling expertise by responding to Self-Check A.

Grammar programs can help you find grammatical errors. They flag punctuation and capitalization errors. They also let you know

Communication Tip:

Do not mix metaphors; e.g., *roar like a cat* is a mixed metaphor.

Chapter 9: Letters, Memos, and Reports

- accesible _____
- accurate _____
- appearence _____
- calender _____
- changeable _____
- comittment _____
- dilema _____
- embarrass _____
- exhorbitant _____
- fourty _____
- harass _____
- maintanence _____
- milage _____
- ninty _____
- occasionally _____
- parallel _____
- priviledge _____
- recieve _____
- succeed _____
- superintendant _____

when you have used the passive voice. A thesaurus helps you develop your vocabulary by suggesting alternatives for words you have used.

LETTERS

Letters are more formal than email or memorandums. A letter represents the company to the outside public—customers, clients, and prospective customers and clients. A well-written letter can win friends and customers. Conversely, a poorly written letter can lose customers and make enemies of prospective customers. One of your tasks as an administrative professional is assisting your employer

with writing effective letters or writing letters yourself for her or his signature. Here are additional suggestions for writing effective letters.

Classify and Organize the Type of Message

Letters can be classified into the following four categories according to the anticipated reader reaction:

Type of Message	*Anticipated Reader Reaction*
Favorable	Positive
Routine	Neutral
Unfavorable	Negative
Persuasive	Interested—Indifferent

Favorable messages are those messages the reader will be pleased to receive. A favorable message might be a letter offering someone a job or a letter congratulating someone on a promotion.

Routine messages have a neutral effect on the receiver. Many letters are routine messages, such as letters requesting information or letters relaying information.

Unfavorable messages include messages that bring a negative reaction from the reader, such as a letter turning down a job applicant.

Persuasive messages attempt to get the reader to take some action. For example, a letter to a busy executive trying to convince him or her to speak at a conference is a persuasive letter.

The type of message determines the organization of the letter or memorandum.

Type of Message	*Organization*
Favorable	Direct
Routine (neutral)	Direct
Unfavorable	Indirect
Persuasive	Indirect (Persuasive Approach)

Direct

If the reader's reaction to your message will be favorable or neutral, you should use the **direct approach.** Much of the routine correspondence you write falls into this category. Direct correspondence should have the following components:

- Begin with the reason for the correspondence. If you are making a request or an inquiry, state that request or inquiry.

    Do you sell a combination PDA and cellular phone?

- Continue with whatever explanation is necessary so the reader will understand the message.

    If so, please provide me with the capabilities of your product and the price. Send me any literature you have, including the price of your product.

- Close the letter with a thank-you for action that has been taken or with a request that action be taken by a specific date.

    I need the information by January 15; please respond using the address given in the letterhead. Thank you for your assistance.

The checklist presented in Figure 9-8 will help you as you begin to write favorable and routine letters.

Indirect

When your message to the reader will cause an unfavorable reaction, your best approach is an **indirect approach.** At times, you must write correspondence refusing a request or an appointment or in some way saying no to a person. Even so, you want the person to accept the decision and to understand that you are concerned. You want to leave the person with a positive impression. Follow these guidelines when writing indirect correspondence:

- Begin with an opening statement that is pleasant but neutral.

    Your plan to build a fund for a new arts center in the community is commendable. I hope you are able to meet your goal.

- Review the circumstances and give the negative information.

    Every year AmeriAsian contributes several thousand dollars to important causes. However, even though your proposal is a worthy one, we have already expended this year's budget. If you are still in need of our help next year, please let me know. We will be happy to consider a proposal from you.

- Close the correspondence on a pleasant and positive note.

    Good luck in your efforts. Our town needs more civic-minded groups such as yours.

An example of an indirect letter is given in Figure 9-9. To help you in writing unfavorable messages, use the checklist presented in Figure 9-10.

Persuasive

The **persuasive approach** is an indirect approach with special characteristics. Use the persuasive approach when you want to

---

FAVORABLE AND ROUTINE MESSAGE CHECKLIST

- Did you begin the first paragraph with the reason for the correspondence?
- Did you continue with whatever explanation was necessary?
- Did you close with a thank-you for action or with a request that action be taken by a particular date?
- Did you use the *you* approach?
- Is the correspondence clear, concise, and simple?
- Is the correspondence complete? Did you ask the W questions?
- Is the correspondence considerate?

- Is the correspondence timely?
- Is the correspondence positive?
- Do the paragraphs have unity, coherence, and parallel structure?
- Is the readability level appropriate for the intended audience?
- Is the format correct?
- Did you proofread carefully?

Figure 9-8

Chapter 9: Letters, Memos, and Reports

AmeriAsian Airlines
5519 Reeds Parkway
Grand Rapids, MI 49509-3295
1-800-555-2347

December 12, 2003

Mr. Steven Marceau
Higgins Association
19 Belmont Avenue
Dallas, TX 75001-4839

Dear Steve:

Your invitation to speak at the conference on October 13 is an honor. Your group is a respected one, and I have enjoyed my association with it.

Unfortunately, the demands on my time at work now are extremely heavy. In addition to a new planning process that I must implement, we have recently employed two new managers who are looking to me for assistance in learning their jobs. As you might expect, I hardly have time to "look up." As I would not want to accept your invitation without having adequate time to prepare, I must say no this time. However, if you need a speaker in the future, please don't forget me. It is always a good experience for me to speak to your group.

Have you met Ramona Stanley, one of our marketing directors? She does an excellent presentation on listening, and she might be available to speak at your conference. Her number is 616-555-4378. Good luck with the program.

Sincerely,

Maria Martin

Maria Martin
Vice President of Human Resources

pjc

Figure 9-9   Indirect Letter

convince someone to do something or change an indifferent or negative reader reaction. By using this approach, you can, hopefully, change the reader's initial negative or indifferent attitude to a positive one. The persuasive correspondence should follow these guidelines:

- Begin with the *you* **approach.** This approach requires the writer to place the reader at the center of the message. Rather than using *I* or *we*, the writer puts himself or herself in the shoes of the reader and uses *you* frequently. More information is given about the *you* approach in the next section of this chapter. Here is an example of an effective beginning for a persuasive approach.

  Your role as an administrative professional is often challenging. You deal with conflict, unhappy customers, changing technology, and numerous other challenges daily. Would you like to know how to handle these challenges effectively and keep your frustration level down?

- Continue by creating interest and desire.

UNFAVORABLE MESSAGE CHECKLIST

- Did you begin with a pleasant but neutral statement?
- Did you review the circumstances and give the negative information as positively as possible?
- Did you close on a pleasant note?
- If you had to say *no* to something, did you offer an alternative, if possible?
- Is the correspondence clear, concise, and simple?
- Is the correspondence complete, considerate, and correct?

- Is the correspondence prompt and positive?
- Do the paragraphs have unity, coherence, and parallel structure?
- Is the format correct?
- Did you proofread well?

Figure 9-10

If you answered "yes" to the question, our monthly publication, The Effective Administrative Professional, *will help you. It is packed with techniques and suggestions for handling office situations.*

■ Close by asking for the desired action.

You can have this publication in your office each month for only $48 per year. That is a very small amount to pay for lowering your frustration level and making your job more fun. Fill in the information on the enclosed card, and return it by January. Your early return will guarantee you one free month of the subscription. We look forward to counting you as one of our many satisfied subscribers.

Use the *You* Approach

With the *you* approach, the reader is uppermost in the mind of the writer. The *you* approach involves the use of **empathy** (mentally entering into the feeling or spirit of a person). If the writer is trying to sell a product or service, he or she must look at the benefits the product or service will offer to the reader, not the amount of sales commission. If the message involves something as routine as setting up a meeting, the writer must stress the benefits of the meeting to the reader. Such writing emphasizes *you* and *your* and de-emphasizes the *I, we, mine,* and *ours.*

To carry out the *you* approach, adhere to two words of caution: Be sincere. Do not overuse the *you* approach to the point of being insincere and even dishonest. Your goal is not to flatter the reader; rather, your goal is to see the situation from the reader's point of view and to respond accordingly. Sincerity dictates that you be genuine. Be honest and empathic with the reader.

Notice how the following examples of writing from the *I-we* viewpoint have been changed to the *you* viewpoint. The changes are small, yet the meaning and tone are quite different.

I-We Viewpoint: *We received your order for 100 seat belts today.*
You Viewpoint: *Your order for 100 seat belts was received June 10.*

I-We Viewpoint: *We sell the seat belts for $25 each.*
You Viewpoint: *Your cost for the seat belts is $25.*
I-We Viewpoint: *I will be glad to attend the conference.*
You Viewpoint: *Thank you for asking me to attend the conference. I am delighted to accept your invitation.*

Take a few minutes now to check your understanding of what you have learned about writing. Rewrite the sentences in Self-Check B so they are effective. When you have finished, check your responses with those given at the end of the chapter.

Ensure Mailability

Since letters represent your company to outside individuals, in addition to writing them well and using correct grammar, spelling, and punctuation, you must also format them correctly. If you need a quick review on letter styles and folding letters, refer to the Reference Guide on page 393.

Your employer may on occasion return a piece of correspondence to you, informing you of an error that must be corrected before it can be mailed. Paying attention to all details will help ensure your effectiveness as an administrative professional.

REPORTS

The administrative professional's role in preparing reports varies. You may have the responsibility of keying the report, producing the final copies, and distributing the report to the appropriate individuals. Or your role may involve assisting with the creation of visuals for the report (charts, graphs, and so on), doing research for your employer, and even drafting some or all portions of the report.

The planning steps involved in the writing of a report include the following:

- Determining the purpose of the report
- Analyzing the audience who will receive the report

Once the initial planning has taken place, the writer begins to determine the content of the report by taking these steps.

- Prepare a summary of what should be included in the report.
- Gather information for the report.
- Prepare an outline of the report. The outline may be a detailed or informal one the writer prepares to get his or her thoughts organized.
- Draft the report. The body of the report should have (1) an introduction to help the reader understand the purpose of the report, (2) a main section that includes all the pertinent information, and (3) a conclusion or findings and recommendations to help the reader understand what to do with the report.
- Prepare any necessary graphs, charts, and tables.
- Read and edit the report.
- Prepare the executive summary.
- Print and distribute the report.

Reference Sources

Most reports involve some type of research. The research may be **primary research**—the collecting of original data through surveys, observations, or experiments. The research also may be **secondary research**—data or material that other people have discovered and reported via the Internet, books, periodicals, and various other publications.

Primary Research

If you are conducting primary research, you must decide how to gather the information. You may decide to take these steps.

- Observe situations and individuals
- Survey or interview groups of individuals
- Perform an experiment

Observational research involves collecting data through observations of an event or of actions. Survey research involves collecting data through some type of survey or interview. An interview is usually done in person; however, it may be done over the telephone. Sometimes **focus groups** are brought together to talk with an interviewer about their opinions of certain events or issues. In recent political campaigns, focus groups were used extensively to learn the opinions of people on various issues. A survey is generally done by mail; however, it also may be administered in person. For example, you may decide to assemble several people in your company and pass out a survey to be completed immediately. You generally get a better **response rate** (the number of people responding to a survey or questionnaire) on surveys administered in person than those done by mail.

Experimental research has generally been used in the sciences; however, it is becoming popular with businesses too. It may involve a researcher selecting two or more sample groups and exposing them to certain treatments. For example, a business may decide to test a marketing strategy before implementing a marketing campaign. Experimental groups may be selected and the marketing strategy implemented with the group. Based on the outcome of the research, the business would proceed with the marketing strategy, modify it, or select another one.

Secondary Research

The library has been the major source for conducting secondary research in the past. Although it is still a major source, the Internet (with the huge collection of information available on the Web) has become another major source. In fact, most libraries today have become virtual ones, with millions of pages of data catalogued and offered on the Web. This approach allows several libraries to be connected to each other and eliminates the necessity for housing a large number of books and other documents on shelves in the library.

With the amount of data now on the Web, the researcher has the task of evaluating the data. Any person, as you are aware, can get on the Web and write almost anything he or she chooses. The information may or may not have any validity or reliability. If you are doing research on the Web, you should evaluate the information carefully. For example, here are some questions you can ask.

- Is the information presented by a credible organization, company, or individual?
- Is adequate support given for the points made in the article?
- If the information is presented solely by an individual, what are the individual's credentials?

When using secondary research in reports, that research must be documented. The Reference Guide of this text includes a section on documentation. Information is provided on **MLA** (Modern Language Association), **APA** (American Psychological Association), Web, and traditional documentation styles.

Parts of the Report

An informal report may have only one or two parts, with those parts being the body and an **executive summary** (a one- or two-page summary of the report). An informal report is written in a conversational style. Personal pronouns such as *I*, *you*, *me*, *we*, and *us* are used. Contractions are also acceptable.

The executive summary is written for the busy executive who

- Wishes to preview the report to determine if there is a portion he or she wants to read in its entirety
- Does not need a detailed understanding of all aspects of the report, but does need to know the major findings and recommendations

The executive summary

- Describes the background—why the report was necessary and what the problem or issue is
- Gives the major findings—what was discovered through the research
- Gives the recommendations that are being made as a result of the discoveries

The formal report normally deals with a more complex subject, is longer than the informal report, and requires more time and preparation. Formal reports are generally written in manuscript format and contain preliminary and supplementary parts. An explanation of each part is provided here.

Title Page

The title page contains the title of the report, the writer's name and title and the organization department or division name, and the date the report is being submitted.

Table of Contents

The table of contents lists each major section of the report and the page number of the first page of that section. A table of contents is not required; however, when a report is long, the table of contents helps the reader find particular parts of the report.

List of Tables and Illustrations

If numerous tables and illustrations are within a report, list the title of each one with the respective page number. This procedure helps the reader quickly locate and scan the data presented.

Body of the Report

The body is divided into the following major sections:

- Introduction
- Problem statement
- Research methods
- Findings and discussion
- Recommendations
- Conclusion

Footnotes/Endnotes/Internal Citations

Footnotes appear at the bottom of the page where the reference is made. Endnotes are grouped at the end of the document. Internal citations appear within the context of the document.

Bibliography or Reference Section

All references used in a report should be included in a bibliography or reference section.

This section includes the complete name of the author(s), the title of the book or periodical, the date of publication, the publishing company, and the page numbers.

Appendix

A formal report may contain an appendix that includes supporting information such as tables, statistics, and other pertinent material. Items in an appendix are listed as Appendix A, Appendix B, and so on. The appendix is the last part of the report.

COLLABORATIVE WRITING

You have learned throughout this text that teams are used extensively in organizations today. Teams may write reports as a group. To be an effective member of a writing team, you need to use the skills presented in Chapter 2, such as listening actively and understanding and accepting cultural, gender, and age differences. Additionally, if you are engaged in a team writing assignment, the guidelines presented in Figure 9-11 on page 238 will help you be successful.

© PhotoDisc, Inc.

Effective team writing requires participants to listen actively and understand individual differences.

- Determine the purpose of the writing assignment. What is the team to produce? What is the deadline? Must certain stipulations be met?
- Determine who the audience is. Who is to receive the final report? What is their background? How much do they know about the subject matter? In other words, determine what your style of writing should be and how much information to give the recipients.
- Select a team leader. The team leader is responsible for setting the procedures for the team writing meetings; facilitating the meetings; and helping the group meet deadlines, solve problems, and produce the document.
- Set a work schedule. Decide when and where you are going to meet. Set timelines and stick to them.
- Allocate the work. Define the tasks of each team member. Determine each team member's writing strengths, and use these strengths when assigning tasks.
- Monitor the progress. The group must stay focused and produce the written product by the deadline established.
- Reduce the chance of conflict by
  - actively listening to each group member
  - paying attention to cultural, age, and gender differences
  - acknowledging the worth of the other group members and their points of view

Figure 9-11

INTERNATIONAL CORRESPONDENCE

Throughout this course, you have been reminded of the global nature of business and what that means for you as an administrative professional. Chances are great that, at some point in your career, you will be communicating in writing with individuals from various countries. This chapter has focused on written communication using the principles appropriate for U.S. firms. However, if you are writing to individuals outside the United States, you must consider the differences in culture. You learned in Chapter 2 about various cultural differences. Although these differences vary from country to country, you need to be aware of them when communicating in writing. The result of such knowledge and understanding will be clear, concise, and appropriate communications with international businesses. Generally, communication must be more formal than what is used with U.S. businesses. To learn the particulars of a country, read about the country and its customs. General principles for international written correspondence are provided in Figure 9-12.

ETHICAL AND LEGAL CONSIDERATIONS

You were introduced to the importance of ethical behavior in Chapter 7. Almost every day we hear on television or read in a newspaper about business ethics. In 2001, a lower court ordered Phillip Morris® to pay $3 billion to a man who had developed cancer. The man claimed he was not aware of the dangers of cigarettes. At the time of publication of this text, Phillip Morris was appealing the suit. Did Phillip Morris behave ethically? According to a jury, the company did not, even though it printed the hazards of smoking on its cigarette packages.

Ethical problems are difficult to resolve precisely because no rules exist to determine when something is ethical or unethical. Each organization and individual must make that determination.

In written correspondence, you, as an employee of an organization, must be honest, must maintain confidentiality (not divulge organizational business outside the organization), and must be loyal (act in the employer's interest). The organization must also act ethically in regard to its public responsibilities. Organizations must tell the truth about their products and services and not mislead the public. For

GENERAL PRINCIPLES FOR INTERNATIONAL WRITTEN CORRESPONDENCE

- Use relatively formal language. Phrases such as *Very Honored Professor Dr. Fruer* and *Your honored servant* are used in some countries.
- Do not use expressions unique to the United States; do not refer to events that are common only to the United States.
- Use the dictionary meanings of words; do not use slang.
- Always use the title of the individual with whom you are corresponding. First names should not be used.
- Be extremely courteous; use *thank you* and *please* often.
- Be complimentary when appropriate (but always sincere).

- Ask questions tactfully.
- Do not use humor; it may be misunderstood.
- Respect all customs of the country (social, religious, and so on).
- Learn all you can about particular countries; read extensively.
- Translate correspondence into the native language of the country.
- Send business cards that are printed in the native language of the country.

Figure 9-12

example, airlines have an ethical obligation to the public to meet the scheduled flight times unless circumstances such as weather or mechanical problems arise. They also have an ethical obligation to be honest with the public as to why a flight is late. Automotive companies have an ethical obligation to the public to present correct written specifications of all vehicles. Not-for-profit organizations have an ethical obligation to present in writing to the public how their dollars are spent in meeting the needs of the underprivileged.

In written correspondence (newspaper ads, TV ads, marketing letters, brochures, and so on), organizations have legal obligations that are covered by various laws, including copyright, trademark, contract, and liability laws. These laws are also applicable to email messages. For example, email users must abide by the fair use rule of copyright law when forwarding copyrighted materials obtained from the Web. The fair use rule is very specific about when something can and cannot be used and provides guidelines about materials used in a commercial or not-for-profit nature, the length of the copied work in comparison to the entire document, and so on. In the Firestone tire situation, Firestone had an obligation under liability law to inform the public of any defects in its tires that could cause personal injury, death, property damage, or financial loss. Tobacco companies today must print the health hazards of tobacco on all of their products. Unless the legal obligations of organizations are carefully observed in all written materials, the organization faces the consequences of costly lawsuits, loss of the public's goodwill, and loss of business.

CHAPTER SUMMARY

The summary will help you remember the important points covered in the chapter.

- The basic business correspondence that the administrative professional prepares includes memorandums, email, letters, and reports.
- Effective correspondence is clear, concise, and simple. This means the sentences are short and the vocabulary is easily understood, a conversational tone is used, unneeded words are deleted, active verbs are used, the writing style is varied, and clichés are avoided.
- Effective correspondence is complete, considerate, correct, prompt, and positive. The paragraphs have unity and coherence. The sentences are parallel in structure. The writer uses the appropriate readability level—usually between 7 and 11.
- When planning correspondence, the writer should determine the objective, consider the reader, and gather the facts.
- Letters and memorandums can be classified as favorable, routine (neutral), unfavorable, and persuasive. If the message is favorable or routine, the direct approach is used. If the message is unfavorable or persuasive, the indirect approach is used.
- The *you* approach should be used when writing letters. With this approach, the reader is uppermost in the mind of the writer. It involves the use of empathy.

- The planning steps involved in the writing of a report include determining the purpose of the report and analyzing the audience who will receive the report.
- Primary research may be essential for a business report. This research may include observational research, survey research, and/or experimental research.
- Secondary research, including sources from the Web and from libraries, is also used.
- The parts of a formal business report include the title page, table of contents, list of tables and illustrations, body, footnotes/endnotes/internal citations, bibliography or reference section, and appendix.
- Reports are often written through a collaborative process.
- International correspondence is usually more formal than correspondence written to individuals within the United States. The writer must be aware of the customs and culture of the country to which he or she is writing.
- The writer and organization are responsible for ensuring that their written correspondence is both ethical and legal.

CHAPTER GLOSSARY

The following terms were used in this chapter. Definitions are provided to help you review the terms.

- **pc** (p. 221)—photocopy.
- **cc** (p. 221)—courtesy copy.
- **Tone** (p. 226)—the manner of expression in writing.
- **Topic sentence** (p. 226)—the sentence that contains the main idea of a paragraph.
- **Parallelism** (p. 228)—grammatically equivalent forms are used consistently.
- **Readability** (p. 229)—the degree of difficulty of the message.
- **Favorable messages** (p. 231)—messages the reader will be pleased to receive.

- **Routine messages** (p. 231)—messages that have a neutral effect on the receiver.
- **Unfavorable messages** (p. 231)—messages that bring a negative reaction from the reader.
- **Persuasive messages** (p. 231)—messages that attempt to get the reader to take some action.
- **Direct approach** (p. 231)—used when the message is favorable or neutral; it begins with the reason for the correspondence, continues with any needed explanation, and closes with a thank-you for the action that has been taken or with a request that action be taken by a specific date.

- **Indirect approach** (p. 232)—used when the message is unfavorable; it begins with an opening statement that is pleasant but neutral, reviews the circumstances and gives the negative information, and closes on a pleasant and positive note.
- **Persuasive approach** (p. 232)—an indirect approach with special characteristics; it begins with the *you* approach, continues by creating an interest and desire, and closes by asking for the desired action.
- *You* **approach** (p. 233)—requires the writer to place the reader at the center of the message; *you* and *your* are used rather than *I* or *we*.
- **Empathy** (p. 234)—mentally entering into the feeling or spirit of a person.
- **Primary research** (p. 235)—the collecting of original data through surveys, observations, or experiments.
- **Secondary research** (p. 235)—data or material other people have discovered and reported via the Internet, books, periodicals, and various other publications.
- **Focus groups** (p. 236)—people brought together to talk with an interviewer about their opinions of certain events or issues.
- **Response rate** (p. 236)—the number of people responding to a survey or questionnaire.
- **MLA** (p. 236)—documentation guidelines established by the Modern Language Association.
- **APA** (p. 236)—documentation guidelines established by the American Psychological Association.
- **Executive summary** (p. 236)—a one- or two-page summary of the report.

DISCUSSION ITEMS

These discussion items provide an opportunity to test your understanding of the chapter through written responses and/or discussion with your classmates and your instructor.

1. Explain what is meant by clear, concise, and simple when referring to effective correspondence.
2. How are letters classified?
3. Identify the parts of a formal business report.
4. Explain why legal and ethical considerations are important in writing.
5. List ten principles you should adhere to when writing for an international audience.

CRITICAL-THINKING ACTIVITY

One of the managers, Martin Helmholdt, asks the administrative assistant to write a letter to Ruth Hart congratulating her on becoming city manager of Dallas. Ruth worked for Mr. Helmholdt a number of years ago and moved to Dallas five years ago. The assistant prepared a draft, but he is not pleased with the letter. He asks that you critique the letter before he gives it to Mr. Helmholdt.

Here is the draft of the letter.

Dear Ms. Hart:

I want to congratulate you on becoming city manager of Dallas. I recognized your talent during the years you worked for me. I know you will do an excellent job for Dallas.

Again, my congratulations on your success.

What suggestions would you make to the administrative assistant?

RESPONSES TO SELF-CHECK A

- accessible
- accurate (correct)
- appearance
- calendar
- changeable (correct)
- commitment
- dilemma
- embarrass (correct)
- exorbitant
- forty

- harass (correct)
- maintenance
- mileage
- ninety
- occasionally (correct)
- parallel (correct)
- privilege
- receive
- succeed (correct)
- superintendent

RESPONSES TO SELF-CHECK B

1. Your October 8 letter was received today.
2. Thank you for your recent order.
3. The modular furniture we received on November 5 is unsatisfactory; the furniture does not match what was ordered. A copy of our purchase order is enclosed.
4. Please send us the information by September 14.
5. You are correct.
6. Your bill has been reviewed carefully by our billing department. We can find no error in the computations. Please give me a call at 555-1500 if the bill is still unclear. I will be happy to discuss it with you.
7. A number of businesspeople were consulted on this matter.
8. People constantly consume goods.
9. You will receive the merchandise by January 10.
10. Our washing machine will be a good investment for your family.

PROJECTS

 Project 9-1 (Objective 1)
Collaborative Project

Work with two of your classmates. Collect six business letters that you have received through the mail. Any type of business letter is acceptable. Using the characteristics of effective letters given in this text, critique the letters. Pick one letter to rewrite. Present your critique to the class along with your revised letter.

Project 9-2 (Objective 1)

Each sentence below is intended to be the beginning sentence of a letter. Rewrite the sentences so they will be effective.

1. I received your order today and wanted to thank you for it.
2. Enclosed please find my check in the amount of $510.36 in payment for your Order 34560.
3. I regret to inform you that the seat belts you ordered are no longer being manufactured.
4. This check affirms my intent to subscribe to your weekly investment publication, *Financial News*.
5. I hope you will send us your subscription renewal today.

Project 9-3 (Objective 2)

Mr. Albertson has been asked by Dr. Marcel Lubbers, president of Grand Haven University, to do a presentation on business ethics at a national conference for business executives scheduled on November 11 from 3:00 to 4:00 p.m. AmeriAsian is having a meeting of its executive management team (from the United States and its international locations) on November 8, 9, 10, and 11. The meeting will conclude at noon on the 11th. Mr. Albertson has decided to ask Yang Su from the China office to join him in the presentation. The presentation will be made by a panel with each participant allotted approximately 20 minutes to discuss international business ethics. A question-and-answer session will follow the presentations.

Write a memorandum to Mr. Su asking him to participate; the memorandum may go out with your name on it. Use the memorandum form on the Student CD, file SCDP9-3.

Project 9-4 (Objective 2)

Mr. Albertson has asked you to write a letter to Dr. Marcel Lubbers, president of Grand Haven University (1800 College Street, Grand Haven, MI 49534), giving him the name of the individual who will be on the panel with him; Yang Su has agreed to be on the panel. Explain the presentation format and the time each individual will be given. Tell Dr. Lubbers you will be sending him a copy of the resumes of both Mr. Albertson and Mr. Su by November 8. Mr. Albertson does not know the room number for the presentation; he does know it will be in the Administrative Building. Ask Dr. Lubbers for this information. Mr. Albertson will sign the letter. Print out your letter on AmeriAsian letterhead. This letterhead is available on the Student CD, file SCDP9-4. Print several copies of the letterhead on high-quality bond paper for your use in this project as well as Projects 9-5 and 9-6; use a color printer if one is available to you. Then print the letter you have written on the letterhead. DO NOT KEY ON THE LETTERHEAD TEMPLATE ON YOUR DISK. You will need to print out the letterhead in other chapters.

Project 9-5 (Objective 2)

Mr. Mike Rowse of Temporary Office Workers, 3986 Ottawa SE, Grand Rapids, MI 49501, asked you to participate in a panel discussion on the topic of effective communications in the workplace. You would like to do so, but your current workload is extremely heavy. Write a letter to Mr. Rowse saying no to his request. Print your letter on the letterhead stationery you printed out in Project 9-4.

Project 9-6 (Objective 2)

One of your friends, Monica Sanchez, has just received a promotion to office manager for Vickers Steel, 1852 Airport Drive SE, Grand Rapids, MI 49502. Write a letter of congratulations to her. Print your letter on the letterhead stationery you printed out in Project 9-4.

Project 9-7 (Objective 3)
Collaborative Project
Online Project

Team with three members of your class. Mr. Albertson asks you to research articles on U.S. and international business ethics for the November 11 panel. He asks that you focus on the ethical responsibility of the company to society. You are to check the Web and your library for information. Once you have completed your research, prepare a detailed summary of your findings in informal report form. Include in the report an introduction (giving the research methods used), a body, and the findings. Also include a bibliography of your resources (use at least three).

Project 9-8 (Objective 3)
Collaborative Project

Team with three of your classmates. Write a formal report about students' use of the Web in your school. You will need to do original research. Develop a survey instrument that asks questions similar to these: Do you use the Web? If so, how often? How do you use the Web? What information do you seek? Do you do research on the Web? Do you use the Web in any of your classes? If so, which ones? Ask the approximate age of the respondents using these categories: 18–25, 26–40, 41–50, above 50. You might want to do the survey in the cafeteria or the student lounge. Survey at least 12 students. Prepare the information obtained from the survey in graph form, categorizing Web use by age. Include the survey form as an appendix to your report. Include a title page with the title and date of the report plus your name and the names of your team members.

Project 9-9 (Objective 4)

While doing research on the Web for Mr. Albertson on the ethics seminar, you discover a copyrighted article that you believe is very relevant. You mention it to one of your friends at AmeriAsian, and he asks you to forward copies via email to his workgroup. What should you do? After you make your decision, write a memorandum to your friend telling him what you will do. Use the memorandum form on the Student CD, file SCDP9-9.

Project 9-10 (Objective 4)

Add to your Professional Growth Plan by determining how you will continue to observe ethical and legal obligations in your written correspondence. Save your plan on your Professional Growth Plan disk as "Progro9-10."

ENGLISH USAGE CHALLENGE DRILL

Correct the following sentences. Cite the grammar rule that is applicable to each sentence. Before you begin, refresh your memory by reviewing the comma rules in the Reference Guide of this text.

1. Everyone wanted to be near a television set to watch the results of the Florida recount that began after the national presidential election on November 14 2000.

2. The jury listened closely to the testimony of Nelson Hemingway M.D. last week.

3. Of the gymnastic team's thirty two received gold metals.

4. Her address is 49,000 State Street.

5. The major news story during May and June, 2001, was the Timothy McVeigh death sentence.

ASSESSMENT OF CHAPTER OBJECTIVES

Now that you have completed the chapter and the projects, take a few minutes to review the chapter learning objectives. For your convenience, the objectives are repeated here. Did you accomplish these objectives? If you were unable to accomplish the objectives, give your reasons for not doing so.

1. Identify the characteristics of effective correspondence.　　　　　　Yes _____　　No _____

_____

_____

_____

2. Compose letters and memos.　　　　　　Yes _____　　No _____

_____

_____

_____

3. Research and write a business report.　　　　　　Yes _____　　No _____

_____

_____

_____

4. Observe ethical and legal obligations in written correspondence.　　　　　　Yes _____　　No _____

_____

_____

_____

You may submit your answers in writing to your instructor, using the memorandum form on the Student CD, SCDAP9-1.

WORKPLACE VISITORS AND PRESENTATIONS

LEARNING OBJECTIVES

1. Develop effective techniques for receiving workplace visitors.
2. *Release your creativity.*
3. Deliver effective verbal and electronic presentations.
4. *Conquer presentation fears.*

Communication, whether it is written or verbal, is a significant part

of the administrative professional's job. In Chapter 9, you began to perfect your written communication skills by composing memorandums, letters, and reports. In this chapter, you will increase your communication skills by learning how to receive workplace visitors and how to make effective individual and group presentations. For years, research has shown that people retain more of what they hear when they both hear and see the information at the same time. Good presenters have always understood the importance of appropriate visuals in getting their message across. Now with the advent of tools such as PowerPoint, we have the ability to produce a relatively sophisticated visual presentation easily. This chapter is not designed to teach you PowerPoint; you probably already know how to use it. However, it is designed to help you build effective PowerPoint presentations and successfully deliver the presentation. Developing verbal communication skills, much like written communication skills, is an ongoing process. You should strive to improve your verbal communication skills every day. Your understanding of and commitment to continual growth in verbal communications will increase your effectiveness in all areas of your life.

WORKPLACE VISITORS

In many large organizations, a receptionist initially greets all visitors. The receptionist may keep a register with the name of the visitor, company affiliation, nature of the visit, person the visitor wishes to see, and date of the visit recorded. After obtaining this information from the visitor, the receptionist notifies the administrative professional that the caller has arrived. If this is a first-time visit for the caller, your job may involve going to the receptionist area and escorting the visitor to your employer's office.

In small companies, you may also serve as the receptionist. In other words, you may have the responsibility of greeting all visitors to the organization and seeing that they are directed to the proper people. Regardless of whether you work in a large or small organization, here are some techniques for receiving workplace visitors.

Know Your Supervisor's Expectations

Generally your supervisor will have definite expectations with regard to handling certain visitors. For example, certain people usually have immediate access to your supervisor. The president of the organization, the chairperson of the board, a valuable client or customer, a distinguished civic official—these people are usually granted immediate access. Here are some questions you can ask your supervisor to learn his or her preferences concerning visitors.

- Will you see certain people immediately, regardless of how busy you are?
- Will you see friends or relatives immediately?
- Will you *not* see certain people under any circumstances? How are job applicants handled? Should they be referred to the human resources department? How are sales representatives handled? Should they be referred to the purchasing department?
- Do you want me to make introductions if you have not met the visitor?
- Do you set aside a particular time of day for seeing visitors?

Greet the Visitor

Even though the visitor may have been greeted by the receptionist, your role as an administrative professional is to welcome the visitor to the organization. Greet the person graciously with a simple "Good morning" or "Good afternoon." Use the visitor's name if you know it. Everyone appreciates being called by name, and it lets the visitor know you care enough to make an effort to remember his or her name.

If you have never met the visitor, rise from your chair, say "Hello. I'm Eleanor Wilkerson, Mr. Albertson's administrative assistant," shake hands, and then ask the client to be seated. As you shake hands, look the person in the eye, smile, and say, "I'm happy to meet you." Always extend your hand first to the visitor. However, if the person seems to back off, do not force a handshake. Simply drop your hand to your side, smile, and say, "I'm happy to meet you."

© PhotoDisc, Inc.

Greet people you have not met with a smile and a handshake.

Do not be embarrassed that the person has not offered his or her hand.

Business greetings in the United States have become relatively informal. This statement, however, is not true for international visitors. A later section of this chapter deals with greeting international visitors. Sometimes greetings for people in the United States begin with a hug if the person is a close friend or long-time acquaintance. You may find that your supervisor greets some individuals in this warm, informal manner. However, as an administrative professional, you do not initiate such an intimate greeting with someone entering your office. If the caller initiates it, do not recoil in surprise or embarrassment; this response is awkward for both parties. If a frequent caller to your office insists on this greeting and you are uncomfortable, you might mention it to your employer. He or she can politely tell the caller that you are uncomfortable with such a greeting.

You might greet a co-worker who has been away from the workplace for a period of time with a more informal greeting such as a hug. However, always take into consideration the occasion and the setting. Never hug someone who is at a higher or lower rank in the company than you are. It can look as if you are currying favor or taking advantage of someone.

Always give a visitor your immediate attention. It is discourteous to leave someone standing at your desk while you finish filing papers, preparing a report, or talking on the phone. If you are on the phone when a visitor arrives, ask the telephone caller to hold while you greet the visitor. Tell the visitor you will assist him or her in just a moment. Return to your telephone call and finish as quickly as possible. Excuse yourself if you must answer the telephone when a visitor is at your desk.

Keep Confidential Information Confidential

If confidential information is on your desk or computer screen when a visitor arrives, be certain the visitor cannot read the information. You may casually place the papers in a folder on your desk or remove the information from your computer screen. You can handle these situations nonchalantly while smiling and greeting the visitor appropriately.

Determine the Purpose of the Visit

When a scheduled visitor (one with an appointment) comes to the workplace, you probably already know the purpose of the visit. When you receive an unscheduled visitor, however, you must find out why the person is calling. Your initial greeting may be "Good morning (or Good afternoon). How may I help you?" Such a greeting gives the person a chance to respond with his or her name and the reason for the call. If the visitor does not volunteer the information you need, ask for it. *Avoid* blunt questions such as:

- What is your name?
- What do you want?
- Where do you work?

Keeping a register of workplace visitors is a polite, proven way to get the information you need. Merely ask the visitor to record the necessary information on the register. The register should have a place for the date, time, visitor's name and affiliation, person visited, and purpose of the call. Most visitors regard registering as routine procedure and do not object to providing the information requested. In fact, some administrative professionals must keep a register of the time their employer spends with clients for billing purposes; e.g., attorneys bill by the hour. If you use a register frequently, you may want to transfer the information to a computer file for ease of use.

Another way to get information about a visitor is to ask for the person's business card. The card will have the visitor's name, title, company name, address, and telephone number. If you proceed in this manner, you still need to determine the purpose of the visit. Once you have the visitor's card, you can say, "May I tell Mr. Albertson the purpose of your visit?"

You will save the visitor and your supervisor time by finding out the purpose of the visit and referring the visitor to the appropriate person. Be considerate if you must refer the visitor to someone else. Call the office of that person to determine her or his availability. If the person can see the visitor immediately, escort the visitor to the other office if possible. If you are unable to leave your desk, give the visitor specific instructions on how to find the office. If an appointment must be made for another day, check with the visitor to set a mutually convenient time.

Remember Names and Faces

As you have already learned, you should use a visitor's name. The following pointers will help you learn names quickly:

- Listen carefully to the person's name when it is pronounced.
- If you do not understand a name, ask the person to repeat it.
- Write the name phonetically if the pronunciation is difficult.
- Use the person's name when you first learn it. For example, you might say, "I'm very happy to meet you, Mr. Aikers."
- Use the person's name again before he or she leaves. Practice helps you remember the name for future meetings.

- Ask the person for a business card. Attach the card to an index card with notations about the visitor. Place the index card in a card file, and refer to it often. Another possibility is to transfer the card information to your computer; include notations that will help you remember the person. For example, you might describe the person's appearance—tall, wears glasses, black hair, slight build.

If you receive a visitor who has been in the office before but whose name you have forgotten, be tactful and say, "It's good to see you again." At least you will let the person know that you remember him or her. If the person has an appointment, however, forgetting the name is unforgivable. Your responsibility is to check all appointments each day on both your calendar and your employer's calendar. By doing so, you identify an appointment that has been scheduled without your awareness, assuring that you know the name of the person, the reason for the appointment, whether or not your supervisor needs an introduction, and so on.

© PhotoDisc, Inc.
Greet all visitors promptly and in a professional manner.

Make the Wait Pleasant

If the visitor must wait, your job is to make that wait as pleasant as possible. If coffee or tea is available, offer the person a cup. Tell the visitor approximately how long the wait will be. If possible, explain the reason for the delay— particularly if the visitor had an appointment. For example, you might say, "I'm sorry, but Mr. Albertson had an unexpected meeting; he will be available in about ten minutes." Such an approach lets the visitor know you are concerned but the delay is unavoidable. Offer the visitor something to read so the wait does not seem so long. *Forbes*™, *Fortune*®, *Business Week*®, or organizational publications are good choices to have on hand.

After the visitor is situated, you are free to go back to your work; you are not expected to chat. The visitor realizes you have other duties. However, if the wait is going to be longer than anticipated, tell the person. He or she may decide to come back later or see someone else in the organization if that can be arranged.

Make Introductions

Have you ever been in a business situation where you were the only person in the group who did not know everyone present and no one introduced you? If you have, you know how awkward it is. The most important rule concerning introductions is this: *Make them.* Do not let someone feel ignored or insignificant because he or she was not introduced. In making introductions, there is one basic rule: *The most important person is named first, regardless of gender.* To help you understand this rule, here are some examples.

- A customer/client is more important than your supervisor.
- A government official is more important than your supervisor.
- Your supervisor is more important than a new employee who is at a lower level on the organizational chart.

If the president of another company visits your supervisor, you would say, "Mr. Poster, this is Mr. Albertson." Or if your supervisor does not know the name of the visitor's company you would say, "Mr. Poster, president of Cortez Equipment, this is Mr. Albertson." If you have some information about the person you are introducing, mention that information when making introductions.

It may not be necessary to use the titles *Mr., Mrs., Miss,* or *Ms.* In other words, you may use the first and last names of the individuals when introducing them. However, be sure of your supervisor's preference. When in doubt, use titles. *Always* use the title *Dr.* and government titles such as *Senator.*

When introducing people of equal rank in business situations, the social rules for introductions apply: A man is introduced to a woman, and a younger person is introduced to an older person.

Follow these steps when introducing people or when being introduced.

- Stand up. (Both men and women should stand.)
- Make eye contact with the person, and move toward the person.
- Use a firm but not crunching handshake.
- Repeat the person's name when you are introduced. For example, you might say, "I'm very glad to meet you, Ms. Edwards" in a formal situation or "Hello, Anne" in a less formal situation.

Handle Interruptions

You may need to interrupt your supervisor with a message when visitors are present. Do so as unobtrusively as possible. You can knock on the door or telephone your supervisor, whichever

she or he prefers. If you knock on the door, hand your supervisor a note; never give the information verbally. The visitor should not be privy to the information. This approach can also be used if a visitor overstays the time allocated. It provides your supervisor with a convenient means of letting the visitor know other people are waiting or other responsibilities require his or her attention.

Handle the Difficult Visitor

It is not always easy to be pleasant to visitors, especially those who are ill-tempered and discourteous. At such times, however, you must keep foremost in your mind your role as an ambassador of goodwill.

Your job is to find out the name of the visitor and why that visitor wants to see your employer. Be wary of a visitor who tries to avoid your inquiries by using evasive answers such as the following:

- It's a personal matter.
- I have reason to believe Mr. Albertson will be interested in what I have to say.

You may respond, "I'm sorry but Mr. Albertson sees callers only by appointment. If you tell me the purpose of your visit, I'll check to see if Mr. Albertson can see you at another time." If the visitor still refuses to reveal the purpose of the visit, you may offer him or her a sheet of paper and suggest that he or she write a note to the executive; then take the note to your supervisor. Your supervisor will let you know if he or she will see the visitor. If your supervisor is in a conference, you might suggest that the visitor write a letter requesting an appointment at a later date.

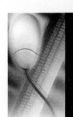

Communication Tip:

When introducing business associates, mention something about the other person. For example, you might say, "Mr. McQuale, I would like you to meet Mr. Greer. He is the head of marketing at Phillips International and a Dallas Cowboys fan."

Do not disclose specific information about the organization or your supervisor to unidentified visitors. If a person comes to your office and asks for specific information, your response should be, "I'm sorry; I don't have that information."

Sometimes a visitor is upset or angry for reasons that have nothing to do with you or the company. Something may have happened on the way to your office, and the person is venting his or her frustrations on you. If you are curt and further provoke the visitor, the situation is aggravated. Let the visitor talk. Listen. Try to understand the visitor's viewpoint. Most of the visitor's anger or frustration will be released through talking. Your role is to be even-tempered and tolerant.

Effectively Communicate with the International Visitor

You learned earlier that organizations are becoming increasingly international in scope. If you have frequent international guests, you need to become aware of their cultures and customs. You can make a poor impression and possibly lose business if you do not make a point to understand international cultures. Do not assume a custom is good or bad just because it is different. For example, we might say that the Irish drive on the wrong side of the road. But do they? No, they merely drive on the opposite side of the road from Americans. Here are some suggestions for communicating with the international visitor.

Greetings

Greetings differ depending on the country. Europeans and South Americans shake hands, although South Americans hug and kiss on the cheek (for both the same and opposite gender) when they know someone. However, women in many other countries do not enjoy the status or prestige of American women. If you are greeting a woman from another country, wait for her to extend her hand. If she does not, you can assume that women do not shake hands in her country.

When greeting people from Asian countries, you may bow. Many Asians have accommodated to the American handshake and do not expect you to bow. However, when an Asian is visiting you, a nice gesture is to bow in recognition of the culture. If you do bow, follow these guidelines.

- Your hands should remain at your sides.
- Your back and neck should be held in a rigid position, with eyes looking downward.
- The person in the inferior position always bows longer and lower.

When greeting people from India, Bangladesh, and Thailand, hold your hands together in front of your chin in a prayerlike position and nod your head.

In Latin America, people commonly greet each other with a full embrace and pats on the back. Other countries engaging in this custom include Greece and Italy. In Russia, it is common to be kissed and hugged. In Saudi Arabia, a male guest may be kissed on both cheeks after shaking hands. Although handshaking is common in France, people also kiss each other on alternate cheeks as a form of greeting.

The general rule for all international callers is not to use first names. Use titles and last names. Remember that in China, the first name is the surname; thus, Zhao Xiyang is Mr. Zhao, not Mr. Xiyang.

During the greetings, your supervisor should offer a business card. You should do the same if you have one. A business card is important with all international visitors, but with Asians, it is almost a ritual. The card is not

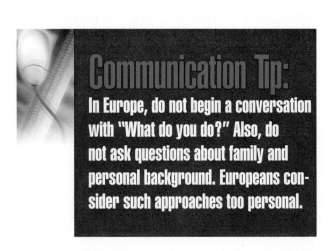

Communication Tip:
In Europe, do not begin a conversation with "What do you do?" Also, do not ask questions about family and personal background. Europeans consider such approaches too personal.

merely handed to the individual; it is presented. You should receive the card gracefully, using both hands.

Welcoming

You may have the responsibility of making arrangements for international visitors to visit your organization. You should read about your visitor's country before the visit. Numerous books are available in local libraries and bookstores. Information is also available on the Web. Additionally, you might talk with people within your organization who have traveled to the particular country of the visitor. Being knowledgeable is the best way to avoid showing any disrespect to the visitor.

When making arrangements, follow these general guidelines.

- Meet (or have someone meet) the guest at the airport and drive him or her to the company or hotel. Remember that language may be a problem. A common practice that works well is to carry a sign with the person's name on it.
- Provide a driver for the individual (if possible) while he or she is in the country.
- Arrange for complementary food and/or flowers to be delivered to the visitor's hotel. However, be certain that you choose the appropriate food and flowers. For example, Muslims and Hindus do not drink alcoholic beverages. Do not send a person from Iran yellow flowers; yellow means you wish the person dead. Do not send Chinese white flowers; white is the color of mourning.
- When arranging for dinners, respect the dietary customs of your guests. Hindus do not eat beef; Muslims and Jews do not eat pork.
- If the international visitor brings family members, offer to arrange outings for the family.

Ongoing Conversations

When talking with international visitors, be sensitive to possible language difficulties. Do not talk in long sentences. Keep slang and **acronyms** (words formed from the initial

letters of other words) out of your vocabulary. Make sure you are being understood. You might ask: "Did I explain that clearly?" However, never talk down to the person; do not assume that the person knows little about America. Most people from other countries know more about American culture than Americans know about other cultures. Language difficulties do not equate to stupidity. In fact, the international visitor has probably prepared for the visit just as much or more than you have. He or she is concerned, just as you are, about making a favorable impression.

Greet Internal Visitors

Co-workers are in and out of each other's offices frequently. However, if you have not met a co-worker, stand and offer your hand when introducing yourself or being introduced. If a co-worker drops by your office for a quick question, you do not need to offer the person a seat; doing so will probably prolong the visit. However, if the person is your superior, do offer him or her a seat. If you are visiting a co-worker who

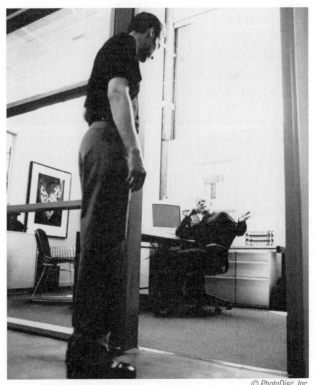

© PhotoDisc, Inc.

As a courtesy to a co-worker, knock or say the person's name from the entrance of the workspace before entering.

has a modular workspace (rather than a standard office), either knock or say the person's name from the entrance to the workspace.

Greet Government Officials

You should greet state or federal government officials using the title of whatever office they hold followed by their last name (for example, Senator Gwynn, Representative Arhar, Secretary of State Holtz). If you are introducing a legislator, present the person within the organization to the legislator; e.g., "Senator Hackett, I would like you to meet Jennifer Farnsworth, our human resources director. Jennifer, this is Senator Hackett of Georgia."

Schedule Appointments

As an administrative professional, you will be responsible for scheduling appointments for your employer and for maintaining a record of the appointments your employer has scheduled. Generally, even in our electronic age, the manual desk calendar still appears on most desks. Both you and your employer will have calendars. You should check your employer's calendar each morning to verify that both calendars contain the same information and that there are no conflicts. In addition to manual calendars, electronic calendars are used extensively. Almost all software packages contain calendaring functions. As you learned in Chapters 4 and 5, many people now use PDAs or cell phone and PDA combination units, allowing them to add to their calendars wherever they are.

Cancel Appointments

If your employer cannot keep an appointment, your responsibility is to cancel it. Appointments may be canceled by a telephone call or by an email (if they are internal). Be sure to give a reason for canceling the appointment and offer to reschedule it. A detailed explanation is not necessary. You may say, "Mr. Albertson has been called out of town unexpectedly, and he will be unable to keep the appointment. May I schedule another appointment for next week?"

PRESENTATION SKILLS

With the team approach commonly being used in business today, administrative professionals frequently are expected to give presentations. These presentations may be informal ones to a small group or more formal ones to a larger group; they may also be group presentations. Not only do you need to understand how to present, you also need to exercise creativity in making a presentation fit the intended audience. The remainder of this chapter is devoted to helping you understand and develop your creativity and to preparing and giving effective individual and group presentations.

Creativity

Creativity is important for producing effective presentations, but it is also important for dealing with the constant change that is occurring in offices today. In fact, creativity and change are closely linked. Creativity is needed to respond successfully to change, and creativity results in change. For example, in giving presentations, you probably have a goal of educating your audience about a certain concept or idea. Assume you are giving a presentation to your workgroup on developing empowered teams. You have two basic goals.

- Help the audience understand the importance of teamwork in today's workplace.
- Help the audience understand how to develop empowered teams.

In other words, through your presentation, you hope to effect change within the organization.

The next few pages are devoted to helping you understand what creativity is and how you may use it in giving presentations. Hopefully, a **serendipitous** (desirable but unsought accidental discovery) benefit will be your ability to think creatively in numerous workplace situations.

Definition

Creativity is defined as "having the ability or the power to cause to exist." Creativity is a process. It is a way of thinking and doing. It is a way of making new connections or new links. It is solving a problem in a new and different way. For example, assume you and your colleagues are going to give a presentation. You suggest that the presentation would be more effective if you used presentation software. Your colleagues think it would be too difficult. You know your idea will work, but it does not have a chance unless you are heard. You decide that rather than trying to talk with them, you will prepare one concept using presentation software and bring it to the next planning meeting. You do so and they agree that your idea is extremely effective and begin planning how software might be used throughout the presentation. You have used your creativity in changing individuals' minds. You did not just present your idea in one way; you thought of another way to present it, and you were successful. You brought about change.

How Creativity Works

Clearly, there are no rigid steps to becoming creative. Remember, it is a process—a process that can be different for each individual. However, here are some steps that can help release the creativity already existing within you.

Have Faith in Your Creativity.
First, have faith in the fact that you are creative. If you have an idea about something that is different from other ideas, do not immediately assume you are wrong. Try it out. Your idea may be the creative spark to solving a complex problem. Always maintain a spirit of inquiry. Ask questions. Do not assume that a question you have is too dumb to ask. Allow yourself the freedom to ask. Do not be uncomfortable when you do not know how something is going to turn out. By experimenting with the unknown, a wonderfully new and creative product can occur. For example, assume that Orville and Wilbur Wright had no faith in their dream of a flying machine. What if they had allowed their idea to die because of all the people who openly laughed and made jokes about their "craziness"?

© Corbis

Imagine the sensations you feel when you are on a roller coaster.

Destroy Judgment. As you are thinking through a problem or an issue, do not be judgmental. Let your thoughts flow freely. Do not discard any of them. Do not let your mind tell you that an idea is "no good" or "ridiculous." To help you destroy judgment (which, by the way, is not easy to do), pay attention to each thought you have. Notice it; hear yourself think it. If you begin to be critical of your thought, attack the judgment. Say to yourself or out loud, "Judgment, get out!" Be firm. Do not let judgment have its say.

Lest you become too judgmental about the importance of creativity in business (and thus this whole section of the book), know that surveys show that one of the skills most wanted by organizations is creative thinking. Employers clearly understand that a successful employee is one who can creatively solve the problems that he or she faces. Kao, in a book entitled *Jamming: The Road to Creativity*, states that creativity is so necessary in the technology world that we either "create or fail."[1] According to Kao, we are going right through the Age of Information to the Age of Creativity. He suggests that companies should be auditing their staff to discover how many new ideas employees generate and who the most creative people are. An article in *Fortune*, June 11, 2001, discusses the creative surge at Microsoft: "Microsoft is getting more creative in large part because it has to." It is impossible to downplay the importance of creativity for all organizations and people in our fast-paced technological world.

Look and Listen. The story is told of a businessman who heard that a Zen master (who lived at the top of a mountain) knew the three basic secrets to life. Anyone who knew these secrets would live a happy, fulfilling life. The businessman climbed for two years to get to the top of the mountain. Once there he approached the old master and asked that he tell him the secrets. The master said, "Yes, I will tell you. The first secret is pay attention, the second secret is pay attention, and the third secret is pay attention."

You may be asking "Pay attention to what?" Pay attention to what you sense, what you think, what you hear, what you see. Pay attention to nature; pay attention to others.

Ask Questions. Michael Ray and Rochelle Myers, in their book, *Creativity in Business*, report writing down the following questions that a four-and-a-half-year-old asked in less than an hour:

- What's behind a rainbow?
- What color is the inside of my brain?
- What's inside of a rock? a tree? a sausage? bones? my throat? a spider?
- Does the sky have an end to it?
- Why are my toes in front of my feet?

We smile when we read these questions. If you have children or younger siblings, they may have asked similar questions. As we grow up, somehow we do not allow ourselves to continue to ask questions. We think we should know all the answers; but obviously, we do not. Our continuing to ask questions (whatever they

---

[1]John Kao, *Jamming: The Road to Creativity* (New York: Harper Business, 1996).

may be) helps us get in touch with our creativity. Do not frighten yourself at first by asking big questions, such as "What is the nature of humans?" Give yourself permission to ask small and even playful questions. Let yourself question things you have never questioned in your adult life.

Bring Your Personal Creativity to the Office. Begin to ask questions in your work environment. Realize that through your asking and finding answers, you may discover a more creative, more productive way to do the work of the organization. As you practice thinking creatively, you will find that you not only have successes but also huge frustrations. However, if you keep up the struggle, you will achieve a breakthrough. Often the breakthrough comes at a higher level of creativity than before. Do not lose your creativity when problems arise. You probably need it more then ever. **Aikido** (the Japanese soft martial art) teaches that you should never meet force with force. The person who breaks harmony by attacking or being aggressive in some way fails. Rather, you should move with the person rather than struggle against him or her. By moving in the same direction of the other person, you are able to effect more change than by attacking.

Consider this example of the Aikido concept in a business situation. Your supervisor (Mr. Albertson) has become obsessed with acquiring the latest technology—whatever it may be. However, he never gets training for himself. He expects you to be able to solve the problem he is having with the technology he has acquired. If you cannot solve it, he gets angry. Rather than your getting angry at him, go with him as Aikido teaches. Tell him you understand his feelings of frustration when he cannot solve a problem. Tell him you will get help for both of you. Contact a technician who knows the new technology, and ask the technician to show you and your supervisor how to handle the problem. Then if your employer is willing, ask the technician to provide both of you with additional training.

Now that you have learned how you might "grow" your creativity, let's look at how you can put creativity into action in developing and delivering presentations.

The Audience

You will generally give presentations to three basic types of audiences.

- Co-workers in your organization
- Workplace teams containing a cross section of people within your organization
- Colleagues within professional organizations to which you belong

The Plan

Planning means gathering and arranging your thoughts, developing your ideas, and finding unique ways to express them. Using your creativity in the process will help you put together a memorable presentation that holds the audience's attention and allows you to get your message across.

As soon as you know you are going to give a presentation, start a folder. Put whatever comes to your mind in the folder—ideas, quotations, and so on. You may even wake up in the middle of the night with an idea. Keep a pad and pencil by your bed to use in jotting down your thoughts. You do not want to forget them.

In the planning process, take these steps.

Begin Early

A good presentation is not prepared 30 minutes before it is given. You may get lucky and be able to deliver a presentation with little or no preparation, but that is a rarity. Do not tempt fate; begin early. You might say, "I don't have time to prepare." If that is the case, then do not agree to give the presentation. Beginning preparation three weeks before the presentation is to be delivered is not too soon. Also, by beginning early, you can spend a few minutes each day thinking about what you want to say and writing down your thoughts. Then you can come back to your ideas at a later point and revise them or throw out material that no longer seems relevant. In other words, you have a chance to mull over your thoughts.

Determine the Purpose

Is your purpose to inform your audience? to persuade? to inform and persuade? Spend some time determining the purpose. If you do not understand what the purpose of your presentation is, certainly no one else will. Once you have determined the purpose, write it down in one clear, concise statement. As you prepare your presentation, review the statement frequently to stay on track.

Visualize the Anticipated Audience

Who will the people be in the audience? For example, if your audience is a group of administrative professionals, you are familiar with their interests. You can use anecdotes or stories that will have meaning for them. Find out the age of your audience. A teenage audience will be very different than an audience in its fifties and sixties. Know something about the educational level and experiences of the audience. For example, if you are giving a presentation on software, you need to know what level of expertise the audience already has. You do not want to bore them by giving them information that is too elementary nor do you want to confuse them by being too technical.

Visualize your audience.

Find out how many people will be in the audience. Will there be 15 or 50? Numbers do make a difference. A small audience allows greater interaction; questions can be used effectively. With a large audience, there is little chance for interaction other than a question-and-answer period at the end. If you have a question-and-answer period, make sure the audience has access to a microphone so everyone can hear the questions or comments.

If you are providing handouts for the audience, you need to know the number of attendees so you have the appropriate number of handouts. Also, it is a good idea to have only the exact number of chairs needed for the audience. Having to add chairs after most of the audience has arrived makes you look as if you were not prepared. Conversely, if you have too many chairs in the audience, it appears as though you did not have a good turnout for your presentation.

Determine the Length of the Presentation

Most presentations should be no longer than 20 minutes, with 30 to 40 minutes the maximum. Part of your task is to manage your topic; do not try to give the audience so much information that you drone on for an hour or more. You will lose your audience; people's attention spans are not that long.

Generally speaking, 175 words (or three-quarters of a keyed, double-spaced page) equals one minute of talking time. A 15- or 20-minute talk will be about 10 to 12 keyed pages.

Gather the Material

Research the topic if necessary in the library or on the Web. Do original research if needed. For example, you may want your audience to know how a certain group feels about a particular idea. If so, send a survey to a targeted group for their responses.

Construct an Outline

An outline should consist of an introduction, a body, and a conclusion. In the introduction, you tell your audience what you are going to say. In the body, you give them the information.

I. INTRODUCTION
   A. Opening Statement to Gain Attention
      1. Development of opening statement
      2. Supporting material
   B. Second Introductory Point (if needed)
II. BODY
   A. First Main Idea
      1. First supporting point
      2. Second supporting point
   B. Second Main Idea
      1. First supporting point
      2. Second supporting point
   C. Third Main Idea
      1. First supporting point
      2. Second supporting point
III. CONCLUSION
   A. Summary
   B. Application or Challenge and Final Statement

Figure 10-1

In the closing, you remind them of what you said by giving a summary. In other words, you tell the audience the important points of your presentation three times. This repetition increases the chances that the audience will understand and remember what you said. Figure 10-1 illustrates a sample outline.

The Written Presentation

Once you have planned adequately, you are ready to begin the writing process. Your writing tasks include

- Developing an opening
- Using language well
- Developing an appropriate conclusion
- Preparing visual aids

Develop an Opening

The opening should immediately get the audience's attention. You might tell a story, use a quotation, ask a question, or refer to a current event. Begin with the unexpected and the unpredictable. Also, know what you do best. If you are a good joke teller, you might open with a joke. However, if you are not, stay away from a joke like you would stay away from poison. Nothing can be worse than starting a presentation with a joke that is in poor taste and offends someone in the audience or a joke that the audience does not think is funny. If you tell stories well, tell one. Not only should the opening get the audience's attention, it should also help you relax with your audience. Plan your opening well and open with something you do well. When you determine how you are going to open your presentation, ask yourself these questions.

- Is there a link between the story and the presentation?
- Is it a new story or joke? (You do not want to relay one the audience has heard numerous times.)
- Am I telling it as succinctly as possible? You do not want to spend one-third of your time on your opening story.
- If it is a joke, am I timing the punch line to elicit a laugh?

Use Language Well

Nothing is more disconcerting than discovering that people are nodding off while you are talking. Obviously, you are not getting your message across in an interesting fashion. One technique that will help you get your message across is to involve the audience. People are always interested in their own concerns. When you know who the audience will be, think about how you can establish a link with them. For example, if the audience is a group of administrative professionals, what concerns does the audience have in common? Make your major points, relating those points to experiences both you and the audience have had.

Another technique that will help you is to refer to people, not to abstractions. Use interesting facts, figures, and quotations. For example, if you are giving a motivational talk on the importance of service, you might use the following quote from Mother Teresa: "Love cannot remain by itself—it has no meaning.

Love has to be put into action and that action is service."

Use active rather than passive voice. Do not say, "It is believed . . ."; say, "I believe . . . ." Talk in a conversational tone. Talk with the audience, not at the audience. Use the same tone you would use when trying to persuade someone who is sitting across the table from you at a dinner party. Be animated; if you do not appear to be interested in what you are saying, the audience certainly will not be. Never speak in a monotone; vary your tone of voice. Vary your expressions. A commanding speaker is

- Sincere
- Credible
- Concerned
- Enthusiastic
- Energetic
- Intense
- Knowledgeable

Develop an Appropriate Conclusion

Your conclusion should summarize the points made in your presentation and leave the audience feeling motivated to respond in the way you intended. Remember, your conclusion is the final impression you will make on the audience. Be forceful and positive. When summarizing, state the points in slightly different ways. You might also suggest a challenge to the audience, propose a solution to a situation, or use a compelling quote.

Prepare Visual Aids

When used properly, visual aids can be very effective. People remember 40 percent more when they hear and see something simultaneously. Many people today use presentation software, such as PowerPoint, to present visuals. This software is easy to use and extremely effective. A section later in this chapter is devoted to the effective use of presentation software.

Once the presentation is written, put it aside for a day or two; then go back over it. Does the speech fit the anticipated audience? Does it meet the purpose? Is the opening creative? Will it get the audience's attention? Have you used stories and quotes appropriately and

spaced them throughout the presentation? Remember, if you involve the audience, they will learn. A well-selected story or quote can involve the audience. Is the presentation the proper length? Remember, it is better to be too brief than too long. Abraham Lincoln delivered one of the nation's most celebrated addresses (the Gettysburg Address) in less than five minutes. Are your visual aids effective? Are you using an appropriate number of visuals? Do you need to rewrite any parts?

The Rehearsal

Rehearse the presentation just as you are going to give it. For example, if you will be standing at a lectern during the presentation, stand at a lectern during your rehearsal. If you are going to be using a microphone, use a microphone during your rehearsal. Ask a respected colleague to listen to your practice session and provide constructive criticism. Go over your presentation completely three or four times. With repeated rehearsals, the text becomes part of your memory; you will be more at ease since you are not likely to forget an important point during the presentation.

© PhotoDisc, Inc.

Rehearse your presentation before a group of respected colleagues; ask for their constructive criticism.

Appropriate Dress

The usual attire for a woman is a suit or dress; for a man, it is a suit and tie. Wear something you are comfortable in and that looks good on you. Bright colors are perfectly okay. Women should avoid necklaces and earrings that are too large and distracting. Rings and bracelets are appropriate, but women should not wear noisy bracelets, which distract audience members. Men may wear colored shirts and bright ties. The color of the suit should look good on the man. Men should not wear gold bracelets and a number of rings; they are distracting to the audience. Hair for both men and women should be well groomed and should not be in the eyes.

Presentation Room Check

If you have not visited the room where you will make your presentation, do so. Know how the room will be set up. Find out where the lectern is going to be if you are using one. Be certain you have the visuals in order. Check out your visuals on the actual equipment you will be using. Be sure you know how to use the equipment. If you are at all uncomfortable with the equipment, ask a colleague to assist you by operating the equipment. If you are giving a presentation with PowerPoint, be sure all the equipment is working properly and is placed so the audience can see your presentation.

Fear Control

First of all, realize that nervousness is normal. Even the professionals experience it. Dean Martin was famous for his stage fright; so is Barbra Streisand. In fact, one of the greatest  fears individuals have (as shown in surveys) is the fear of speaking before an audience. Some of the things you have already learned to do will help you control nervousness—preparation and rehearsal. A well-prepared and well-rehearsed presentation can eliminate many of your fears. You know who your audience is, what you intend to say, and how you will say it. Here are other suggestions for controlling nervousness.

The Day Before the Presentation

Remind yourself that you have prepared well. You have followed all of the steps mentioned previously; that is, beginning early, determining the purpose of the presentation, rehearsing, and so on. Burn off some of your nervousness by exercising. Try not to push yourself to the limit with work responsibilities the few days before your presentation; when you are overly tired, you increase your chances of not doing a good job.

© PhotoDisc, Inc.
Burn off nervousness by exercising the day before your presentation.

The Day of the Presentation

Arrive early enough to check out the microphone, the equipment, and the layout of the room. If changes need to be made, find someone who can assist you in making the changes.

In the 10 or 15 minutes before your presentation is to begin, find a private place (maybe a small room away from the gathering audience) and try these relaxation techniques.

- Say these four sentences several times to yourself.
  1. I'm glad I'm here.
  2. I'm glad you're here.
  3. I care about you.
  4. I know that I know.[2]
- Sit in a straight chair, carry your rib cage high, and breathe deeply. As you exhale, push the air over your lower teeth in a *ssss* sound. Focus your efforts entirely on your breathing.
- Walk around. Take a brisk walk for a minute or two. Do some jumping jacks.
- Realize that some nervousness can help you. You can channel this nervousness into your talk, and it will become a positive energy source that adds to your effectiveness.
- Compose your thoughts.
- Right before you enter the room, swing your arms a few times.

As You Begin Your Presentation

- Walk slowly to the lectern. Arrange your note cards, look at the audience for a few seconds, and then begin.
- Realize that the audience is much less aware of your nervousness than you are. Also, realize that the audience is your friend; the audience wants you to succeed.
- Do not draw attention to your hands, which may be shaking as you begin. For example, instead of holding a hand microphone, leave the mike on a stand. Do not hold a glass of water. Leave your notes on the lectern; you do not want to call attention to shaking papers.

During the Presentation

During the presentation, observe the nonverbal feedback from the audience. Puzzled looks or blank stares are cues that the audience does not understand what you are saying. You may need to modify the rate of your voice or give another example or two to clarify what you mean. Smiles and nodding heads are positive reactions.

Maintain eye contact with the audience. If you are in a small group, look at each individual briefly. When you are in a large group, move your eyes from one side of the room to the other, concentrating for a period of time on each portion of the room. Use natural gestures. You may use your arms and hands to emphasize points. However, avoid too many arm and hand gestures; they can be distracting to the audience. Be natural; do not perform. Speak in a normal tone of voice; vary your tone; do not speak too fast. However, do not speak too slowly either; speaking too slowly can result in a bored listener. Articulate carefully. For example, do not drop your *g's*; say *learning*, not *learnin*.

Electronic Presentations

You have already learned that individuals remember 40 percent more of a presentation when they both hear and see the information that is presented. Presentation software allows you to provide images for the audience.

PowerPoint is a widely used Microsoft software presentation package. Other software packages are available that assist you in creating visuals for your presentation, such as Photoshop, CorelDRAW™, Acrobat®, and MediaPro®. Also, free presentation software is available on the Web. However, since PowerPoint is used so extensively and comes bundled with Microsoft's Office Suite package, which you may have on your computer, it is the package referenced here. You can produce the following types of materials with PowerPoint:

- Slides
- Handouts
- Speaker's notes
- Outlines
- Sounds and images
- Charts and spreadsheets

Your PowerPoint materials are displayed to the audience on a computer screen or a projection system. Unless your audience is very small (three or four people who can gather around a

---

[2]Dorothy Sarnoff, *Never Be Nervous Again* (New York: Crown Publishers, Inc., 1987).

computer), you should use a large projection screen.

You can also establish links to Websites within your presentation. For example, assume you are doing a presentation on Chinese culture. You can use a Web link to show some of the historical sites in China. You can also use PowerPoint to establish a virtual seminar by placing a number of PowerPoint presentations from various presenters on the Web.

Here are some of the features PowerPoint offers in helping to make your presentation a powerful visual one.

- Color—The use of color adds interest to your presentation. PowerPoint has hundreds of color schemes you can use to make professional-looking slides.
- Clip art—PowerPoint includes a clip-art collection. However, if you do not find what you need there, you can purchase clip-art software or download clip art from the Web.
- Through the use of Media Player, Power-Point accepts movies and sound clips, thus allowing you to see and hear a movie image on the screen.

Although preparing a PowerPoint presentation is more time-consuming than merely preparing a presentation without visuals, doing so is well worth the effort if it is done well. Effective visuals will ensure that your audience learns and retains more from your presentation. Tips for preparing your PowerPoint visuals are given in Figure 10-2.

Presentation Critique

After you have finished delivering your presentation, critique what happened. Either evaluate yourself or have someone else evaluate you. You might want to videotape your presentation to help you in the critiquing process. You may also want to provide evaluation forms for the people in the audience. In critiquing yourself

- Be kind. List the good along with the not-so-good.
- Do not try to solve too many problems at once. Pick one or two things to improve each time.
- Realize evaluation is an ongoing process.
- Build yourself up by thinking about how much you have improved.
- Get feedback from other people; really listen to the feedback. If someone compliments you, believe it.

TIPS FOR PREPARING POWERPOINT VISUALS

- Keep the text to a minimum on each slide. Make your points in as few words as possible. Do not put more than three or four points on each slide.
- Determine how many graphics you should have. You want to have enough graphics but not too many. Generally, you should not have more than one graphic for each slide.
- Use color to enhance the slide; however, do not use a very dark color. Dark colors make it more difficult to see the material.
- The visual presentation should be consistent. For example, typestyles should be the same for all major points; minor points may be in a different typestyle. However, do not use more than two different typestyles. (A slide looks cluttered when you use too many.)

- Make certain the visual can be seen and read from all parts of the room. If your audience is large, you may need two screens, with one screen on one side of the room and the other screen on the other side of the room.
- Proofread the slide carefully. Errors are embarrassing, and they detract from your presentation, making the audience wonder about your attention to detail.
- Practice using the PowerPoint slides before the presentation.
- Make certain all equipment is in good working order.
- Make certain you know how to operate all equipment.
- Talk to the audience—not to the PowerPoint slide.
- Stand to the side of the slide when showing it.

Figure 10-2

- Say each idea aloud as it occurs to you.
- Have a recorder jot down each idea.
- Listen attentively to others' ideas.
- Piggyback on the ideas of others.
- Suspend judgment. Do not critique ideas as they are presented.

- Encourage an uninterrupted flow of ideas.
- Expect the outrageous to surface, which is perfectly okay in the brainstorming process; it encourages creativity.

Figure 10-3

Team Presentations

You have already learned that team presentations are being used extensively in businesses today. The techniques presented in the previous section still apply, but team presentations require collaborative planning. In addition to knowing the purpose of your presentation, the people who will be in attendance, and how long the presentation should be, you need to take these steps.

- **Brainstorm** (engage in problem solving) what the presentation should include and how it will be presented. (See Figure 10-3 for how to brainstorm.)
- Decide who will present which part of the presentation.

- Determine how you will make the transition from one speaker to another. It is usually a good idea for the speaker finishing to mention the next speaker's name.
- Practice your presentation as a group.
- If a PowerPoint presentation is going to be done, determine who will be in charge of it and who will actually key the presentation.
- Determine what the attire will be; each speaker should dress in a similar fashion.
- Determine how the group will be seated before the presentation begins and after each presentation is finished. For example, will there be a table with chairs for the speakers or will the speakers sit on a stage? In what order should the speakers sit? Generally the first speaker should be closest to the podium.

CHAPTER SUMMARY

The summary will help you remember the important points covered in the chapter.

- When receiving workplace callers, know your employer's expectations. Your employer will usually see certain people without an appointment. Your employer may also decide not to see certain people.
- Appropriate techniques for receiving office callers include the following:
  - Greet the visitor with a handshake if you have not met him or her previously.
  - Determine the purpose of the caller's visit.
  - Call the visitor by name.
  - Make the wait pleasant by offering the caller coffee or tea and reading material.
  - Introduce the caller to your supervisor if appropriate.
  - Do not be discourteous to callers—even the difficult ones.
- When dealing with international guests, know their cultures and customs. Use the appropriate greeting; be sensitive to language difficulties.
- Develop and use your creativity when preparing presentations.
- These steps will help you release your creativity: Have faith in your creativity, destroy judgment, look and listen, ask questions, and bring your personal creativity to the office.

- When planning presentations: Begin early, determine the purpose, visualize the anticipated audience, determine the length of the presentation, gather the material, and construct an outline.
- When writing presentations, develop an opening, use language well, develop an appropriate conclusion, and prepare visual aids.
- Before giving the presentation, rehearse it several times.
- Conquer your fears. Realize that nervousness is normal. However, you should always take steps to conquer your fears. Be well prepared and well rehearsed.
- During the presentation, watch for nonverbal feedback from the audience and maintain eye contact with the audience throughout the presentation.
- Use PowerPoint or some other presentation software to prepare a visual presentation. By providing the audience with images, you will help them remember 40 percent more of what you say.
- Once the presentation is over, do your own critique of it or have a trusted friend evaluate you.
- Team presentations require collaborative planning; this collaborative planning should include brainstorming to release the creativity of the group.

CHAPTER GLOSSARY

The following terms were used in this chapter. Definitions are provided to help you review the terms.

- **Acronym** (p. 251)—a word formed from the initial letters of other words.
- **Serendipitous** (p. 252)—desirable but unsought accidental discovery.
- **Creativity** (p. 252)—having the ability or the power to cause to exist.
- **Aikido** (p. 255)—the Japanese soft martial art.
- **Brainstorm** (p. 262)—engage in problem solving.

DISCUSSION ITEMS

These discussion items provide an opportunity to test your understanding of the chapter through written responses and/or discussion with your classmates and your instructor.

1. List eight techniques for effectively handling the workplace visitor.
2. Explain how you would treat an international visitor.
3. List the planning steps involved in developing a presentation.
4. Define creativity and give four steps for helping to release the creativity that exists within you.
5. List five steps you might take to conquer your presentation fears.

CRITICAL-THINKING ACTIVITY

Numerous groups of Chinese administrators from the Beijing office of AmeriAsian visit the Grand Rapids office. Mr. Albertson is often host for these groups. Mr. Albertson has asked you to visit China with Maria Sergio, vice president of Human Resources, to learn more about the Chinese culture so you can be of greater assistance to him when he hosts these groups. You will be in the Beijing office for a week. In preparation for your trip, you do some reading about culture and talk with one of the administrative professionals (who was born in China) about the culture. You think you are fairly well prepared. However, during the trip, numerous situations occur that make you feel embarrassed about your lack of preparation. Here are a few of those situations.

- The Chinese officials always offer you their business cards. You notice immediately that their cards have their names, addresses, and so on, in Chinese on one side of the card and in English on the other side. You do have business cards, but your name and pertinent information is only in English. You notice that Ms. Sergio has her business cards imprinted with the information in English on one side and the information in Chinese on the other side.
- Small gifts are given to you in each office. You did not bring any gifts, so you have nothing to offer in return.
- The Chinese officials take many photos of your visit; as you leave, they present both you and Ms. Sergio with photo albums.
- Since the trip was a week in length, you took three bags with you. However, you were embarrassed as you went from the airport to the hotel because the Chinese host who met you insisted on carrying your bags; you felt that three bags were too many. You notice that Ms. Sergio only has one bag, which she is able to carry herself.
- In the first meeting that you had at the AmeriAsian office, you immediately extended your hand in greeting to each of the members of the Chinese group. Although they were very polite, you noticed that Ms. Sergio waited until the Chinese had spoken before she responded to their greeting; her response was a bow.
- In an effort to show your friendliness, you immediately made small talk with the Chinese. There was an interpreter present at all sessions. People were polite to you, but you knew you must have done something wrong.
- The Chinese hosted you for all lunches and dinners. The tables were filled with food. You were not familiar with many of the dishes; the food was much different than the Chinese food that you had eaten in America. You politely refused several dishes that were offered to you. You noticed that no one else refused any dish. You wonder if you made an error.

Respond to these questions. Before you do, read the information on the Student CD, SCDCTA-10. Additionally, discuss your answers with your classmates.

- What errors did you make, and what should have been done?
- What could you have done to prevent these errors from occurring?

PROJECTS

Project 10-1 (Objective 1)

You receive the following visitors in your office today. How would you handle each situation? Write a memorandum to your instructor, use the memorandum form on the Student CD, file SCDP10-1, and state how each situation should be handled.

1. A sales representative comes in and asks for an appointment to see your supervisor; your supervisor has told you he does not like to see sales representatives.
2. Your supervisor has been called out of town unexpectedly. He scheduled an appointment with Mr. Scheen for 11 a.m. but failed to tell you about this appointment. You forgot to check his calendar. Mr. Scheen comes in at 10:50 for his appointment.
3. A woman comes in to see your supervisor. She refuses to give her name or the purpose of her visit. However, she says the matter is urgent. She seems upset.
4. Ms. Nicole Botha comes in to see your supervisor. Ms. Botha has an appointment at 11 a.m., and it is now 10:55 a.m. Your supervisor has had an extremely busy morning, and he is now in a conference that will last until 11:20 a.m.
5. R. T. Arlston is in your supervisor's office. He had an appointment at 2 p.m. It is now 3 p.m., and your supervisor has an appointment with Ms. Carol Haile. Ms. Haile has arrived.
6. George O'Casey arrives at 3 p.m. for his appointment with your supervisor. Upon checking your appointment book, you find that Mr. O'Casey's appointment really is for 3 p.m. tomorrow.

 ## Project 10-2 (Objective 2)
Collaborative Project

Divide up into groups of four or five. Decide who will be the "starter" for the group. For example, the starter may be the person with the longest hair, the bluest eyes, or the youngest person. The purpose of this activity is to learn to release your creativity. Once the starter is determined, he or she begins a story. As a departure point, use this starter: "Everyone knows that Dorothy (in the Wizard of Oz) traveled down the yellow brick road to the land of Oz. However, did you know that the land of Oz was actually on the moon and the yellow brick road was made of

numerous moon crystals that glistened and even 'spoke' to Dorothy, giving her directions as she made her way to the land of Oz? In fact, these crystals sang a song in 'moon language' that went like this: 'Dorothy, Dorothy, follow this path. Run with us into the unknown. You can do it, you can, you can.'

From this point, each person within the group is to add a little-known fact about Dorothy to the story. Tape your story if a recorder is available, and play it for the class.

Once you have finished the story, each person should discuss how he or she felt during this process. Was it difficult to be spontaneous? If so, why? Did you have trouble thinking of little-known facts? If so, why? Listen to each other carefully. Develop a list as a group of how creativity can be encouraged and released.

 ## Project 10-3 (Objectives 3 and 4)
Collaborative Project

Work in groups of four or five on this team presentation, which is to be on a topic of the team's choosing. Use the brainstorming techniques listed in this chapter to brainstorm topics and how the presentation will be presented. To get your creative juices flowing, here are three general topics you can choose from: Women in Management, Diversity in the United States (or another area), or The Future Workplace. The presentation is to be from 15 to 20 minutes in length; each team member is responsible for a portion of the presentation that is to be delivered verbally to the class. If you have PowerPoint available to you, prepare a PowerPoint presentation. Your class members are to evaluate your presentation. An evaluation form appears on the Student CD, file SCDP10-3a. Run copies for your classmates, and distribute them before you begin your presentation. Your instructor will collect the evaluation forms at the end of your presentation and give them to you for review. What can you learn from the evaluation forms? Write a memorandum to your instructor, using the memorandum form on the Student CD, file SCDP10-3b. Detail the strengths and weaknesses of your presentation as revealed by the evaluation forms and as seen by your group. Use these headings in your memorandum: (1) Group Opinion of Strengths and Weaknesses of Presentation, and (2) Class Members' Opinion of Strengths and Weaknesses of Presentation.

PROJECTS

(continued)

Project 10-4 (Objectives 2 and 4)

Add to your Professional Growth Plan by describing how you will continue to work on releasing your creativity and conquering presentation fears. If you are giving verbal presentations in other classes this semester, you might mention how you are transferring the skills learned in this chapter to presenting in other situations. Save your plan on your Professional Growth Plan disk as "Progro10-4."

ENGLISH USAGE CHALLENGE DRILL

Correct the following sentences. Cite the grammar rule that is applicable to each sentence. Before you begin, refresh your memory of grammar rules by reviewing parallelism in writing in the Reference Guide of this text. Parallelism calls for the use of equivalent grammatical forms when expressing ideas of equal importance.

1. The automotive workers had tried pleas, threatening, and striking to make their demands known.
2. The committee discussed the petition, analyzed its major points, and the decision was made to reject it.
3. Having a solid friendship with one or two individuals can be more rewarding than the acquisition of possessions.
4. Differing expectations for a friendship not only can lead to disappointment but also to frustration and even anger.
5. Difficult supervisors not only affect their employees' performances but their personal lives may be affected as well.

ASSESSMENT OF CHAPTER OBJECTIVES

Now that you have completed the chapter and the projects, take a few minutes to review the chapter learning objectives. For your convenience, the objectives are repeated here. Did you accomplish these objectives? If you were unable to accomplish the objectives, give your reasons for not doing so.

1. Develop effective techniques for receiving workplace visitors.   Yes _____   No _____

_____

_____

_____

2. Release your creativity.   Yes _____   No _____

_____

_____

_____

3. Deliver effective verbal and electronic presentations.   Yes _____   No _____

_____

_____

_____

4. Conquer presentation fears. Yes _____ No _____

_____

_____

_____

You may submit your answers in writing to your instructor, using the memorandum form on the Student CD, SCDAP10-1.

BARBARA GRIGGS' CASE SOLUTION

I believed I needed to pay attention to his style of management and his style of communication. I spoke with another assistant in the organization who was successful in her job. She helped me see things in a different light, thinking long term. She helped me to look at the executive's calendar to consider what might be needed for an upcoming trip or meeting (perhaps a report or a presentation that would need to be prepared by a member of his staff or me). I sought ways to organize his mail. I first organized it by subject; but when this method did not work, I sorted it by the sender's name. I learned to present the mail and messages so as not to overwhelm him on his first day back in the office after a trip. I read and responded to his email when he could not access it. Reading someone else's email was new to me. In my past position, we did not read each other's mail. As a result, I considered this to be an invasion of privacy (by me!).

I would master one task and get a well-done stamp of approval—only to be faced by something else that needed to be conquered.

I had no sense of ease or well being. Overall I was very uncomfortable in this position. I knew I could go back to my previous position at any time, but I was not ready to do that. I decided to speak to a good friend, who also worked for the company, about my dilemma. To my surprise, not many weeks later when she received a promotion, she recommended me for her job, which is now my present position.

Fortunately, this story ended happily. But it just as easily could have gone another way. Perceptions that other people have of you can play a big part in your success or failure. Only those closest to me knew how unhappy I was, mainly my family.

Sometime in your career you will be involved in a working relationship where there is a difference of style or opinion. You must maintain a positive attitude and be willing to learn and improve yourself in order to persevere. You must also portray a professional demeanor at all times. I am sure if I had conducted myself in any other way, I would not be where I am now—growing and thriving at Pharmacia Corporation.

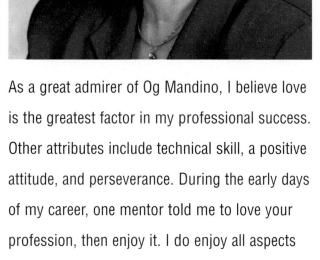

A
Success
Profile

Nilda Campbell

Personal Assistant to the National President

New Zealand Educational Institute (NZEI)

As a great admirer of Og Mandino, I believe love is the greatest factor in my professional success. Other attributes include technical skill, a positive attitude, and perseverance. During the early days of my career, one mentor told me to love your profession, then enjoy it. I do enjoy all aspects of my job.

I graduated from the University of the East, Philippines. I have a bachelor's degree in Business Administration with a major in Management. While working on my degree, I was active in campus activities. I was an honor student but missed out on graduating cum laude because I started working in the last semester and was unable to maintain the grades necessary.

My parents wanted me to become a doctor, but my decision to pursue business management was influenced by an uncle who was then working at the university. When I started working, I discovered the interesting nature and diverse role of an administrative professional. Since then I have stuck to it and made it a career.

While in the Philippines, I was involved with the Philippine Association of Secretaries and served in different capacities. The company I worked for at that time conducted in-house seminars and encouraged professional development by allowing staff to attend seminars and workshops. The company also supported my attendance at international conferences abroad.

When I migrated to New Zealand, I was told I would have difficulty getting a job at the same level I had in the Philippines as confidential secretary to the chairman of the board and president of the biggest real estate company in the country. Local experience was required and academic qualifications were essential. To get started, I accepted a job as a telex operator. My skills and competence in the job surfaced immediately, and my employers believed I should be given more responsibilities. I received training on computers and began doing more in the accounts department, overseeing accounts payable and receivables. After I had been with the company for five years, its New Zealand operations closed.

At this point, equipped with local experience, I found a job as an administrative secretary at the New Zealand Educational Institute (NZEI). After

three years in this position, the personal assistant to the national president resigned. I applied for and was granted this position.

My responsibilities include providing secretarial and personal assistance to the national president in all aspects of the organization and administration of the office. My duties involve communicating with other national executive members, communicating with staff and outside organizations, assisting in the preparation of executive meetings, organizing travel bookings, diarying meetings and appointments, hiring catering services, processing correspondence and other documents, and maintaining the mail flow to and from the office of the president.

The most stressful part of my job is having several things to do that are all required "yesterday." I am fortunate to have an executive who understands my responsibilities and empathizes with me. Having a good relationship, communicating effectively, and understanding each other's role are important.

The position of national president is elected on an annual basis. Therefore, I have a new executive every year unless he or she is reelected for a second term. As personal assistant to the national president, I must adapt to my executive's personality.

A newcomer in the administrative field should have a good attitude, good communi-

cation and human relations skills, and a willingness to keep abreast of technology. Spirituality also helps me a lot. I believe you should have faith in your ability to perform well at your job.

In this modern day, continuing education is important. One can achieve this through membership in professional organizations, such as the International Association of Administrative Professionals (IAAP) or a local professional group. As a member, you meet many people who help you grow both personally and professionally.

I enjoy reading, creating tapestry, doing community work, and traveling with my husband when we have free time. I am a member of IAAP and recently won the inaugural seat as International Affiliate Representative. I am a member of the Association of Administrative Professionals, New Zealand (AAPNZ) and was national president of the organization from 1999 to 2000. I received the National President's award in 1998 and a Fellow of the Association. Additionally, I am involved with our local Ethnic Council.

NILDA CAMPBELL'S CASE

New Zealand is a bicultural country with two languages. When I joined the company, only a few of the staff knew or had an interest in learning the second language, which is

Maori. I was working then for three executives, one of whom was involved with Maori education. To be able to understand my job and relate to the indigenous people, I believed I needed to learn the language. Because of my desire to do well on my job and demonstrate my skills to the executive, I privately read books and learned some of the language. One day a 30-page document in Maori needed to be typed. The executive said he would have it done by a translation service pool. He added that it could be done in a week's time and, of course, for a fee.

I knew I had a decision to make. Should I tell him I thought I could do the job and save him both time and money? Should I just let the job go to the translation service? After all, it would be another task on top of my regular responsibilities.

What would you have done? Bear in mind that I am a migrant and speak a different language. Decide how you would have handled the situation. Then turn to the end of Part 5 (page 343) to see how I solved the situation.

TRAVEL ARRANGEMENTS

Travel is a way of life for most business executives; and with our global economy, the amount of international travel has increased dramatically. Many U.S. businesses now are multinational, having locations both within the United States and abroad. Conversely, many companies abroad now have locations within the United States. Additionally, mergers between U.S. companies and companies abroad continue to occur. The car industry is a good example of international locations and mergers. For example, Honda®, Mazda®, Toyota®, Mitsibushi™, and Nissan® are some of the car manufacturers from abroad who have assembly plants in the United States. The merger of Chrysler® with Daimler-Benz™ in 1998 was a megamerger of two large automobile makers into one company. The United States and other countries take advantage of land, labor, and technical expertise available in other parts of the world to decide where to produce and/or assemble a product.

Due to the global nature of our economy, executives often make trips abroad for businesses purposes. As an administrative professional, you also may travel occasionally. Or if you are working for a company who has subsidiaries abroad, you may have the opportunity to work in one of the international locations for a period of time.

In order to handle travel arrangements effectively, you must become familiar with the types of services available. This chapter will help you understand your options when making travel arrangements. It also will help you know how to handle other travel-related responsibilities.

DOMESTIC AIR TRAVEL

Since time is an extremely important commodity for busy executives, almost all their travel is done by air. They usually do not have the time required to travel by car or rail. Thus, the emphasis in this section is on air travel.

© PhotoDisc, Inc.

PDAs and laptops allow us to continue to be productive as we travel across the United States and the world.

An air traveler today can fly from New York to California in approximately five hours or fly from Chicago to Germany in approximately eight hours. During a flight, travelers can use their time productively by taking advantage of available technology. For example, executives can read and send email, write letters and reports, and stay current on news or investments through the Internet. Computers and cell phones may not be used during takeoff or landing due to possible interference with the electronics of the airplane. (A flight attendant announces when they may and may not be used.) With our technological expertise, air travel has the potential of not only saving travel time but also allowing executives to continue to be productive.

Flight Classifications

There are three classes of flight—first class, business class, and coach. Some flights offer all three classes, with business class being offered mainly on international flights. All large planes offer first class and coach. Today a number of airlines have added regional jets, smaller in size than the planes that fly longer routes within the United States or internationally. These regional jets also fly shorter distances (for example, from Grand Rapids to Chicago or from Grand Rapids to Dallas). Regional jets generally have 30–100 seats and only one class of flight—coach. They may offer drinks and snacks or small boxed lunches.

At the opposite end of the spectrum from the regional jet is the luxury jet, which transports small groups of people (approximately 40–90) in "country club" style to almost all parts of the world. These luxury jets are very expensive and provide many amenities, including numerous attendants to handle the needs of the travelers, concierge service, spacious seating, and lavish food and beverages. Obviously, only a small portion of the population is able to utilize luxury jet transportation.

First-Class Accommodations

First-class accommodations are the most expensive of the three classes and the most luxurious. The seats are wider and farther apart, and services are greater. For example, the quantity and quality of food is better. More attention is paid to presentation of the meal. Cloth napkins, tablecloths, silverware, and china dinnerware are used. Alcoholic beverages are offered without additional cost. Some airlines allow you to eat at a time of your choosing. Headsets for listening to music are provided, the seats are generally wider, and more legroom is provided. There are more flight attendants per customer than in coach or business, which means greater attention is given to each flyer. First-class customers are allowed to board and exit first. Attendants take passengers' coats and hang them up; they also store passengers' parcels in overhead bins.

Business-Class Accommodations

Business-class accommodations are slightly more expensive than coach. The business-class section is located in front of the coach class—directly behind first class or at the front of the plane if first class is not offered. Accommodations may include more spacious seating than coach, complimentary alcoholic beverages, headsets for listening to music, recliner seats, more legroom, and better food than coach class.

Coach-Class Accommodations

Coach-class accommodations provide complimentary snacks, soft drinks, fruit juice, tea or coffee, and meals. Seats are closer together; however, one airline, American, has committed to increasing legroom for its passengers by removing some of the seats. Fewer flight attendants are available to serve the needs of the customers. Food is served with plastic dinnerware and paper napkins. Since there are fewer flight attendants, service is slower than in first class.

Company-Owned Planes

Large companies may have their own plane or fleet of planes if the amount of travel within the company makes it advantageous to do so. Pilots employed by the company generally fly these planes, which are housed at local airports. Executives may be driven to the airport by company employees and picked up at the airport upon returning from a trip.

Special Services

Some airlines offer membership in an airline club. These clubs offer a comfortable lounge for passengers who may have a layover between flights. The lounge area is equipped with computer workstations, telephones, reading material (newspapers and periodicals), comfortable chairs, drinks, snacks, and restrooms.

Large airports generally provide free shuttle service from a parking or rental car location to the airport gate. However, you are charged for parking your car, with the fee based on how long your car is parked. Since parking at an airport for an extended period of time can become expensive, large cities generally provide private shuttle services to the airport from locations around the city.

Ticketing

Gone are the days of having only one type of airline ticket, the standard paper one that contains tickets for both your departure and return. Although paper tickets are still available, the e-ticket is a common form of ticketing. Some people prefer paper tickets in case they have to change airlines because of a strike or miss a connection. However, some airlines, such as American, charge an additional fee for issuing paper tickets.

Generally, you receive an e-ticket by email or fax. This ticket is a one-page document that gives only the basic information you need—your departure and arrival times. You present your e-ticket at the counter or gate of the airline, at which time you are issued a boarding pass.

Changes or Cancellations

You may need to cancel or change a flight reservation. Generally, there is a charge for changing a flight, with most major airlines charging $100. Clearly, you should ask when making the original reservation if there is a charge for changes and, if so, how much it is. When you do cancel a flight, ask if you can use the ticket at a later time to either the same or a different location.

Ground Transportation

Once executives arrive at their destination, they may need some type of ground transportation to their hotel. That transportation may be a taxi or shuttle bus. When making arrangements, check taxi costs and the availability of shuttle services. Some hotels provide free shuttle service to and from the airport. Shuttle services are also available from private vendors, which may be less expensive than taxi service. Limousine service is also available at many airports, with the cost being approximately the same as taxi service.

If executives must attend meetings at several locations during their stay, renting a car may be the most economical and convenient method of ground transportation. Toll-free numbers for car rental agencies are listed in the telephone directory. Cars may also be rented through airlines or travel agents or over the Internet. (More information on this topic is provided later in the chapter in the section Online Reservations.) When renting a car, specify the make and model preferred and the date and time the car will be picked up and returned.

When arriving at the destination airport, executives pick up their cars from the rental location, which may be in the same building as the airport gates or in a separate building. If the car rental is in a separate location, a free shuttle service is available to take them there. The cost of a rental car is determined two ways—either by a daily rate plus an amount for each mile driven or by a daily rate with unlimited mileage. (The daily rate with unlimited mileage is the most common.) Company policy may dictate that executives rent a car no larger than midsize. Prices from rental agencies are determined by the size of the car, with the classifications being full-size (the most expensive), midsize (moderately priced), and economy (the least expensive). Insurance is available upon rental of a car. (Insurance is not mandatory if executives have their own coverage through a business or personal policy.) The executives are asked if they wish to purchase extended insurance coverage. Personnel at the rental agency fill out necessary authorization forms; the executives then sign the forms.

The car will have a full tank of gas when it is rented. The executive should fill the car up with gas before returning it since the rental agency will charge for gas (generally at a higher price than can be obtained at a local gas station) if the tank is not full when the car is returned. The executive usually carries a company credit card, which can be used to purchase gas and rent a car. Some companies prefer to deal with only one car rental agency; you should know your organization's policy before reserving a car. Most car rental agencies provide maps and assist in planning the best route to the destination. They also supply information about hotels, restaurants, and tourist attractions. However, you can also use the Internet to find

a map of the area the executive is visiting and information about hotels, restaurants, and tourist attractions.

CAR TRAVEL

If an executive is traveling only a few hundred miles, he or she may prefer to travel by car. Most top-level executives use cars furnished by the company; gasoline expenses are paid by the company. Other executives are reimbursed on a per-mile basis for any job-related travel. Your responsibilities for a trip by car may include determining the best route to follow, making hotel reservations, and identifying restaurants along the way. You may use the Internet to find this information. However, if your employer is a member of the American Automobile Association (AAA®), you may choose to obtain map, hotel, and restaurant information from them rather than the Internet.

RAIL TRAVEL

Rail travel is also an option for the executive if the trip is a fairly short distance. Travel by train allows the executive the freedom to work during a trip. He or she can use a laptop computer, a PDA, and a cell phone on the train, just as can be done on a plane. Train stations are generally centrally located within a city, and their fares are usually less expensive than airfares. First-class and sleeping accommodations are available on trains, along with coach accommodations for more economical travel. Dining cars are also available; meals may be delivered in first-class accommodations. To find out about train travel in your area, look under "Railroads" in the Yellow Pages.

OFFICE SERVICES

If the executive chooses not to take a computer, a cell phone, and so on, on a trip, he or she may need office services while away. These services are available at most hotels in large cities. The services include access to computers, printers, office supplies, fax equipment, and even administrative assistance. Some hotel rooms are equipped with desks and certain other equipment, such as fax machines. When services are not available at the hotel, most concierges can find assistance for the traveler.

INTERNATIONAL TRAVEL

As you learned earlier, many businesses now have international interests. Those interests may involve subsidiaries of the firm, separate firms, or partnerships with firms in other countries. Whatever the interests may be, travel abroad is quite common for executives in many companies.

Cultural Differences

Travelers need to be knowledgeable about and sensitive to the customs and culture of the country they are visiting. Information about other countries may be obtained from a variety of sources, with some listed here.

- Consulates of the country to be visited. (Look in the Yellow Pages under "Consulates.") These offices usually have printed materials available. They are also willing to answer questions about local customs and culture.
- Travel books. Available at libraries and bookstores, these books generally contain information about local customs and business practices.

- Books about doing business with a particular country being visited. These books are also available at libraries and bookstores.
- Seminars and short courses. The company may arrange for consultants to assist personnel in understanding the culture abroad. Additionally, local colleges and universities often provide short courses on doing business with particular countries.
- The Web. Numerous articles are available that review cultural differences internationally. Also, the Web is a good source for finding books concerning cultural differences.

Consider this example of errors that are sometimes made when visiting China.

Roger Schmiedicke visited China for the first time to negotiate a contract for his company. Roger is 35 years old. The Chinese president with whom he was negotiating was much older. After a few amenities with the Chinese were taken care of, Roger submitted the contract. The contract was written in precise language with all contingencies covered. His presentation of the contract was extremely clear; he considered himself an effective communicator. After presenting the contract, he asked the Chinese official to sign it within 30 days. He then thanked the Chinese individuals in the meeting, shook hands with everyone, and left. After 30 days had passed, Roger called the president of the Chinese company and asked him if the contract was going to be signed. The president responded, through an interpreter, that they were considering the contract. Another 30 days passed, and there was still no signed contract.

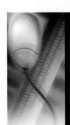

Communication Tip:

When your supervisor brings back business cards from an international trip, file the cards according to the name of the trip. For example, if the trip was to Japan, set up a card file with the first card following the Japan tab including the date of the trip and the places visited. Place the business cards behind this card.

SOCIETAL AND INSTITUTIONAL DIFFERENCES BETWEEN CHINA AND THE UNITED STATES

- China is in transition from a planned economy to a market economy. The United States is a market-driven economy.
- In China, the culture is centered around relationships; in the United States, the culture is centered around individuals.
- In China, trust is placed in the people close to you; in the United States, trust is placed in the written contract.
- The Chinese are quiet and reserved as a rule; the people of the United States are more outspoken.

- In China, relationships come first; in the United States, economics come first.
- In China, respect comes from seniority, wisdom, and ability; in the United States, respect comes from success, achievement, and wealth.
- Time has a much different connotation in China, with accountability marked by generations; in contrast, accountability in the United States is often marked by weeks or months.

Figure 11-1

What assumptions did Roger make about the Chinese? What should he have known about the Chinese culture that would have helped him in negotiating a contract?

Figure 11-1 lists several important societal and institutional differences between China and the United States that Roger should have considered. Also, you may want to refer back to Chapter 2, which lists several cultural differences among nations.

Here are some general rules that apply to international travel.

- Learn the appropriate greeting for the country you will be visiting.
- Learn how to say *please* and *thank you* in the language of the country.
- Have business cards printed with your name and your company name in both English and the language of the country you are visiting.
- Do not criticize the people or customs of the country you are visiting. Show appreciation for the music, art, and culture of the country.
- Remember that business generally is more formal in other countries than it is in the United States.
- Dress appropriately; this generally means business suits for men and conservative dresses or suits for women. Although dress in the United States has become more casual than in the past, you cannot assume that is true for international organizations. Casual business dress generally does not

imply a professional image. It may be seen as sloppy dress. It is also important to be well groomed.
- Eat the food that is offered you; do not ask what you are being served; show appreciation to your host.
- Be courteous and respectful at all times.

Appointments

If you are involved in setting up appointments or meetings for the executive, remember time zone differences. **Jet lag** (the feeling of exhaustion following a flight through several time zones) can limit an executive's effectiveness. Since it takes the body about a day to adapt to the new environment for each time zone crossed, give the executive an extra day to recover from the trip before scheduling meetings.

If executives do not have the luxury of a full day before attending appointments, they can take advantage of certain techniques to help with jet lag. For example, if they are traveling west, they can postpone the time they usually go to bed by two or three hours for two days before the flight. If they are traveling east, they can retire a couple of hours earlier than usual. At the same time, they can also start shifting mealtimes to those of the destination city. Their body clock will not be fully adapted to the new time when they land, but they will have made a start in the right direction.

You should not schedule appointments the day before the executive leaves on a trip or the day the executive returns from a trip. The day before a trip is usually a busy one in preparation for the trip. When the executive returns from a trip, he or she must again contend with time zone changes.

Business Gifts

Generally, a gift is appropriate, particularly if the executive is meeting officials for the first time. The gift should be a small one, a nice pen or some memento representative of the United States. However, executives must be aware of customs and taboos when giving gifts to avoid offending someone without knowing it. Figure 11-2 lists some gift taboos.

Flight Classifications

International flight classifications are the same as domestic air travel. Classes of flight are first class and coach, with business class available on most international flights. Weight and size restrictions for luggage may vary slightly from one airline to another. When traveling abroad, executives must arrive at the airport earlier than normal; most airlines suggest arriving two hours before the flight. This allows time for check-in, which is more involved than when traveling within the United States.

Passports

A **passport** is an official government document that certifies the identity and citizenship of an individual and grants the person permission to travel abroad. A passport is required in most countries outside the United States. Check with a local travel agent to determine if the country being visited requires a passport. For example, Canada and Mexico do not require passports. However, even if a country does not require a passport, having one is a good idea since it shows proof of citizenship.

Passport application forms can be obtained from the Web, a travel agency, a passport office, or the post office. You can find your local passport office telephone number by looking under "United States Government, Passport Information" in the Blue Pages or under "Passports" in the Yellow Pages. To obtain a passport for the first time, you must appear in person before an agent of the passport office and present the items listed in Figure 11-3.

UNDERSTANDING GIFT ETIQUETTE

- In English-speaking countries, including Britain, Ireland, Canada, and Australia, gifts are not expected and might even be considered inappropriate. Business gifts are also rarely exchanged in Spain and France.
- Gift giving is important in China, Japan, the Philippines, Russia, and Eastern European countries.
- When visiting China, present your gift to the Chinese official at your first meeting.
- In Korea, it is considered rude to open a gift in front of the donor.
- When giving gifts, be certain the gift is made in the United States. For example, it would be inappropriate to give a gift to an individual from China that was made in his or her country.
- Appropriate gifts include pens or pen-and-pencil sets. Items from your home state and books of historical areas of your state are also appropriate.

- Photo albums containing pictures of the people you met on your trip are appropriate gifts.
- Flowers are not a universally acceptable gift to take to someone's home as a gift to the host. If flowers are acceptable, the color and type of flower are important. For example, in Italy, chrysanthemums are displayed mainly at funerals. In Brazil, purple flowers signify death.
- In France, flowers are appropriate to take to a dinner host. However, chrysanthemums (primarily funeral flowers) or red roses (indicating romantic intent) should not be sent. Chocolates are also an acceptable gift for the French dinner host.

Figure 11-2

- A completed application
- Proof of U.S. citizenship through a certified copy of a birth certificate, Consular Report of Birth Abroad or Certification of Birth, Naturalization Certificate, or Certificate of Citizenship—if such proof is not available, the applicant must submit a notice that no birth record exists and provide secondary evidence, such as a baptismal certificate, a hospital birth certificate, a census record, a family bible record, or an early school record.

- Proof of identity through such documents as a driver's license, Naturalization Certificate, or Certificate of Citizenship
- Two signed duplicate photographs taken by a photographer within the past six months
- Social Security number
- Applicable fee payment

Figure 11-3

A passport is valid for ten years from the date of issue. As soon as the passport is received, it should be signed, rendering it valid. Also, the information in the front pages should be filled out, which includes the address of the bearer and names to be contacted in case of an emergency. The traveler should carry the passport with him or her while abroad; it should never be left in a hotel room.

Visas

A **visa** is a document granted by a government abroad that permits a traveler to enter and travel within a particular country. A visa usually appears as a stamped notation on a passport indicating that the bearer may enter the country for a certain period of time.

Currency

Before leaving the United States, the executive can exchange money from certain banks and currency exchange offices for the currency of the country being visited. The rate of exchange for various countries is published in the newspaper. If the executive prefers, he or she can exchange a small amount of money in the United States and exchange more money upon arrival at the country of destination. Any currency left over at the end of a trip can be exchanged for U.S. currency. It is always a good idea to be aware of the exchange rates before traveling to another country and to pay attention to the exchange rates once in the

country. Exchange rates are not always the same; for example, the exchange rate at a bank may be more favorable than the exchange rate at an airport.

The **euro** became the standard currency of Belgium, Germany, Spain, France, Ireland, Italy, Luxembourg, the Netherlands, Austria, Portugal, and Finland on January 1, 1999. By July 2002, the euro will gradually displace national currencies in the form of seven euro notes and eight euro coins. A businessperson traveling to any of these countries will no longer have to worry about currency exchange.

Health Precautions

Before leaving for a country abroad, the executive should check with a physician concerning any medications or vaccinations needed. The

© PhotoDisc, Inc.

Check with a physician about medications that can be taken for stomach-related illnesses or colds when traveling abroad.

environmental factors are usually different from those in the United States; and it is easy to develop some type of illness as a result of the food, water, or climate of the country. A physician can prescribe medications for stomach-related illnesses or colds. Also, vaccinations may be required before traveling to certain countries.

Travel agencies have information about possible health precautions. In some countries, you should not drink the water unless it has been boiled or purified. Another health precaution may be not to eat any type of raw fruit or vegetable unless it has been peeled.

Transportation Arrangements

Local arrangements within a country may include hotel, car, and rail accommodations. Hotel and rail arrangements should be made before arriving in a country. Car arrangements may be made after arriving.

Hotel Reservations

Hotel reservations can be made through travel agents or airlines at no additional cost. Hotel reservations may also be made online. A section entitled Online Reservations presented later in this chapter gives additional information. Some hotels provide breakfast at no additional charge. If administrative assistance or a meeting room is needed at a hotel, a travel agent can arrange for these services; these arrangements can also be made directly with the hotel. However, making arrangements directly may be difficult, particularly if there is a language difference. When making hotel reservations, let the hotel reservations clerk know if the executive will arrive late. You simply ask the hotel to guarantee the room for late arrival; this procedure ensures that the hotel room is not released to someone else if the executive is arriving late in the evening.

Car Rental

Cars are readily available to rent. Travel agencies can arrange for car rentals before executives arrive in a country, or the executives can rent their cars after they have arrived. In most countries, a U.S. driver's license is sufficient. You may obtain an International Driver's License from AAA. Travelers must have appropriate insurance. Travelers should also familiarize themselves with the driving regulations of the country they are visiting. Conditions are often quite different from those in the United States. For example, the steering wheel

Self-Check A

Take a few minutes now to check your understanding of what you have learned about international travel. Respond to these questions.

1. What contributes to the increase in international travel?

   _____

   _____

   _____

2. Where can you find information concerning customs and culture of a country an executive plans to visit?

   _____

   _____

   _____

3. What are six general rules that apply to international travel?

   _____

   _____

   _____

4. What is the relationship between jet lag and setting appointment times?

   _____

   _____

   _____

5. How should business cards be handled when traveling abroad?

   _____

   _____

   _____

Check your answers with those at the end of the chapter.

may be mounted on a different side of the car or you may drive on the opposite side of the road.

Rail Transportation

Many countries have excellent rail service (particularly in Europe). Frequent service is relatively inexpensive. A traveler can get from one city in Europe to another in a relatively short period of time with a limited amount of inconvenience. The trains are generally clean, and the accommodations are comfortable. Underground rail and bus transportation is also convenient and an inexpensive way to travel.

TRAVEL ARRANGEMENTS

How travel arrangements are made depends on the company where you work. Many companies use one travel agency to schedule all travel. This agency becomes knowledgeable about the needs of the company, thereby providing the unique services the company requires. Other companies, particularly small ones, ask that individuals make their own travel arrangements. Whatever method the company uses, as an administrative professional, you will have a role in making travel arrangements.

Before an executive takes his or her first trip (whether that trip is by plane, car, or rail),

talk with the person about travel preferences. If you are to be an effective agent, you must have the information listed in Figure 11-4.

If an executive is traveling by air, you need to know:

- The name of the preferred airline (if the executive has a preference) along with the frequent flyer number. (A **frequent flyer program** is an incentive program offered by most airlines that provides a variety of awards after the accumulation of a certain number of mileage points. Awards may include upgrades from coach to first class and free airline tickets.)
- Whether the flight is to be a direct one (if possible) or whether the executive is willing to change planes. (Less expensive flights are sometime available if the executive is willing to change planes. The downside of changing planes is the hassle of getting from one flight to another and the increase in travel time.)
- The class of flight—first class, business class, or coach.
- Preference as to an aisle or window seat.
- Meal preferences. (Low-calorie meals, low-cholesterol meals, salt-free meals, and other special needs are available upon request.)
- The timeline for arriving at the airport. (One hour prior to departure is standard for domestic flights; two hours prior to departure is standard for international flights.)

INFORMATION NEEDED FROM YOUR EMPLOYER ON TRIP PREFERENCES

- Dates and times of travel
- Cities to be visited
- Hotel preferences—price range, number of nights, single or double room, size of bed (full, queen, king), smoking or nonsmoking room
- Car rental preferences—type of car, size, make, model, number of days of usage, pick-up and drop-off locations
- Reimbursement—reimbursement policies of the company (**per diem** [per day] for meals and other travel expenses)
- Arrangements for transportation to airport or train station

- Appointments to be made and where and when
- Materials—computer, business cards, and so on
- Person in charge while the executive is away
- Correspondence and calls—how they will be handled in the executive's absence
- Executive's credit card number or company account number for charging tickets, hotel, car rental, and so on

Figure 11-4

- If you are making arrangements for more than one top-level executive to travel to the same location at the same time, company policy may dictate that the executives fly on separate airlines. In case of a serious accident, both executives would not be lost to the company.

If an executive is traveling by rail, you need to have this information.

- Type of accommodations—coach or first-class
- Sleeping accommodations if the executive is going to be on the train for more than one day
- Ticket delivery. (How will tickets be obtained? Are they to be picked up at the train station, mailed, or delivered?)

It is a good idea to set up a folder when the executive first tells you about an upcoming trip. Then you can place all notes and information relating to the trip in the folder. It is available for instant referral when needed.

Travel Agency Arrangements

Travel agencies perform complete travel services for a company; i.e., schedule flights, obtain tickets, make hotel reservations, arrange car rentals, and perform specialized services that the executives may need (such as obtaining workspace or meeting space at the destination). They also provide an itinerary, which lists flight numbers, departure and arrival times, hotel reservations, and car rentals. Figure 11-5 shows an itinerary prepared by a travel agency. Also, travel agencies (through the use of computer software) can provide a list of all airlines leaving at the approximate time the executive wishes to travel and provide an analysis of fares. Travel agencies usually bill the company directly for tickets and other arrangements; travel agencies do not charge the business for their service. They receive commissions from airlines, hotels, and other service industries when services are sold.

Ask the travel agency to determine the least expensive flight available. Companies are cost-conscious; they want to keep travel costs as low as possible. Since airlines are so competitive

today, reduced fares may be available on a particular airline. If that airline is not one the executive usually uses, ask if he or she is interested in getting a lower fare rate. Also, reduced rates are usually available for traveling over a weekend. However, the reduced rate has to be considered in light of the cost of additional hotel rooms and meals due to the longer stay. The reduced fare, considering other costs, may not prove to be cost-effective.

Administrative Professional Arrangements

If you do not work with a travel agency, you have the responsibility of making the travel arrangements directly. You may choose to telephone the airlines, hotels, and car rental agencies. However, telephoning can be time consuming since airline and hotel lines are busy, and you often have to hold for an agent. Another method of making reservations is on the Web. Information is given about online reservations in the next section. Whatever method you use, you should compare prices. The travel industry is a competitive one. By taking the time to telephone several airlines and hotels or check several Websites, you generally can save money.

ONLINE RESERVATIONS

More and more people are using the Web to make airline reservations, book hotels, and reserve rental cars. According to PhoCusWright®, a market research organization, online travel sales rose from $6.9 billion in 1999 to $14.5 billion in 2000. It is expected that the figure will rise to $40.1 billion in 2003.[1] According to Greenfield Online®, 28 percent of all business travelers now regularly make airline reservations online, compared with 33 percent who book using the telephone.[2] Most airlines now state when you telephone to get reservation information that you may find a less expensive

[1]Michael Shapiro, "Click & Go," *The Dallas Morning News*, Sunday, May 20, 2001.
[2]"Using the Internet to Travel the Real World," accessed July 20, 2001; available from www.carolinacountry.com.

Prepared on 06/19/—11:20:26
Passenger: MONAGHAN/THOMAS M 4228250001/MONAGHAN
CALKINS/RICHARD 4228250001

08JUL SUN 341P		**AIR** American Airlines flight no: 4058 class: Q no seat info. Grand Rapids, MI(GRR) to Chicago/O Hare, IL(ORD) arrival: 344P equipment: ER4 flight duration: 1:03 NONSMOKING OPERATED BY AMERICAN EAGLE ARRIVES ORD TERMINAL 3 EXIT ROW SEATS PENDING
	455P	**AIR** American Airlines flight no: 4157 class: Q no seat info. Chicago/O Hare, IL(ORD) to Evansville, IN(EVV) arrival: 608P equipment: ER4 flight duration: 1:13 NONSMOKING OPERATED BY AMERICAN EAGLE DEPARTS ORD TERMINAL 3 EXIT ROW SEATS PENDING
		CAR Pickup at Evansville, IN drop off 09JUL MON National Car Rental type: Inter 4dr Car Auto A/C confirmation no: 96959103COUNT rate guaranteed $21.59 per day, unlimited free miles extra day $34.24, unlimited free miles
		HOTEL Hampton Inn in Evansville, IN check out: 09JUL MON HAMPTON INN EVANSVILLE IN 8000 EAGLE CREST BLVD EVANSVILLE IN 47715 Voice: 812 473-5000 Fax: 812 479-1664 confirmation no: 87312737 Room guaranteed to credit card rate: $65.00 Rate guaranteed CHECK-OUT DATE: 09JUL 1 ROOM(S) RESERVED HOTEL GUARANTEED TO AMEX CANCEL BY 6PM TO AVOID BILLING NONSMOKING REQUESTED
		HOTEL Hampton Inn in Evansville, IN check out: 09JUL MON HAMPTON INN EVANSVILLE IN 8000 EAGLE CREST BLVD EVANSVILLE IN 47715 Voice: 812 473-5000 Fax: 812 479-1664 confirmation no: 86002177 Room guaranteed to credit card rate: $65.00 Rate guaranteed CHECK-OUT DATE: 09JUL 1 ROOM(S) RESERVED HOTEL GUARANTEED TO AMEX CANCEL BY 6PM TO AVOID BILLING NONSMOKING REQUESTED
09JUL MON 1154A		**AIR** American Airlines flight no: 4208 class: Q no seat info. Evansville, IN(EVV) to Chicago/O Hare, IL(ORD) arrival: 107P equipment: ER4 flight duration: 1:13 NONSMOKING OPERATED BY AMERICAN EAGLE ARRIVES ORD TERMINAL 3
	246P	**AIR** American Airlines flight no: 4177 class: Q no seat info. Chicago/O Hare, IL(ORD) to Grand Rapids, MI(GRR) arrival: 446P equipment: ER4 flight duration: 1:00 NONSMOKING OPERATED BY AMERICAN EAGLE DEPARTS ORD TERMINAL 3

Figure 11-5 A Travel Agency Prepares an Itinerary.

ADVANTAGES OF MAKING ONLINE TRAVEL ARRANGEMENTS

- Virtual travel agents are available any hour of the day or night and on weekends. There is no "holding" on the Internet.
- Fares of different airlines can be compared.
- Last-minute specials on airfare are given.
- Hotels and cars may be booked online.
- International travel advice and information is available on some sites, such as passport and visa

information, political instability in foreign countries, health scares, and natural disasters.
- Frequent flyer bonus miles are available on some sites if tickets are purchased online.
- Weather information is given on some sites.

Figure 11-6

flight on their Website. Some advantages of making travel arrangements online are listed in Figure 11-6.

Two major one-stop online travel-booking sites are www.expedia.com and www.travelocity.com. Both sites negotiate fares directly with major airlines and offer below-market deals to consumers. However, there are some disadvantages to special fares.

- They cannot be changed or upgraded.
- They are not valid for standby on other flights.
- No frequent flier miles are awarded.

An additional one-stop travel-booking site is www.orbitz.com, which came online in 2001. Its early success suggests it will do well in the travel market. In addition to the one-stop travel-booking sites available, all major airlines have a Website. Website addresses for several of the one-stops, plus several individual airline sites, are given in Figure 11-7.

WEBSITE ADDRESSES

- www.travelocity.com
- www.expedia.com
- www.orbitz.com
- www.southwest.com
- www.ual.com
- www.hotwire.com
- www.priceline.com
- www.delta.com
- www.AA.com
- www.northwest.com

Figure 11-7

RESPONSIBILITIES BEFORE THE TRIP

In addition to the duties already mentioned that you have in assisting the executive with travel arrangements, other responsibilities include:

- Preparing a complete itinerary
- Obtaining travel funds
- Preparing materials for the trip
- Checking the calendar
- Confirming appointments
- Understanding how matters are to be handled while the executive is away

Prepare the Itinerary

Once you have determined where and when the executive wants to travel and after you have made the appropriate travel arrangements, you need to prepare an itinerary. The **itinerary,** a detailed outline of the trip, is a record of all trip arrangements for you and the executive. An itinerary should include information on flight numbers, airports, departure and arrival times, hotel arrangements, car rental information, appointments, and any other pertinent information. You have already learned that a travel agency will provide an itinerary that includes flight, hotel, and car information. However, an agency does not have the information on appointments and other special information. The executive needs to have an itinerary that reflects all the activities on the trip.

You will want to prepare multiple copies of the itinerary.

- One for the executive
- One for the executive's family
- One for the person who will be in charge while the executive is away
- One for your files

Figure 11-8 shows an itinerary prepared by the administrative professional. Time zones are included on the itinerary since the executive is traveling from one time zone to another. Otherwise, they are not necessary.

Obtain Travel Funds

Companies differ in how they handle funds for trips. Most of the time, airline tickets are charged directly to the company. Hotel, meals, and car rental may be charged on a credit card provided by the company. Another practice is for the individual to get a cash advance to cover all expenses of the trip. To do so, the individual fills out a travel form before leaving, indicating how much money he or she will need for lodging, meals, and so on. The company advances the money to the employee before he or she leaves on the trip. Another practice is for the executive to pay the expenses; he or she is then reimbursed by the company upon returning from the trip. Most company policies require employees to turn in a receipt for an expense above a certain amount.

If an executive is traveling abroad, he or she may take traveler's checks. Traveler's checks may be purchased from most local banks and travel agencies. However, since credit cards are readily acceptable in almost all international locations, it may be easier for the executive to use a credit card. He or she may want to take a limited amount of money in traveler's checks. Traveler's checks come with two receipts, which serve as records of the checks' serial numbers. One copy of the receipt should be kept in the files at the office, and the other copy should be given to the executive. If checks are lost, the individual is reimbursed by producing the receipt. Therefore, the receipts should not be kept with the checks.

Prepare and Organize Materials

Any number of items may be needed for a trip. If it is an international trip, items such as passports, medications, business cards, and small gifts may be necessary. Whether the trip is

---

Itinerary for Paul Forrest Mr. G

March 1–2, 2004 Nov

Trip to San Francisco China

central > chicago standard time

Monday, March 1 (Dallas to San Francisco) Chicago

CST Leave Dallas—DFW Regional Airport, American Flight 55; tickets are in briefcase.	9:30 a.m.
PST Arrive San Francisco—San Francisco International Airport; arrangements have been made for car at Hertz; hotel reservations are at the Airport Hilton, telephone: 555-0145.	10:30 a.m.
PST Appointment with Peter Nelson of Nelson & Nelson in his office, 1214 Harwood Avenue, telephone: 555-0116; correspondence file in briefcase.	2:00 p.m.

Tuesday, March 2 (San Francisco to Dallas)

PST Appointment with Roger Hall of San Francisco office; reports in briefcase.	10:00 a.m.
PST Appointment with Carla Hampton of San Francisco office; reports in briefcase.	2:00 p.m.
PST Leave San Francisco International Airport on American Flight 43.	5:00 p.m.
CST Arrive Dallas—DFW Regional Airport.	10:00 p.m.

Figure 11-8 Detailed Itinerary Prepared by the Administrative Professional.

domestic or international, several items usually must be prepared, such as reports for meetings and presentation materials.

Here is a list of items that may be included in a briefcase.

- E-ticket or plane ticket
- Itinerary
- Credit cards, traveler's checks
- Hotel confirmation
- Special materials, reports, or contracts for appointments
- Presentation notes
- Office equipment and supplies; for example, laptop and disks
- Reading materials
- Business cards
- Passport (for international trips)

Check the Calendar

Check your employer's electronic and desk calendars, along with your calendar, to see if any appointments have been scheduled for the period in which the executive will be gone. If so, find out if they are to be canceled or if someone else in the company will handle them. Then notify the people involved. Also check other files, such as tickler files or pending files, to see if there are matters that should be handled before the executive leaves.

Confirm Trip Appointments

Write or call people the executive plans to see during the trip to confirm the appointments. It is wise to do this before preparing the itinerary. Get correct addresses and directions from the hotel to the location of all meetings. Make a note of these addresses and directions on the itinerary.

Know How Matters Are to Be Handled

Find out who will be in charge during your employer's absence. Check to see if your employer is expecting any important papers that should be forwarded. Be sure you understand how to handle all incoming mail. For example, your employer may want you to refer all mail that must be answered immediately to another executive within the office. Or your employer may ask that you answer the routine mail (signing the employer's name with your initials) and refer the nonroutine mail to a designated executive.

YOUR ROLE DURING THE EXECUTIVE'S ABSENCE

You may be tempted to tell yourself that you have worked hard in getting the executive ready for the trip so you deserve a little time off. However, such is not the case. It may be a more relaxed pace for you while the executive is away, but certain responsibilities are ongoing. Here are a few of them.

Handle Messages, Appointments, and Correspondence

Executives often call in to the office on a daily basis while they are away on trips. If possible, determine the time of day the executive may be calling so you can have all messages and items of importance ready to discuss with him or her. Always keep urgent messages and correspondence in a certain place on your desk so you can refer to them quickly.

Communication Tip:

Prepare a folder for special materials that are to be taken on a trip. Label the folder appropriately, and place it in the executive's briefcase. Be certain you make copies of any information needed.

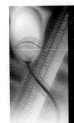

While the executive is away, you may need to set up appointments for people who want to see him or her after the trip. Remember that the executive will probably already have a full day of work to handle on the first day back. Thus, it is not a good idea to schedule appointments for that day. If you must do so, however, remember to schedule as few appointments as possible and keep the timing convenient for the executive.

It is important that correspondence be handled. You may be responsible for seeing that all mail is given to the person in charge; you also may be required to assist the person in answering the mail. You may have the responsibility for answering routine correspondence. If so, keep a copy of the correspondence and response for your employer to review after she or he returns. So your employer will know of the visitors and telephone callers, you may wish to keep a log.

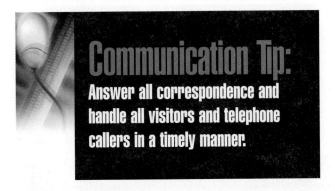

Make Decisions

You have the responsibility of making wise decisions within the scope of your responsibility during the executive's absence. You should know what matters to refer to someone else in the company and what matters to refer directly to the executive through an email, a fax, or a telephone call. Certainly you do not want to place an excessive number of calls to the executive while she or he is away, but there may be matters that the executive must be informed of immediately.

Maintain a Positive Attitude

Sometimes when a manager is away and we are not sure how to handle something, we find ourselves thinking we cannot do the job. We may even become frustrated and negative about our abilities. Remember that a soft skill has been stressed in each chapter of this book. Why? From years of research, we know that people lose their jobs most often due to lack of "soft skills" rather than lack of knowledge or technological skills. We also know from research that one of the most significant differences between high and low achievers is their attitude. High achievers maintain a positive attitude. They believe they can perform their job well, make a difference on the job, and solve problems. Conversely, people with a negative attitude often believe they cannot perform their job well so they do not really try. Do not confuse a positive attitude with a **Pollyanna attitude** (a foolishly or blindly optimistic attitude). People who have a positive attitude do not see everything in life as wonderful. However, they do see ways to change a bad situation.

Think now about your attitude. Is it generally positive or generally negative? Answer the questions in Self-Check B on page 288.

1. Do you think of yourself as successful in most situations?

_____

_____

_____

_____

2. Do you expect to do a good job?

_____

_____

_____

3. Do you think about your failures often?

_____

_____

_____

_____

4. Are your best friends positive or negative people?

_____

_____

_____

_____

5. Now think of a time in which you had a negative expectation of an action or event. List that negative expectation. Did that negative expectation come true?

_____

_____

_____

_____

© PhotoDisc, Inc.

Seek out positive people; negative people sap your energy and positive resolve.

tion." A positive attitude merely means that you believe in yourself; you believe that you have the power to make positive things happen in your life. Even though you might believe you have a positive attitude, consider these situations.

■ Do you procrastinate in your course work, putting off to the last minute your homework and then doing a poor job?
■ Do you engage in activities that are harmful to your health even though research shows the behavior to be harmful?
■ Are you extremely critical of everyone, including yourself?

If you answered yes to any of these questions, chances are your actions do not always reflect what you believe is a positive attitude. So how do you go about achieving and maintaining a positive attitude? Here are some suggestions.

■ Practice visualization. Picture yourself in positive situations where you are achieving your goals and solving your problems.

Assuming you accept the importance of achieving and maintaining a positive attitude, answer the following questions:

■ What is a positive attitude?
■ How do you go about achieving and maintaining a positive attitude?

Attitude is defined as "a state of mind or feeling with regard to some matter or posi-

- Listen to yourself talk. Do you often say: "I don't think I can do that well" or "I know I won't be successful on that job"? Control your inner voice. Say to yourself silently or out loud "I didn't mean that. I know I can do the job well and be successful, and here is how I will be successful." Then think through the ways that will make you successful in the particular situation you are confronting.
- Remind yourself often of past successes.
- Surround yourself with positive people and ideas. Do not spend time with negative people. They can sap your energy and positive resolve.
- Keep trying to achieve whatever is important to you until you are successful.

Use Time Wisely

The slower work pace that generally occurs while the executive is traveling gives you time to plan and organize your work. Perhaps you need to organize your desk, clean out the files, prepare new labels for folders, plan your work for the next two weeks, or catch up on your professional reading. While the executive is gone, you have the opportunity to do so. Use the time wisely.

POSTTRIP BRIEFING

When the executive returns, you must brief him or her on what occurred in the office during the trip, providing all necessary information. You should also inform the executive of the appointments you set up, the telephone calls and correspondence you received, and other items that require his or her attention.

Additionally, the executive may need to write several follow-up letters as a result of the trip. Thank-you letters are often sent. Information on products or services may need to be sent to customers. The executive may tell you what needs to be said and ask that you write or draft the correspondence. The executive may also need to answer correspondence that accumulated during his or her absence; he or she may ask that you respond to the correspondence. You may be handed several receipts (meals and incidental expenses) that need to be included on the expense report, in addition to flight and hotel expenses. Expense forms are provided by the company and should be filled in correctly with the amounts totaled. You should complete the expense report carefully, double-checking all figures and totals. You should also be sure that the necessary receipts are attached and that the figures on the expense report match the figures on the receipts.

CHAPTER SUMMARY

The summary will help you remember the important points covered in the chapter.

- There are three classes of flight—first class, business class, and coach.
- First-class accommodations are the most expensive and the most luxurious of the three classes, offering wider seats, more legroom, better food, better service, and complimentary alcoholic beverages.
- Business-class accommodations are slightly more expensive than coach and offer more spacious seating, complimentary alcoholic beverages, headsets, recliner seats, and more legroom.
- Coach-class accommodations provide complimentary snacks, soft drinks, fruit juice, tea or coffee, and meals. Seats are closer together and less service is provided. Coach class is the least expensive class.
- In addition to flying, the executive may travel by car or by rail. AAA can provide information for car travel, and the appropriate railroad can provide information about rail travel.
- When traveling internationally, the executive needs to be sensitive to different customs and cultures. The executive should take business cards printed with his or her name and the company name printed in both English and the language of the country being visited.
- Jet lag can be a factor in international travel; it should be considered when scheduling appointments.
- Small business gifts are appropriate for business associates when traveling abroad.
- A passport is necessary when traveling to countries other than Canada or Mexico.
- A visa is a document granted by a government abroad that permits a traveler to enter and travel within a particular country.
- The euro has become the standard currency for Belgium, Germany, Spain, France, Ireland, Italy, Luxembourg, the Netherlands, Austria, Portugal, and Finland.
- Before leaving for a trip abroad, the executive should check with a physician about health problems that may occur due to the food, water, or climate of the country.
- Rail and bus transportation are other alternatives to renting a car.
- In helping the executive to schedule travel, the administrative professional must know the dates and times of travel, the cities to be visited, hotel preferences, car rental preferences, appointments to be scheduled, materials needed, and so on.
- If the executive is traveling by air, the administrative professional must know the name of the preferred airline, the class of flight, preferences as to an aisle or window seat, meal preferences, and so on.
- Arrangements for travel can be made through travel agencies or by the administrative professional using the Internet or calling the airline, hotel, and car rental agency directly.
- The administrative professional has several responsibilities before the trip, including purchasing the tickets, preparing an itinerary, obtaining travel funds, preparing materials for the trip, checking the calendar, confirming appointments, and understanding how matters are to be handled while the executive is away.
- While the executive is away, the administrative professional should handle messages, appointments, and correspondence; make the appropriate decisions; maintain a positive attitude; and use time wisely.
- When the executive returns, the administrative professional must bring the executive up to date on significant happenings while he or she was away and assist with any correspondence and reports that need to be prepared as a result of the trip.

CHAPTER GLOSSARY

The following terms were used in this chapter. Definitions are provided to help you review the terms.

- **First-class accommodations** (p. 273)—the most expensive of the three classes of airline flights and the most luxurious.
- **Business-class accommodations** (p. 273)—slightly more expensive than coach but less expensive than first class; located in front of coach class or directly behind first class.
- **Coach-class accommodations** (p. 274)—the least expensive of the three classes of flight; seats are closer together, there is less legroom, and service is not as good as in first class or business class.
- **Jet lag** (p. 277)—the feeling of exhaustion following a flight through several time zones.
- **Passport** (p. 278)—an official government document that certifies the identity and citizenship of an individual and grants the person permission to travel abroad.
- **Visa** (p. 279)—a document granted by a government abroad that permits a traveler to enter and travel within a particular country.
- **Euro** (p. 279)—the standard currency of Belgium, Germany, Spain, France, Ireland, Italy, Luxembourg, the Netherlands, Austria, Portugal, and Finland.
- **Frequent flyer program** (p. 281)—an incentive program offered by most airlines that provides a variety of awards after the accumulation of a certain number of mileage points.
- **Per diem** (p. 281, Figure 11-4)—means "per day"; it is used in conjunction with how much a company is willing to reimburse an individual for travel.
- **Itinerary** (p. 284)—a detailed outline of a trip showing all trip arrangements, including flight numbers, airports, departure and arrival times, hotel arrangements, car rental information, appointments, and so on.
- **Pollyanna attitude** (p. 287)—a foolishly or blindly optimistic attitude.
- **Attitude** (p. 288)—a state of mind or feeling with regard to some matter or position.

DISCUSSION ITEMS

These discussion items provide an opportunity to test your understanding of the chapter through written responses and/or discussion with your classmates and your instructor.

1. List and explain the three main classes of domestic flights.
2. List eight general rules that apply to traveling internationally.
3. What are some of the advantages of making travel arrangements online?
4. List four responsibilities of the administrative professional during trip preparation.
5. Explain why a positive attitude is important, and list five steps to achieving a positive attitude.

CRITICAL-THINKING ACTIVITY

Juan Mercado, one of your two assistants, has been working for AmeriAsian for almost two years. Luyin Wu, your other assistant, has been working for AmeriAsian for almost a year. Although Juan is Puerto Rican, he was born in New York and came to Michigan to go to college. He is fluent in both English and Spanish. Juan is extremely outgoing and will grab you in a bear hug when things are going well. Although Juan is proud of his heritage, he believes he is a blend of Spanish and American cultures. Luyin is from China and has been in the United States only two years. She learned English in school in China, but she does not always understand slang expressions. She is quiet and reserved. Both are good employees; both enjoy their jobs. Luyin lives with a married sister who came to the United States five years ago. Juan is married and has his own home.

CRITICAL-THINKING ACTIVITY

(continued)

When Mr. Albertson found out he would be traveling to China, he talked with Luyin on several occasions about the culture. She had never seemed willing to talk about her life before, but she seemed eager to share certain things with Mr. Albertson. She said that in her culture, older people are greatly respected. She said she was shocked when she came to the United States and heard young people talk disrespectfully to their elders. She also said that she did not like public displays of affection. When Juan heard about this, he became embarrassed. He decided he must have offended Luyin on numerous occasions without realizing that he was doing so. He did not say anything to her, but the next day he asked you how he should handle the situation. What advice would you give Juan?

RESPONSES TO SELF-CHECK A

1. Contributions to the increase in international travel include the global economy; countries taking advantage of land, labor, and technical expertise available in all parts of the world; international markets; and technology.

2. You can find information concerning customs and cultures of other countries through consulates of the country to be visited, travel books, books about a particular country, seminars and short courses offered at local colleges, and the Web.

3. Six general rules that apply to international travel are given below (students may list any six of the following).
   - Learn the appropriate greeting for the country you will be visiting.
   - Learn how to say *please* and *thank you* in the language of the country.
   - Have business cards printed with your name and your company name in both English and the language of the country you are visiting.
   - Do not criticize the people or customs of the country. Show appreciation for the music, art, and culture of the country.
   - Remember that business generally is more formal in other countries than it is in the United States.
   - Dress appropriately; this generally means business suits for men and conservative dresses or suits for women. Also be well groomed.
   - Eat the food that is offered you; do not ask what you are being served; show appreciation to your host.
   - Be courteous and respectful at all times.

4. Since it generally takes the body about a day to adapt to the new environment for each time zone crossed, give the executive an extra day to recover from the trip before scheduling meetings.

5. Business cards should be given to all representatives of a company; the cards should be printed in English and in the language of the country being visited.

PROJECTS

Project 11-1 (Objectives 1 and 2)
Online Project

Mr. Albertson is visiting AmeriAsian's China office in Beijing from November 11 through November 18. Determine flight times and hotel arrangements by checking a Website. The executive vice president of the Beijing office, Pai Ying, will pick Mr. Albertson up at the airport. He will not need a car. He wants to leave the morning of November 11 and return the afternoon/evening of November 18. He will fly first class and prefers low-calorie meals. He wants a nice hotel that includes a queen-size bed, a room for nonsmokers, and exercise facilities. Mr. Albertson does not speak Chinese. His appointments while in China include the following:

November 13, 9 a.m., appointment with Chan Yi

November 13, 2 p.m., appointment with Sheng Mo

November 15, 10 a.m., appointment with Kuo Lu

November 15, 1 p.m., appointment with Niu Chih

You may want to use one of the these Web addresses to determine the most appropriate flight times and hotel: www.travelocity.com, www.expedia.com, or www.orbitz.com. Prepare a travel itinerary, listing the appointments. Note the number of hours on the itinerary for travel time; also note the time difference from Michigan to China. Turn in the itinerary to your instructor.

Project 11-2 (Objectives 3 and 4)

While Mr. Albertson is in China, you ask one of your assistants, Luyin Wu, to sort the mail each day and the other assistant, Juan Mercado, to take care of telephone calls. You are devoting your time to a report that will take you several days to complete; you must have it finished by the time Mr. Albertson returns. Mr. Albertson calls in after being gone three days to see what important items may need his attention. You tell him there is nothing. However, after hanging up, you decide to check the mail

and the telephone calls. You discover that he should have been informed of two calls and three letters. You thought you were clear in your instructions to both Luyin and Juan that they should call your attention to any important items. You are upset with them and call them in to voice your concerns. "I should have known you two would make a mess of the job." Both Luyin and Juan say they did not understand your instructions. You tell them you will take care of the mail and phone calls yourself. They are both concerned; Juan apologizes profusely and Luyin looks down and says nothing. The situation is tense in the office for the next few days.

Answer these questions:

How should you have handled the situation?

Did you demonstrate a positive attitude?

Once you have answered those questions, describe your role during Mr. Albertson's absence.

Project 11-3 (Objective 4)

Add to your Professional Growth Plan by describing how you will continue to work on developing a positive attitude. File your plan on your Professional Growth Disk under "Progro11-3."

ENGLISH USAGE CHALLENGE DRILL

Correct the following sentences. Cite the grammar rule that is applicable to each sentence. Before you begin, review semicolon and colon punctuation rules, collective nouns, and often misused words in the Reference Guide of this text.

1. The board is divided on their opinions.
2. Hand me all of the books.
3. If you want to lose weight, you need to give up three things eating fatty snacks, eating large portions of food at meal times, and being a couch potato.
4. I use this quotation from Theodore Roosevelt frequently when making speeches; "It is not the critic who counts, not the man who points out how the strong man stumbled, or where the doer of deeds could have done them better. The credit belongs to the man who is actually in the arena; whose face is marred by dust and sweat and blood; who strives valiantly; who errs and comes short again and again; who knows the great enthusiasms, the great devotions, and spends himself in a worthy cause; who, at the best, knows in the end the triumph of high achievement; and who, at worst, if he fails, at least fails while daring greatly, so that his place shall never be with those cold and timid souls who know neither victory nor defeat."
5. The students' demands included the following better food in the cafeteria, free parking, and less markup on textbooks in the bookstore.

ASSESSMENT OF CHAPTER OBJECTIVES

Now that you have completed the chapter and the projects, take a few minutes to review the chapter learning objectives. For your convenience, the objectives are repeated here. Did you accomplish these objectives? If you were unable to accomplish the objectives, give your reasons for not doing so.

1. Make travel arrangements. Yes _____ No _____

_____

_____

_____

2. Prepare an itinerary. Yes _____ No _____

_____

_____

_____

3. Describe the responsibilities of administrative professionals
regarding their executives' trips. Yes _____ No _____

_____

_____

_____

4. Maintain a positive attitude. Yes _____ No _____

_____

_____

_____

You may submit your answers in writing to your instructor, using the memorandum form on the Student CD, SCDAP11-1.

MEETINGS AND CONFERENCES

LEARNING OBJECTIVES

1. Identify the responsibilities of the administrative professional for meetings and conferences.
2. Become familiar with the types of meetings—audio, online, and video.
3. Prepare meeting notices.
4. Prepare agendas and minutes.
5. *Develop conflict resolution skills.*

Meetings are a way of life in the workplace. In a business environment that is downsized, multinational, and driven by technology (with email, faxes, and computers providing for quick communication throughout our world), you might expect fewer meetings. However, in reality, the opposite is true. As more work is handled by teams, the number of meetings is increasing rather than decreasing. Even estimating conservatively, administrative professionals average four hours a week in meetings. This average increases the higher a person's position in the organization. Management may spend as much as 50 percent or more of each week in meetings. Obviously, these meetings are costly to business. In fact, estimates show that organizations spend between 7 and 15 percent of their personnel budgets on meetings. Thus, the meeting time must be spent as productively as possible. This chapter will help you develop the knowledge and skills needed to assist your supervisor in planning, organizing, and facilitating productive meetings. Additionally, you will learn more about how to manage conflict.

NECESSARY MEETINGS

Meetings are a good means of generating ideas, sharing information, and making decisions. Calling a meeting can be appropriate in the following situations:

■ Advice is needed from a group of people.
■ A group needs to be involved in solving a problem or making a decision.
■ An issue needs clarification.
■ Information needs to be given to a group.
■ A problem exists but it is not clear what the problem is or who is responsible for dealing with it.
■ Quick communication is necessary with a large number of people.

UNNECESSARY MEETINGS

Unfortunately, unnecessary and unproductive meetings are held daily in organizations. These meetings generally occur when no clear purpose or agenda is defined or when no follow-up takes place. These meetings are not only a waste of an individual's time but also a waste of the organization's time. Everyone has been to such meetings. Sometimes the major purpose of meetings seems to be one of these.

- Consume large quantities of coffee and doughnuts at the company's expense
- Engage in small talk with co-workers
- Get away from work responsibilities for a while
- Ask others' opinions about a subject
- Avoid making a decision

Clearly, if the person or team calling the meeting has not thought through the importance of the meeting, the agenda to be discussed, and the manner in which the meeting will be conducted, such inane meetings can occur. These meetings often result in the participants wondering why a meeting was called in the first place. Meetings are generally not a good idea in these situations.

- Confidential or sensitive personnel matters must be addressed.
- There is inadequate data for the meeting.
- There is insufficient time to prepare for the meeting.

- The information could be better communicated by memo, fax, email, or telephone.
- Group members feel considerable anger or hostility among themselves, with individuals needing time to calm down before coming together.

Human Relations Tip:

Schedule meetings only when absolutely necessary. A poorly structured meeting with no apparent purpose results in a waste of employees' time, frustration for many, and unnecessary costs for the organization.

TYPES OF MEETINGS

For years, meetings were traditional in nature; that is, the participants gathered in face-to-face meetings at a common location. Now with the technology that is available, we can choose the type of meeting to have. The traditional meeting and the electronic meeting have certain advantages and disadvantages. By carefully analyzing the purpose of the meeting and the outcomes expected, you can determine which type of meeting will be most appropriate.

Meetings are not a good idea when the purpose of the meeting is not clear.

Chapter 12: Meetings and Conferences

Traditional Meetings

The traditional meeting where people gather for face-to-face discussion of an issue or a problem at one location has a number of advantages.

- All individuals have a chance to talk informally with other participants before, during, and after the meeting.
- The body language of the participants can be closely observed.
- People generally feel more relaxed with the informal setting.
- If the issue to be discussed is a difficult one, the atmosphere allows attendees to deal more effectively with the issue.
- A creative, interactive group discussion is more likely.
- Widespread participation among group members is more likely.

Clearly, there are disadvantages to the face-to-face meeting. Some of these disadvantages are listed in Figure 12-1.

Electronic Meetings

Telecommunication technology provides alternatives to face-to-face meetings through several electronic options referred to as **teleconfer-**

encing. Teleconferencing is a general term applied to a variety of technology-assisted two-way (interactive) communications via telephone lines, DSL, cable modems, and other high-bandwidth connections. You learned about these high-bandwidth connections in Chapter 5. If you do not recall the specifics of bandwidth, you may want to review that chapter now. There are three main types of teleconferencing: audioconferencing, online conferencing, and videoconferencing.

Audioconferencing

Audioconferencing in its simplest form is a type of conference in which participants talk with each other using standard telephones or speakerphones. Many telephones now allow you to add additional callers to your line by pressing the appropriate button on your telephone (usually labeled "conference"). If your phone does not have this capability, you can access a conference operator through your telephone service provider, who will set up the call for you and make sure all callers are on the line at the appropriate time. Additionally, a number of communications companies (such as NuVox Communications®, WorldCom™, and Gentner®) can assist you with audioconferencing. Additional services available from these companies include the following:

DISADVANTAGES OF FACE-TO-FACE MEETINGS

- Travel to and from a face-to-face meeting can be costly, particularly if the travel is from another city, state, or country. Cost includes not only transportation to and from the meeting and/or hotel rooms if the meeting requires an overnight stay, but also the time lost in travel. A study done by InfoCom of Greenwich, Connecticut, and sponsored by MCI WorldCom revealed that the typical executive flies to 4.6 meetings a month, taking at least a day of travel time for sessions that last an average of only 3.2 hours.
- The meeting room may be costly; or if the meeting is held within the company, finding a vacant room or tying up a room that is used for multiple purposes can be a problem.

- Coffee, lunches, and other refreshments for the participants are needed if the meeting is a fairly long one. Individuals need breaks in long meetings.
- The face-to-face meeting can be harder to control since people are freer to interact with each other.
- Socializing can consume a major part of the meeting time if it is not controlled by the leader.
- Time can be lost through waiting for people who are late.
- Individuals (particularly those who work together daily) may tend to rely on their colleagues' suggestions or solutions; thus, creativity can suffer.

Figure 12-1

- On-demand conferencing from any touch-tone phone with no reservation and no operator required
- Simplification of material distribution through faxes and voice mail
- Phone-add capabilities for videoconferencing, enabling audio-only participation in a videoconference using a telephone
- The ability to take your audioconferences onto the Internet.

You can review the services provided by audioconferencing companies by accessing their Websites. If you do not have a company name, use the keyword *audioconferencing* to locate companies who provide these services.

Advantages of audioconferencing include the following:

- Assembling individuals on short notice (assuming their schedules allow)

© Image 100

Audioconferencing allows several people at locations around the world to talk with each other at one time through telephone technology.

- Connecting individuals at any location
- Using familiar and readily available telephone technology
- Reducing travel time and expense
- Reducing the administrative overhead involved in meetings
- Broadening meeting participation
- Receiving digital recordings of meetings

One of the primary disadvantages of an audioconference is the lack of visual input. However, visual input can be achieved through an ordinary fax machine to transmit reports, spreadsheets, graphs, and so on. In addition, visual messages can be written on an **electronic whiteboard.** This whiteboard is a display screen on which multiple users write or draw. Participants in the audioconference can see what is written on the whiteboard by viewing it on a video screen and can add or change the visual input. In other words, the whiteboards allow for **interactivity** (information transmitted from one location to another and acted on by participants at any location). Whiteboards can also be used as **stand-alone conventional dry-erase boards** or as **electronic dry-erase whiteboards.** The conventional whiteboard is used without connection to a computer or a projector—as a standard classroom whiteboard is used. The electronic dry-erase whiteboard is connected to a computer, but without a projector. All annotations made on the board can be saved to the computer, printed out, and emailed or faxed to participants.

Online Conferencing

Online meetings link individual participants via a computer. A variety of terms are used to describe these meetings, including computer conferencing, keyboard conferencing, Web conferencing, and data conferencing. The term *online meetings* is used in this textbook since it describes the exact nature of the meeting. Online meetings may have a video portion; however, currently most do not. Videoconferencing is dealt with as a separate topic in the next section.

Online meetings utilize techniques that allow groups of people anywhere in the world to exchange ideas via the computer. This technology allows people to work successfully and productively. For example, a group of people can work in **real time,** simultaneously creating electronically produced documents such as presentations, spreadsheets, reports, and proposals. An **outside** or **remote facilitator** (a person trained in facilitation techniques who is not part of the decision making of a meeting and whose role is to keep the meetings productive, positive, and efficient) may be used. Online meetings, as explained earlier, may have a video portion. For example, if participants do not know each other, cameras used at the beginning of the meeting allow each person to introduce himself or herself and provide background information. Additionally, computers can be connected to the Internet.

In setting up online meetings, you have two basic options.

- Have your meetings fully hosted on a vendor's Website and pay a per-use or monthly fee
- Purchase software for use on your own Website

Companies who provide Website service include the following:

- WebEx Meeting Center℠
- Contigo™ i2I
- PlaceWare® Web Conferencing
- SneakerLabs™ iMeet
- Gentner
- MCI™ WorldCom
- Sprint®

Software packages available include NetMeeting® and HelpMeeting LLC™. With these and other similar software packages, you can engage in these activities.

- Share files
- Show presentations
- Conduct chats
- Utilize whiteboarding

Videoconferencing

Videoconferencing is a system of transmitting audio and video between individuals at distant locations. Individuals can see and hear each other. Videoconferencing is also referred to as **virtual conferencing** since it allows participants to enter and move around rooms electronically. For example, virtual conferences can be set up that allow participants to enter a conference room and view the speaker, post questions for the speaker, and enter a chat room to talk with other conference participants.

One of the largest obstacles to videoconferencing in the past was the amount of bandwidth needed. However, the technology is steadily improving, especially for organizations that utilize DSL, cable modems, T1 lines, and other high-bandwidth connections. Videoconferencing also has limits as to picture quality. Vendors continue to work on ways to make videoconferencing more attractive. For example, Vianet Technologies® is using the company's Wavelet™ compression technology to eliminate portions of images, such as a background, that are not crucial. This procedure helps reduce the bulk of data needed for video frames, improves speed, and clarifies details in the parts of the image that remain. With advances in technology, expectations are that videoconferencing will become a more productive tool.

Videoconferencing may be accomplished through the use of Web conferencing software or through vendors who provide videoconferencing services. Video software includes Webcam32™, CUseeMe®, CorelVIDEO™, and shareware Webcam32. Service providers include such organizations as MediaOnDemand.com℠ and MShow.com™.

Advantages and Disadvantages of Electronic Meetings

Just as face-to-face meetings have advantages and disadvantages, so do electronic meetings.

Some of the advantages are as follows:

- Simplicity—participants can join a meeting or conference anytime anywhere
- Savings in travel time, meals, and hotel rooms
- Ability to take care of the concerns of multinational organizations without expensive travel and resultant time commitments

Electronic meetings allow for individuals at distant locations to discuss issues without having to spend time and money traveling.

© PhotoDisc, Inc.

- Ability to present a considerable amount of information concisely through sophisticated audio and video technology
- Ability to bring together people with expertise in different areas to discuss problems of mutual concern with a minimum of effort
- Availability of software packages and service providers

Some of the disadvantages are as follows:

- Less spontaneity between individuals due to a fairly structured environment
- Inability to see body language of all participants at any one time
- Inability to pick up small nuances of body language over the monitor
- No or relatively little socialization between participants
- Less chance for effective brainstorming on issues

ORGANIZATIONAL MEETINGS

Several types of meetings are held within an organization. Executives usually meet on a regular basis with the people who report to them. These meetings are generally referred to as staff meetings. Meetings are often held with customers and clients of the business, generally involving only two or three people. Other types of meetings, which may be more formal in nature, include board meetings, committee meetings, and meetings of special task forces or project teams.

The Executive's Role

The executive has certain roles in planning meetings. He or she must determine the purpose of the meeting, determine who should attend, and determine the number of attendees. The executive may work closely with the administrative professional in accomplishing these tasks.

Determining the Purpose of the Meeting

Unless the administrative professional is calling the meeting, it is generally not his or her responsibility to determine the purpose of the meeting. However, the administrative professional must understand the purpose of the meeting in order to make appropriate arrangements. If your supervisor does not tell you the purpose of the meeting, ask. Your asking may help your supervisor define the purpose; in other words, it may help crystallize his or her thinking regarding the meeting.

Determining Who Should Attend

The decision as to who will attend a meeting is generally not the prerogative of the administrative professional. However, you may be asked for input if you have worked for a company for a considerable amount of time. Also, you may, through total quality management initiatives, be calling a meeting yourself. In either situation, you can use the ideas presented here to help determine who should be at a meeting.

If it is a problem-solving meeting, individuals who have knowledge of the problem and who will be involved in implementation of the solution should attend. For example, if the issue is to establish a strategic plan for the business, the top-level executives of the business should be involved—the president, the vice presidents, and possibly the board of trustees.

In determining who should attend, consider who is most affected by the problem or issue and who can contribute to the solution. Also, you need to think about the backgrounds of the people. For example a **heterogeneous group** (a group having dissimilar backgrounds and experiences) can often solve problems more satisfactorily than a **homogeneous group** (a group with similar backgrounds and experiences). A heterogeneous group can bring varying views to the problem and encourage creative thinking through the diversity that is present. However, a more heterogeneous group demands a skilled facilitator in order to make the meeting productive.

Determining the Number of Attendees

The ideal number of attendees is based on the purpose of the meeting and the number of people who can best achieve the purpose. The best size for a problem-solving and decision-making group is from 7 to 15 people. This size group allows for creative **synergy** (the ideas and products of a group of people developed through interaction with each other). There are enough people to generate divergent points of view and to challenge each other's thinking.

Small groups of seven people or less may be necessary at times. For example, if the purpose of the meeting is to discuss a personnel matter, the human resources director and the supervisor may be the only people in attendance. If the purpose of the meeting is to discuss a faulty product design, the product engineer, the manager of the engineering department, and the line technician may be the only people in attendance. Advantages to having only a few people in a meeting are as follows:

- Participants may be assembled more quickly since there are fewer.

- The meeting can be informal and thus provide for more spontaneity and creativity.
- Group dynamics are easier to manage.

The disadvantages of a small group include the following:

- Points of view are limited due to the size of the group.
- There may not be enough ideas to create the best solution to the problem.
- Participants may not be willing to challenge each other's point of view if they are a close-knit group.

The Administrative Professional's Responsibilities

In planning meetings (whether they are face to face or some type of electronic meeting), the administrative professional has a number of responsibilities. As you have just learned, you must work closely with your supervisor to determine the purpose of the meeting, who will attend, and the appropriate number of attendees. There are other responsibilities you can handle on your own; however, you must understand your supervisor's preferences in these areas. When you first join an organization or begin to work with a supervisor, take time before each meeting to learn his or her needs and preferences. Once you have spent time with a particular supervisor, you will have less need to discuss the details with him or her. However, you should always discuss the purpose of the meeting and general expectations with your supervisor. Otherwise, you may waste

Communication Tip:
Set up a folder for each meeting you are planning; keep all materials about the meeting in the folder. Once the meeting is over, file the folder for a period of time for future reference.

your time taking care of details only to find that your supervisor is not pleased with the direction you have taken.

Selecting and Preparing the Room

A room can impact what happens during a meeting. You probably have attended meetings where these problems occurred.

- The room was too large or too small for the group.
- The participants could not be heard.
- The room was too cold or too hot.
- The lighting in the room was not adequate.
- The ventilation was poor.

Room inadequacies can start a meeting off in a negative manner. As you have learned already, meetings are expensive. Meeting arrangements should allow for maximum effectiveness from the participants. If you carefully plan the room arrangements, you can help the meeting begin in a positive way.

When you know how many people are going to attend the meeting, look for a room that is the proper size to accommodate the group. Most businesses will have several conference rooms of varying sizes available. If someone schedules the conference rooms, contact this individual to reserve the room. If you have to choose between a room that is too large or too small, generally choose the smaller room. For example, 20 people in a room that accommodates 80 can make the group feel intimidated because of the empty space. However, you do not want to attempt to put 40 people in a room that accommodates 20. In addition to the room being too crowded, you may be violating restrictions established by the local fire department concerning the number of people allowed in a room. If you must take a room that is too large for the number of participants, you can make the room appear smaller. For example, you set up chairs or tables in one corner of the room. If there are movable partitions, arrange them around the actual meeting space.

Check the temperature controls before a meeting. Remember that bodies give off heat, so the room will be warmer with people in it.

A standard rule is to aim for about 68 degrees. Be sure you know who to call if the temperature gets too hot or too cold during the meeting. You do not want a room that is hot and stuffy or a room that is icy cold when you are trying to make important decisions.

Check the ventilation. Is the air flow adequate? Is the lighting bright enough? If visuals are going to be used, can they be seen? If you have any questions about the temperature, ventilation, or lighting, check with the building maintenance personnel well before the meeting begins. Give them a chance to correct the problem. Avoid calling at the last minute.

If you are selecting a room for an electronic meeting, be certain the room is large enough to accommodate the equipment needed for the meeting. The seating arrangement must allow all individuals to see the monitors, electronic whiteboards, or whatever other equipment is used. With a videoconference, the meeting is usually held in a room that is permanently maintained with the special equipment. Check the electrical outlets in the room. Are there enough? Are they positioned so you do not have to string extension cords across the room? Doing so can be a safety hazard.

Determining the Seating Arrangement

The seating arrangement of a room depends on the objectives of the meeting. The four basic seating arrangements are rectangular, circular, semicircular, and U-shaped. Figure 12-2 shows these arrangements.

The **rectangular arrangement** allows the leader to maintain control since he or she sits at the head of the table. Conversation is usually directed to the leader. The rectangular arrangement is also appropriate if the purpose is to have individuals talk in groups of twos or threes. Individuals seated next to or opposite each other are able to talk among themselves. If discussion is important, the table should not be too long. A long table may make communication difficult due to the inability to see the nonverbal behavior of all participants. A long table can also prevent the leader from taking part in discussions if he or she is at a distance from participants.

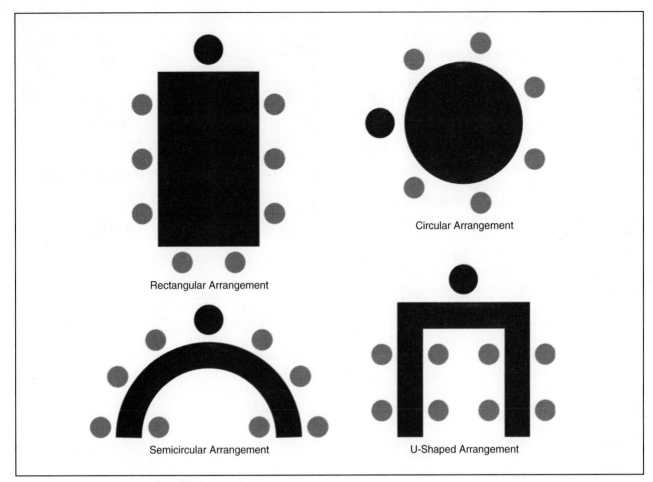

Figure 12-2 Four Basic Seating Arrangements

The **circular arrangement** is effective for minimizing status positions. In a circle, it is difficult to determine the leader since no one sits in a position of control. The arrangement encourages a sense of warmth and togetherness. The leader has less control in a circle than in any other arrangement. If the circular arrangement is used, communication channels should be fairly equal among all members since no one assumes a position of dominance.

The **semicircular** and **u-shaped arrangements** work well for small groups of from six to eight people. The leader has moderate control since he or she can sit in a fairly dominant position. These two arrangements work well for showing visuals since the visuals can be set up at the front of the configuration. The u-shaped and semicircular arrangements are desirable for semiformal meetings. The circular arrangement is most effective for informal meetings; the rectangular arrangement, for formal meetings.

Sending Meeting Notices

The most effective way to notify participants within an organization of a meeting is by email. Since many people now keep their calendars on the computer, you may be able to check when participants are available. Another way to inform internal participants is by interoffice memorandum. When notifying participants of a meeting, include the following information:

- Purpose of the meeting
- Topics to be considered at the meeting
- Materials that should be read before the meeting and brought to the meeting
- Date of the meeting
- Start and end times
- Location

- Name of the person to whom the addressee should respond and when the response should be made as to attendance

When considering the time of the meeting, generally avoid Monday mornings, meetings immediately after lunch, and meetings near the end of the day. Meetings should generally last no longer than two hours. When people have to sit for longer than two hours, they get restless and lose interest in the topic. When a meeting is two hours in length or longer, short five-to-ten minute breaks should be given every 40 or 45 minutes, depending on the participants. By being observant, you will know when it is time for a break. Signals include lack of participation, individuals leaving the room, and individuals losing their focus. Breaks allow people to move around a little; generally, they will return to the meeting ready to concentrate and get back to the task at hand. An example of a meeting notification is given in Figure 12-3.

It is important to begin and end meetings on time. If the meeting notice states that the meeting will begin at 9 a.m., begin sharply at 9. Do not wait for stragglers. People will soon get

© PhotoDisc, Inc.

Always begin meetings on time.

the message that you start on time, and they will be there. The same holds true for ending meetings; end them on time. People appreciate your being respectful of their time constraints. Also, by stating an end time, the leader of the meeting can help the group accomplish its objectives in the time allocated.

As an administrative professional, you may also have the responsibility of following up to determine if people are planning to attend the meeting. Although you ask people to let you know, some may not respond. The usual method of follow-up is a telephone call or an email reminder. A good idea is to contact the administrative professionals who work with the individuals invited; they can remind their co-workers of the meeting. Let your supervisor know who will be attending the meeting and who might be late. You can write this information directly on a copy of the memo or email that went out announcing the meeting and give it to your supervisor. Another alternative is to prepare a special form for noting attendees. If a number of people are unable to attend the meeting, let your supervisor know so he or she can decide whether to cancel the meeting. Although canceling a meeting is not generally a good idea, it is best to do so if key individuals cannot attend.

AMERIASIAN AIRLINES

Memorandum

TO: All Managers

FROM: Martin Albertson *MA*

DATE: November 12, 2004

SUBJECT: Meeting Notice

A meeting will be held on November 22 from 9 a.m. until 11 a.m. The meeting will be held in Conference Room A, with the purpose being to

- Discuss accomplishment of objectives for this year
- Review goals and budget for next year

Please send a summary of your accomplishments to the other managers by November 20 and bring a copy to the meeting.

It is important that everyone be in attendance. If you cannot attend, please let me know by November 16.

Figure 12-3   Meeting Notification

Preparing the Agenda

Everyone should know what to expect before coming to a meeting, and an agenda does this. An **agenda** is an outline of what will occur at the meeting. Participants should receive a detailed agenda at least a day (preferably a week) before the meeting. The agenda should include the following information:

- Name of the meeting or the group
- Date of the meeting
- Start and end times
- Location
- Order of agenda items
- Person responsible for presenting each agenda item
- Action expected on each agenda item
- Background materials (if needed)

In addition, you might also allocate a particular time period for the presentation of each agenda item. Although this process is not essential, it does remind people of the importance of time and adhering to a schedule. If time frames are not listed, the facilitator of the meeting may need to move the meeting along. The order of the agenda items can vary. Some people think the most difficult items should be presented first so participants can deal with them while they are fresh. Other people think the difficult items should be presented last. Check with your supervisor to find out which order he or she prefers. An agenda is shown in Figure 12-4.

Notice that the word *ACTION* is listed after certain agenda items. This word indicates that a decision should be made. Such an approach helps participants know what is expected of

them. If they are to make a decision, they can come prepared to do so. If a decision is not going to be made on an item, the individual in charge of the meeting should let the group know what will happen to the item being discussed. Will it be discussed again at a later date? Will it be referred to another group to deal with? When participants understand what is expected of them, they are better contributors.

When sending out materials prior to a meeting, keep them as concise as possible. Most people will not take the time to read verbose materials.

Determining the Procedures

Highly structured procedures generally are not appropriate for small committee meetings, departmental meetings, informational meetings, and other informal meetings. For a formal meeting, you may need to adhere to Robert's Rules of Order. For example, parliamentary procedure is essential at a meeting of the board of directors of a corporation or at an annual business meeting of a professional organization. You should become familiar with parliamentary procedures. Check your local bookstore or library for information; you will find a number of books available.

Preparing Materials for Your Supervisor

You should prepare a folder for each meeting your supervisor will attend or lead. The folder should include the following:

- Meeting notice with a list of the people who will be in attendance
  - Materials that have been sent out before the meeting
  - Notes that are needed at the meeting
  - Visuals or handouts

If your supervisor is participating in an offsite meeting, you may also need to include directions to the meeting site. Through the use of such online sites as www.mapquest.com, you can get maps, driving directions, and even traffic reports.

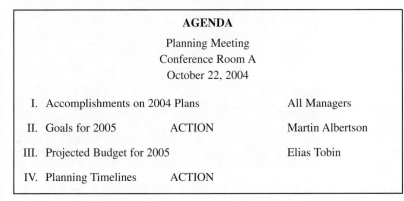

AGENDA

Planning Meeting
Conference Room A
October 22, 2004

I. Accomplishments on 2004 Plans		All Managers
II. Goals for 2005	ACTION	Martin Albertson
III. Projected Budget for 2005		Elias Tobin
IV. Planning Timelines	ACTION	

Figure 12-4 Meeting Agenda

By using online sites such as www.mapquest.com, you can obtain driving directions for your employer.

Preparing Materials for Attendees

If handouts are to be distributed during the meeting, prepare them well in advance of the meeting. If there are several pages, place the handouts in individual folders. Sometimes attendees are expected to take notes. If so, you might provide a pad of paper in the folder and make extra pens and/or pencils available in case attendees need them.

Ordering Equipment

Determine what equipment, if any, is needed for the meeting. Then follow through to see that it is available. You might make a list of the equipment needed and note on the list what arrangements have been made. List the person responsible for obtaining each item. If something is your responsibility, note that. Before the meeting begins, take your list to the room and check it against the equipment.

Ordering Food and Beverages

For a morning meeting, coffee, tea, and juice can be provided for the participants. Water should also be available. For an afternoon meeting, you may want to provide coffee and/or soft drinks. Providing beverages is not mandatory, however. Check with your supervisor to see what he or she prefers to do.

For a luncheon meeting, you may have the responsibility of selecting the menu, calling the caterer, and arranging for the meal to be served. Avoid a heavy lunch if you are expecting people to work afterward. A salad or light entree is more appropriate for a working lunch. For a dinner meeting, you may have the responsibility of working with an outside caterer. Sometimes there are health issues to consider. If you know the attendees, provide food that meets their needs. If you do not know the attendees, ask the caterer to recommend several meals to you; then select from one of these meals. Be certain to ask your supervisor what the budget allocation is for the meal.

For a dinner meeting at a hotel, you can expect assistance from the hotel staff. You will usually be responsible for selecting the menu. If the event is formal, you might wish to have table decorations and place cards. You should know the group when selecting the seating arrangement; your supervisor can help you with this. You want to avoid seating two people next to each other who do not get along well.

Handling Duties During the Meeting

The administrative professional's responsibilities during the meeting are varied. You may be expected to greet the participants and to

Be attentive to the seating arrangements when planning dinner meetings.

introduce individuals if they do not know each other. Your courteousness, warmth, and friendliness can go a long way toward making people feel comfortable and getting the meeting off to a good start.

Your main responsibility during the meeting will probably be to take the **minutes** (a record of the meeting). Sit near the leader so you can clearly hear what he or she says. You may wish to use a laptop computer to take notes. The computer can save you time. After the meeting is over, all you have to do is read over your notes and make necessary changes to the file. Such an approach is faster than taking notes by hand or recording the meeting on tape and then having to key everything after the meeting.

Minutes should contain a record of the important matters that were presented in the meeting. You do not need to record the minutes verbatim (with the exception of motions), but you do need to record all pertinent information. Items that should be included in the minutes are given in Figure 12-5.

Minutes are not necessary for all meetings; however, they do remind attendees of what happened and what responsibilities they might have after the meeting. Minutes are needed in the following situations:

- When decisions are made that affect a large number of people
- In formal meetings, such as board of directors' meetings
- When attendees act upon a list of different topics and a record is necessary to recall the events

- When the same type of meeting is held on a regular basis and a record is needed of the continual activities of the group
- When meeting results need to be reported to the president or other officers of the organization

Following Up After the Meeting

Your duties after the meeting include seeing that the meeting room is left in order, preparing the minutes, and handling other details.

Routine Tasks. These routine tasks are essential after a meeting.

- Return all equipment. See that additional tables and chairs are removed from the room. Clean up any food or beverage leftovers, or notify the cleaning staff if the room needs a general cleaning.
- Write items on your calendar that require future attention by you or your employer.
- Send out any necessary follow-up memos.
- Evaluate the meeting. Review what happened; consider how you might improve the arrangements for the next meeting. Make notes for your files to review before the next meeting. If you used a caterer, make notes about the quality of the food, the helpfulness of the staff, and so on.
- Keep files on meetings long enough to refer to them when planning the next similar meeting. Your notes will help ensure future success. You might also keep names and telephone numbers of contact people.

ITEMS TO BE INCLUDED IN MEETING MINUTES

- The date, time, and place of the meeting
- The type of meeting (regular, special, monthly, and so forth)
- The name of the group
- The name of the person presiding
- The members present and absent
- Approval or correction of the minutes from the previous meeting
- Reports of committees, officers, or individuals

- Actions taken and/or motions made
- Items on which action needs to be taken and the person responsible for taking the action
- The date and time of the next meeting (if there is one)
- Time of adjournment
- The signature of the secretary for the group

Figure 12-5

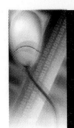

Preparation of Minutes. If minutes are necessary, they should be prepared and distributed within 24–48 hours of a meeting. Prompt preparation and distribution of minutes reminds attendees of what they must do before the next meeting. Nonparticipants may also get copies of minutes from a meeting. For example, minutes from a company board meeting may be made available to all executives within a company.

Minutes from a meeting are shown in Figure 12-6. Although there is no set format for writing minutes, general guidelines are given here.

- Minutes are single-spaced. Margins should be at least 1 inch. If the minutes are to be placed in a bound book, the left margin should be 1½ inches.
- The heading should be keyed in all capital letters and centered.
- Subject captions should be used as paragraph headings; subject captions usually correspond to the agenda topics.
- Minutes may or may not be signed. Minutes of board meetings and professional organizations are generally signed. If minutes are to be signed, a signature line should be provided.
- Minutes should be stored for future reference. Minutes may be stored in hard-copy form, on a disk, or on a microrecord. In addition, the agenda and all pertinent materials presented in the meeting should be stored with the minutes.

Organizing—The Key

Regardless of what your responsibilities are, the key is organization. Know what you have to do, and stay organized in doing it. As you plan a meeting, continue through the process of the meeting, and oversee the follow-up activities, ask yourself these questions.

- How can I best organize my time and efforts?

BOARD OF DIRECTORS MEETING
MANAGEMENT ASSOCIATION

Grand Rapids Chapter
November 16, 2004

TIME AND PLACE OF MEETING

The regular monthly meeting of the Board of Directors of the Management Association was held on November 16 at the Regent Hotel at 6:30 p.m. The meeting was called to order by the President, Aretha Edwards. All 12 Board members were present.

READING OF THE MINUTES

The minutes of the October meeting were approved without reading since each member received a copy prior to the meeting.

TREASURER'S REPORT

Margaret Mustoe reported that she received acceptance from Harold McLean to speak at the December meeting and that his picture and vita have been turned over to the Publicity Committee.

NEW BUSINESS

Membership Committee: The application of Theresa Pulliams for membership was unanimously approved.

Service Committee: It was suggested that the merit award qualifications be included in the Chapter Bulletin for the first week of December.

Program Committee: William Farr, Chairperson of the Speakers Bureau, reported that he and the committee are planning to increase the number of programs at the winter seminar. He also reported that the committee agreed on "Ethics in International Business" as the theme for the seminar.

ADJOURNMENT

The meeting was adjourned at 8:30 p.m.

Rebecca M. Wylie
Rebecca M. Wylie
Secretary, Grand Rapids Chapter
Management Association

Figure 12-6 Meeting Minutes

- When should each task be completed?
- Who is responsible for each activity?
- What should I discuss with my supervisor? What can I do on my own?

The Leader's Responsibilities

The leader of a meeting at which you are assisting is generally your supervisor. However, as you work on teams within the company, you may be the meeting leader on occasion. If a meeting is to go well, the leader must fulfill certain responsibilities.

Adhering to the Agenda

As you have learned, the purpose of a meeting must be clearly established and that purpose made clear in writing to the participants when the meeting is announced. When the meeting begins, the leader should reiterate the purpose of the meeting. The leader should also let the participants know what outcomes are expected. For example, if the purpose of a meeting is to establish a direction for the department for the next two years, the expected outcomes of the meeting may be to determine at least two departmental objectives.

If participants stray from the agenda, the leader is responsible for sensitively but firmly bringing them back to the topic at hand. The leader might say "Thank you for your comments. We can put that issue on the agenda for a future meeting. Now let's continue discussing the departmental objectives we must set."

Managing Time

You already know that meetings should begin on time, even if several people are late in arriving. Waiting for others is not fair to the individuals who have made an effort to be on time. The leader is responsible for beginning and ending meetings on time. The leader must be sensitive to other commitments participants may have made. Time frames (both beginning and ending) should have been established when the meeting notice was sent out.

Encouraging Participation

Before participants are invited to a meeting, the leader should give considerable thought to who should be at the meeting. The people in attendance should be the best people in the organization to discuss the issues, determine the direction, or solve the problem. Once the meeting begins, the leader is responsible for seeing that all individuals participate. The leader should help individuals feel secure enough to say what they really think. If, as the meeting gets under way, several people have not spoken, the leader may make statements similar to these.

- "Inez, what direction do you think we should take to satisfy our needs in the twenty-first century?"
- "Juan, we haven't heard from you on this issue. What is your opinion?"

Let each participant know that you and the group value his or her opinion. Encourage everyone to contribute. Respect participants and the comments they make. You might make statements such as these.

- "Thank you for that contribution."
- "That's a great idea."
- "Thanks. Can you expand on your idea? It may have possibilities for us."

The leader is also responsible for seeing that one or two people do not dominate the conversation, even if their contributions are beneficial. The leader can use statements similar to the ones here.

- "Diana, that is an excellent idea. Eduardo, how could it be implemented in your area?"
- "Thanks, Diana; Eduardo, what do you think about the direction?"

The leader has the following responsibilities:

- Keep the participants focused on the agenda.
- Encourage participation from everyone in the meeting.
- Limit the domination of any one person in the meeting.

© PhotoDisc, Inc.

One of the leader's responsibilities in a meeting is to encourage participation by all individuals.

- Positively reinforce all individuals for their contributions.
- Keep the discussion moving toward the outcomes determined.

Reaching Decisions

The leader is responsible for helping the participants reach a decision about the issue, problem, or direction if a decision is needed. The leader must carefully assess if all alternatives have been discussed. Then the leader needs to push for a decision on the issue. For example, the leader might say "We seem to have identified each issue and the possible solutions. Does anyone else have anything to add?" Then the leader can move to resolution by saying "Now let's determine which solution will work best in our present situation." Once a resolution is reached, the leader can check to see if all participants agree by asking "Now that we have reached a resolution, is everyone in the room comfortable with it? Are we overlooking anything? Are there problems we haven't seen?"

Evaluating the Meeting

Generally, with informal meetings within an organization, no formal evaluation is necessary. However, an informal evaluation by the leader (and possibly the participants) should be done. The attendees are usually very forthright. They may tell the leader they found the meeting to be a waste of time. When attendees make such a statement, the leader should seek clarification on exactly what they meant. The leader may also want to ask individual participants how the meeting went. In either case, the leader should ask these questions of herself or himself.

- Were the attendees participatory?
- Was the nonverbal behavior positive?
- Were the participants creative problem solvers?
- Did the participants exhibit a high energy level?
- Was the purpose of the meeting satisfied?
- Were appropriate decisions made?
- Can I improve in how I handled the issues, the people, or the meeting in general?

MEETING EVALUATION FORM

Place a check mark in the "yes" or "no" column. Write in any comments you may have in the space provided.

		YES	NO
1.	Was the purpose of the meeting accomplished?	☐	☐
2.	Was the agenda received in time to prepare for the meeting?	☐	☐
3.	Was the room arrangement satisfactory?	☐	☐
4.	Did the leader help the group accomplish the goals of the meeting?	☐	☐
5.	Did the leader adhere to the agenda?	☐	☐
6.	Were the appropriate people included in the meeting?	☐	☐
7.	Did all attendees participate in the discussion?	☐	☐
8.	Did attendees listen to each other?	☐	☐
9.	Did the leader encourage participation?	☐	☐
10.	Did the meeting begin on time?	☐	☐
11.	Did the meeting end on time?	☐	☐
12.	Were decisions that were made consistent with the purpose of the meeting?	☐	☐

Figure 12-7

If the meeting is a relatively formal one, the leader may ask participants to fill out an evaluation form. If so, the administrative professional's role may be to prepare and administer the evaluation. A meeting evaluation form is shown in Figure 12-7.

Participants' Responsibilities

Just as a leader has responsibilities, so do the participants. Their role is much broader than attending the meeting. Their responsibilities begin before the meeting and continue after the meeting.

Before the Meeting

Participants are responsible for reading the meeting notice, responding to it promptly, and reading any materials sent out before the meeting. Participants are also responsible for understanding the purpose of the meeting and analytically evaluating the materials in relation to the purpose of the meeting. Participants must understand that they have been asked to the meeting because the leader believes they have something to offer. Each participant must take seriously his or her responsibility to contribute to the success of the meeting, which means being prepared. No one appreciates the person who comes to a meeting late and opens up the pack of materials for the first time—clearly not having read the material beforehand.

During the Meeting

During the meeting, participants are responsible for

- Being on time
- Adhering to the agenda
- Making contributions
- Listening thoughtfully to other participants' contributions and responding if they have something to add
- Respecting the leader's role
- Not dominating the discussion
- Not being judgmental of others' comments
- Being courteous to each individual in the meeting
- Taking notes, if necessary

It is not always easy to listen carefully to others, to be nonjudgmental, and to make contributions. Your mind tends to wander, focusing on other work-related tasks you need to complete or on your plans after work. However, your contributions can be the very ones that get the meeting back on track if individuals stray or help the leader keep the meeting focused. Your obligation is to help the meeting get better.

After the Meeting

Once the meeting is over, a participant's responsibilities do not necessarily end. The participant may have been asked to do some research or take some action before the next meeting, or the participant may have been asked to work with one or two other people to bring back a recommendation to the next meeting. The participant must fulfill all obligations by the designated time; others are depending on him or her to do so.

INTERNATIONAL MEETINGS

Your supervisor, with your assistance, may be responsible for setting up an international meeting, either electronic or face-to-face. In international meetings, remember that cultural differences do exist and these differences must be understood and respected. Otherwise, you may be dealing with an international incident rather than getting a resolution on an important contract or issue. Do your homework before the meeting. Find out as much as you can about the culture or cultures that will be represented. Then be sensitive to the needs of the individuals in the meeting.

International meetings are always more formal in nature. You must understand hierarchical considerations and use proper greetings and

Communication Tip:

Meeting participants must be good listeners; they must hear and acknowledge all contributions. The adage "Seek first to understand and then to be understood" is appropriate.

amenities. Figure 12-8 gives several suggestions for what to do and not to do in international meetings.

CONFERENCES

A conference is much larger in scope and has more participants than a meeting. Executives may belong to a professional organization in a particular field of expertise, such as accounting, engineering, or human resources. Many of these organizations hold at least one major conference each year. Most companies encourage their executives to participate in conferences as a means of broadening their knowledge. Your role as an administrative professional may be to assist your supervisor in planning a conference.

As an administrative professional, you may be a member of the International Association of Administrative Professionals (IAAP), the National Association of Legal Secretaries (NALS), the American Association for Medical Transcription (AAMT), ARMA International, the Association for Information Management Professionals, or another organization. As a member, you may attend or help to plan some of their conferences.

Before the Conference

Preparing for a regional or national conference takes months of work. Good planning ensures a smooth, successful conference. Poor planning results in a disorganized, ineffective conference. One of the major responsibilities of planning is to determine the location and meeting facilities for the conference. Contact the chamber of commerce in the city being considered. Ask for information about the city and appropriate conference facilities. Request conference planning guides from the hotels and conference centers that give floor plans of the facilities, dining and catering services, price list of rooms, and layout of meeting rooms. Figure 12-9 on page 314 shows a portion of a hotel floor plan. Once the city and hotel have been selected, detailed arrangements need to be made for meeting rooms, guest rooms, meal arrangements, and so on.

You must contact presenters and make travel and lodging arrangements before the conference. If you are responsible for making arrangements for a presenter, you should determine the type of accommodations required—room (single or double, queen- or king-size bed), flight preferences, arrival and departure times, rental car needs, and so on.

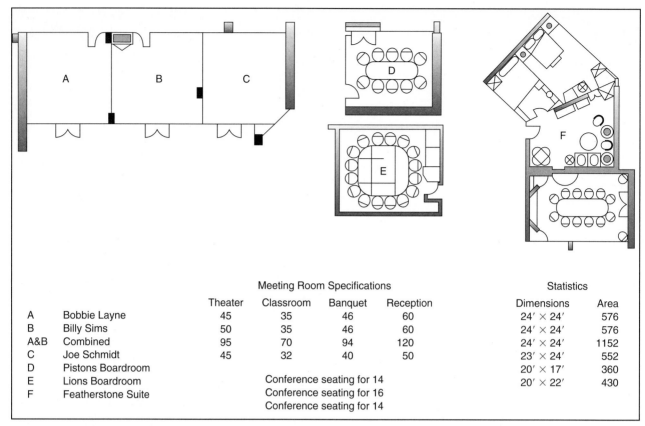

		Meeting Room Specifications				Statistics	
		Theater	Classroom	Banquet	Reception	Dimensions	Area
A	Bobbie Layne	45	35	46	60	24′ × 24′	576
B	Billy Sims	50	35	46	60	24′ × 24′	576
A&B	Combined	95	70	94	120	24′ × 24′	1152
C	Joe Schmidt	45	32	40	50	23′ × 24′	552
D	Pistons Boardroom					20′ × 17′	360
E	Lions Boardroom		Conference seating for 14			20′ × 22′	430
F	Featherstone Suite		Conference seating for 16				
			Conference seating for 14				

Figure 12-9 Hotel Floor Plan

Some type of preregistration is usually held before a conference with registration taking place during the conference. You may be responsible for mailing out and processing returned preregistration forms. You also may be responsible for assisting with registration at the conference. If the conference is a large one, several people will be needed to staff the registration tables.

During the Conference

Your responsibilities during the conference may include running errands, delivering messages to participants, and solving problems that may occur. Other responsibilities may include checking room arrangements, equipment needs, meal arrangements, and so on. At a conference, you are a representative of the company for which you work or the organization of which you are a member. Therefore, you should present a positive image at all times. Keep a smile on your face, and handle even the most difficult situations with **aplomb** (self-assurance).

After the Conference

After the conference, your basic duties involve cleaning up and following up. These responsibilities include seeing that all equipment is returned, presenters are assisted with transportation to the airport, letters of appreciation are sent to presenters and others, expense reports are filled out, and bills are paid. You may also be responsible for seeing that the proceedings of the conference are published and mailed to participants. You may not be responsible for writing the report, but you may be responsible for working with the conference reporters in assembling and mailing the report. At some conferences, the sessions are recorded and attendees may purchase these audiotapes.

Those who have worked on a conference should have a meeting to evaluate the conference. They should ask these questions.

- What went right?
- What went wrong?
- Was the facility adequate?

- Was the registration process smooth?
- Were the meals good and served on time?
- Were the presenters effective?

A formal evaluation of the conference is usually filled out by attendees. This evaluation may be of the conference as a whole and/or of individual sessions.

Keep a record of the evaluations to refer to before the next conference. These evaluations will remind you of what did and did not work at the previous conference. Also, keep all files containing information about the conference preparation. These files can be valuable in planning future conferences.

CONFLICT RESOLUTION

Conflict resolution skills are always important in workplace situations. Individuals and groups frequently face conflicts they must resolve. As an administrative profes-

sional, you should develop these important skills. Certainly, in meetings and conferences, conflict can arise. Although you are not generally responsible for solving the problem unless you are conducting the meeting or conference, you can become one of the people who helps resolve the conflict. Also, you may be confronted with conflict as you are planning meetings and conferences, in which case, you are responsible for its resolution. When you are faced with conflict, address it. Suggestions for resolving conflict are given in Figure 12-10. Read these suggestions carefully, and implement them as you work with others. Engage in **conflict resolution** (addressing and dealing with issues in a positive manner). Too many people try to avoid conflict. However, it usually does not go away; it merely gets worse. Here are some attitudes that help resolve conflict.

Openness

Be open to what others think and feel. Also, state your feelings and thoughts openly without being negative. In other words, use "I"

SUGGESTIONS FOR RESOLVING CONFLICT

- Identify what is causing the conflict. Is it power, resources, recognition, or acceptance? Many times our needs for these items are at the heart of the conflict.
- Determine what each person needs or wants. Ask questions to determine what the other person wants. Be willing to listen to the other person. Everyone feels a deep need to be understood. By satisfying that need in the other person, you may be able to lessen the conflict. If you do not understand what the other person is saying, paraphrase what you think you hear and ask for clarification. Be open to what the other person tells you.
- Identify points of agreement. Work from these points first. Then identify the points of disagreement.
- Create a safe environment. Establish a neutral location; establish a tone that is accepting of the other person's views and feelings. Acknowledge the other person's feelings. Behind anger may be fear. Let the other person tell you how he or she is feeling. Watch how you position yourself physically in the

room. Remember, you have a more difficult time competing with someone who is sitting next to you than with someone who is across the table or room. A circular seating arrangement may be appropriate if you have several individuals involved in a conflict.
- Do not react. Many times individuals act too quickly when a conflict occurs. Step back, collect your thoughts, and try to see the situation as objectively as possible.
- Do not seek to win during a confrontation. Negotiate the issues, and translate the negotiation into a lasting agreement.
- Actively listen. Watch the individual's eyes; notice his or her body language.
- Separate people from the issue. When the people and the problem are tangled together, the problem becomes difficult to solve. Talk in specific rather than general terms.

Figure 12-10

statements about how you feel and what you think should happen. For example, if a conflict erupts about the type of meeting that should be held, you might say, "I think the meeting should be a videoconference rather than a face-to-face meeting. It will save both money and time." You should not say, "You're not thinking! A face-to-face meeting would not be productive in this situation. Twenty people would have to travel from all over the United States, costing both time and money."

Do you see the difference between these two statements? In the first one, you have used an "I" statement and you have stated your reason for why a videoconference is preferable. In the second statement, you began by accusing the others involved of not thinking. Such a statement immediately puts the individuals on the defensive. After all, you have suggested that they do not have the ability to think through a situation and come up with a logical conclusion.

Empathy

Listen with **empathy** (identification with and understanding of another's situation, feelings, and motives) to what others are saying. Express your concern and support for the other person's opinions. Be willing to change your position if others present appropriate reasons for doing so. In other words, do not be closed to the opinions of others.

Equality

Give other people time to express their feelings. Evaluate all ideas equally. Do not base your opinion of an idea on whether the person is a friend of yours or whether you like or dislike the individual. Disagreements where openness, empathy, and equality are present provide growth opportunities for all involved. We learn from hearing what others think and feel. We close ourselves to learning when we ignore the ideas of others.

CHAPTER SUMMARY

The summary will help you remember the important points covered in the chapter.

- Management spends as much as 50 percent or more of each week in meetings. Due to the frequency and cost of meetings, meeting time must be spent as productively as possible.
- Meetings are a good means of generating ideas; however, unnecessary and unproductive meetings are held daily in organizations. Meetings are not a good idea when there is inadequate data; when there is insufficient time to prepare for the meeting; when information could be better communicated by memo, fax, email or telephone; or when there is a considerable amount of anger or hostility in the group.
- Meetings may be face-to-face or electronic, which includes audioconferencing, online conferencing, or videoconferencing.
- The executive's role in meeting preparation usually involves determining the purpose of the meeting, determining who should attend, and determining the number of attendees. The administrative professional may assist with these roles.
- The administrative professional's role, in consultation with the executive, includes selecting and preparing the room, determining the seating arrangement, sending meeting notices, preparing the agenda, determining the procedures, preparing materials for the supervisor, preparing materials for attendees, ordering equipment, ordering food and beverages,

handling duties during the meeting, and following up after the meeting.
- The leader's responsibilities during the meeting include adhering to the agenda, managing time, encouraging participation, reaching decisions, and evaluating the meeting.
- The participant's responsibilities during the meeting include reading material before the meeting, being on time, adhering to the agenda, making contributions, listening thoughtfully to other participants, and carrying out any responsibilities assigned during the meeting.
- In planning and conducting international meetings, the leader and administrative professional should become familiar with the customs and culture of the participants.
- Conferences are much larger in scope and have more participants than meetings. The administrative professional may be involved in planning a conference; carrying out duties during the conference, such as solving problems, running errands, and assisting with registration; and writing letters of appreciation, filling out expense reports, paying bills, and numerous other follow-up activities.
- Conflict resolution skills are always important in workplace situations. Attitudes that help resolve conflicts include openness, empathy, and equality.

CHAPTER GLOSSARY

The following terms were used in this chapter. Definitions are provided to help you review the terms.

- **Teleconferencing** (p. 297)—a general term applied to a variety of technology-assisted two-way (interactive) communications via telephone lines, DSL, cable modems, and other high-bandwidth connections.
- **Audioconferencing** (p. 297)—a type of conference in which participants talk with each other using standard telephones or speakerphones.
- **Electronic whiteboard** (p. 298)—a display screen connected to a computer on which multiple users write or draw; allows for visual and interactive input during a teleconference.

- **Interactivity** (p. 298)—information transmitted from one location to another and acted on by participants at any location.
- **Stand-alone conventional dry-erase boards** (p. 298)—whiteboards used without connection to a computer or a projector; similar to a standard classroom whiteboard.
- **Electronic dry-erase whiteboards** (p. 298)—connected to a computer but without a projector.

CHAPTER GLOSSARY

(continued)

- **Online meetings** (p. 298)—link individual participants via a computer; also referred to as computer conferencing, keyboard conferencing, Web conferencing, and data conferencing.
- **Real time** (p. 299)—when individuals simultaneously create electronically produced documents such as presentations, spreadsheets, reports, and proposals.
- **Outside** or **remote facilitator** (p. 299)—a person trained in facilitation techniques who is not part of the decision making of a meeting and whose role is to keep the meetings productive, positive, and efficient.
- **Videoconferencing** (p. 299)—a system of transmitting audio and video between individuals at distant locations.
- **Virtual conferencing** (p. 299)—another term for videoconferencing since it allows participants to enter and move around rooms electronically.
- **Heterogeneous group** (p. 301)—a group having dissimilar backgrounds and experiences.
- **Homogeneous group** (p. 301)—a group with similar backgrounds and experiences.

- **Synergy** (p. 301)—the ideas and products of a group of people developed through interaction with each other.
- **Rectangular arrangement** (p. 302)—a seating arrangement that allows the leader to maintain control.
- **Circular arrangement** (p. 303)—an effective seating arrangement for minimizing status positions.
- **Semicircular arrangement** (p. 303)—another seating arrangement that works well for small groups of from six to eight people.
- **U-shaped arrangement** (p. 303)—a seating arrangement that works well for small groups of from six to eight people.
- **Agenda** (p. 305)—an outline of what will occur at a meeting.
- **Minutes** (p. 307)—a record of the meeting.
- **Aplomb** (p. 314)—self-assurance.
- **Conflict resolution** (p. 315)—addressing and dealing with issues in a positive manner.
- **Empathy** (p. 316)—identification with and understanding of another's situation, feelings, and motives.

DISCUSSION ITEMS

These discussion items provide an opportunity to test your understanding of the chapter through written responses and/or discussion with your classmates and your instructor.

1. When is a meeting unnecessary?
2. List and define three types of electronic meetings.
3. List ten responsibilities that an administrative professional has when meetings are being held.

4. List and explain three attitudes that help resolve conflicts.
5. List ten appropriate behaviors when conducting an international meeting.

CRITICAL-THINKING ACTIVITY

AmeriAsian Airlines is planning an online conference for its Grand Rapids and Beijing executives. The meeting is being held to begin discussion of the strategic direction of the airlines for the next five years. You have been asked to coordinate with the various offices on agenda items. Once you receive the agenda items, you will be working with Mr. Albertson to send out the necessary materials and the agenda. You have contacted the appropriate administrative professional in each office to discuss these details. To date, you have received agenda items from two of the three executives in the Grand Rapids office and one of the three executives in the Beijing office. You have emailed a reminder to the administrative professional in each office, asking for the executive's agenda; you have received no response. Copies of the emails you wrote are on the Student CD at SCDCTA12-1, -2, and -3. The meeting is only a month away, and you are becoming anxious. You know you must get the agenda out soon. You do not want to go to Mr. Albertson with the situation, but you do not know how to handle it. What should you do?

RESPONSES TO SELF-CHECK

1. Consider its size, arrangement, temperature, and ventilation and whether the room is large enough to accommodate the equipment needed.
2. U-shaped and semicircular are the most effective arrangements for semiformal meetings.
3. An agenda should include the name of the meeting or the group, date of the meeting, start and end times, location, order of agenda items, person responsible for presenting each agenda item, action expected on each agenda item, and background materials (if necessary).

4. Minutes should include the date, time, and place of the meeting; the type of meeting; the name of the group; the name of the person presiding; the members present and absent; approval or correction of minutes from the previous meeting; reports of committees, officers, or individuals; actions taken and/or motions made; items on which action needs to be taken and the person responsible for taking the action; the date and time of the next meeting; time of adjournment; and the signature of the secretary for the group.

PROJECTS

Project 12-1 (Objectives 1, 2, 3, 4, and 5)
Collaborative Project

Mr. Albertson is planning a meeting with not-for-profit groups and several large businesses within the Grand Rapids community to consider ways in which the organizations might work together on these major issues impacting the city: transportation, crime, inner-city housing, and public education. The not-for-profit groups involved in this meeting are the Department of Social Services, The Grand Rapids Foundation, the Chamber of Commerce, the Hispanic Coalition, the Urban League, and the Native American Council. The businesses are Kowski International, VonDer Health Care, Clark Associates, Inc., Godwin Tools, and Lowell Granite. The group's work will take approximately one year; recommendations from this group after one year of operation will go to the mayor for action.

The first meeting will be an organizational one to develop a mission statement and to establish goals for the group. Mr. Albertson has already contacted the community leaders, and they have agreed to serve on the task force. Mr. Albertson has asked you to handle several of the arrangements for him. Since this project is a fairly extensive one, you ask your two assistants to work with you. (Assemble a group of three for this project—you and two

of your classmates.) Mr. Albertson is considering an electronic meeting. He asks you to use the Internet to research the advantages and disadvantages of audioconferencing and online meetings. Prepare a memorandum to Mr. Albertson, using the memorandum form on the Student CD, SCDP12-1a, summarizing the results of your findings. Then draft a letter for Mr. Albertson, inviting participants to the first meeting; use a copy of the letterhead on the Student CD, SCDP9-4 (run copies of the letterhead and print out your letter, using the letterhead). The meeting will be held two days—Thursday, November 15, beginning with lunch at noon and ending at 4 p.m., and Friday, November 16, beginning with breakfast at 8:30 a.m. and ending at 11 a.m.

Prepare an agenda. The agenda on November 15 should include a welcome to the group from Mr. Albertson; lunch; an introduction of the participants; and a videoconference with Dr. Peter Sigman, who has been working with inner-city issues for over 15 years. Dr. Sigman will be in Chicago; the participants at the meeting will have a chance to interact with him after his presentation. The remainder of Thursday afternoon will be devoted to writing a mission statement for the group. On Friday morning, the group will begin to develop their goals. Mr. Albertson will facilitate both sessions.

PROJECTS

(continued)

Have a team meeting with your two classmates to determine who will be responsible for each task. Determine how you will work together as a team. Print out a copy of the team evaluation form from your Student CD, SCDP12-1c. Discuss it with your teammates so everyone understands what evaluation criteria are being used. Once you have completed the project, each member of your team should complete the evaluation form.

1. Refer back to the section in Chapter 12 that presents the administrative professional's responsibilities in assisting with meetings. Make a list of the things your group must do. Include menus for lunch and breakfast.
2. Write a memorandum to Mr. Albertson summarizing your research on the Internet; include copies of the articles you found.
3. Prepare a draft of a letter inviting the not-for-profit groups and the businesses to the meeting. Include an agenda. Give the draft to your supervisor for approval. The meeting will be held in the Board Conference Room at AmeriAsian. (In this case, the supervisor will be your instructor.) Once your instructor has approved the letter and the agenda, prepare letters and envelopes for the invitees. Include the agenda for the two days. Addresses are given on the Student CD at SCDP12-1b.

4. Complete the team evaluation form separately, and then discuss your evaluation with your team members. Next, prepare a team evaluation that consolidates the opinions given by each team member. Turn in your team evaluation to your instructor. Use the team evaluation form given on the Student CD at SCDP12-1c. (Print four copies of the form—one for each member of the team and one for your collective evaluation.)

Project 12-2 (Objective 4)

Attend a meeting of a professional organization—either a club you are a member of at school or another organization. Take notes at the meeting, and key your notes in the form of minutes. Turn in the minutes to your instructor.

Project 12-3 (Objective 5)

Describe how you will continue to develop your conflict resolution skills. If you are presently employed, describe a conflict you may have participated in and how you might change your behaviors. This project is a continuation of your Professional Growth Plan. Save a copy on your Professional Growth disk under "Progro12-3."

ENGLISH USAGE CHALLENGE DRILL

Correct the spelling errors in the following sentences. Cite the spelling rule that is applicable to each sentence. Before you begin, refresh your memory of spelling rules by reviewing them in the Reference Guide of this text.

1. The cieling of the room needs some paint.
2. The speech is forgetable.
3. Happyness can be a state of mind—one that has to be worked at to be achieved.

4. The beachs on the shores of Lake Michigan are beautiful.
5. The office stationary is 75 percent cotton content.

ASSESSMENT OF CHAPTER OBJECTIVES

Now that you have completed the chapter and the projects, take a few minutes to review the chapter learning objectives. For your convenience, the objectives are repeated below. Did you accomplish these objectives? If you were unable to accomplish the objectives, give your reasons for not doing so.

1. Identify the responsibilities of the administrative professional
   for meetings and conferences.   Yes _____   No _____

   _____

   _____

   _____

2. Become familiar with the types of meetings—audio, online, and video.   Yes _____   No _____

   _____

   _____

   _____

3. Prepare meeting notices.   Yes _____   No _____

   _____

   _____

   _____

4. Prepare agendas and minutes.   Yes _____   No _____

   _____

   _____

   _____

5. Develop conflict resolution skills.   Yes _____   No _____

   _____

   _____

   _____

You may submit your answers in writing to your instructor, using the memorandum form on the Student CD, SCDAP12-1.

MAIL AND WORKPLACE COPIERS

▼

LEARNING OBJECTIVES

1. Identify USPS classes of mail and special services.
2. Explain how to process both incoming and outgoing mail.
3. Explain the types of copiers and their functions.
4. *Develop teamwork skills.*

For years mail could be defined with a fairly simple statement. Mail was written information sent via the **USPS**^{SM} (United States Postal Service) to locations both within the United States and abroad. Then came electronic communications—fax, email, intranets and extranets that allow people within organizations to exchange data internally and externally, the Internet, and software packages that allow the user to determine postage and print it out on a document without ever entering a post office. Additionally, express services, such as FedEx® (Federal Express), UPS® (United Parcel Service), DHL Worldwide Express™, and Airborne Express®, have become big business as organizations expect their paper products to be delivered almost as quickly as electronic mail. Today the meaning of mail is much broader, with electronic mail (email and fax) and mail delivery systems that include numerous private express companies in addition to the USPS.

The result of the huge increase in electronic mail has been a significant drop in the volume of first-class mail coming in to organizations and a resultant drop in revenue for the USPS. In fact, the USPS is now looking at its business differently. It has introduced a number of electronic options for customers, including PC postage and PC-generated evidence of postage that is printed on the user's PC printer. The USPS now offers numerous other electronic services, including a service called NetPost Mailing Online™, which is a convenient way to send mail via computer to a receiver's mailbox. You can learn more about these services through the USPS Website at www.usps.com.

Does this mean we are sending less mail than in the past? Absolutely not. In fact, we are sending more. What it does mean is that the way we communicate with each other has changed drastically. Electronic communication is here to stay and is a routine part of our everyday existence. Does this information mean that paper mail can now be ignored? Certainly not. Paper mail, even though it may continue to drop in volume, is still extremely important to organizations.

"Nothing important—nothing on fax, nothing on voice mail, nothing on the Internet. Just, you know, handwritten stuff."

This chapter will help you, an administrative professional, understand your role and responsibilities in regard to traditional mail. Your mail duties may include preparing incoming mail for your employer to review and preparing outgoing correspondence to be mailed. After studying this chapter, you will be able to process mail more effectively. You will also become more knowledgeable about copiers and their functions. The soft skill you will focus on in this chapter is teamwork.

SERVICES THROUGH USPS

Even though the way we send and receive mail has changed drastically with the advent of electronic technology, the main provider of mail services in the United States remains the USPS (a governmental entity). Regular and special mail services provided by the USPS, private mail services, and international mail are presented in the next section.

Postal Service Classifications

Domestic mail (mail delivered within the United States) is divided into several classifications; the major ones are presented here.

First-Class Mail

Although we think of First-Class Mail as basically letters and other types of business correspondence, it is any type of mail that weighs 13 ounces or less. It includes bills, statements, all matter sealed or otherwise closed against inspection, and matter wholly or partly keyed or handwritten.

Priority Mail

Mail that weighs more than 13 ounces may be sent as **priority mail.** Priority Mail offers two-day service to most domestic destinations. Items cannot exceed 70 pounds in weight, and the maximum size for any item is 108 inches in combined length and **girth** (a measurement around the thickest part). Priority mail envelopes, labels, and boxes are available at no additional charge at USPS locations. Pickup service is also available for a fee.

Express Mail

Express Mail is the fastest mail service available from the USPS, with next-day delivery by noon to most destinations. Express Mail is delivered 365 days a year. Items must weigh 70 pounds or less and measure 108 inches or less in combined length and girth.

Parcel Post

Parcel Post is used for mailing items such as books, circulars, catalogs, and other printed matter that weighs no more than 70 pounds. Parcel Post must measure 130 inches or less in combined length and girth. Pieces exceeding 108 inches but not more than 130 inches in combined length and girth can be mailed at Parcel Post oversized rates.

Bound Printed Matter

The maximum weight for Bound Printed Matter is 15 pounds. Rates are based on the weight of the piece and the zone (distance from origin to destination). Bound Printed Matter must consist of advertising, promotional, directory, or editorial materials (or a combination of such materials).

Media Mail (Book Rate)

Media Mail is generally used for books, film, printed test materials, sound recordings, play scripts, printed educational charts, and binders consisting of medical information. Certain advertising restrictions apply.

Special Mail Services

The USPS offers several services that are beneficial in special situations. These services include delivery confirmation, certificate of mailing, certified mail, collect on delivery, insured mail, return receipt, and registered

mail. Additional special services of the USPS are listed on their Website, www.usps.com.

Delivery Confirmation

This service provides the sender with information about the date and time of delivery or attempted delivery. Delivery confirmation may be purchased at the time of mailing only. This service is available for Priority Mail, Parcel Post, Bound Printed Matter, and Media Mail.

Certificate of Mailing

A certificate of mailing provides evidence of mailing to the sender; it must be purchased at the time of mailing and is available for First-Class Mail, Priority Mail, Parcel Post, Bound Printed Matter, and Media Mail.

Certified Mail

Certified mail provides the sender with a mailing receipt. The USPS maintains a delivery record. No insurance is provided. It is available with First-Class Mail and Priority Mail.

Collect on Delivery (COD)

This service allows mailers to collect the price of goods and/or postage on merchandise ordered by the addressee when the item is delivered. The amount to be collected from the recipient may not exceed $1,000.

Insured Mail

This service provides coverage against loss or damage. Coverage up to $5,000 is available for Parcel Post, Bound Printed Matter, Media Mail, and First-Class Mail. Items may not be insured for more than their value.

Registered Mail

Registered mail provides maximum protection and security for valuables. The sender is given a receipt for the item mailed, and the USPS maintains a delivery record. It is available only for Priority Mail and First-Class Mail.

Return Receipt

With this service, the mailer is provided evidence of delivery. This receipt may be requested before or after delivery. It is available only for Express Mail, certified mail, registered mail, and mail insured for more than $50.

Self-Check

Take a few minutes now to check your understanding of what you have learned to this point about USPS mail classifications. Answer the following questions:

1. Describe the following types of mail: First-Class Mail and Priority Mail.

_____

_____

_____

2. Describe these special services offered by the USPS: certificate of mailing, COD, insured mail, and registered mail.

_____

_____

_____

How did you do? Check your answers with the ones provided at the end of this chapter.

INTERNATIONAL MAIL

With organizations continuing to expand into international markets, you may need to send paper mail internationally. The principal categories of international mail provided by the USPS are as follows:

- Global Express Guaranteed (GXG)
- Global Express Mail (EMS)
- Global Priority Mail (GPM)

Global Express Guaranteed (GXG)

Global Express Guaranteed (GXG) is an expedited delivery service for both documents and nondocuments (merchandise items). It is the product of a business alliance between the USPS and DHL Worldwide Express Inc. It provides senders with reliable, high-speed, time-definite service from designated U.S. ZIP Code areas to principal locations in more than 200 countries and territorial possessions.

Global Express Mail (EMS)

Global Express Mail (EMS) is a high-speed service for mailing time-sensitive items to more than 175 countries and territorial possessions. It provides customers with expeditious handling and delivery. Shipments are insured for up to $500 at no additional cost. Optional insurance coverage is available for an additional fee.

Global Priority Mail (GPM)

Global Priority Mail (GPM) is an accelerated airmail service that provides customers with a reliable and economical means of sending correspondence and lightweight merchandise items to Canada, Mexico, and specified destination countries in Western Europe, the Caribbean, Central and South America, the Pacific Rim, the Middle East, and Africa.

Other categories of international mail are available from the USPS. If you are involved in sending a large amount of mail internationally, you may want to check the USPS Website at www.usps.com.

PRIVATE MAIL SERVICES

Several private companies across the United States offer mail services. In addition to service within the United States, many of these private companies offer international service. Four major companies are FedEx, United Parcel Service (UPS), DHL Worldwide Express, and Airborne Express.

You can find information about each of these companies on their Websites.

- fedex.com
- www.ups.com
- www.dhl.com
- www.airborneexpress.com

FedEx service marks used by permission.

Private mail services such as FedEx offer fast service both within the United States and abroad.

Here are some of the services offered by UPS. Other companies offer similar services.

- Document exchange that is an electronic delivery service, enabling customers to send time-sensitive documents, images, and software for immediate worldwide delivery via the Internet
- Same-day delivery service to virtually anywhere in the continental United States as well as from many international business centers 24 hours a day, 365 days a year
- Overnight delivery of letters, documents, and packages
- Daily pickup services
- Online tools that allow users to select services, calculate rates, look up addresses, validate and print labels, and track shipping history using criteria defined by the user

ADDITIONAL DELIVERY SERVICES

Most large cities also have messenger or courier services available. For example, if you wish to have a document delivered to a customer across town, you can call the messenger service to pick up the document and deliver it to the receiver.

In addition, a number of private companies, such as Mail Boxes, Etc.℠ and Pak Mail®, pro-

vide packing and shipping services for businesses and individuals. These companies pack the material, ship it, insure it, and make certain it reaches its final destination anywhere in the world. These businesses also stuff envelopes, meter mail, accept CODs, and hold and forward your mail while you are away.

INCOMING AND OUTGOING MAIL

An administrative professional has numerous responsibilities regarding the handling of both outgoing and incoming mail. Unanswered or misplaced mail can be a significant cost to an organization in lost business. Your job as an administrative professional is to make certain that incoming mail is well organized and presented to the executive and that outgoing mail leaves the office in a timely manner by way of the most expeditious service.

Outgoing Mail

An administrative professional's responsibilities for handling outgoing mail will vary. The administrative professional in a large company is responsible for preparing the mail for processing by mailroom employees. Mailroom employees may pick up the mail at various times during the day, or the administrative professional may be responsible for taking the outgoing mail to the mailroom.

Mailrooms today are automated. In large companies, mailrooms may be **outsourced** (handled by an outside firm) as a cost-saving measure. Such firms as Kelly Management Services®, Pitney Bowes Management Services®, and Xerox® Business Systems are a few of the firms that handle mail services for organizations. The Internet is used extensively to access postage (More information on electronic postage will be given in a separate section), gather postal-related information, access postal-related associations, and keep track of delivery status (with express carriers such as Airborne Express and FedEx providing online delivery information). Multifunctional equipment is used to fold, sort, label, and attach postage. Software is used in such functions as maintaining mailing lists. Incoming mail may also be processed via computer imaging and integrated into an electronic communication system.

Courtesy of Pitney Bowes

Mailrooms today use a wide variety of electronic equipment in processing the mail.

PC-based software allows mailrooms easy check-in of **accountable items** (express items), including items sent via FedEx, UPS, DHL, and registered and certified mail. Using a wand, the mailroom attendant scans the bar code on each incoming piece to establish its identity and enters the recipient's name. Mail can then be easily sorted by whatever delivery scheme is used in the organization—floor, building, department, and so on. Mailrooms also use software to track mail expenditures by departments or divisions within the organization. Such tracking allows budget managers to control their postal budgets more effectively.

In a small company, the administrative professional usually has the responsibility of preparing and processing the mail, which may even include taking the mail to the local postal office or calling the mailing service to arrange pickup. Whether you work in a large or small company, certain standard responsibilities are a part of processing outgoing mail. These responsibilities are discussed here.

Preparing Correspondence for Mailing

By following these procedures consistently and carefully, you can save your organization both time and money.

- Address envelopes carefully. Using software packages today, you only key the address once; you may then either address an envelope or prepare a label without rekeying. Your task is to be certain the address is keyed correctly the first time. Check it carefully against your records. When an address of an organization changes, be sure to correct your mailing list.
- Check each letter or memorandum to see that it is signed.
- Make sure special mailing notations are noted on the envelope.
- Make certain all enclosures are included.
- If enclosures are sent in a separate large envelope (because they are too large to send with the letter), be sure the address on the large envelope is correct. Mark the large envelope with the appropriate class of mail. For example, if the enclosures are to go first-class, indicate that on the envelope.
- Place all interoffice correspondence in appropriate envelopes with the name and department of the addressee listed on the envelope.
- If a mailroom employee applies postage and seals your mail, neatly stack your correspondence for the employee who picks it up.

© PhotoDisc, Inc.

Key addresses carefully; check the keyed address against your records to be certain it is correct.

Adhering to Automation Requirements

As an administrative professional, you are responsible for seeing that outgoing mail is properly prepared for automated sorting equipment. The USPS and private services use automated equipment. Envelopes that are not legible or that do not contain a ZIP Code are removed for hand sorting, taking longer to process. In addition to being sorted by ZIP Code, mail is also sorted by bar codes. Check your utility statement the next time you receive one. Many utility companies now have bar codes on their return envelopes, which allow fast sorting with a **BCS** (bar code sorter). Private mail services, such as FedEx and UPS, also use bar codes to sort their huge volumes of mail.

With the five-digit ZIP Code system, the United States and its possessions are divided into ten geographic areas. Each area consists of three or more states or possessions, and each is assigned a number between 0 and 9. The national area is the first digit of the ZIP Code. The remaining four numbers in the five-digit code also designate areas of the country. For example, in the ZIP Code 49503, 4 designates the national area, 9 designates a subdivision within the region, 5 designates a section center, and 03 designates a specific post office or delivery area within a multi-ZIP coded city. The ZIP 49503 is a delivery area in Grand Rapids, Michigan.

The ZIP + 4 is an expanded designation to improve service. The additional four digits further identify the destination of correspondence and permit even greater mailing productivity. When addressing envelopes or packages using the ZIP + 4 code, the following guidelines should be used:

- Key the address in all capital letters.
- Key an attention line as the second line of the address.
- Use no punctuation except the hyphen in the ZIP Code.

Sealing and Stamping

If you work in a medium to large office, you may not be responsible for sealing and stamping the mail. The outgoing mail is sent to a mailroom where sealing and stamping is done with automated equipment. If you work in a small office, you may seal and stamp envelopes using a postage meter. Envelopes are fed into the meter and are stacked, sealed, weighed, meter-stamped, and counted in one continuous operation. The metered mail imprint serves as postage payment, a postmark, and a cancellation mark. A postage meter either prints directly on envelopes or on adhesive strips that are then affixed to packages.

Using Electronic Postage

E-stamps (electronic postage, also referred to as **PC Postage**), is a fairly recent innovation that allows you to generate postage via the Web to your PC. This type of postage is rapidly gaining users due to its convenience, particularly in small offices and home offices. Larger organizations will also be able to take advantage of electronic postage as PC postage vendors develop better ways to control postage expenditures. Before you can start sending PC postage, you must apply for a postal license, which you can get online in just a few hours. With e-stamps, you can print postage on envelopes, packages, mailing tubes, or anything else that needs mailing. Two software packages available are Stamps.Com (www.stamps.com) and Simply Postage (www.simplypostage.com).

The idea for Stamps.com was born late one night in 1996 when UCLA graduate student Jim McDermott ran out of stamps and no post office was open to buy stamps. He and two classmates founded a company that replaced

Courtesy of Pitney Bowes

PC postage is gaining users due to its convenience.

post office trips with mouse clicks. With a computer, printer, and Internet connection, businesses can

- Print USPS approved postage for letters and packages
- Import addresses from address book programs
- Track mailings and postage expenditures
- Charge back mailing costs to clients or company departments

Electronic postage companies such as Stamps.com and Simply Postage are approved and regulated by the USPS.

Maintaining Mailing Lists

Most companies have correspondence they send to certain groups of individuals. As an administrative professional, your responsibility is to maintain a current mailing list. You must periodically update addresses as well as occasionally add new names to the mailing list. By maintaining mailing lists on your computer, you can update them quickly and easily. You can print address labels and envelopes from your mailing lists.

Incoming Mail

In a large office, mail comes into a central mailroom where it is sorted according to the company's departments. In addition to sorting, the mailroom may offer additional services, such as opening the mail. If the mail is opened, correspondence is not taken from the envelope, since the envelope may have information the receiver needs to know. Mail that is opened in mailrooms is processed through automatic mail openers that not only open the mail but also count the pieces of mail. This counting process helps a company analyze mail costs. Mail generally is delivered at set times twice each day (in the morning and the afternoon) so employees know when to expect their mail. Methods of delivery vary, with several possibilities given here.

- Delivered by a mailroom attendant
- Picked up at the mailroom by the administrative professional

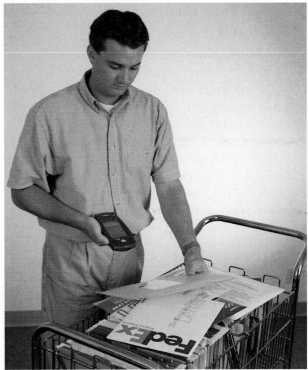

Courtesy of Pitney Bowes

Electronic devices are used in large organizations to deliver mail.

- Delivered by an electronic cart—A self-powered, unattended robotlike cart uses a photoelectric guidance system to follow invisible chemical paths painted on carpeting, floor tile, or other surfaces. The cart is programmed to make stops at particular locations, where the office professional can retrieve the mail from the cart.

In small offices, a USPS carrier may deliver the mail directly to the office or the company may maintain a mailbox at the post office. If the organization maintains a post office box, you may have the responsibility for picking up the mail.

Sorting

Once you receive the mail in your office or department, you must do a preliminary mail sort. If several individuals work in the department, sort the mail according to the addressee. An alphabetical sorter is handy if you are sorting mail for a number of individuals. Once the mail is sorted, place the mail for each individual into separate stacks.

When this preliminary sort is completed, sort each person's mail in this order.

- **Personal and confidential.** The administrative professional should not open mail marked "personal" or "confidential." Place this mail to one side so you do not inadvertently open it.
- **Special delivery, registered, or certified.** This mail is important and should be placed so the individual to whom it is addressed sees it first.
- **Regular business mail (First-Class Mail).** Mail from customers, clients, and suppliers is also considered important and should be sorted so it receives top priority.
- **Interoffice communications.** This mail generally is received in a distinctive interoffice envelope.
- **Advertisements and circulars.** Advertisements and circulars are considered relatively unimportant and can be handled after the other correspondence is answered.
- **Newspapers, magazines, and catalogs.** These materials should be placed at the bottom of the correspondence stack since they may be read at the executive's convenience.

Communication Tip:
Set aside a certain time each day for processing incoming mail.

Opening

Mail may be opened in the mailroom (as you have previously learned), or it may be opened in the individual's office. Mail opened in an individual's office is usually opened by hand, using an envelope opener. When opening mail, follow the procedures given here.

- Have necessary supplies readily available. These supplies include an envelope opener, a date and time stamp, routing and action slips, a stapler, paper clips, and a pen or pencil.

- Before opening an envelope, tap the lower edge of the envelope on the desk so the contents fall to the bottom and are not cut when the envelope is opened.
- After the correspondence is opened, check the envelope carefully to be certain all items have been removed.
- Fasten any enclosures to the correspondence. Attach small enclosures to the front of the correspondence. Attach enclosures larger than the correspondence to the back.
- Mend any torn paper with tape.
- If a personal or confidential letter is opened by mistake, do not remove it from the envelope. Write "Opened by Mistake" on the front of the envelope, add your initials, and reseal the envelope with tape.
- Stack the envelopes on the desk in the same order as the opened mail in case it becomes necessary to refer to the envelopes. A good practice is to save all envelopes for at least one day in case they are needed for reference. Then they may be thrown away.

Keeping Selected Envelopes

Certain envelopes should be retained. Keep the envelope when one or more of the following situations exist:

- An incorrectly addressed envelope—You or your supervisor may want to call attention to this fact when answering the correspondence.
- A letter with no return address—The envelope usually will have the return address.
- A letter written on letterhead with a different return address than that on the envelope—For example, a person may write a letter on hotel letterhead and write the business address on the envelope.
- A letter without a signature—The envelope may contain the writer's name.
- An envelope that has a significantly different postmark from the date on the document—The document date may be compared with the postmark date to determine the delay in receiving the document.
- A letter specifying an enclosure that is not enclosed—Write "No Enclosure" on the letter and attach the envelope.

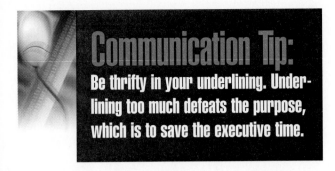

- A letter containing a bid, an offer, or an acceptance of a contract—The postmark date may be needed as legal evidence.

Dating and Time Stamping

Although all organizations do not use date and time stamping procedures, it can be an important step. It furnishes a record of when the correspondence was received. For example, a letter may arrive too late to handle the matter mentioned in the letter. Therefore, the stamped date of receipt is a recorded confirmation of the day the letter was received and of the resultant inability to take care of the matter. Or the correspondence may not be dated. Therefore, the date stamped on the letter shows approximately when the correspondence was written. Date and time stamping may be done with either a hand stamp or a small machine that prints the date and time of day.

Reading and Annotating

Busy executives need help with the large amount of mail that crosses their desk each day. As an administrative professional, you can help by scanning the mail for the executive and noting important parts of the correspondence. You can underline the important words and phrases with a colored pen or pencil. You should also check mathematical calculations and verify dates that appear in correspondence.

The next step is to **annotate** (to make notations about previous action taken or facts that will assist the reader). You can annotate by writing notes in the margin of the correspondence or by using sticky notes. The advantage of sticky notes is that they can be peeled off and destroyed when you and the executive are finished with them. If an enclosure is missing

from the letter, make an annotation. If a bill is received, check the computations. Note any discrepancies by annotating. If the correspondence refers to a previous piece of correspondence written by the executive, pull that correspondence and attach it to the new correspondence. Note that the previous correspondence is being attached. Annotations may also be used to remind the executive of a previous commitment. For example, the executive might have agreed to have lunch with the person who signed the correspondence. When answering the letter, the executive may want to refer to their lunch plans.

Organizing

After you have completed the preliminary mail sorts and have opened, date and time stamped, read, and annotated, you are ready to do a final sort. Here is one arrangement that may be used.

- Immediate action. This mail must be handled on the day of receipt or shortly thereafter.
- Routine correspondence. Such mail would include memorandums and other types of nonurgent mail.
- Informational mail. Periodicals, newspapers, advertisements, and other types of mail that do not require answering but are for the executive's reading should be included here.

Notice another method of sorting mail provided in the Communication Tip below.

After you have organized the mail, you are ready to place it in folders with labels indicating the categories established. A good practice is to color code the folders. For example, the

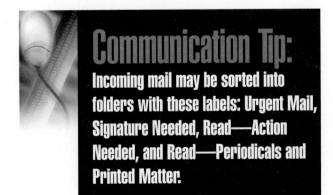

immediate action folder might be red, the routine correspondence folder might be blue, and the informational mail folder might be yellow. Color coding helps the executive see at a glance what mail needs to be handled first. Folders also help maintain the confidentiality of mail. For example, someone walking into the executive's office cannot easily read the material in folders. The folders should be placed on the executive's desk in a predetermined area. He or she may have an inbox for mail. Whatever the procedure, it should meet the executive's needs.

The executive may also ask that you present the mail two times a day. For example, if outside mail is received in the morning and afternoon, the executive may ask that you organize and present it approximately 30 minutes after you receive it.

You may handle a large portion of the mail yourself if the executive does not need to see it. This is especially true if you have been working for the company and the executive for a period of time and are familiar with the procedures and the executive's style. However, never destroy mail (even what you might consider junk mail) unless you have a clear agreement with the executive about making decisions in this regard.

Routing

At times, more than one person may need to read a piece of correspondence. In that case, make photocopies of the correspondence and send a copy to each individual on the list or route the correspondence to all individuals, using a routing slip. When determining whether to make photocopies, ask yourself if it is urgent that all individuals receive the information contained in the correspondence immediately. If so, it is best to photocopy the document. If not, it generally is best to use a routing slip, particularly if the correspondence is lengthy. You save copying costs by routing. You can purchase routing slips or create your own. For example, if you route correspondence to the same individuals regularly, you can create a routing slip that already has the individuals' names printed on it.

Handling During the Executive's Absence

You learned in Chapter 11 that one of your responsibilities while the executive is traveling is to handle the mail. In that case, follow these general guidelines.

- Talk with the executive before he or she leaves about your responsibilities in handling the mail. Be specific with any questions so you have a clear understanding. Mistakes in handling mail can be costly to the company.
- When urgent mail comes in, handle it immediately according to the executive's directions. For example, you may give it to the person who is in charge or you may fax it to the executive.
- Answer mail that falls within your area of responsibility in a timely manner.
- Maintain mail that has been answered (with the answer attached) in a separate folder; the executive may want to review it when he or she returns.
- Maintain mail that can wait for the executive's return in a separate folder. Retrieve any previous correspondence that the executive will need when reviewing the mail. Place this correspondence in the folder also.

OFFICE COPIERS

The advent of copiers and multifunction units (combination copiers, scanners, fax, and printers) has made the job of the administrative professional much easier. Rather than having to rekey a document, he or she can simply save or scan it into the computer, make any needed changes, and print it. Copiers are used constantly in offices. However, the convenience of copiers has also brought with it abuses by employees. We make too many copies and end up throwing away an inordinate amount of paper. It is **ecologically** (pertaining to the relationships between human groups and their physical and social environments) important to conserve paper rather than to increase the amount of paper being used. As an administrative professional, you will be using copiers daily.

Your task, in addition to making and distributing copies, also includes making ethical decisions when using copiers. This section will help you understand the types of copiers available and remind you of the importance of ethical copying. An all-inclusive term used to refer to the copying process is **reprographics.** Reprographics refers not only to the process of making copies but also to any piece of equipment that produces multiple copies of an original.

© PhotoDisc, Inc.

The administrative professional must be conscious of ecological issues when making copies; conserving paper is an ecologically sound practice.

Types of Copiers

Copiers are available in two types—analog and digital. Although digital technology is rapidly overtaking the copier market, analog copiers are still used and may be the best choice for small offices and teleworkers. Analog copiers, while making the first copy at a fast rate, take longer to produce multiple copies than do digital copiers. Since digital copiers have fewer moving parts than analog copiers, they are less likely to jam. Analog copiers are generally less expensive than digital machines, with the cost per copy being lower too. However, digital copier prices are dropping, and many believe analog copiers will be obsolete in the not-too-distant future.

Another way to categorize copiers is by the number of copies they make. **Low-volume copiers** typically produce from 12 to 30 **cpm (copies per minute)** and run from 500 to 4,000 copies per month. **Mid-volume copiers** run from 5,000 to 85,000 copies per month, and **high-volume copiers** run from 100,000 to 400,000 copies per month.

Copier Features

Copier features vary, depending on the size and price of the copier. Some of the features are given here. If you are involved in helping to select a copier for your organization, you need to carefully analyze the various features offered by different copiers and compare those features with the needs of your organization. Figure 13-1 on page 334 lists a number of questions you should ask when selecting a copier.

Paper Capacity

Paper capacity is controlled by the amount of paper the copier can hold in the paper tray. Low-volume copiers hold from 100 to 999 sheets of paper, medium-volume copiers hold from 1,000 to 1,999 sheets of paper, and high-volume copiers hold from 2,000 to 5,000 sheets of paper.

Duplexing

Copying on both sides of a sheet of paper is known as **duplexing.** This feature saves paper and reduces the number of sheets of paper to be stored in files. An operator makes copies on both sides of the paper by merely pushing the proper buttons, requiring no other intervention by the operator.

Document or Digital Editing

Copiers that have an editing function scan the image and convert it to digital signals. Then using control keys or a wand (similar to a wand used in retail stores to scan letters and numbers on price tags), the operator can mask (delete copy by covering), move, and manipulate the copy to alter the image.

Questions for the Organization
- How many people will be using the copier?
- How many copies will be made per month?
- Is there a projected increase or decrease in copy volume over the next three years?
- What features are needed?
- Will color copying be needed?
- What materials will be copied? What percentage of copying will be on letter-size paper? What percentage of copying will be on legal-size paper? What percentage of copying will be stapled?
- What space limitations exist for the copier? (If there are space limitations, the size of the copier becomes an issue.)
- Should a maintenance contract be purchased?

Questions to be Answered During a Demonstration
- What is the quality of the copy?
- Are the copies clean and crisp?
- If it is a color copier, are the colors clear?
- Is the machine easy to operate?
- Is the interior easily accessible for removing jammed paper and replacing toner?

Questions to be Answered About the Dealer/Vendor's Background
- Is the vendor authorized to sell and service the model being considered?
- How long has the dealer/vendor been in business?
- Have any complaints been filed against the vendor with the Better Business Bureau?

Questions to Ask of the Dealer/Vendor
- What is the purchase price of the machine?
- What is the cost of supplies, especially toner?
- Do you carry parts for the brand?
- What is your response time on a typical service request?
- What is the cost of the service?
- Are maintenance contracts available? If so, what is the cost?
- Is key operator training available?
- How long have you been in business?

Figure 13-1

Collate and Staple

Depending on your needs, you can program copiers to collate only or to collate and staple sets of materials.

Automatic Folding

Some copiers fold 11 × 17-inch copies to an 8½ × 11-inch size. This feature allows drawings and schematics to be kept in a convenient format for handling and distribution. The fold can also be **offset** (not folded to the edge of the paper) so folded materials can be placed in three-ring binders.

Environmentally Friendly Features

Many copiers incorporate organic photoconductors, recyclable materials, toner-save modes, and energy-save modes. Some vendors offer their own brands of recycled paper as well as programs that allow customers to recycle their toner cartridges.

Control Systems

If you have worked in an office at all, you are probably aware of the copying abuses that persist. Employees often make ten copies of a document when only eight are actually needed. The additional copies are made "just in case." More often than not the extra copies are thrown away. Unfortunately, another widespread abuse is the copying of materials for personal use. Such behavior is clearly an ethical violation.

In order to curb copying abuses, many organizations use copy control devices. Each system operates somewhat differently, but the same basic features exist in all systems. For example, with a keypad system, the user enters an account number onto a keypad to gain access to the copier. With a card system, the user inserts a card into the machine to gain access. The card is good only for a set number of copies, and copying costs are automatically charged back to the appropriate department or division. Each department or division can then check copy costs against a specific account. If abuses are occurring, appropriate action can be taken.

Ethical Considerations

Each employee in a company should be ethical in the use of copying machines. Each employee should also be aware of the legal restrictions on the copying of certain documents. Behaving ethically when copying means that **YOU DO NOT** engage in the following activities.

- Copy documents for your own personal use
- Copy cartoons, jokes, and similar types of information to be distributed to your friends and co-workers
- Make copies of documents that you need for an outside professional group, such as a service club, unless you have approval from your organization to do so
- Copy materials restricted by Copyright Law, such as birth certificates, passports, driver's licenses, and so on. (If you have questions about what is legal to copy, check with your organization's attorney or check the Copyright Law.)

In addition to ethical considerations, etiquette is an issue when a number of individuals use the same copier. Figure 13-2 gives several etiquette considerations.

SHREDDERS

For those times when a machine malfunctions and copies must be destroyed, businesses often place a shredder in proximity to the copier. A **shredder** is a machine that cuts paper into strips or confetti-like material. Today shredded paper is recycled by many businesses as packing material. Since mailrooms process a large amount of paper and often pack materials for shipping, they use shredders too.

The shredder market has increased over the last few years due primarily to the impact of technology. Unfortunately, additional copies are often made that are not needed. These copies, often containing confidential or sensitive information, are tossed into wastebaskets. People with unethical agendas can use this information to the detriment of the company. Consider these very real possibilities within an organization when sensitive data is tossed into wastebaskets.

- Social Security numbers and birth dates can be used to create false identity papers and open fake checking accounts.

ETIQUETTE CONSIDERATIONS WHEN COPYING MATERIALS

When sharing a copier with several people, be considerate of their time. Observe the basic courtesies listed here.

- If you are involved in an extensive copying job, let your colleagues interrupt when they have only a few pages to copy.
- If the machine malfunctions while you are copying, try to fix the problem. If you cannot do so, call the key operator in your company or call a service repairperson. **Do not** walk away, leaving the problem for the next person to handle.
- When toner runs out, refill it.
- When paper runs out, add more.

- When paper jams, remove it.
- If you are using additional supplies such as paper clips, scissors, and so on, return them to their location before leaving the copier.
- If you have run copies that are not usable, destroy them. Put them in a shredder and/or a recycle bin. Do not leave a messy work area for the next person to clean up.
- Return the copier to its standard settings.

Figure 13-2

- Company competitors can retrieve sensitive documents, using this information to damage the company. For example, a company bid placed in the trash may get in the hands of a competitor who then underbids another company.
- Information about new technology being developed by the company may get into the hands of information criminals who use it to the detriment of society.

Help save our trees—recycle!

© PhotoDisc, Inc..

You have certain responsibilities as an administrative professional in shredding papers.

- Know your company policies on shredding
- Know when a document is confidential or sensitive
- Never toss unneeded copies in the trash without questioning if they are confidential or sensitive
- Shred all appropriate, unneeded copies

RECYCLING

Our technological age is spawning the use of more paper rather than less, even considering the number of electronic messages that are sent and received. This increase in the use of paper has some serious repercussions for our environment. We are losing valuable forests and land (in establishing landfills). Here are a few facts about paper use within offices.

- Typical businesses generate about 1.5 pounds of wastepaper per employee per day.

- Financial businesses generate over 2 pounds per employee per day.
- Nearly half of typical office paper waste is comprised of high-grade office paper, for which there is strong recycling demand.
- Recycling one ton of paper saves about 6.7 cubic yards of landfill space.
- Every recycled ton of paper saves approximately 17 trees.
- Recycling paper reduces the air and water pollution due to paper manufacturing.[1]

Because so much paper is used, resulting in serious environmental issues, recycling programs are becoming common in businesses. Such programs can save millions of tons of paper each year. Organizations often provide recycling bins for paper and outsource the collection and shredding of paper to private vendors.

In addition to recycling paper, organizations need to use recycled paper products. Recycled paper uses 64 percent less energy and 58 percent less water in its production than does the production of virgin papers. In addition, manufacturing recycled paper produces 74 percent less air pollution and 35 percent less water pollution than virgin paper production processes.

Additionally, organizations need to look at how they can reduce the use of paper in the office. Here are several suggestions.

- Use both sides of the page (duplex documents).
- Convert scratch paper into memo pads, telephone answering slips, and similar items.
- Print only the number of copies needed.
- Send interoffice mail via email.
- Shred used paper and use to package materials instead of using plastic pellets.

TEAMWORK

You have been introduced to the importance of teamwork in collaborative writing and for team presentations in Chapters 9 and 10, respectively. However, in almost all workplace situations,

---

[1]"Fact Sheet: Reducing Office Paper Waste," accessed August 5, 2001; available from www.es.epa.gov/techinfo/facts.

teamwork is vitally important to your success. You learned in Chapter 1 that the word *team* can be traced back to the Indo-European word *deuk*, meaning "to pull together." A truly effective team consists of two or more people who need each other to accomplish the best results possible.

In this chapter, you have learned the importance of working closely with your employer in processing incoming and outgoing mail. You must understand your employer's needs when processing mail—how it is to be sorted, organized, and routed. If the two of you fail to work together in setting parameters, the results may be angry clients or customers who have not received prompt responses to their requests or inquiries. Obviously, this example is merely one important team situation in the workplace. You work with a number of individuals—your workgroup, other administrative assistants, your employer, and your administrators—on a daily basis in various types of teams.

If you are to be an effective team member or team leader, you must understand what it  takes to make an effective team. Then you must work to build effective teams within the organization. Most of us understand effective teams in sports. We watch championship basketball and football teams, and we notice a team of specialists. However, these specialists do not act independently of each other. Their success depends not only on individual excellence but also on their ability to work together. Team members must complement each other's specialties. They must come together as a highly skilled team, concentrating on doing

their best to win the game they are playing. This team analogy also holds true in the workplace. The effective workforce team is a group of people, each with his or her own special talents and skills, who come together to produce the best product or outcome.

Characteristics of an effective team include the following:

- Team members are skillful in discussion. They pay attention not only to the words said but also to the tone of voice and what is not said.
- Team members have excellent inquiry skills. They ask appropriate questions of each other.
- The team encourages an atmosphere of openness and trust.
- Team members encourage new ideas.
- The team creates a safe haven for all participants to be honest in their statements and actions pertaining to the goals of the team.
- Team members actively listen to each other. They do not interrupt.
- Team members resist the temptation to criticize each other or each other's ideas.
- Each team member builds his or her own self-awareness. When a team member is frustrated or confused, he or she silently asks these questions: What am I thinking? What am I feeling? What do I want at this moment?
- Team members explore impasses. They ask these questions of each other: What exactly has happened? What is our objective? What does the data reveal? What do we need to do? What is the best decision consistent with organizational goals?

CHAPTER SUMMARY

The summary will help you remember the important points covered in the chapter.

- USPS classifications of mail include First-Class Mail, Priority Mail, Express Mail, Parcel Post, Bound Printed Matter, and Media Mail.
- First-Class Mail is any type of mail that weighs 13 ounces or less.
- Mail that weighs more than 13 ounces may be sent as Priority Mail. Items cannot exceed 70 pounds in weight, and the maximum size for any item is 108 inches in combined length and girth.
- Express Mail is the fastest mail service available from the USPS, with next-day delivery by noon to most destinations.
- Special Mail services include delivery confirmation, certificate of mailing, certified mail, collect on delivery, insured mail, registered mail, and return receipt.
- The principal categories of international mail provided by the USPS are Global Express Guaranteed (GXG), Global Express Mail (EMS), and Global Priority Mail (GPM).
- A number of private mail services offer fast and efficient delivery of mail, including FedEx, UPS, DHL, and Airborne.
- The administrative professional's responsibilities for outgoing mail include preparing correspondence for mailing, adhering to automation requirements, sealing and stamping, using electronic postage, and maintaining mailing lists.

- The administrative professional's responsibilities for incoming mail include sorting, opening, keeping selected envelopes, date and time stamping, reading and annotating, organizing, routing, and handling during the executive's absence.
- The administrative professional uses copiers daily and should be knowledgeable about the types of copiers and their basic features. Copiers are available in two types—analog and digital. Digital technology is rapidly overtaking the copier market; however, many analog copiers are still in operation.
- When making copies, the administrative professional should be ethical; i.e., not copy documents for personal use, not copy information such as cartoons and jokes to be distributed to friends and co-workers, and not copy materials restricted by Copyright Law.
- Shredding a document is important when the information is confidential or might be used to harm the organization.
- In order to save costs and help protect the environment, businesses are instituting recycling programs.
- The effective administrative professional understands the importance of teamwork and is constantly developing team skills.

CHAPTER GLOSSARY

The following terms were used in this chapter. Definitions are provided to help you review the terms.

- **USPS** (p. 322)—United States Postal Service.
- **Priority mail** (p. 323)—mail that weighs more than 13 ounces but does not exceed 70 pounds in weight, with the maximum size for any item being 108 inches in combined length and girth.
- **Girth** (p. 323)—a measurement around the thickest part of a parcel.
- **Outsourced** (p. 326)—handled by an outside firm.

- **Accountable items** (p. 327)—express items; e.g., items sent via FedEx, UPS, DHL, and Registered and Certified mail.
- **BCS** (p. 328)—bar code sorter.
- **E-stamps** or **PC postage** (p. 328)—postage via the Web to the PC.
- **Annotate** (p. 331)—to make notations on a piece of mail concerning a previous action taken or facts that will assist the reader.

- **Ecologically** (p. 332)—pertaining to the relationship between human groups and their physical and social environment.
- **Reprographics** (p. 333)—an inclusive term used to refer to the copying process.
- **Low-volume copiers** (p. 333)—copiers that typically produce from 12 to 30 copies per minute.
- **CPM** (p. 333)—copies per minute.

- **Mid-volume copiers** (p. 333)—copiers that run from 5,000 to 85,000 copies per month.
- **High-volume copiers** (p. 333)—copiers that run from 100,000 to 400,000 copies per month.
- **Duplexing** (p. 333)—copying on both sides of a sheet of paper.
- **Offset** (p. 334)—not folded to the edge of the paper.
- **Shredder** (p. 335)—a machine that cuts paper into strips or confetti-like material.

DISCUSSION ITEMS

These items provide an opportunity to test your understanding of the chapter through written responses and discussion with your classmates and your instructor.

1. Identify the classes of USPS mail.
2. List and explain the types of special mail services offered by the USPS.
3. What are the administrative professional's responsibilities in preparing incoming mail?
4. List and explain the two major types of copiers. Explain the differences between low-volume, mid-volume, and high-volume copiers.
5. List six characteristics of an effective team.

CRITICAL-THINKING ACTIVITY

Roger Martin is a clerk in the mailroom. He has been with the company for six months. He seems like a nice young man who is eager to succeed on his job, but he has made several mistakes. You have also heard other employees complain about the errors he is making. The mistakes you have noticed are these.

- You had an important item to mail, and you requested that it be insured for $500. Roger failed to have the package insured.
- You asked that a certificate of mailing be provided for a piece of correspondence. Roger sent the mail without requesting the certificate of mailing.
- On several occasions, when picking up your mail, Roger inadvertently left your outgoing mail on other desks in the building. The employees at these desks returned the mail to you.

- One afternoon this week Roger was an hour late picking up the mail. That meant you had to take a piece of correspondence that Mr. Albertson wanted sent by Express Mail to the post office yourself in order to get it out the same day. Mr. Albertson was not happy; he needed you for some additional assignments.
- Two mornings this week (and on several previous occasions) Roger missed you on his mail run; he neither picked up your outgoing mail nor brought you the incoming mail.

Each time Roger made a mistake, you talked with him about the error. He was very apologetic and made the excuse that he still has a lot to learn. However, the last time you called a mistake to his attention, he became defensive. What should you do now?

RESPONSES TO SELF-CHECK

1. First-Class Mail is any type of mail that weighs 13 ounces or less, including bills, statements, all matter sealed or otherwise closed against inspection, and matter wholly or partly keyed or handwritten.

   Priority Mail is mail that weighs more than 13 ounces but does not exceed 70 pounds in weight, with the maximum size for any item being 108 inches in combined length and girth.

2. A certificate of mailing provides evidence of mailing to the sender. It must be purchased at the time of mailing and is available for First-Class Mail, Priority Mail, Parcel Post, Bound Printed Matter, and Media Mail.

COD (Collect on Delivery) is a service that allows mailers to collect the price of goods and/or postage on merchandise ordered by the addressee when the item is delivered.

Insured mail is a service that provides coverage against loss or damage. Coverage up to $5,000 is available for Parcel Post, Bound Printed Matter, Media Mail, and First-Class Mail.

Registered Mail provides maximum protection and security for valuables. The sender is given a receipt for the item mailed, and the USPS maintains a delivery record.

PROJECTS

Project 13-1 (Objective 1)
Online Project

Using the USPS Website at www.usps.com, determine what class of mail and what mail services you would use to send the following items:

1. A package weighing 5 pounds that must be at its destination within two days. The package is valued at $3,000.
2. A letter that must be to the addressee before noon on the date after it is written.
3. Three books that weigh a total of 5 pounds.
4. A package that weighs 10 pounds, is worth $400, and must be to the addressee by the next day.
5. A letter for which you need evidence of delivery and that must reach its destination the next day.
6. A package weighing 10 pounds that must be received in Japan within two days.
7. Valuables that are worth $15,000.
8. A letter that must reach China within three days.

Project 13-2 (Objective 2)

Student CD, SCDP13-2 contains a mailing list of 30 names and a letter that is to be sent to the names on the list. Add the eight names that are given here to the mailing list. Here are a few changes to make to the letter. (1) The session has been moved to March 21. (2) The session will be held in the Galaxy Room of AmeriAsian.

Once you have made the changes, prepare letters for the 38 individuals and address envelopes. Print out letterhead from the Student CD, SCDP9-4. Print out a copy of the new mailing list, putting it in alphabetical order. Sign the letters for Mr. Albertson with your initials under the signature, fold the letters, and place them in the envelopes. Bundle the 38 envelopes together in alphabetical order; place one copy of the letter on top of the envelopes. Submit the package to your instructor.

Mary Valdez, Hunt Manufacturing Corporation, 3345 Edna SE, Grand Rapids 49546

Wayne Tuftee, Robinson Drugs, 2798 Lowell SE, Grand Rapids 49502

Lynn Knouf, Manley Roofing, 323 Harcourt NE, Grand Rapids 49502

Jack Kemp, Kaczmarski Services, Inc., 2520 Normandy NE, Grand Rapids 49502

Jackson McDougall, Soft Warehouse, 850 Powell NW, Grand Rapids 49503

Bruce VanDamm, Bell Atlantic Business Systems, 7620 Lime Hollow SE, Grand Rapids 49546

Richard Espinosa, Dodds Grocery, 2370 Valleywood SE, Grand Rapids 49546

Theodore Ethridge, Computers Unlimited, 5135 28th Street NE, Grand Rapids 49501

Project 13-3 (Objective 2)

Here is a list of Mr. Albertson's incoming mail that you are to handle. Explain how you would sort and place items in folders. Prepare a list of the mail as it is to be arranged, listing the folder you would place each piece in. If there are problems, explain how you would handle them. Submit your work to your instructor.

1. A confidential letter to Mr. Albertson
2. The *Wall Street Journal*
3. A new product advertisement
4. A letter with enclosures
5. A letter sent by Express Mail
6. A letter from China sent by Global Priority Mail
7. A catalog of computer supplies
8. A letter with no letterhead address
9. A letter stating a check is enclosed; no check is enclosed
10. A letter referring to a letter written two weeks ago by Mr. Albertson
11. *Fortune*
12. A letter sent by FedEx for next-day delivery

Project 13-4 (Objectives 3 and 4)
Collaborative Project

Work with two of your classmates on this task. Search the Web for the types of copiers available from two manufacturers; e.g., copiers made by Xerox and Canon™. You are working for AmeriAsian; the copier is for your work area.

Approximately 300 are copies made each week. Recommend which copier the company should purchase and give your reasons. Submit your recommendations in memorandum form to your instructor, citing your Web references. Use the memorandum form on the Student CD, file SCDP13-4. As you work on this assignment, use the effective teamwork characteristics you learned in this chapter. In your memorandum to your instructor, include a statement describing how you worked together as an effective team.

Project 13-5 (Objective 4)

Recently, your two assistants, Juan Mercado and Luyin Wu, have not been getting along well. Almost every day one of them comes to you with a complaint about the other. You do not understand the problems; they seem to be petty and a waste of time. For example, Juan complained one day that Luyin was five minutes late getting back from lunch, which caused him to be five minutes late in taking his lunch. Luyin complained that Juan was pushing his work off on her. Your advice to both of them was to work together to handle the problem situations. However, the situation is getting worse, not better. You decide you need to help. You know they must work together as a team and with you as a team. What suggestions would you make to them? Submit your suggestions in a memorandum to your instructor. Use the memorandum form on the Student CD, file SCDP13-5.

ENGLISH USAGE CHALLENGE DRILL

Correct the following sentences. Cite the grammar rule that is applicable to each sentence. Before you begin, refresh your memory of commonly misused words by reviewing the Reference Guide of this text.

1. I shall be happy to assist you in anyway I can.
2. She was pleased to discover that her dog was alright.
3. The advise received from the counselor was helpful in finding a job.
4. The affect of the decision was negative.
5. The dentist's office was further than I thought.

ASSESSMENT OF CHAPTER OBJECTIVES

Now that you have completed the chapter and the projects, take a few minutes to review the learning objectives. For your convenience, the objectives are repeated below. Did you accomplish these objectives? If you were unable to accomplish the objectives, give your reasons for not doing so.

1. Identify the classes of USPS mail and special mail services.　　　　Yes _____　No _____

_____

_____

_____

2. Explain how to process both incoming and outgoing mail.　　　　Yes _____　No _____

_____

_____

_____

3. Explain the types of copiers and their functions.　　　　Yes _____　No _____

_____

_____

_____

4. Develop teamwork skills.　　　　Yes _____　No _____

_____

_____

_____

You may submit your answers in writing to your instructor, using the memorandum form on the Student CD, SCDAP13-1.

NILDA CAMPBELL'S CASE SOLUTION

With courage, I offered to type it, and the executive reluctantly agreed. I finished the task in a couple of days, impressing the executive with my efficiency. I had proven that my knowledge of another language was an asset and had saved the company the cost of having the job outsourced. Since then I have been able to attend Maori classes at the local university at the company's expense, which is part of its professional development program. Also, the company now requires new employees to be proficient in Maori.

A Success Profile

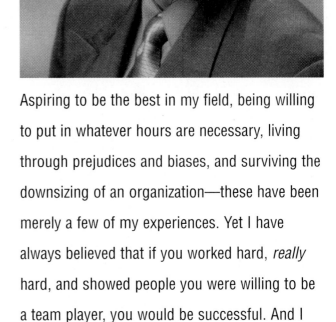

José Rego
Course Leader
Langevin Learning Services
Miami, Florida

Aspiring to be the best in my field, being willing to put in whatever hours are necessary, living through prejudices and biases, and surviving the downsizing of an organization—these have been merely a few of my experiences. Yet I have always believed that if you worked hard, *really* hard, and showed people you were willing to be a team player, you would be successful. And I have found this to be true in my career.

My first job (right out of high school at the age of 18 with four years of French and

PLANNING AND MANAGING YOUR CAREER

the ability to type 92 wpm) was as an assistant to my father's assistant. My father reached the position of vice president of a major soft drink distributor in Puerto Rico based on his hard work, perseverance, and impeccable word of honor. Many of the principles my father taught me have been the solid rocks upon which I have built my career. Any successes I have today are due to a combination of influential factors that continue to play an important role in my day-to-day life.

After nearly 20 years, I realized I had never done a serious self-assessment to find out what I really love to do. For years, I dedicated myself to the administrative profession, only to realize a few years ago that it was not to be the "main event" in my career, but the one essential stepping stone to where I am today. During my years as an administrative professional, I came to understand

aspects of the business world that allow me today to establish a common ground with and feel empathy toward my audiences in the training field.

As an administrative professional, I learned about strategic planning, contract administration, legal procedures, project coordination, and marketing techniques. I became a member of the International Association of Administrative Professionals (IAAP). I prepared for and passed the Certified Professional Secretary (CPS) exam and eventually held the presidency of the Miami-Dade chapter. This was the final step in my administrative career that thrust me forward into my life mission and passion—training and development. With the guidance of a sponsor and friend, I was able to focus on my true calling and begin preparing for a training career. I became a member of the American Society of Training and Development

(ASTD) and attended a National Speakers Association convention in Philadelphia.

Having a sponsor/mentor is not a luxury, but a necessity for success. My mentor never advised me on what to do, but rather what *not* to do—especially in those instances when I was about to take on more than I could handle. My mentor is a trainer and speaker who tailors her efforts and programs strictly to the administrative profession. She invested time and energy into our friendship and guided me through the process of realizing my life calling. While she helped me see what my career path opportunities were, she also helped me understand that the knowledge and skills I had gained through the administrative profession where not to be taken for granted. These days I look for the opportunity to sponsor or mentor people at different stages of their career, in the hope they can find the same satisfaction in their work that I have found.

I clearly recall December 31, 1999. It was the only time I made a New Year's resolution. I committed myself to finding my place in the training industry and to do so no later than December 31, 2000. In January 2000, my local IAAP chapter had a dinner meeting presentation on "How to Set and Achieve Goals." This one-hour presentation proved to be the key to opening my door to the training field. I applied the step-by-step process. I updated my resume to reflect all

the knowledge and skills the administrative profession had provided me relevant to my mission.

Less than three months later I was an instructor with the world's largest train-the-trainer company, which I have the honor and pleasure to represent today. I still work hard, very hard, but I have a smile on my face at the end of the workday. About 50 percent of my time is spent traveling around the world. The rest of the time I work from my office at home, preparing lesson plans, customizing workshop agendas for private clients, and helping other instructors in the company prepare for their new workshops. The background I acquired through my many years in the administrative profession was a key element to helping me find my calling. Without this background and the experiences it provided, I would not be able to stay organized and handle the stacks of paperwork on my desk.

I have the most fun when I encounter a challenge in the training class, which motivates me to work even harder. I know I will receive the same positive energy back in return for my effort. I have learned that life is like a boomerang and what you send will return to you ten fold. When you do something you love, it stops being work and becomes an adventure. This realization helps me deal with a stressful travel schedule. If I could give you only one piece of advice for

the future, it would be to do something you love to do—something that fulfills you and that complements your values.

JOSÉ REGO'S CASE

I recently conducted a three-day workshop. As I started to get acquainted with the participants, it became clear that this was a group of extroverts and highly participative people. They enjoyed discussions and voicing their opinions.

One of the participants had a substantial amount of experience, resulting in his undermining the perspectives and opinions of the other participants at his table. All of his comments were about "when I did this" or "what I did was that."

The other participants at his table believed he was being too controlling, unwilling to consider anybody else's perspectives. The group dynamics at his table became so difficult for other people to handle that I had to change seating arrangements three times on the first day of the workshop. I even approached him individually. I explained how valuable his years of experience were to the process and asked him to allow others to participate as well. He agreed but the situation did not change much. Basically, he was determined to voice his "expertise" at all times (including breaks).

On the second day of the workshop, he was at a new table—again. This time one of the younger and less experienced participants, who was determined to get the most out of the workshop experience, was sitting at his table. While the group was debriefing an exercise, our "expert" had a comment or rebuttal about anything anyone said. When it came time for his table to participate in the debriefing, the young woman sitting in the group attempted time and time again to voice her perspective, each time being interrupted by our "expert." After noticing her frustration over and over, I made a point to address her attempts to voice her opinion. I looked straight at her and asked, "What was the perspective you wanted to offer?" She promptly replied, "Well, I was going to say something, but I've been interrupted so many times, I forgot." And with that said, I called a ten-minute break.

Although our "expert" continued to grace the rest of the workshop with his insights, he kept his comments brief and relevant, seeming to keep in his mind everyone else's need to participate and contribute to the learning.

What happened? What turned the "expert" around? Turn to the end of Part 6 (page 388) to see José Rego's explanation of the change.

CHAPTER 14
YOUR CAREER PATH

LEARNING OBJECTIVES

1. Determine sources of job information.
2. Prepare a letter of application and a resume.
3. Develop job interview skills.
4. Discover how to advance your professional career.
5. *Commit to living your values in the workplace.*

It is time to stop and reflect. You have almost completed this course. As you study the next two chapters, you need to think carefully about your skills and abilities, what you have learned in this course, and how you can most effectively use your knowledge and skills as you apply for a job and advance in your chosen profession.

First of all, consider the workplace you are entering or may already be in. It is probably not the workforce of your parents, and it is certainly not the workforce of your grandparents. In Chapter 1, you learned that the workforce is changing in these ways.

- More diverse than ever with more women, more older workers, and more cultural and ethnic diversity
- Increasing globalization of our economy, merger mania, downsizing, outsourcing, telework, and the constant growth of technology

You also learned that the National Association of Colleges and Employers (NACE) identified important skills that employers seek in new hires. The top seven skills listed by employers are as follows:

- Interpersonal skills
- Teamwork skills
- Verbal communication skills
- Critical-thinking skills
- Technology/computer skills
- Written communication skills
- Leadership skills

Throughout this course, these and other soft skills have been identified as extremely important in the workplace: value clarification, self-management, ethical behaviors, decision-making, positive attitudes, creativity, continual learning, conflict resolution, and anger and stress management.

As you reflect on both your hard skills (computer competency, English competency, and so on) and your soft skills, you need to analyze what all of this means for your career path. Where do you want your career path to go? What type of organization interests you? Where do you think your hard skills and soft skills will fit best? The days when an organization took care of its employees' career development are over. Your grandparents and possibly your parents may have worked for one organization all of their lives. However, it is highly unlikely you will work for one organization your entire career. You will be responsible for your own growth and career path; sometimes changing jobs is a part of that growth.

Self-Check A

As you reflect on your skills, ask yourself these questions.

- What are my strengths?
- What are my weaknesses?
- What have I achieved?
- What do I enjoy doing?
- Where do I want to be in five years? in ten years?
- Do I enjoy my work more when I am working with others?
- Do I enjoy working with people but also enjoy working independently?

Now you are ready to begin thinking about what steps you must take to identify a job that fits your skills and interests, apply for that job, and succeed at that job.

DETERMINE SOURCES OF JOB INFORMATION

One of the first things to do as you look for a job is to get all the information you can about available job opportunities. Information is available through the sources listed here.

- The Web
- Personal networks
- College placement offices
- Newspaper advertisements
- Public employment agencies
- Private employment agencies
- Temporary employment agencies
- Professional organizations
- Direct canvass

The Web

A variety of resources for job seekers are available on the Web, including tips for resume and cover letter preparation and interviewing. You may also research companies in which you have an interest and actually post your resume on the Web for employers' review. Here are several Websites that provide helpful information.

- www.jobweb.com—Provides information related to the job search.
- www.monster.com—Allows you to search for positions and post your resume; also offers career advice and tips on preparing a resume and interviewing.
- http://careers.yahoo.com and www.flipdog.com— Allows you to post your resume; recruiters can scan resumes without paying a fee.
- www.yourmissinglink.com—Sends your resume to human resource departments and provides a list of employers who receive it.
- www.rileyguide.com—Provides information on researching companies and other job search tips.
- www.headhunter.net—Allows you to post your resume and search for a job.
- www.ajb.dni.us—Lists over a million jobs.
- www.hotjobs.com—Lists over a thousand jobs.
- www.careerjournal.com—Is the *Wall Street Journal's*® free site for job seekers, offering job-hunting advice and salary tables.

You can also find sites aimed at a particular field by using a search engine such as www.google.com and keywords such as *jobs— administrative professional*.

Personal Networks

Networking is defined as "the process of identifying and establishing a group of acquaintances, friends, and relatives who can assist you in the job search process." This approach is one of the best strategies for finding a job. In fact, some studies have shown that as many as 80 percent of jobs are obtained through some form of networking. Why? Consider this example. If someone in an organization tells you about a job vacancy, that person has some knowledge of your skills and abilities. Employing and training a new employee costs an organization a considerable amount of money, so the organization wants to hire the right person. When personnel directors hear about possible employees from respected employees, they are more confident of the applicants' abilities. Employers are not always able to tell from a resume whether a person

© PhotoDisc, Inc.

Networking is an excellent way to obtain job information. As many as 80 percent of jobs are obtained through some form of networking.

has the skills and abilities necessary for the job. Due to networking, an organization can hire an excellent employee with limited risk.

How do you go about networking? If you have a part-time job, let management know you are ready for a full-time position. If you take part in an internship program, let the organization know you are interested in a full-time job. Talk with friends in your community or church, or with associates in professional organizations to which you belong. You also might give them a copy of your resume. A later section in this chapter deals with resume preparation.

College Placement Offices

Many colleges maintain a placement office. Visit this office. Your school may not receive enough calls from employers to provide positions for all students, but counselors are usually well informed about job opportunities in the community. They know the employers who need entry-level workers, and they can match a job to your qualifications and abilities.

Newspaper Advertisements

Employers and employment agencies list available positions in local newspapers. These ads describe the positions and the qualifications required and may provide information about the salaries offered.

Employment Agencies

There are two types of employment agencies: public and private. Public employment agencies are known as **state employment services.** You can find these services listed in the state government section of your telephone book. An advantage of a state service is that it is free to the individual using the service. The state in which the employment agency resides funds the agency.

Private employment agencies charge a fee for their services. Either you or the employing firm pay for these services. Most private agencies are paid by the organization hiring the employee. However, if you choose to use a private agency, you need to ask how the fee is paid. If you pay the fee, it is usually 5 to 10 percent of your first year's salary. Generally, you must sign a contract with private employment agencies. Information regarding how their fee is determined should be included in the contract. Read a contract carefully before signing it. When private employment agencies advertise jobs that are **fee-paid,** the employer pays the fee when the applicant is hired.

You should be prepared to take tests for both public and private employment agencies. The types of tests include the following:

- Specific software packages, such as Microsoft Word, Excel, and PowerPoint
- Keyboarding speed and accuracy
- Grammar, punctuation, and proofreading skills
- Mathematical aptitude

Temporary Agencies

With the downsizing that is occurring today, many organizations hire temporary workers. These workers can be a cost-saving measure for a company since fewer dollars are tied up in staffing and limited organizational perks are provided. Greater flexibility is another advantage for the organization since there is no long-term commitment to the employees.

A **temporary agency** (one that offers temporary work) is not a source of job information in the usual sense. However, a temporary agency can help you know more about where you want to work. If you are not clear about the type or size of company you want to work for, you might try working for a temporary agency for a period of time. A temporary agency can place you in a number of different companies. Without any long-term commitment, you can gain an understanding of where you want to work as a full-time employee.

Some organizations also use temporary agencies to get first-hand knowledge of employees. For example, a business may hire an individual from a temporary agency, be extremely pleased with the employee's work, and offer the employee a full-time job.

Professional Organizations

If you are a member of a professional organization, check to see if it maintains a listing of jobs in your area. You should also ask individual members if they are aware of any openings.

Direct Canvass

If you are interested in obtaining a position with a certain company or in a particular type of business, the **direct canvass** or **cold canvass** (going directly to an organization without having an appointment or without knowing if a job is available) is sometimes successful. If you have a gift for selling yourself, you might find this approach beneficial. However, before you engage in the direct canvass approach, find out as much as you can about the company. Never restrict your job search to walk-ins only. It can be a time-consuming process, often with little success.

LEARN ABOUT THE ORGANIZATION

Once you have identified organizations with which you are interested in applying, spend time learning more about the organization—its mission and vision, its financial history, its reputation, the length of time it has been in business, and how it treats its employees. How do you do this? There are several ways.

- Ask friends, relatives, and acquaintances what they know about the organization.
- Check the organization's Website for information. Many organizations have Web pages that provide the history of the organization, its philosophy, its strategic direction, and information about its products or services.
- Read periodicals, such as *Fortune*, which often profile some of the largest businesses in the United States.
- Obtain an annual report of the company; most companies will send you one upon request.

© PhotoDisc, Inc.

To find out about local companies, visit the chamber of commerce.

- Consult your local chamber of commerce.
- Ask your college placement office for information.

When evaluating an organization, here are some questions to consider.

- What is the organization's service or product?
- Is the organization multinational? Does the organization have branches in other states?
- What has been the profit picture of the organization for the last several years?
- Is the organization financially secure?
- Is the organization growing?
- Does the organization have a good reputation in the community?
- Is there a good relationship between the employer and employees?
- Is the organization an equal opportunity employer?
- Are there opportunities for advancement?

WRITE A LETTER OF APPLICATION

Once you are interested in an organization, your next step is to obtain an interview. The **letter of application** is the key to obtaining that interview. It is basically a sales letter because it attempts to sell your abilities.

Prepare your letter thoughtfully. Its appearance, format, arrangement, and content are extremely important in your making a good impression and obtaining your objective, an interview.

The three basic goals of a letter of application are as follows:

- Introduce yourself to the organization and arouse its interest in you.
- Present your most relevant selling points, including your skills and your background.
- Transmit your resume and request an interview.

Introduce Yourself

In the opening, provide a brief statement of your qualifications. Let the person know you are interested in the organization and what you can do for them. Consider the following examples of effective beginnings:

Example 1

The position you have advertised sounds challenging. My associate of arts degree in Business Information Systems and my part-time experience as an administrative assistant while attending college have given me the skills necessary to perform the job well.

Example 2

Your employment announcement calls for an administrative assistant who is interested in learning the latest technology and has good computer skills. My training at Grand Haven College for the last two years has provided me with these skills.

In both cases, you let the prospective employer know you are interested in the position and you have the skills needed for the job.

Describe Your Abilities

The next paragraph of the letter should describe in more detail the abilities you have. It should also call attention to your enclosed resume.

In May of this year, I will graduate from Grand Haven College. During my two years at Grand Haven, I have taken courses in administrative

2445 Rivercrest Drive
Grand Rapids, MI 49546-1655
May 21, 2004

Ms. Rebecca Edwards
Human Resource Department
AmeriAsian Airlines
5519 Reeds Parkway
Grand Rapids, MI 49509-3295

Dear Ms. Edwards:

Your announcement for an administrative assistant posted on the Employment Opportunities
page of your Website is most appealing to me. After reading the qualifications you are
seeking, I believe my skills and experience make me a strong candidate. My associate
degree in Administrative Systems from Grand Haven College and my one year of work
experience have given me the skills and knowledge needed to perform the job well. I am
interested in working for AmeriAsian Airlines, and I am willing to work hard to demonstrate
my capabilities.

My courses included business communications, organizational behavior, management,
accounting, administrative procedures, English, and computer science. Additionally,
I gained valuable, practical experience through an internship program where I worked
20 hours a week in the Admissions Department of the college. I prepared spreadsheets
using Excel, keyed correspondence using Microsoft Word, and handled student inquiries
concerning admission to the college. In addition to improving my computer skills, this
experience also helped me improve my communication skills. I learned how to deal with
upset people, solving their problems and calming them down. Prior to beginning college,
I worked as a receptionist for one year at Martin Paper Company.

My resume, giving further details concerning my qualifications and experience, is enclosed.
May I have the opportunity to discuss my qualifications with you? I will call within a week
to check the status of my application. You may also reach me at 555-0113. Thank you for
your consideration.

Sincerely,

Martha A. Zipinski

Martha A. Zipinski

Enclosure

Figure 14-1   Letter of Application

*procedures, accounting, management, business
communications, computer software, and organizational behavior. I have strong computer
skills and an excellent working knowledge of
Microsoft Word, Excel, and PowerPoint. My
resume, detailing my school and work experience, is enclosed.*

Request an Interview

Remember that the purpose of the letter is to
get an interview. Therefore, you should ask
directly for the interview.

*Please give me an opportunity to dis-
cuss my qualifications with you. My
telephone number is 555-0157.*

A letter of application is
shown in Figure 14-1. Additional
hints on writing a letter of application are given in Figure 14-2 on
page 354. Carefully reading these
hints will help you write effective
application letters.

PREPARE A RESUME

The **resume**, a concise statement
of your background, education,
skills, and experience, is an
important part of your job application packet. Just as the letter of
application is a sales letter, so is
the resume. It represents a very
important product—you.

Chronological Resume

The resume may be **chronological** (listing the jobs you have had
in reverse chronological order) or
functional (highlighting and
emphasizing skills) or a combination of the two. Figure 14-3 on
page 355 illustrates the format
and style of a typical resume in
chronological order. Notice that
the education and experience are
listed in date order with the most recent education and experience listed first. Figure 14-4
on page 355 provides advantages and disadvantages of the chronological resume.

Functional Resume

The functional resume allows you to concentrate on those skills and abilities that are more
applicable to the job you are seeking. You clus-
ter your education, experiences, and activities
into categories that support your career goals.

- Research the organization before writing your letter. One good source of information for most organizations is their Web page.
- Key the letter in proper form using an acceptable letter style.
- Print your letter on high-quality bond paper. Most office supply stores sell paper recommended for use in writing letters of application and resumes.
- Use correct spelling, punctuation, capitalization, and grammar. Always use the spell checker and grammar checker on your computer.
- Keep the letter short—one page. Put details in the resume.
- Address the letter to a specific person. Never address an application letter "To Whom It May Concern." If you do not have a name, call the company or check with the placement office, agency, or person who told you about the job.

- Send an original letter for each application. Do not send photocopies. Do not assume one letter will be appropriate for all organizations. Personalize each letter by reading and writing to the job notice published by the organization.
- Do not copy a letter of application from a book. Make your letter representative of your personality.
- Use three paragraphs—an opening paragraph in which you provide a brief statement of your interest and qualifications, a middle paragraph in which you describe your abilities in more detail, and a closing paragraph in which you request an interview.
- If you do not own a printer that produces quality work, have your cover letter and resume professionally printed.

Figure 14-2

This type of approach is usually appropriate for the individual who has developed skills that are more relevant to the job than organizational names. It also works well if you have periods of time when you did not work; for example, you took a break from your career to have a child. It allows you to de-emphasize these gaps and emphasize your skill sets. The functional resume is shown in Figure 14-5 on page 356. Other advantages and disadvantages of the functional resume are shown on page 356 in Figure 14-6.

Combination Style Resume

The **combination style** resume allows you to present your experiences in reverse chronological skill set order. This style works best for the experienced worker who has held a number of different jobs. This style also works well when skills, titles, and organizational names are equally impressive. It does not work well if you do not have numerous experiences that match a number of skills. It also does not work well if you have multiple skills but a small number of different experiences (job titles or organizations for which you have worked).

Electronic Resume

In addition to the job seeker using technology, human resource departments and recruiters also use it extensively. A study done of 100 employers indicated that 85 percent of them accepted **electronic resumes** (online statement of background and experiences).[1] Other findings of this study reveal the following statistics:

- Seventy-seven percent of the employers accepted electronically submitted resumes for any position within their organization.
- Sixty-eight percent of the employers reported that they used an online resume service to actively search for applicants.
- Seventy-eight percent of the employers indicated that electronically submitted thank-you and follow-up letters (to be discussed in a later section) were acceptable.

In addition to using online services to search for prospective employees, organizations are now adding sections to their home page that

[1]Myrena S. Jennings, Lana W. Carnes, and Vicki K. Whitaker, "Online Employment Applications: Employer Preferences and Instructional Implications," *Business Education Forum*, February 2001, 34–35.

allow you to submit your resume online. Also, many organizations use computer-tracking systems to search through resumes and narrow the search to a few individuals. If your resume is not easy for the computer to scan, errors can be made. When preparing a resume that is to be scanned by the computer or submitted on line, follow these guidelines. (Remember, you are not creating a different resume from the one you may be sending by mail; however, you are altering the presentation of the resume.)

- Use a basic font (Times New Roman or Courier).
- Use a standard size font (12 points).
- Use all caps or bold.
- Use plain fonts (i.e., Courier, Arial, or Times New Roman)
- Do not use italics, script, or underlining.
- Do not use abbreviations.
- Do not use bullets.
- Use keywords. The computer is often programmed to pick up certain keywords. Many times these words are listed in the advertisement. You should use them in your resume. For example, an administrative assistant should list specific software programs that he or she can operate—Microsoft Word, Excel, PowerPoint, and so on. Since human relations skills are often part of the skills sought, use human relations as a keyword in your resume.

MARTHA A. ZIPINSKI

2445 Rivercrest Drive
Grand Rapids, MI 49546-1655

616-555-0113
email: tbaz3@tt.com

CAREER OBJECTIVE
A position as an administrative assistant with the opportunity to use technology and human relations skills

COMPUTER SKILLS
Keyboarding at 90 wpm; proficient in Windows, Word, Excel, PowerPoint, Access, Internet research, and Web page design

EDUCATION
Grand Haven College, Grand Rapids, Michigan, September 2002 to May 2004
Associate Degree in Administrative Systems

Courses studied: Business communications, organizational behavior, management, English, psychology, administrative procedures, and computer software

EXPERIENCE
 Intern, Admissions Department, Grand Haven College, September 2003 to May 2004
 - Prepared spreadsheets using Excel
 - Keyed correspondence using Microsoft Word
 - Prepared first draft of letters to students
 - Filed correspondence on hard drive and disks
 - Handled student inquiries
 - Answered the telephone
 - Assisted in designing schedule

 Receptionist, Martin Paper Company, June 2002 to August 2003
 - Greeted visitors
 - Answered the telephone
 - Keyed correspondence

HONORS
 - Phi Theta Kappa
 - Dean's List
 - Most Outstanding Student in the Business Department

Figure 14-3 Chronological Resume

ADVANTAGES AND DISADVANTAGES OF THE CHRONOLOGICAL RESUME

Advantages
- Highlights titles and company names; advantageous when the names or titles are relevant or impressive
- Highlights consistent progress from one position to another
- Highlights length of time in each organization

Disadvantages
- Readily shows gaps in work history
- Shows frequent changes of jobs
- Does not show most impressive or relevant work experience first if that is not the most recent

Figure 14-4

- Use standard-size paper—8½ × 11, white only. Print on one side of the paper.
- Do not use graphics, shading, boxes, or lines.
- Make certain your name is the first item on your resume.

MARTHA A. ZIPINSKI

2445 Rivercrest Drive
Grand Rapids, MI 49546-1655

616-555-0113
email: tbaz3@tt.com

EDUCATION
Grand Haven College, Associate Degree in Administrative Systems, September 2002 to May 2004

SKILLS
- Computer—Windows, Word, Excel, PowerPoint, Access, Internet research, Web page design
- Keyboarding—90 wpm with high level of accuracy
- Human relations—handled student complaints, successfully worked in teams to produce products such as class schedules, answered the telephone
- Writing—drafted correspondence for supervisor's review; prepared final document
- Spreadsheet—prepared student enrollment numbers each semester; determined increases or decreases from previous semester
- Graphics—assisted in designing schedules, suggested graphics to be used

EXPERIENCE
- Intern, Admissions Department, Grand Haven College, September 2003 to May 2004
- Receptionist, Martin Paper Company, June 2002 to August 2003

HONORS
- Phi Theta Kappa
- Dean's List
- Most Outstanding Student in the Business Department

REFERENCES
Furnished upon request

Figure 14-5 Functional Resume

Resume Sections

The sections of a resume may vary; there is no one perfect model. How you set up your resume depends on your situation and how you want to present your qualifications. However, certain parts are common to most resumes. The parts are discussed here.

Career Objective

This section lets the reader know what your present career goals are. For example:

Career Objective: A position as an administrative professional in a challenging business with opportunities to use my technology and human relations skills.

Notice that this objective did not specify a particular type of organization. If you are interested in a specialized field, you may note that in the objective. You also might list your long-term goal. In that case, your objective might be stated as follows:

ADVANTAGES AND DISADVANTAGES OF THE FUNCTIONAL RESUME

Advantages
- Highlights skills
- De-emphasizes gaps between jobs
- Is more appropriate when changing career fields since skills are highlighted over positions held

Disadvantages
- Is not a good style if skill areas are not relevant to targeted position
- Does not show advancement from one job to another
- Does not show organizations and titles held
- Is more difficult to review since progression from one position to another is not apparent

Figure 14-6

Career Objective: A position as an administrative professional in a law firm, with a long-range goal of being a law office manager.

Relevant Skills

This section gives you a chance to identify your skill strengths. For example, you can list your computer skills, including the various software packages in which you are proficient and your keyboarding skill.

Education

In this section, list the schools you have attended and the degrees you have obtained (if applicable). You might also list the courses or programs you have taken that pertain to the position.

Employment History

List the companies where you have worked, the dates of employment, and your duties. You may want to reverse the order of education and experience on your resume. For example, if you have experience that directly relates to the job for which you are applying, you might list the experience first. Remember that the resume is a sales piece. You want to call attention to your best selling features first.

Accomplishments

If you have participated in special activities, maintained memberships in professional organizations, or achieved honors, you may wish to list these. Such activities illustrate that you have many interests and leadership qualities. Employers are usually impressed with such characteristics. This involvement and recognition can provide an added advantage for you.

References

Do not list references on your resume. The resume is a place to highlight work experiences and skills. However, you may choose to include a section with the statement "References will be furnished on request." Both are acceptable choices; it is a matter of preference and style.

On the resume in Figure 14-3 notice that the reference section is omitted; in Figure 14-5 the reference section is included with the statement that they will be furnished if requested.

You need to think through your reference choices before sending out resumes or going on job interviews. Generally, if the employer is interested in hiring you, you will be asked to provide between three and five references. The most effective references are previous employers and instructors. Personal references are considered to be less effective. Do not use the names of close relatives or religious leaders (unless it is a church-related job).

Choose your references carefully. Select those individuals who know your qualifications well and will take the time to respond to a reference request. Before you list someone as a reference, obtain his or her permission. Once you have determined who your references will be, prepare a separate reference sheet, listing their names, telephone numbers, and addresses. You then have your list of references available if you are asked for it during the job application process.

Personal Information

To a certain degree, a resume reflects what is important in the changing business world. For example, prior to the antidiscrimination legislation of the 1960s and 1970s, almost all resumes included a section labeled "Personal Data." This section included such information as age, marital status, number of children, height, weight, and hobbies. Our laws now state that it is illegal to discriminate on the basis of national origin, ethnic group, gender, creed, age, or race. Therefore, authorities recommend that personal items be left off the resume. What the prospective employer needs to know is whether you have the qualifications for the job.

Resume Length

If you are an inexperienced job seeker, keep your resume to one page. If you are an experienced job seeker, your resume may be two pages due to your background and experience. However, generally a resume should not be longer than two pages. Exceptions exist in certain fields, such as education, where research and publishing are important.

FILL OUT THE EMPLOYMENT APPLICATION

You will be asked to fill out an **employment application** (a form used by organizations to obtain information about prospective employees). You may do this before or after being interviewed. In some organizations, all applicants fill out a form. Other firms ask only those people who are seriously being considered for a position to fill out a form. Most organizations request that applicants print the information requested on the form. Read each question carefully before answering it. Avoid asking unnecessary questions of the individual who gave you the form. Take the time to print legibly. Spell correctly. Carry a pocket dictionary in case you need to look up a word. Fill in all blanks. If you have no response, print *none* or *not applicable*. Have all the information with you that you need, such as your social security number, dates you attended schools, dates of employment, and complete addresses of previous employers and references. Be certain that the information you provide is consistent with what is in your resume.

Be careful not to spoil the form since you do not want to ask for another one. A standard question included on the application is the reason for leaving your last position. State your reason in its most positive light. For example, if you were fired from your job, you might say, "My skills did not match those needed by the organization." Answer all questions truthfully. The final portion is usually a statement that the information you provided is accurate and that any misrepresentation is grounds for immediate dismissal. Some firms may discharge you, even after months of satisfactory work, if they discover you were untruthful on the application. You will be asked to sign and date the form.

PREPARE FOR THE INTERVIEW

The interview will not be an ordeal if you adequately prepare for it. Knowing what to do and what to say help eliminate a great deal of nervousness. In the interview, the employer will judge your appearance, personality, human relation skills, self-confidence, and other traits. The interviewer will question you about your experience and abilities, as identified in your letter of application and resume. The interview is an opportunity for the prospective employer to get to know you and for you to get to know him or her. Although it may be a new experience for you, approach it with confidence.

If you have not had much experience in interviewing, you might accept interviews for positions you do not think you are interested in to give you much-needed practice. In fact, you may find you were wrong; the job may turn out to be of interest to you.

Answer all questions truthfully on an employment application.

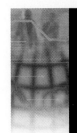

Portfolio Information

You may wish to prepare a portfolio of your work to take with you to the interview. A **portfolio** is a compilation of samples of your work. The work should be arranged attractively in a binder. Some possible items for inclusion are as follows:

- Letters you have written, which demonstrate your writing style
- Spreadsheets you have prepared
- Reports, including graphics
- PowerPoint slides

Preparing and presenting a portfolio during the job interview allows you to show what you can do rather than merely talk about it.

Location of Interview

Be sure you know the exact time and location of the interview. Do not rely on your memory. Write down the time, address, and person's name you are to see; and take it with you. When traveling to the interview location, allow time for unexpected delays. You do not want to be late for an interview. Excuses for being late will not change the poor impression you have made by your lateness.

Number of Interviews

You may have more than one interview for a particular position. For example, a human resources professional may interview you first. Next, you may interview with your prospective supervisor. Finally, you may have a group interview with your prospective team members.

Team Interviews

A team interview may be with five or six people. Although this type of interview sounds intimidating, it need not be. Tips for a successful team interview are as follows:

- Pay careful attention to the individuals' names as they are introduced.
- Remember to focus on each individual as the person asks a question.
- Listen carefully to the question and answer it succinctly.
- When you ask a question, ask it of the group unless one person has said something about which you need more information.
- Make eye contact with all individuals if the question or statement is meant for the entire group.

© PhotoDisc, Inc.

You may be interviewed by a team of people.

The Virtual Interview

Occasionally organizations will conduct a **virtual interview** (an employee is interviewed via technology by an interviewer at a distant location). Here is how the virtual interview works.

Assume you are applying for a job in Canada. Rather than flying to Canada for the interview, you are interviewed in Grand Rapids,

Michigan, where you live. The company makes arrangements for you to go to a facility that has teleconferencing capabilities. The room in Grand Rapids is linked electronically to a room in Canada.

If you are going to take part in a virtual interview, you need to be well prepared. When a camera is involved, most people get a little nervous. However, your goal is to relax and treat the situation as if the person interviewing you were in the same room. Since the situation is unique, here are some suggestions for a successful virtual interview.

- Greet the interviewer warmly and with a smile, just as you would in person. Repeat the interviewer's name. For example, say, "I'm happy to meet you, Mr. VanDoss."
- Sit in the chair provided; sit back in the chair, not on the edge of your seat. Sitting on the edge of the chair can connote nervousness.
- Try to forget the camera is there; do not concentrate on it. Concentrate on the interviewer and the questions you are asked.
- Dress in colors that look good on you. Black or gray generally does not come across well on camera. Do not wear jewelry that jingles. The noise on camera is even more noticeable than in person.
- Pay attention to body language and small nuances of the interviewer. Do not spend an inordinate amount of time answering any one question. Be warm and informative but also be concise.
- Enunciate carefully. Poor enunciation is more pronounced on camera than in person.
- Once the interview is over, thank the person and leave the teleconferencing room.
- Keep in mind the hints for traditional interviews (given in the next section). Many of these also apply to the virtual interview.

Helpful Interview Hints

Observe these suggestions to help you make a good impression during the interview.

- Dress appropriately, which means dressing conservatively, even if you are applying for a position in a creative line of work, such as art and design. For both men and women, a suit is appropriate attire; wear a color that looks good on you. Keep your jewelry to a minimum.
- If you wear an overcoat, hang it in the reception area. Do not take it into the office where you are being interviewed. You do not want to be burdened with numerous belongings.
- Be well-groomed. Women may wish to have their hair done professionally the day before the interview; men should have an appropriate haircut.
- Get a good night's rest before the interview so you will be alert.
- Carry a briefcase. Women should try to do without a handbag, resulting in one less item to juggle. Have an extra copy of your resume in your briefcase in case the interviewer has misplaced the one you mailed. Have a pad and pen in your briefcase in case you need to take notes. Also have your list of references ready if you need to fill out an employment application.
- Greet the receptionist with a friendly smile, stating your name and the purpose of your visit.
- Shake the interviewer's hand with a firm (but not tight) grip.
- Wait to sit down until invited to do so.
- Maintain appropriate eye contact.
- Try not to act nervous; avoid nervous gestures such as playing with your hair or jewelry.
- Display good humor and a ready smile.
- Show genuine interest in what the interviewer says, and be alert to all questions.
- Do not talk too much. Answer questions carefully.
- Be enthusiastic; demonstrate pride in your skills and abilities.
- Be positive. Do not criticize former employers, instructors, schools, or colleagues.
- Try to understand your prospective employer's needs, and describe how you can fill them.
- Be prepared to tell the interviewer something about yourself, a commonly asked question at the start of the interview.
- Express yourself clearly with a well-modulated voice.

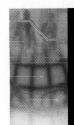

- Do not smoke even if you are invited to do so.
- Do not chew gum.
- Be prepared to ask questions. The interviewer will usually give you a chance at the end of the interview to do so. Often-asked questions are given below. Listen carefully to the answers to your questions.
- Be prepared to take tests. Expect to take tests pertaining to basic skills, such as keyboarding, spelling, math, proofreading, vocabulary, and reasoning ability. The law demands that any test given must relate to the job for which you are applying.
- At the close of the interview, attempt to determine what the next step will be. Will there be another interview? When can you expect to hear the results of the interview?
- Reiterate your interest in the job (that is, if you are still interested).
- Smile pleasantly and thank the interviewer for his or her time.
- Smile and thank the receptionist as you leave.

Questions the Interviewer Might Ask

Take a few minutes to read the questions in Figure 14-7 on page 362. Using Self-Check B, formulate answers to five of these questions. If you have concerns about the appropriateness of your answers, read the tips provided at the end of the chapter.

Questions You Might Ask

If given the opportunity by the interviewer, you might ask a couple of these questions.

- Could you describe the specific duties of the job?

- Could you tell me about the people with whom I will be working if I were accepted for the position?
- I read on your Web page that your organization has grown tremendously over the last few years. To what do you attribute this growth? Do you expect it to continue?
- Can you tell me about advancement opportunities in your organization?
- When will you make a decision about hiring?

Self-Check B

Answer these frequently asked interview questions.

1. What can you tell me about yourself?

_____

_____

2. How would your previous employers and co-workers describe you?

_____

_____

3. How have the classes you completed as part of your major helped you prepare for your career?

_____

_____

4. How would you describe your personality?

_____

_____

5. What skills do you possess that will help you excel in this position?

_____

_____

Questions Relating to Your Interest in the Company and the Job

- How did you learn about this position?
- Are you familiar with our company?
- Why are you interested in our company?
- Why do you think you are qualified for the position?
- Why do you want this job?
- What is the ideal job for you?

Questions Regarding Your Ability to Do the Job

- What are your greatest strengths?
- What is your major weakness?
- Why should I hire you?
- If I talked to your former employer, what would the person say about you?
- What in your past job did you enjoy the most? Why?
- What in your last job did you enjoy the least? Why?
- If I talked with your former colleagues, what would they say about you?
- What can you tell me about yourself?

Questions Regarding Education

- Why did you choose your major area of study?
- What was your academic average in school?
- What honors did you earn?
- In what extracurricular activities were you involved?
- Which courses did you like best? least? Why?
- How have the classes you completed as part of your major helped you prepare for your career?

Questions Regarding Your Ability to Fit into the Organization

- If you disagreed with something your supervisor asked you to do, what would you do?
- What type of work atmosphere do you prefer?
- Is a sense of humor important at work? Why or why not?

- Tell me about a conflict you have had with someone. How did you handle that conflict?
- What is your definition of diversity?
- How do you handle pressure?
- How would your previous employers and co-workers describe you?

Questions Regarding Experience

- Have you ever been fired or asked to resign from a position?
- Why did you leave your previous job?
- Have you had any problems with previous supervisors?
- What are your greatest strengths?
- What do you not do well?
- Why should I hire you?
- What salary do you expect?

Note on Salary: You should have an idea of an appropriate salary before going to an interview. You can check the job advertisements of your local newspaper for area salaries. Your placement office is another good source for local salary information.

You can ask the interviewer the starting rate for the company. If you are willing to accept that amount, merely respond that the rate is appropriate. If you think the starting salary is below average for that type of work, you can reply that you had hoped to start at a slightly higher salary but that you are interested in an opportunity to show what you can do and in taking advantage of opportunities for promotion (if this is true). If not, you can say you are not interested in the salary offered. However, be certain before you respond that you are not interested. Your chances of getting additional salary may not be good, and you may well lose out on a job offer.

Figure 14-7

What Not to Do in an Interview

Up to this point, you have been given suggestions about what to do during an interview. Here are some suggestions for what not to do.

- Avoid nervous gestures and movements, such as fidgeting, tugging at your clothes, and stroking your chin.

- Do not place personal belongings or your hands on the interviewer's desk.
- Do not argue. You are not participating in the interview to prove a point.
- Do not interrupt. Let the interviewer complete all questions or statements before you speak.
- Do not ask too many questions. Ask important questions only. If you ask when you

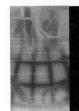

Human Relations Tip:
Know when to leave the interview. Take your signal from the interviewer. Do not take up his or her time with needless chatter once the interview is over.

can expect your first raise, when you might be promoted, or when you can expect a vacation, the interviewer may decide you are not interested in working.

- Do not tell jokes. Let the interviewer do that if he or she wishes.
- Do not comment on the furnishings of the interviewer's office.
- Do not brag. If the company hires you, you may have to live up to your boasts.
- Do not criticize. If you are hired, you will have ample time and opportunity to make constructive suggestions for improvement.
- Do not smoke. Most companies have no-smoking policies, and many people find smoking offensive.
- Do not chew gum.

Interview Follow-Up

Promptly after the interview, write a **follow-up letter** thanking the employer for the interview and reviewing points of special interest. A sample letter is given in Figure 14-8. Notice that the letter begins by thanking the interviewer.

A second follow-up letter may be advisable a week or two after the first one is sent. You should not annoy the employer unnecessarily. However, if no action is taken in regard to your application within a reasonable time, a short letter is not out of place. The second letter should merely remind the employer of your having filed

a letter of application and express a willingness to return for another interview if necessary.

Of course, after an interview, you may decide you are not interested in the position. In this case, you should promptly send a letter in which you express your appreciation for having been considered and explain why you do not want the position. Although you are not

---

2445 Rivercrest Drive
Grand Rapids, MI 49546-1655
June 15, 2004

Ms. Rebecca Edwards
Human Resource Department
AmeriAsian Airlines
5519 Reeds Parkway
Grand Rapids, MI 49509-3295

Dear Ms. Edwards:

Thank you for giving me the opportunity to interview for the administrative assistant position that is open in the Human Resource Department. I appreciate the time you spent with me, and I enjoyed learning more about AmeriAsian Airlines.

Because of my education and experience, I am confident I can be an asset to the company. My skills in technology, communications, and human relations will help me perform at a high level. The interview today reinforced my interest in joining your team; I was extremely impressed with what I heard from you about AmeriAsian's philosophy of management and the directions the company is taking. I welcome the chance to become a part of the organization.

You may reach me at home by calling 555-0113 or by email at tbaz3@tt.com. Thank you again for your graciousness, and I look forward to hearing from you.

Sincerely,

Martha A. Zipinski

Martha A. Zipinski

Figure 14-8 Interview Thank-You Letter

interested in the present position, you may at a later time be interested in another position with the company. If so, the courteous way in which you declined the first position may help you when being considered a second time. You want to keep all doors open if possible.

SUCCEED ON THE JOB

Once you have successfully completed the interviewing process and have been hired, your task is to combine the skills and knowledge you have to perform the job well. Listen to what co-workers and supervisors tell you. Observe and learn what is expected and accepted in the office. Make sure you have a clear understanding of your job duties and how you will be evaluated. Most companies provide job descriptions that detail the responsibilities of particular jobs. If you are not given one, ask for it. If a job description does not exist, ask your supervisor to go over your duties with you.

Live Your Values

In Chapter 2, you spent some time clarifying your values. Think back now to the values you identified as most important to you. In Project 2-1, you were asked to keep a list of your values. You may want to look back at that list now. Ask yourself this question: How can I live my values on the job I have now or on a future

job? For example, assume you identified dependability as one of your values. How do you live that value on the job? You report to work on time. If your job requires eight hours of work each day, you work all of those eight hours. You do not spend an hour and a half for lunch each day when the organization allows an hour. You complete all projects in the time frame given you. If you know you will have trouble completing a project on time, you immediately let your supervisor know your reservations. You establish a plan for getting the work done when it is needed.

Consider two more values you may have identified—cooperation and tolerance. How do you live cooperation at work? You cooperate with your supervisor and your co-workers. If an assignment requires overtime, you put in the hours graciously. You do not complain or look for excuses. How do you live tolerance at work? You do not judge other people. You listen openly to what they have to say. You do not evaluate people based on their gender, age, or ethnicity.

Think about your own values and how you will live them on the job by responding to Self-Check C.

Self-Check C

List three of your values. How will you daily live these values on a job? If you determine it is impossible to live your values, what steps will you take?

1. _____

_____

_____

2. _____

_____

_____

3. _____

_____

_____

Prepare Performance Appraisals

Usually, your job performance is evaluated formally once or twice each year. These evaluations are called **performance appraisals.** For the beginning employee, this evaluation may occur during the first three to six months with annual or semiannual evaluations thereafter. When you are first employed, you may be asked to establish short-range goals. If so, you will then be evaluated on whether you accomplished these goals. Your employer may also use a performance appraisal form, one that is the same for all employees in your classification

Advance on the Job

Advancing on the job may mean doing your present job more effectively and efficiently. Your first job, in all likelihood, will be at an entry level. You must learn your job well, work well with others, and learn new ways of doing your job better. Remain current on new equipment, software, and procedures related to your job. Increase your verbal, nonverbal, and written communication skills. Remember that you gain valuable work experience from whatever job you are assigned. Concentrate on doing each task of your job to the best of your ability.

Advancing on the job may also mean taking advantage of promotional opportunities that come your way. Remember that promotions usually come to those individuals who have performed well at their position in the company. Be ready for a promotion should the opportunity present itself. Learn as much as

© PhotoDisc, Inc.

Be open to constructive criticism during the evaluation process. Commit to improving your performance.

within the company. Figure 14-9 shows a portion of a performance appraisal form. Another method of evaluation may be a meeting with your supervisor in which your work performance is discussed and a formal written evaluation document is prepared, becoming part of your personnel file. Whatever method of evaluation is used, you are usually evaluated on whether you

- Perform job assignments
- Maintain good working relationships with your employer and other employees
- Adhere to company policies regarding attendance, punctuality, sick leave, and so on
- Contribute to overall company goals

Remember, during your evaluation, your job performance is being evaluated. Be open to criticism and how you can perform better. Do not take the statements of the evaluator personally. Assume the evaluator is trying to help you improve, not hurt you. Figure 14-10 on page 366 offers some tips to help you during the evaluation process.

AMERIASIAN AIRLINES

PERFORMANCE APPRAISAL

Employee Name_____
Job Title_____
Supervisor_____

Assessment
4   Performance demonstrates consistent and important contributions that surpass defined expectations of the position.
3   Performance demonstrates attainment of the defined expectations of the position.
2   Performance has not reached a satisfactory level. Improvement is needed.
1   Performance demonstrates deficiencies that seriously interfere with the attainment of the defined expectations of the position.

Skills	Assessment
Organization	
Prioritizes tasks	
Plans steps to accomplish tasks	
Meets deadlines	
Attends to detail	
Communication	
Conveys ideas effectively	
Responds to ideas conveyed by others	
Demonstrates appropriate professional courtesy	
Demonstrates sensitivity to a diverse staff	
Problem-Solving Skills	
Demonstrates ability to identify problem	
Demonstrates ability to select best solution	
Follows through on chosen solution	
Takes action to prevent future problems	

Figure 14-9 Sample Performance Appraisal Form

you can about other jobs in the company. Know how your present position fits into the organizational structure of the company. Stay informed about job openings in the company.

LEAVE A JOB

You may decide to leave a job voluntarily, or you may be given no choice. Whatever your reasons for leaving (whether you are unhappy with a position and decide to leave on your own, you are looking for greater opportunities than you are being provided, or you are forced to leave for whatever reason), you must be professional in how you handle your departure.

The Exit Interview

Most companies conduct an **exit interview** with the employee. A sample exit interview form is shown in Figure 14-11. An impartial party (such as a staff member in the human resource department) generally conducts the interview. Your immediate supervisor is not involved.

This exit interview is not a time to get even, to make derogatory remarks about your supervisor, or to unduly criticize the company. Keep in mind the old adage about not burning your bridges. If you are leaving on your own, you may wish to return some day. Regardless of your reason for leaving, you will probably need a reference from the company. Be honest but not vindictive in the exit interview. For example, if you are leaving for a job that has greater opportunities for growth, say, "I've decided to accept a position with greater responsibilities." You do not need to give all the reasons for your move.

A Layoff or Termination

You may have to face the situation of being laid off or fired. Assume first you are being laid off. The situation may be a downsizing of the company where other jobs are being eliminated in addition to your own. Keep in mind that you did not cause the situation. Even though the situation is difficult, the skills, abilities, and experience you gained from your job will help you to find another one. Remain positive and begin to think about what you want to do next.

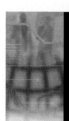

Human Relations Tip:

Do not join the complainers in the organization. Remember that most complainers spend their time talking rather than doing. Be an action-oriented worker; do your job well and look for opportunities to grow and learn.

EXIT INTERVIEW/TERMINATION FORM

TO BE COMPLETED BY SUPERVISOR

Name _____   Social Security No. _____
　　　　Last　　　　　　　First　　　　　　M.

Job Title _____   Eligible for Rehire _____ Yes _____ No

Date of Hire _____ Termination Date _____   Comments _____

_____

TO BE COMPLETED BY EMPLOYEE LEAVING

	Satisfactory	Unsatisfactory	No Opinion	Comments
1. Work load/ responsibilities				
2. Working conditions				
3. Satisfaction received from work				
4. Attention to employee ideas				
5. Supervision				
6. Employer benefits				
7. Advancement opportunities				
8. Other				

Reason for Termination _____

_____

Postemployment Plans _____

_____

_____

Additional Comments _____

_____

_____

Supervisor's Signature _____ Date _____

Employee's Signature _____ Date _____

Figure 14-11　Exit Interview Form

Now assume you have been fired. Your feelings of fear, rejection, and insecurity are normal. However, it is not a time to blame yourself. It is time to take a hard look at what skills you have. Listen to what your employer tells you about your performance. What can you learn for the future? What steps do you need to take to ensure that you do not find yourself in the same situation again? In what areas do you need to improve? Talk with family, friends, and your closest advisers. Realize that the job may not have been the best one for you. Commit to finding a job that will better match your skills and abilities.

CHAPTER SUMMARY

The summary will help you remember the important points covered in the chapter.

- Sources of job information include the Internet, personal networks, college placement offices, newspaper advertisements, public employment agencies, private employment agencies, temporary employment agencies, professional organizations, and direct canvass.
- When you identify an organization with which you are interested in applying, learn as much as you can about the organization. Ask friends, relatives, and acquaintances about the organization, check out Websites, read periodicals, obtain annual reports, consult the local chamber of commerce, and talk to college placement office personnel.
- The goals of a letter of application are to introduce you to the organization, describe your skills and background, and transmit your resume and request an interview.
- The resume is a concise statement of your background, education, skills, and experience. Resume styles include chronological and functional or a combination of the two.
- You can post your resume on the Web for review by prospective employers. You can also send your resume over the Web directly to selected employers.
- Resume sections include career objective, relevant skills, education, employment history, and accomplishments.
- Read an employment application form carefully before filling in each blank. Be truthful; reflect your background and experience accurately.
- The interview is extremely important. Most interviews are in person; however, you may be involved in a virtual interview. You must carefully prepare for an interview and present yourself to the best of your ability.
- Once the interview is over, send a follow-up letter thanking the employer for the interview and reviewing points of special interest.

- When you obtain a job, you must combine your skills and knowledge to perform well. You must listen to what co-workers and supervisors tell you, observe and learn what is expected and accepted in the office, and find out what your job duties are and how you will be evaluated.
- It is important that you live your values at work.
- Formal performance appraisals are usually done within three to six months after you begin work. After that time, appraisals are done on an annual or semiannual basis. You are evaluated on whether you can perform job assignments; maintain good working relationships with your employer and other employees; adhere to company policies regarding attendance, punctuality, sick leave, and so on; and contribute to overall company goals.
- To advance on the job, you must do each task assigned to you extremely well; increase your verbal, nonverbal, and written communication skills; learn as much as you can about other jobs in the company; know how your present position fits into the organizational structure of the company; and stay informed about job openings in the company.
- If you decide to leave a job (either on your own or due to a layoff or termination), handle the situation professionally. Do not make negative comments about your supervisor, the job, or the company.
- If you are fired, remember that feelings of fear, rejection, and insecurity are normal. Take some time to analyze your skills. Listen to what your employer tells you about your performance. Learn from your mistakes.

CHAPTER GLOSSARY

The following terms were used in this chapter. Definitions are provided to help you review the terms.

- **Networking** (p. 350)—the process of identifying and establishing a group of acquaintances, friends, and relatives who can assist you in the job search process.
- **State employment services** (p. 350)—public employment agencies whose services are provided to customers free of charge.
- **Private employment agencies** (p. 350)— privately owned employment agencies that charge a fee (either of the employer or the client) when providing services.
- **Fee-paid** (p. 351)—jobs for which the employer pays the fee.
- **Temporary agency** (p. 351)—one that offers temporary work.
- **Direct canvass** or **cold canvass** (p. 351)—going directly to an organization without having an appointment or without knowing if a job is available.
- **Letter of application** (p. 352)—letter applying for a job with the goals of the letter being to arouse the prospective employer's interest, describe the abilities of the person writing the letter, and request an interview.
- **Resume** (p. 353)—a concise statement of background, education, skills, and experience that is sent with the letter of application when seeking a job.
- **Chronological** (p. 353)—a resume that lists a person's credentials in reverse chronological order.

- **Functional** (p. 353)—a resume that highlights and emphasizes skills; chronological order is not a consideration.
- **Combination style** (p. 354)—a resume that presents experiences in reverse chronological skill set order.
- **Electronic resume** (p. 354)—online statement of background and experiences.
- **Employment application** (p. 358)—a form used by companies to obtain information about prospective employees' education, background, and experience.
- **Portfolio** (p. 359)—a compilation of samples of an individual's work.
- **Virtual interview** (p. 359)—an interview via technology with an interviewer at a distant location.
- **Follow-up letter** (p. 363)—a letter thanking the prospective employer for an interview and reviewing points of special interest.
- **Performance appraisals** (p. 364)—evaluations of employees done by the employer.
- **Exit interview** (p. 366)—an interview done by the employer when an employee leaves the company.

DISCUSSION ITEMS

These discussion items provide an opportunity to test your understanding of the chapter through written responses and discussion with your classmates and your instructor.

1. List five sources of job information.
2. Explain what should be included in a resume.
3. List ten helpful hints for making a good impression during the interview.

4. Explain the importance of living your values on a job.
5. What is the purpose of performance appraisals? What might you be evaluated on in a performance evaluation?

CRITICAL-THINKING ACTIVITY

Arturo Herrera has just finished a two-year business course in college. He has done well in school. He is proficient in Microsoft Word, Excel, and PowerPoint. His math and English skills are good, and he works well with people. He has applied at five different companies for administrative assistant positions, but he has been turned down for all of them. Arturo knows he has the skills necessary to handle the jobs; he does not understand why he has not been hired. Here is what happened on his last job interview.

Arturo was ten minutes late for the interview. He left home in time to get to the interview, but he had trouble finding a parking place. When he went in, he told the receptionist he was sorry he was late but he could not find a parking place. Arturo was anxious over being ten minutes late, so

he decided to have a cigarette while waiting for his interview. He did not see the no-smoking sign until after he had lit a cigarette. He did put out his cigarette immediately.

The first question the interviewer asked him was, "Could you tell me a little about yourself?" Arturo thought he did a thorough job with the question. He spent ten minutes telling the interviewer about his life, starting from grade school. When the interviewer asked him if he had worked before, he said he had only had summer jobs. He told the interviewer he had recently been on four interviews and he believed the interviewers were unfair when they did not offer him the job.

What mistakes did Arturo make? How can he correct these mistakes in the future? How should he prepare for the next job interview?

RESPONSES TO SELF-CHECK B

Here are suggested answers for Self-Check B.

1. Briefly talk about your education and job experiences. Do not spend more than a minute or two on your answer. Be concise; this question should not take up much time in the interview process.
2. Make several positive statements, such as "My previous employer would say I am a hard worker and I complete my tasks in a timely manner. My co-workers would say I am easy to work with and I care about them."
3. Briefly describe the computer courses you took and the software packages in which you are proficient. Talk about how your English and communication courses improved your writing skills and your ability to interact with others.
4. You might say you have an outgoing personality and you enjoy working with people.
5. You might mention your computer skills, writing skills, human relation skills, critical-thinking skills, and problem-solving skills.

PROJECTS

Project 14-1 (Objective 1)
Online Project

Using the Web, identify three sources of job information; one site is to include jobs available for administrative assistants. Report your findings, including your sources,

in a memorandum to your instructor. Include the information available on each Website. List several administrative assistant job openings, including the city, state, company, and salary (if given). Use the memorandum form provided on the Student CD, file SCDP14-1 to report your findings to your instructor.

Project 14-2 (Objective 2)

Using one of the administrative assistant jobs you found in Project 14-1, apply for the position. Prepare a resume and a letter of application. Use either a chronological or functional format, whichever best fits your background and experience. Save your resume on a disk; label it RES14-2. Print out a copy. Then prepare that same resume as an electronic resume, making the necessary changes to fit the online format. Print out a copy of your electronic resume. Submit your chronological or functional resume, your electronic resume, and your letter of application to your instructor.

Project 14-3 (Objective 3)
Collaborative Project

Work in teams of four on this project. Review the pages in your text on interviewing before beginning this task. Using the position you applied for in Project 14-2, assume you are going on an interview. Role-play that interview with your classmates with one of you being the employer, one being the interviewee, and the other two observing. When you have finished, the two observers are to critique your performance. Go through the steps again until each member of the team has played every role.

Project 14-4 (Objective 4)
Collaborative Project

As a team of three or four, interview an employed administrative professional. The interview may take place by email rather than in person. Ask the individual these questions.

- To what do you contribute your success in this position?
- What advancement opportunities are available in your company?
- What skills do you believe are necessary in order to be promoted?

Report your findings to the class.

Project 14-5 (Objective 5)

Before beginning this project, review the values you listed in Chapter 2 and saved on your Professional Growth Plan disk under "Progro2-4." Now list your major values and explain how you will commit to living those values in the workplace. Save the file as "Progro14-5."

ENGLISH USAGE CHALLENGE DRILL

Correct the following sentences. Cite the grammar rule that is applicable to each sentence. Before you begin, refresh your memory of grammar rules by reviewing pronouns in the Reference Guide of this text.

1. The eclipse of the sun was an astonishing sight for both him and I.
2. The instructor spoke with her and I about the project that is due next week.
3. The winner of the speech contest was me.
4. I wondered whom would go to the polls in the presidential election.
5. Alicia admires who?

ASSESSMENT OF CHAPTER OBJECTIVES

Now that you have completed the chapter and the projects, take a few minutes to review the learning objectives. For your convenience, the objectives are repeated below. Did you accomplish these objectives? If you were unable to accomplish the objectives, give your reasons for not doing so.

1. Determine sources of job information.   Yes _____   No _____

_____

_____

_____

2. Prepare a letter of application and a resume.   Yes _____   No _____

_____

_____

_____

3. Develop job interview skills.   Yes _____   No _____

_____

_____

_____

4. Discover how to advance your professional career.   Yes _____   No _____

_____

_____

_____

5. Commit to living your values in the workplace.   Yes _____   No _____

_____

_____

_____

You may submit your answers in writing to your instructor, using the memorandum form on the Student CD, SCDAP14-1.

LEARNING OBJECTIVES

1. Describe the characteristics of effective leaders.
2. Define the essential management responsibilities.
3. *Determine your own leadership values.*

As you assume positions of greater responsibility in the workplace,
you may have one or more people reporting to you. Being an effective manager, one
who is able to inspire people to produce at their maximum, means that you understand
and apply basic leadership and management theory. Even if you do not become a manager or supervisor, you may have the opportunity to assume leadership roles in other
areas. For example, you may assume these leadership roles.

- Leading teams within the workplace
- Serving as an officer in a professional organization
- Taking on responsible roles in civic and church organizations

Whatever form leadership takes, most of us find ourselves in leadership roles or have
the opportunity to take on leadership roles at numerous times in our lives. By studying
this chapter, you will understand some of the important aspects of leadership.

LEADERSHIP IN THE TWENTY-FIRST CENTURY

Throughout this course, you have learned that change will be constant in the twenty-
first century due to technology, the multinational nature of organizations, a diverse population (with increased diversity expected in the future), and e-commerce. In addition,
you have learned that we must consider ourselves part of a global community. Even if we
wanted to think of the United States in isolation, we cannot do so. Technology allows us
to communicate on a worldwide basis, pulling together people of diverse backgrounds
and cultures. Leadership in the twenty-first century demands two unique skills—skills
that were not essential in the past but are imperative now. These skills are change mastery and an international perspective.

Change Mastery

The leader in the twenty-first century not only understands change but also embraces change, which is not easy. Change can be scary and even threatening to some people. The successful leader sees change as challenging but filled with opportunity. This kind of leader expects the future to be filled with shifting variables and understands that disruptions are an inevitable part of our changing world. The twenty-first-century leader is cognizant of these facts.

- Long-term results are more important than short-term results.
- Effectiveness, in addition to efficiency, is stressed.
- Strategic thinking is crucial.
- Actions to situations must be proactive rather than reactive.
- Organizations must be driven by plans rather than problems.

International Perspective

The organization of the twenty-first century will draw resources—financial, human, and technical—from all over the world. In order to be effective, the leader must understand and be able to function in an **interdependent** (mutually dependent on each other) world. This interdependent world is made possible by almost instantaneous communication available through email, faxes, television, computers, the Web, and global transportation systems. The effective organization of the twenty-first century cannot think and act independently. Additionally, the effective organization not only is aware of the necessity of global interdependence but also cultivates that interdependency.

CHARACTERISTICS OF AN EFFECTIVE LEADER

What are the characteristics of an effective leader in this global world of constant change? Here are a few important ones.

Understands Self

If leaders are to be effective, they must understand themselves (not just superficially, but deeply). We are all shaped by our background and experiences. Our families, our friends, the schools we attended, and society in general have told us how we should behave and what we should value. If we truly are to understand ourselves, however, we must at some point in our lives decide for ourselves what is important. How can we really know who we are? These ideas will help you.

- Understand that self-knowledge is a lifetime process. Just as the world changes, individuals change as a result of new experiences and new knowledge. If we are going to understand ourselves, we must commit to continuing the process through life. We must continue to explore our own potential, to reflect on our experiences, and to seek new challenges.
- Be willing to accept responsibility. Life is about accepting responsibility for our own actions. Have you ever known someone who never made a mistake, never made an error, never admitted to being wrong? Most of us have had some experience with this type of individual. Unfortunately, this person usually has very little understanding of self. Knowing self means that we recognize our strengths and our weaknesses. We know what we can and cannot do. We know that all human beings make mistakes, and we are willing to admit when we make one. To make an error is not unique or even unforgivable. What is unforgivable, however, is to continue to make the same error and to refuse to learn from it. Knowing ourselves means that we accept our humanness, that we do make mistakes but we do not attempt to pass blame on to others.

Builds a Shared Vision

The ethical organization is visionary. The effective leader is able to build a shared vision of the organization with employees. Building this vision means employees at all levels of the organization must be involved. It means that leaders help employees consider these questions.

- What products or services does the organization produce? What should it produce?
- What values does the organization have? What values should it have?
- What contributions should the organization make to the community?
- What reputation does the organization have? What reputation should it have?
- Who are the clients and customers of the organization?
- How do people work together within the organization?
- Do the values of the individuals within the organization match the values of the organization?
- What contributions do individuals within the organization make to the community?

Effective leaders help employees understand the organization's vision and how their individual goals and objectives support that vision. Effective leaders publish the organization's vision statement so employees are aware of it. Additionally, a number of organizations today publish their value/vision statement on the Web to inform the general public about what is important to the organization.

Lives by a Set of Values

When we look back over history, we discover that values have been important topics of discussion among many leaders and philosophers. The writings and teachings of both Socrates and Plato asserted that virtue and ethical behavior were associated with wisdom. After the rise of Christianity, Catholic theologians such as St. Augustine and St. Thomas Aquinas dominated ethical thinking. Correct behavior in both personal and business dealings was necessary to achieve salvation and life after death.

Today ethical behavior in business remains the accepted practice. The tough part becomes how that ethical behavior is lived in the business organization. What practices are ethical? What practices are not ethical? Even though it

can be difficult to determine what is and is not ethical in specific instances, few of us would disagree that our leaders must stand firmly on moral principles. Leaders must work within the organization to identify and define those principles and then ensure that they are carried out in the daily activities of the organization. When difficult decisions must be made, leaders must stand on their espoused values; they must *walk the talk*. Effective leaders understand this principle. They understand that establishing and living a set of values must begin with the top leaders and that living the organizational values must permeate every level of the organization.

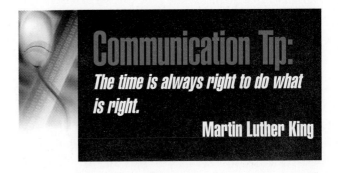

Communication Tip:
The time is always right to do what is right.

Martin Luther King

Commits to Service

Effective leaders consider service to others as primary. In other words, effective leaders are not concerned first with building a career for themselves, but in understanding how they can serve the organization and its employees as well

© PhotoDisc, Inc.

The effective leader has a commitment to the community.

as the external community. For example, a leader's values may include a commitment to helping people grow, a commitment to diversity, and a commitment to helping the world become a better place. Figure 15-1 provides General Electric's statement about its commitment to the community.

Empowers Others

Power is defined as "the ability or official capacity to exercise control; authority." Because the prefix *em* means "to put on to" or "to cover with," **empowering** means the passing on of authority or responsibility.

Leaders empower people when they take these actions.

- Provide employees with access to information that will help them increase their productivity and effectiveness
- Allow employees to take on more responsibility
- Allow employees a voice in decision making

Empowered employees feel a sense of ownership and control over their jobs. They understand they are responsible for getting their jobs done. Empowered employees usually are happier individuals; they trust the organization, feel a part of it, and enjoy the rewards the job provides.

The leader who empowers people has a core belief in people, believing that people are basically good, honest, and well intentioned. The leader believes that people will do the right thing when they have the resources available to accomplish a task. The leader under-

stands that leadership is operating from a central core of values, even in the most difficult situations.

Rewards Risk-Taking

The organization of the twenty-first century, with change as a constant, will face risks daily. Ignoring the risks does not make them go away. The organization cannot take refuge in status quo, conformity to the norm, or security in the past. None of these stances make sense if the organization is to be successful. The organization must be willing to seek new answers to problems, try new approaches, and be flexible. If the organization is to be successful, it must have leaders who not only take risks themselves but also encourage others to take risks. Wise leaders who take risks demonstrate a number of characteristics, some of which are listed in Figure 15-2.

Here are some keys to successful risk-taking.

- Trust your own abilities. Do not place limits on your ability to learn and improve. As a small child you did not doubt yourself because you could not read, knowing you would soon learn that skill in school. Therefore, you should not doubt your ability to learn and try new things when you are 30, 50, or even 70.
- Be open-minded. Our assumptions can prevent us from seeing new possibilities. When analyzing situations that need solving, we need to discard our old assumptions. Where would we be today if Columbus and his colleagues had believed the world was flat, as

CHARACTERISTICS OF LEADERS WHO TAKE RISKS

Wise leaders who take risks engage in the following behaviors:

- Gather information wisely
- Risk from strength
- Prepare thoroughly
- Display flexibility
- Envision what can be gained
- Understand what is at stake

- Stay on mission
- Possess the right motives
- Give their followers wins
- March forward with confidence

Figure 15-2

Source: John C. Maxwell, *The Right to Lead* (Nashville: Thomas Nelson, Inc., 2001), 66.

did almost everyone in the world at that time? Where would we be today if Wilbur and Orville Wright had not believed they could build a *flying machine?*

- Develop your intuitive powers. Subconsciously we take note of many things our conscious mind does not realize. However, these subconscious thoughts can be brought to the surface of our consciousness if we listen carefully to ourselves (our intuition).
- Overcome the fear of making mistakes. Certainly when trying something new, you make mistakes. What you need to consider when taking risks is the likelihood of success. For example, you would not jump off a ten-story building thinking you would live through it. That would be a foolish and senseless risk. Most people know intuitively when a risk makes sense and when it does not. Sam Walton, in building Wal-Mart, went through many failures and difficult times. Yet his vision was so clear and his understanding of what would yield success so deep that he endured the risks and temporary failures to achieve his dream.
- Develop a support team. Supportive colleagues can help you analyze a situation when you believe you have made a mistake. They can look at the situation more objectively than you can; they can help you determine what to do next. When your colleagues make mistakes, you can return that objectivity and support by helping them analyze their situations.

The task of the effective manager is to build an environment that supports risk-taking. Employees need to know they will not be pun-

ished for taking appropriate risks. They need to know that the organization will support their risk-taking ventures and reward their successes.

Communication Tip:
Develop a risk-taker award to be given to employees who take risks.

Moves Through Chaos

The effective leader learns from the chaos in the world and, in fact, is often shaped by the chaos. In this case, *shaping* means that the leader learns from both the good and bad experiences that happen during times of chaos. You have already learned that when you take risks, you often make mistakes. Mistakes are an inevitable outcome of continued risk taking. The effective leader takes these mistakes, learns from them, and builds on the lessons learned from failure so success will be more likely the next time. For example, many highly successful people have been fired from jobs but they do not let that fact keep them from being successful in their next venture. They learn what they can from the experience, discard what is not meaningful, and continue to try to make a difference in the world. In other words, they are driven by their own inner beliefs.

Chaos is an inevitable part of being a leader in the twenty-first century. The successful leader accepts this inevitability. The successful leader practices the art of meeting individuals and situations where they are and moving them forward to bring about the desired outcomes.

Knows How to Follow

The effective leader knows the importance of stepping back and being a follower when the situation demands it. This person understands that leaders are sometimes followers and followers are sometimes leaders. A **bilateralness** (affecting two sides equally) exists, with the leader not only understanding the importance of following but also having the trust in others to know that they, given the proper opportunities and training, can be leaders too.

The men and women who lead at the highest level are extraordinary. They have many extraordinary characteristics, and they continue to develop these characteristics throughout their lives. Figure 15-3 lists some additional characteristics of these leaders.

Self-Check

Stop for a few minutes, and consider the characteristics of an effective leader you believe you already possess.

Now list the characteristics you would like to work on during the remainder of this course.

_____

_____

_____

_____

LEADERSHIP AND MANAGEMENT CONTRASTED

Leadership is doing the right thing, while **management** is doing things right. The effective leader operates around a clearly defined set of values, with those values centering on what is right for an organization and its employees. Effective leadership relies on the leader bringing the appropriate set of values to the work environment. There is no real way to assess the values of the leader in isolation. They become apparent only as the leader guides an organization to accomplish its goals, which benefit not only the organization but also the external community and the individuals within the organization. The importance of leadership cannot be diminished, and the numerous books written on the subject attest to the fact that true leadership is to be valued and respected.

By contrast, management can be considered a subset of leadership. The functions of management include planning, organizing, recruiting, training, controlling, and evaluating. These activities are relatively concrete and can be quantified, measured, and assessed. If an organization is to be successful, these functions must be understood and carried out effectively. Although the characteristics of effective leaders and the responsibilities of effective managers are presented separately here, understand that the most effective managers are also effective leaders. Conversely, effective leaders are also effective managers.

CHARACTERISTICS OF UNCOMMON LEADERS

The men and women who lead at the highest level have these traits.

- Futurists—Their dreams are bigger than their memories.
- Catalysts—They initiate movement and momentum for others.
- Optimists—They believe in their cause and their people beyond reason.
- Activists—They are doers and empower others by their actions.

- Strategists—They plan how to use every resource available to be successful.
- Pragmatists—Their legacy is that they solve the practical problems people face.

Figure 15-3

Source: John C. Maxwell, *The Right to Lead* (Nashville: Thomas Nelson, Inc., 2001), 22.

MANAGEMENT RESPONSIBILITIES

If you are to be successful in a supervisory role, you need to understand how to effectively perform the basic management responsibilities, including planning, organizing, recruiting and employing, training, motivating, delegating, and evaluating. These functions are presented here.

Plan

Planning is a crucial function of management. Without proper planning, an organization and its employees do not know where they are going. A major part of the planning process is setting goals and objectives. Although all organizations have goals and objectives, they may be very loosely defined or not defined at all. Defining them in writing and establishing measurable results is a process that was recommended by Peter Drucker[1] over 30 years ago. In a seminal work entitled *The Practice of Management*, Drucker set forth the process that came to be known as **MBO** (management by objectives). Although it has taken on numerous forms and variations, it is still used today; MBO is implemented through the planning process described here.

The planning process in which goals and objectives are set is usually done for a one-year period, which is called **tactical planning**, and for a three- to five-year period, which is called **long-range planning.** Many times the overall goals of a company are set by top-level administrators; i.e., the board of directors, the president, and the executive vice presidents. Once these goals have been determined, they are distributed to the managers in the organization. Then the managers set objectives for their work units. In most organizations today, managers also involve their workgroups in setting objectives. Managers are held responsible by upper administration for achieving the objectives defined. In some organizations, bonuses are awarded based on the accomplishment of objectives.

Think about what your role in the planning process might be as an administrative profes-

© PhotoDisc, Inc.

One of the tasks of managers is to plan.

sional supervising support staff. You may help set the objectives for your department or division. However, even if you do not, you will engage in planning the activities of your unit, which includes setting objectives. The employees who report to you must know what they are expected to produce. You should have a planning session at least once a year, preferably every six months, to look at what your unit should be accomplishing for the year. During this planning session, you and your employees determine what objectives should be accomplished, when they should be accomplished, the costs of accomplishing them, and how they will be measured. For example, assume that one of your objectives is to revise the document management system within your division. The objective might be written as follows:

> Revise the document management system from a manual system to an electronic system by April 15. After two months of use, users will evaluate the system. The cost of the revision is in software, approximately $3,000.

Organize

Once the planning has been done, the work must be organized. Organization involves bringing together all resources—people, time, money, and equipment—in the most effective

---

[1]Peter Drucker, *The Practice of Management* (New York: Harper and Row, 1954).

way to accomplish the goals. The three factors that affect how the work is organized are span of control, job analysis, and work periods.

Span of Control

Span of control refers to the number of employees who are directly supervised by one person. No formula rigidly defines the span of control; the number is determined more by the philosophy of management. Organizations are flatter today than in the past, with fewer levels of hierarchy. A flattened organizational structure usually means a greater span of control for supervisors. For example, rather than supervising 5 individuals, a manager may supervise as many as 30. Here are some questions that need to be asked when considering span of control.

- Is the organization committed to a hierarchical structure or a flattened structure?
- Is the manager highly skilled and experienced? Does the manager have the skills needed to assume the responsibilities of an expanded reporting structure?
- Are the work-group members highly skilled and knowledgeable?
- Is the work the group is performing similar in nature?
- Is the work group given a great degree of autonomy? Is the work group allowed to make decisions without checking with the supervisor?

Job Analysis

A second factor in the organization of work is job analysis. To perform a job analysis, a supervisor must determine the requirements of a job and the qualifications needed by personnel to get the job done. Once this information is determined, it is usually compiled into a job description, such as the one in Figure 15-4. The job description includes skills, training, and education necessary for the job and a list of the job duties. Most companies have job descriptions for all employees, which not only are helpful in the hiring process but also in letting employees know what they are expected to do.

Work Periods

A third factor to consider in organizing work is the time in which the work is to be performed. The workweek is traditionally from 8 or 9 a.m. to 5 p.m. five days per week. However, factors such as flextime, four-day weeks, job sharing, and telework make the workweek different from that of the past.

Recruit and Employ

Organizations usually establish procedures through their human resources departments that outline how they will recruit employees. There are certain legal considerations. For

---

JOB DESCRIPTION

Job Title: Administrative Assistant
Company: AmeriAsian Airlines
Reports to: Martin Albertson

Skills and Training

The position of Administrative Assistant requires excellent organizational and human relations skills. The ability to establish priorities on projects and to supervise administrative support staff is required. Excellent verbal and written communication skills are necessary.

Basic skills include computer (word processing, spreadsheet, and graphics software), document management, grammar and composition, and accurate keyboarding at 90 wpm.

Education and Experience

Four years of experience in an administrative profession role; an associate degree in business

Duties

- Composing letters, emails, and reports
- Keying correspondence and reports
- Maintaining an electronic document management system
- Planning meetings and conferences
- Handling requests from the external community
- Supervising administrative support staff

Figure 15-4

example, when placing advertisements, companies must ensure that the wording of the advertisement does not conflict with fair employment practice laws. Discrimination statutes prohibit advertisements that show preferences in terms of race, religion, gender, age, or physical disabilities. An employer cannot advertise for a particular age group. Thus, expressions such as *young person* or *retired person* cannot be used in advertisements. If you are recruiting employees, check with the appropriate individuals within your company to make sure you are observing the company rules and legal guidelines.

Once applicants are recruited, three major tools are used for screening and selection.

- Written applications
- Personal interviews
- Testing procedures

The manager or a team of people may review the applications. If you are part of that team, when reviewing the applications, you should be very clear about the skills, education, and experience you are seeking. These questions will help.

- What type of person are we seeking?
- What qualifications does that person need to have?
- What education and experience does the person need?

With your criteria in mind, screen the applications and select the most qualified individuals to interview.

You may choose to conduct one-on-one interviews, team interviews, or a combination of the two. Before the interviewing process begins, compile a list of questions to ask of each candidate. Such a list keeps you and the team on target as you begin the interviewing process and helps you treat all interviewees with fairness and consistency. Additionally, the list helps remind you that certain questions are not legal. The following questions are unlawful to ask during the interview:

- Are you married? single? divorced? separated?
- What is the date of your birth?
- Is your spouse a U.S. citizen?
- Where were you born?

- To what clubs do you belong?
- What are the ages of your children?
- What church do you attend?

You must keep up with the latest laws concerning discrimination and interviewing procedures. Otherwise, you may inadvertently place your company in jeopardy of a discrimination suit.

Set aside enough time for a thorough interview. You will probably need to spend an hour or more with each applicant. Do not consider this time wasted. Hiring the right person for a job is one of the most important things you will do as a manager.

The third screening tool is the test. Here, too, legal considerations are important. The use of tests in selecting administrative professionals is not prohibited, but testing practices that have discriminatory effects are. Keep in mind that the test must measure the person's qualifications for the job, not the person as an individual. If you are employing an administrative professional, for example, and a requirement of the job is that the person be able to key at a certain rate with an established degree of accuracy, you can give the person a keyboarding test. You can also give an administrative professional grammar and spelling tests since the individual will be required to produce documents that are free of grammatical and spelling errors. You cannot ask a person to take a math proficiency test unless the use of math is necessary in performing the job.

Train

The manager is responsible for two kinds of training—individual training and team training. Both types are discussed here.

Individual Training

Once a person is employed, the next step is to assist that person in gaining the knowledge necessary to be successful on the job. Certainly the individual comes in with a set of skills; however, remember that the person probably knows little or nothing about how your organization works. To be successful, that person must learn about proper company procedures. As a manager, you have an obligation in this area.

In addition to entry-level training, ongoing training for administrative professionals must also be provided as a result of the rapid changes in technology. The company, for example, may purchase a new software program. A new employee will also need training to become proficient on this software. Individuals within the organization or outside trainers may provide the training.

Another type of training for which a supervisor may be responsible is preparing employees for promotion. Company programs for promoting qualified workers can improve employee morale. Supervisors should watch for promising employees and use every opportunity to encourage and develop these employees. Additional training may be available through company-sponsored seminars, tuition-reimbursed courses at local colleges, or job internships where an employee spends a period of time learning various jobs.

© PhotoDisc, Inc.

Ongoing training is essential.

Team Training

The use of teams within the office demands that the manager be involved in team training. Teams often cannot function at their highest degree of productivity without acquiring some interpersonal skill development. These skills are generally necessary for all team members as they work together.

- Listening—summarizing, checking for understanding, and giving and receiving feedback
- Resolving conflicts—identifying and resolving conflicts within the team or with individuals outside the team
- Influencing others—gaining respect as a team and as individuals
- Developing solutions—creatively generating and sorting through alternative solutions to issues
- Ensuring ongoing quality—determining how results will be measured

In addition, a manager working with teams must take on the following responsibilities for the team to be successful.

- Empower the team; give them the information needed to get the job done.
- Trust the team. Once the team has the information it needs, trust the team to produce the best possible solutions to problems.
- Take a strong stand with the team when needed. If the team is not accomplishing the task and is getting bogged down in personality issues, let them know that such behaviors are not acceptable.
- Check on the team's development. Are team members communicating with and trusting each other? Do they understand the goals of the team? Do they understand individual roles? Is each member involved in the process and product?
- Do not **micromanage** (attempt to tell individuals every step to take).

Motivate

Motivation comes from the Latin word meaning "to move." Motivation may be **extrinsic** (relying on factors such as salary increases or promotions) or **intrinsic** (coming from within the person—something gets done because it is right, fits the individual's values, and so on). Figure 15-5 lists both intrinsic and extrinsic motivational factors that will help motivate others.

Delegate

Delegation means assigning tasks to others and then empowering them by providing the necessary information to get the job done. Delegation can be difficult for a manager, particularly one who has a need to control all aspects of a job. Yet no manager can possibly do it all. One widely accepted definition of management is "getting work done through others." Managers must delegate. Obviously, delegation means

employees receive the proper information and training before being given a task. Once a task is delegated, employees should be trusted to perform.

© PhotoDisc, Inc.

The effective manager delegates.

MOTIVATIONAL TECHNIQUES

- Set objectives. Help the employees you supervise establish challenging, measurable objectives. Then, help them commit themselves to achieving the objectives. This approach requires follow-through and planning on the part of the supervisor. You must not only know the objectives, but also follow up to see that the employee has achieved the objectives.
- Give recognition. As a supervisor, you need to become sensitive to the accomplishments of others. You can give recognition in a number of ways: verbal praise for a job well done, a thank-you letter written to an employee, and recognition in the organization's newsletter.

- Develop a team. Individuals need to be an accepted member of a group. As a supervisor, you can capitalize on this need by building a team of people who work together well. Productivity can be increased when each person in the group contributes to the overall effectiveness of the team.
- Pay for the job. As a supervisor, know what your employees do and then pay them fairly for their work. Reward employees who consistently give you outstanding performance with good salary increases.
- Delegate work. Employees enjoy doing meaningful and challenging work. Provide them this opportunity by delegating important projects to them.

Figure 15-5

Evaluate

Performance evaluation occurs whether or not there is a formal evaluation program. It is a consequence of the way jobs are designed and organizations are structured. Supervisors constantly observe the way people are performing. Most companies have formal evaluation periods in which personnel are evaluated every six months or every year. These evaluations may be individual evaluations, team evaluations, or work-group evaluations.

Individual Evaluation

Individual evaluations are essential even if team evaluations occur. Most companies use forms and processes developed for evaluations that come from the human resource department. This department may use a team within the company to develop the evaluation system. Once the evaluation process is developed, it should be consistently followed throughout the organization. Usually, the process involves an employee completing a self-evaluation and the supervisor preparing an evaluation. At the evaluation conference, both evaluations are discussed and a final evaluation document is prepared. If the employee gives the supervisor new information that applies to the evaluation, the supervisor should accept that information and note it on the evaluation form. Read Figure 15-6 carefully; the techniques provided will help you understand how to effectively evaluate employees.

EVALUATION TECHNIQUES

- Evaluate performance on a day-to-day basis. Employees should always know how they are doing. If a report or letter is not written or formatted correctly, let the employee know immediately. Praise a job well done. Give employees immediate feedback as to their performance. Do not save all criticism or all praise for a yearly evaluation session.
- Allow adequate time for the evaluation. The performance evaluation is important for both you and the employee. Set aside enough time on your calendar to do it well. You need to spend an hour or two with each employee. Hold the evaluation conference in an appropriate place. If you are using your office, ask that you not be interrupted and close the door to ensure privacy.
- Give credit where credit is due. Praise the employee for work well done. Too many managers consider an evaluation period a time for criticism only. It is not. It is a time to look at the total work of the employee. In what areas is the employee performing in an exemplary manner? in an average manner? below expectations?
- Be fair. Analyze the employee's work based on established criteria of performance, not on how well you like or dislike the employee. Stay away from personality traits. Stress job performance. When discussing errors, suggest how the work could have been performed satisfactorily. Give the employee an opportunity to suggest possible alternatives. Word your comments as positively as possible. Do not say, for example, "Your performance is a problem." Instead, say, "You are doing well in . . . , but you need to improve in . . . ."
- Listen to what the employee is saying. Too often we listen to others with only half an ear. An employee may come to an evaluation session with a certain amount of anxiety and perhaps hostility. Let the person talk. By talking, the employee will release much of his or her anxiety and thus be more receptive to constructive criticism.
- Avoid personal areas. Sometimes a supervisor, with the best of intentions, will become too involved in the employee's personal life. Do not try to counsel an employee about problems that should be handled by a qualified professional.
- Establish attainable objectives for improvement. Help the employee set realistic objectives. A plan of action for improvement may be developed, including dates set for the accomplishment of each objective. Remember, this plan of action is a growth plan for improvement. Praise the employee for improvement.

Figure 15-6

Team Evaluation

Some companies use team evaluations in which employees who work together as a team are asked to evaluate each other. These team evaluations may be given by the supervisors of the people involved in the team or discussed among the team members only. If the team members discuss the evaluation, the team leader needs to take a strong position in the process to ensure that the team evaluation session does not become one of fault-finding or blaming others. Guidelines should be given to the team before the evaluation occurs. The team leader should stress that the evaluation is to determine whether the team completed their tasks successfully and what contributions were made by individual members to the task.

Work-Group Evaluation

Work-group evaluations may also be a part of the evaluation process. Work groups should set measurable objectives that are related to the overall goals established by the organization. The manager and the work group might also evaluate what needs to be improved during the next six months or year by using a total quality approach. Here are some questions they might ask.

- What needs to be improved?
- What actions should the work group take to improve the areas identified?
- Who does what and when is it done? This stage is when the action plan is developed. The **action plan** should include specific tasks to be achieved, including who is responsible for each task identified and when the task will be completed.
- How do we know the action is working? Once the action plan is implemented, it is monitored to determine if the desired results are achieved.
- How can we ensure that the problem will not reoccur? Once results are achieved, procedures, training, and other necessary measures are taken to ensure that the problem does not happen again.
- What have we learned? Areas where difficulties occurred should be reviewed so performance can improve.

THE RIGHT TO LEAD

You have learned in this chapter that the effective leader has certain characteristics and is willing to follow a set of values to help the organization and its employees to learn and grow. You have learned that a number of management responsibilities are necessary in order for an organization to function efficiently. You have learned that there is a definite link between good leaders and good managers. Although management tasks are more concrete, each manager (in order to be the most effective) must have leadership characteristics—characteristics that keep the organization focused on doing what is right.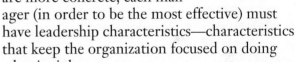

Needless to say, not all individuals have the characteristics mentioned in this chapter and not all individuals are interested in developing these traits. The process of learning how to lead is a continual one. No one person is born with the right to lead. Leadership is earned. Individuals who consistently demonstrate a commitment to the skills defined in this chapter earn the right to lead.

CHAPTER SUMMARY

The summary will help you remember the important points covered in the chapter.

- Leadership in the twenty-first century requires two unique skills—change mastery and an international perspective.
- An effective leader has these characteristics: understands self, builds a shared vision, lives by a set of values, commits to service, empowers others, rewards risk taking, moves through chaos, and knows how to follow.
- Leadership is doing the right thing; management is doing things right.

- Although management responsibilities are more concrete and can be quantified, measured, and assessed, effective management and effective leadership are a blend. The effective manager is also an effective leader.
- Management responsibilities include planning, organizing, recruiting and employing, training, motivating, delegating, and evaluating.
- The process of learning how to lead is continual. No one person is born with the right to lead. Individuals who demonstrate a commitment to develop needed leadership characteristics earn the right to lead.

CHAPTER GLOSSARY

The following terms were used in this chapter. Definitions are provided to help you review the terms.

- **Interdependent** (p. 374)—mutually dependent on each other.
- **Power** (p. 376)—the ability or official capacity to exercise control.
- **Empowering** (p. 376)—the passing on of authority or responsibility.
- **Bilateralness** (p. 378)—affecting two sides equally.
- **Leadership** (p. 378)—doing the right thing.
- **Management** (p. 378)—doing things right.
- **MBO** (p. 379)—management by objectives.
- **Tactical planning** (p. 379)—setting goals and objectives for a one-year period.
- **Long-range planning** (p. 379)—setting goals and objectives for a three- to five-year period.
- **Span of control** (p. 380)—the number of employees who are directly supervised by one person.

- **Micromanage** (p. 382)—attempt to tell individuals every step to take in performing a task.
- **Motivation** (p. 382)—to move individuals to accomplish a task.
- **Extrinsic motivation** (p. 382)—relying on factors such as salary increases or promotions to motivate.
- **Intrinsic motivation** (p. 383)— coming from within the person.
- **Delegation** (p. 383)—assigning tasks to others and then empowering them by providing the necessary information to get the job done.
- **Action plan** (p. 385)—includes specific tasks to be achieved, including who is responsible for each task identified and when the task will be completed.

DISCUSSION ITEMS

These discussion items provide an opportunity to test your understanding of the chapter through written responses and/or discussion with your classmates and your instructor.

1. List the characteristics of an effective leader.
2. Explain the difference between leadership and management.
3. Define the essential functions of management.
4. What is meant by MBO? Explain how it is used within an organization.
5. List five motivational factors.

CRITICAL-THINKING ACTIVITY

Two months ago AmeriAsian offered you a position as records manager. You accepted the offer since the position matches your skills and career goals. Five individuals report to you. During the two months, two staff members have committed what you believe to be serious ethical violations. The situations are these.

SITUATION 1

One of your first responsibilities was to develop an electronic document system for personnel records. You asked two of your staff (Joanna and Theodore) to work with you on the project. As your team started to work, you reminded them of the confidential nature of the project, stating that no information could be shared with *anyone*. Two weeks into the project, Joanna reported she overheard Theodore discussing project details with two administrative professionals in the accounting department. He gave them details (including salaries, ages, and employment history) of three executives in the company.

SITUATION 2

Kami, one of the five members of your staff, worked overtime one evening on a project you assigned. You left the office at 5 p.m., but returned at 8 p.m. Kami was not working. She turned in the completed assignment the next morning. When Kami turned in her overtime for the week, she claimed overtime from 5 p.m. until 11 p.m. on that evening; overtime is paid at time and a half.

How should you handle each situation? As you respond, ask yourself if you are living your values.

PROJECTS

Project 15-1 (Objectives 1 and 2)
Collaborative Project

Work as a team with four of your classmates on this assignment. Interview two top-level executives (presidents or vice presidents, if possible). Ask the executives the following questions:

- What are the characteristics of an effective leader?
- How did you develop your leadership skills?
- How is planning conducted in your organization?
- Do you provide ongoing training for your employees? If so, what types of opportunities do you provide?
- What process do you use to evaluate employees?

Summarize your findings and report them to the class.

Project 15-2 (Objective 3)

Assume you are in a leadership position, and identify the leadership values you would uphold and demonstrate to your employees. Add these values to your Professional Growth Plan disk, and save it under "Progro15-2."

Next, review all the professional growth plans you developed this semester. Have you met your professional growth plan objectives? Did you successfully complete all of the items listed on your plans? Write a summary of what you intended to accomplish. Include an evaluation of your actual accomplishments and your future plans for professional growth. Submit this summary to your instructor.

ENGLISH USAGE CHALLENGE DRILL

Correct the following sentences. Cite the grammar rule that is applicable to each sentence. Before you begin, refresh your memory by reviewing possessives in the Reference Guide of this text.

1. Jane Withers's coat was lost.
2. I will be going to the doctors tomorrow.
3. Mavis' pet lizard likes to eat flies.
4. The childrens talking bothered me.
5. The CEOs office was extremely large.

ASSESSMENT OF CHAPTER OBJECTIVES

Now that you have completed the chapter and the projects, take a few minutes to review the chapter learning objectives. For your convenience, the objectives are repeated here. Did you accomplish these objectives? If you were unable to accomplish the objectives, give your reasons for not doing so.

1. Describe the characteristics of effective leaders.   Yes _____   No _____

_____

_____

_____

2. Define the essential management responsibilities.   Yes _____   No _____

_____

_____

_____

3. Determine your own leadership values.   Yes _____   No _____

_____

_____

_____

You may submit your answers in writing to your instructor, using the memorandum form on the Student CD, SCDAP15-1.

JOSÉ REGO'S CASE SOLUTION

Our "expert" realized beyond the shadow of any doubt that the comment made by the young woman was directed at him. I often find that after a trainer has done everything possible to control group dynamics, the participants may choose to handle situations on their own by taking the initiative to address issues directly. I believe this is a result of the trainer carefully but skillfully reminding people that a workshop is only as effective as they want it to be and that participants must take ownership of their personal experiences if they are to gain the most from the workshop.

One of the lessons I learned in my years of administrative work is that sometimes the best thing to do is nothing at all—except to provide opportunities where others can become empowered and handle the situation themselves.

I wonder if anyone in the group noticed after that break that our "expert" consumed most of my free time. However, it was worth what it took from me. The participants were freed from the all-consuming experiences of the "expert," and everyone walked away feeling that someone had listened to what he or she said.

REFERENCE GUIDE

The Reference Guide provides grammar and punctuation rules and basic formats for letters and reports that you use daily in written and verbal communication. To help you review the basics, read through the Reference Guide at the beginning of the course. You can also refer to it as questions arise when you are preparing materials for this course. Additionally, as you complete the English Usage Challenge Drill in each chapter, use the materials to review specific rules. The parts of the Reference Guide are as follows:

- Abbreviations
- Bias-Free Language
- Capitalization
- Collective Nouns
- Letters and Envelopes
- Number Usage
- Often Misused Words and Phrases
- Parallel Construction
- Plurals and Possessives
- Pronouns
- Proofreaders' Marks
- Punctuation
- Report Format
- Spelling Rules
- Subject and Verb Agreement
- Word Division

ABBREVIATIONS

1. Use standard abbreviations for titles immediately before and after proper names.

   Before the Name
   Periods are used in abbreviations before the name.

   Dr. Cindy Bos
   Mr. Michael Khirallah
   Rev. Thomas McIntrye

   After the Name
   Academic, military, and civil honors follow a name and are preceded with a comma. Academic degrees are abbreviated in uppercase with periods, or the periods may be eliminated. The titles *Reverend* and *Honorable* are spelled out if preceded by *the*.

   The Honorable Marjorie Popham
   Patricia LaFaver, Ph.D.
   Nathan Portello, MS
   Bryant McAnnelley, J.D.
   Helene Chen, PhD
   Bryon Edwards, MD

   Civil titles are abbreviated in uppercase with no periods.

   J. Hansel LeFevre, CLU

   Personal titles such as *Rev.*, *Hon.*, *Prof.*, *Gen.*, *Col.*, *Capt.*, and *Lieut.* may be abbreviated when they precede a surname and a given name. When only the surname is used, these titles should be spelled out.

   Prof. Mark Huddleston
   Professor Huddleston

2. Many companies and professional organizations are known by abbreviated names. These abbreviated names are keyed in capital letters with no periods and no spaces between the letters.

IBM	International Business Machines
YMCA	Young Men's Christian Association

3. Certain expressions are abbreviated.

e.g.	exempli gratia (for example)
etc.	et cetera (and so forth)
i.e.	id est (that is)

4. Names of countries should be abbreviated only in tabulations or enumerations and should be written in capital letters; periods may or may not be used in these abbreviations.

U.S.A. or USA
U.S. or US

Note: *United States* may be spelled out as a noun and abbreviated as an adjective.

The United States 2000 Census gave us updated statistics concerning our population.
The median age of the U.S. population is 35.6 years.

5. Abbreviations for government agencies are usually written in capital letters with no periods and no spaces between the letters.

FTC   Federal Trade Commission
CIA   Central Intelligence Agency

6. Abbreviations containing a period falling at the end of a sentence use only one period. In sentences ending with a question mark or an exclamation mark, place the punctuation mark directly after the period.

The play began at 8:15 p.m.
Does the class start at 9:30 a.m.?

7. The following categories of words should not be abbreviated unless these words appear in tabulations or enumerations.

- Names of territories and possessions of the United States, countries, states, and cities
- Names of months
- Days of the week
- Given names, such as *Wm.* for *William*
- Words such as *Avenue, Boulevard, Court, Street, Drive, Road, Building*
- Parts of company names (such as *Bros., Co., Corp.*) unless the words are abbreviated in the official company name
- Compass directions when they are part of an address; use *North, South, East, West. NW, NE, SE,* and *SW* may be abbreviated after a street name, however.
- The word *number* unless it is followed by a numeral.

BIAS-FREE LANGUAGE

In the last few years, we have become aware of the effects language can have when used to describe characteristics such as gender, race, and physical characteristics. As we speak and write, we must carefully consider the words we use. This section offers suggestions for avoiding communication biases in three areas—gender, race, and physical characteristics.

Gender Bias

Inclusive usage in language (incorporating both sexes) is extremely important in writing. Exclusive language (words that by their form or meaning, discriminate on the basis of gender) should be avoided. Examples of exclusive language include words such as *craftsman, weatherman, fireman, policeman,* and so on. Other examples of exclusive language include such statements as these.

The teacher asked everyone to state his name.
The executive answered his phone.

In writing and speaking, gender bias statements should be eliminated. For example, *weatherman* becomes *weatherperson, policeman* becomes *police officer.*

The teacher asked everyone to give his or her name.
The executive answered the phone.

Strategies for avoiding pronoun gender problems include the following:

- Use the plural of the noun and pronoun.
- Delete the pronoun altogether.
- Replace the masculine pronoun with an article (*the*).
- Use *he* or *she* (but only sparingly).

Ethnic and Racial Bias

Acceptable terms for various races and ethnicities change over time. It is the writer's and speaker's responsibility to be aware of the most acceptable terms. Presently these terms are the ones to use.

- *African American* (Some African Americans prefer *black*.)
- *Native Americans* or *American Indians*
- *Hispanic* (Some individuals prefer *Latinos/ Latinas*, with the masculine form ending in *o* and the feminine form ending in *a*.)
- *Asian* may be used as a general term when referring to people from the Far Eastern region of the world. Citizens of China are *Chinese*, never Orientals.

Biases Based on Physical Characteristics

The most recent term for individuals with disabilities is *physically challenged*. Some groups (but certainly not all) prefer to use *visually impaired* for the blind and *hearing impaired* for the deaf. Since terms do change, you must be aware of current usage.

CAPITALIZATION

1. The first word of every sentence should be capitalized.

2. The first word of a complete direct quotation should be capitalized. The first word of an indirect quotation is not capitalized. (The word *that* frequently introduces indirect quotations.)

   Mary reported that "the group is angry over the intolerance of several group members."

   If words like *yes* and *no* are not direct quotations, they are not placed in quotes.

   He answered no to every question he was asked.

3. The first word of a salutation and all nouns used in the salutation should be capitalized.

4. The first word in a complimentary close should be capitalized.

5. The first word after a colon is capitalized when the colon introduces a complete passage or sentence having independent meaning.

   Jacques made this statement: "The survey shows that consumers are satisfied with the product."

   If the material following a colon is dependent on the preceding clause, the first word after the colon is not capitalized.

   I present the following three reasons for changing: the volume of business does not justify the expense; we are short of people; the product is decreasing in popularity.

6. The names of associations, buildings, churches, hotels, streets, organizations, and clubs are capitalized.

   The Business Club, Merchandise Mart, Central Christian Church, Peabody Hotel, Seventh Avenue, Administrative Management Society, Chicago Chamber of Commerce

7. All proper names should be capitalized.

   Great Britain, John G. Hammitt, Mexico

8. Capitalize names derived from proper names.

   American, Chinese

   Do not, however, capitalize words derived from proper nouns that have developed a special meaning.

   pasteurized milk, china dishes, moroccan leather

9. Capitalize special names for regions and localities.

   North Central States, the Far East, the East Side, the Hoosier State

   Do not, however, capitalize adjectives derived from such names or localities used as directional parts of states and countries: far eastern lands, the southern United States, southern Illinois

10. Capitalize names of government boards, agencies, bureaus, departments, and commissions.

    Civil Service Commission, Social Security Board, Bureau of Navigation

11. Capitalize names of the deity, the Bible, holy days, and religious denominations.

    God, Easter, Yom Kippur, Genesis, Church of Christ

12. Capitalize the names of holidays.

    Memorial Day, Labor Day

13. Capitalize words used before numbers and numerals, with the exception of common words, such as *page*, *line*, and *verse*.

    We are on Flight 1683.
    He found the material on page 15.

14. Any title that signifies rank, honor, and respect and that immediately precedes an individual's name should be capitalized. Do not capitalize a title that follows a name.

    She asked President Harry G. Sanders to preside.
    Dr. Carter is president of the company.

15. Capitalize titles of high-ranking government officers when the title is used in place of the proper name in referring to a specific person.

    Our Senator invited us to visit him in Washington.
    The President will return to Washington soon.

16. Capitalize military and naval titles signifying rank.

    Captain Meyers, Lieutenant White, Lieutenant Commander Murphy

17. Capitalize the first words of list items when they are set apart from the text; do not capitalize the first words of list items in running text.

    The appendix includes the following parts:
    • Abbreviations
    • Capitalization

    Before preparing a presentation, the presenter should consider these areas: the intended audience, the age of the audience, the number of people who are anticipated, and the interests of the audience.

18. Personifications of abstractions are usually capitalized.

    In the autumn, Nature treats us to beautiful colors of gold, orange, and auburn.

19. Names of buildings, monuments, and public places are usually capitalized.

    Buckingham Palace

the Statue of Liberty
the Great Wall of China

20. Titles of laws, bills, and historical documents are capitalized when the full title is used.

    the Gettysburg Address
    the Constitution
    the Declaration of Independence
    the Civil Rights Act

21. Proper nouns referring to a supreme being and other deities are capitalized.

    the Messiah
    Buddha
    Jehovah
    the Prophet Mohammed
    Jesus

22. Proper names of clubs, societies, associations, and institutions are capitalized.

    Girl Scouts of America
    Better Business Bureau

23. Names of teams, leagues, divisions, and conferences are capitalized.

    the Dallas Cowboys
    the Olympic Games
    the Davis Cup
    the World Series

COLLECTIVE NOUNS

A collective noun is a word that is singular in form but represents a group of persons or things. For example, the following words are collective nouns: *committee*, *company*, *department*, *public*, *class*, and *board*. These rules determine the form of the verb to be used with a collective noun.

When the members of a group are thought of as one unit, the verb should be singular.

The *committee has* voted unanimously to begin the study.

When members of the group are thought of as separate units, the verb should be plural.

The *staff are* not in agreement on the decision that should be made.

If the sentence seems unclear or awkward, you may address the problem by inserting the word *members* after the collective noun and using a plural verb.

> The *staff members are* not in agreement on the decision that should be made.

LETTERS AND ENVELOPES

This section provides a review of letter and punctuation styles, placement of letter parts, envelope addresses, and letter insertion.

Letter and Punctuation Styles

Letters may be keyed in block or modified block style. Figure 1 shows block style with blocked paragraphs. (When using block letter style, the paragraphs must be flush left.) Notice in the block letter style that every line begins at the left margin. Figure 2 shows modified block style with indented paragraphs. (When using modified block style, the paragraphs may be blocked or indented.) Notice in the modified block style that the date line and the closing lines begin at the center point.

With open punctuation, no punctuation appears after the salutation or complimentary close. With mixed punctuation, a colon appears after the salutation and a comma appears after the complimentary close. Notice the open punctuation style in Figure 1 below and the mixed punctuation style in Figure 2 on page 394.

Placement of Letter Parts

- Date line—Key a double space below the last line of the letterhead.
- Inside address—Key up to 9 lines below the date, depending on the letter's length.

Tricounty Building Corporation
Attention Mr. Harold Chad
2395 36th Street
Ada, MI 49301

Ladies and Gentlemen

Thank you for your order for three executive chairs and three desks. The order will be shipped to you on March 5. I understand you are interested in working with one of our designers on furniture for a new building that you anticipate completing in October. As manager of the department, I will be calling your office in the next week to schedule an appointment with you.

We are pleased you are using our furniture, and I look forward to working with you on furniture designs for the new building.

Sincerely

Allen McGregory

Allen McGregory
Manager, Interior Design

lc

Figure 1   Block Letter Style, Open Punctuation

December 21, 2004

Mrs. Helena Andrews
Fetzer Foundation
2356 Old Kent Road
Kalamazoo, MI 49003

Dear Mrs. Andrews:

The National Management Association is sponsoring a community seminar on management techniques for not-for-profit organizations. Would you be interested in speaking at this seminar? I know your expertise would add greatly to the quality of the seminar.

I will be calling you within the next week to talk about this possibility.

Sincerely,

Eduardo Heminez

Eduardo Heminez
Vice President, Community Relations

lc

Figure 2   Modified Block Letter Style, Mixed Punctuation

- Attention line—Key a double space below the address and a double space above the salutation.
- Salutation—Key a double space below the address or a double space below the attention line.
- Subject or reference line—Key a double space below the salutation.
- Body—Key a double space below the salutation or a double space below the subject line.
- Second-page heading—Key approximately 1" from the top. Key the addressee's name, the page number, and the date in a three-line block at the left margin. Or use a one-line arrangement, and key the addressee's name at the left margin, center the page number, and position the date flush at the right margin.
- Complimentary close—Key a double space below the last line of the body.

- Name and title of writer—Key a quadruple space below the complimentary close.
- Reference initials—Key a double space below the name and title.
- Enclosure—Key a double space below the reference initials.
- Postscript—Key a double space below the reference initials or the last keyed line.
- Copy notation—Key a double space below the reference initials or the last keyed line. If a copy notation and a postscript are both used, the postscript is a double space below the copy notation.

Envelope Addressing

Software packages have envelope addressing tools that allow for correct placement of both the letter address and return address on an envelope. However, you should be aware of the correct placement in case you need to key an envelope address manually.

OCRs (optical character readers) used by the U.S. Postal Service are programmed to scan a specific area, so the address must be placed appropriately. With a No. 10 envelope (the standard size used in offices), the address is placed 2 1/2" from the top of the envelope and 4" from the left edge. The address is keyed in all capital letters with no punctuation. Two-letter state abbreviations should be used, along with the nine-digit ZIP Code.

Notations to the post office, such as REGISTERED, should be keyed in all capital letters below the stamp at least three lines above the address.

Notations such as HOLD FOR ARRIVAL, CONFIDENTIAL, and PLEASE FORWARD should be keyed in all capital letters a triple space below the return address and three spaces from the left edge of the envelope

Letter Insertion

Standard Size Envelopes (No. 10—9½" × 4⅛")

Fold in the following manner:

Small Envelope (No. 6¾—6½" × 3⅜")

Fold in the following manner:

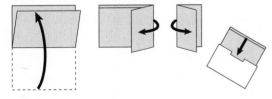

NUMBER USAGE

1. Spell out numbers 1 through 9; use figures for numbers 10 and above.

   We ordered nine coats and four dresses.
   About 60 letters were keyed.

2. If a sentence contains numbers above and below nine, either spell out all numbers or key all numbers in figures. If most of the numbers are below nine, use words. If most are above nine, use in figures.

   Please order 12 memo pads, 2 reams of paper, and 11 boxes of envelopes.

3. Numbers in the millions or higher may be expressed in the following manner in order to aid comprehension.

   3 billion (rather than 3,000,000,000)

4. Numbers are spelled out at the beginning of a sentence.

   Five hundred books were ordered.

5. If the numbers are large, rearrange the wording of the sentence so the number is not the first word of the sentence.

   We had a good year in 2003.
   Not: Two thousand and three was a good year.

6. Indefinite numbers and amounts are spelled out.

   A few hundred voters turned out for the local election.

7. All ordinals (first, second, third, and so on) that can be expressed in words are spelled out.

   The store's twenty-fifth anniversary was held this week.

8. When adjacent numbers are written in words or figures, use a comma to separate them.

   On car 33, 450 cartons are being shipped.

9. House or building numbers are written in figures. However, when the number one appears by itself, it is spelled out. Numbers one through nine in street names are spelled out. Numbers ten and above are written in figures. When figures are used for both the house number and the street name, use a hyphen preceded and followed by a space.

   101 Building
   One Main Place
   21301 Fifth Avenue
   122 - 33d Street

10. Ages are usually spelled out except when the age is stated exactly in years, months,

and days. When ages are presented in tabular form, they are written in figures.

She is eighteen years old.
He is 2 years, 10 months, and 18 days old.

Name	Age
Jones, Edward	19
King, Ruth	21

11. Use figures to express dates written in normal month-day-year order. Do not use *th*, *nd*, or *rd* following the date.

May 3, 2005
Not: May 8th, 2005

12. Fractions should be spelled out unless they are part of mixed numbers. Use a hyphen to separate the numerator and denominator of fractions written in words when the fraction is used as an adjective.

three-fourths   5¾

13. Amounts of money are usually expressed in figures. Indefinite money amounts are written in words.

$1,000
$3.27
several hundred dollars

14. In legal documents, numbers may be written in both words and figures.

One hundred thirty-four dollars ($134)

15. Express percentages in figures; spell out the word *percent*.

10 percent

16. To form the plural of figures, add *s*.

The 2000s will be challenging.

17. In times of day, use figures with *a.m.* and *p.m.*; spell out numbers with the word *o'clock*. In formal usage, spell out all times.

9 a.m.
10 p.m.
eight o'clock in the evening

OFTEN MISUSED WORDS AND PHRASES

1. *A* or *an* before the letter *h*

A is used before all consonant sounds, including *h* when sounded.

An is used before all vowel sounds, except long *u* and before words beginning with a silent *h*.

a historic event
an honor
a hotel

2. Awhile, a while

A while is a noun meaning a short time; *awhile* is an adverb meaning a short time.

We plan to go home in a while.
She wrote the poem awhile ago.

3. About, at

Use either *about* or *at*, not both.

He will leave about noon.
He will leave at noon.

4. Accept, except

To *accept* an assignment is to agree to undertake it.

To *except* someone from an activity is to excuse that person from the activity.

5. Accessible, assessable

If something is *accessible*, it can be reached or attained.

An object whose value can be estimated is *assessable*.

6. Advice, advise

Advice is a noun meaning a recommendation; *advise* is a verb meaning to counsel.

She did not follow my advice.
The counselor will advise you.

7. All, all of

Use *all*; *of* is redundant. If a pronoun follows *all*, reword the sentence.

Check all the items.
They are all going.

8. All right, alright

All right is the only correct usage; *alright* is incorrect.

9. Among, between

Among is used when referring to three or more persons or things; *between* is used when referring to two persons or things.

The inheritance was divided among the four relatives.
The choice is between you and me.

10. Appraise, apprise

Appraise means to set a value on; *apprise* means to inform.

The house was appraised at $300,000.
I was apprised of the situation by Jack.

11. Bad, badly

Bad is an adjective; *badly* is an adverb.

He feels bad about losing.
The football team played badly tonight.

12. Biannual, biennial

Biannual means occurring twice a year; *biennial* means occurring once every two years.

The Conseco Board meets biannually.
Tactical planning occurs biennially.

13. Bimonthly, semimonthly

Bimonthly means every two months; *semimonthly* means twice a month.

Our IAAP chapter meets bimonthly.
We put plant food on our flowers semimonthly.

14. Can, may

Can means to be able to; *may* means to have permission.

The diskette can be copied.
You may leave when you finish your work.

15. Capital, capitol

Capital is used unless you are referring to a building that houses a government.

Austin is the capital of Texas.
We toured the United States Capitol in Washington.

16. Cite, sight, site

Cite means to quote; *sight* means vision; *site* means location.

She cited the correct reference.
That is a pleasant sight.
They sighted a whale.
The site for the new building will be determined soon.

17. Complement, compliment

Complement means to complete, fill, or make perfect; *compliment* means to praise.

His thorough report complemented the presentation.
I complimented Jane on her new dress.

18. Council, counsel

Council is a noun meaning a governing body.

Counsel can be a noun or a verb. As a noun, *counsel* means a person with whom one consults about a matter. As a verb, *counsel* means to advise.

The council meets today.
Dr. Baker's counsel helped Chris overcome her fears.
Counsel was consulted on the case.
He is there to counsel you.

19. Desert, dessert

Desert, as a noun, means a barren or arid region with low rainfall; *desert*, as a verb, means to abandon.

Dessert is a confection often served at the end of a meal.

We traveled through the desert of Arizona.
He deserted his family.
We had ice cream for dessert.

20. Farther, further

Farther refers to distance; *further* refers to a greater degree or extent.

The store is a mile farther down the road.
We will discuss the matter further on Saturday.

21. Good, well

Good is an adjective. *Well* is typically used as an adverb but may be used as an adjective when referring to the state of a person's health.

I feel well. (adjective)
I will perform the task as well as I can. (adverb)
She feels good about her job.

22. Got, gotten

Got is preferred to *gotten* as the past participle of get. It is informal when used for *must* or *ought*.

I've got to get up at 6 a.m.
Improved: I must get up at 6 a.m.

23. In, into

In means located inside an area or limits; *into* means in the direction of the interior or toward something.

She went into the room.
She is sitting in the room.

24. Its, it's

    Its is the possessive form of *it*; *it's* is the contraction of *it is*.

    The family had its reunion yesterday.
    It's probably going to rain.

25. Percent, per cent, percentage

    Percent is always spelled as one word; *per cent* is incorrect.

    Percentage is also one word and is the preferred word when a number is not used.

    He received 56 percent of the vote.
    The percentage of votes he received is not known.

26. Principal, principle

    Principal as an adjective means *main*; as a noun, *principal* means the main person or a capital sum.

    Principle is a noun meaning a rule, guide, truth; it never refers to a person directly.

    The principal character in the play was John.
    The principals in the case are present.
    She held steadfast to her principles.

27. Respectfully, respectively

    Respectfully means in a courteous manner; *respectively* refers to being considered singly in a particular order.

    She respectfully asked for her grade report.
    The first, second, and third awards will go to Richard, Sarah, and Christine, respectively.

28. Stationary, stationery

    Stationary means stable or fixed; *stationery* is writing paper.

    The ladder seems stationary.
    Order three boxes of stationery.

29. That, which

    Both *which* and *that* are relative pronouns used to refer to places, animals, objects, ideas, and qualities. To improve clarity, many writers make this distinction: The word *which* is used to introduce nonessential information, and a comma is placed before the word. The word *that* is used to introduce a clause containing essential information, and no comma is used.

    In ten minutes, Harry solved the problem that I had been working on for hours. The presentation, which would have worked well for managers, had little appeal to the teachers.

30. Who, whom

    Who is used as the subject of a verb; *whom* is used as an object of a verb or as a preposition.

    Ken is the one who will be at the meeting.
    Ken is the one whom I will hire.
    It does not matter who did what to whom.

PARALLEL CONSTRUCTION

Parts of a sentence that are parallel in meaning should be parallel in structure. Writers should balance a word with a word, a phrase with a phrase, a clause with a clause, and a sentence with a sentence. Notice the examples given below.

Incorrect: The parents tried pleading, threats, and shouting.

Correct: The parents tried pleading, threatening, and shouting.

Incorrect: In undeveloped countries, don't drink the water; in developed countries, the air is dangerous to your health.

Correct: In undeveloped countries, don't drink the water; in developed countries, don't breathe the air.

PLURALS AND POSSESSIVES

1. When a compound word contains a noun and is hyphenated or made up of two or more words, the principal word takes an *s* to form the plural. If there is no principal word, add an *s* to the end of the compound word.

    commanders-in-chief
    runners-up
    write-ins

2. The plural of letters is formed by adding *s* or *'s*. The apostrophe is unnecessary except where confusion might result.

    CPAs
    dotting the i's

3. Singular nouns form the possessive by adding 's. If a singular noun has two or more syllables and if the last syllable is not accented and is preceded by a sibilant sound (s, x, z), add only the apostrophe for ease of pronunciation.

the person's computer   The boss's office
the department's rules   for goodness' sake

4. Plural nouns form the possessive by adding an apostrophe if the plural ends in *s* or by adding 's when the plural does not end in *s*.

ladies' wear
the children's bicycles

5. When a verb form ending in *ing* is used as a noun (gerund), a noun or pronoun before it takes the possessive form.

Mr. Ware's talking was not anticipated.

6. To form the possessive of a compound word, add the possessive ending to the last syllable.

Her mother-in-law's gift arrived.
The commander-in-chief's address was well received.

7. Joint possession is indicated by adding the possessive end to the last noun.

We are near Jan and Mike's store.
Drs. Edison and Martin's article was published this week.

8. In idiomatic construction, possessive form is often used.

a day's work   two weeks' vacation

9. The possessive form is used in cases where the noun modified is not expressed.

Take it to the plumber's. (shop)

10. The possessive form of personal pronouns is written without an apostrophe.

This book is hers.
She will deliver yours tomorrow.

PRONOUNS

1. A pronoun agrees with its antecedent (the word for which the pronoun stands) in number, gender, and person.

Roger wants to know if *his* book is at your house.

2. A plural pronoun is used when the antecedent consists of two nouns joined by *and*.

Mary and *Tomie* are bringing *their* stereo.

3. A singular pronoun is used when the antecedent consists of two singular nouns joined by *or* or *nor*. A plural pronoun is used when the antecedent consists of two plural nouns joined by *or* or *nor*.

Neither *Elizabeth* nor *Johann* wants to do *her* part.
Either the *men* or the *women* will do *their* share.

4. Do not confuse certain possessive pronouns with contractions that sound alike.

Possessive	*Contraction*
its	it's (it is)
their	they're (they are)
theirs	there's (there is)
your	you're (you are)
whose	who's (who is)

As a test for the use of a possessive pronoun or a contraction, try to substitute *it is, they are, it has, there has, there is,* or *you are.* Use the corresponding possessive form if the substitution does not make sense.

Your wording is correct.
You're wording that sentence incorrectly.
Whose book is it?
Who's the owner of the laptop?

5. Use *who* and *that* when referring to persons. *Who* refers to an individual person or group; *that* refers to a class or type.

He is the boy *who* does well in history.
She is the type of *person that we* like to employ.

6. Use *which* and *that* when referring to places, objects, and animals.

The card *that I* sent you was mailed last week.
The fox, *which* is very sly, caught the skunk.

7. A pronoun in the objective case functions as a direct object, an indirect object, or an object of a preposition. Objective pronouns include *me, you, him, her, it, us, them, whom,* and *whomever*.

The movie was an emotional experience for *her* and *me*. (The pronouns *her* and *me* are in the objective case since they function as the object of a preposition.)

8. A linking verb connects a subject to a word that renames it. Linking verbs indicate a

state of being (*am, is, are, was, were*), related to the senses, or indicate a condition. A pronoun following a linking verb renames the subject, so it must be in the subjective case. Subjective pronouns include *I, you, she, he, it, we, they, who,* and *whoever.*

It is *I* who will attend the play.

9. The pronouns *who* and *whoever* are in the subjective case and are used as the subject of a sentence or clause.

Whoever is in charge will be required to stay late.

10. At the beginning of questions, use *who* if the question is about the subject and *whom* if the question is about the object.

Who is going to the party?
Whom can we expect to give the welcoming address?

11. Reflexive pronouns reflect back to the antecedent. Reflexive pronouns include *myself, herself, himself, themselves,* and other *self* or *selves* words.

I intend to do the painting *myself.*

PROOFREADERS' MARKS

Symbol	Meaning	Marked Copy	Corrected Copy
∧	Insert	two people or three	two or three people
ℒ	Delete	the man and the woman	the man
⊏	Move left	human relations	human relations
#	Add space	follow these	follow these
/	Lowercase letter	in the Fall on 2002	in the fall on 2002
⌒	Close up space	sum mer	summer
∼	Transpose	when is it	when it is
⊐	Move right	skills for living	skills for living
∨́	Insert apostrophe	Macs book	Mac's book
∨̋	Insert quotation marks	She said, No.	She said, "No."
⊔	Move down	falle	fallen
⊓	Move up	straigh t	straight
¶	Paragraph	¶ The first and third page	The first and third page
No ¶	No new paragraph	No ¶ The first and third page	The first and third page
◯ SP	Spell out	Dr. SP	Doctor
stet or	Let it stand; ignore correction	most efficient worker	most efficient worker
___	Underline or italics	Business World	Business World
⊙	Insert period	the last word	the last word.

PUNCTUATION

Correct punctuation is based on accepted rules and principles rather than on the whims of the writer. Punctuation is also important if the reader is to correctly interpret the writer's thoughts. The summary of rules given provided here will be helpful in using correct punctuation.

The Period

The period indicates a full stop and is used in the following ways:

1. At the end of a complete declarative or imperative sentence.

2. After abbreviations and after a initials that represent a word.

   acct.   etc.   Ph.D.
   U.S.   p.m.
   Jr.   i.e.   pp.

   However, some abbreviations made up of several initial letters do not require periods.

   FDIC (Federal Deposit Insurance Corporation)
   FEPC (Fair Employment Practices Committee)
   AAA (American Automobile Association)
   YWCA (Young Women's Christian Association)

3. Between dollars and cents. A period and cipher are not required when an amount in even dollars is expressed in figures.

   $42.65 $1.47 $25

4. To indicate a decimal.

   3.5 bushels   12.65 percent   6.25 feet

The Comma

Use the comma:

1. To separate coordinate clauses that are connected by conjunctions (such as *and, but, or, for, neither, nor*) unless the clauses are short and closely connected.

   We have a supply on hand, but I think we should order an additional quantity.
   She had to work late, for the auditors were examining the books.

2. To set off a subordinate clause that precedes the main clause.

   Assuming no changes will be needed, I suggest you proceed with your instructions.

3. After an introductory phrase containing a verb form. If an introductory phrase does not contain a verb, it usually is not followed by a comma.

   To finish his work, he remained at the office after hours.
   After planning the program, she proceeded to put it into effect.
   After much deliberation, the plan was revoked.
   Because of the vacation period we have been extremely busy.

4. To set off a nonrestrictive clause.

   Our group, which had never lost a debate, won the grand prize.

5. To set off a nonrestrictive phrase.

   The beacon, rising proudly toward the sky, guided the pilots safely home.

6. To separate from the rest of the sentence a word or group of words that breaks the continuity of a sentence.

   The administrative professional, even though his work was completed, was always willing to help others.

7. To separate parenthetical expressions from the rest of the sentence.

   We have, as you know, two people who can handle the reorganization.

8. To set off names used in direct address or to set off explanatory phrases or clauses.

   I think you, Mr. Bennett, will agree with the statement.
   Ms. Linda Tom, our vice president, will be in your city soon.

9. To separate from the rest of the sentence expressions that, without punctuation, might be interpreted incorrectly.

   Misleading: Ever since we have filed our reports monthly.
   Better: Ever since, we have filed our reports monthly.

10. To separate words or groups of words when they are used in a series of three or more.

    Most executives agree that dependability, trustworthiness, ambition, and judgment are required of workers.

11. To set off introductory words.

> For example, the musical was not as lyrical as the last one I saw.
> Thus, both the man and the boy felt a degree of discrimination.

12. To separate coordinate adjectives. Coordinate adjectives are two or more adjectives that equally modify a noun.

> The large, insensitive audience laughed loudly at the mistake.

13. To set off short quotations from the rest of the sentence.

> He said, "I shall be there."
> "The committees have agreed," he said, "to work together on the project."

14. To separate the name of a city from the name of a state.

> Our southern branch is located in Atlanta, Georgia.

15. To separate abbreviations of titles from the name.

> William R. Warner, Jr.
> Ramona Sanchez, Ph.D.

16. To set off conjunctive adverbs such as *however* and *therefore*.

> I, however, do not agree with the statement.
> According to the rule, therefore, we must not penalize the student for this infraction.

17. To separate the date from the year. Within a sentence, use a comma on both sides of the year in a full date.

> The anniversary party was planned for June 18, 2005.
> He plans to attend the management seminar scheduled for April 15, 2004, at the Hill Hotel.

18. Do not use a comma in numbers in an address even when there are four are more digits.

> The house number was 3100 Edmonds Drive.

19. Do not use a comma in a date that contains the month with only a day or the month with only a year.

> The accident occurred on June 10.
> The major event for June 2003 was the ethics seminar.

The Semicolon

The semicolon should be used in the following instances:

1. Between independent clauses when either of the clauses contains a comma.

> He was outstanding in his knowledge of technology, including telecommunications and computers; but he was lacking in many desirable personal qualities.

2. Between compound sentences when the conjunction is omitted.

> All individuals in the group enjoyed the meal; many of the group did not enjoy the movie.

3. To precede expressions (such as *namely, for example* or *e.g., that is* or *i.e.*) used to introduce a clause.

> We selected the machine for two reasons; namely, it is reasonably priced and it has the necessary features.
> There are several reasons for changing the routine of handling mail; i.e., to reduce postage, to conserve time, and to place responsibility.

4. In a series of well-defined units when special emphasis is desired.

> *Emphatic:* Prudent administrative professionals consider the future; they use their talents to successfully attain their desired goals.
> *Less emphatic:* Prudent administrative professionals consider the future and use their talents to successfully attain their desired goals.

The Colon

The colon is recommended in the following instances:

1. After the salutation in a business letter except when open punctuation is used.

> Ladies and Gentlemen:
> Dear Ms. Carroll:

2. Following introductory expressions (such as *the following, thus, as follows,* and other expressions) that precede enumerations.

> Please send the following by parcel post: books, magazines, newspapers.
> Officers were elected as follows: president, Helen Edwards; vice president, Mark Turnball; treasurer, Ralph Moline.

3. To separate hours and minutes when indicating time.

2:10 p.m.   4:45 p.m.   12:15 a.m.

4. To introduce a quotation of more than one sentence.

This quote from Theodore Roosevelt is a favorite of mine: "No man needs sympathy because he has to work. Far and away the best prize that life offers is the chance to work hard."

5. To introduce a list after phrases such as *the following*.

His holiday gifts included the following: a cruise, a computer, a new suit, and ten books.

The Question Mark

The question mark should be used in the following instances:

1. After a direct question.

When do you expect to arrive in Philadelphia?
An exception to the foregoing rule is a sentence phrased in the form of a question when it is actually a courteous request.
Will you please send us an up-to-date statement of our account.

2. After each question in a series of questions within a sentence.

What is your opinion of the Orlando division? the Phoenix division? the Boston division?

Exclamation Point

The exclamation point is used to express command, strong feeling, emotion, or exclamation.

Don't waste supplies!
It can't be done!
Stop!

The Dash

The dash is used in the following instances:

1. To indicate an omission of letters or figures.

Dear Mr. —   The dollar amounts are —

2. To indicate a definite stop or as emphasis.

This book is not a revision of an old book—it is a totally new book.

3. To separate parenthetical expressions when unusual emphasis is desired.

These sales arguments—and every one of them is important—should result in getting the order.

4. Around appositives if the use of commas might cause confusion.

Concern over terrorism—biological warfare, attacks on cities, and attacks on government buildings and personnel—is demanding much media attention.

The Apostrophe

The apostrophe should be used in the following instances:

1. To indicate possession.

the boy's coat
the ladies' dresses
the girl's book

To the possessive singular, add *'s* to the noun.

man's work
bird's wing
hostess's plans

An exception to this rule is made when the word following the possessive begins with an *s* sound.

for goodness' sake   for conscience' sakes

To form the possessive of a plural noun ending in an *s* or *z* sound, add only the apostrophe (') to the plural noun.

workers' rights   hostesses' duties

If the plural noun does not end in an *s* or *z* sound, add *'s* to the plural noun.

women's clothes   alumni's donations

Proper names that end in an *s* sound form the possessive singular by adding *'s*.

Williams's house   Fox's automobile

Proper names ending in *s* form the possessive plural by adding the apostrophe only.

The Walters' property faces the Jones' swimming pool.

2. To indicate the omission of a letter or letters in a contraction.

it's (it is)
you're (you are)
we'll (we will, we shall)

3. To indicate the plurals of uncapitalized letters and uncapitalized abbreviations.

Don't forget to dot your i's and cross your t's.
The girls wore their Christmas pj's.

Quotation Marks

The following rules should be applied to the use of quotation marks:

1. When a quotation mark is used with a comma or a period, the comma or period is inside the quotation mark.

   She said, "I plan to complete my program in college before seeking a position."

2. When a quotation mark is used with a semicolon or a colon, the semicolon or colon is placed outside the quotation mark.

   The treasurer said, "I plan to go by train"; others in the group stated they would go by plane.

3. When more than one paragraph of quoted material is used, quotation marks should appear at the beginning of each paragraph and at the end of the last paragraph.

4. Quotation marks are used in the following instances:

   Before and after direct quotations.

   The author states, "Too frequent use of certain words weakens the appeal."

   To indicate the title of a published article.

   Have you read the article "Anger in the Workplace"?

   To indicate a quotation within a quotation, use single quotation marks.

   The instructor said, "Read the chapter 'The Art of Listening' to prepare for tomorrow's discussion."

Omission Marks or Ellipses

Ellipses marks (. . .) are frequently used to denote the omission of letters or words in quoted material. If the material omitted ends in a period, four omission marks are used (. . . .). If the material omitted does not end in a period, three omission marks are used (. . .).

   He quoted the proverb, "A soft answer turneth away wrath, but. . . ."

She quoted Plato, "Nothing is more unworthy of a wise man . . . than to have allowed more time for trifling and useless things than they deserved."

Parentheses

Although parentheses are frequently used as a catchall in writing, they are correctly used in the following instances:

1. When amounts expressed in words are followed by figures.

   He agreed to pay twenty-five dollars ($25) as soon as possible.

2. Around words that are used as parenthetical expressions.

   Our personnel costs (including benefits) are much too high.

3. To indicate technical references.

   Sodium chloride (NaCl) is the chemical name for common table salt.

4. When enumerations are included in narrative form.

   The reasons for his resignation were three: (1) advanced age, (2) failing health, and (3) a desire to travel.

REPORT FORMAT

Title Page

Include the title of the report, the name and title of the person writing the report, and the date of the report. Center all items on the page. Key the title of the report in all caps approximately one-third from the top of the page. Space down 2–2½ inches, and key the name and title of the person writing the report. Space down another 2–2½ additional inches and key the date.

Table of Contents

Center *Table of Contents* approximately 2 inches from the top of the page. Key main headings and subheadings in order, using leaders (periods every other space) to the page number. Use a combination of double and single spacing. Center the page number 1 inch from the bottom of the page using lowercase Roman numerals.

Body of the Report

Center the title of the report 1½–2 inches from the top of the page. Set the left margin for 1½ inches if leftbound, 1 inch if unbound; use 1 inch top and bottom margins. Number the first page of the body 1 inch from the bottom at the center, or do not number at all. Number all other pages of the report using Arabic numerals keyed 1 inch from the top of the page at the right margin or centered 1 inch from the bottom. The report may be double or single spaced.

Footnotes/Endnotes

Follow an acceptable style for formatting endnotes/footnotes.

Endnote (Chicago Style)

The endnote style requires a superscript number when the reference is noted in the text. However, no information about the work is given until the end of the paper in a section referred to as "Works Cited."

Footnote (Chicago Style)

At the point where the reference is mentioned, a superscript number is placed in the text and a footnote is placed on the same page as the superscript number.

> Your body sends messages to your mind to meet its needs. One of the most important signals the body sends is that of hunger.[1]

APA and MLA Documentation Style

Both the APA (American Psychological Association) and the MLA (Modern Language Association) format style use internal citations. These citations are placed in the report itself within parentheses. The details of the source are then given in a section titled "Works Cited" or "References."

In the report itself, the documentation is given in the following ways:

> APA Style: According to Chopra (2001), the essence of flexibility is the willingness to let go.
> MLA Style: Deepak Chopra suggests that the essence of flexibility is the willingness to let go (15).

Note: When the authority is first introduced, the first name and the surname are used. In subsequent citations by the same authority, only the surname is used.

References/Works Cited Section

1. At the end of the report (APA documentation style), a section entitled "References" gives information on all sources quoted. The format of the section is as follows:

   Chopra, Deepak. (2001). Grow Younger, Live Longer. New York: Harmony Books.

2. At the end of the report (MLA documentation style), a section entitled "Works Cited" gives information on all sources quoted. The format of the section is as follows:

   Chopra, Deepak. Grow Younger, Live Longer. New York: Harmony Books, 2001.

3. At the end of the report (Chicago style) with footnotes or endnotes, a section entitled "Works Cited" gives information on all sources quoted. The format of the section is as follows:

   Chopra, Deepak. Grow Younger, Live Longer. New York: Harmony Books, 2001.

Tables, Charts, and Graphs

Number the tables, charts, and graphs consecutively throughout a report. Identify all tables, charts, and graphs with the word *Figure* followed by the number. Give each graphic a title.

SPELLING RULES

1. Put *i* before *e* except after *c* or when sounded like *a* as in *neighbor* or *weigh*. Exceptions: *either, neither, seize, weird, leisure, financier, conscience*

---

[1] Deepak Chopra, *Grow Younger, Live Longer* (New York: Harmony Books, 2001), 77.

2. When a one-syllable word ends in a single consonant and when that final consonant is preceded by a single vowel, double the final consonant before a suffix that begins with a vowel or the suffix *y*.

run	running
drop	dropped
bag	baggage
skin	skinny

3. When a word of more than one syllable ends in a single consonant, when that final consonant is preceded by a single vowel, and when the word is accented on the last syllable, double the final consonant before a suffix that begins with a vowel.

begin	beginning
concur	concurrent

When the accent does not fall on the last syllable, do not double the final consonant before a suffix that begins with a vowel.

travel	traveler
differ	differing

4. When the final consonant in a word of one or more syllables is preceded by another consonant or by two vowels, do not double the final consonant before any suffix.

look	looked
deceit	deceitful
act	acting
warm	warmly

5. When a words ends in a silent *e*, generally drop the *e* before a suffix that begins with a vowel.

guide	guidance
use	usable

6. When a word ends in a silent *e*, generally retain the *e* before a suffix that begins with a consonant unless another vowel precedes the final *e*.

hate	hateful
due	duly
excite	excitement
argue	argument

7. When a word ends in *ie*, drop the *e* and change the *i* to *y* before adding *ing*.

lie	lying
die	dying

8. When a word ends *ce* or *ge*, generally retain the final *e* before the suffixes *able* and *ous* but drop the final *e* before the suffixes *ible* and *ing*.

manage	manageable
force	forcible

9. When a word ends in *c*, insert a *k* before adding a suffix beginning with *e*, *i*, or *y*.

picnic	picnicking

10. When a word ends in *y* preceded by a consonant, generally change the *y* to *i* before a suffix except one beginning with *i*.

modify	modifying	modifier
lonely	lonelier	

11. When a word ends in *o* preceded by a vowel, form the plural by adding *s*. When a word ends in *o* preceded by a consonant, generally form the plural by adding *es*.

folio	folios
potato	potatoes

12. When a word ends in *y* preceded by a vowel, form the plural by adding *s*. When a word ends in *y* preceded by a consonant, change the *y* to *i* and add *es* to form the plural.

attorney	attorneys
lady	ladies

SUBJECT AND VERB AGREEMENT

This section presents a review of basic rules concerning subject-verb agreement.

1. When the subject consists of two singular nouns and/or pronouns connected by *or*, *either . . . or*, *neither . . . nor*, or *not only . . . but also*, a singular verb is required.

   Jane or *Bob has* the letter.
   Either *Ruth or Marge plans* to attend.
   Not only a *book* but also *paper is* needed.

2. When the subject consists of two plural nouns and/or pronouns connected by *or*; *either . . . or*, *neither . . . nor*; or *not only . . . but also*, a plural verb is required.

   Neither the *managers* nor the *administrative assistants have* access to that information.

3. When the subject is made up of both singular and plural nouns and/or pronouns connected by *or, either . . . or, neither . . . nor,* or *not only . . . but also,* the verb agrees with the noun or pronoun closest to the verb.

Either *Ms. Rogers* or the *assistants have* access to that information.
Neither the *men* nor *Jo* is working.

4. Disregard intervening phrases and clauses when establishing agreement between subject and verb.

One of the men *wants* to go to the convention.
The *request* for new computers *is* on Mr. Woo's desk.

5. The words *each, every, either, neither, one, another,* and *much* are singular. When they are used as subjects or as adjectives modifying subjects, a singular verb is required.

Each person *is* deserving of the award.
Neither boy *rides* the bicycle well.

6. The following pronouns are always singular and require a singular verb:

anybody	everybody	nobody	somebody
anyone	everyone	no one	someone
anything	everything	nothing	something

Everyone plans to attend the meeting.
Anyone is welcome at the concert.

7. *Both, few, many, others,* and *several* are always plural. When they are used as subjects or adjectives modifying subjects, a plural verb is required.

Several members *were* asked to make presentations.
Both women *are* going to apply.

8. *All, none, any, some, more,* and *most* may be singular or plural, depending on the noun to which they refer.

Some of the supplies *are* missing.
Some of that paper *is* needed.

9. *The number* has a singular meaning and requires a singular verb; *a number* has a plural meaning and requires a plural verb.

A number of people *are* planning to attend.
The number of requests *is* surprising.

10. Geographic locations are considered singular and used with a singular verb when referring to one location. When reference is made to separate islands, the plural form is used with a plural verb.

The Hawaiian Islands has been my vacation spot for years.
The Caribbean Islands have distinct cultures.

WORD DIVISION

1. Divide words between syllables.
   moun-tain
   base-ment

2. Do not divide words of five or fewer letters (preferably six or fewer).
   apple
   among
   finger

3. Do not divide one-syllable words.
   helped
   eighth

4. If a single-letter syllable falls within a word, divide the word after the single-letter syllable.
   regu-late
   sepa-rate

5. If two single-letter syllables occur together within a word, divide between the single-letter syllables.
   continu-ation
   radi-ator

6. Divide between double consonants that appear within a word. Also, when the final consonant of a base word is doubled to add a suffix, divide between the double consonants.
   neces-sary
   commit-ted

7. When a base word ends in a double consonant, divide between the base word and the suffix.
   tell-ing
   careless-ness

8. Divide hyphenated compound words at existing hyphens only.
   two-thirds
   self-control

9. Avoid dividing a date, a personal name, or an address. If it is absolutely necessary, maximize readability by doing the following:

Divide a date between the day and the year.
Divide a personal name between the first name and surname.
Divide an address between the city and state.

10. Do not divide figures, abbreviations, and symbols.

$20,000
YMCA
#109

11. Do not divide contractions.

he'll
wouldn't

12. Divide no more than three or four words on a page.

13. Avoid dividing words at the end of the first and last lines of a paragraph.

14. Do not divide the last word on a page.

15. Do not divide a word when a one-letter syllable is the first syllable. Do not divide a word when the last syllable contains only two letters.

around (not a-round)
lately (not late-ly)

INDEX

Flextime, 14
Flight classifications, 273–274, 290
  for international travel, 278
Floppy disks, 91
Focus groups, 236
Folding, automatic, 334
Follow-up
  after interviews, 363–364
  after meetings, 307–308
Follow-up letters, 363
Food, ordering for meetings, 306
Footnotes, in a report, 237
Fortune magazine, 351
Free software, 98
Frequent flyer programs, 281
Frequently called numbers, list of, 124
Friendliness, on the telephone, 124
Friends, talking to, 200
Fry, William, 196
Fujiwara, Bernice, 2–5
  case solution for, 53
Functional resumes, 353–354
  advantages and disadvantages of, 356
Funding, for travel, 285–286
Furniture. *See also* Equipment
  home-office, 71
  in the workplace, 179
Future Shock (Toffler), 100

G

Gender bias, 200
  on the telephone, 124
Gender differences, communication and, 42
Gender discrimination, 172
Gender issues, 36–37, 48
Gender roles, 36
  in the workplace, 10
General Electric, statement of community commitment
  by, 376
General Motors Corporation, 13
Generation X, 37
Genome projects, 83
Gentner Corporation, 297
Geographic filing, 138–139
Gifts, business, 278, 290
Gigabytes (GB), 89
Girth, 323
Global "chat groups," 36
Global economy, travel and, 272
Global express guaranteed (GXG) mail, 325
Global express mail (EMS), 325
Globalization, economy and, 11
Global priority mail (GPM), 325
Global world, 32
Goals, attributes of, 204–205
Goal setting, 204–205
GoldMine, 209
Government names, indexing, 151–154
Government officials, greeting, 252
Government publications, on records management, 145
Grammar, correct, 224–225
Grammar software packages, 230–231

Greatest Generation, The (Brokaw), 37
Greeting, of international visitors, 250–251
Griggs, Barbara D., 216–219
  case solution for, 267
Grooming, 21. *See also* Attire
  for interviews, 360
Ground transportation, 274–275, 290
Group rewards, 186
Growing Up Digital (Tapscott), 37
Gunning Fog Index, 229

H

Hard copy, 92
Health. *See also* Safety
  ergonomics and, 86–87
  in the work environment, 176–178
Health benefits, for teleworkers, 72
Health precautions, for international travel, 279–280
Herman Miller Corporation, 176
Heterogeneous groups, 301
High-end protein analyzers, 83
High-volume copiers, 333
Home-based work. *See* Telework
Home workspace, 70–72
Homogeneous groups, 301
Honesty, 20
  employee, 182
  in the workplace, 179
Hotel floor plan, 314
Hotel reservations, during international travel, 280
Hotels, dinner meetings at, 306
Housecleaning needs, 69
Humor consultants, 196
Hygiene, 21. *See also* Attire; Grooming

I

IBM Corporation, 13, 84
Identical names, indexing, 151
Illustrations, in a report, 237
Important records, 146
Incoming calls, techniques for, 124–126
Incoming mail, 329–332
Indexing. *See also* Cross-referencing
  as a manual filing procedure, 140
  rules for, 141–142, 147–155, 157
Indian visitors, greeting, 250
Indirect approach, in letter writing, 232
Individual evaluation, 384
Individual Retirement Accounts (IRAs), 72
Individuals
  labeling of, 185
  rewarding, 186
Individual training, 381–382
Ineffective communication, 202
Ineffective listeners, 40–41
Inference, 41–42
InfoPro, 141
InfoPro Online, 142
Information, confidentiality of, 20
Information Age, 7–14
  stress and, 192

U

V

Visionary organizations, 179
Vision building, by leaders, 374–375
Visitor interruptions, 208
Visitors, improper handling of, 202–203. *See also* Workplace callers
Visual aids, for presentations, 258
Visualization, 288
Vital records, 146, 157
Voice mail, 129
Voice over Internet Protocol (VoIP), 117
Voice quality, 46–47
Voice recognition systems, 88
Voice technology, 119–120, 128

W

"Walking the walk," 375
Wavelet compression technology, 299
Web browser, 94–95
Web search engines, 95
Website service companies, 299
Web terminology, 94
Wide area networks (WANs), 94
Windows 2002, 97
Wireless local loop (WLL) technology, 110–112, 128
Women. *See also* Gender issues; Sexual harassment
   gender roles of, 36
   as teleworkers, 62
   in the workforce, 8–9, 25
Word barriers, 42
Words
   positive and negative, 226
   study of, 41
Work area, organizing, 207
Work computers, personal use of, 99
Work conditions, distressing, 194
Work environment. *See also* Workplace
   changes in, 11–14
   ergonomically sound, 178–179
   personal creativity in, 255
   safe and healthy, 176–178
Workers. *See also* Teleworkers
   advantages of telework to, 59–60
   disadvantages of telework to, 60–61
   senior, 9
   women, 8–9
Workforce
   twenty-first century, 25
   women in, 8–9
Work-group evaluation, 385
Work/life balance, 69–70
Work overload, stress and, 193
Work periods, 380
Workplace. *See also* Work environment
   anger and violence in, 194–195
   gender roles in, 10
   sexual harassment in, 174

Workplace callers
   difficult, 249–250
   ensuring a pleasant wait for, 248
   greeting, 246–247
   international, 250–251
   making introductions for, 248–249
   purpose of, 247
   receiving, 245–252, 263
   supervisor expectations for, 246
Workplace politics, awareness of, 181
Workplace safety, for teleworkers, 72. *See also* Safety
Work/play balance, 195–196
Workspace, home, 70–72
Workstation Checklist, 179
Workstation computers, 84
Workweek, 14, 25
WorldCom, 297
World Wide Web (Web), 82, 94, 101
   ethics of, 94–95
   making travel arrangements on, 282–284
   as a source of job information, 349–350
WORM technology, 144
"W" questions, 224
Writing, principles of, 223. *See also* Business writing; Written communication
Written communication, 220–240
   collaborative writing, 237–238
   the correspondence plan, 231
   effective correspondence, 222–229
   ethical and legal considerations for, 238–239
   international correspondence, 238
   letters, 231–235
   reports, 235–237
   types of written messages, 220–222
Written presentations, 257–258, 263

X

Xerox Business Systems, 326
Xerox Corporation, 13

Y

You approach, in letter writing, 233, 234–235, 240

Z

ZDNet Software Library, 209
ZIP Codes, 328
Zip disks, 90
Zip drives, 89, 90
Zoot, 209

SOUTHWEST
COOKING

BEEKMAN HOUSE

Louis Weber, C.E.O.
Publications International, Ltd.
7373 North Cicero Avenue
Lincolnwood, Illinois 60646

Permission is never granted for commercial purposes.

ISBN 0-517-68757-7

Library of Congress Catalog Card Number: 90-60185

This edition published by:
Beekman House
Distributed by Crown Publishers, Inc.
225 Park Avenue South
New York, NY 10003

Recipe Development: Jan Nix

Photography and Food Styling: Burke/Triolo Studio

Pictured on front cover: Arizona Cheese Crisp (page 17).

Pictured on back cover from top to bottom: Green Enchiladas with Chicken (page 71); Biscochitos (page 92) and New Mexican Hot Chocolate (page 92); Salsa Fresca (page 6), Guacamole (page 14) and Tomatillo Salsa (page 15).

Printed in Yugoslavia.

h g f e d c b a

SOUTHWEST COOKING

Introduction

Earthy. Zesty. Festive and full-flavored. That's Southwestern cooking. Its origins are Spanish, Mexican and Native Indian. Later, cowboy, pioneer and settler cooking broadened its base. Today, contemporary cooks use Southwestern inspirations to focus on lighter fare. The blend is a kaleidoscopic and mouth-watering cuisine for you to enjoy at your own table. To help you get started, here is a glossary of ingredients that might be unfamiliar to you.

GLOSSARY OF INGREDIENTS

Herbs & Spices

Chili Powder. Dried chilies are the main ingredients in this blend of ground spices commonly associated with "a bowl of red." Depending on the chilies used, the powder varies in color, from reddish to dark brown, and in flavor, from spicy and slightly sweet to very peppery.

Cilantro. Also known as coriander or Chinese parsley, cilantro looks like green broadleaf parsley, but the flavor is pungent, aromatic and peppery. Coarsely chop cilantro leaves and tender stem tips to add a unique flavor or use whole sprigs as a garnish. To store, stand in a jar of water, loosely cover with a plastic bag and refrigerate.

Coriander seeds. Dried, roasted seeds of the fresh cilantro plant are packaged whole or ground. Although the same plant produces cilantro and coriander, the coriander seed has a warmer, less pungent flavor than the cilantro leaf and is therefore not a substitute for the fresh herb.

Cumin. Sold as whole seeds or ground. Similar in taste to caraway seeds, cumin has a warm, slightly bitter flavor. It is commonly used in chili powder blends.

Oregano. Available fresh, dried or ground. Also called wild marjoram, this is a strong aromatic herb with a pleasant bitter undertone.

Fruits & Vegetables

Chayote *(vegetable pear).* A tropical summer squash, the female chayote has a pale green skin and corrugated surface. The male chayote, more commonly found in home gardens, is often covered with spines. If the chayote skin is not tough or spiny, there's no need to peel before cooking. When cooked, the seed is edible.

Jicama. This root vegetable, which looks like a giant-size turnip with brown skin, can be eaten raw or cooked. Cut off the peel with a knife to reach the crisp, white, slightly sweet flesh. Chinese cooks often use jicama as a substitute for water chestnuts.

Nopales. These leaves of the prickly pear cactus taste similar to pickled green beans. Look for ready-to-eat, diced nopales in jars or cans in the Mexican food section of well-stocked markets.

Tomatillos. Similar in appearance to green cherry tomatoes enclosed in a papery husk, tomatillos have a mild acidic flavor. Remove husks and wash the sticky-skinned fruit before using. Both fresh and canned tomatillos are sold in well-stocked markets.

Chilies.

Chilies are the fiery soul of Southwestern cooking. While dozens of varieties are grown, the chilies necessary for the recipes in this book are limited to those readily available in well-stocked markets. **A note of caution:** Chilies contain volatile oils which may burn your skin and make your eyes smart. When handling them, it is best to wear rubber gloves and avoid touching your face or eyes. Thoroughly wash any skin that comes into contact with chili oil.

Dried red chilies. These are more important in Southwestern cooking than fresh ones because they are less seasonal. Look for cellophane bags of the 6- to 7-inch whole dried red New Mexico or California chilies or the shorter Ancho chilies in a Mexican grocery store or in the Mexican products section of a well-stocked market. Dried chilies are simmered or soaked in hot water before using. These chilies are also sold ground in small cellophane bags if you prefer to use pure ground chili rather than a blended chili powder.

Green chilies. These 6- to 7-inch mild chilies are widely available canned, either whole or diced. Or you can buy fresh Anaheim or California green chilies and prepare them for cooking in the following way: Cut a small slit near the stem end of each chili. Place in a shallow-rimmed pan, 2 inches below preheated broiler, and broil, turning frequently, until blistered and lightly charred. Immediately place chilies in a plastic bag; seal. Let sweat until cool enough to handle. Peel off the skins, then remove and discard the stems, seeds and veins. Chilies may be refrigerated for up to 3 days or frozen.

Jalapeño peppers and Serrano chilies. These small green garnish chilies can be used interchangeably to give food a fiery punch. Although available canned or pickled, they are generally used fresh with the stems, seeds and membranes removed to make them less hot.

Appetizers & Snacks

SALSA FRESCA

This chunky sauce has a fresh flavor that makes a perfect accompaniment to almost every kind of Southwest food.

4 medium tomatoes
1 small onion, finely chopped
2 to 3 fresh jalapeño peppers or serrano chilies, stemmed, seeded and minced
¼ cup chopped cilantro
1 small clove garlic, minced
2 tablespoons lime juice
Salt
Ground black pepper

Cut tomatoes in half; remove seeds. Coarsely chop tomatoes. Combine tomatoes, onion, jalapeño peppers, cilantro, garlic and lime juice in medium bowl. Add salt and black pepper to taste. Cover and refrigerate 1 hour or up to 3 days for flavors to blend.

Makes about 2½ cups

Clockwise from left: Salsa Fresca, Guacamole (page 14) and Tomatillo Salsa (page 15)

Spanish Potato Omelet

SPANISH POTATO OMELET

Cut this cook-ahead omelet into thin wedges to serve as an appetizer. It is sturdy enough to pick up with your fingers and traditionally is served at room temperature.

¼ cup olive oil
¼ cup vegetable oil
1 pound thin-skinned red or white potatoes, cut into ⅛-inch slices
½ teaspoon salt, divided
1 small onion, cut in half lengthwise, thinly sliced crosswise
¼ cup chopped green bell pepper
¼ cup chopped red bell pepper
3 eggs

Heat oils in large skillet over medium-high heat. Add potatoes to hot oil. Turn with spatula several times to coat all slices with oil. Sprinkle with ¼ teaspoon of the salt. Cook 6 to 9 minutes or until potatoes become translucent, turning occasionally. Add onion and peppers. Reduce heat to medium. Cook 10 minutes or until potatoes are tender, turning occasionally. Drain mixture in colander placed in large bowl; reserve oil. Let potato mixture stand until cool. Beat eggs with the remaining ¼ teaspoon salt in large bowl. Gently stir in potato mixture; lightly press into bowl until mixture is covered with eggs. Let stand 15 minutes.

Heat 2 teaspoons of the reserved oil in 6-inch nonstick skillet over medium-high heat. Spread potato mixture in pan to form a solid layer. Cook until egg on bottom and side of pan has set but top still looks moist. Cover pan with plate. Flip omelet onto plate, then slide omelet back into pan. Continue to cook until bottom is lightly browned. Slide omelet onto serving plate. Let stand 30 minutes before serving. Serve in wedges.

Makes 8 servings

CARNITAS

2 to 2½ pounds pork butt
2 bay leaves
2 cloves garlic, minced
1 teaspoon chili powder
¾ teaspoon salt
½ teaspoon pepper
½ teaspoon dried oregano, crushed
½ teaspoon ground cumin
½ cup water
Guacamole (page 14) *or* 2 cups salsa

Preheat oven to 350°F. Trim external fat from meat; cut meat into 1-inch cubes. Combine bay leaves, garlic, chili powder, salt, pepper, oregano and cumin in large shallow roasting pan (pan should be large enough to hold meat in single layer). Gradually add water; mix well. Place meat in pan; stir until well coated. Cover with foil. Bake 45 minutes. Remove foil; continue baking 45 to 60 minutes or until most of the liquid has evaporated and meat begins to brown. Discard bay leaves. Transfer meat to fondue pot or chafing dish; keep warm over heat source. Serve with Guacamole.

Makes 12 to 14 servings

NACHOS

When time is short, use purchased tortilla chips.

½ cup Salsa Fresca (page 6) *or*
  ¼ cup sliced fresh or canned
  jalapeño peppers
  Crisp Tortilla Chips (page 15)
  made from 6 corn tortillas,
  6- to 7-inch diameter
1 cup refried beans (optional)
2 cups (8 ounces) shredded Colby
  or Cheddar cheese

Prepare Salsa Fresca and Crisp Tortilla Chips. Preheat oven to 350°F. Place tortilla chips in single layer on ungreased baking sheet. If using refried beans, top each chip with small amount of beans. Cover each with about 1 teaspoon cheese; top with a little salsa. Bake 10 to 12 minutes or until cheese is melted.

Makes 3 dozen

Variation

Nachos with Artichoke Hearts: Drain 1 can (14 ounces) artichoke hearts; cut into quarters. Place in medium bowl; stir in ½ cup picante sauce. Cover and refrigerate 8 hours or up to 3 days. Place tortilla chips in solid layer in quiche dish or other rimmed ovenproof serving dish. Top with half of the artichoke mixture; reserve remaining mixture for later use. Sprinkle with 2 cups shredded Cheddar cheese. Bake, following directions for Nachos. Garnish with cilantro sprigs.

MARINATED MUSSELS ON THE HALF SHELL

½ cup Tomatillo Salsa (page 15)
36 mussels *or* small hard-shell clams
  Boiling water
1 tablespoon olive oil
1 tablespoon lime juice
  Salt

Prepare Tomatillo Salsa. Scrub mussels (*or* clams) under cold water with stiff brush; discard any with open shells or with shells that don't close when tapped. If using mussels, pull out and discard brown, hairlike beards. Arrange half of the mussels in large skillet; pour in boiling water to depth of about ½ inch. Cover and simmer over medium heat 5 to 8 minutes or until shells open. As their shells open, remove mussels with slotted spoon; set aside to cool. Discard any unopened mussels. Repeat cooking with remaining mussels. Remove mussels from shells with small knife. Separate shells; save half. Cover shells and refrigerate. Combine salsa, oil and lime juice in large bowl. Add mussels; stir to coat. Season with salt to taste. Cover and refrigerate up to 24 hours. Remove mussels from marinade; place one in each shell. Arrange on platter. Spoon any remaining marinade over mussels.

Makes 3 dozen

CHILI CON QUESO

2 tablespoons butter or margarine
1/4 cup finely chopped onion
1 clove garlic, minced
1 can (8 ounces) tomato sauce
1 can (4 ounces) diced green chilies
2 cups (8 ounces) shredded
    Cheddar cheese
2 cups (8 ounces) shredded
    Monterey Jack cheese with
    jalapeño peppers
Tortilla chips and crisp raw
    vegetable dippers

Melt butter in 3- to 4-quart pan over medium heat. Add onion and garlic; cook until onion is tender. Stir in tomato sauce and chilies; reduce heat to low. Simmer 3 minutes. Gradually add cheeses, stirring until cheeses are melted and mixture is evenly blended. Transfer to fondue pot or chafing dish; keep warm over heat source. Serve with tortilla chips and vegetable dippers.

Makes 3 cups, about 12 servings

SALSA VERDE DIP

Serve this creamy, mild sauce as a topping for tacos, tostados, burritos or as a dip for tortilla chips.

1/2 cup Green Chili Salsa (page 15)
1 cup (1/2 pint) sour cream
    Salt
    Pepper

Prepare Green Chili Salsa. Combine salsa and sour cream in small bowl; mix well. Add salt and pepper to taste. Cover and refrigerate 1 hour or up to 2 days for flavors to blend.

Makes 1 1/2 cups

CHILI-BEAN DIP

Crisp Tortilla Chips (page 15) or
    purchased tortilla chips
1 tablespoon vegetable oil
1/4 cup chopped onion
1 clove garlic, minced
1 can (about 16 ounces) refried
    beans
1 can (8 ounces) tomatoes, drained
    and chopped
1/4 cup canned diced green chilies
2 cups (8 ounces) shredded
    Cheddar or Monterey Jack
    cheese

Prepare Crisp Tortilla Chips. Heat oil in large skillet over medium heat. Add onion and garlic; cook until onion is tender. Add refried beans, tomatoes and chilies; mix well. Heat until mixture is bubbly. Reduce heat to low; stir in cheese. Cook, stirring occasionally, until cheese is melted. Transfer to fondue pot or chafing dish; keep warm over heat source. Serve with tortilla chips.

Makes 3 cups, about 12 servings

Variation
Five-Minute Dip: Heat 1 can (15 ounces) chili without beans in 2-quart pan over medium heat until bubbly. Stir in 1/2 pound chopped process cheese. Reduce heat to low; cook, stirring occasionally, until cheese is melted. Serve with tortilla chips.

Makes 2 1/2 cups, about 8 servings

TORTILLA PINWHEELS

*For the best flavor, have the beef and
turkey freshly sliced in the deli section
of your supermarket.*

1 package (8 ounces) cream cheese,
  softened
2 teaspoons milk
1/8 teaspoon garlic powder
1 can (4 ounces) diced green
  chilies, drained
1 tablespoon minced onion
  Dash of salt
8 flour tortillas, 8- to 10-inch
  diameter
1/4 pound very thinly sliced roast
  beef
1/4 pound very thinly sliced roast
  turkey
3 tablespoons cilantro leaves
1 can (2 1/4 ounces) sliced pitted
  ripe olives, drained

Beat cream cheese, milk and garlic
powder in medium bowl until light and
fluffy. Stir in chilies, onion and salt.
Lightly moisten both sides of each tortilla with water. Spread a heaping 2 tablespoons cream cheese mixture onto
each tortilla. Evenly layer roast beef on
half of the tortillas, layer turkey on remaining tortillas. Sprinkle about 1 teaspoon cilantro over each tortilla; top
with olives. Roll up; wrap each roll in
plastic wrap. Refrigerate 1 hour or up
to 8 hours. To serve, trim 1/2 inch from
each end; discard. Cut each roll into 6
slices.

Makes 4 dozen appetizers

PICO DE GALLO

*Also known as Rooster's Beak, this
light, refreshing appetizer can be
assembled on the spur of the moment.*

1 small jicama
3 oranges
1/4 cup lime juice
  Lime wedges for garnish
  Cilantro sprigs for garnish
  Salt
  Chili powder

Peel jicama; cut into 3-inch julienne
strips. Peel oranges. Cut in half lengthwise; cut halves crosswise into thin
slices. Arrange jicama and oranges on a
serving plate; brush with lime juice.
Garnish with lime wedges and cilantro.
To serve, sprinkle with salt and chili
powder to taste. Top with additional
lime juice, if desired.

Makes 6 to 8 servings

Top: Tortilla Pinwheels; bottom: Pico de Gallo

EMPANADITAS

Chicken Filling (recipe follows)
Beef Filling (recipe follows)
Pastry for double-crust 9-inch pie
1 egg yolk mixed with 1 teaspoon
    water

Preheat oven to 375°F. Prepare Chicken and Beef Fillings. Roll out pastry, one half at a time, on floured board, to a thickness of about ⅛ inch; cut into 2½-inch circles. Place about 1 teaspoon filling on each circle. Fold dough over to make half moons; seal edges with fork. Prick tops; brush with egg mixture. Place, slightly apart, on ungreased baking sheets. Bake 12 to 15 minutes or until golden brown. Serve warm.

Makes about 3 dozen

CHICKEN FILLING

2 teaspoons butter or margarine
½ cup finely chopped onion
1 cup finely chopped cooked
    chicken
2 tablespoons canned diced green
    chilies
2 teaspoons capers, drained and
    coarsely chopped
¼ teaspoon salt
½ cup (2 ounces) shredded
    Monterey Jack cheese

Melt butter in medium skillet over medium heat. Add onion; cook until tender. Stir in chicken, chilies, capers and salt; cook 1 minute. Remove from heat and let cool; stir in cheese.

BEEF FILLING

¼ pound lean ground beef
¼ cup chopped onion
2 tablespoons canned diced green
    chilies
2 teaspoons all-purpose flour
¼ teaspoon salt
¼ teaspoon ground cumin
¼ teaspoon chili powder
½ cup water
½ cup (2 ounces) shredded
    Cheddar cheese

Crumble meat into medium skillet; stir over medium-high heat until browned. Drain. Add onion; reduce heat to medium. Cook until onion is tender. Stir in chilies, flour, salt, cumin and chili powder. Cook 1 minute, stirring occasionally. Add water; cook until sauce thickens, stirring occasionally. Remove from heat and let cool; stir in cheese.

GUACAMOLE

To ripen hard avocados, store them in a loosely closed paper bag at room temperature.

2 large avocados, peeled and pitted
¼ cup finely chopped tomato
2 tablespoons lime juice or lemon
    juice
2 tablespoons grated onion with
    juice
½ teaspoon salt
¼ teaspoon hot pepper sauce
    Ground black pepper

Place avocados in medium bowl; mash coarsely with fork. Stir in tomato, lime juice, onion, salt and hot pepper sauce; mix well. Add black pepper to taste. Spoon into serving container. Serve immediately or cover and refrigerate up to 2 hours. Garnish with additional chopped tomatoes if desired.

Makes 2 cups

GREEN CHILI SALSA

This mild salsa, using canned tomatoes, is a perfect recipe to make when vine-ripened tomatoes are out of season.

1 can (14½ ounces) tomatoes
1 can (4 ounces) diced green chilies, drained
½ cup chopped green onions with tops
1 clove garlic, minced
2 tablespoons chopped cilantro
1 fresh serrano chili or jalapeño pepper, stemmed, seeded and minced
1 tablespoon lime juice
1 teaspoon vegetable oil
Salt

Drain tomatoes, reserving liquid. Coarsely chop tomatoes. Combine tomatoes, green chilies, green onions, garlic, cilantro, serrano chili, lime juice and oil in medium bowl. Stir in ¼ cup of the reserved tomato liquid; discard remaining liquid. Add salt to taste. Cover and refrigerate 1 hour or up to 3 days for flavors to blend.

Makes about 2 cups

CRISP TORTILLA CHIPS

A fresh-tasting treat to scoop up guacamole, chili con queso or your favorite salsa.

Corn tortillas
Flour tortillas
Whole Wheat Tortillas (page 38)
Vegetable oil for deep-frying
Salt (optional)

Use tortilla of your choice, or make chips from several kinds of tortillas. Depending on size of tortilla, with kitchen scissors, cut each into 6 to 8 wedge-shaped pieces. Pour oil into deep 2- to 3-quart pan to depth of 1 inch. Place over medium-high heat until oil reaches 360°F on deep-frying thermometer. Add tortilla pieces, a few at a time, and deep-fry, turning occasionally, until crisp and lightly browned. Allow about 45 seconds for flour tortillas and 1 minute for corn tortillas. Remove from oil with slotted spoon; drain on paper towels. Sprinkle lightly with salt if desired. Chips can be made up to 2 days in advance. Let cool and store in plastic bags at room temperature.

TOMATILLO SALSA

Fresh tomatillos give you a crunchy salsa; canned tomatillos make a juicier relish.

1 pound tomatillos (about 12 large) or 1 can (13 ounces) tomatillos
½ cup finely chopped red onion
¼ cup coarsely chopped cilantro
2 fresh jalapeño peppers or serrano chilies, stemmed, seeded and minced
1 tablespoon lime juice
1 teaspoon olive oil
½ teaspoon salt

If using fresh tomatillos, remove papery husks; wash tomatillos and finely chop. If using canned tomatillos, drain; coarsely chop. Combine all ingredients in medium bowl. Cover and refrigerate 1 hour or up to 3 days for flavors to blend.

Makes about 1½ cups

Arizona Cheese Crisp

ARIZONA CHEESE CRISP

*The sloping sides of a wok allow
you to easily curl the edges of the
tortilla as it deep-fries. If you wish,
you may deep-fry the tortilla flat
in a large skillet.*

½ cup Salsa Fresca (page 6) or
    picante sauce
    Vegetable oil for deep-frying
2 flour tortillas, 10- to 12-inch
    diameter
1 to 1½ cups (4 to 6 ounces)
    shredded Cheddar or
    Monterey Jack cheese
¼ cup grated Parmesan cheese

Prepare Salsa Fresca. Pour oil into wok
to depth of 1 inch. Place over medium-
high heat until oil registers 360°F on
deep-frying thermometer. (You can also
test oil by standing wooden chopstick
on bottom of wok; oil should bubble
gently around base of chopstick.) Slide
1 tortilla into oil. Using 2 slotted
spoons, gently hold center of tortilla
down so oil flows over edges. When
tortilla is crisp and golden on bottom,
carefully tilt wok, holding tortilla in
place with spoon, to cover edge of tortilla with oil; cook until lightly browned.
Rotate tortilla as needed so entire edge
is lightly browned. Remove from oil
and drain on paper towels, curled side
down. Repeat with second tortilla. Tortillas can be made up to 8 hours in advance. Cover loosely and let stand at
room temperature.

Preheat oven to 350°F. Place shells,
curled side up, on baking sheet. Sprinkle each with half of the Cheddar
cheese; top each with half of the salsa.
Sprinkle with Parmesan cheese. Bake,
uncovered, 8 to 10 minutes or until
cheeses melt. To serve, break into
pieces to eat out of hand.

Makes 4 to 6 servings

Variations

Chorizo Cheese Crisp: Remove casing
from ¼ pound chorizo sausage. Crumble sausage into large skillet; stir over
medium-high heat until browned.
Drain fat. Follow directions for Arizona
Cheese Crisp but substitute chorizo
for Parmesan cheese.

Olive Cheese Crisp: Follow directions
for Arizona Cheese Crisp but omit
salsa and Parmesan cheese. Sprinkle ⅓
cup sliced pitted ripe olives and ⅓ cup
diced green chilies over Cheddar
cheese.

Soups, Stews & Chili

TORTILLA SOUP

3 corn tortillas, 6- to 7-inch
   diameter
Vegetable oil for deep-frying
2 teaspoons vegetable oil
1/2 cup chopped onion
1 small clove garlic, minced
1 can (14 1/2 ounces) tomatoes,
   undrained
2 cans (14 1/2 ounces each) ready-to-
   serve chicken broth or
   3 1/2 cups Chicken Stock
   (page 73)
1 cup shredded cooked chicken
2 teaspoons lime juice
1 small avocado, peeled and pitted
2 tablespoons cilantro leaves

Cut tortillas in half, then cut crosswise into 1/2-inch strips. Pour oil to depth of 1/2 inch in small skillet. Place over medium-high heat until oil reaches 360°F on deep-frying thermometer. Add tortilla pieces, a few at a time, and deep-fry 1 minute or until crisp and lightly browned. Remove with slotted spoon; drain on paper towels.

Heat the 2 teaspoons oil in 3-quart pan over medium heat. Add onion and garlic; cook until onion is tender. Coarsely chop tomatoes; add to pan. Add chicken broth. Bring to a boil. Cover; reduce heat and simmer 15 minutes. Add chicken and lime juice. Simmer 5 minutes. Dice avocado. Serve soup in individual bowls. Top with avocado, tortilla strips and cilantro.

Makes 4 servings

Top: Sheepherder's Bread (page 34); bottom: Tortilla Soup

NAVAJO LAMB STEW WITH CORNMEAL DUMPLINGS

This stew thickens as the dumplings cook in the bubbling gravy.

- 2 pounds lean lamb stew meat with bones, cut into 2-inch pieces, or 1½ pounds lean boneless lamb, cut into 1½-inch cubes
- 1 teaspoon salt
- ½ teaspoon pepper
- 2½ tablespoons vegetable oil, divided
- 1 large onion, chopped
- 1 clove garlic, minced
- 2 tablespoons tomato paste
- 2 teaspoons chili powder
- 1 teaspoon ground coriander
- 4 cups water
- 3 small potatoes, cut into 1½-inch chunks
- 2 large carrots, cut into 1-inch pieces
- 1 package (10 ounces) frozen whole kernel corn
- ⅓ cup coarsely chopped celery leaves
  Cornmeal Dumplings (recipe follows)
  Whole celery leaves for garnish

Sprinkle meat with salt and pepper. Heat 2 tablespoons of the oil in 5-quart kettle over medium-high heat. Add meat, a few pieces at a time, and cook until browned on all sides. Transfer meat to a medium bowl. Heat the remaining ½ tablespoon oil over medium heat. Add onion and garlic; cook until onion is tender. Stir in tomato paste, chili powder, coriander and water. Return meat to kettle. Add potatoes, carrots, corn and chopped celery leaves. Bring to a boil. Cover; reduce heat and simmer 1 hour and 15 minutes or until meat is tender. During last 15 minutes of cooking, prepare Cornmeal Dumplings. Drop dough onto stew to make 6 dumplings. Cover and simmer 18 minutes or until dumplings are firm to the touch and a wooden pick inserted in center comes out clean. To serve, spoon stew onto individual plates; serve with dumplings. Garnish with whole celery leaves.

Makes 6 servings

CORNMEAL DUMPLINGS

- ½ cup yellow cornmeal
- ½ cup all-purpose flour
- 1 teaspoon baking powder
- ¼ teaspoon salt
- 2½ tablespoons cold butter or margarine
- ½ cup milk

Combine cornmeal, flour, baking powder and salt in medium bowl. Cut in butter with fingers, pastry blender or 2 knives until mixture resembles coarse crumbs. Make a well in center; pour in milk all at once and stir with fork until mixture forms dough.

Navajo Lamb Stew with Cornmeal Dumplings

container with tight-fitting lid. Stir in olives, wine vinegar, oil, salt and oregano. Add hot pepper sauce to taste. Stir in up to 1/2 cup of the remaining vegetable juice cocktail to make soup desired consistency. Cover and refrigerate 4 hours or up to 2 days. Serve cold in individual bowls.

Makes 6 servings

POTATO SOUP WITH GREEN CHILIES & CHEESE

2 tablespoons vegetable oil
1 medium onion, chopped
1 clove garlic, minced
2 cups chopped potatoes
1 tablespoon all-purpose flour
1 1/2 cups ready-to-serve chicken broth
2 cups milk
1 can (4 ounces) diced green chilies
1/2 teaspoon celery salt
3/4 cup (3 ounces) shredded
    Monterey Jack cheese
3/4 cup (3 ounces) shredded Colby
    or Cheddar cheese
    White pepper
    Chopped celery leaves for
    garnish

Heat oil in 3-quart pan over medium heat. Add onion and garlic; cook until onion is tender. Stir in potatoes; cook 1 minute. Stir in flour; continue cooking 1 minute. Stir in broth. Bring to a boil. Cover; reduce heat and simmer 20 minutes or until potatoes are tender. Stir in milk, chilies and celery salt; heat to simmering. Add cheeses; stir and heat just until cheeses melt. Do not boil. Add pepper to taste. Serve in individual bowls. Garnish with celery leaves.

Makes 6 servings

TURKEY SOUP, TAOS STYLE

In early Southwest cooking, a full-meal soup such as this bubbled in a cast-iron pot suspended over the fire.

2 turkey legs (2 to 3 pounds total)
1 large carrot, coarsely chopped
1 medium onion, coarsely chopped
8 cups water
1 bay leaf
1 teaspoon cumin seeds
1/4 teaspoon black peppercorns
1 can (15 1/2 ounces) garbanzo
    beans, drained
1/2 cup uncooked small pasta shells
1 teaspoon dried oregano, crushed
1/4 cup canned diced green chilies
1/4 cup cilantro leaves, divided
    Salt
    Ground black pepper

Place turkey legs, carrot, onion and water in 8-quart kettle. Combine bay leaf, cumin seeds and peppercorns in cheesecloth bag or tea ball. Add to kettle. Bring to a boil over high heat. Cover; reduce heat and simmer 1 1/2 to 2 hours or until turkey is very tender. Remove turkey to plate with slotted spoon; let cool. Reserve vegetables and broth. Discard skin and bones from turkey; cut meat into bite-size pieces. Reserve. Discard seasoning bag. Place reserved vegetables, broth and beans, a portion at a time, in blender or food processor container fitted with metal blade; process until smooth. Return to kettle. Reheat soup to boiling. Stir in pasta shells and oregano. Simmer, uncovered, 10 minutes or until pasta is tender but firm to the bite. Return meat to soup. Add chilies and 2 tablespoons of the cilantro. Season with salt and pepper to taste. Heat to simmering. Serve in individual bowls. Garnish with the remaining 2 tablespoons cilantro.

Makes 6 servings

Top: Chilled Avocado Soup; bottom: Corn & Red Pepper Soup

CORN & RED PEPPER SOUP

If you wish to make this with fresh corn, cut the raw kernels from four large ears of yellow or white corn.

2 tablespoons butter or margarine
2 cups seeded and coarsely chopped red bell peppers
1 medium onion, thinly sliced
1 can (14½ ounces) ready-to-serve chicken broth or 1¾ cups Chicken Stock (page 73)
1 package (10 ounces) frozen whole kernel corn
½ teaspoon ground cumin
½ cup sour cream
    Salt
    White pepper
    Sunflower seeds or popped corn for garnish

Melt butter in 3-quart pan over medium heat. Add bell peppers and onion; cook until tender. Add chicken broth, corn and cumin. Bring to a boil. Cover; reduce heat and simmer 20 minutes or until corn is tender. Pour into blender or food processor container fitted with metal blade; process until smooth. Pour into sieve set over bowl; press mixture with rubber spatula to extract all liquid. Discard pulp. Return liquid to pan; whisk in sour cream until evenly blended. Add salt and pepper to taste. Reheat but do not boil. Serve in individual bowls. Garnish as desired.

Makes 4 servings

CHILLED AVOCADO SOUP

3 small onion slices, each ¼ inch thick, divided
1 can (14½ ounces) ready-to-serve chicken broth or 1¾ cups Chicken Stock (page 73)
½ cup plain yogurt
1½ tablespoons lemon juice
1 large ripe avocado, halved and pitted
3 to 5 drops hot pepper sauce
    Salt
    White pepper
¼ cup finely chopped tomato
¼ cup finely chopped cucumber
    Cilantro sprigs for garnish

Place 1 onion slice, chicken broth, yogurt and lemon juice in blender or food processor container fitted with metal blade; process until well blended. Remove pulp from avocado; spoon into blender. Process until smooth. Pour into medium container with tight-fitting lid. Add hot pepper sauce and salt and pepper to taste. Finely chop the remaining 2 onion slices; add to soup. Stir in tomato and cucumber. Cover and refrigerate 2 hours or up to 24 hours. Serve in individual bowls. Garnish with cilantro and additional chopped tomato and cucumber if desired.

Makes 6 servings

BLACK BEAN CHILI

Mellow-flavored and spicy-sweet, you wouldn't guess that this chili doesn't contain meat.

1 pound uncooked dried black beans
  Cold water
6 cups water
1 bay leaf
3 tablespoons vegetable oil
2 large onions, chopped
3 cloves garlic, minced
1 can (14½ ounces) tomatoes, undrained
2 to 3 fresh or canned jalapeño peppers, stemmed, seeded and minced
2 tablespoons chili powder
1½ teaspoons salt
1 teaspoon paprika
1 teaspoon dried oregano, crushed
1 teaspoon unsweetened cocoa powder
½ teaspoon ground cumin
¼ teaspoon ground cinnamon
1 tablespoon red wine vinegar

Condiments
1 cup plain yogurt *or* sour cream
  Salsa Fresca (page 6) or picante sauce
½ cup coarsely chopped cilantro sprigs

Sort beans, discarding any foreign material. Place beans in 8-quart kettle. Add enough cold water to cover beans by 2 inches. Cover; bring to a boil over high heat. Boil 2 minutes. Remove from heat; let soak, covered, 1 hour. Drain. Add the 6 cups water and bay leaf to beans in kettle. Return to heat. Bring to a boil. Reduce heat and simmer, partially covered, 2 hours.

Meanwhile, heat oil in large skillet over medium heat. Add onions and garlic; cook until onions are tender. Coarsely chop tomatoes; add to skillet. Add jalapeño peppers, chili powder, salt, paprika, oregano, cocoa powder, cumin and cinnamon. Simmer 15 minutes. Add tomato mixture to beans. Stir in wine vinegar. Continue simmering 30 minutes or until beans are very tender and chili has thickened slightly. Discard bay leaf. Ladle chili into individual bowls. Serve with condiments.

Makes 6 servings

POZOLE

Canned hominy replaces the hard-to-find dried hominy traditionally used in this stew.

1½ pounds lean boneless pork butt
1 large onion, coarsely chopped
2 cloves garlic, minced
1 bay leaf
1 dried red New Mexico or California chili, seeds removed, *or* 1 teaspoon chili powder
1 teaspoon dried oregano, crushed
½ teaspoon cumin seeds
½ teaspoon coriander seeds
½ teaspoon black peppercorns
10 cups water
3 chicken legs with thighs attached
1 can (29 ounces) yellow or white hominy, drained

Condiments
3 limes, cut into wedges
1 package (3 ounces) cream cheese, cut into cubes
½ head iceberg lettuce, shredded
1 bunch radishes, thinly sliced
6 green onions with tops, thinly sliced
1 avocado, peeled, pitted and finely chopped

Combine pork, onion, garlic, bay leaf, chili, oregano, cumin seeds, coriander seeds, peppercorns and water in 5-quart kettle. Bring to a boil. Cover; reduce heat and simmer 45 minutes. Add chicken. Simmer 1 hour or until meat is tender. Remove meat with slotted spoon to pan; let cool. Pour broth through sieve set over large bowl; discard solids. Return broth to kettle. Skim fat, or if made ahead, cool, cover and refrigerate overnight; remove fat. When meat is cool enough to handle, discard skin and bones; shred meat. Cover and refrigerate until needed. Reheat broth to simmering. Add hominy. Cover and simmer 30 minutes. Return meat to broth; heat to simmering. Spoon pozole into individual bowls. Serve with condiments.

Makes 6 servings

CHUNKY ANCHO CHILI WITH BEANS

Dried anchos give the traditional chili flavor; jalapeño peppers provide the bite.

5 dried ancho chilies
2 cups water
2 tablespoons lard or vegetable oil
1 large onion, chopped
2 cloves garlic, minced
1 pound lean boneless beef, cut into 1-inch cubes
1 pound lean boneless pork, cut into 1-inch cubes
1 to 2 fresh or canned jalapeño peppers, stemmed, seeded and minced
1 teaspoon salt
1 teaspoon dried oregano, crushed
1 teaspoon ground cumin
½ cup dry red wine
3 cups cooked pinto beans or 2 cans (15 ounces each) pinto or kidney beans, drained

Rinse ancho chilies; remove stems, seeds and veins. Place in 2-quart pan with water. Bring to a boil; turn off heat and let stand, covered, 30 minutes or until chilies are soft. Pour chilies with liquid into blender or food processor container fitted with metal blade. Process until smooth; reserve.

Melt lard in 5-quart kettle over medium heat. Add onion and garlic; cook until onion is tender. Add beef and pork; cook, stirring frequently, until meat is lightly colored. Add jalapeño peppers, salt, oregano, cumin, wine and ancho chili puree. Bring to a boil. Cover; reduce heat and simmer 1½ to 2 hours or until meat is very tender. Stir in beans. Simmer, uncovered, 30 minutes or until chili has thickened slightly. Serve in individual bowls.

Makes 8 servings

Variation
To make chili with chili powder, use ⅓ cup chili powder and 1½ cups water in place of ancho chili puree. Reduce salt and cumin to ½ teaspoon each.

ALBONDIGAS SOUP

In Spanish, albondigas means meatballs. A favorite way to cook them is in a hearty soup chock-full of vegetables.

1 pound lean ground beef
2 eggs, slightly beaten
¼ cup blue cornmeal or fine dry bread crumbs
1 clove garlic, minced
1 tablespoon chopped fresh mint or 1 teaspoon crumbled dried mint
½ teaspoon salt
¼ teaspoon ground cumin
   Dash of pepper
6 cups water
3 cans (10¾ ounces each) condensed beef broth
1 small onion, chopped
¼ cup sliced celery
1 carrot, chopped
1 zucchini, chopped
1 yellow crookneck squash, chopped
½ bunch spinach, stems removed, leaves cut into ½-inch slices
   Cilantro sprigs for garnish
2 limes, cut into wedges

To make meatballs, combine meat, eggs, cornmeal, garlic, mint, salt, cumin and pepper. Shape mixture into 1-inch balls; reserve. To make soup, combine water, beef broth, onion and celery in 5-quart kettle. Bring to a boil. Reduce heat; simmer, uncovered, 10 minutes. Add meatballs to broth. Cook, uncovered, 5 minutes. Spoon off fat and foam from surface of broth. Add carrot, zucchini and squash; simmer, uncovered, 20 minutes or until vegetables are tender. Add spinach to soup; cook, uncovered, 5 minutes. Serve in individual bowls. Garnish with cilantro. Pass lime wedges at the table to squeeze onto individual servings.

Makes 6 servings

TEX-MEX CHILI

Bold is the best way to describe this "bowl of red." Use the minimum amount of red pepper unless you like three-alarm heat.

4 bacon slices, diced
2 pounds beef round steak, trimmed and cut into ½-inch cubes
1 medium onion, chopped
2 cloves garlic, minced
¼ cup chili powder
1 teaspoon dried oregano, crushed
1 teaspoon ground cumin
1 teaspoon salt
½ to 1 teaspoon ground red pepper
½ teaspoon hot pepper sauce
4 cups water
   Chopped onion for garnish

Cook bacon in 5-quart kettle over medium-high heat until crisp. Remove with slotted spoon; drain on paper towels. Add half of the steak to bacon drippings in kettle; cook until lightly browned. Remove steak from kettle. Repeat with remaining steak. Reduce heat to medium. Cook medium onion and garlic in pan drippings until onion is tender. Reduce heat to medium. Return steak and bacon to kettle. Add chili powder, oregano, cumin, salt, ground red pepper, hot pepper sauce and water. Bring to a boil. Cover; reduce heat and simmer 1½ hours. Skim fat. Simmer, uncovered, 30 minutes or until steak is very tender and chili has thickened slightly. Serve in individual bowls. Garnish with chopped onion.

Makes 6 servings

Albondigas Soup

Breads, Beans & Rice

ARIZONA RANCH BEANS

Long simmering gives a smooth, melting quality to these beans.

1 pound uncooked, dried pinto
   beans
Cold water
8 cups water
½ pound bacon, diced
1 can (14½ ounces) tomatoes,
   undrained
2 medium onions, chopped
2 cloves garlic, minced
1 can (4 ounces) diced green chilies
1 teaspoon chili powder
½ teaspoon dried oregano, crushed
¼ teaspoon ground cumin
Salt
Fresh oregano for garnish
   (optional)
2 limes

Sort beans, discarding any foreign material. Place beans in large kettle. Add enough cold water to cover beans by 2 inches. Cover; bring to a boil over high heat. Boil 2 minutes. Remove from heat; let soak, covered, 1 hour. Drain. Add the 8 cups water. Simmer, partially covered, 1 hour. Cook bacon in large skillet until crisp. Add bacon and 2 tablespoons of the drippings to beans. Coarsely chop tomatoes; add to beans. Add onions, garlic, chilies, chili powder, dried oregano and cumin. Simmer, partially covered, 3 hours or until beans are very tender. At end of cooking, beans should have a little liquid. If beans become too dry, add more water. If beans have more liquid than you like, uncover and boil over medium heat, stirring more frequently as mixture thickens. Season with salt to taste. Garnish with fresh oregano if desired. Cut lime into wedges; pass at the table to squeeze over each serving.

Makes 6 to 8 servings

FRIJOLES

Follow this method to cook any type of dried beans.

1 pound uncooked dried pinto, pink, red or black beans
Cold water
½ cup (¼ pound) finely diced salt pork *or* 2 tablespoons bacon drippings
8 cups water
1 small onion, finely chopped
1 clove garlic, minced
Salt

Sort beans, discarding any foreign material. Place beans in large kettle. Add enough cold water to cover beans by 2 inches. Cover. Bring to a boil over high heat. Boil 2 minutes. Remove from heat; let soak, covered, 1 hour. Drain. If using salt pork, cook pork in small skillet until fat begins to melt. Add pork and drippings (or bacon drippings) to beans. Add the 8 cups water, the onion and garlic. Simmer, partially covered, until beans are tender, 1½ to 2 hours for pinto, pink or red beans, 2½ hours for black beans. If beans have more liquid than you like, uncover and boil over medium heat until desired consistency, stirring more frequently as mixture thickens. Season with salt to taste.

Makes 6 to 8 servings

Variations

Fiesta Beans: Follow directions for Frijoles but use 1½ pounds ham shank in place of salt pork. When beans are cooked, remove meat; cut into bite-size pieces, discarding bone. Return meat to kettle; heat to simmering.

Refried Beans: Remove 4 cups Frijoles with slotted spoon. Mash beans with potato masher or process in blender or food processor container fitted with metal blade until coarsely mashed. Heat 2 tablespoons bacon drippings in large skillet. Add mashed beans. Cook over medium heat until thick and bubbly. Top with 1 cup (4 ounces) shredded Cheddar or Colby cheese. Let cheese melt before serving.

Makes 4 to 6 servings

SPANISH RICE WITH AVOCADO

Add the avocado just minutes before serving. If overheated, avocado loses its buttery sweetness.

1 tablespoon butter or margarine
1 tablespoon olive oil
1 small onion, finely chopped
1 clove garlic, minced
1 cup uncooked rice
¼ teaspoon salt
¼ teaspoon dried oregano, crushed
¼ teaspoon ground cumin
¼ teaspoon ground turmeric
1 can (14½ ounces) ready-to-serve chicken broth or 1¾ cups Chicken Stock (page 73)
1 small avocado

Place butter and oil in 2-quart pan over medium heat. When butter is melted, add onion and garlic; cook until onion is tender. Add rice; cook, stirring constantly, 3 minutes or until rice looks milky and opaque. Add salt, oregano, cumin, turmeric and chicken broth. Bring to a boil. Cover; reduce heat and simmer 20 to 25 minutes or until rice is tender and all liquid is absorbed. Peel and pit avocado; dice. Fluff up rice with fork; add avocado and toss gently. Turn off heat; let stand 5 minutes before serving. Serve with grilled steak and tomato slices if desired.

Makes 4 to 6 servings

Spanish Rice with Avocado

SHEEPHERDER'S BREAD

Basque sheepherders traditionally bake this puffy white bread in Dutch ovens buried in pits. Using a conventional oven eliminates the guesswork.

1/2 cup butter or margarine, softened
1/2 cup sugar
2 teaspoons salt
3 cups boiling water
2 packages (1/4 ounce each) active dry yeast
9 to 10 cups all-purpose flour, divided
Shortening

Combine butter, sugar, salt and boiling water in large bowl of electric mixer; stir until butter is melted. Let cool to 110°F. Sprinkle yeast over mixture; stir until dissolved. Let stand 10 minutes or until small bubbles form. Beat in 6 cups of the flour, 1 cup at a time, on low speed until blended. Beat 5 minutes on medium speed. Stir in an additional 3 cups flour to make a stiff dough. Turn out onto lightly floured board; knead 10 minutes or until dough is smooth and satiny, adding as little remaining flour as necessary to prevent sticking. Place dough in greased large bowl; turn dough to coat evenly. Cover loosely with plastic wrap; let stand in warm place until doubled in bulk, about 1 hour.

Punch down dough and knead briefly to release air. Shape into a smooth ball. Grease the side and inside lid of 5-quart Dutch oven with shortening. Cover bottom of Dutch oven with circle of foil. Place dough in Dutch oven; cover with lid. Let stand in warm place until dough raises lid by 1/2 inch, about 1 hour. Preheat oven to 375°F.

Bake, covered, 20 minutes. Remove lid. Continue baking, uncovered, 45 to 60 minutes or until golden brown. Turn out onto rack; bread should sound hollow when tapped on bottom. Peel off foil; turn loaf upright and cool.

Makes 1 large loaf

BLUE CORN MUFFINS

Blue cornmeal, beloved by Indians of the Southwest, has a deep, earthy flavor. Look for it in health food stores.

1 cup all-purpose flour
3/4 cup blue cornmeal
2 tablespoons sugar
1 1/2 teaspoons baking powder
1/2 teaspoon baking soda
1/4 teaspoon salt
2 eggs
1 cup buttermilk or sour cream
1/4 cup butter or margarine, melted
Honey Butter (recipe follows)

Preheat oven to 400°F. Grease 12 (2 1/2-inch) muffin cups. Combine flour, cornmeal, sugar, baking powder, baking soda and salt. Beat eggs, buttermilk and butter in small bowl until blended. Pour liquid mixture into dry ingredients; stir just until moistened. Fill each prepared muffin cup 2/3 full with batter. Bake 15 to 20 minutes or until a wooden pick inserted in centers comes out clean. Remove muffins from pan to wire rack; cool 5 minutes. Meanwhile, prepare Honey Butter; serve with warm muffins.

Makes 12 muffins

Variation

Blue Corn Sticks: Preheat corn stick pans in 400°F oven 5 minutes. Melt ½ teaspoon butter in each section. Fill each section ¾ full with batter. Bake 12 to 15 minutes or until wooden pick inserted in centers comes out clean.

Makes about 1½ dozen

HONEY BUTTER

½ cup butter or margarine,
    softened
⅓ cup honey
1 teaspoon grated orange peel

Whip butter until fluffy. Add honey and whip until well blended. Stir in orange peel.

Makes about ¾ cup

ANGEL BISCUITS

In Southwestern ranch kitchens, cooks whip up a large batch of this biscuit dough, which can be stored in the refrigerator or freezer. The result is a ready-to-bake biscuit that is feather light.

⅓ cup warm water (110°F)
1 package (¼ ounce) active dry
    yeast
5 cups all-purpose flour
3 tablespoons sugar
1 tablespoon baking powder
1 teaspoon baking soda
1 teaspoon salt
1 cup shortening
2 cups buttermilk

Preheat oven to 450°F. Pour warm water into small bowl. Sprinkle yeast over water and stir until dissolved. Let stand 10 minutes or until small bubbles form.

Combine flour, sugar, baking powder, baking soda and salt in large bowl. Add shortening. With fingers, pastry blender or 2 knives, rub or cut in shortening until mixture resembles fine crumbs. Make a well in center. Pour in yeast mixture and buttermilk; stir with fork until mixture forms dough.

Turn dough out onto lightly floured board. Knead 30 seconds or until dough feels light and soft but not sticky. Roll out desired amount of dough to ½-inch thickness. Cut biscuit rounds with 2-inch cutter. Place biscuits close together (for soft sides) or ½ inch apart (for crispy sides) on ungreased baking sheet. Bake 15 to 18 minutes or until tops are lightly browned.

Place remaining dough in airtight bag; refrigerate up to 3 days. Or roll out and cut remaining dough into rounds; place on baking sheet and freeze. Transfer frozen rounds to airtight bags; return to freezer. At baking time, place frozen rounds on ungreased baking sheet. Let stand 20 minutes or until thawed before baking. Bake as directed.

Makes about 5 dozen biscuits

Variation

Red Devil Biscuits: Prepare Angel Biscuits but add 2 tablespoons mild red chili powder to flour mixture. Cut biscuits regular size to serve as a hot bread. To serve as an appetizer, cut biscuits miniature size. Serve with your favorite cheese spread or with softened butter and thinly sliced roast beef or turkey.

Top: Jalapeño-Bacon Corn Bread; bottom: Tex-Mex Corn Bread

JALAPEÑO-BACON CORN BREAD

Moist and flavorful, this corn bread reheats beautifully in the microwave oven.

4 slices bacon
¼ cup minced green onions with tops
2 jalapeño peppers, stemmed, seeded and minced
1 cup yellow cornmeal
1 cup all-purpose flour
2½ teaspoons baking powder
½ teaspoon baking soda
½ teaspoon salt
1 egg
¾ cup plain yogurt
¾ cup milk
¼ cup butter or margarine, melted
½ cup (2 ounces) shredded Cheddar cheese

Preheat oven to 400°F. Cook bacon in skillet until crisp; drain on paper towels. Pour 2 tablespoons of the bacon drippings into 9-inch cast-iron skillet or 9-inch square baking pan. Crumble bacon into small bowl; add green onions and peppers.

Combine cornmeal, flour, baking powder, baking soda and salt in large bowl. Beat egg slightly in medium bowl; add yogurt and whisk until smooth. Whisk in milk and butter. Pour liquid mixture into dry ingredients; stir just until moistened. Stir in bacon mixture. Pour into skillet; sprinkle with cheese. Bake 20 to 25 minutes or until a wooden pick inserted in center comes out clean. Cut into wedges or squares; serve hot.

Makes 9 to 12 servings

TEX-MEX CORN BREAD

For a ranch-style breakfast, serve this alongside scrambled eggs and bacon.

1 cup yellow cornmeal
¼ cup all-purpose flour
1 teaspoon baking powder
½ teaspoon baking soda
½ teaspoon salt
2 eggs
¾ cup milk
¼ cup vegetable oil
1 can (17 ounces) cream-style corn
¼ cup minced onion
1½ cups (6 ounces) shredded Cheddar cheese
1 can (4 ounces) diced green chilies, drained

Preheat oven to 400°F. Grease 9-inch square pan. Combine cornmeal, flour, baking powder, baking soda and salt in large bowl. Beat eggs, milk and oil until blended in medium bowl. Stir in corn and onion. Pour liquid mixture into dry ingredients; stir just until moistened. Spoon half of the batter into prepared pan. Sprinkle with half of the cheese and half of the chilies. Cover with remaining batter; top with remaining cheese and chilies. Bake 30 to 35 minutes or until a wooden pick inserted in center comes out clean. Cut into squares; serve hot.

Makes 9 to 12 servings

WHOLE WHEAT TORTILLAS

Good white flour tortillas are easily purchased; hard-to-find whole wheat tortillas are quick to make at home.

1½ cups whole wheat flour
½ cup all-purpose flour
1 teaspoon baking powder
½ teaspoon salt
¼ cup shortening
½ cup warm water

Combine flours, baking powder and salt in medium bowl. With fingers, pastry blender or 2 knives, rub or cut in shortening until mixture resembles fine crumbs. Gradually add water; stir with fork until mixture forms dough. Turn out onto lightly floured board; knead 2 minutes or until smooth. Shape into a ball; cover with bowl and let rest 30 minutes.

Divide dough into 8 equal portions for 9-inch tortillas, 12 portions for 6-inch tortillas. Keep dough covered to prevent it from drying out. Roll out one portion at a time on lightly floured board to make ⅛-inch-thick circle. To cook, place tortilla in preheated ungreased heavy skillet or griddle over medium-high heat. Cook 2 to 3 minutes on each side or until bubbly and browned. Stack cooked tortillas in tightly covered dish or wrap in foil to keep them soft. Serve warm. (If desired, tortillas may be made ahead for later use. Cool tortillas; wrap airtight and refrigerate. To reheat tortillas, wrap with foil and heat in 350°F oven 12 minutes.)

Makes 8 large or 12 small tortillas

HONEY SOPAIPILLAS

Easy-to-make flat dough pieces billow into crisp-shelled, puffy bread that tastes superb with honey.

¼ cup plus 2 teaspoons sugar, divided
½ teaspoon ground cinnamon
2 cups all-purpose flour
½ teaspoon salt
2 teaspoons baking powder
2 tablespoons shortening
¾ cup warm water
   Vegetable oil for deep-frying
   Honey

Combine ¼ cup of the sugar and the cinnamon in small bowl; set aside. Combine the remaining 2 teaspoons sugar, the flour, salt and baking powder. Add shortening. With fingers, pastry blender or 2 knives, rub or cut in shortening until mixture resembles fine crumbs. Gradually add water; stir with fork until mixture forms dough. Turn out onto lightly floured board; knead 2 minutes or until smooth. Shape into a ball; cover with bowl and let rest 30 minutes.

Divide dough into 4 equal portions; shape each into a ball. Flatten each ball to form a circle about 8 inches in diameter and ⅛ inch thick. Cut each round into 4 wedges.

Pour oil into electric skillet or deep heavy pan to depth of 1½ inches. Heat to 360°F. Cook dough, 2 pieces at a time, 2 minutes or until puffed and golden brown, turning once during cooking. Remove from oil with slotted spoon; drain on paper towels. Sprinkle with cinnamon-sugar mixture. Repeat with remaining sopaipillas. Serve hot with honey.

Makes 16 sopaipillas

Variation

Sopaipillas for Stuffing: Omit the cinnamon-sugar mixture. Cut each round of dough into half circles; deep-fry as directed above. Cut a slit to open each sopaipilla. Stuff with your favorite bean, cheese or meat filling.

MEXICAN RICE

This is the traditional partner to serve with beans.

- 2 tablespoons bacon drippings or vegetable oil
- 1 small onion, finely chopped
- 2 tablespoons minced green bell pepper
- 1 clove garlic, minced
- 1 cup uncooked rice
- 1½ cups ready-to-serve chicken broth or Chicken Stock (page 73)
- ½ cup tomato sauce
- ¼ teaspoon salt
- ⅛ teaspoon ground black pepper
- 1 tablespoon chopped parsley (optional)

Heat bacon drippings in 2-quart pan over medium heat. Add onion, bell pepper and garlic; cook until vegetables are tender. Add rice; cook, stirring constantly, 3 minutes or until rice looks milky and opaque. Add chicken broth, tomato sauce, salt and black pepper. Bring to a boil. Cover; reduce heat and simmer 20 to 25 minutes or until rice is tender and all liquid is absorbed. Fluff up rice with fork; add parsley and toss gently. Turn off heat; let stand 5 minutes before serving.

Makes 4 to 6 servings

INDIAN FRY BREAD

Serve as a sweet bread dusted with powdered sugar or drizzled with honey.

- 2 cups all-purpose flour
- ⅓ cup instant nonfat dry milk
- 2 teaspoons baking powder
- ½ teaspoon salt
- 2 tablespoons lard or shortening
- ¾ cup warm water
  Vegetable oil for deep-frying

Combine flour, dry milk powder, baking powder and salt in medium bowl. Add lard. With fingers, pastry blender or 2 knives, rub or cut in lard until mixture resembles fine crumbs. Gradually add water; stir with fork until mixture forms dough. Turn out onto lightly floured board; knead 2 minutes or until smooth. Shape into a ball; cover with bowl and let rest 30 minutes.

Divide dough into 8 equal portions; shape each into a ball. Flatten each ball to form a circle about 7 inches in diameter and ⅛ inch thick. Cut two 2-inch slashes, 1 inch apart, in center of each round or poke a hole in center of each round with finger.

Pour oil into electric skillet or deep heavy pan to depth of 1½ inches. Heat to 360°F. Cook bread rounds, one at a time, 2 minutes or until puffy and golden brown, turning once during cooking. Remove from oil with slotted spoon; drain on paper towels. Repeat until all breads are fried. Serve hot. To reheat, place in a single layer on baking sheet. Bake in 350°F oven 5 minutes.

Makes 8 bread rounds

CHUCK WAGON PANCAKES

Drizzle creamy vanilla syrup over light, fluffy pancakes for a breakfast or brunch treat.

Vanilla Cream Syrup (recipe follows)
1 cup all-purpose flour
2 tablespoons sugar
1 teaspoon baking powder
½ teaspoon baking soda
½ teaspoon salt
2 eggs
½ cup plain yogurt
½ cup water
2 tablespoons butter or margarine, melted

Prepare Vanilla Cream Syrup; reserve. Combine flour, sugar, baking powder, baking soda and salt in large bowl. Beat eggs slightly in medium bowl. Add yogurt and water; whisk until well blended. Whisk in butter. Pour liquid, all at once, into dry ingredients; stir until all flour is moistened. Preheat griddle or large skillet over medium heat; grease lightly. Spoon about ¼ cup batter onto griddle for each pancake, spreading batter to make 5-inch circles. Cook until tops of pancakes are bubbly and appear dry; turn and cook other side until browned.

Makes 8 pancakes

VANILLA CREAM SYRUP

½ cup sugar
½ cup light corn syrup
½ cup whipping cream
1 teaspoon vanilla
1 nectarine, diced (optional)

Combine sugar, corn syrup and cream in 1-quart pan. Cook, stirring constantly, over medium heat until sugar is dissolved. Simmer 2 minutes or until syrup thickens slightly. Remove from heat. Stir in vanilla and nectarine.

Makes 1 cup

RICE CHILI VERDE

For variety, try the new white and brown rice blend.

1 tablespoon butter or margarine
¼ cup finely chopped onion
1 cup small-curd cottage cheese
1 cup (½ pint) sour cream
½ teaspoon salt
⅛ teaspoon white pepper
1 can (7 ounces) whole green chilies, drained and cut into 1-inch pieces
3 cups cooked rice
1 cup (4 ounces) shredded Monterey Jack cheese
1 cup (4 ounces) shredded Cheddar cheese

Preheat oven to 350°F. Melt butter in small skillet over medium heat. Add onion; cook until tender. Combine onion, cottage cheese, sour cream, salt and pepper in medium bowl; mix well. Stir in chilies. Butter 1½-quart casserole dish. Spoon in half of the rice; cover with half of the cottage cheese mixture. Top with half of the Monterey Jack cheese and half of the Cheddar cheese. Repeat layering with remaining ingredients. Bake 25 to 30 minutes or until rice is hot and cheese is melted.

Makes 6 servings

Chuck Wagon Pancakes

Vegetables & Salads

THREE BEAN SALAD WITH NOPALITOS

Nopalitos, diced leaves of the prickly pear cactus, taste something like pickled green beans. Look for them in jars in the Mexican section of the supermarket.

1 can (17 ounces) green lima beans, drained
1 can (15½ ounces) garbanzo beans, drained
1 can (15½ ounces) kidney beans, drained
1 cup canned nopalitos, drained
1 cup thinly sliced celery
¼ cup thinly sliced green onions with tops
½ cup olive oil
3 tablespoons sherry wine vinegar or red wine vinegar
1 teaspoon grated lemon peel
1 teaspoon lemon juice
¾ teaspoon salt
½ teaspoon paprika
¼ teaspoon pepper
¼ cup chopped parsley

Combine beans, nopalitos, celery and green onions in large bowl. Whisk oil, vinegar, lemon peel, lemon juice, salt, paprika and pepper in small bowl until well blended; stir in parsley. Pour over bean mixture; toss gently until vegetables are well coated. Cover; refrigerate 2 hours or overnight for flavors to blend.

Makes 6 to 8 servings

Top: Cimarron Slaw (page 47); bottom: Three Bean Salad with Nopalitos

CALABACITAS

In Spanish, calabacita means "little squash."

2 tablespoons vegetable oil
2 medium yellow crookneck
    squash, cut into ¼-inch slices
2 medium zucchini, cut into
    ¼-inch slices
1 medium onion, coarsely chopped
1 clove garlic, minced
1 can (8 ounces) whole kernel
    corn, drained
¼ cup diced green chilies
½ teaspoon salt
¼ teaspoon dried oregano, crushed
⅛ teaspoon pepper
½ cup (2 ounces) shredded mild
    Cheddar cheese

Heat oil in large skillet over medium heat. Add squash, zucchini, onion and garlic. Cook, stirring occasionally, until onion is tender. Reduce heat. Cover; continue cooking 10 minutes or until squash are barely tender. Add corn, chilies, salt, oregano and pepper. Cook 3 minutes or until hot. Sprinkle with cheese; heat just until cheese melts.

Makes 4 to 6 servings

SAN JUAN TACO SALAD

This picnic salad is a specialty of San Juan River rafting trips. The precooked meat and shredded cheese are transported in plastic bags; the final assembly takes place on the river bank.

1 pound lean ground beef
1 jar (8 ounces) mild or medium
    picante sauce, divided
½ teaspoon dried oregano, crushed
½ teaspoon salt
1 can (15½ ounces) kidney beans,
    drained
1 can (2¼ ounces) sliced pitted
    ripe olives, drained
1 medium head iceberg lettuce,
    shredded
2 medium tomatoes, diced
½ small red onion, chopped
1 cup (4 ounces) shredded
    Cheddar cheese
1 large avocado, peeled and pitted
½ cup sour cream
½ cup French dressing
1 teaspoon cumin seeds
1 bag (16 ounces) tortilla chips

Crumble meat into large skillet; stir over medium-high heat until browned. Spoon off and discard pan drippings. Add 2 tablespoons of the picante sauce, the oregano and salt. Cook 2 minutes, stirring constantly; let cool. Combine meat mixture, beans, olives, lettuce, tomatoes, onion and cheese. Chop avocado; add to salad. Whisk sour cream, French dressing and ½ cup of the picante sauce in small bowl until well blended, reserving any remaining picante sauce for another use. Pour dressing over salad; sprinkle with cumin seeds. Toss gently to mix. Place 6 to 8 tortilla chips on each serving plate; top with salad. Serve with additional tortilla chips.

Makes 6 servings

WINTER FRUIT SALAD WITH AVOCADO DRESSING

Dramatize your buffet table with a pineapple boat piled high with luscious fruit.

Avocado Dressing (recipe follows)
1 pineapple
1 papaya
2 pink grapefruits
2 oranges
1/4 cup pomegranate seeds

Prepare Avocado Dressing. Slice pineapple lengthwise, just to one side of crown, cutting off about 1/3 of the pineapple. Remove pineapple from shells with curved grapefruit knife, leaving 1/2-inch shells. Remove core; cut fruit into bite-size pieces. Place in large bowl. Pare and seed papaya; cut into bite-size pieces. Add to pineapple. Pare grapefruits and oranges, removing white membrane; cut segments between membranes to remove. Add to pineapple mixture; gently stir fruit. Cover and refrigerate 2 hours. Cover and refrigerate larger pineapple shell until serving time; discard smaller shell. To serve, spoon fruit into pineapple shell, using slotted spoon. (Or serve fruit from bowl.) Sprinkle with pomegranate seeds. Pass dressing at the table to spoon over individual servings.

Makes 6 servings

AVOCADO DRESSING

1 small avocado, peeled and pitted
1/2 cup sour cream
1/3 cup vegetable oil
1 1/2 tablespoons lemon juice
3/4 teaspoon sugar
1/4 teaspoon salt
1/4 teaspoon hot pepper sauce

Place avocado in blender or food processor container fitted with metal blade. Add remaining ingredients. Blend until smooth and creamy. Transfer to serving bowl; cover and refrigerate 2 hours or up to 2 days for flavors to blend.

Makes about 1 cup

MINT-ROASTED ONIONS

In the Southwest, the Texas sweet onion is preferred, but you can use any mild-flavored yellow onion.

2 medium onions
2 1/2 tablespoons white wine vinegar
2 tablespoons water
1 tablespoon olive oil
3/4 teaspoon sugar
1/2 teaspoon dried leaf mint, crushed
1/2 teaspoon dried oregano, crushed
1/4 teaspoon salt
1/8 teaspoon pepper

Preheat oven to 400°F. Line bottom of 8-inch square baking pan with foil. Cut onions in half crosswise; remove skins. Place, cut side down, in pan. Whisk remaining ingredients in small bowl until well blended; drizzle over onions. Lift onions and swirl in liquid so cut sides are moistened. Bake, uncovered, for 1 hour or until onions are tender and golden brown, basting with pan drippings several times during roasting. (During end of baking, liquid evaporates and cut sides of onions become glazed.) Serve onion halves cut side up.

Makes 4 servings

Spinach-Orange Salad with Lime Vinaigrette

SPINACH-ORANGE SALAD WITH LIME VINAIGRETTE

1 large bunch spinach, stems removed
2 oranges
1/2 small jicama, peeled, cut into matchsticklike pieces (about 1 cup)
1/4 cup toasted pecan halves
Lime Vinaigrette (recipe follows)

Wash and dry spinach; chill until very crisp. Tear into bite-size pieces; place in large bowl. Pare oranges, removing white membrane. Cut segments between membranes to remove; chop. Add oranges, jicama and pecans to spinach. Prepare Lime Vinaigrette; pour over spinach mixture and toss gently until well mixed.

Makes 6 servings

LIME VINAIGRETTE

3 tablespoons lime juice
2 tablespoons vegetable oil
2 tablespoons sour cream
2 1/4 teaspoons sugar
1/4 teaspoon salt
1/8 teaspoon crushed red chili pepper
Dash of white pepper

Whisk ingredients in small bowl until well blended.

Makes about 1/2 cup

CIMARRON SLAW

Jicama looks like a giant-size brown turnip. Peel the skin before cutting the crisp, slightly sweet flesh into matchsticklike pieces.

2 cups finely shredded green cabbage
2 cups finely shredded red cabbage
1 cup jicama strips
1/4 cup diced green bell pepper
1/4 cup thinly sliced green onions with tops
1/4 cup vegetable oil
1/4 cup lime juice
3/4 teaspoon salt
1/8 teaspoon ground black pepper
2 tablespoons coarsely chopped cilantro leaves

Combine cabbages, jicama, bell pepper and green onions in large bowl. Whisk oil, lime juice, salt and black pepper in small bowl until well blended. Stir in cilantro. Pour over cabbage mixture; toss lightly. Cover; refrigerate 2 hours or up to 6 hours for flavors to blend.

Makes 4 to 6 servings

STUFFED CHAYOTES

Also known as vegetable pear, the pale green chayote is a tropical summer squash.

2 large chayotes, cut in half
    lengthwise
Boiling water
2 tablespoons butter or margarine
½ cup chopped onion
1 clove garlic, minced
1 large tomato, peeled, seeded and
    chopped
2 tablespoons chopped parsley
½ cup cooked whole kernel corn
½ teaspoon salt
⅛ teaspoon pepper
½ cup (2 ounces) shredded
    Cheddar cheese

Cook chayote halves in 1 inch boiling water in large covered skillet 20 to 25 minutes or until tender; drain. When cool, remove pulp, leaving ½-inch shells; coarsely chop pulp and edible seeds. Melt butter in large skillet over medium heat. Brush half of the butter inside chayote shells. Add onion and garlic to remaining butter in skillet; cook until onion is tender. Add tomato and parsley; simmer 5 minutes or until liquid has evaporated. Remove from heat; stir in corn, salt, pepper and chayote pulp.

Preheat oven to 375°F. Place chayote shells in greased shallow baking pan. Evenly fill shells with corn mixture; top with cheese. Bake, uncovered, 15 minutes or until chayotes are hot and cheese is melted.

Makes 4 servings

Variation

Stuffed Summer Squash: Follow directions for Stuffed Chayotes but use 8 large pattypan squash or 8 zucchini (each about 6 inches long) in place of chayotes. Boil whole squash 8 to 10 minutes or until barely tender. After scooping out pulp, turn shells upside down on paper towels to drain before filling.

Makes 8 servings

Stuffed Chayotes

Colache

COLACHE

Pumpkin is the traditional squash used in this dish, but butternut squash has a less stringy texture and is easier to cut and peel. This is a colorful harvest dish to serve with roast turkey.

 2 tablespoons vegetable oil
 1 butternut squash (about
        2 pounds) peeled, seeded and
        diced
 1 medium onion, coarsely chopped
 1 clove garlic, minced
 1 can (16 ounces) tomatoes,
        undrained
 1 green bell pepper, seeded and
        cut into 1-inch pieces
 1 can (14½ ounces) whole kernel
        corn, drained
 1 canned green chili, coarsely
        chopped (optional)
 ½ teaspoon salt
 ¼ teaspoon ground black pepper

Heat oil in large skillet over medium heat. Add squash, onion and garlic; cook 5 minutes or until onion is tender. Coarsely cut up tomatoes; add tomatoes and bell pepper to skillet. Bring to a boil over high heat. Cover; reduce heat and simmer 15 minutes. Add remaining ingredients. Simmer, covered, 5 minutes or until squash is tender. Uncover; increase heat to high. Continue cooking a few minutes or until most of liquid has evaporated.

Makes 6 to 8 servings

JICAMA SALAD

Crisp and crunchy, this makes a delicious contrast to any spicy dish.

 1 cucumber
 1 small jicama
 ½ red bell pepper, seeded and cut
        into 1-inch strips
 ½ green bell pepper, seeded and
        cut into 1-inch strips
 ½ small onion, thinly sliced
        crosswise
 ¼ cup olive oil
 3 tablespoons lime juice
 ½ teaspoon dried oregano, crushed
 ¼ teaspoon salt
 ¼ teaspoon chili powder
 ⅛ teaspoon ground black pepper
        Small romaine lettuce leaves for
        garnish

Peel cucumber; cut in half lengthwise. Scoop out and discard seeds; cut crosswise into ¼-inch slices. Place in large bowl. Peel jicama; cut into ¼-inch slices, then cut slices into matchstick-like pieces. Add to cucumber. Add bell peppers and onion. Whisk oil, lime juice, oregano, salt, chili powder and black pepper in small bowl until well blended. Pour over salad; toss until vegetables are evenly coated. Place salad in serving bowl. Serve immediately or cover and refrigerate up to 4 hours. Tuck lettuce leaves around edge of bowl just before serving.

Makes 6 servings

GREEN BEANS WITH PINE NUTS

1 pound green beans, ends
   removed
2 tablespoons butter or margarine
2 tablespoons pine nuts
   Salt
   Pepper

Cook beans in 1 inch water in covered 3-quart pan 4 to 8 minutes or until crisp-tender; drain. Melt butter in large skillet over medium heat. Add pine nuts; cook, stirring frequently, until golden. Add beans; stir gently to coat beans with butter. Season with salt and pepper to taste.

Makes 4 servings

FRESH CORN WITH ADOBE BUTTER

Chili powder and lime juice make sweet corn taste even sweeter.

$1/2$ teaspoon chili powder
1 teaspoon lime juice
$1/4$ cup butter or margarine,
   softened
   Salt
4 ears yellow or white corn, husks
   and silk removed

Moisten chili powder with lime juice in small bowl. Add butter; stir until well blended. Season with salt to taste. Place in small crock or bowl. Place corn in 5-quart pan; cover with cold water. Cover pan and bring to a boil. Boil 1 minute. Turn off heat; let stand 2 minutes or until corn is tender. Drain. Serve with butter mixture.

Makes 4 servings

Top: Green Beans with Pine Nuts; bottom: Fresh Corn with Adobe Butter

Southwestern Entrees

GRILLED FISH WITH CHILI-CORN SALSA

To prevent fish from sticking, cook on a clean, well-oiled, preheated grill.

1 cup cooked whole kernel corn
1 large tomato, seeded and diced
¼ cup thinly sliced green onions
　　with tops
¼ cup canned diced green chilies
1 tablespoon coarsely chopped
　　cilantro
⅛ teaspoon ground cumin
1 tablespoon lime juice
4 teaspoons olive oil, divided
　　Salt
　　Pepper
1½ pounds firm-textured fish steaks
　　or fillets such as salmon,
　　halibut, sea bass or swordfish,
　　each 1 inch thick
　　Cilantro sprigs for garnish

Combine corn, tomato, green onions, green chilies, cilantro, cumin, lime juice and 2 teaspoons of the oil in small bowl; mix well. Add salt and pepper to taste. Let stand at room temperature 30 minutes for flavors to blend. Brush fish with the remaining 2 teaspoons oil; season with salt and pepper. Preheat charcoal grill and grease grill rack. Place fish on grill 4 to 6 inches above solid bed of coals (coals should be evenly covered with grey ashes). Cook, turning once, 4 to 5 minutes on each side or until fish turns opaque and just begins to flake. Serve with salsa. Garnish with cilantro.

Makes 4 servings

CHILIES RELLENOS EN CASSEROLE

For a weekend brunch, bake this in individual baking dishes, then lavish with your choice of condiments.

3 eggs, separated
³/₄ cup milk
³/₄ cup all-purpose flour
¹/₂ teaspoon salt
1 tablespoon butter or margarine
¹/₂ cup chopped onion
8 whole roasted, peeled chilies (page 3) or 2 cans (7 ounces each) whole green chilies, drained
8 ounces Monterey Jack cheese, cut into 8 slices

Condiments
Sour cream
Sliced green onions
Pitted ripe olive slices
Guacamole (page 14)
Salsa

Preheat oven to 350°F. Place egg yolks, milk, flour and salt in blender or food processor container fitted with metal blade; process until smooth. Pour into bowl and let stand. Melt butter in small skillet over medium heat. Add onion; cook until tender. If using canned chilies, pat dry with paper towels. Slit each chili lengthwise and carefully remove seeds. Place 1 strip cheese and 1 tablespoon onion in each chili; reshape chilies to cover cheese. Place 2 chilies in each of 4 greased 1¹/₂-cup gratin dishes or place in single layer in 13 × 9-inch baking dish. Beat egg whites until soft peaks form; fold into yolk mixture. Dividing mixture evenly, pour over chilies in gratin dishes (or pour entire mixture over casserole). Bake 20 to 25 minutes or until topping is puffed and a knife inserted in center comes out clean. Broil 4 inches below heat 30 seconds or until topping is golden brown. Serve with condiments.

Makes 4 servings

KEAM'S CANYON CHICKEN

4 cups tortilla chips
1 chicken (3 to 3¹/₂ pounds), cut into pieces
¹/₄ cup butter or margarine, melted
1 package (1¹/₄ ounces) taco seasoning mix
2 to 3 cups shredded iceberg lettuce
¹/₂ cup sour cream
1 medium avocado
1 lemon, cut into wedges
Green chili salsa

Preheat oven to 350°F. Place tortilla chips in food processor container fitted with metal blade; process to make coarse crumbs. (Or place chips in heavy plastic bag; crush with rolling pin.) Place crumbs on large plate. Rinse chicken and pat dry. Combine butter and seasoning mix in pie plate. Roll each piece of chicken in butter mixture, then coat with crumbs. Arrange chicken pieces, skin side up, slightly apart in 13 × 9-inch baking pan. Bake, uncovered, 1 hour or until meat near thigh bone is no longer pink when slashed. Arrange chicken on bed of shredded lettuce; top with sour cream. Peel, pit and slice avocado. Garnish chicken with avocado and lemon wedges. Serve with salsa.

Makes 4 servings

CHILI-CORN QUICHE

1 9-inch pastry shell, 1½ inches
    deep
1 can (8¾ ounces) whole kernel
    corn, drained, or 1 cup frozen
    whole kernel corn, cooked
1 can (4 ounces) diced green
    chilies, drained
¼ cup thinly sliced green onions
    with tops
1 cup (4 ounces) shredded
    Monterey Jack cheese
3 eggs
1½ cups half-and-half
½ teaspoon salt
½ teaspoon ground cumin

Preheat oven to 450°F. Line pastry
shell with aluminum foil; partially fill
with uncooked beans or rice to weight
shell. Bake 10 minutes. Remove foil
and beans; continue baking pastry 5
minutes or until lightly browned. Let
cool. Reduce oven temperature to
375°F.

Combine corn, green chilies and green
onions in small bowl. Spoon into pastry
shell; top with cheese. Whisk eggs,
half-and-half, salt and cumin in medium bowl. Pour over cheese. Bake 35
to 45 minutes or until filling is puffed
and knife inserted in center comes out
clean. Let stand 10 minutes before cutting to serve.

Makes 6 servings

ARROZ CON POLLO

*Subtle seasonings make this chicken
and rice dish a favorite with all ages.*

4 boneless chicken breast halves
    (about 1½ pounds total)
    Salt
    Ground black pepper
3 tablespoons olive oil
1 medium onion, chopped
¼ cup chopped green bell pepper
1 clove garlic, minced
1 cup uncooked rice
½ teaspoon ground cumin
¼ teaspoon ground turmeric
2 medium tomatoes, seeded and
    chopped
1 fresh or canned jalapeño pepper,
    stemmed, seeded and minced
1½ cups ready-to-serve chicken broth
    or Chicken Stock (page 73)
½ cup frozen peas, thawed
¼ cup pimiento-stuffed olives, sliced
2 teaspoons capers, rinsed and
    drained

Sprinkle chicken with salt and black
pepper. Heat oil in 3-quart pan over
medium-high heat. Add chicken; cook
4 minutes on each side or until lightly
browned. Remove chicken and set
aside. Reduce heat to medium. Add onion, bell pepper and garlic; cook until
vegetables are tender. Add rice; stir to
coat with drippings. Add cumin, turmeric, tomatoes, jalapeño pepper and
chicken broth. Bring to a boil. Place
chicken on rice. Cover; reduce heat
and simmer 25 minutes or until rice is
tender and all liquid is absorbed.
Sprinkle remaining ingredients over
chicken. Turn off heat. Let stand, covered, 10 minutes.

Makes 4 servings

Huevos Rancheros

HUEVOS RANCHEROS

Ranch-style eggs are traditionally served with refried beans.

Ranchero Sauce (recipe follows)
4 to 8 corn tortillas, 6- to 7-inch diameter
Vegetable oil for frying (optional)
4 to 8 fried eggs
Peeled avocado slices for garnish
Cilantro sprigs for garnish

Prepare Ranchero Sauce. For soft tortillas, heat ungreased skillet over medium-high heat. Place tortillas, one at a time, in pan and heat 30 seconds on each side or until soft and hot. Immediately place in covered ovenproof container or foil packet; keep warm in 200°F oven. For fried tortillas, heat ½ inch oil in 8-inch skillet over medium-high heat. When oil is hot, add tortillas, one at a time. Cook 5 seconds on each side or until limp; drain on paper towels.

For each serving, place 1 or 2 tortillas on plate, top with 1 or 2 fried eggs and about ½ cup Ranchero Sauce. Garnish as desired.

Makes 4 servings

RANCHERO SAUCE

3 tablespoons vegetable oil
1 medium onion, chopped
2 cloves garlic, minced
2 tablespoons all-purpose flour
1 can (14½ ounces) ready-to-serve chicken broth or 1¾ cups Chicken Stock (page 73)
1 can (8 ounces) tomatoes, drained and chopped
2 tablespoons chili powder
½ teaspoon dried oregano, crushed
Salt

Heat oil in 3-quart pan over medium heat. Add onion and garlic; cook until onion is tender. Add flour and cook, stirring constantly, until bubbling and foamy. Stir in chicken broth, tomatoes, chili powder and oregano. Cook until sauce is thick and boiling, stirring constantly. Reduce heat; simmer, uncovered, until sauce is reduced to about 2 cups. Season with salt to taste. Keep sauce warm.

SCRAMBLED EGGS WITH TAMALES

1 can (15 ounces) tamales
8 eggs
2 tablespoons milk
½ teaspoon salt
2 tablespoons butter or margarine
1 large tomato, chopped
2 tablespoons minced onion
2 tablespoons diced green chilies
1 cup (4 ounces) shredded Monterey Jack cheese
Cilantro sprigs for garnish

Preheat oven to 350°F. Drain tamales, reserving half of the sauce from the can. Remove paper wrappings from tamales; place tamales in single layer in 10 × 6-inch baking dish. Cover with reserved sauce. Place in 350°F oven 10 minutes to heat through. Meanwhile, whisk eggs, milk and salt in medium bowl. Melt butter in large skillet over medium heat. Add tomato, onion and chilies. Cook 2 minutes or until vegetables are heated through but still crisp. Add eggs. Cook, stirring gently, until eggs are soft set. Remove tamales from oven. Spoon eggs over tamales; sprinkle with cheese. Broil 4 inches below heat 30 seconds or just until cheese melts. Garnish with cilantro sprigs.

Makes 4 to 6 servings

BROILED TROUT WITH PIÑON BUTTER

If you prefer to barbecue trout, place fish in a hinged wire broiler and grill, uncovered, 4 to 6 inches above low-glowing coals.

4 whole trout (each about 8 ounces), cleaned
¼ cup vegetable oil
¼ cup dry white wine
2 tablespoons minced chives
2 tablespoons chopped parsley
½ teaspoon salt
⅛ teaspoon pepper
¼ cup butter or margarine, softened
¼ cup pine nuts, finely chopped
1 lemon, cut into wedges, for garnish

Place trout in heavy self-sealing plastic bag. Whisk oil, wine, chives, parsley, salt and pepper in small bowl. Pour over fish; seal bag. Marinate 30 minutes or refrigerate up to 2 hours, turning bag occasionally to distribute marinade. Combine butter and pine nuts; stir until well blended. Cover and let stand at room temperature until ready to use.

Preheat broiler and greased broiling pan. Remove fish from marinade and drain briefly; reserve marinade. Place fish on broiling pan. Broil 4 to 6 inches from heat 4 minutes; turn fish over. Brush with marinade; continue broiling 4 to 6 minutes or until fish turns opaque and just begins to flake. Transfer fish to serving platter. Place a dollop of reserved butter mixture on each fish. Garnish with lemon wedges.

Makes 4 servings

CARNE ADOVADA

In Chimayo, New Mexico, this specialty is served with pinto beans or rice. It's muy bueno for those who like things hot!

8 to 10 dried red New Mexico or California chilies
2 cups water
⅓ cup finely chopped onion
1 clove garlic, minced
1 teaspoon dried oregano, crushed
½ teaspoon salt
½ teaspoon ground cumin
1½ pounds lean boneless pork butt or 2 pounds pork chops, cut ½ inch thick

Wash chilies; remove stems and seeds. Place in 3-quart pan with water. Cover and simmer 20 minutes or until chilies are very soft. Pour chilies and liquid into blender or food processor container fitted with metal blade; process until pureed. Push puree through wire strainer; discard pulp. Add onion, garlic, oregano, salt and cumin to chili mixture.

If using pork butt, trim excess fat. Cut meat into ½-inch slices, then cut into strips about 1 inch wide and 3 inches long. If using pork chops, trim fat.

Place meat in heavy self-sealing plastic bag. Pour chili mixture over meat; seal bag. Refrigerate 1 to 2 days. Preheat oven to 325°F. Transfer meat and chili mixture to 2½-quart casserole dish; cover. Bake 2 to 2½ hours or until meat is very tender. Skim and discard fat before serving.

Makes 4 to 6 servings

RANCH-STYLE SAUSAGE & APPLE QUICHE

1   9-inch pastry shell, 1½ inches deep
½   pound bulk spicy pork sausage
½   cup chopped onion
¾   cup shredded, peeled tart apple
1   tablespoon lemon juice
1   tablespoon sugar
⅛   teaspoon crushed red chili pepper
1   cup (4 ounces) shredded Cheddar cheese
3   eggs
1½ cups half-and-half
¼   teaspoon salt
    Dash of ground black pepper

Preheat oven to 450°F. Line pastry shell with aluminum foil; partially fill with uncooked beans or rice to weight shell. Bake 10 minutes. Remove foil and beans; continue baking pastry 5 minutes or until lightly browned. Let cool. Reduce oven temperature to 375°F.

Crumble sausage into large skillet; add onion. Stir over medium heat until sausage is browned and onion is tender. Spoon off and discard pan drippings. Add apple, lemon juice, sugar and chili pepper. Cook on medium-high heat 4 minutes or until apple is barely tender and all liquid is evaporated, stirring constantly. Let cool. Spoon sausage mixture into pastry shell; top with cheese. Whisk eggs, half-and-half, salt and black pepper in medium bowl. Pour over sausage mixture. Bake 35 to 45 minutes or until filling is puffed and knife inserted in center comes out clean. Let stand 10 minutes before cutting to serve.

Makes 6 servings

HIGH-COUNTRY LAMB

Lamb or kid goat that's been cooked over the coals tastes marvelous when wrapped in a warm flour tortilla and splashed with salsa.

1   leg of lamb (6 to 7 pounds), boned and butterflied
¼   cup olive oil
¼   cup lemon juice
¼   cup dry vermouth
1   teaspoon dried oregano, crushed
1   clove garlic, minced
1   teaspoon salt
½   teaspoon pepper
½   teaspoon ground cumin
⅛   teaspoon hot pepper sauce

Place lamb in heavy self-sealing plastic bag. Combine remaining ingredients in small bowl. Pour over meat; seal bag. Refrigerate 4 to 6 hours or overnight, turning bag occasionally to distribute marinade.

Preheat charcoal grill and grease grill rack. Remove meat from refrigerator and bring to room temperature. Remove meat from marinade and drain briefly; reserve marinade. Place meat on grill 4 to 6 inches above solid bed of coals (coals should be evenly covered with gray ashes). Cook, uncovered, 50 minutes or until a meat thermometer inserted in thickest part registers 140°F for rare, 160°F for medium or 170°F for well-done, basting frequently and turning as needed to brown evenly. To serve, slice meat across grain.

Makes 8 to 10 servings

FAJITAS

¼ cup lime juice
¼ cup tequila
2 tablespoons vegetable oil
2 cloves garlic, minced
1 fresh or canned jalapeño pepper,
    stemmed, seeded and minced
1 tablespoon chopped cilantro
¼ teaspoon salt
¼ teaspoon ground black pepper
1½ pounds beef flank steak
2 cans (about 16 ounces each)
    refried beans
8 to 12 flour tortillas, 8-inch
    diameter

Condiments
2 avocados or Guacamole (page 14)
    Lime juice
    Salsa
    Sour cream

To prepare marinade, combine lime juice, tequila, oil, garlic, jalapeño pepper, cilantro, salt and black pepper in small bowl. Trim any visible fat from meat; place in heavy self-sealing plastic bag. Pour marinade over meat; seal bag. Refrigerate 8 hours or up to 2 days, turning bag occasionally to distribute marinade.

Preheat charcoal grill and grease grill rack. Place refried beans in large skillet and heat through; keep warm. Stack and wrap tortillas in foil; place tortillas on side of grill to heat. Remove meat from marinade; reserve marinade. Place meat on grill 4 to 6 inches above solid bed of coals (coals should be medium-glowing). Cook, basting frequently with reserved marinade, 4 minutes on each side for rare or until meat is brown on the outside but still pink when slashed in thickest part. To serve, cut meat across the grain into thin slices; place on warm platter. Peel, pit and chop avocados; sprinkle with lime juice. Place tortillas, refried beans, avocados, salsa and sour cream in separate serving dishes. Wrap the meat and condiments in tortilla and eat out of hand.
Makes 4 to 6 servings

Variation
Shrimp or Chicken Fajitas: Follow directions for Fajitas but use 2 pounds raw medium shrimp, shelled and deveined, *or* 2 pounds chicken breasts, boned and skinned, in place of flank steak. Marinate 2 to 3 hours. To cook, thread shrimp or chicken on skewers. Place on greased grill 4 to 6 inches above a solid bed of coals (coals should be low-glowing). Cook shrimp, turning and basting frequently with reserved marinade, 3 to 4 minutes on each side or until pink. Cook chicken, turning and basting frequently with reserved marinade, 3 to 4 minutes on each side or until meat is no longer pink when slashed in thickest part.

Fajitas

MESQUITE-GRILLED CHICKEN QUARTERS

Extra care should be taken when grilling foods over mesquite charcoal since it burns hotter (and cooks food faster) than other types of charcoal. Let it burn until it is covered with gray ash before putting the chicken on the grill.

    2 chickens (about 3½ pounds
        each), cut into quarters
    2 tablespoons vegetable oil
    1 small onion, chopped
    1 clove garlic, minced
    ½ cup ketchup
    2 tablespoons brown sugar
    2 teaspoons chili powder
    1 teaspoon dry mustard
    ¼ teaspoon salt
    ¼ teaspoon pepper
    1 can (12 ounces) beer
    ½ cup tomato juice
    ¼ cup Worcestershire sauce
    1 tablespoon lemon juice

Preheat oven to 350°F. Place chickens in 1 large or 2 medium baking pans; cover tightly with foil. Bake 30 minutes. Remove from oven; uncover. Cool. Heat oil in 3-quart pan over medium heat. Add onion and garlic; cook until onion is tender. Combine ketchup, brown sugar, chili powder, dry mustard, salt and pepper in medium bowl. Add remaining ingredients; whisk until well blended. Pour into pan. Bring to a boil. Reduce heat and simmer, stirring occasionally, 20 minutes or until sauce has thickened slightly and is reduced to about 2 cups. Let cool.

Place chickens into 2 heavy self-sealing plastic bags. Dividing marinade equally, pour over chicken in each bag; seal bags. Refrigerate 8 hours or up to 2 days.

Preheat charcoal grill and grease grill rack. Remove chickens from refrigerator and bring to room temperature. Remove chickens from marinade and drain well; reserve marinade. (Because marinade contains sugar, it will burn if cooked too long.) Hook wing tips back behind body joint on breast pieces of chicken. Place leg and thigh quarters on hottest part of grill 4 to 6 inches above solid bed of coals (coals should be evenly covered with gray ashes); place breast pieces on cooler edges of grill. Cook, turning occasionally, 20 to 25 minutes or until meat near thigh bone is no longer pink when slashed. Brush chicken generously with marinade during the last 10 minutes of cooking.

Makes 8 servings

TEXAS-STYLE BARBECUED BRISKET

The classic Texas barbecue is cooked in a pit; our delicious home version is more easily made in the oven. If you have leftover meat, simmer thin slices in the barbecue sauce and serve between toasted crusty rolls.

    1 beef brisket (3 to 4 pounds)
    3 tablespoons Worcestershire sauce
    1 teaspoon liquid smoke
    1 tablespoon ground mild red chili
        or chili powder
    1 teaspoon celery salt
    1 teaspoon coarsely ground black
        pepper
    2 cloves garlic, minced
    2 bay leaves
      Barbecue Sauce (recipe follows)

Trim and discard excess fat from meat; place in heavy self-sealing plastic bag. Combine Worcestershire sauce, liquid smoke, ground chili, celery salt, pepper, garlic and bay leaves in small bowl. Spread half of the mixture onto each side of meat with large spoon; seal bag. Refrigerate 24 hours. Preheat oven to 300°F. Remove meat from bag and place on large piece of heavy-duty foil. Pour marinade over meat; seal foil. Place in large roasting pan. Bake 4 hours. Prepare Barbecue Sauce during last ½ hour of baking.

Remove meat from oven. Open foil; carefully pour juices into 2-cup measure. Discard bay leaves; skim fat from juices. Stir 1 cup of juices into Barbecue Sauce. Save remaining juices for other use or discard. Pour barbecue sauce mixture over meat. Reseal foil; continue baking 1 hour. Remove meat from foil; cut across the grain into ¼-inch slices. Serve 2 to 3 tablespoons barbecue sauce mixture over each serving.

Makes 10 to 12 servings

BARBECUE SAUCE

    3 tablespoons vegetable oil
    1 medium onion, chopped
    2 cloves garlic, minced
    1 cup ketchup
    ½ cup molasses
    ¼ cup cider vinegar
    2 teaspoons ground mild red chili
        or chili powder
    ½ teaspoon dry mustard

Heat oil in 3-quart pan over medium heat. Add onion and garlic; cook until onion is tender. Add remaining ingredients. Simmer 5 minutes, then remove from heat until needed.

GRILLED BEEF WITH CREAMY JALAPEÑO SAUCE

    2 egg yolks
    1 to 1½ teaspoons chopped fresh
        or canned jalapeño peppers
    1 tablespoon coarsely chopped
        cilantro
    2 tablespoons lemon juice
    ¾ cup butter, melted and warm
    2 to 3 drops hot pepper sauce
    6 ground beef patties, about 1 inch
        thick, *or* 6 small New York or
        club steaks, 1 inch thick
    Salt
    Ground black pepper
    3 tomatoes, sliced, for garnish
    Cilantro sprigs for garnish

To prepare sauce ahead, process egg yolks, jalapeño peppers and chopped cilantro in blender container until seasonings are finely chopped. Heat lemon juice in small pan to simmering. Add to egg yolk mixture; blend 45 seconds. With motor on medium speed, add butter, a few drops at a time in the beginning but increase to a thin, regular stream as mixture begins to thicken. (Sauce will be consistency of a creamy salad dressing.) Stir in hot pepper sauce. Pour into jar; cover. Let stand at room temperature up to 1 hour. While meat is cooking, place jar in hot water; stir until sauce is warm, not hot.

Preheat charcoal grill and grease grill rack. Place meat on grill 4 to 6 inches above solid bed of coals (coals should be evenly covered with gray ashes). Cook, turning once, 3 to 5 minutes on each side for rare or to desired doneness. Season with salt and black pepper to taste. Spoon sauce over meat; garnish with tomato slices and cilantro sprigs.

Makes 6 servings

Tequila-Lime Prawns

SOUTHWEST SCALLOPINI

The cooking technique is Italian and the seasoning is Mexican. The result is a delicious example of modern Southwestern cooking.

1½ pounds boneless skinless turkey breast, sliced ¼ inch thick
¼ cup all-purpose flour
½ teaspoon chili powder
¼ teaspoon ground cinnamon
⅛ teaspoon white pepper
⅓ cup butter or margarine, divided
2 green onions, white parts only, minced
1 clove garlic, minced
½ cup orange juice
¼ cup ready-to-serve chicken broth or Chicken Stock (page 73)
2 tablespoons raisins
1 tablespoon capers, drained
2 oranges
2 tablespoons toasted slivered almonds

Place turkey slices slightly apart between 2 sheets of waxed paper; pound with mallet to ⅛-inch thickness. Combine flour, chili powder, cinnamon and white pepper on plate. Dredge each turkey slice in flour mixture; gently shake off excess. Melt 2 tablespoons of the butter in large skillet over medium-high heat. Add as many slices of turkey as will fit in skillet without crowding. Cook 30 seconds or until lightly browned. Turn slices over; repeat. Transfer to platter and keep warm. Repeat with remaining turkey, adding more butter to skillet as needed.

When all slices are browned, add green onions and garlic to pan drippings; cook 2 minutes. Add orange juice, chicken broth, raisins and capers, stirring to scrape up browned bits from bottom of pan. Bring to a boil. Turn off heat; add the remaining butter (about 2 tablespoons) and stir until completely blended. Pare oranges, removing white membrane; cut into slices. Pour sauce over turkey; sprinkle with almonds. Garnish with orange slices.

Makes 6 servings

TEQUILA-LIME PRAWNS

1 pound medium shrimp, shelled and deveined
3 tablespoons butter or margarine
1 tablespoon olive oil
2 large garlic cloves, minced
2 tablespoons tequila
1 tablespoon lime juice
¼ teaspoon salt
¼ teaspoon crushed red chili pepper
3 tablespoons coarsely chopped cilantro
Hot cooked rice (optional)
Lime wedges for garnish

Pat shrimp dry with paper towels. Heat butter and oil in large skillet over medium heat. When butter is melted, add garlic; cook 30 seconds. Add shrimp; cook 2 minutes, stirring occasionally. Stir in tequila, lime juice, salt and chili pepper. Cook 2 minutes or until most of liquid evaporates and shrimp are pink and glazed. Add cilantro; cook 10 seconds. Serve over hot cooked rice if desired. Garnish with lime wedges.

Makes 3 or 4 servings

Tortilla Dishes

TOSTADAS

Spiced Meat Filling (page 72) or
    2 cups Carnitas (page 9)
1 cup Salsa Fresca (page 6) or
    picante sauce
1 can (about 16 ounces) refried
    beans
8 crisp-fried corn tortillas, 6- to
    7-inch diameter
2 cups shredded lettuce
1 cup (4 ounces) shredded
    Cheddar or Monterey Jack
    cheese
1 large avocado, peeled, pitted and
    sliced
2 tomatoes, cut into wedges or
    chopped
1 small onion, thinly sliced
    crosswise, separated into rings
    Cilantro sprigs for garnish

Prepare Spiced Meat Filling and Salsa Fresca; heat meat filling. (If using Carnitas, shred cubes of meat with fingers; place in skillet and stir over low heat until hot.) Heat refried beans in large skillet. To assemble each tostada, place a tortilla on dinner plate and spread with about ¼ cup refried beans. Cover with meat filling, lettuce, cheese, avocado, tomatoes and onion. Drizzle with salsa. Garnish with cilantro.

Makes 8 tostadas

Green Enchiladas with Chicken

GREEN ENCHILADAS
WITH CHICKEN

1 pound fresh tomatillos or 2 cans
    (13 ounces each) tomatillos,
    drained
1 can (7 ounces) diced green
    chilies, undrained
2 tablespoons vegetable oil
1 medium onion, finely chopped
1 clove garlic, minced
1 can (14½ ounces) ready-to-serve
    chicken broth or 1¾ cups
    Chicken Stock (page 73)
    Vegetable oil for frying
12 corn tortillas, 6- to 7-inch
    diameter
3 cups shredded cooked chicken
2½ cups (10 ounces) shredded
    Monterey Jack cheese
1 cup (½ pint) sour cream
4 green onions with tops, thinly
    sliced
    Cilantro sprigs for garnish

Preheat oven to 350°F. If using fresh tomatillos, remove husks; wash thoroughly. Place tomatillos in 2-quart pan; add ½ inch water. Bring to a boil. Cover; reduce heat and simmer 10 minutes or until tender. Drain. Place tomatillos and chilies in blender or food processor container fitted with metal blade; process until pureed. Heat the 2 tablespoons oil in large skillet over medium heat. Add onion and garlic; cook until onion is tender. Stir in puree and chicken broth. Simmer, uncovered, until sauce has reduced to about 2½ cups and is consistency of canned tomato sauce.

Heat ½ inch oil in 7- to 8-inch skillet over medium-high heat. Place 1 tortilla in hot oil; cook 2 seconds on each side or just until limp. Drain briefly on paper towels, then dip softened tortilla into tomatillo sauce. Transfer sauced tortilla to a plate. Place about ¼ cup of the chicken and 2 tablespoons of the cheese across center of tortilla; roll to enclose. Place enchilada, seam side down, in 15 × 10-inch baking pan. Repeat until all tortillas are filled. Spoon remaining sauce over enchiladas, making sure all ends are moistened; reserve remaining cheese. Cover. Bake 20 to 30 minutes or until hot in center. Uncover and top with reserved cheese. Continue baking, uncovered, 10 minutes or until cheese is melted. Spoon sour cream down center of enchiladas; sprinkle with green onions. Garnish with cilantro.

Makes 6 servings

CHIMICHANGAS

Spiced Meat Filling (recipe follows)
1 cup refried beans
1 cup (4 ounces) shredded Monterey Jack cheese
8 flour tortillas, 10- to 12-inch diameter
Vegetable oil for deep-frying

Condiments
1 small head lettuce, shredded
2 tomatoes, diced
1 cup (1/2 pint) sour cream
1 cup Salsa Fresca (page 6) or picante sauce
1 can (2 1/4 ounces) sliced pitted ripe olives, drained
8 radishes, sliced

Prepare Spiced Meat Filling. To assemble each chimichanga, spoon about 2 tablespoons of the beans, 2 tablespoons of the cheese and 1/4 cup of the meat filling into center of each tortilla. Fold 1 side of tortilla over filling; fold in ends, then roll to enclose ends and filling. Secure open edge with wooden pick. Pour oil into large, deep skillet to depth of 1 inch. Place over medium heat until oil registers 350°F on deep-frying thermometer. Lower 1 chimichanga into oil, seam side down. Add second chimichanga. Cook 1 minute or until golden brown. Carefully turn over; continue cooking 1 minute or until golden. Remove from oil; drain on paper towels. Keep warm in 200°F oven; repeat until all chimichangas are cooked. To serve, place 1 chimichanga on dinner plate; remove wooden pick. Serve with condiments as desired.

Makes 8 chimichangas

SPICED MEAT FILLING

1/2 pound lean ground beef
1/4 pound lean ground pork
1/2 cup chopped onion
1 clove garlic, minced
1 fresh or canned jalapeño pepper, stemmed, seeded and minced
1 teaspoon brown sugar
1 teaspoon chili powder
1/4 teaspoon salt
1/4 teaspoon dried oregano, crushed
1/4 teaspoon ground cumin
1/8 teaspoon ground cinnamon
1/2 cup canned tomatoes, drained and finely chopped
1 tablespoon cider vinegar

Crumble beef and pork into large skillet; stir over medium-high heat until browned. Add onion, garlic and jalapeño pepper. Reduce heat to medium; cook until onion is tender. Spoon off and discard pan drippings. Add remaining ingredients. Simmer, stirring occasionally, 15 minutes or until most of liquid has evaporated.

CHILAQUILES

Assemble this casserole just before it goes into the oven so the chips will not become too soft.

8 cups Crisp Tortilla Chips (page 15) or taco chips
1 can (10 3/4 ounces) condensed cream of chicken soup
1/2 cup mild green chili salsa
1 can (4 ounces) diced green chilies, undrained
2 to 3 cups shredded cooked chicken or turkey
2 cups (8 ounces) shredded Cheddar cheese
Sliced pitted ripe olives for garnish
Cilantro sprigs for garnish

Prepare Crisp Tortilla Chips. Preheat oven to 350°F. Combine soup and salsa in medium bowl; stir in green chilies. Place 1/3 of the tortilla chips in 2- to 2 1/2-quart casserole dish; top with 1/3 of the chicken. Spread 1/3 of the soup mixture over chicken; sprinkle with 1/3 of the cheese. Repeat layering. Bake, uncovered, 15 minutes or until casserole is heated through and cheese is melted. Garnish with olives and cilantro.

Makes 6 servings

CHICKEN ENCHILADAS

Shredded chicken from Chicken Stock (recipe follows)
Red Chili Sauce (page 76) or 2 cups enchilada sauce, divided
Vegetable oil for frying
12 corn tortillas, 6- to 7-inch diameter
3 green onions with tops, thinly sliced
1 1/2 cups (6 ounces) shredded Monterey Jack cheese
1 can (2 1/4 ounces) sliced pitted ripe olives, drained

Prepare Chicken Stock and Red Chili Sauce. Preheat oven to 350°F. Heat half of the chili sauce in 7- to 8-inch skillet until bubbly; remove from heat. Heat 1/2 inch oil in another 7- to 8-inch skillet over medium-high heat. Place 1 tortilla in hot oil; cook 2 seconds on each side or just until limp. Drain briefly on paper towels, then dip softened tortilla into chili sauce. Transfer sauced tortilla to a plate. Place about 1/4 cup chicken and 2 teaspoons green onions across center of tortilla; roll to enclose. Place, seam side down, in 15 × 10-inch baking pan. Repeat until all tortillas are filled. Spoon remaining chili sauce over enchiladas, making sure ends are moistened. Sprinkle with cheese. Bake, covered, 20 to 30 minutes or until hot in center. Sprinkle with olives before serving.

Makes 6 servings

CHICKEN STOCK

1 chicken (3 to 4 pounds), cut in half
1 small onion, cut into quarters
1 clove garlic, cut in half
1 bay leaf
3 parsley sprigs
1/2 teaspoon salt
1/4 teaspoon ground cumin
1/8 teaspoon black peppercorns
4 cups water

Place chicken in 5-quart pan. Add remaining ingredients. Bring to a boil. Cover; reduce heat and simmer 45 minutes or until meat near thigh bone is no longer pink when slashed. Transfer chicken to a plate with slotted spoon; let cool. Strain stock; discard solids. Save for any recipe that calls for Chicken Stock. Remove chicken from bones; discard skin and bones. Shred chicken.

Makes about 3 cups stock

Variation
Beef Enchiladas: Follow directions for Chicken Enchiladas but omit chicken. Instead, crumble 1 pound lean ground beef and 1/4 pound chorizo sausage (casing removed) into large skillet; stir over medium-high heat until browned. Add 1 medium onion, chopped; 1 clove garlic, minced; and 1/4 teaspoon salt. Reduce heat to medium; cook until onion is tender. Spoon off and discard pan drippings before filling tortillas.

QUESADILLA

Cook this Southwestern "sandwich" in a dry skillet if you like a soft tortilla; use butter if you prefer the tortilla to have a crispy finish.

1 teaspoon butter or margarine (optional)
1 flour tortilla, 8-inch diameter
1/2 cup (2 ounces) shredded Colby or Cheddar cheese
1 tablespoon minced green onion with top
1 tablespoon canned diced green chili
Salsa

Place large nonstick skillet over medium heat. If using butter, melt in skillet. Add tortilla. Place cheese, green onion and chili on half of tortilla; fold in half. Cook, turning once or twice, 4 minutes or until cheese is melted and tortilla is lightly browned. Cut into wedges. Serve with salsa.

Makes 1 serving

Variation
Quesadilla with Potato: Combine 1/4 cup mashed potato, 1 tablespoon canned diced green chili and 1 tablespoon minced green onion in small bowl. Spread mixture onto half of an 8-inch flour or Whole Wheat Tortilla (page 38); top with 1/3 cup shredded Colby cheese. Fold tortilla in half. Cook as directed above.

Makes 1 serving

SOFT TACOS WITH CHICKEN

This filling may also be used to fill crisp taco shells.

8 corn tortillas, 6- to 7-inch diameter
2 tablespoons butter or margarine
1 medium onion, chopped
1 1/2 cups shredded cooked chicken
1 can (4 ounces) diced green chilies, drained
2 tablespoons chopped cilantro
1 cup (1/2 pint) sour cream
Salt
Pepper
1 1/2 cups (6 ounces) shredded Monterey Jack cheese
1 large avocado, peeled, pitted and diced
Green taco sauce

Stack and wrap tortillas in foil. Warm in 350°F oven 15 minutes or until heated through. Melt butter in large skillet over medium heat. Add onion; cook until tender. Add chicken, green chilies and cilantro. Cook 3 minutes or until mixture is hot. Reduce heat to low. Stir in sour cream; add salt and pepper to taste. Heat gently; do not boil. To assemble each taco, spoon about 3 tablespoons of the chicken mixture into center of each tortilla; sprinkle with 2 tablespoons of the cheese. Top with avocado; drizzle with 1 to 2 teaspoons taco sauce. Sprinkle tacos with remaining cheese. Roll tortilla into cone shape or fold in half and eat out of hand.

Makes 8 tacos

Soft Tacos with Chicken

CHEESE ENCHILADAS

Red chili sauce, also called enchilada sauce or chili colorado, is very easy to make and tastes far better than anything you can buy in a can. For best flavor, use any mild packaged chili, not the commercial chili powder designed to season chili con carne.

Red Chili Sauce (recipe follows)
Vegetable oil for frying
12 corn tortillas, 6- to 7-inch
    diameter
3 cups (12 ounces) shredded
    Monterey Jack cheese
1 medium onion, chopped
3 green onions with tops, thinly
    sliced

Prepare Red Chili Sauce. Preheat oven to 350°F. Heat ½ inch oil in 7- to 8-inch skillet over medium-high heat. Place 1 tortilla in hot oil; cook 2 seconds on each side or just until limp. Drain briefly on paper towels, then dip softened tortilla into chili sauce. Transfer sauced tortilla to a plate. Place about 3 tablespoons of the cheese and 2 teaspoons of the chopped onion across center of tortilla; roll to enclose. Place enchiladas, seam side down, in 15 × 10-inch baking pan. Repeat until all tortillas are filled. Spoon remaining chili sauce over enchiladas, making sure ends are moistened. Sprinkle with the remaining cheese. Bake, covered, 20 to 30 minutes or until hot in center. Sprinkle with green onions just before serving.

Makes 6 servings

RED CHILI SAUCE

3 tablespoons olive oil or vegetable
    oil
1 clove garlic, minced
2 tablespoons all-purpose flour
⅓ cup mild chili powder
2 cups water
1 teaspoon dried oregano, crushed
½ teaspoon salt

Heat oil in 3-quart pan over low heat. Add garlic; cook 2 minutes or just until golden. Add flour and cook, stirring constantly, until mixture is bubbling and a light golden color. Blend in chili powder. Stir in water; add oregano and salt. Increase heat to medium; cook, stirring constantly, until sauce is thick and boiling. Reduce heat to low so sauce stays warm but does not boil.

Makes 2 cups

Variations

Quick Enchiladas: Use 1 large can (19 ounces) and 1 small can (10 ounces) enchilada sauce in place of Red Chili Sauce. Omit step of dipping tortillas into hot oil; instead dip each tortilla directly into enough warm enchilada sauce to soften tortilla so it rolls easily. Fill and bake as directed above.

Red Chili Sauce from dried red chilies: Wash 16 to 20 dried red New Mexico or California chilies; remove stems and seeds. Place in 3-quart pan with 3 cups water. Cover and simmer 20 minutes or until chilies are very soft. Pour chilies and liquid into blender or food processor container fitted with metal blade; process until pureed. Push puree through wire strainer; discard pulp. Heat 1 tablespoon vegetable oil in large skillet over medium heat. Add ⅓ cup finely chopped onion and 1 clove garlic, minced; cook until onion is tender. Add chili puree, 1 teaspoon dried oregano, crushed, and ¾ teaspoon salt. Simmer 10 minutes.

Makes about 2½ cups

FLAT BLUE ENCHILADAS

Easily made blue corn crepes can stand in for hard-to-find blue corn tortillas.

¾ **cup milk**
1 **egg**
½ **cup blue cornmeal**
½ **cup all-purpose flour**
⅛ **teaspoon salt**
  Vegetable oil
1½ **cups (6 ounces) shredded Monterey Jack cheese**
1 **can (4 ounces) diced green chilies, drained**
1 **cup (½ pint) sour cream**
3 **green onions with tops, thinly sliced**
  Salsa

To make crepes, place milk, egg, cornmeal, flour and salt in blender or food processor container fitted with metal blade; process until smooth. Pour into bowl; let batter rest at room temperature 1 hour. Heat 6- to 7-inch skillet over medium-high heat; brush lightly with oil. Stir batter; pour 2 to 2½ tablespoons batter into pan. Immediately tilt pan to coat evenly. Cook crepe until top side is dry and underside is lightly browned. Turn and cook other side about 10 seconds. Slide out of pan onto paper towel. Repeat, oiling pan and stirring batter before making each crepe. (Recipe should yield nine crepes.) When all crepes are cooked, stack on a plate; cover with plastic wrap and refrigerate until needed, up to 2 days.

To assemble enchiladas, combine cheese and chilies in small bowl. Combine sour cream and green onions in another small bowl. Preheat oven to 300°F. Stack 3 crepes on each of 3 ovenproof plates; cover with foil. Bake 10 minutes to heat through. Remove plates from oven; increase oven temperature to 350°F. Remove top 2 crepes from each plate. Dividing mixture equally, cover bottom crepes with ½ of the cheese mixture. Top each stack with a second crepe; spread each stack with ⅓ of the sour cream mixture. Top each with a third crepe; cover with remaining cheese mixture. Bake, uncovered, 10 minutes or until cheese is melted. Serve 1 stack per person for entree servings or cut stacks into wedges for appetizers. Serve with salsa.
Makes 3 servings

Variation
Rolled Shrimp Enchiladas: Prepare Blue Corn Crepes. Combine ½ pound cooked deveined small shrimp, ¾ cup (3 ounces) shredded Monterey Jack cheese and ¼ cup diced green chilies in medium bowl. Spoon equal amount of shrimp mixture down center of each crepe; roll to enclose. Arrange enchiladas, seam side down, in greased 13 × 9-inch baking pan. Bake, uncovered, in 350°F oven 15 minutes or until cheese is melted. Spoon ¾ cup sour cream down center of enchiladas; sprinkle with 3 tablespoons sliced green onions.
Makes 4 servings

Beef & Bean Burritos

BEEF & BEAN BURRITOS

Burritos are soft flour tortillas wrapped around a variety of savory fillings. For an easy meal, provide the ingredients and let each diner do the assembling.

½ cup **Red Chili Sauce (page 76)** or enchilada sauce
1 cup **Guacamole (page 14)** or purchased guacamole
1 pound **lean ground beef**
½ cup **chopped onion**
¼ teaspoon **salt**
1 can (about 16 ounces) **refried beans**
8 **flour tortillas, 10- to 12-inch diameter**

Condiments
1 cup (4 ounces) **shredded Monterey Jack cheese**
2 cups **shredded lettuce**
1 cup (½ pint) **sour cream**

Prepare Red Chili Sauce and Guacamole. Crumble meat into large skillet; stir over medium-high heat until browned. Add onion; reduce heat to medium. Cook until onion is tender. Spoon off and discard pan drippings. Stir in chili sauce and salt. Cover; simmer 10 minutes for flavors to blend. Keep warm. Place refried beans in another large skillet and heat through; keep warm. To heat tortillas, place them, one at a time, in large ungreased skillet placed over medium-high heat. Turn frequently until soft and hot, about 30 seconds. Immediately wrap in cloth or foil to keep warm. Serve tortillas in towel-lined basket. Serve meat mixture, beans, cheese, lettuce, sour cream and Guacamole in separate bowls. To assemble each burrito, place about ¼ cup each of the meat filling and refried beans on each tortilla; top with condiments and Guacamole as desired. Roll up and eat out of hand.

Makes 8 burritos

Tip:
To heat tortillas in microwave oven, stack and wrap tortillas in paper towels. Microwave 50 seconds to 1 minute or until hot.

QUESADILLA GRANDE

2 **flour tortillas, 8-inch diameter**
2 to 3 **large fresh spinach leaves, stems removed, rinsed and patted dry**
2 to 3 slices **cooked chicken breast**
2 tablespoons **salsa**
1 tablespoon **chopped cilantro leaves**
¼ cup (1 ounce) **shredded Monterey Jack cheese**
2 teaspoons **butter or margarine (optional)**

Place 1 tortilla in large nonstick skillet; cover tortilla with spinach leaves. Place chicken in single layer over spinach. Spoon salsa over chicken. Sprinkle with cilantro; top with cheese. Place remaining tortilla on top, pressing tortilla down so filling becomes compact. Cook over medium heat 4 to 5 minutes or until bottom tortilla is lightly browned. Holding top tortilla in place, gently turn over. Continue cooking 4 minutes or until bottom tortilla is browned and cheese is melted. For a crispy finish, place butter in skillet to melt; lift quesadilla to let butter flow into center of skillet. Cook 30 seconds. Turn over; continue cooking 30 seconds. Cut into wedges to serve.

Makes 1 serving

Desserts & Beverages

FRUIT TRAY WITH HONEY-LIME SAUCE

1 cantaloupe, seeded and peeled
1 papaya, seeded and peeled
1 small fresh pineapple, peeled, cored and cut into triangles or short spears
1½ cups strawberries, hulled, or 6 fresh figs, cut in half
2 kiwifruit, peeled and thinly sliced
1 cup (½ pint) whipping cream
3 tablespoons honey
1 teaspoon grated lime peel
2 teaspoons lime juice
2 bananas
1 egg white (room temperature)*
Mint sprig for garnish

Cut cantaloupe and papaya into ½-inch crescents. Arrange cantaloupe, papaya, pineapple, strawberries and kiwifruit on large serving platter. Cover and chill up to 4 hours. Whip cream in medium bowl until soft peaks form. Fold in honey, lime peel and lime juice. Cover and refrigerate 2 hours for flavors to blend.

To serve, slice bananas crosswise; arrange on fruit platter. Beat egg white in small bowl until stiff peaks form; fold into whipped cream mixture. Spoon into serving bowl; serve with fruit. Garnish with mint.

Makes about 8 servings

*Use only Grade A, clean, uncracked eggs.

Celia's Flat Fruit Pie

CELIA'S FLAT FRUIT PIE

2 packages (8 ounces each) mixed
    dried fruit (pitted prunes,
    pears, apples, apricots and
    peaches)
3 cups water
1/2 cup sugar
1/2 teaspoon ground cinnamon
1/4 teaspoon ground cloves
1 teaspoon lemon juice
    Flaky Pastry (recipe follows)

Combine fruit, water, sugar, cinnamon and cloves in 3-quart pan. Cook, stirring occasionally, over medium heat until sugar is dissolved. Cover; reduce heat and simmer 45 minutes or until fruit is tender. Pour fruit and liquid into blender or food processor container fitted with metal blade; process to make coarse puree. (Puree should measure 3 cups. If puree measures more, return to pan and cook, stirring frequently, to reduce to 3 cups.) Stir in lemon juice. Let cool. While fruit is cooling, prepare Flaky Pastry.

Preheat oven to 400°F. Roll one pastry ball on lightly floured board to 13-inch circle about 1/8 inch thick. Fold pastry into quarters. Place in 12-inch pizza pan; unfold. Trim edge of pastry to leave 1/2-inch overhang. Spread fruit puree in even layer over pastry. Roll out second ball to 13-inch circle; place over filling. Cut slits or design in center. Fold edge of top crust under edge of bottom crust; flute edge. Bake 35 to 40 minutes or until pastry is golden brown. Place pie on rack. Let cool 1 hour before cutting into thin wedges.

Makes 12 servings

FLAKY PASTRY

3 1/3 cups all-purpose flour
3/4 teaspoon salt
1 cup shortening or lard
6 to 8 tablespoons cold water

Combine flour and salt in medium bowl. With fingers, pastry blender or 2 knives, rub or cut shortening into flour mixture until it resembles fine crumbs. Gradually add water; stir with fork until mixture forms dough. Shape into 2 balls. Wrap in plastic wrap; refrigerate 30 minutes.

SPICED ORANGE TEA

A refreshing, tangy beverage—served hot or cold.

3 cups water
1 cup orange juice
2 tablespoons lemon juice
1/4 cup sugar
1 cinnamon stick
1/2 teaspoon whole cloves
2 tea bags
    Ice cubes (optional)
    Mint sprigs (optional)

Combine water, orange juice, lemon juice, sugar, cinnamon stick, cloves and tea bags in 2-quart pan. Cook over medium heat, stirring occasionally, until sugar is dissolved. Cover pan when mixture just begins to steam. Turn off heat; let steep 5 minutes. Strain tea into preheated teapot; serve hot. Or to serve cold, strain tea into 1 1/2-quart container with tight-fitting lid. Cover when cool and refrigerate until very cold. Serve in ice-filled tumblers. Garnish each serving with mint.

Makes 4 servings

SANGRIA COMPOTE

Let the season dictate your choice of fruits and berries.

½ cup sugar
½ cup water
1 cinnamon stick
3 whole cloves
⅛ teaspoon ground nutmeg
2 (1-inch-wide) strips orange peel
2 (1-inch-wide) strips lemon peel
6 cups assorted fruits and berries:
    sliced, peeled fresh or
    unsweetened frozen peaches;
    pitted Bing cherries;
    blueberries; small, hulled
    strawberries; red and green
    seedless grapes; cantaloupe
    and honeydew melon balls;
    peeled, cored and diced pears
1 cup dry red wine or rosé wine
¼ cup orange juice
1 teaspoon lemon juice
    Mint sprigs for garnish

Combine sugar, water, cinnamon stick, cloves, nutmeg, orange peel and lemon peel in small pan. Cook, stirring occasionally, over medium heat until sugar is dissolved. Cover; reduce heat and simmer 5 minutes. Let cool.

Place fruits and berries in large bowl. Pour sugar mixture through strainer over fruit. Discard spices and peels. Add wine, orange juice and lemon juice. Stir gently to mix. Cover and refrigerate 1 hour or up to 2 days for flavors to blend. To serve, spoon about ¾ cup fruit into each of 8 bowls. Pour about ¼ cup wine mixture over each serving. Garnish with mint sprigs.

Makes 8 servings

MOCHA DESSERT

2 tablespoons cornstarch
½ cup cold water
2 teaspoons instant espresso coffee
    powder dissolved in ½ cup
    boiling water
1 cup (6 ounces) semi-sweet
    chocolate chips
2 tablespoons butter or margarine
6 eggs, separated
½ cup sugar, divided
1 teaspoon vanilla extract
1 cup chocolate wafer crumbs (half
    of 8½ ounce package chocolate
    wafers, crushed)

Dissolve cornstarch in cold water in top of double boiler. Add coffee mixture, chocolate chips and butter. Cook, stirring constantly, over simmering water until chocolate chips and butter melt and mixture is smooth. Remove from water; cool slightly.

Beat egg yolks in large bowl of electric mixer on medium speed until light and lemon colored. Gradually beat in ¼ cup of the sugar, 2 tablespoons at a time, until mixture falls from spoon in a thick ribbon. Beat a small amount of the chocolate mixture into yolks, then return to chocolate mixture in top of double boiler. Cook, stirring constantly, over simmering water until mixture has thickened enough to lightly coat metal spoon. Stir in vanilla. Let cool.

Beat egg whites with clean beaters and bowl until frothy. Gradually add the remaining ¼ cup sugar, 1 tablespoon at a time, beating well after each addition. Beat until stiff peaks form; fold into cooled chocolate mixture.

Butter 8-inch square baking pan. Sprinkle ⅓ of the crumbs onto bottom of greased pan. Pour in half of the chocolate mixture; gently spread over crumbs. Repeat layers; sprinkle with remaining crumbs. Freeze until firm. To store for more than 1 day, wrap tightly before freezing. Let dessert soften 5 minutes before cutting into serving-size pieces.

Makes 8 servings

ORANGE BREAD PUDDING WITH RUM SAUCE

This is a contemporary version of a classic Southwest dessert.

Rum Sauce (recipe follows)
1/2 loaf (1 pound) day-old French bread
5 eggs
1 egg white
2/3 cup granulated sugar
1/3 cup packed brown sugar
1/4 teaspoon ground cinnamon
2 cups milk
1 cup orange juice
1 tablespoon vanilla extract
1/2 cup raisins
1/4 cup pine nuts
3 tablespoons butter
Boiling water

Prepare Rum Sauce; refrigerate until ready to use. Preheat oven to 350°F. Cut bread into 1-inch slices; cut each slice, with crust, into 1-inch cubes to make 8 cups. Beat eggs and egg white in large bowl of electric mixer on medium speed until foamy. Gradually beat in granulated sugar, brown sugar and cinnamon. Stir in milk, orange juice, vanilla, raisins and pine nuts. Add bread cubes; mix well, pushing bread into liquid so each piece is moistened. Butter 3-quart baking dish or casserole dish with 1 tablespoon of the butter. Pour bread mixture into dish. Dot top with the remaining 2 tablespoons but-

ter. Set dish in larger pan. Pour boiling water into larger pan to depth of 1 1/2 inches. Bake, uncovered, 45 minutes or until top of pudding is golden brown and knife inserted in center comes out clean. Remove pudding from water bath and place on rack to cool 30 minutes. Serve warm with Rum Sauce. To reheat cake, bake, covered, in 350°F oven 15 minutes or until warmed.

Makes 8 servings

RUM SAUCE

1/4 cup butter or margarine, softened
1 egg yolk
1 1/2 cups powdered sugar
2 tablespoons rum
1 teaspoon grated orange peel

Beat butter in small bowl of electric mixer on medium speed until creamy. Beat in egg yolk. Add powdered sugar; beat until light and fluffy. Add rum; beat until well blended. Stir in orange peel. Cover and refrigerate up to 2 days. Serve chilled sauce over warm pudding.

Makes about 1 cup

SPANISH COFFEE

Use regular or decaffeinated coffee.

3/4 cup coffee-flavored liqueur
1 tablespoon plus 1 teaspoon sugar
4 cups hot brewed coffee
Whipped cream
Chocolate curls for garnish

Stir coffee-flavored liqueur and sugar into hot coffee. Pour into 4 heatproof glasses or mugs. Top each serving with dollop of whipped cream. Garnish with chocolate curls.

Makes 4 servings

MANGO-ORANGE MOUSSE

This tropical-flavored dessert also tastes good when served in a baked pie shell.

1 large can (28 ounces) mangoes or 2 small cans (15 ounces each) mangoes, drained
1 envelope (1 tablespoon) unflavored gelatin
1/4 cup cold water
3 eggs (room temperature), separated
1/2 cup sugar, divided
3/4 cup orange juice
1 tablespoon lemon juice
Dash of salt
2 tablespoons rum
1 cup (1/2 pint) whipping cream, divided
Shredded orange peel for garnish
Mint sprig for garnish

Process enough of the mangoes in blender or food processor container fitted with metal blade to make 1 cup puree. Thinly slice remaining mangoes; cover. Refrigerate; reserve for garnish.

Sprinkle gelatin over cold water in small bowl; let stand 1 minute to soften. Beat egg yolks with whisk in heavy 1-quart pan. Whisk in 1/4 cup of the sugar, the orange juice, lemon juice and salt. Cook over medium-low heat, stirring constantly, until mixture has thickened enough to lightly coat metal spoon. Remove from heat; add softened gelatin and stir until dissolved. Stir in mango puree and rum. Refrigerate (or stir over ice water) until mixture mounds slightly when dropped from spoon.

Beat egg whites in large bowl of electric mixer on high speed until frothy. Gradually add the remaining 1/4 cup sugar, 1 tablespoon at a time, beating well after each addition. Beat until stiff peaks form; fold into mango mixture. Without washing bowl or beaters, whip 1/2 cup of the cream until soft peaks form. Fold into mango mixture. Spoon into glass serving bowl. Refrigerate until firm, 3 to 4 hours or up to 24 hours. Just before serving, whip the remaining 1/2 cup cream until soft peaks form. Garnish mousse with reserved mango slices, whipped cream, orange peel and mint.

Makes 6 to 8 servings

PINK GRAPEFRUIT ICE

Tart-sweet and refreshing—the perfect conclusion to a spicy-hot meal.

2/3 cup sugar
1 1/3 cups water
Dash of salt
1 2/3 cups fresh pink grapefruit juice (about 3 grapefruits)
1 teaspoon grated orange peel
Mint sprigs for garnish

Combine sugar, water and salt in 2-quart pan. Cook, stirring occasionally, over medium heat until sugar is dissolved. Let cool. Stir in grapefruit juice and orange peel. Pour into 2 divided ice cube trays; freeze 2 hours or until almost firm. Transfer cubes to blender or food processor container fitted with metal blade or large bowl of electric mixer; process until smooth and slushy. Spoon into 1-quart container with lid. Cover and freeze until firm, about 3 hours or up to 2 weeks. Let stand at room temperature 10 minutes or until slightly softened before serving. Garnish with mint sprigs.

Makes 6 servings

Mango-Orange Mousse

Clockwise from left: Sangria Blush, Sangrita and Margaritas, Albuquerque Style

SANGRITA

Similar in name to the Spanish and Mexican wine drink, sangria, sangrita contains no alcohol.

1 can (12 ounces) tomato juice
1½ cups orange juice
¼ cup lime or lemon juice
1 tablespoon finely minced onion
⅛ teaspoon salt
¼ teaspoon hot pepper sauce
  Ice cubes
4 small celery stalks with leafy tops

Combine juices, onion, salt and hot pepper sauce in 1-quart container with tight-fitting lid. Cover; refrigerate 2 hours for flavors to blend. Pour into ice-filled tumblers. Add celery stalk to each glass for stirrer.

Makes 4 servings

MARGARITAS, ALBUQUERQUE STYLE

This refreshing slush is very easy to prepare for a crowd.

1 lime, cut into wedges
  Coarse salt
1 can (6 ounces) frozen lime
    concentrate
¾ cup tequila
6 tablespoons Triple Sec
1 can (12 ounces) lemon-lime or
    grapefruit soda
3 to 4 cups ice cubes
  Lime twist for garnish
  Lime peel for garnish

Rub rim of each cocktail glass with lime wedge; swirl glass in salt to coat rim. Combine half of each of the remaining ingredients, except garnishes, in blender container; process until ice is finely chopped and mixture is slushy. Pour into salt-rimmed glasses. Repeat with the remaining ingredients. Garnish as desired.

Makes 7 to 8 servings

SANGRIA BLUSH

Lighter than the typical wine drink made with red wine, this makes a refreshing accompaniment to spicy food.

1 cup orange juice
½ cup sugar
1 bottle (1.5 liters) white zinfandel
    wine
¼ cup lime or lemon juice
1 orange, thinly sliced and seeded
1 lime, thinly sliced and seeded
16 to 20 ice cubes

Combine orange juice and sugar in small pan. Cook over medium heat, stirring occasionally, until sugar is dissolved. Pour into 2-quart container with tight-fitting lid. Add wine, lime juice and sliced fruits. Cover; refrigerate 2 hours for flavors to blend. Place ice cubes in small punch bowl or large pitcher. Pour wine mixture over ice.

Makes 8 servings

SWEETWATER RANCH SPICE CAKE

Texas-grown pecans and a brown sugar meringue form the frosting as the cake bakes.

2½ cups all-purpose flour
1 teaspoon baking powder
1 teaspoon ground cinnamon
½ teaspoon salt
½ teaspoon ground allspice
½ teaspoon ground ginger
½ teaspoon ground nutmeg
½ cup butter or margarine, softened
1½ cups packed brown sugar
2 egg yolks
1 teaspoon baking soda
1¼ cups buttermilk
1 teaspoon vanilla extract
Meringue Frosting (recipe follows)
⅔ cup coarsely chopped pecans

Preheat oven to 350°F. Grease 13 × 9-inch baking pan; set aside. Sift together flour, baking powder, cinnamon, salt, allspice, ginger and nutmeg. Beat butter in large bowl of electric mixer on medium speed until creamy. Add brown sugar; beat until fluffy. Beat in egg yolks. Dissolve baking soda in buttermilk. Add flour mixture to butter mixture alternately with buttermilk mixture, starting and ending with flour mixture. Stir in vanilla. Pour batter evenly into prepared pan. Prepare Meringue Frosting; spread over cake batter. Sprinkle with pecans. Bake 45 minutes or until wooden pick inserted in center comes out clean. Transfer to rack; let cool completely in pan.

Makes 12 servings

MERINGUE FROSTING

2 egg whites
½ cup packed brown sugar

Beat egg whites, using clean beaters and bowl, in medium bowl of electric mixer until stiff peaks form. Gradually add brown sugar, 2 tablespoons at a time, beating well after each addition. Beat until stiff peaks form.

BOURBON PECAN PIE

Use your favorite recipe for pastry or purchase a 1½-inch-deep, 9-inch frozen pie shell.

Pastry for a single-crust 9-inch pie
¼ cup butter or margarine, softened
½ cup sugar
3 eggs
1½ cups light or dark corn syrup
2 tablespoons bourbon
1 teaspoon vanilla extract
1 cup pecan halves

Preheat oven to 350°F. Roll out pastry and line 9-inch pie pan; flute edge. Beat butter in large bowl of electric mixer on medium speed until creamy. Add sugar; beat until fluffy. Add eggs, one at a time, beating well after each addition. Add corn syrup, bourbon and vanilla; beat until well blended. Pour filling into pastry shell. Arrange pecan halves on top. Bake on lowest oven rack 50 to 55 minutes or until knife inserted slightly off center comes out clean (filling will be puffy). Place on rack and cool. Serve at room temperature or refrigerate up to 24 hours.

Makes 6 to 8 servings

CARAMEL PUMPKIN FLAN

Pumpkin and spices give this flan a Southwest accent.

3/4 cup sugar, divided
4 eggs
1 cup canned pumpkin
1 teaspoon ground cinnamon
1/4 teaspoon salt
1/4 teaspoon ground ginger
1/4 teaspoon ground allspice
1/4 teaspoon ground nutmeg
1 cup half-and-half
1/2 teaspoon vanilla extract
    Boiling water

Preheat oven to 350°F. Melt 1/2 cup of the sugar in 8-inch skillet over medium heat, stirring constantly, until sugar is caramelized. Immediately pour caramel syrup into 1-quart soufflé dish or other baking dish 7 to 8 inches in diameter. Tilt dish so syrup flows over bottom and slightly up sides. Let cool 10 minutes.

Beat eggs slightly on medium speed in large bowl of electric mixer. Add the remaining 1/4 cup sugar, pumpkin, cinnamon, salt, ginger, allspice and nutmeg. Beat to blend thoroughly. Add half-and-half and vanilla; beat until smooth. Pour into caramel-lined dish. Set dish in larger pan. Pour boiling water into larger pan to depth of 1 1/2 inches. Bake 45 to 50 minutes or until knife inserted in center comes out clean. Remove from water bath and place on rack to cool. Refrigerate, loosely covered, 6 hours or until next day.

To unmold, run knife around edge of dish; cover with rimmed serving plate. Holding plate in place, invert dish. Flan and caramel will slide onto plate. Cut into wedges to serve; spoon caramel over top.

Makes 6 servings

SNOW CAPS

A double chocolate bite to enjoy with after-dinner coffee.

3 egg whites, room temperature
1/4 teaspoon cream of tartar
3/4 cup sugar
1/2 teaspoon vanilla extract
1 cup (6 ounces) semi-sweet chocolate chips
4 ounces white chocolate, grated

Preheat oven to 200°F. Line baking sheets with plain ungreased brown paper such as heavy brown paper bags (not recycled). Combine egg whites and cream of tartar in large bowl of electric mixer. Beat at highest speed until mixture is just frothy. Add sugar, 1 tablespoon at a time, beating well after each addition. Beat until stiff peaks form. Add vanilla; beat 1 minute. Fold in chocolate chips. Drop mixture by teaspoonfuls onto prepared baking sheets. Bake 2 hours or until meringues are thoroughly dry to touch but not browned, rotating baking sheets halfway through baking. Turn off heat and leave in closed oven 3 to 4 hours or until completely dry. Remove from oven and cool completely. Carefully remove meringues from paper.

Bring water in bottom of double boiler to a boil; turn off heat. Place white chocolate in top of double boiler; place over hot water. Stir constantly until chocolate melts. Dip top of each meringue into melted chocolate. Place on waxed paper to dry. Store at room temperature in a tightly covered container.

Makes about 6 dozen

NEW MEXICAN HOT CHOCOLATE

This recipe duplicates the traditional flavors of Mexican chocolate using easy-to-find ingredients.

¼ cup unsweetened cocoa powder
¼ cup sugar
½ teaspoon ground cinnamon
¼ teaspoon ground nutmeg
  Dash of salt
⅔ cup water
3⅓ cups milk
1 teaspoon vanilla extract
4 cinnamon sticks or ground nutmeg

Combine cocoa powder, sugar, cinnamon, nutmeg, salt and water in 3-quart pan. Cook, stirring occasionally, over medium heat until cocoa powder and sugar are dissolved. Add milk and vanilla. Heat to simmering. Whip mixture with rotary beater or portable electric mixer until frothy. Pour into mugs. Place cinnamon stick in each mug or sprinkle each serving lightly with nutmeg.

Makes 4 servings

Traditional recipe: Omit sugar, ground cinnamon, nutmeg, salt, water and vanilla. Substitute 1 round (3.7 ounces) of Mexican chocolate, broken into wedges, for cocoa powder. Combine chocolate and milk in 3-quart pan. Cook, stirring occasionally, over medium heat until chocolate is melted. Continue as directed.

BISCOCHITOS

A favorite treat at Christmas, these cookies are usually served with New Mexican Hot Chocolate.

3 cups all-purpose flour
2 teaspoons anise seed
1½ teaspoons baking powder
½ teaspoon salt
1 cup lard or butter
¾ cup sugar, divided
1 egg
¼ cup orange juice
2 teaspoons ground cinnamon

Preheat oven to 350°F. Combine flour, anise seed, baking powder and salt in medium bowl; set aside. Beat lard in large bowl of electric mixer on medium speed until creamy. Add ½ cup of the sugar; beat until fluffy. Blend in egg. Gradually add flour mixture alternately with orange juice, mixing well after each addition.

Divide dough in half; roll out one portion at a time on lightly floured surface to ¼-inch thickness; cover remaining dough to prevent drying. Cut out cookies with fancy cookie cutters 2 to 2½ inches in diameter. As you cut cookies, add scraps to remaining dough. If dough becomes too soft to handle, refrigerate briefly. Place cookies, slightly apart, on ungreased baking sheet.

To prepare cinnamon topping, combine the remaining ¼ cup sugar and the cinnamon; lightly sprinkle over cookies. Bake 8 to 10 minutes or until edges are lightly browned. Let cool on racks, then store in airtight container.

Makes 4 to 5 dozen

Top: New Mexican Hot Chocolate; bottom: Biscochitos

Index